An exploration of the unconscious
mind below the surface

Frans Cilliers

Being a
SYSTEMS
PSYCHODYNAMIC
Scholar

compiled by
Sanchen Henning

Being a Systems Pyscohdynamic Scholar

Published by AFRICAN SUN MeDIA under the SUN MeDIA imprint

First edition 2019

ISBN 978-1-928314-63-9
ISBN 978-1-928314-64-6 (e-book)
https://doi.org/10.18820/9781928314646

Set in Fire Sans (OTF) Thin 10/14

Cover design, typesetting and production by AFRICAN SUN MeDIA

SUN MeDIA is an imprint of AFRICAN SUN MeDIA. Academic and general works are published under this imprint in print and electronic formats.

This publication can be ordered from:
orders@africansunmedia.co.za
Takealot: bit.ly/2monsfl
Google Books: bit.ly/2k1Uilm
africansunmedia.store.it.si *(e-books)*
Amazon Kindle: amzn.to/2ktL.pkL

Visit africansunmedia.co.za for more information.

Table of Contents

Theme 2 I Systems Psychodynamics in Postgraduate Academic Work

Dedication

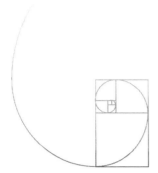

I dedicate my work to my parents, Dr Dawie and Mrs Marie Cilliers of Potchefstroom. They have provided me and my siblings with an emotionally well-contained childhood where self and academic development were always encouraged. Thank you to my older brother, Professor Charl Cilliers of Pretoria, and my younger sister, Professor Landa Terblanche of Vancouver, Canada, for their love and support through the years.

Thank you to my former academic colleagues at the Potchefstroom University for their profound impact on my development as a student and a lecturer early in my academic career. Hereafter, I spent 30 years of quality academic time at UNISA with many colleagues, working on various tasks and projects. Thank you for supporting and respecting my tuition and research interests. I especially learned a lot in working with those colleagues with whom I could join in the systems psychodynamic quest to study and understand the depth psychology of organisations and consulting.

My gratitude goes to my friends, Prof Sanchen Henning, Wilma Pienaar, Johan Venter and my sister, Prof Landa Terblanche, for their initiative, contributions and hard work in bringing this Festschrift to life.

Frans Cilliers
November 2019

Introduction

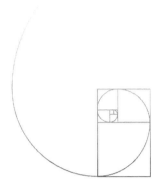

I see my role in being a systems psychodynamic scholar as consisting of three interdependent parts – (1) an academic involved in research and teaching in and supervision of research projects, (2) a psychologist consulting to organisations on complex and unconscious human behavioural matters, and (3) as a human being intrigued by my own unconscious.

My formal academic training comprised the traditional industrial and organisational psychology content, mostly informed by humanistic thinking and quantitative research methodology. My doctorate degree focussed on self-actualisation and 'sensitive relationship forming' based on the work of Dr Carl Rogers and others. I attended many international person-centred psychology training and growth events which provided very meaningful learning opportunities about myself.

The application of my person-centred knowledge made me realise that, although I may experience high levels of self-development, I do not have the vocabulary or the insight to understand and explain complex, dynamic and below the surface organisational and systemic psychological behaviour. I redirected my academic training and research focus towards becoming a systems psychodynamically informed academic, researcher and consultant. This enriched my work and personal life tremendously towards realising, for example, the importance of psychobiography in the understanding of the self and the other, the unconscious positioning of the self and being positioned, the interplay between relationships and relatedness, the-self-and-the-world-in-the-mind as a point of departure in studying organisational behaviour, the importance of using myself as a psychological instrument and to listen without memory, desire and judgement.

My journey towards becoming a systems psychodynamic instrument, was supported by UNISA as my employer for 30 years. I made use of the available resources such as academic freedom, time, grants to attend international training events and conferences. Systems psychodynamics became my preferred field of focus. As staff, we could include systems psychodynamics into the curricula of master's and doctorate students. Many Masters and Doctoral students chose systems psychodynamics as their research focus. I am grateful towards them for allowing me many insights into this field and into myself as instrument in supervision.

The included articles in this Festschrift represents a selection of what kept me academically and personally occupied over years. I thank those psychology colleagues with whom I could co-publish to hopefully add to our collective systems psychodynamic knowledge, insight and competence.

Theme 1 | **Systems Psychodynamics in Leadership Coaching**

Article 1

Executive Coaching Experience: A Systems Psychodynamic Perspective[1]

F Cilliers

Abstract

The Integrated Executive Experiential Learning Coaching model was applied in an information technology organisation. The aim of the research was to analyse and interpret the experiences of seven executives in the form of written essays from the systems psychodynamic perspective. The manifesting themes were, experiential learning facilitates the working through of defences; interdependency facilitates taking responsibility for the self; flight reactions inhibit owning and learning; transcending defences is needed to authorise the self in role; the difficulty of moving from the paranoid-schizoid to the depressive position and valuing all parts of the self; and containment facilitates self-authorisation. Recommendations towards more effective executive coaching are presented.

The post-modern work environment is associated with various new constructs such as the new economy, globalisation, change, transformation, diversity management, mergers, acquisitions, increased competition and complexity (Clutterbuck, 2003). These constructs facilitate heightened levels of anxiety because of changes in the nature of psychological boundaries within and between systems (individual, teams, organisation), and the demand to take up multiple (especially leadership) roles in complex matrix systems (Huffington, Armstrong, Halton, Hoyle & Pooley, 2004). According to Price (2003a; 2004d; 2004e), executive coaching is one of the new management tools to cope with

1   Cilliers, F. (2005). Executive coaching experiences. A systems psychodynamic perspective. *South African Journal of Industrial Psychology*, 31(3):23-30.

these changes and complexities. It offers a highly focussed and fast learning opportunity to compensate for lengthy training sessions and its methods where learning content is becoming obsolete at an increasingly fast rate.

Although organisational coaching can be traced back to the 1940s (Lowman, 2002), its broader application has only gained momentum in the late 1990s. Internationally, the American Psychological Society (Division 14) layed down standards for executive coaching (Stern, 2001) which is supported by substantial – especially North American – research results (for example by Brotman, Liberi & Wasylyshyn, 1998; Garman, Whiston & Zlatoper, 2000; Goldsmith, Lyons & Freas, 2000; King & Eaton, 1999; Peltier, 2001; Peterson, 1996; Sperry, 2004; Witherspoon & White, 1998). Almost all articles and chapters start with the definition of executive coaching as compared to mentoring, counselling and therapy, and how coaching should be 'rolled-out' in different organisations. This finding as well as the lack of clear empirical evidence of behavioural and organisational change could be indicative of the still unclear identity boundaries of executive coaching as a new organisational endeavour.

In South Africa, coaching enjoys professional recognition in the existence of the South African Council of Coaches and Mentors (SACCM) (Bjorkman & Van Niekerk, 2003). The South African literature on executive coaching is mainly found in popular journals on general and human resources management (Clutterbuck, 2003; Meyer & Fourie, 2004a; 2004b; Price, 2003a; 2003b). These articles focus on the practical 'how to do' executive coaching and claims that its practice will result in increased management and leadership competence, strategic thinking, intellectual capacity, wisdom, empowerment, relationship management as well as the solving of business problems (Johnson & Cohen, 2004; Knouldts, 2003; Price, 2003c; 2004b; 2004c; Van Wyk, 2003; Will & Codrington, 2004; Willem, 2002; 2004). Unfortunately, no South African academic and scientific research with reference to the psychological effects of executive coaching could thus far be found as evidence of the above claims.

Executive Coaching Described

Many definitions of executive coaching exist (see Brotman, Liberi & Wasylyshyn, 1998; Clutterbuck, 2003; Garman, Whiston & Zlatoper, 2000; Goldsmith, Lyons & Freas, 2000; Kilburg, 2000; King & Eaton, 1999; Meyer & Fourie, 2004b; Peltier, 2001; Peterson, 1996; Sperry, 2004; Witherspoon & White, 1998). All these definitions refer to the core of executive coaching as a specific form of organisational and staff development and a specific kind of interpersonal relationship. Some refer to the stimulation of and personal process of growth in the executive, while others refer to outcomes such as enhanced performance in leadership and transformation roles.

For purposes of this research executive coaching is defined as a form of consultation, namely a formal, ongoing relationship between (1) an individual or team having executive (including managerial and leadership) authority and responsibility in an organisation, and (2) a consultant who possesses in-depth knowledge of behaviour change and organisational functioning from various psychological perspectives and paradigms (Hall & Duval, 2004; Hillary, 2003; Huffington, Armstrong, Halton, Hoyle & Pooley, 2004; Lowman, 2002; Peltier, 2001; Schein, 2005; Sperry, 2004; Tönsing, 2003). The underlying facilitative process involves the provision of learning opportunities towards self-awareness, self-esteem and increased quality in the communication with colleagues, peers and subordinates, especially with regards to the individual's leadership role and accompanying authorisation. The techniques include giving direct behaviourally based feedback and interpretations about the executive's impact on others, both within and outside of the organisation, thus creating opportunities for change and demanding accountability for the outcome. It is believed that the measurable behavioural change in the individual or team will result in increased performance on the individual, team and organisational levels.

The Efficacy of Executive Coaching

On the macro-level studies on the efficacy of executive coaching (Lowman, 2002) claim the enhancement of organisational morale, productivity and profits. Unfortunately, these studies mostly hypothesis about the outcomes without it being substantiated by empirical designs and methods. On the micro and individual level the research suggests that (1) the executive finds the experience beneficial and believes that he/she receives a high return on investment, and (2) that various types of executive coaching approaches do impact positively on self-awareness, self-development, improved relationships with superiors, subordinates and clients, leadership effectiveness, teamwork, conflict reduction, commitment, satisfaction, performance and productivity (Peltier, 2001). Yet, these results do not refer to the individual's learning about his/her own behavioural dynamics and its effect on the rest of the system.

According to Kampa and White (in Lowman, 2002), executive coaching efficacy depends on three variables, namely the growth in the executive, the coach's skills and the quality of the interpersonal relationship. Further investigation of this literature showed the following:

5

∞ The growth of the executive is described in most of the literature in terms of his/her self-efficacy, referring to what Bandura's 1997; Wood & Bandura, 1989 concept and defined from the behaviouristic perspective as having the belief that one has the capabilities to mobilise the motivational and cognitive resources, and courses of action needed to meet given situation-demands. Price (2004a; 2004b) for example, described the growth in terms of wellness and strengths, but without giving a scientific and psychological conceptualisation of the nature of these terms.

∞ The coach's skills are described in most of the literature as a special kind of communication style, including active listening as the necessary core quality to facilitate learning in and for the executive (Lowman, 2002). Peltier (2001) refers to executive coaching as a mainstream leadership skill including management functions (such as planning, decision making, chairing a meeting, writing skills, delegation, dealing with difficulty, project and conflict management, team building and coping with diversity), interpersonal communication (listening, assertiveness, giving feedback), and the understanding of and working with organisation culture.

∞ The quality of the relationship between the two roles is described as the most critical component of executive coaching. Almost all the literature conceptualises the relationship referring to aspects of the person-centered facilitation perspective (Cilliers, 1995; 1996; 2000). This includes listening supported by the core dimensions of realness, openness, honesty, respect and empathy, which, according to Rogers (1982), will facilitate a meaningful experiential encounter of the other. Unfortunately, the executive coaching literature does not operationalise the relationship to the depth as researched by Rogers and operationalised in existing helping models (e.g. Carkhuff, Ivey, Egan – see Cilliers, 2000). Actually, Rogers (1982, in Schneider, Bugental & Pierson, 2001) cautioned that his work should not be trivialised in organisational applications. In this context, Kramer (1995) illustrated how active listening is easily forced into a tool to enhance productivity (rather than a skill to build relationships) and Cilliers (1991; 1992; 1995) illustrated how the concepts of facilitation and empathy are used superficially in training, management and organisational development. Using these facilitative conditions in executive coaching will require a high level of training to provide a trusting and respectful environment for the executive to experience the freedom to learn as well as the coach's continuous development towards self-actualisation.

Paradigms in Studying Executive Coaching

An analysis of the above literature indicated that executive coaching is generally studied from the behaviouristic (e.g. self-efficacy) and humanistic paradigms in psychology (e.g. client-centered facilitation). Price's (2004a; 2004b) references to wellness and strengths could refer to what is being studied in the positive psychology paradigm (Sheldon & King, 2001; Snyder & Lopez, 2002). Unfortunately, these descriptions are vague in terms of psychological functioning (compared to how well it is explicated in Lindley & Joseph, 2004). On the one hand, the study of executive coaching from the above paradigms ensure that the interpersonal relationship and its outcomes are understood from a cognitive and immediate relationship perspective. On the other hand, it avoids understanding the dynamic and unconscious nature of the coaching relationship, as well as the individual's dynamic team and organisational relationships and relatednesses (as was the aim in this research).

The Integrated Executive Experiential Learning Coaching Model (IEELC)

This model designed by Chapman (2004) was used in this research. It conceptualises executive coaching as a form of a consulting, combining the Wilber Integrative (interior/exterior and individual/collective) and Kolb Experiential Learning models (monologue/dialogue I/we/it), while integrating the hierarchical evolution of consciousness. It operationalised coaching as the facilitation of self-organised learning in adults through experiential learning conversations in order to grow and improve performance. The technique of self-organised learning is the conversational construction, reconstruction and exchange of personally significant, relevant and viable meaning with awareness and controlled purposiveness. This is applied to the one-on-one coaching situation and includes strategy formulation, implementation via the balance scorecard from an architectural approach, organisational complexity and Jaques' Leadership Competency model – including cognitive processes and power, knowledge and skills, personality, temperament and style. It distinguishes between the styles of the master, the dabbler, the obsessive and the hacker.

From a research point of view, the IEELC model offers opportunities to study specific organisational constructs such as management, leadership, personal growth, commitment and involvement on the conscious level. At the same time, it offers the opportunity to study the dynamic nature of the executive's relationships and relatedness on the unconscious level from a systemic point of view (from the intra-personal to the collective) by means of experiential learning. This includes the struggle to take up and authorise the self in role as a leader, to offer containment in this role to the self, others and the organisation, to move from dependence to interdependence, and to investigate defensive reactions, which all make this model appropriate for inclusion in this research.

The Systems Psychodynamic Perspective

The conceptual origins of the systems psychodynamic perspective stems from classic psychoanalysis (Freud, 1921), group relations theory and open systems theory (De Board, 1978; French & Vince, 1999; Hirschhorn, 1993; Miller, 1993; Obholzer & Roberts, 1994). This perspective is based upon the following five basic assumptions acting as the cornerstones for studying relationships in organisational systems (López-Corvo, 2003; Miller, 1993; Rice, 1965): Dependency (the group's unconscious projection for attention and help onto an authority figure as parental object); fight/flight (a defence mechanisms in trying to cope with discomfort, involving the authority figure for example management or leadership); pairing (unconsciously connecting with perceived powerful others such as the manager or leader, or splitting the authority figure(s) as an individual or as a pair in order to be able to identify with one part as a saviour – Bion, 1961; 1970; Lipgar & Pines, 2003); one-ness (also referred to as me-ness by Turquet, 1974) (the individual's escape into his/her own fantasy and inner safe, comfortable and good world, whilst denying the presence of the group, seen as the disturbing and bad part); and we-ness (the opposite of me-ness, and the unconscious need to join into a powerful union with and absorption into an omnipotent force, surrendering the self in passive participation – Lawrence, Bain & Gould, 1996).

The Systems Psychodynamic Consulting Stance

The systems psychodynamic perspective is a developmentally focused, psycho-educational process for the understanding of the deep and covert behaviour in the system. Its primary task is formulated as pushing the boundaries of awareness to better understand the deeper and covert meaning of organisational behaviour, including the challenges of management and leadership (Koortzen & Cilliers, 2002; Miller & Rice, 1976).

The systems psychodynamic consultant engages in an analysis of the interrelationships of some or all the following: boundaries, roles and role configurations, structure, organisational design, work culture and group process (Miller, 1993; Neumann, Kellner & Dawson-Shepherd, 1997). The consultant is alert to, hypothesises about and interprets the covert and dynamic aspects of the organisation and the work group that comprise it, with the focus on relatedness, representation and how authority is psychologically distributed, exercised and enacted, in contrast to how it is formally invested (see Haslebo & Nielsen, 2000). This work includes a consideration of attitudes, beliefs, fantasies, conflicts, core anxieties, social defences, patterns of relationships and collaboration, and how these in turn may influence task performance; how unwanted feelings and experiences are split off and projected onto particular parts (individuals or groups who may have the valence for receiving and carrying the specific projections), that contain them on behalf of the system (their projective identifications and process roles as distinct from their formally sanctioned roles); and how work roles are taken up, especially leadership and followership. Menzies (1993) emphasised the analysis of social defence aspects of structure and its relationship to task and process, thus trying to understand how unconscious anxieties are reflected in organisational structures and design (which function as a defence mechanism). The stance studies the system as a reality as well as 'a system in the mind' in its totality (group- as-whole), and its dynamic movement from basic assumption group functioning and the paranoid-schizoid position towards interdependence, characterised by work group functioning and the depressive position (Colman & Bexton, 1975; Colman & Geller, 1985; Cytrynbaum & Lee, 1993; Czander, 1993; Gabelnick & Carr, 1989; Gould, Stapley & Stein, 2001; Neumann, Kellner & Dawson-Shepherd, 1997; Shapiro & Carr, 1991; Stapley, 1996; Wells, 1980).

Thus, the stance studies the emotional task of the organisation which is filled with chaos, a lack of control and difficult experiences such as competition, rivalry, jealousy, envy, hate, hostility and aggression (Miller, 1976; 1993). As a result, leadership (as the focus in executive coaching) becomes difficult (if not impossible) and the relationships and relatedness between subsystems as well as the containment of these, become increasingly complex. As a result, mistrust and distrust increase (indicating the prevalence of paranoid fear, and a lack of meaning and hope in the system). Because leaders seem to find themselves de-authorised to negotiate new roles within their organisations directly, the system creates new mechanisms as a defensive compensation for the loss of control (Huffington, Armstrong, Halton, Hoyle & Pooley, 2004). The systems psychodynamic approach believes coaching to be one of the modern defences against the increasing organisational complexity, role ambiguity, high levels of anxiety and loneliness.

This research endeavoured to integrate the above systems dynamic behaviours as an interpretive stance towards exploring executive coaching experiences operationalised in the IEELC model. As an argument towards relevance and compatibility between the stance and the model, the following is offered: Both the interpretive stance and the operational model are based upon well-grounded, structured and contained scientific backgrounds, both focus on conscious and unconscious behaviour from a system perspective, and on how the individual takes up the role towards higher levels of functioning. One major difference is the focus within the systems psychodynamic stance on object relations based on Klein's (1959; 1975) theory of how objects could have representative value for one another (which were included in this research).

Problem Statement and Aim

The conceptual and operational identity of executive coaching as a new organisational endeavour is still unclear. Conceptually it struggles to find its place somewhere between training, development, mentoring, counselling and therapy. Operationally, its research is based upon popular and untested assumptions about its effect and influence on the executive, especially in the long term, as well as on the organisation. In practice, various helping models are used in executive coaching, but there is limited evidence of the effect of different paradigms on outcomes.

The aim of this research was to offer a systems psychodynamic interpretation of executive coaching experiences amongst a group of IT specialists/executives to offer this stance's view on behavioural change during executive coaching.

Research Design

Research Approach

The approach was qualitative and explorative in nature. More specifically, the social phenomenological approach was used (Higgs & Smith, 2003). This entails that the researcher will not be intimidated by social power or status and will be concerned with the relevant values and ethics. The researcher asks the question, 'what is actually happening', while exploring, 'looking again' and then reflecting in ruthless honesty. Thus, the researcher attempts "to penetrate the illusion in order to get to the reality underlying the illusion" (Higgs & Smith, 2003:67).

Research Methodology

Participants

The research was done in an international information technology organisation. An executive coaching programme was introduced in 2001 for a two-year period consisting of individual, bi-monthly, two-hour sessions, using the Integrated Experiential Learning Coaching Model. A sample of seven executives being coached by the same coach was used.

Data Collection Technique

Data was collected by means of essays written by participants. The essays were transcriptions representing the experience of each participant (Camic, Rhodes & Yardley, 2003:82-83).

Data Collection Procedure

Each participant was asked to: 'Write an essay of about 5 pages on your experiences of the coaching and the coaching relationship'. The essays were received electronically and then printed out.

Data Analysis

To best accommodate the explorative nature of the approach, content analyses was used (Camic, Rhodes & Yardley, 2003), consisting of breaking down, examining, comparing, conceptualising and categorising of data. Firstly, the responses were read through a couple of times for familiarisation of content. Thereafter, true to the systems psychodynamic interpretive stance, Schafer's (2003) guidelines were used towards the formulation of working hypotheses (also see Haslebo & Nielsen, 2000) on the manifestation of the basic assumptions and its associated anxieties and conflicts (see Menzies, 1993; Neumann, Kellner & Dawson-Shepherd, 1997). Different examples were clustered (see Brewerton & Millward, 2004; Clarkson & Nuttall, 2000) leading to the prominent themes. Trustworthiness was ensured (as defined by De Vos, 2002) by having the findings examined by a psychologist, to whom this research method and interpretive stance were well known.

Findings

The Following Six Themes Manifested

1. Experiential learning facilitates the working through of defences

   Participants expressed their need to be instructed and taught by the coach, and not to be 'facilitated in this open and vague' manner. It seemed that the nature and method of experiential discovery as a way of learning and thus explicating inner experiences in order to develop shared models of reality (Bion, 2003; Gould, Stapley & Stein, 2001), created a high level of anxiety amongst this group of IT executives. Using Stapley's (1996) description of organisational culture as the personality of the organisation, it was interpreted that this anxiety reflects the existing organisational culture where anxiety is contained in structure and procedure. This scenario has led to rigidity and a mechanistic way of operating, rather than to dynamically investigate evidence in the here-and-now as learning opportunities. There is also a lack of trusting in one's own experience or to freely explore and discover the nature of dynamic relationships in the system.

The participant's anxiety manifested in various ego defences, namely intellectualisation (trying to keep their learning on the cognitive level and not make contact with difficult and disturbing feelings), rationalisation (giving intellectual explanations for their behaviour), denial (not wanting to work with the difficulty of introspection and 'soul searching'), regression (referring to childhood experiences suggesting that the coach represented a parental figure – not realising their own transferences) and projection (of incompetence onto the coach for 'not helping' them). These defences represented the participant's immaturity at the beginning of the executive coaching relationship (see Gabelnick & Carr, 1989).

As the work continued, the experiential nature of the executive coaching model made an appeal on the participant's ego strength to stay with and work through their anxieties and difficulties. Towards the end of the coaching contract the neurotic agendas of moaning (about management) and blaming (the organisation) used by most participants, diminished and were replaced by self-authorisation and working towards openness and a shared reality in the coaching relationship. Generalising from Menzies' (1993) theory, this could be interpreted as happening because the individuals experienced containment in the executive coaching relationship, the climate and its culture. According to Horney's theory (1950; 1957) the participant's behaviour moved from (only) working against the coach and what he represented, towards integrating the three neurotic tendencies of moving towards, away from and against their objects, in exploring their relationship and work behaviour.

2. Interdependency facilitates taking responsibility for the self

Many participants expressed dependence on the coach as a parental and authority figure, an experienced expert, director and guide of their development. This means that they expect him to 'help them to become more successful as employees and leaders in this organisation'. Unconsciously, he represented the object of wisdom and the accompanying fantasy was that he will take charge of their learning and instruct them 'what to do'. This transferential relationship tries to pull the coach into a rescue mentality (Huffington, Armstrong, Halton, Hoyle & Pooley, 2004) while the participants split off their own competence, and project this onto the experienced expert. This behaviour also represents their attempt to seduce the coach out of his authorised role into carrying and containing the participant's immaturity and incompetence (Shapiro & Carr, 1991).

Despite the above transferences and projections, the coach stayed in his authorised role. This may be an indication of the level of organisational authorisation given to him from above (see Obholzer & Roberts, 1994), specifically from the human resources director who acted as custodian for executive coaching and who contracted this role with him.

The participants reacted with intense feelings of frustration, anger and hostility as a manifestation of their counter dependence (see Bion, 2003) and rebellious child ego state (Berne, 1961). This behaviour was an attempt to take up their roles in the coaching relationship, but with pseudo authority, because it was still filled with transferences and projections – as if they were playing the game of 'getting-my-own-way' (Bennett, 1976).

Most participants did not stay in this counter dependent position for long. This was interpreted as therapeutic movement (see Czander, 1993), based on the knowledge that the group was especially selected on the grounds of their intelligence and high potential for development. Hereafter all participants moved to the independent position, where some stayed for some time and two participants never moved out of. This was interpreted as a manifestation of me-ness – it was as if the participants found a new independent position where he/she can show of strength and power and stay separate and unattached from others (see Turquet, 1974). This behaviour could also be a defence (for example compensation) for the lack of an experienced independence in their functional roles and in the organisational culture. The core of this defence could be the need to hang on to power and to serve the narcissism which normally forms part of a power play (Peltier, 2001).

Most of the participants moved to the interdependence position where they could work productively, experiencing their own needs, thoughts, feelings and drives without defending as strongly as in the beginning. This position does not imply that the individual 'has arrived', but the position supplied him/her with the resilience to explore and address deeper experiences and integrate these into his/her ego functioning (Gould, Stapley & Stein, 2001). The underlying process implies that the participants increasingly took responsibility for themselves in owning their behaviour as it enters consciousness (Cytrynbaum & Lee, 1993).

3. Flight reactions inhibit owning and learning

The initial discomfort in coping with the limited structure in the experiential executive coaching design has lead to flight reactions as a defence mechanism. Initially, participants referred to many past and 'out there' events and situations, which lessened as the coaching sessions progressed. This was interpreted as the participants getting used to taking up their authority in their roles as learners (Clarkson & Nuttall, 2000) and in exploring the content and intensity of the here-and-now situation. This implied a letting go of defences and game playing. When this happened, the learning became more personalised and owed as if the participant had to go through some kind of psychological birth process in trusting the coach as an outsider looking inside towards their environments, situations and personal experiences. The resulting trusting relationship showed clear evidence of self-empowerment amongst the participants. Sievers (2002) referred to the dynamics of trust being embedded in the level of meaning the participant experiences in the relationship and the accompanying hope to sustain the interaction and the learning. This was evident in their references to finding deep meaning in the here-and-now of the learning event as well as the application of the learning in their work teams.

4. Transcending defences is needed to authorise the self in role

Initially, splits manifested between what the participants apparently experienced and felt, versus what they verbally communicated, which resulted in the many defences being used. Because of the inner turmoil, it was difficult to trust and therefore to be honest and open in their experience of themselves. It took some time for most participants to realise that their experience of 'I do not trust the coach' was a projection of their distrust towards themselves for confronting the self with seemingly threatening information. In general, this behaviour is linked with authorisation to take up a leadership role (French & Vince, 1999). Three participants referred to the realisation that 'putting the parts of the self together' is important for learning, growth, self-integration and taking up the leadership role. This is what Peltier (2001) referred to as self-management and Miller (1993) as wisdom, which is needed for the participant to authorise the self in a role, especially of a leader in complex matrix systems.

5. It is difficult to move from the paranoid-schizoid to the depressive position and valuing all parts of the self

During the initial and immature stage of the relationship between the participant and coach, many schizoid splits occurred. This is seen as typical in many types of immature organisational relationships (Hirschhorn, 1993). For example, participants tried to split off and project the parts of themselves they perceived as bad. These were their fears of being part of this competitive organisation, colleagues they do not get along with, people in the organisation seen as dangerous or strict, and their incompetence and non-coping with specific organisational demands. In many occasions the participants unconsciously used the coach to carry these anxieties on their behalf. Thus, external figures and structures were created who are both hated and feared, for the insider (the participant) to feel safe and secure (Colman & Bexton, 1975; Colman & Geller, 1985). The projection of badness to the outside of the self was used to simplify psychic complexities in the self and the organisation and to produce a state of illusionary goodness and self-idealisation. This led to the experience of fragmentation in the participant, because contact was lost between parts of the self – which needed to connect in order to act as a whole person (see Menzies, 1993).

The above anxiety were prosecutory in nature (see Lipgar & Pines, 2003) and resulted in paranoia-genesis (see Gould, Stapley & Stein, 2001) where the individual is experiencing the bad parts of the self as situated within the other, who becomes 'the enemy' and the receiver of unwanted projections. It took some time for participants to work through and finding out who his/her 'enemy' was and how he/she related towards the enemy, before a satisfactory level of insight and understanding could be reached. De Jager, Cilliers and Veldsman (2004) referred to the unconscious collusions happening in cases such as the above, especially in organisations where anxiety is contained in having many structures, rules and procedures. This defence structure occurred amongst most of these participants. It was interpreted that participants got stuck within their safe boundaries and did not manage to integrate both parts of the split into their own ego boundary.

On the other hand, there were two participants who showed some resilience towards movement to the depressive position (see Colman & Bexton, 1975; Colman & Geller, 1985), indicating their maturity to recognise that their painful feelings come from their own projections, and not an outside source. This was followed by being brave enough to own their projected material and to return their received projections to its source, saying for example, 'these are my feelings, not yours/those are your feelings and not mine'. The two mentioned participants stayed within this position where projections are ricocheting back and forth for quite a while, during which the coach respectfully reflected and interpreted the behaviour, until there was enough evidence to let go of the feelings and to reflect on them. The maturity aspect in this action lies in the re-owning of parts of the self which lead to decreased splitting, polarisation and antagonism. Why only two participants reported on having this sense of integration within their own egos, could relate to many aspects, such as the individual's valence for development towards maturity (French & Vince, 1999) or the experiential nature of the coaching relationship (Peltier, 2001; Stapley, 1996).

6. Containment facilitates self-authorisation

Many participants ended their essays referring to the nature and quality of the relationship between themselves and the coach. This could refer to their experience of containment, defined as a state of integration in terms of a reciprocity between two parts – a containing function and a contained function, in this case a coach and a participant (Huffington, Armstrong, Halton, Hoyle & Pooley, 2004). When this function breaks down, the individual could experience catastrophic anxiety, and when it is held up, the individual can integrate. These participants experienced the holding quality of the containment which lead to their taking up of their authority to learn and integrate the learning into their organisational roles, especially their leadership roles. This meant that participants could manage the boundaries between the inside and the outside – which is how leadership is defined in this stance (Obholzer & Roberts, 1994). It was interpreted that the participants experienced being authorised from above (firstly by the organisational system in selecting them to be part of the executive coaching programme and secondly by the coach during the sessions), and from within (by allowing the self to integrate the learning about the self and their relationships). This self-authorisation facilitated their increased understanding of their role(s) as well as its demands on the self (inside the own boundary) and others (across the boundary). They reported being recognised by their superiors as someone who has a valuable place in the larger organisational system, that they had more effective interpersonal and supervisory communication with colleagues and followers, and more awareness of their own team's dynamic behaviour.

Discussion

The findings showed that this specific executive coaching relationship has empowered and authorised the executives in taking up their organisational leadership roles. They started the sessions with being dependent on a 'guru' whilst projecting their own insecurities and incompetence on him, with the unconscious expectation that he will teach them and help them carry the psychological burden of learning. Through the exploratory and experiential learning process, they realised that this position of dependence with all its accompanying immature splits, was withholding them from moving towards maturity and interdependent functioning. The individual process of growth seems to be filled with lots of effort and difficult learning – yet the outcome seemed to be successful in providing opportunities to work through personal defences, towards the owning of some unconscious behaviour (see Obholzer & Roberts, 1994).

Most participants could work through their basic assumption behaviour (of dependence and flight) but not all participants could move beyond the paranoid-schizoid position. This is not surprising, seeing that a system never completely transcends this position (French & Vince, 1999; Miller & Rice, 1976) and the depressive position is never attained for long (Colman & Bexton, 1975; Colman & Geller, 1985).

The findings showed how executive coaching resembles the family dynamic of children acting towards parental figures and using them as objects for projections and projective identification (Miller & Rice, 1976). This emphasised the importance for executive coaches to contain anxiety on behalf of participants, especially during the initial phase of the contract and the relationship. It seems that this model as applied to these executives offered them the opportunity to explore the meaning attached to their various organisational roles in the here-and-now, as well as what is hoped for in future – in short how trust manifests in his/her work relationships.

Conclusion

It was concluded that this executive coaching model of integrated systems learning, facilitated psychodynamic insight and wisdom in individual participants. They understood and owned important behavioural dynamics inside of themselves, between themselves and other significant colleagues. This underlines the possibilities of executive coaching as a staff development intervention to facilitate self authorisation by working through own splits and projections. It was hypothesised that executive coaching presented from this model empowered individual employees to work towards their own cognitive insight, the experience of emotional meaningfulness and the taking of responsibility for their own growth and career development.

These findings link with all three types or functions of executive coaching mentioned by Sperry (2004), namely, skill-focussed, performance-focussed and development-focussed coaching. Participants reported enhanced functioning in terms of skills (relating to the process and method for learning used, operational leadership, analytical ability, awareness of dynamic behaviour in human relations and relatedness, strategy and self-management), in terms of performance (functioning significantly more empowered and authorised as leaders and executives), and in terms of development (having clear steps implemented towards personal and professional transformation and career development).

It seemed that executive coaching is a powerful organisational learning opportunity (see Price, 2003a), which could be approached from different psychological perspectives and paradigms. But this means that the different views need to be scientifically investigated before general claims of its effectiveness can be made. This research indicated that the systems psychodynamic consultancy stance facilitated awareness around its basic assumptions and empowered the executive to effectively take up the role of leader.

Because executive coaching is a new organisational endeavour, its long-term effect on the individual's growth and career is not yet clear, as is the effects on the larger organisational system, for example morale, productivity and profits. It is suggested that continued research is done within the systems psychodynamic consultancy stance to ascertain this effect on organisational climate, culture and trust relationships

References

Bandura, A. (1997). *Self-efficacy: the exercise of control.* New York: Freeman.

Berne, E. (1961). *Transactional analysis in psychotherapy.* New York: Ballentine.

Bennett, D. (1976). *TA and the manager.* New York: Amacom.

Bion, W.R. (1961). *Experiences in groups.* London: Tavistock Publications.

Bion, W.R. (1970). *Attention and interpretation.* London: Tavistock Publications.

Bion, W.R. (2003). *Learning from experience.* London: Karnac.

Bjorkman, D. & Van Niekerk, P. (2003). Coaching and mentoring gains professional status. *Management Today,* 19(5):41-42.

Brewerton, P. & Millward, L. (2004). *Organisational research methods. A guide for students and researchers.* London: Sage.

Brotman, L.E.; Liberi, W.P. & Wasylyshn, K.M. (1998). Executive coaching. The needs for standards of competence. *Consulting Psychology Journal: Practice and Research,* 50(1):40-46.

Camic, P.M., Rhodes, J.E. & Yardley, L. (2003). *Qualitative research in Psychology.* Washington: APA.

Chapman, L. (2004). An exploration of executive coaching as an experiential learning process. Paper presented at 7th Industrial Psychology Conference, SIOPSA, Pretoria, 25 June.

Cilliers, F. (1991). Facilitating: Making a process available. *Human Resource Management,* 7(2),February.

Cilliers, F. (1992). The (ir)relevance of empathy as concept in management. *Human Resource Management,* 8(3),April.

Cilliers, F. (1995). *Facilitator training. Journal for Industrial Psychology,* 21(3):7-11.

Cilliers, F. (1996). Facilitator training in South Africa. In: R. Hutterer, G. Pawlowsky, P.F. Schmid & R. Stipsits. (eds.), *Client Centred and Experiential Psychotherapy.* Frankfurt am Main: Peter Lang.

Cilliers, F. (2000). Facilitation skills for trainers. *Journal of Industrial Psychology,* 26(3):21-26.

Clarkson, P. & Nuttall, J. (2000). Working with countertransference. *Psychodynamic Counselling,* 6:359-379.

Clutterbuck, D. (2003). Coaching and mentoring at the top. *Management Today,* 19(5):38-40.

Colman, A.D. & Bexton, W.H. (1975). *Group Relations Reader 1.* Jupiter: The A.K. Rice Institute.

Colman, A.D. & Geller, M.H. (1985). *Group Relations Reader 2.* Jupiter: The A.K. Rice Institute.

Cytrynbaum, S. & Lee, S.A. (1993). *Transformations in global and organizational systems.* Jupiter: A.K. Rice Institute.

Czander, W.M. (1993). *The psychodynamics of work and organizations.* New York: Guilford Press.

De Board, R. (1978). *The psychoanalysis of organisations.* London: Routledge.

De Jager, W., Cilliers, F. & Veldsman, T. (2004). Leadership development from a systems psychodynamic consultancy stance. *SA Journal of Human Resource Management,* 1(3):85-92.

De Vos, A.S. (2002). *Research at grass roots.* Pretoria: Van Schaik.

French, R. & Vince, R. (1999). *Group relations, management, and organization.* New York: Oxford University Press

Freud, F. (1921). *Group psychology and the analysis of the ego. Complete works of Sigmund Freud.* London: Hogarth.

Gabelnick, F. & Carr, A.W. (1989). *Contributions to social and political science.* Jupiter: A.K. Rice Institute.

Garman, A.N., Whiston, D.L. & Zlatoper, K.W. (2000). Media perceptions of executive coaching and formal preparation of coaches. *Consulting Psychology Journal. Practice and Research,* 52(3):201-205.

Goldsmith, M., Lyons, L. & Freas, A. (2000). *Coaching for leadership: How the world's greatest coaches help leaders learn.* San Francisco: Jossey-Bass.

Gould, L.J., Stapley, L.F. & Stein, M. (2001). *The systems psychodynamics of organisations.* London: Karnac.

Hall L.M. & Duval, M. (2004). Neurosemantic coaching. *HR Future,* 4-7 January.

Higgs, P. & Smith, J. (2003). *Rethinking truth.* Landsdown: Juta.

Hillary, D. (2003). Executive coaching. *HR Future,* 10-11 October.

Hirschhorn, L. (1993). *The Workplace Within: psychodynamics of organizational life.* Cambridge: MIT Press.

Horney, K. (1950). *Neurosis and human growth. The struggle towards self-realisation.* New York: Norton:

Horney, K. (1957). *Our inner conflicts.* London: Routledge & Kegan Paul.

Huffington, C., Armstrong, A., Halton, W., Hoyle, L. & Pooley, J. (2004). *Working below the surface. The emotional life of contemporary organisations.* London: Karnac.

Johnson, A. & Cohen, D. (2004). Coaching: Adding value to a business relationship. *Management Today,* 20(5):45-46.

Kilburg, R.R. (2000). *Executive coaching: Developing managerial wisdom in a world of chaos.* Washington: APA.

King, P. & Eaton, J. (1999). Coaching for results. *Industrial and Commercial Training,* 31(4):145-148.

Klein, M. (1959). Our adult world and its roots in infancy. *Human Relations,* 12:291-303.

Klein, M. (1975). *Envy and Gratitude and Other Essays, 1946-1963.* London: Hogarth Press.

Knouldts, F. (2004). Coaching: The internal realities of leaders. *Management Today,* 20(6):49-51.

Koortzen, P. & Cilliers, F. (2002). The psychoanalytical approach to team development. In: R.L. Lowman (ed.), *Handbook of organizational consulting psychology.* San Francisco: Jossey- Bass.

Kramer, R. (1995). Carl Rogers meets Otto Rank: The discovery of relationship. In: T. Pauchant & Associates (eds.), *In search of meaning.* San Francisco: Jossey-Bass.

Lawrence, W.G, Bain, A. & Gould, L. (1996). *The fifth basic assumption.* London: Occasional paper.

Linley, P.A. & Joseph, S. (2004). *Positive psychology in practice.* Hoboken: Wiley.

Lipgar, R.M. & Pines, M. (2003). *Building on Bion: Branches.* London: Jessica Kingsley.

López-Corvo, R.E. (2003). *The dictionary of the work of WR Bion*. London: Karnac.

Lowman, R.L. (2002). *The handbook of organizational consulting Psychology*. San Francisco: Jossey-Bass.

Menzies, I.E.P. (1993). *The functioning of social systems as a defence against anxiety*. London: The Tavistock Institute of Human Relations.

Meyer, M. & Fourie, L. (2004a). Coaching and mentoring: Business tool of the 21st century. *Management Today*, 20(9):48-52.

Meyer, M. & Fourie, L. (2004b). *Mentoring and coaching. Tool and techniques for implementation*. Randburg: Knowres.

Miller, E.J. (1976). *Task and Organisation*. New York: Wiley.

Miller, E.J. (1993). *From dependency to autonomy: Studies in organization and change*. London: Free Association Books.

Miller, E.J. & Rice, A.K. (1976). *Systems of organisation*. London: Tavistock Publications.

Neumann, J.E., Kellner, K. & Dawson-Shepherd, A. (1997). *Developing organisational consultancy*. London: Routledge.

Obholzer, A. & Roberts, V.Z. (1994). *The unconscious at work*. London: Routledge.

Peltier, B. (2001). *The psychology of executive coaching. Theory and application*. New York: Brunner-Routledge.

Peterson, D.B. (1996). Executive coaching at work. The art of one-on-one change. *Consulting Psychology Journal: Practice and Research*, 48(2):78-86.

Price, B. (2003a). Coaching and mentoring: A perspective. *Management Today*, 19(5):44-47.

Price, B. (2003b). Coaching: Critical for the new demands of business. *Management Today*, 19(4):34-36.

Price, B. (2003c). Coaching options. Solving a wide variety of business problems. *Management today*, 19(9):48-50.

Price, B. (2004a). Coaching and mentoring. It's about concentrating on the strengths. *Management Today*, 20(8):42-45.

Price, B. (2004b). Coaching and mentoring: Part of the company psyche. *Management Today*, 19(10):63-65.

Price, B. (2004c). Coaching sustainability, wellness and performance. *Management Today*, 20(4):46-49.

Price, B. (2004d). Coaching wisdom and magic. *Management Today*, 20(3):51-52.

Price, B. (2004e). Director of operations: A coaching experience. *Management Today*, 20(2):54-56.

Rice, A.K. (1965). *Learning for leadership*. London: Tavistock Publications.

Richard, J.T. (1999). Multimodal therapy. A useful model for the executive coach. *Consulting Psychology Journal: Practice and Research*, 51(1):24-30

Rogers, C.R. (1982). *Freedom to learn for the 80's*. Columbus: Merrill.

Schafer, R. (2003). *Insight and interpretation. The essential tools of psychoanalysis*. London: Karnac.

Schein, E. (2005). *Course in career and executive coaching*. Pretoria: UNISA.

Schneider, K.J., Bugental, J.F.T. & Pierson, J.F. (2001). *The handbook of humanistic psychology. leading edges in theory, research and practice*. Thousand Oaks: Sage.

Shapiro, E.R. & Carr, A.W. (1991). *Lost in familiar places: Creating new connections between the individual and society.* London: Yale University Press.

Sheldon, K.M. & King, L. (2001). Why positive psychology is necessary. *American Psychologist,* 56(3):216-217.

Sievers, B. (2002). Against all reason: Trusting in trust. Paper at International Society for the Psychoanalytic Study of Organisations, Melbourne.

Snyder, C.R. & Lopez, S.J. (2002). *Handbook of positive psychology.* Oxford, UK: Oxford University Press.

Sperry, L. (2004). *Executive coaching. The essential guide for mental health professionals.* New York: Brunner-Routledge.

Stapley, L.F. (1996). *The personality of the organisation.* London: Free Association Books.

Stern, L. (2001). *Executive coaching handbook: Principles and guidelines for a successful coaching partnership.* Boston: Executive Coaching Forum

Tonsing, T. (2003). Coaching skills training. *HR Future,* 26-29 April.

Turquet, P.M. (1974). Leadership – the individual in the group. In: G.S. Gibbard, J.J. Hartman & R.D. Mann (eds.), *Analysis of groups.* San Francisco: Jossey-Bass.

Van Wyk, L. (2003). Coaching has to deliver measurable results. *Management Today,* 19(7):49-50.

Wells, L. (1980). The group-as-a-whole: A systemic socio-analytical perspective on interpersonal and group relations. In: C.P. Alderfer & C.L. Cooper (eds.), *Advances in experiential social processes,* 2:165-198.

Will, B. & Codrington, G. (2004). Coaching: Perspectives on leadership. *Management Today,* 20(7):51-53.

Willem, A. (2002). Coaching: Extracting intellectual capital. *Management Today,* 18(9):34-35.

Willem, A. (2003). Coaching: Obtaining wisdom from the relationship, *Management Today,* 18(10):50-51.

Witherspoon, R. & White, R.P. (1998). *Four essential ways that coaching can help executives.* Greensboro: Center for Creative Leadership.

Wood, R. & Bandura, A. (1989). Social cognitive theory of organisational management. *Academy of Management Review,* 14(3):36.

Article 2

Leader and Team Behaviour During Organisational Change: A Systems Psychodynamic Stance[1]

Abstract

The aim of this research was to explore the dynamic nature of leader and team behaviour during organisational change, using five different organisational constellations or neurotic personality styles, namely the paranoid, schizoid, depressive, compulsive and histrionic styles. Qualitative research was conducted, comprising of two focus groups with eight psychologists consulting regularly to organisational change. The data was content analysed and interpreted from the systems psychodynamic stance. Each style's leader and team behavioural manifestations are discussed. The findings and recommendations can be used by consulting psychologists towards understanding and implementing organisational change dynamics.

It is generally accepted that all organisations are influenced by change (Campbell, 1995; Drucker, 2004; Kemp & De Villiers, 2004; McLagan, 2002a), that change may manifest uniquely in every organisation (McLagan, 2002b; Nel, 2004), and that change management is one of the greatest challenges to the modern organisation (Haslebo & Nielsen, 2000). Organisational change is generally defined in a reactive manner with reference to the planning and implementation of mechanistic organisational development inputs and expected outputs (McLagan, 2002c; 2003). The focus is for example on restructuring, re-engineering

---

1   Cilliers, F. (2006). Leader and team behaviour during organisational change: A systems psychodynamic stance. *South African Journal of Industrial Psychology*, 32(1):33-41.

and enhancing employee's coping skills in difficult times of adaptation to newness and/or difference.

For purposes of this research organisational change is defined in dynamic terms based on the belief that all organisations and its members are constantly undergoing change (Haslebo & Nielsen, 2000). Change itself is not the problem – rather, the problem is seen as the meaning or interpretation that staff members attribute to change. For example, team members may experience management's or leadership's plans to restructure as a disparagement of their efforts and performance. The organisation is seen as a complex network of relationships between people, their ideas, mental models, values, attitudes and future dreams. Change is seen as being determined by the structure of the system and is always directed from within (far more as being controlled from the outside). Change management is not seen as linear (where one stage depends on the outcome of the previous one), but rather as a rational process that the manager or leader can think out, plan and assist staff or team members through, thus achieving the desired outcome. Change is therefore defined as any demand to operate differently in any facet of the organisation as a system (Peltier, 2001; Sperry, 2004), and which is experienced as disruptive to both the organisation and its members. A demand may originate from the macro environment, outside of the boundary of the system (such as from a turbulent economy, the professional or operational field, changes in clients and product structures) or from the micro environment inside the boundary of the system (such as from technology, structures, procedures, policies, job content, role design, culture and climate) (Gould, Stapley & Stein, 2001). The disruptive effect on the people refers to the individual's readiness and willingness to cope with the demands of change entering his/her personal and work boundaries, versus being so filled up with anxiety that defence mechanisms are used to feel safe (Schafer, 2003). For example, Prochaska, Norcross and DiClemente (1994) identified and discussed six stages whereby the individual progresses in his/her coping with change, namely pre-contemplation, contemplation, decision, action, maintenance and recycling. This progress requires the individual's continuous awareness of the level of anxiety in the self, and how this is coped with by exploring the interaction between the self and the various objects of change (Lawrence, 1999; Miller, 1993).

Most theories and research link organisational change to leadership (see Holburn, 2003; Horth, 2003; Kotter, 2003; Nel, 2004; Nkomo, 2003), which is the organisational construct presently being referred to most in the popular as well as the academic journals (Verwey, 2003). Many grand theories and models on leadership and its roles in change management exist and are still developing.

This includes seeing leadership as a property (Kets De Vries, 2005), a skill (Ellis, 2004; Giuliani, 2004; Kotter, 2003), a task (Roodt, 2003), a belief and value system (Holburn, 2003), a competence (Horth, 2003; Steyn, 2004), a situational variable depending on the follower and a process (Robbins, Odendaal & Roodt, 2001). There is even reference to a leadership gene determining one's effectiveness (Vermeulen, 2004). The new economy demands new leadership styles because of the everchanging intra and inter organisational relationships and the wisdom it requires to explore new ways of coping and managing. Examples are transformational (De Jager, Cilliers & Veldsman, 2004), people (Schmikl, 2004), charismatic (Robbins et al., 2001), servant (Makwana, 2003), community (Khambula, 2003), visionary and complexity leadership (Verwey, 2003). Added to this list is containment leadership, referred to by the systems psychodynamic stance which is used in this research (Huffington, Armstrong, Halton, Hoyle & Pooley, 2004).

For purposes of this research leadership is defined in dynamic terms as managing the boundary between what is inside versus what is outside (Miller, 1993). This implies that leadership belongs to the system that is the organisation, the individual in the designated leadership role as well as to followership – "the person who most clearly could discover and articulate the task in any particular situation becomes the leader" (Miller, 1993:183).

Over the last decade many change leadership programmes have been implemented to counteract the negative effects of change (Pretorius, 2004; Steyn, 2004). An analysis of this literature showed that most of these programmes are based upon either the functionalistic (Schmikl, 2003) or humanistic (Pretorius, 2004) views on organisational behaviour. The functionalistic view (Morgan, 1980) approaches change in a normative, concrete, tangible, regulative, ordered, structured and pragmatic manner, with the focus on policy, structure, and quickly removing the symptoms of discomfort. This view is mechanistic in its measurement of expected outcomes (Schmikl, 2003) while prescribing expected behaviours to employees. The humanistic view (Quitmann, 1985; Schneider, Bugental & Pierson, 2001) approaches change in a sensitive manner, with the focus on the individual and the group, its humility, integrity, respect and shared values (Pretorius, 2004). This orientation is seen as positive (Snyder & Lopez, 2002) in its focus on growth towards self-actualisation, awareness about choices and interpersonal effectiveness (Rogers, 1975; 1982) and more dynamic (than the first) in the sense that human interaction during the process of change, as well as individual coping skills, are valued (Bergh & Theron, 1999). If organisational change is to be defined and approached as a whole system phenomenon (Sperry, 2004), it could be said that both the above views fail in addressing organisational change effectively. According to Kets de Vries (1991) and Miller (1993) the functionalistic view stimulates dependence on outside authority, which is experienced as disempowering by most employees.

The Systems Psychodynamic Stance

Argued from the assumptions of the systems psychodynamic stance, the above-mentioned views on leadership during organisational change oversimplify organisational behaviour. It denies the complexity of organisational systemic functioning, its deep struggle with change and the expectancy that leadership will contain the anxiety and defensive reactions, such as resistance, denial and projection (Menzies, 1993; Miller, 1976; 1993; Neumann, Kellner & Dawson- Shepherd, 1997; Obholzer & Roberts, 1994; Huffington et al., 2004). Furthermore, it makes no provision for the complex and dynamic relationship between on the one hand strategy, structure (Miller, Kets de Vries & Toulouse, 1982) and organisational culture (Kets de Vries, 1989, 1991; Zaleznik & Kets de Vries, 1980) and on the other hand the personality of the top leader (Jaques, 1951, 1970; Kernberg, 1979; Kets de Vries, 1980; 1984, Zaleznik & Kets de Vries, 1980). It is hypothesised that the traditional views towards change management defend against organisational complexity by framing leadership and its role in change in mechanistic terms, and contains the anxiety in structured inputs and recipes – as if coping with change manifests similarly in all organisational systems and personality plays no role in the behavioural process.

The systems psychodynamic stance originated at the Tavistock Institute in the UK (Miller, 1989; 1993) and incorporates Freudian system psychoanalysis, the work of Klein on child and family psychology, Ferenczi on object relations and Bertalanffy on systems thinking (Colman & Bexton, 1975; Colman & Geller, 1985; Czander, 1993; De Board, 1978; Gould, Stapley & Stein, 2004; Hirshhorn, 1993; Hugg, Carson & Lipgar, 1993; Kernberg, 1979). The stance has been used in group relations working conferences for over 50 years (Cytrynbaum & Lee, 1993), and it developed into an organisational theory (Bion, 1961; 1970; Miller, 1976; 1983; 1993) as well as an organisational consultancy stance (Gabelnick & Carr, 1989; Neumann et al., 1997).

Research on leadership during organisational change using this stance was reported by Gould, Stapley and Stein (2004), Haslebo and Nielsen (2000), Kets de Vries (1991), Klein (2005), Lawrence (2000), Menzies (1993), Miller (1993), Obholzer and Roberts (1994). The findings indicate that employees, managers and leaders have insight into the organisation in terms of its complex inter-related systems, understand its unconscious manifestations of change behaviour (e.g. resistance to change because of past experiences and pain), have acquired a dynamic and pro-active change coping style, and realise the role of the leader in containing anxiety and giving authorisation. The concept and role of the leader are used here to refer to any person in an appointed position of authority, such as a manager, executive or CEO (as defined by Miller, 1993). Although the literature refers to the culture and fantasies associated with organisational change, limited reference is made to the dynamic leader and team behaviour manifesting during organisational change.

The Systems Psychodynamic Leadership Style Typology

The leadership typology used in this research was developed by Kets de Vries (1991), based on the work by Shapiro (1965). It was intended for use by organisational consultants to study a range of unobserved and frequently related organisational behavioural manifestations, in order to consider appropriate change interventions. This typology enjoys face validity and is highly regarded amongst the systems psychodynamic fraternity (Czander, 1993; Gould, Stapley & Stein, 2001; Merry & Brown, 1990; Miller, 1993; Stapley, 1996). Unfortunately, the work was not explored in his further publications (e.g. Kets de Vries, 2001; 2005). It is therefore not sure whether the typology applies in the post-modern, new economy world of work and the complex demands on leadership and followership to change, especially in the South African political and social change scenario. In this research the typology is extended into the domain of leadership's relatedness with team behaviour.

Shapiro (1965) argued that everyone has a specific way of thinking, perceiving and experiencing emotion. These are modes of subjective experience in general and modes of activity that are associated with various pathologies. The individual's way of dealing with the environment and deeply embedded patterns are likely to endure. He referred to the fantasies that make up the individual's inner world, defined as the stereotyped, well-rehearsed, constantly repeated ways of behaving and acting that determine the individual's cognitive and affective behaviour. According to Kets de Vries (1991), human functioning is generally characterised by a mixture of styles derived from these fantasies. The same individual may possess elements of many different styles, each of which is triggered by different circumstances. Among a group of individuals, however, one specific style will dominate and consistently come to the fore in situations of change. Extreme manifestations of any one style can signal significant psychopathology that seriously impairs functioning (Freedman, Kaplan & Sadock, 1975; Nivid, Rathus & Greene, 2003).

According to Kets de Vries (1991) all organisations contain a mixture of these personality styles (where personality is seen as a large system phenomenon – see Stapley, 1996), which characterise and motivate organisational behaviour. The more centralised the organisation in terms of decision-making power being in the hands of either a top leader or a small, homogeneous, dominant coalition, the more pronounced and purer the personality type of the leader. The more power the leader has, the greater impact this personality style (in terms of fantasy and neurotic style) will have on structure, culture and strategy. Where power is broadly distributed throughout the organisation, its culture and strategies will be determined by many leaders. Also, then the relationship between style and organisational pathology becomes more complex. Although neurotic styles can have an impact at all levels of the organisation, it is easier to start with the understanding of leadership behaviour. Typically, top leaders show resistance to change, especially when they hold very powerful positions.

Research Approach

Research Design

Many times, adapting to change in the organisation would only occur after dramatic failure has eroded the power base of the top leader, or when he/she is replaced by another person (Merry & Brown, 1990).

It seems that the stable and global psychological orientations of the organisation's leader(s) are major determinants of the 'neurotic styles' of the organisation (Klein, 1948; Mahler, Pine & Bergman, 1975; Sandler & Rosenblatt, 1962). The leader creates shared fantasies that permeate all levels, influence organisational culture, and underlie a dominant organisational adaptive style (Kernberg, 1976). This style again influences decisions about strategy and structure (Kets de Vries & Miller, 1984a; 1984b; 1984c; 1987). Parallels can be drawn between common neurotic styles or dysfunctions of behaviour and common modes of organisational failure and pathological organisational styles. (Organisational pathology does not necessarily require the leader to exhibit these neurotic styles – some organisations might manifest such styles for completely different reasons.)

A number of common, well established organisational fantasies and neurotic styles have been identified (Merry & Brown, 1990; Nicholi, 1988; Shapiro, 1965; Sperry, 2004), based on personality disorders as defined in the Diagnostic and Statistical Manual of Mental Disorders (DSM 1V:TR) (American Psychiatric Association, 2000). This included hypotheses about each style's predominant motivating fantasy, its emerging organisational culture, and the manifesting strategy and structure of the organisation. The study of these styles in organisational context, becomes quite complex because of its dynamic nature. Kets de Vries (1991) hypothesised that movement across organisational styles often occur depending on who is in power and the stage of the organisation's life cycle. The style of the leader may also become modified through interactions with the evolving organisation. The more extreme the style manifests in a leader and team, the more pathological the behaviour. Furthermore, a mutual causation exists – the personality of the leader can influence the organisation, and vice versa. For example, an organisation that fails in reaching its goals and feels disappointment can cause a leader to become depressed, and competition in the system can stimulate the leader's paranoia.

The Five Organisational Constellations/leadership Styles

Kets de Vries (1991) and Shapiro (1965) identified for each organisational constellation, a leadership style, culture and fantasy, namely:

1. The paranoid style and culture are suspicious and the fantasy about persecution.
2. The schizoid style is detached, the culture politicised and the fantasy about detachment.
3. The depressive style is dependent, the culture avoiding and the fantasy about helplessness.
4. The compulsive style is rigid, the culture bureaucratic and the fantasy about control.
5. The histrionic style is dramatic and narcissistic, the culture charismatic and the fantasy about grandiosity.

Research Question and Aim

The research question was formulated as: Given the five organisational constellations and leadership styles above, what are the typical system psychodynamic behaviour manifesting amongst each leadership style and team during organisational change? The aim was to explore the nature of the dynamic behaviour of each of these styles between the leader and the team during organisational change.

The design was qualitative, explorative and descriptive in nature (Higgs & Smith, 2003).

Research Methodology

Participants

Eight psychologists were chosen who regularly consult to organisations undergoing change. They were all trained in the systems psychodynamic stance (the Tavistock group relations model).

Data Collection Technique

Focus groups were used, defined as a carefully planned and organised discussion designed to obtain perceptions on a defined area of interest in a permissive, non-threatening environment, by a selected group of participants sharing and responding to views, experiences, ideas, feelings and perceptions (Brewerton & Millward, 2004; Litosseliti, 2003). Its purpose is to gain information, perspectives and empirical field texts about a specific research topic, and its rationale is to provide a socially-oriented interaction, similar to a real life situation, where participants freely influence one another, build on one another's responses and thus stimulate a collective and synergistically generated thought, feeling and experience.

Data Collection and Analysis Procedure

Two 120-minute focus groups with the researcher in the role of facilitator were conducted. Each session started with a brief overview of the organisational constellations and leadership styles. The task of the group was to generate answers to the following question: 'In your experience as a psychologist and consultant to organisations undergoing change, what specific systems psychodynamic behaviour do you see manifesting within and between each leadership style and its team'. Both sessions were tape recorded and the content transcribed. The data analysis procedure and interpretation were done according to the systems psychodynamic stance (Clarkson & Nuttall, 2000; Czander, 1993; Hirschhorn, 1993). The procedure comprised firstly, of reading through of all responses a couple of times for familiarisation. Secondly, the responses were read through again according to Schafer's (1970) systems psychodynamic interpretive stance. Thirdly, the responses were categorised into cognitive, affective, motivational, interpersonal and leader-team behaviour. To ensure trustworthiness (as defined by Camic, Rhodes & Yardley, 2003), the interpreted findings were discussed with half of the participants and their suggestions were incorporated into the findings.

Findings

The following leader and team behaviours were identified. For each style the characteristics of the leaders are given in terms of cognitive, affective, motivational and interpersonal behaviour, followed by the nature of the leader-team relationship (which is presented in a free-flowing narrative manner). (For the sake of convenience, the leader will be referred to in the masculine singular – he/him/his, and the team in the plural.)

The Paranoid Style

Characteristics of the Leader

1. **Cognitive behaviour.** He has a narrow attention span; uses facts to confirm his own worst expectations; is inclined to misread or distort facts.

2. **Affective behaviour.** He experiences fear (real or fantasised) and acts defensively towards his own fragility; denies the needs for change; is compulsive and rigid; has a strong need to control which may manifest in thought and action; is afraid to confront change because of the risk for exposure it holds; splits change into good and bad parts; then he becomes suspicious and blames something or someone (as the enemy); sometimes this enemy becomes larger in his own head; he distrusts anything new such as change initiatives; experiences anger, hostility and envy, while at the same time appearing cold and unemotional to others.

3. **Motivational behaviour.** He acts on his guard; protect his own boundaries; makes plans to attack the real or imagined secretive object that represent change (in order to counter any perceived threats); he has to keep the enemy at bay; is preoccupied with hidden motives and special meanings; minor issues become magnified; to have an enemy implies that everything needs to be done correctly; he does not allow himself to make mistakes.

4. **Interpersonal behaviour.** He acts with intensity; is hypersensitive and hyper-alert; is mistrustful and envious; takes offence easily; expects deception; he may be very careful to hire, reward or promote any idea or person.

Leader-team Relationship

Although some suspicion in a work situation is good (for example to be aware of behavioural dynamics in the system), he brings the suspicion towards change into the team which leads to distrust; it jeopardises intra team relationships; the result is that team members feel unsafe, distrustful and un-contained; he directs his suspicion towards any object or person within or without the boundary of the team; his need is to seek for and to label an instigator of change outside of himself; he experiences change as being forced down from a powerful force outside of himself or even the team; he shows resistance towards change and what it represents; then he fights any change object and projects his fear and anxiety onto objects that represent the change for him (such as management, the union, the board, the government, the economy); he becomes the carrier of the suspicion which implies that others don't have to carry it; he acts it out on behalf of the others (such as his team); he transfers and injects his suspicion onto and into the team; which the team experiences intensely; he may then even use this team experience as evidence of paranoia in the system (as if he was not the originator and instigator); the team fears him – they feel the criticism; they feel not good-enough to live up to his requirements and expectations; sometimes he becomes depressed to the extent that the team has to take care of him emotionally; thus the team becomes the container of his anxiety; he generates competition with a strong element of fear; team members fear being 'stabbed from and in the back'; he sets himself up to continuously check out the competition; this leads to the team becoming more defensive and then they compensate by working harder to show him that he has reason to trust them; this consumes unnecessary psychological energy; he is giving the message that no one is good-enough; this view is based on his fear that someone just may be good-enough or just better than himself; his script is 'maybe you are better than me and that would be terrible'; his role becomes to ensure that no one in the team or no other team is better; often he would do an environment scan ('like a "verspieder" in an army') to inform the team what is going on, who the enemy is, who is worse off; he handles the politics and fighting on behalf of the team and thus becomes the container of the survival anxiety, leaving the team members to be free of that role; the team could easily fall apart under this anxiety; next the relationships across the team boundary (such as with other managers, leaders, teams) suffer; his fear is projected across the boundary onto and sometimes into other departments (projective identification).

The Schizoid Style

Characteristics of the Leader

1. **Cognitive behaviour**. His cognitive deficits lead to poor performance; he is more interested in politics and social issues than work issues.
2. **Affective behaviour**. He is emotionally bland and schizoid; he has an inability to express enthusiasm and pleasure; his emotional deficits (such as fear) lead to a lack of concern and caring; he is cold and aloof; often bored; he defends against his hurt by isolating himself.
3. **Motivational behaviour**. He is unavailable; tries to avoid; does not show interest in the daily work routine.
4. **Interpersonal behaviour**. He fears being and feels rejected; he defends against the pain of rejection by keeping to himself; he seems to ignore the outside world,

its demands and needs for change; he has little need to communicate; he avoids closeness; seems distant, hesitant, detached, withdrawn, uninvolved, unconcerned, mistrustful and unresponsive; he believes that interactions will harm him or they will fail; he acts indifferently to praise and to criticism; he seems unable to engage in reciprocal relationships.

Leader-team Relationship

He is better at managing individuals (which he may do with some warmth) than the team; 'he is not a team player'; managing the team (or collective behaviour) is difficult for him because of its complexity; he isolates himself; he creates a sense of absence, detachment, withdrawal, avoidance and passivity; he creates an impression of incompetence in terms of not producing or having effective relationships; he does not link rationally with the team, yet he sometimes links emotionally and experientially; this means that he does not speak out or address change issues; he makes or initiates no plans for change; takes no responsibility except perhaps when he can personally gain from the venture; the result is often that the group creates fantasies about what is going on; even about their performance, future and careers; in this manner he hold some power over others (even if it is by avoidance and withholding); he fears group pressure; he mistrust the team; he alienates team members from himself and from one another; he injects fear onto and into the team; the team members realise that he is not performing well; yet they keep supporting him because of the (sometimes fantasised) emotional link; he may in a manipulative way set up a shadow leader or sub-team to manage the work as well as the relationships as in building trust, facilitating meaning and hope on his behalf; this is convenient for him as a cop-out, but the danger is that the shadow has no official authority to act on behalf of others; this could even lead to this individual or sub-system 'falling on its face' and 'burn its fingers'; this implies a (not consciously planned) set-up by the leader; leading to a split in leadership with some members experiencing being close to him while others feel excluded; this can also manifest in some people having resources (such as knowledge, power) and some not; dynamically this means that one part contains the power, knowledge and trust, while the other contains the not knowing, dis-empowerment and distrust; the team does not identify with the leader and what he represents; the team feels ashamed when he represents them across the team boundary; the team climate is one of limited interaction, cohesion and trust.

The Depressive Style

Characteristics of the Leader

1. **Cognitive behaviour.** He shows a lack of ability and talent; he sees the organisation as a machine; he feeds the team with routine input; there is a sense of futility; he reduces his own contributions to the minimum required; he is negative and lethargic.

2. **Affective behaviour.** He has low self-esteem and confidence; feels worthless, insecure, inadequate, powerless, inferior, incapacitated, incompetent, helplessness, angry and guilty; doubts and downgrades himself; contains the not good enough in the system; practices a type of moral masochism (hostility turned inward); feels lonely, not loved and liked; experiences pain as a redemptive act; sees defeat as a just reward; he fears change and denies its need and reason.

3. **Motivational behaviour.** He is passive and acts purposeless; abdicates most of his responsibilities; comes across as helplessness and hopelessness; will combat his insecurity through external sources; submerges his own individuality; acts rigidly and makes use of routines and rituals even when he is in trouble; resists change in policy, as well as planning; sees change efforts as hopeless, not adding value ('it has not worked in the past, why will it now?'); experiences a lack of power to change; puts structures in place to not transform because he does not have enough energy and ego strength to cope with and contain its demands; when requested to implement change he will postpone the demand; when forced to implement change he may put in place an unimaginative and mechanical plan, without believing in it, and causing its failure; he is in competition with change.

4. **Interpersonal behaviour.** He is very dependent on the team to assume the responsibility; experiences strong needs for affection, to being nurtured and protected; he shows a wariness towards others; can adapt his behaviour to please others; his reactions may stem from unpleasant past relationships; his subordinates may lose their sense of control, authority, self-esteem, initiative and become unmotivated; he is emotionally and/or physically absent and unmotivated; he passively waits for others to change and then idealise those who do change; he can be mean to others behind their backs if they upset the status quo or work against him.

Leader-team Relationship

He experiences the team members not liking him; his own anger leads to confusion in the team; he denies change ('I'm so depressed, I cannot think about this now, or spend energy on this'); the denial of change in his own life, his depressed state and lack of energy to embrace change leads to him dumping (projecting the anxiety thereof) on the team; he is competitive believing that 'if I don't get ahead, nobody will get ahead'; he often refers to how unreachable change is or how unready the workforce is; this confuses the team to such an extent that they may act out his anger and guilt; because of his lack of energy and depression, the team may start looking after him, giving him support, caring and nurturing; it is as if the team is taking on his paranoid thoughts (that forms part of his depression); this leaves the team with his projected sadness, helplessness and hopelessness - a projective identification; this keeps the system stuck which could be seen as a self-fulfilling prophecy of his own incompetence and negative beliefs about change; if he is clever enough to work beyond the depression and get into a caring position, the energy may be used to cope with change; normally the realisation comes too late, for example after the change should have been implemented already.

The Compulsive Style

Characteristics of the Leader

1. **Cognitive behaviour.** He is industrious and indecisive; rigid in thinking and problem solving
2. **Affective behaviour.** He is unrestful; acts out his anxiety in a compulsive and repetitive manner; fears making mistakes and being at the mercy of events outside of his control; is upset by unfamiliar situations and events; has strong needs for control, perfection, order, familiarity and efficiency; revels in this anal behaviour; experiences high levels of anxiety when he has to invent something new or deviate from the known; he denies himself pleasure; uses work as defence to feel good and in control; even more so when his stress level is high.
3. **Motivational behaviour.** He counteracts his fear by a preoccupation to master and control events; focuses on routine, repetition and his own set ways, detail, rules and regulations; for him form is more important than substance; he lacks spontaneity; is devoted to his work; may procrastinate outcomes; is preoccupied with success because of strong fear of failure; denies himself the pleasure of change.
4. **Interpersonal behaviour.** He acts deferentially to superiors, sometimes also with submission; is autocratic and dominant towards subordinates; demanding that they work according to his way.

Leader-team Relationship

He regularly confronts himself in a masochistic manner, but he does not own the pain involved – he rather projects this on the team; this lack of owning means that he finds it extreme difficulty to change anything in himself, in the team or the larger organisational system; he can be sadistic in getting back at the team in case of high stress levels and if they disobey his demands and requirements; this happens because he is inclined to operate more cognitive than affective; is less open for projections from the team; when he plans for change he does so well in advance, making sure that he understands it, that it makes sense and represents good management; he finds simple tasks easy and complexity anxiety provoking; his plans for change are mechanistic, controlled, detailed, sometimes far-fetched and unreal; he over-structures as a fight reaction (changing structures such as organigrams, job descriptions); blames management and other authority figures for the uncertainty; the structuring makes him feel in control; thus, he does not have to deal with difficult feelings, conflicts, complexity and chaos in his relationships; he may use change to suit himself while not having strong concerns about the team; he passively resists change, as long as he doesn't have to change any behaviour in himself; team members experience his style as enforced, controlled, bureaucratic, dis- empowering and frustrating; it allows them less opportunity for creativity, autonomy and ownership; if he owns the control, none is left for the team to work with; it seems as if the more he controls, the more the rebelliousness in the team will come to the fore; being so effective as a leader stimulates the "not good enough" in the team; he may be easily seduced by the team's positive feedback; then he may take responsibility for not finishing a task because of his need to always be perfect; he can be quite successful in tasks where little emotions and their containment are involved; also when he can trust the team and delegate authority clearly; his attention to detail can be very helpful in the team.

The Histrionic Style

Characteristics of the Leader

1. **Cognitive behaviour.** He struggles with concentration and alternate between extremes of idealisation and devaluation.
2. **Affective behaviour.** He experiences emotions very intensely (from excitement to anger and rage); he acts impulsively and panicky; he idolises himself.
3. **Motivational behaviour.** He acts out (sometimes overreact) in a narcissistic, grandiose, dramatic, immature, exhibitionistic manner with strong emotion; has a strong need for attention, to look good, to be in the limelight, to impress, be accepted; he prefers action, excitement and stimulation, often without substance or self-discipline.
4. **Interpersonal behaviour.** He has a strong need for attention and to impress others; exaggerates especially about his talents and achievements; does not allow resistance or dissent from subordinates easily; need to impress and get attention; can be (although superficially) warm and charming; yet he comes across as insincere, inconsiderate, exploitative, lacking empathy and taking others for granted; has unstable relationships and often attracts dependent personalities; wants quick decisions, reactions and results.

Leader-team Relationship

He has an idealised and unrealistic concept of change; this acts as a defence against his resistance to change because of his natural high level of anxiety and his panic reactions; when he does plan for change his efforts are grandiose and charismatic (such as 'putting the best ever programme on the table, better than any competitor and everybody must love it!'); he needs to impress authority figures; yet his efforts are superficial (not authentic) and shallow; his impulsive, panicky and exhibitionistic behaviour is accompanied by his demanding quick results from the team; this again may result in the team making mistakes; he needs to look good and to impress others, be in limelight; he is self-absorbed; from this narcissism and self-protection position, he demands credit for implementing change as if he is the sole actor in the change drama; he acts for the sake of acting and own survival and not for the sake of change; he is emotionally not available for the team (because of his obsession with himself); takes up most of the available energy for change; does not care about the team; does not act as a container for the team to explore options; his immaturity leads to him doing all the work himself; needs to look active and busy; often he loses energy by attending to more fluff than essence; is insincere in his motives; often introduces and enforces change with little planning; thus he politically manipulates and seduces others and off-loads his anxiety; he projects his incompetence onto the team in order for him to look good; he positions himself to be the saviour; his change initiatives have a destabilising effect; it incapacitates the team; even 'sadistically killing them off in order to be the king'; internally he has little interest in the change or empathy towards the team members; he gets frustrated and angry when team members offer first or 'better' solutions for change; his narcissism inhibits him from letting others flourish or succeed; he gets stuck in his own dependency; he knows he can't do the task alone and then manipulates others to do it (while not having enough resources); this makes his predictions true of 'I told you it was impossible to do'.

Discussion

The findings showed that each organisational constellation and leadership style reacts in a distinctly different manner to organisational change:

> The paranoid style approaches change with suspicion, distrust and blaming. The leader projects fear, suspicion and competition about change onto and into the team; the team experiences themselves as not being good enough to handle and implement change; in order to not fall apart, the team works harder in a pseudo competition to succeed and convince leadership that the work is successful; this dynamic can also cross the boundary into other teams or departments in the organisation.

The schizoid style approaches change with detachment, avoidance and withdrawal. The leader does not make contact with the team; he introjects fear, mistrust and isolation into the team; the team needs to make assumptions and fantasies about their roles, tasks and performance; the team is set up to do the work alone and to even support the leader in his emotional absence; the team struggles to identify with and feel proud of their leader.

The depressive style approaches change with dependence and helplessness. The leader is passive, unmotivated and feels rejected; he projects confusion onto and into the team; the team easily identifies with his projected feelings leading to anger, shame, guilt and sadness and feeling ashamed of the leader.

The compulsive style approaches change with mechanistic structure and control. The leader passively resists change initiatives by over structuring and controlling the planning and implementing of change in order to feel safe; he ensures that change is designed neatly and mechanistically according to his own ideas and needs; he avoids complexity and own involvement in change; the team experience being forced into the leader's views and actions, which is frustrating and disempowering; the team has no opportunity for autonomy or creativity.

The histrionic style approaches change with grandiosity to impress others. The leader may refer to his good efforts but it may not have substance; change efforts are idealised and unrealistic; his narcissism leads to him doing the work alone, leaving the team with little to think about or do; the team does not experience being contained by the leader; they feel seduced and manipulated into making the leader look good.

The findings supported Kets de Vries' typology in terms of the profound effect of the leader in determining the organisational culture (as the personality of the organisation – Stapley, 1996), and furthermore indicated the leader's influential role on the team's dynamic functioning relating to change. Based on these findings, the following hypothesis about leadership dynamics during change was presented (as the concept was defined by Haslebo & Nielsen, 2000):

> The leader's construct of leadership is based upon his past experiences in general and specifically with significant authority figures as role models. These experiences were ingrained into his personality – the conscious as well as the unconscious, deeply embedded patterns, needs and fantasies – from where his cognitive, affective and motivational behaviour originate and which become visible in his stereotyped, well-rehearsed, constantly repeated ways of behaving and acting.

Because of the inherent anxiety associated with change, the team is more than naturally dependent on the leader for the direction, management and containment of its primary task, including its cognitive, affective, motivational and interpersonal behaviour.

The leader crosses the interpersonal boundary (also with its inherent anxiety) into the space and realm of the team, bringing in his inner world as an individual as well as his authority and style as leader, it being paranoid, schizoid, depressive, compulsive or histrionic.

In the dynamic relationship between leader and team, the leader influences the team's relatedness with change as an object representing the unknown. The leader functioning purely and for a long time in any of the above five leadership styles, will not provide the necessary containment for the team to engage with change in a constructive and productive manner.

This scenario keeps the team at an impasse in terms of planning and implementing change, which is characterised by a phobic attitude of avoidance and incapability to break out of its catatonic paralysis into new possibilities of the fertile void (see Merry & Brown, 1990).

Leadership style in itself and its deconstructive effect on the team becomes the defence against change and the unconscious collusion towards the implementation of change management initiatives (see De Jager, Cilliers & Veldsman, 2004).

Recommendations

Linking the findings to the literature review, the following recommendations were formulated in order to assist the psychologist in understanding and implementing organisational change effectively.

If all organisations cope with change, similarly, implementing change management from the outside by introducing a grand plan for structural changes and re-engineering the business, may not lead to insight and understanding of the dynamic behaviour around change and the successful implementation of a change management programme.

Change from within, assuming that each organisation, its leadership's and team's coping with change is unique, complex and largely influenced by the personality and interactional style of the leader as conceptualised within the systems psychodynamic stance, would lead to in-depth insight into and understanding of the dynamic behaviour around change (see Obholzer & Roberts, 1994).

The change management consultant does not act as the change guru, helping leadership to control change and to change the team directly. Instead, the consultant would work with the processes of change. The purpose of the consultation is to find ways of creating new contexts, for people to claim ownership of new ideas and to investigate possibilities to incorporate them into existing relationships (Haslebo & Nielsen, 2000).

These new contexts are co-created in a series of well-planned and structured sessions which acts as containment for, firstly, understanding own dynamics and, secondly, leading to implementing change initiatives. Inclusiveness is practised by consulting to the whole system, for example, the leader with his/her team or subsections thereof (see Wells, 1980).

During the sessions, the consultant engages in an analysis of what change means for the system and what such experiences it has had in the past, and what the anticipated gains and losses are (see Campbell, 1995). On a more abstract level, the consultant engages in an analysis of the interrelationships of the primary task, boundaries, roles and role configurations, structure, organisational design, work culture and group processes (Miller, 1993; Neumann et al.,1997). Overt and covert dynamics and social anxieties (Menzies, 1993; Obholzer & Roberts, 1994) are interpreted as it manifests between the leader and the team in the here-and-now of the consultation, for example the relatedness between objects and its boundary management (see Lawrence, 199), its representative value and how authority is psychologically distributed, exercised and enacted, in contrast to how it is formally invested. This implies the study of the emotional task of the leader and the team which is inherently filled with chaos, a lack of control and difficult experiences such as competition, rivalry, jealousy, envy, hate and aggression (Miller, 1976; 1993). As a result, leadership becomes difficult if not impossible especially if the leader gets caught up in the 'change missionary position' (French & Vince, 1999). Hirschhorn (1997) referred to the difference between the leader as person (the need for vulnerability) and the leader as role (the need for organisational authority) which needs to be worked with and integrated.

French and Vince (1999) referred to the dynamic in change management as working from envy to desire as an integral part of the constructive and destructive processes underlying organisational life in these difficult times. If the desire to change is too strong, it becomes destructive to creativity. If desire is too weak, the system becomes stagnant. The consultant then assists the leader and team to work on balancing the desire for change. Envy, on the other hand, harbours destruction because it contains anger and hate. It is defined as the desire to break down something good, simply because it is good and does not belong to the self (Huffington et al., 2004). Envy has an inherent projective nature and is connected to narcissism and guilt. If the leader is overwhelmed by the envy, he/

she is placed in a position of omnipotence, continually imposing on others a guilt-engendering point of reference which again has an impact on the whole team. The activity of holding, exercised through this implosion of the leader's ego ideal, impedes the working of desire within the team. Then the team lives under the illusion that it can only change through the action of the leader. Thus, the unconscious dynamics of desire and envy needs to be processed with the leader and team in order to move beyond these stumbling blocks towards change.

If the leader's behaviour and its effect on the team are not addressed during change initiatives, the system will stay in the social unconscious (Hopper, 2003). This means that it will exist as a constraint of social, cultural and communicational arrangements of which the system (the leader, the team and the organisation) is unaware – unaware in so far as these behaviours are not perceived (not known), and if perceived not acknowledged (denied), and if acknowledged, not taken as problematic (given), and if taken as problematic, not considered with an optional degree of detachment and objectivity.

Another model to be used is the CIBART (Cilliers & Koortzen, in press) which offers a systematic and diagnostic way to work through the system's (individual, leadership and team) dynamic behaviour, namely its conflicts, identity, boundaries, authority, roles and tasks. This endeavours to help the leader to be more 'psychologically present' (Hirsschhorn, 1997) in his managing of the boundaries with his followers.

The ideal outcome would be for the system (the leader and the team) to realise the leader's significant position to serve as a role model in culture and team-building. Therein, the focus is on pointing out the relevance of the team as a whole (consisting of individual members and subgroups, each with a unique contribution), to identify emergent processes as they take shape and to refer back to the team's cultural articulations in times of crises and opportunity, thereby acknowledging a shared history while fostering institutional memory and encouraging further transformations (Lipgar & Pines, 2003).

On a meta-level it is important to remember the notion of homeostasis (see Campbell, 1995) which could be an indication of wellness. Therefore, the consultation endeavours to balance change and stability, care and control, conflict and collaboration, and to develop a spirit of enquiry (Cilliers, 2004; Obholzer & Roberts, 1994).

More research is needed to determine the effect of the different leadership styles in different organisations and scenarios.

References

American Psychiatric Association. (2000). *Diagnostic and Statistical Manual of Mental Disorders (DSM 1V:TR). (4th Ed.) Text Revision.* Washington: American Psychiatric Association.

Bergh, Z.C. & Theron, A.L. (1999). *Psychology in the work context.* Johannesburg: International Thompson. https://doi.org/10.1037/001990

Bion, W.R. (1961). *Experiences in Groups.* London: Tavistock Publications.

Bion, W.R. (1970). *Attention and interpretation.* London: Tavistock Publications.

Brewerton, P. & Millward, L. (2004). *Organisational research methods. A guide for students and researchers.* London: Sage.

Camic, P.M.; Rhodes, J.E. & Yardley, L. (2003). *Qualitative research in psychology.* Washington: APA.

Campbell, D. (1995). *Learning consultation. A systemic framework.* London: Karnac.

Cilliers, F. (2004). *Organisational wellness conceptualised from the systems psychodynamic paradigm.* 2nd South African Work Wellness Conference, North-West University, Potchefstroom.

Cilliers, F & Koortzen, P. (in press). *The CIBART model of organisational diagnosis.*

Colman, A.D. & Bexton, W.H. (1975). *Group Relations Reader 1.* Jupiter: The A.K. Rice Institute.

Colman, A.D. & Geller, M.H. (1985). *Group Relations Reader 2.* Jupiter: The A.K. Rice Institute.

Cytrynbaum, S. & Lee, S.A. (1993). *Transformations in global and organizational systems.* Jupiter: A.K. Rice Institute.

Czander, W.M. (1993). *The psychodynamics of work and organizations.* New York: Guilford Press.

De Board, R. (1978). *The psychoanalysis of organisations.* London: Routledge. https://doi.org/10.4324/9780203321812

De Jager, W.; Cilliers, F. & Veldsman, T. (2004). Leadership development from a systems psychodynamic consultancy stance. *SA Journal of Human Resource Management,* 1(3):85-92. https://doi.org/10.4102/sajhrm.v1i3.23

Drucker, P. (2004). Leadership. The new economy and Shakespeare. *Management Today,* 20(3):6.

Ellis, L. (2004). Would you follow me. Developing effective leadership behaviour. *Management Today,* 20(8):32.

Freedman, A.M.; Kaplan, H.J. & Sadock, B.J. (1975). *Comprehensive Textbook of Psychiatry.* 1&2. Baltimore: Williams & Wilkins.

French, R. & Vince, R. (1999). *Group relations, management and organisation.* New York: Oxford.

Gabelnick, F. & Carr, A.W. (1989). *Contributions to social and political science.* Jupiter: A.K. Rice Institute.

Gould, L.J.; Stapley, L.F. & Stein, M. (2001). *The systems psychodynamics of organisations.* London: Karnac.

Gould, L.J., Stapley, L.F. & Stein, M. (2004). *Experiential learning in organisations. Applications of the Tavistock group relations approach.* London: Karnac.

Guiliani, R. (2004). Leadership. Six skills to become a strong leader. *Management Today,* 20(9):6-7. https://doi.org/10.1002/ltl.72

Haslebo, G. & Nielsen, K.S. (2000). *Systems and meaning. Consulting in organisations.* London: Karnac.

Hirschhorn, L. (1993). *The Workplace Within: psychodynamics of organizational life.* Cambridge: MIT Press.

Hirschhorn, L. (1997). *Reworking authority. Leading and following in the post-modern organisation.* London: MIT Press.

Holburn, P. (2003). The work of leadership in unpredictable times. *Management Today,* 19(9):16-17.

Hopper, E. (2003). *The social unconscious. Selected papers.* London: Jessica Kingsley.

Horth, D.M. (2003). Leadership. Competencies for navigating complex challenges. *Management Today,* 19(10):4-6.

Huffington, C.; Armstrong, A.; Halton, W.; Hoyle, L. & Pooley, J. (2004). *Working below the surface. The emotional life of contemporary organisations.* London: Karnac.

Hugg, T.W.; Carson, N.M. & Lipgar, R.M. (1993). *Changing group relations. The next twenty-five years in America.* Jupiter: A K Rice Institute.

Jaques, E. (1951). *The changing culture of a factory.* London: Tavistock.

Jaques, E. (1970). *Work, creativity and social justice.* New York: International Universities Press.

Kemp, N. & De Villiers, B. (2004). The language of transformation. *Management Today,* 20(2):34.

Kernberg, O. (1976). *Borderline conditions and pathological narcissism.* New York: Aronson.

Kernberg, O. (1979). *Object relations theory and clinical psychoanalysis.* New York: Aronson.

Kets de Vries, M. F. R. (1980). *Organizational paradoxes: Clinical approaches to management.* London: Tavistock.

Kets de Vries, M.F.R. (1984). *The irrational executive: Psychoanalytic studies in management.* New York: International Universities Press.

Kets de Vries, M.F.R. (1989). *Prisoners of leadership.* New York: Wiley.

Kets De Vries, M.F.R. (1991). *Organizations on the Couch: Handbook of Psychoanalysis and Management.* New York: Jossey-Bass.

Kets De Vries, M.F.R. (2001). *The leadership mystique. A user's manual for the human enterprise.* London: Prentice-Hall.

Kets De Vries, M.F.R. (2005). Characteristics of effective leadership. *Management Today,* 20(10):14-16.

Kets de Vries, M.F.R. & Miller, D. (1984a). Group fantasies and organizational functioning. *Human Relations,* 37:111-134. https://doi.org/10.1177/001872678403700201

Kets de Vries, M.F.R. & Miller, D. (1984b). *The neurotic organization: Diagnosing and changing counterproductive styles of management.* San Francisco: Jossey Bass.

Kets de Vries, M. F. R. & Miller, D. (1984c). Neurotic style and organizational pathology. *Strategic Management Journal,* 5:35-55. https://doi.org/10.1002/smj.4250050104

Kets de Vries, M.F.R. & Miller, D. (1987). *Unstable at the top: Inside the troubled organization.* New York: New American Library.

Khambula, C. (2003). Leadership is as much a community activity as a business one. *Management Today,* 19(9):12-13.

Klein, L. (2005). *Working across the gap. The practice of social science in organisations.* London: Karnac.

Klein, M. (1948). *Contributions to psychoanalysis, 1921-1945.* London: Hogarth Press.

Kotter, J. (2003). Leading change. What leaders really do. *Management Today,* 19(3):4-7.

Lawrence, W.G. (1999). *Exploring individual and organisational boundaries. A Tavistock open systems approach.* London: Karnac.

Lawrence W.G. (2000). *Tongued with fire. Groups in experience.* London: Karnac.

Lipgar, R.M. & Pines, M. (2003). *Building on Bion: Branches.* London: Jessica Kingsley.

Litosseliti, L. (2003). *Using focus groups in research.* London: Continuum.

Mahler, M.S.; Pine, F. & Bergman, A. (1975). *The psychological birth of the human infant.* New York: Basic Books.

Makwana, M. (2003). True leadership. Leading with the heart of a servant. *Management Today,* 19(9):10.

Menzies, I.E.P. (1993). *The functioning of social systems as a defence against anxiety.* London: The Tavistock Institute of Human Relations.

McLagan, P. (2002a). Change leadership: Creating a change capable organisation. *Management Today,* 18(9):28-31.

McLagan, P. (2002b). Change leadership: Success with change. *Management Today,* 18(8):8-13.

McLagan, P. (2002c). Change leadership today. Why we need to rethink change. *Management Today,* 18(7):4-6.

McLagan, P. (2003). Change leadership: Making change everybody's business. *Management Today,* 18(10):18-20.

Merry, U. & Brown, G.I. (1990). *The neurotic behaviour of organisations.* New York: Gardner.

Miller, E.J. (1976). *Task and Organisation.* New York: Wiley.

Miller, E.J. (1983). *Work and Creativity. Occasional Paper No. 6.* London: Tavistock Institute of Human Relations.

Miller, E.J. (1989). *The "Leicester" Model: experiential study of group and organisational processes. Occasional Paper No. 10.* London: Tavistock Institute of Human Relations.

Miller, E.J. (1993). *From Dependency to Autonomy: Studies in Organisation and Change.* London: Free Association Books.

Miller, D., Kets de Vries, M.F.R. & Toulouse, J.M. (1982). Top executive locus of control and its relationship to strategy making, structure and environment. *Academy of Management Journal,* 25:237-253. https://doi.org/10.5465/255988

Morgan, G. (1980). Paradigms, metaphors and puzzle solving in organisational theory. *Administrative Science Quarterly,* 25 (4)-605-622. https://doi.org/10.2307/2392283

Nel, C. (2004). High impact leadership and learning create sustainable change. *Management Today,* 20(2):16-17.

Neumann, J.E.; Kellner, K. & Dawson-Shepherd, A. (1997). *Developing organisational consultancy.* London: Routledge.

Nivid, J.S., Rathus, S.A. & Greene. B. (2003). *Abnormal psychology in a changing world.* Upper Saddle River: Prentice-Hall.

Nicholi, A.M. (1988). *The new Harvard guide to modern psychiatry.* Cambridge: Harvard University Press.

Nkomo, S. (2003). Sustainable leadership development, Developing leadership not just leaders. *Management Today,* 19(9):8.

Obholzer, A. & Roberts, V.Z. (1994). *The unconscious at work.* London: Routledge.

Peltier, B. (2001). *The psychology of coaching. Theory and application.* New York: Brunner-Routledge.

Pretorius, B. (2004). Effective leadership. A guide through challenging times. *Management Today,* 20(4):10-13.

Prochaska, J.; Norcross, J. & DiClemente, C. (1994). *Changing for good.* New York: Morrow.

Quitmann, H. (1985). *Humanistische Psychologie.* Gottingen: Verlag fur Psychologie.

Robbins, S.P.; Odendaal, A. & Roodt, G. (2001). *Organisational behaviour: Global and South African perspectives.* Cape Town: Pearson Education.

Rogers, C.R. (1975). *Encounter groups.* London: Penguin.

Rogers, C.R. (1982). *Freedom to learn for the 80's.* Columbus: Charles E. Merrill.

Roodt, A. (2003). Leadership: Lessons from termites. *Management Today,* 19(5):12-13.

Sandler, J. & Rosenblatt, B. (1962). The concept of the representational world. *Psychoanalytic Study of the Child,* 17:128-145. https://doi.org/10.1080/00797308.1962.11822842

Schafer, R. (2003). *Insight and interpretation. The essential tools of psychoanalysis.* London: Karnac.

Schmikl, E. (2003). Strategy centered leadership using the leadership scorecard. *Management Today,* 19(9):27-29.

Schmikl, W. (2004). Are you a good leader-manager of people. *Management Today,* 19(10):34-35

Schneider, K.J.; Bugental, J.F.T. & Pierson, J.F. (2001). *The handbook of humanistic psychology.* Thousand Oaks, CA: Sage.

Shapiro, D. (1965). *Neurotic Styles.* New York: Basic Books.

Snyder, C.R. & Lopez, S.J. (2002). *Handbook of positive psychology.* Oxford, UK: Oxford University Press.

Sperry, L. (2004). *Executive coaching. The essential guide for mental health professionals.* New York: Brunner-Routledge. https://doi.org/10.4324/9780203483466

Stapley, L.F. (1996). *The personality of the organisation.* London: Free Association.

Steyn, P. (2004). Organisational strategy. Leadership excellence needed. *Management Today,* 19(10):46.

Vermeulen, J. (2004). Making sense of leadership. *Management Today,* 20(9):22-24.

Verwey, A. (2003). Why is leadership suddenly such a big issue? *Management Today,* 19(8):8-9.

Wells, L. (1980). The group-as-a-whole: A systemic socio- analytical perspective on interpersonal and group relations. In: C.P. Alderfer & C.L. Cooper (eds.), *Advances in experiential social processes,* 2:165-198.

Zaleznik, A. & Kets de Vries, M.F.R. (1980). Power and the corporate mind. Chicago: Bonus Books.

Article 3

The Systems Psychodynamic Leadership Coaching Experiences of Nursing Managers[1]

F Cilliers & L Terblanche

Abstract

The mostly linear and mechanistic nature of the nursing manager role is rapidly becoming more dynamic and systemic. The change involves task and people management within a constantly changing organisational identity, taking up multiple leadership roles, having to authorise oneself and others in a complex matrix system, and managing conscious and unconscious psychological boundaries within and between conflicting systems. The aim of this study was to describe the systems psychodynamic learning experiences of nursing managers during leadership coaching. The coaching task was to provide learning opportunities to the individual leader, towards gaining insight into conscious and unconscious leadership dynamics in terms of anxiety, task, role, authorisation, boundaries and identity. A qualitative research design was used. Six nursing managers attended ten leadership coaching sessions over ten weeks. Field notes and reflective essays were analysed using systems psychodynamic discourse analysis. The findings indicated clarity and authorisation in the participants' primary task and normative roles; anxiety and de-authorisation in their experiential and phenomenal roles; anxiety in boundary management related to the misuse of power by others; and the continuous exploration of their leadership role identity towards achieving integration. Participants' learning experiences were evaluated in terms of criteria for organisational learning, after which a general hypothesis was formulated.

---

1   Cilliers, F. & Terblanche, L. (2010). The systems psychodynamic leadership coaching experiences of nursing managers. *Health SA Gesondheid*, 15(1):Art #457, 9 pages. https://doi.org/10.4102/hsag.v15i1.457

Introduction

The post-modern world of work demands that leadership be aware of and stay involved in increasingly competitive and complex technical and interpersonal organisational systems (Clutterbuck, 2003; Willem, 2003). These systems contain constant change, conflict, chaos, paradox and limited resources (Meyer & Boninelli, 2007; Will & Codrington, 2004). As a result, leaders experience high levels of survival and performance anxiety, they feel disorientated, lost, lonely, doubtful, not 'good-enough', vulnerable and under constant pressure to perform their task and manage their relationships effectively (Huffington et al., 2004; Kets de Vries, 1991; 2001; Levinson, 2006). In health care in South Africa, these demands manifest as the depletion of emotional resources, feelings of depersonalisation and a weak sense of coherence, as well as a lack of experienced organisational support (Van der Colff & Rothmann, 2009).

Worldwide, leadership or executive coaching is increasingly used to assist leaders to adapt to the demands mentioned above and their manifestations. Coaching is generally defined as a regular, short-term and highly focused organisational learning opportunity (compared to therapy and traditional training), involving a helping relationship between a client who has managerial authority and responsibility in an organisation and a consultant who uses behavioural techniques and methods to help the client to improve personal insight towards effective leadership performance and, consequently, to improve the effectiveness of the client's organisation, all within the boundaries of a formally defined coaching agreement (Kets de Vries, 2007; Kilburg & Diedrich, 2007; McKenna & Davis, 2009). The goal of coaching is to optimise leadership competence in the individual, and indirectly, in their teams and organisation (Lowman, 2002; Sperry, 2004). Most of the coaching studies mentioned in management and organisational psychology (Coutu & Kaufman, 2009; Goldsmith, Lyons & Freas, 2000; Harvard Business Essentials, 2004; McGovern et al., 2001; Peterson, 1996; Stern, 2001), as well as in nursing (Orenstein, 2007; Savage, 2001), approach coaching from a mechanistic perspective and report results on cognitive learning about leadership. Coaching studies from a humanistic perspective (Stout Rostron, 2009) make use of respect and empathy as constructs and report on the facilitation of self-awareness. Studies that approach coaching from a systemic and psychodynamic perspective, including experiential learning methods (Chapman & Cilliers, 2008; Cilliers, 2005), reported comparatively deeper levels of self-awareness and insight in the role of leader and a compelling and dynamic connective quality in the human relationships in view of the organisation's vision, mission, culture and structure. These outcomes are linked to what Kets de Vries and Engellau (2007:32) refer to as creating the 'authentizotic organisation'.

Systems Psychodynamic Leadership Coaching

The systems psychodynamic perspective was developed at the Tavistock Institute in London (Miller, 1993) based on its annual international group relations training events over 60 years (Brunner, Nutkevitch & Sher, 2006; Fraher, 2004). It consists of a depth psychology organisational theory (Armstrong, 2005; Gould, Stapley & Stein, 2001) and an organisational development consultancy stance (Neumann, Keller & Dawson-Shepherd, 1997). The perspective is based on Freudian systemic psychoanalysis, group relations theory, object relations and open systems theory (Colman & Bexton, 1975; Colman & Geller, 1985; Cytrynbaum & Noumair, 2004) and is theoretically informed by five basic behavioural assumptions – namely, dependency, fight/flight, pairing (Bion, 1961; 2003), me-ness (Turquet, 1974) and one-ness/we-ness (Lawrence, Bain & Gould, 1996).

The primary task of the systems psychodynamic leadership coaching model is to provide developmentally and psycho-educationally focused reflection and learning opportunities to the individual leader, to study, become aware of and gain insight into how task and organisational performance are influenced by both conscious and unconscious behaviour (Brunning, 2006; Huffington et al., 2004; Kets de Vries, 2007; Newton, Long & Sievers, 2006). Consciousness refers to objectivity and rational behaviour, and unconsciousness to 'the organisation in the mind' which contains the system's unconscious defences and irrational behaviours (Armstrong, 2005).

In service of the primary task, the systems psychodynamic leadership coaching model experientially investigates how the following behavioural constructs manifest in the leader's work life (Cilliers & Koortzen, 2005; Czander, 1993; Gould et al., 2001; Klein, 2005; Hirschhorn, 1993):

- **anxiety** – defined as the fear of the future, acting as the driving force ('dynamo') of the relationship and relatedness between leadership and followership.
- **task** – the basic component of work, with the leader's adherence to the primary task indicating contained anxiety, and diversions into off-task and anti-task behaviour indicating confusion and free-floating anxiety.
- **role** – the boundary surrounding work and position, and between leader/follower/organisation, where leadership is defined as managing the boundaries between what is inside and what is outside the role, and where role dynamics differentiate between the normative, experiential and phenomenal.
- **authority** – the formal and official right to perform the task, bestowed from above (the organisation, manager, leader), the side (colleagues), below (subordinates) and within (self-authorisation).
- **boundaries** – such as task, time, territory, which acts as the space around and between parts of the system, keeping it safe and contained.

∞ **identity** – the nature of the leader's role behaviour and the branding, climate and culture of the organisational system.

Operationally, the first leadership coaching session starts with role analysis, which provides the behavioural dynamics for the whole coaching procedure (Newton et al., 2006). The focus is not solely on the person (as in psychotherapy – McKenna & Davis, 2009) or on the organisation, but rather on the leader in role within the person-role-organisation interaction (Huffington et al., 2004). This means that the effect of the organisation on the role is also being studied. Leaders are asked to describe their normative (the objective job description/content, measured according to performance management), existential (how they believe they are performing) and phenomenal roles (how they believe they are performing as experienced by colleagues around them) (Brunning, 2006; Obholzer & Roberts, 1994). The rationale is that the incongruence between the three role parts indicates role anxiety, which is worth studying for the purposes of insight and change (Newton et al., 2006). Each subsequent session starts with the open question, 'what is happening with you in your role as leader at the moment'. There are no specific aims for each session, in order to ensure the flow of the discourse in the here-and-now, which is different from using training methodologies (Kets de Vries, 2007). The coach negotiates with the leader to make short notes during the session, which the leader also sometimes does.

The coach-leader relationship involves an intense discourse (Campbell & Gronbaek, 2006). The role of the coach is to take a reflective stance from a meta-position, alert to the leader's behaviour, interpreting the manifestation of the basic assumptions and behavioural concepts referred to above without judgement, memory or desire (Campbell & Huffington, 2008). This is done by formulating working hypotheses, defined as an integrative statement of 'searching into' (Schafer, 2003) the leader's experiences and by constantly re-visiting this content in the light of further and new manifesting evidence (Campbell, 2007). Leaders are encouraged to be curious, to associate freely, to explore a variety of related feelings, patterns, defences and representations (including the transferences between coach and leader) and to move between different levels of abstraction in thought (Jaques, 1990; Kegan, 1994). Thus, such leaders can access their own unexplored conscious and unconscious role experiences, attitudes, beliefs, fantasies, wishes, conflicts, social defences, preferences, competition, rivalry, jealousy, envy, hostility, aggression as well as patterns of relationships and collaboration. They can investigate how parts of the self are split off and projected onto and into other parts of the organisational system (individuals, groups) who may have the valence for receiving and carrying the specific projections and who contain them on behalf of the system (projective identification). They can also consider what can be done to take back the projections and reclaim the lost parts of the self (Blackman, 2004; Neumann et al., 1997; Shapiro & Carr, 1991; Stapley, 1996, 2006).

Problem Statement, Research Question and Aim of the Research

The manifestation of the above organisational and behavioural demands in health care implies that the role of the nursing manager is also being transformed. The movement is from a traditional focus on the professional/ technical, educational, administration and research fields, and the fairly mechanistic, linear and compartmentalised management of these, towards taking up a dynamic and systemic leadership role (Grossman & Valiga, 2009; Sullivan & Decker, 2009). Porter-O'Grady and Malloch (2007) refer to this movement as quantum leadership for health care innovation.

Operationally, the new role includes task and people management within a constantly changing organisational identity, taking up multiple roles, having to authorise self and others in a complex matrix system and managing conscious and unconscious psychological boundaries within and between conflicting systems (Kets de Vries, 2007). Because nursing managers are generally not educated, either formally or in-service, to understand and adapt to the these complex organisational and leadership demands, this study suggests bridging the gap by means of leadership coaching as an organisational development input. As a coaching model, a systems psychodynamic perspective is suggested here to address the implied behavioural depth and complexity (see Peltier, 2001).

The research question was formulated as follows: what are the manifesting systems psychodynamic learning experiences of nursing managers during leadership coaching that focus on the awareness of their dynamic role behaviour, their authorisation, boundary management and continuous identity formation? The aim was to describe the systems psychodynamic learning experiences of nursing managers during leadership coaching.

Research Method and Design

Research Approach

The research design was qualitative and descriptive in nature (Breverton & Milward, 2004; Camic, Rhodes & Yardley, 2003). This implies that the researcher is interested in, and concerned about, socially relevant values and ethics, without being intimidated by power or status. The researcher asks the question 'what is actually happening', while exploring by means of continuous reflection and then describing the behaviour in the context of the theoretical framework – namely, systems psychodynamics. In this research study, a depth psychology perspective, which includes the manifestation of unconscious behaviour, was chosen in order to 'penetrate the illusion' (Higgs & Smith, 2003:67) that leadership is only about conscious behaviour. Thus, the leadership reality, comprising conscious and unconscious behaviour, could be explained.

Population and Sampling

The population consisted of nine senior nursing managers in a private hospital group working in different hospitals in Gauteng. They were informed about the researchers' leadership coaching project at a head office meeting. The project was framed as follows: it would be voluntary; the coaching would take place in their individual hospitals; since coaching is not a performance assessment intervention no coaching feedback would be given to their management, and there would be no cost involved for the individual manager or hospital. Head office agreed to pay the coach's travel expenses per coaching session to the different hospitals. Interested managers could phone the first author for an appointment for a chemistry meeting (a typical custom in coaching to allow both parties to ascertain whether they will be able to work with the other in a coaching relationship). All nine managers made appointments and during the meeting, they were informed about the rationale, method and logistics of the leadership coaching programme. Six managers declared themselves willing for coaching while three withdrew from the procedure because of practical reasons and time constraints.

Thus, the voluntary and convenient sample (Henning, Van Rensburg & Smit, 2004) consisted of four White and two Black females, all responsible for a hospital unit with its nursing staff in a large hospital. This situation created a potential problem in terms of saturation because up to this point the sample was a given in the sampling method. The researchers decided to accept the sample of six with the probability to enlarge the sample in case the material was not rich enough for interpretation.

Procedure

The sample of six nursing managers received 10 hours of individual leadership coaching, arranged as one-hour sessions over 10 weeks, held in the office of the participant. The aim of the sessions was to work on the primary task of systems psychodynamic leadership coaching, as described above. The first author conducted the sessions as described below. He is a psychologist (category industry) with a doctoral degree in Industrial and Organisational Psychology. His specific training of 12 years in systems psychodynamic coaching was congruent to the requirements described by Brunner et al. (2006) – namely, a solid theoretical systems psychodynamic knowledge, experience in systems psychodynamic consultancy and coaching through 'Tavistock' training by attending, being trained in and directing experiential group relations events, being coached and continuously being supervised whilst coaching clients.

Data Collection

The data collection was carried out during and after the coaching sessions. During the sessions, the coach made field notes about the topics and themes which the leaders addressed and the manner in which they responded to the working hypotheses offered verbally by the coach. After the last session, the participants were asked to write an essay of about five pages on their experiences of coaching with special reference to how they take up their normative, existential and phenomenal roles. These reflective essays were regarded as transcriptions representing the experience of each leader (Camic et al., 2003). Thus, the data consisted of the coach's field notes and the leaders' essays.

Data Analysis and Interpretation

System psychodynamic discourse analysis was used (Smit & Cilliers, 2006). This discourse is defined as the idea that concepts serve as the basis of thinking and are expressed by words, located in language (Campbell & Huffington, 2008). This speech-act forms the central engagement point in the interaction. Thus, one may ascertain what discourses frame the language action, the way in which leaders make sense of their reality and how this discourse is produced and maintained in the social context (Terre Blanche et al., 2006; Van Manen, 1990). The discourse markers related to the leaders' conceptions, values and beliefs about their experiences of the three different parts of their roles. In systems psychodynamic terms the unit of analysis is the individual leader and 'the organisation in her mind' (Armstrong, 2005).

In interpreting the data, the researchers drew on their theoretical knowledge about the above-mentioned basic assumptions and relevant behavioural constructs which were being manifested, as well as on their subjective capacity to make sense of the dynamic leadership world of the nursing manager. The interpretations resulted in a second level of working hypotheses (after those used in the coaching sessions). Thus, the systems psychodynamic data were sorted (Terre Blanche et al., 2006) to best describe the constructions presented by the data resources (Haslebo, 2000). The aim was to arrive at a systemic general hypothesis that connects the behaviour of the individual participants with the collective (Cilliers & Smit, 2006).

At this point, the researchers thoroughly explored the data in terms of saturation in ensuring that they 'have acquired a satisfactory sense of what is going on' (Terre Blanche et al., 2006:422). The data provided a richness that would ensure the clear description of the systems psychodynamic theory. It was therefore not necessary to extend the sample beyond the six participants.

Ethical Considerations

Ethicality (Terre Blanche, Durrheim & Painter, 2006) was ensured by having the leadership coaching programme approved by the hospital authorities. This was followed by authorisation letters to the nursing managers to attend coaching during office hours. During the coaching chemistry meeting, the leadership coaching relationship and logistics were explained to the nursing managers. This was followed up by a jointly signed agreement pertaining to their informed consent, voluntary participation, their withdrawal at any time, a guarantee of their privacy and confidentiality in terms of participation and content of the coaching sessions.

Trustworthiness

The notion of trustworthiness is based on credibility and validity (Denzin, 1989; Denzin & Lincoln, 1994). Credibility was assured in terms of the competence of both authors as professionally trained in psychology and psychiatric nursing and as researchers who have been trained in this leadership coaching model. The study evidenced strong and believable validity in its in-depth (psychological) description, which revealed the complexities of the variables and their interactions from the systemic and psychodynamic perspectives.

The interpretations were peer-reviewed (Breverton & Milward, 2004; Camic et al., 2003). Two independent psychologists, to whom the theoretical model is well known, were asked to investigate the dependability of the findings (which were found to be positive). In the discussion with one psychologist, reflexivity was discussed in terms of the coach being a white male working with a largely white and exclusively female group of participants. Afterwards, she concluded that the findings were free of disturbances in terms of cross-diversity dimensions. Both peer reviewers agreed that the data reached a point of saturation.

Findings and Discussion

The findings are presented according to the participants' coaching experiences as they manifested within the six core behavioural constructs, namely anxiety, task, role, authorisation, boundaries and identity.

1. Anxiety

Participants described their coaching experience as follows: 'it was initially strange, until you understand what it is about', 'an intense way of learning about yourself', 'something I have never experienced at work', 'thought-provoking', 'emotionally challenging and rewarding', 'the greatest learning experience I have ever had', and 'something I would recommend to all nursing staff'. The coach's task and style were described as follows: 'initially weird', 'intensely attentive', 'a very good listener – to the deep stuff', 'making connections that gave me many aha-moments', 'I now understand what coaching is' and 'what it could add to the quality of relationships and leadership in the hospital'. The interpretation was made that participants could significantly move from projecting their anxiety onto the coach and coaching as containing and transitional objects, towards becoming more aware of their own dynamics, owning their learning and integrating the coaching style into their leadership repertoire (Czander, 1993).

Participants defended against their experienced anxiety, as described by Bion (1970). Their dependence anxiety manifested in survival and performance anxiety. One participant remarked that 'coaching challenged my comfort zone big time'. This represented a split between what was expected (which participants described as 'that he will tell me how to do my job' and 'I thought it was going to be like a training session') and reality ('I now realise that coaching is about finding out for myself what works for me'). This was accompanied by flight responses such as their occasional avoidance of working on the coaching task. One participant said that 'I soon realised that coaching is about my leadership role and not about gossiping about the other people in my life'. The above behaviour was driven by high levels of frustration and anger which triggered their counter-dependence, directed at the coach as their object of anger as well as of envy. They used projection ('I was so mad at him'), regression ('If he could only tell me what to do') and envious attack ('I was blaming the coach for not doing his job'). Their flight defences were also manifested in some of them blaming the coach for his incompetence – 'his inability' to 'control my anxiety'.

This was interpreted as their persecutory transference against the intimacy of the here-and-now coaching relationship (Stapley, 2006). Participants reported on their 'profound learning' while working through these experiences. One participant remarked that 'I now realise that without frustration, learning is limited'. Some participants added that the coach exhibited an important leadership dynamic by staying in role and containing the anxiety without judging, memory or desire (Brunner et al., 2006). Another participant added that 'I never thought leaders need to contain behaviour on behalf of others'.

Participants became aware of what their work systems are projecting onto them and how they take the projections in – their valences and projective identifications (Obholzer & Roberts, 1994). Working through their anxiety and confusion led the way towards taking up an independent position in which they started to own their own behaviour and take responsibility for structuring the coaching sessions themselves. One participant said that 'I made an excellent – at least I thought so – hypothesis about how I deny my anger towards that doctor who bullies me'. Another added that 'at the start of the third-last session I told the coach what I wanted to explore and I gave my own interpretations of my experiences'. Towards the end of the coaching sessions, two participants moved towards interdependence when they started to report back on 'testing my new behaviour with others' and processing the implications of how others experience them. It was the authors' experience that this movement took longer compared to other reported cases (such as the case concerning Information Technology staff mentioned in Cilliers, 2005). This was interpreted as an indication of how the nursing managers were caught up in the hospital system domain (Bain, 1998), with its strict rules and strong defences in the relationships between the different authority levels – the nursing staff, administration and doctors.

Participants reported on their learning about how their (mostly unconscious) anxiety acts as a driving force of their own behaviour in their leadership roles. One participant expressed it thus: 'I realise that I defend against anxiety to stay safe and uninvolved when the doctors shunt me around'. They reported on their insight that this dynamic between themselves and the coach (as the authority figure in the session) mirrored (Campbell & Huffington, 2008) their relationships with their direct reports as well as with the hospital administration in terms of the authority dynamics.

This led to working hypothesis 1. Participants experienced anxiety which manifested in basic assumption functioning dependency and fight/flight, accompanied by splitting, projection and regression as defences. Coaching allowed them to work through the process of exploring these defences, to develop a curiosity about their own feeling and thinking behaviour and eventually to own that which belongs to them and give up that which does not. They learned that these coaching behavioural processes are mirrored in their role as leaders towards colleagues and that they need to contain the anxiety of their co-workers and manage the projections in a more conscious manner.

2. Task

Participants described their structured, nursing manager primary task with clarity and pride. As evidence, they referred to their many thick and detailed files containing their job content (job descriptions, key performance areas, rules, procedures, structures). The interpretation was made that the linear nature (input, throughput, output) of their structured task acted as a container for their performance anxiety against the complexity of taking up a dynamic leadership role (see Huffington et al., 2004). Their defences were the following: avoidance (which manifested in their preference to speak about how their direct reports did not behave correctly), denial (which was expressed as 'I thought that leadership can be prescribed in a how-to-do-it file'), simplification (manifested in expression such as 'I realise that I keep myself busy with files', 'I am so busy with administration', 'so office-bound' that 'I do not get involved in people matters', 'I do not walk the floors/do not connect with my people as a leader') and isolation (one participant said 'I get so tired of the difficulties of dealing with people that I lock myself in the office and just do administration'). Participants realised that their defences led to anti-task behaviour and detachment from their primary task (Klein, 2005), which is to connect with their direct reports and colleagues.

Consequently, working hypothesis 2 emerged. Participants split their nursing manager task between the mechanics and dynamics of the task. They preferred to attach themselves to the simplicity of the task as contained in their files and detach from the complexity of demanding interpersonal relationships with subordinates and colleagues. Coaching allowed them to shift their competence towards including and balancing both parts.

3. Role

Participants were clear on their normative roles (the rational job content), but less so on their experiential and phenomenal roles (Obholzer & Roberts, 1994). In exploring their experiential role (the individual's own perception of her performance), participants initially struggled to talk about themselves. Examples of avoiding defences against being honest and open with the self were, 'I am not used to talking about my own performance' and 'I am afraid people will think I brag'. They reported how they continuously, subjectively introject the objective (normative) role. The comment, 'I realise how I only do the parts of the role that I like and just ignore the parts I don't' serves as an example. They expressed their difficulty in taking up the leadership role: 'maybe leadership is far more demanding than I thought'. In exploring their phenomenal role (the individual's perception of how others see her performance), most participants reported their reluctance to know others' views of them. Their avoidance manifested in comments such as, 'people don't give honest feedback' and 'they only gossip about everyone'. They later realised that their reluctance acted as a defence against (on one level) knowing and being vulnerable and (on a deeper level) taking on and taking in the projections of the other.

The theme concerning the reluctance of becoming aware of others' projections exhibited greater depth. In the exploration of their experiential role, some participants referred to their fear of physical contamination by germs and viruses in the hospital. In the subsequent exploration of their phenomenal role, they gave evidence of being exposed to emotional-toxicogenic practices (Fox & Spector, 2005) and bullying (Babiak & Hare, 2006). Examples mentioned were inconsistency, a lack of respect, anti-social behaviour and the abuse of power (manifesting in manipulation and shouting). According to Porter-O'Grady and Malloch (2007), this toxicity in the culture of health care organisations stimulates unconscious forces of control, conflict, hostility and rigidity – extremely irrational and dysfunctional behaviour, which can eventually destroy the vitality of the organisation. The above behaviour was interpreted as indicative of the participants' fear of psychological and specifically emotional contamination in a hospital system, experienced as emotionally toxic.

The incongruence between the three role parts highlighted above indicated high levels of role anxiety (Newton et al., 2006). Most of the coaching was spent on the deconstruction, alignment and reconstruction of these parts. The participants' learning concerned the complexity of taking up the leadership role and managing the boundaries between the rational and the perceptions of self and other. This was expressed in the comments 'I never realised the importance of how I feel about myself as leader' and 'how others see me, assess what I do and how'. Most participants reported their learning to be related to how they can use themselves as instruments (French & Vince, 1999) and objects (Klein, 1988) in connecting more effectively with their direct reports. Participants' commented that 'I now realise how people project their own stuff onto me' and 'their feedback possibly says more about them and their needs, than about me'.

Working hypothesis 3 consequently evolved. Participants initially attached themselves to and found comfort in the rational part of their role and detached from the complex dynamics of working with their introjections and received projections. Coaching allowed them to explore this incongruence and to work towards the integration of the parts of their roles.

4. Authorisation

Initially, most participants were unclear about the meaning of authorisation. After an intervention about how she seemed to be de-authorised in the system, one participant said 'but I am not the authority on the subject' – confusing being authorised with being knowledgeable. The concept was also often confused with power and destruction. The concept needed to be explained according to Hirschhorn's (1997) description – namely, the energy relevant to the performance of the task.

All the participants experienced being formally authorised from above (Haslebo, 2000) by their leaders, hospital administration and head office in their normative role. They gave evidence of how their competence was respected in terms of their knowledge (through their academic qualifications), skills (extensive in-service training and experience) and positive attitudes (being employed in a competitive hospital and recognised as an expert). They experienced informal authority in being liked and appreciated by most colleagues and direct reports. Thus, they were able to self-authorise (Brunning, 2006).

On the other hand, many experiences of being unconsciously de-authorised were explored (Lawrence, 1999; 2000). These experiences led to a sense of not being 'good-enough', low self-regard and a feeling of poor performance. The following serve as examples:

- Participants were authorised in staff meetings with authority figures to deliver on specific projects, only to find out later that authority was being taken back. For instance, it happened that resources such as finances, time or assistance were promised but not delivered in practice. When participants investigated the matter, they were told 'it was not budgeted for', 'you have to do it yourself', or 'make another plan'.

- Participants explained the difficulties in working in a matrix organisational design and how their managers 'don't know what they want from whom' because 'they are confused about what matrix means'.

- Doctors used their status to bully the nursing staff, by threatening to take their expertise elsewhere, which might lead to the discontinuation of that specific type of surgery in the hospital. The interpretation was reached that although the nursing manager feels humiliated, confused and may loathe the doctors' behaviour, she stays obedient to the legitimacy of the authority figure (Burger, 2009) as an object of power in the system. The projection of submission by the authority figure onto the participant is so strong that she can only take it in, which became her projective identification (Klein, 1988). This explains how the nursing manager is emotionally seduced (Cytrenbaum & Noumair, 2004) into 'playing along with the behaviour and not reporting them'. Thus, the power games are sustained while the participant contains the de-authorisation and the 'messiness' on behalf of the whole hospital system (Wells, 1980).

Working hypothesis 4 emerged. Participants experienced being consciously authorised from above, the side and below in their normative role in acknowledgement of their competence. On the other hand, they experienced being unconsciously de-authorised by the power of people in management and leadership positions. Coaching allowed them to understand the dynamics underlying these complex systemic behaviours, how they play along with the power games according to their personal and systemic valences (Czander, 1993) and how they could move from a position of victim to wisdom.

5. Boundaries

Participants found the boundary concept the most 'valuable' and 'amazing' in the coaching model, especially the realisation that boundary management serves the institution on the conscious and unconscious levels (Lawrence, 1999). On the conscious level boundary management contributes towards an effectively managed institution according to practical, management and professional (medical and nursing) requirements. Participants explored and processed their boundary position with the hospital administration (upwards) and their direct reports (downwards).

This was expressed in the following comments: 'we need the policies, rules, administrative and medical procedures', 'I realise that everything in my work is about boundaries and how I manage them!', 'the management of my personal boundaries is essential for having effective working relationships' and 'poor boundary management create [sic] ambiguous situations harming both sides of the relationship'.

On the unconscious level their 'profound learning' related to the unconscious meaning, usage and effect of boundaries on the micro, meso- and macro-systemic levels.

On the micro-level, participants learned how their personal boundary is often compromised in the larger hospital system by their being obliged to work long and extended hours, 'be available 24/7', 'know everything about everything and everyone'. Participants reported that the challenge of the coaching became one of not dwelling on the rights and wrongs of past practices, but instead to move forward, creating conditions in which personal boundaries are acknowledged and respected. On the meso-level, they learned about time boundaries (as in shift work, visiting hours), space (offices, wards, ICU, germ-free zones), task (how to make a bed, give an injection, who may hand out medication, procedures) and relationship boundaries (the structures of how to deal with head office, doctors, specialists, patients, the public). They explored how the hospital as a 'place of distress, illness and death' needs to manage its boundaries tightly as a defence against the anxiety of pain (Menzies, 1993). They realised that command and control emotional outbursts (Porter-O'Grady & Malloch, 2007) and attacks by doctors represent poor boundary management: the projections evident in physicians' irrational outbursts are violations of the nursing manager's boundary. They learned that the doctor 'is saying more about himself than about me' and that they need to manage their boundary in such a way as to 'not let him enter my personal space'. On the macro level, participants became aware of their system domain defences (Bain, 1998; Kilburg, 2006), which refer to health care as practised in a large hospital, its structures, processes and content, as well as its well-established, but unconscious, methods of dealing with physical and emotional anxiety. Their learning on all three systemic levels was congruent with Menzies' (1993) research into how socially constructed defence systems operate in hospitals to preserve and contain the high levels of anxiety.

Working hypothesis 5 was now formulated. Participants became aware of how the hospital requires strict boundary management to contain the intensity of the system's survival anxiety, of the importance and nature of the interpersonal boundaries between themselves and their leaders, colleagues and direct reports, and of how they manage their personal boundaries towards becoming more authorised in their role as nursing managers.

6. Identity

Convincing evidence was processed to deduce the effectiveness of participants' job performance in terms of outputs and agreement in their performance management discussions with hospital administrators. It was interpreted that all the participants' work identities were (on the conscious level) intact with reference to being professionally well trained, technically competent, organisationally authorised in their role, and personally authorised on the intellectual, emotional and motivational levels.

Despite this evidence, most participants referred to their constant dissatisfaction with their own performance. They compulsively asked questions about what they were doing wrong. Speaking from their experiential roles, they were always pressuring themselves to do more, perform better and to be more attentive to their staff and patients. One participant said that 'something is driving me towards ... I don't know what'. They reported that work had become more important than their personal lives. Three participants reported that they experienced nervousness and guilt when they were not actively involved in something. For them, it is as if 'it is important to be seen to be busy'. Three reported that their hospital work has caused them ill health (constant flu, migraines) and even 'negatively interfered' with and 'messed up' their private lives. They reported using private time to study further and/or read about hospital and nursing issues and added that when they take a vacation, they derive little pleasure from it. Speaking in terms of their phenomenal roles, they reported that they think their co-workers also regard their performance as below average. Some participants reported feeling insecure about their jobs, unappreciated and unrecognised. Some felt left out at times of promotion and generally conveyed a message of performance anxiety to comply with the demands in the system. They were motivated by approval, feared rejection and worried that others might perceive them as inferior. Some participants used their free time for shopping (as a flight and compulsive response) – 'but then again, we earn so little that I get frustrated because I cannot buy anything expensive'.

The above was interpreted as identity-based conflict (Porter-O'Grady & Malloch, 2007 – as opposed to interest-based conflict), which is circumstantial and rooted in the unconscious need for dignity, recognition, safety, control, purpose and efficiency. The containment of caring and nurturing being projected by the system (Klein, 1988) onto the role of nursing manager – 'to carry the hospital's emotional stuff' – becomes the impossible task (Campbell & Gronbaek, 2006). 'It is [an] unbearable' and 'overwhelming' task for which no one will ever be good enough (Klein, 1988).

In terms of forming attachments (Huffington et al., 2004), most participants shifted from the initial defence against their fear of intimacy (using avoidance and resistance) towards forming more secure and deeper attachment relationships with the coach, themselves and their colleagues. This was evident in how their self-confidence grew, how they became more realistically involved in their work, how their job satisfaction increased and how they started to challenge their own styles – taking up opportunities to explore instead of staying in the hopeless and helpless positions. Most participants reported moving towards balancing their personal and work lives, which indicated using less defensive behaviour and a movement towards more optimal attachment formation (Campbell, 2007). The coaching process facilitated participants in facing their implicit identity demands and attempting to discover ways to differentiate between 'what is mine and what is not mine', and therefore to take up their role with more realism.

Working hypothesis 6 consequently evolved. Participants' work identity was clear in terms of their conscious job performance but burdened by the organisational expectations that they must unconsciously contain systemic anxiety. Because this irrational content does not belong to them, it creates incomprehensible anxiety which the individuals cannot process by themselves. Coaching allowed them to explore, disentangle and differentiate between illusion, fantasy and their reality with the aim of understanding the intricacies of the projections. They were brave enough to give up their ignorance in favour of heightened awareness – they experienced 'a mini-death of a known way of being' (Bain, 1998:416).

Congruent to the aim of the research referring to the learning experiences of participants, the nature and depth of their learning were investigated. With reference to the theories of Argyris (1994) and Taylor (2007), it could be said that this study provided evidence of unlearning, evolution and adaptation. Unlearning was evident in that participants stopped their immediate defensive responses by asking the self 'what is going on here?' Evolution was evident in that participants moved from being unconscious about the impact of their leadership role towards awareness of how their self-authorisation leads to impactful interpersonal relationships. Adaptation was evident in that participants took up their leadership role in a growing awareness of their boundaries and their impact on others in the hospital system.

Next, the criteria for organisational learning according to the systems psychodynamic perspective were investigated (Bain, 1998; Campbell & Huffington, 2008:78; French & Vince, 1999:7-19; Meznar & Nicolini, 1995).

Reflection Space and Containment

The coaching sessions served as a space for reflection in which participants took up their roles as learners with respect to their psychodynamic primary task as nursing managers. This occurred while the coach was acting as a container of the anxiety and its defences. This process was characterised by eagerness, curiosity and intensity in exploring new possibilities of which they were previously unaware. Participants crossed the boundary out of the project with significantly more 'executive wisdom' (Kilburg, 2006; Kilburg & Diedrich, 2007), which is defined as taking up the leadership role with an openness to experience and a creative exploration of own, team and organisational behaviours towards a cognitive understanding, a strong sense of self, and a systemic awareness of process and dynamics.

The Evolution of the Organisational Container and the Contained

On the macro level participants showed insight into the dynamics of the system domain defences in health care; on the meso-level they showed insight into the socially constructed defences in their own hospitals; while on the micro-level they explored and understood the complexities of their own defensive leadership behaviour – the behaviours that existed below the surface and were as such controlling and determining their and others' behaviour. They developed their containment leadership competence (Bion, 1970).

Interdependence

Participants moved from dependence and non-ownership towards independence and partial ownership in their leadership roles, with some evidence of interdependence (see Stapley, 2006). Their experience of their work seemed less fragmented and more inclusive of the system domain's primary task. They became more robust in their support for themselves as well as for their colleagues as they overcame their defensive behaviours.

Exploration of the Dynamic Primary Task

Participants applied the concepts of primary task, off-task and anti-task behaviour to their coaching learning as well as their leadership roles. They learned to differentiate between what is relevant and appropriately complex (those aspects of the leadership role that are congruent to their primary task), and what is irrelevantly simplistic (those aspects that made them defend against anxiety, for instance by using fight and flight responses). They learned to self-regulate (see Campbell, 2007) and to respond to the rational aspects of their primary task with insight and understanding, and in terms of maintaining effective relationships between themselves and the hospital administration, their colleagues, their direct reports and other professionals (such as the doctors).

Boundary Management

Awareness of the dynamic meaning of personal, interpersonal and organisational boundaries facilitated participants' effective management of the boundaries of their leadership role in the here-and-now (see Lawrence, 1999).

Taking up the Leadership Role with Authority

Participants learned the cognitive meaning of leadership and its appropriate levels of authorisation (see Kets de Vries, 2007). They took up their leadership role experientially, which enlarged their leadership spectrum and behavioural repertoire. They could differentiate between rational and irrational leadership behaviour as well as the accompanying defensive behaviours such as denial, introjections, projections and projective identifications. This enhanced their competence in self-authorisation and capacity for making decisions and taking action.

Conclusion and Recommendation

The reported leadership coaching experiences of the nursing manager indicated individual (micro-level), team (meso-level) and organisational (macro level) learning. The generated working hypotheses were integrated into the following general systems psychodynamic hypothesis: coaching created a reflective space for the development of leadership awareness. Participants moved from being mostly ignorant and unconscious containers of system domain, socially constructed and personal defences, to containers of personal and leadership awareness. They took up their leadership roles with significantly more self-authorisation. While being aware of and managing their personal and organisational boundaries, they started to integrate their normative, experiential and phenomenal roles. These were manifested in their capacity for creating new thoughts, processed feelings and responsible actions. Their depth and the nature of the learning and behavioural change could be seen as the first steps towards building an authentizotic organisation.

Thus, through leadership coaching, the nursing manager developed a dynamic awareness of her individual identity, how she relates to others and what she represents in the hospital system as well as the competence to ask questions about her dynamic experiences. She took up her leadership role according to the definition of managing the boundaries between what is inside and what is outside.

Although the researchers tried to minimise subjectivity in the study, it played a role in conducting the coaching sessions as well as in the data analysis and interpretation of the data. This happened on occasion when the coach strongly identified with the hospital environment, unconsciously wanting to defend nursing staff (having close family members trained in the nursing sciences) and the doctors (having had a doctor as a father). These transference dynamics were discussed and contained by the authors.

It is recommended that these participants' learning be followed up regularly, to ensure that the effect of the learning and skills is not diluted by system domain defences. This leadership coaching model should be further researched and refined amongst all nursing and administrative staff and on different levels in hospitals and health care. It is also recommended that emotional toxicity in hospitals is investigated further.

References

Argyris, C. (1994). *On organisational learning.* Blackwell: Oxford.

Armstrong, D. (2005). *Organisation in the mind. Psychoanalysis, group relations and organisational consultancy.* London: Karnac.

Babiak, P. & Hare, R. (2006). *Snakes in suits. When psychopaths go to work.* New York: Harper Collins.

Bain, A. (1998). Social defences against organisational learning. *Human Relations,* 51(3):413-429. https://doi.org/10.1023/A:1016952722628

Bion, W.R. (1961). *Experiences in groups.* London: Tavistock.

Bion, W.R. (1970). *Attention and interpretation.* London: Tavistock.

Bion, W.R. (2003). *Learning from experience.* London: Karnac.

Blackman, J.S. (2004). *101 Defenses. How the mind shields itself.* New York: Brunner-Routledge. https://doi.org/10.4324/9780203492369

Breverton, P. & Millward, L. (2004). *Organisational research methods. A guide for students and researchers.* London: Sage.

Brunner, L.D.; Nutkevitch, A. & Sher, M. (2006). *Group relations conferences. Reviewing and exploring theory, design, role-taking and application.* London: Karnac.

Brunning, H. (2006). *Executive coaching. Systems-psychodynamic perspective.* London: Karnac.

Burger, J.M. (2009). Replicating Milgram. Would people still obey today? *American Psychologist,* 64(1):1-11. https://doi.org/10.1037/a0010932

Camic, P.M.; Rhodes, J.E. & Yardley, L. (2003). *Qualitative research in psychology.* Washington: American Psychological Association.

Campbell, D. (2007). *The socially constructed organisation.* London: Karnac.

Campbell, D. & Gronbaek, M. (2006). *Taking positions in the organisation.* London: Karnac.

Campbell, D. & Huffington, C. (2008). *Organisations connected. A handbook of systemic consultation.* London: Karnac.

Chapman, L. & Cilliers, F. (2008). The integrated experiential executive coaching model: A qualitative exploration. *South African Journal of Labour Relations,* 32(1):63-80.

Cilliers, F. (2005.) Executive coaching experiences. A systems psychodynamic perspective. *South African Journal of Industrial Psychology,* 31(3):23-30. https://doi.org/10.4102/sajip.v31i3.205

Cilliers, F. & Koortzen, P. (2005). Conflict in groups. The CIBART model. *HR Future,* October:52-53.

Cilliers, F. & Smit, B. (2006). A systems psychodynamic interpretation of South African diversity dynamics: a comparative study. *South African Journal of Labour Relations,* 30(2):5-18.

Clutterbuck, D. (2003). Coaching and mentoring at the top. *Management Today,* 19(5):38-40.

Colman, A.D. & Bexton, W.H. (1975) *Group relations reader 1.* Jupiter: A.K. Rice Institute.

Colman, A.D. & Geller, M.H. (1985). *Group relations reader 2.* Jupiter: A.K. Rice Institute.

Coutu, D. & Kaufman, C. (2009). What can coaches do for you? *Harvard Business Review*, January:91-97.

Cytrynbaum, S. & Noumair, A. (2004). *Group relations reader 3*. Jupiter: A.K. Rice Institute.

Czander, W.M. (1993). *The psychodynamics of work and organizations*. New York: Guilford.

Denzin, N.K. (1989). *The research act*. Englewood Cliffs: Prentice-Hall.

Denzin, N.K. & Lincoln, Y.S. (1994). *Handbook of qualitative research*. Thousand Oaks: Sage.

Fox, S. & Spector, P.E. (2005). *Counterproductive work behaviour. Investigations of actors and targets*. Washington: American Psychological Association. https://doi.org/10.1037/10893-000

Fraher, A. (2004). *A history of group study and psychodynamic organisations*. London: Free Association.

French, R. & Vince, R. (1999). *Group relations, management, and organization*. New York: Oxford University Press.

Goldsmith, M.; Lyons, L. & Freas, A. (2000). *Coaching for leadership: How the world's greatest coaches help leaders learn*. San Francisco: Jossey-Bass.

Gould, L.J.; Stapley, L.F. & Stein, M. (2001). *The systems psychodynamics of organisations*. London: Karnac.

Grossman, S.C. & Valiga, T.M. (2009). *The new leadership challenge. Creating the future of nursing*. Philadelphia: Davis.

Harvard Business Essentials. (2004). *Coaching and mentoring. How to develop top talent and achieve stronger performance*. Boston: Harvard Business School.

Haslebo, G. (2000). *Systems and meaning. Consulting in organisations*. London: Karnac.

Henning, E.; Van Rensburg, W. & Smit, B. (2004). *Finding your way in qualitative research*. Pretoria: Van Schaik.

Higgs, P. & Smith, J. (2003). *Rethinking truth*. Lansdowne: Juta.

Hirschhorn, L. (1993). *The workplace within: Psychodynamics of organizational life*. Cambridge: MIT.

Hirschhorn, L. (1997). *Reworking authority. Leading and following in the post-modern organization*. London: MIT.

Huffington, C.; Armstrong, A.; Halton, W.; Hoyle, L. & Pooley, J. (2004). *Working below the surface. The emotional life of contemporary organisations*. London. Karnac.

Jaques, E. (1990). *Creativity and work*. Madison: International Universities.

Kegan, R. (1994). *In over our heads. The mental demands of modern life*. Cambridge: Harvard University.

Kets de Vries, M.F.R. (1991). *Organisations on the coach. Clinical perspectives on organisational behaviour and change*. San Francisco: Jossey-Bass.

Kets de Vries, M.F.R. (2001). *The leadership mystique*. London: Prentice-Hall.

Kets de Vries, M.F.R. (2007). *Coach and couch*. London: Palgrave.

Kets de Vries, M.F.R. & Engellau, E. (2007). Organisational dynamics in action. In: R.R. Kilburg (ed.), *Executive wisdom. Coaching and the emergence of virtuous leaders*, pp.25-34. Washington: American Psychological Association.

Kilburg, R. (2006). *Executive wisdom*. Washington: American Psychological Association.

Kilburg, R. & Diedrich, R. (2007). *The wisdom of coaching: Essential papers in consulting psychology for a world of change.* Washington: American Psychological Association. https://doi.org/10.1037/11570-000

Klein, L. (2005). *Working across the gap. The practice of social science in organisations.* London: Karnac.

Klein, M. (1988). *Envy and gratitude and other works, 1946–1963.* London: Hogarth.

Lawrence, W.G. (1999). *Exploring individual and organizational boundaries. A Tavistock open systems approach.* London: Karnac.

Lawrence, W.G. (2000). *Tongued with fire. Group in experience.* London: Karnac.

Lawrence, W.G.; Bain, A. & Gould, L. (1996). *The fifth basic assumption.* London. Tavistock.

Levinson, H. (2006). *The psychology of leadership.* Boston: Harvard Business School.

Lowman, R L. (2002). *The handbook of organizational consulting psychology.* San Francisco: Jossey-Bass. https://doi.org/10.1037/e331292004-005

McGovern, J.; Lindemann, M.; Vergara, M., Murphy, S.; Barker, L. & Warrenfeltz, R. (2001). Maximizing the impact of executive coaching. Behavioural change, organizational outcomes and return on investment. *The Manchester Review,* 6(1):1–10.

McKenna, D.D. & Davis, S.L. (2009). Hidden in plain sight: The active ingredient of executive coaching. *Industrial and Organisational Psychology,* 2(3):244–260. https://doi.org/10.1111/j.1754-9434.2009.01143.x

Menzies, I.E.P. (1993). *The functioning of social systems as a defence against anxiety.* London: Tavistock.

Meyer, T.N.A. & Boninelli, I. (2007). *Conversations in leadership. South African perspectives.* Randburg: Knowres.

Meznar, M.B. & Nicolini, D. (1995). The social construction of organisational learning. *Human Relations,* 48(7):24–36. https://doi.org/10.1177/001872679504800701

Miller, E.J. (1993). *From dependency to autonomy: Studies in organization and change.* London: Free Association.

Neumann, J.E.; Keller, K. & Dawson-Shepherd, A. (1997). *Developing organisational consultancy.* London: Routledge.

Newton, J.; Long, S. & Sievers, B. (2006). *Coaching in depth. The organisational role analysis approach.* London: Karnac.

Obholzer, A. & Roberts, V.Z. (1994). *The unconscious at work.* London: Routledge.

Orenstein, R.L. (2007). *Multidimensional executive coaching.* New York: Wiley. https://doi.org/10.1037/t01761-000

Peltier, B. (2001). *The psychology of executive coaching. Theory and application.* New York: Brunner-Routledge.

Peterson, D.B. (1996). Executive coaching at work. The art of one-on-one change. *Consulting Psychology Journal: Practice and Research,* 48(2):78–86. https://doi.org/10.1037//1061-4087.48.2.78

Porter-O'Grady, T. & Malloch, K. (2007). *Quantum leadership. A resource for health care innovation.* Boston. Jones & Bartlett.

Savage, C.M. (2001). Executive coaching: Professional self-care for nursing leaders. *Nursing Economics,* July:25–31.

Schafer, R. (2003). *Insight and interpretation. The essential tools of psychoanalysis*. London: Karnac.

Shapiro, E.R. & Carr, A.W. (1991). *Lost in familiar places: Creating new connections between the individual and society*. London: Yale University.

Smit, B. & Cilliers, F. (2006). Understanding implicit texts in focus groups from a systems psychodynamic perspective. *The Qualitative Report*, 11(2):302–316, http://www.nova.edu/ssss/QR/QR11-2/smit.pdf [Accessed 27 March 2010].

Sperry, L. (2004). *Executive coaching. The essential guide for mental health professionals*. New York: Brunner-Routledge. https://doi.org/10.4324/9780203483466

Stapley, L.F. (1996). *The personality of the organisation. A psychodynamic explanation of culture and change*. London: Free Association.

Stapley, L.F. (2006). *Individuals, groups and organisations beneath the surface*. London: Karnac.

Stern, L. (2001). *Executive coaching handbook: Principles and guidelines for a successful coaching partnership*. Boston: Executive Coaching Forum.

Stout Rostron, S. (2009). *Business coaching. Wisdom and practice. Unlocking the secrets of business coaching*. Randburg. Knowledge Resources

Sullivan, E.J. & Decker, P.J. (2009). *Effective leadership and management in nursing*. Upper Saddle River: Pearson Prentice Hall.

Taylor, R.G. (2007). Learning in uncertain times. In: T.N.A. Meyer & I. Boninelli (eds.), *Conversations in leadership. South African perspectives*, pp.162–179. Randburg: Knowledge resources.

Terre Blanche, M.; Durrheim, K. & Painter, D. (2006). *Research in practice. Applied methods for the social sciences*. Cape Town: UCT Press.

Turquet, P.M. (1974). Leadership – the individual in the group. In: G.S. Gibbard, J.J. Hartman & R.D. Mann (eds.), *Analysis of groups*, pp.15-26. San Francisco: Jossey-Bass.

Van der Colff, J.J. & Rothmann, S. (2009). Occupational stress, sense of coherence, coping, burnout and work engagement of registered nurses in South Africa. *South African Journal for Industrial Psychology*, 35(1):Art. #423, 10 pages. https://doi.org/10.4102/sajip.v35i1.423

Van Manen, M. (1990). *Researching lived experience*. Toronto: State University of New York.

Wells, L. (1980). The group-as-a-whole: A systemic socio-analytical perspective on interpersonal and group relations. In C.P. Alderfer & C.L. Cooper (eds.), *Advances in experiential social processes*, 2:165-198. London: Karnac.

Will, B. & Codrington, G. (2004). Coaching: Perspectives on leadership. *Management Today*, 20(7):51-53.

Willem, A. (2003). Coaching: Obtaining wisdom from the relationship. *Management Today*, 18(10):50-51. https://doi.org/10.1353/at.2003.0061

Article 4

The Experienced Impact of Systems Psychodynamic Leadership Coaching Amongst Professionals in a Financial Services Organisation[1]

F Cilliers

Background

Systems psychodynamic leadership coaching is a depth psychology perspective that provides opportunities for coachees to explore their leadership identity as it manifests in their conscious and unconscious role behaviour.

Aim

The research aim was to explore the experienced impact of systems psychodynamic leadership coaching amongst professionals in a financial services organisation and to report on how this impact can be understood in the context of the literature guidelines on coaching and leadership effectiveness.

Setting

The research was undertaken in a large South African financial services organisation where individual leadership coaching forms part of the leadership development programme (LDP).

[1]   Cilliers, F. (2018). The experienced impact of systems psychodynamic leadership coaching amongst professionals in a financial services organisation. *South African Journal of Economic and Management Sciences*, 21(1):a2091. https://doi.org/10.4102/sajems.v21i1.2091

Methods

The research was qualitative, explorative and descriptive in nature. A multi-case approach was used. Sampling was convenient and opportunistic and comprised of 15 charted accountants who attended six 90-min coaching sessions over 12 weeks. Data gathering comprised field notes and coachee essays during and after coaching. Hermeneutic phenomenology was used as the interpretive stance.

Results

Anxiety, task, role, boundaries, authorisation and identity manifested as themes. Coachees explored how their leadership identity was informed by their anxiety and defence mechanisms, how they took up their leadership role, authorised themselves and their colleagues, and managed their boundaries effectively. Compared to the general guidelines for leadership coaching effectiveness and the general indicators for effective leadership, systems psychodynamic leadership coaching seems to add value to leadership effectiveness.

Conclusion

Professionals in this financial services organisation experienced systems psychodynamic leadership coaching as demanding, challenging and yet fulfilling towards the exploration of their leadership identity. It seems that systems psychodynamics, as coaching stance, created a safe and good-enough container for these financial professionals to explore their own unconscious leadership behaviour and to gain a significant level of understanding and awareness of their own anxiety and defensive behaviours in their interaction with followers.

Introduction

As a field of study, leadership has an extensive and voluminous 100-year old literature base, containing an overwhelming proliferation of paradigms, definitions, models, theories, concepts, terms, outcomes, competencies and measurement instruments (Nohria & Khurana, 2010; Northouse, 2014; Veldsman & Johnson, 2016). According to Bennis (2007), this gives evidence of the complexity, dynamics and elusiveness associated with leadership, which creates confusion amongst researchers and practitioners. In general, leadership can be defined as the activity to willingly involve oneself, influence, coordinate and guide people's organisational activities towards attaining positive goals and outcomes for the organisation, according to the existing context and set strategy (Cooper, 2005; Leonard et al., 2013; Meyer & Boninelli, 2007). Research on the psychology of leadership is mostly informed by a humanistic conceptualisation and positivist operationalisation. Leadership research gives evidence of the psychometric relationship between leadership styles and behaviours, and organisational outcomes (Kaiser, Hogan & Craig, 2008). For example, a task orientation is applicable where there is control over a situation, a people orientation where control is moderate, consideration where job satisfaction is desirable, structure where effectiveness and containment are needed and a transformational stance where inspiration and commitment are needed. Presently, the leadership literature focuses strongly on transformational leadership in a quest to understand how leaders need to cope in the 21st century and postmodern era (Veldsman & Johnson, 2016), amidst never-before-experienced complexity such as the new economy, globalisation, mergers and acquisitions, chaos, paradox, diversity, power, risk and limited resources (Bennis & Sample, 2015; Crevani & Endrissat, 2016; Elkington & Booysen, 2015; Klein, Rice & Schermer, 2009).

Leadership coaching has developed as a way of assisting leadership in coping with its complexity (Passmore, Peterson & Freire, 2013). Coaching's importance is reflected in it being referred to as the fastest-growing profession and the single most influential input in the modern organisational and corporate environment (Kahn, 2014). Leadership coaching is generally defined as a regular, short-term, highly focussed, contractual organisational learning opportunity. It involves a facilitating (helping) relationship between a coachee, who has managerial and leadership authority and responsibility in an organisation, and a coach, who uses psychological and behavioural paradigms, models, techniques and methods to assist the coachee to develop relevant leadership behaviours and thereby improve organisational effectiveness (Brunning, 2006; Hawkins & Smith, 2013; Kets de Vries, Korotov & Florent-Treacy, 2007; McKenna & Davis, 2009; Paice, 2012). Of the demands on leadership (Nohria & Khurana, 2010), coaching focuses on the people aspects of insight, learning, growth and change in the self and between the self and the other. Thus, the goal of leadership coaching can be framed as to significantly optimise the leader 's effectiveness on the intra-personal and interpersonal levels. This refers to self-leadership, leadership of the other (colleagues and followers in dyads and teams) and leadership in the organisation as a system (Greif, 2007). Coaching effectiveness is seldom linked to indicators for effective leadership, such as those formulated by the Kellogg Foundation (Development Guild, 2015).

Although the merit and value of leadership coaching are accepted in practice (Page & De Haan, 2014), it lacks solid research evidence to establish its identity as a scientific intervention in the field of organisational development (OD) (Kahn, 2014). Theoretically, all the major psychological paradigms have been applied to leadership coaching, for example, psychodynamics, behaviourism, cognitive psychology, humanism, existentialism and neuropsychology (Bachkirova, 2011; Bluckert, 2006; Brown & Brown, 2012; Passmore et al., 2013; Peltier, 2009). However, in practice, research mostly reports on coaching programmes linked to positive psychology constructs (Cilliers, 2011; Page & De Haan, 2014; Western, 2012), such as those applied in the goal, reality, options, will (GROW) model (Stout Rostron, 2009). Specifically, emotional intelligence (Dippenaar & Schaap, 2017), happiness (Biswas-Diener & Dean, 2007), resilience (Maddi & Khoshaba, 2005) and flourishing (Grant, 2007) are included in positive psychology coaching programmes. The published coaching research on the aforementioned positive psychology constructs show face validity in terms of enhancing the behavioural constructs it sets out to develop (Dippenaar & Schaap, 2017).

In the present research project, the authorities of a financial services organisation wanted to extend their leadership coaching offering with (amongst others) a model that 'helps leaders understand the complexity of leadership's individual and organisational systemic role identity explored from an unconscious perspective'. The researcher was invited to make a presentation on systems psychodynamic leadership coaching (SPLC), which was accepted with the request to report back to the organisation about the impact of this coaching stance. Thus, the problem statement of this research project was formulated as follows: what is the experienced impact of SPLC amongst professionals in a financial services organisation, and how can this impact be understood in the context of literature guidelines on coaching and leadership effectiveness?

The Motivation for Systems Psychodynamic Leadership Coaching

Because of the huge pressure on and insecurities in financial services organisations in terms of performance and ethics (Kahn, 2014), it is difficult to single out one of the mainstream leadership theories (Kets de Vries et al., 2007) as the most appropriate basis for the coaching of its leaders. Mainstream theories include the contingency, personal attribute, trait, competency, situational and transactional or transformational leadership perspectives (Nohria & Khurana, 2010). Systems psychodynamic leadership coaching offers an open-systems approach focussing on the exploration of conscious and unconscious behaviour relevant to how the coachee takes up the role of leader as part of the larger systemic dynamic, while authorising the self and others and managing the relevant boundaries in service of the leadership task (Newton, Long & Sievers, 2006). Next, SPLC was contrasted to other leadership coaching models with the following arguments. Many leadership coaching programmes are not based on any informing leadership framework or definition (Beck, 2012). The learning approach in the mainstream leadership coaching programmes is simplistic, linear (working from normal to optimal), reductionist (focussing on evidence-based outcomes) (Western, 2012) and focussing on behavioural change, thus excluding the holistic, systemic, existential experiences, characteristic of the complexity of human experience in organisational and social systems (Western, 2012). Furthermore, traditional models focus mostly on rational and conscious behaviour, thus ignoring the impact of irrational and unconscious behaviour (Nohria & Khurana, 2010). A structured stepwise approach is followed, thereby limiting the coachee's movement towards their specific learning dynamic (Passmore et al., 2013). Especially in programmes presented from a positive psychology perspective, leadership is defined from one selected theory and then framed as an individual phenomenon, thus ignoring leadership as a systemic phenomenon (Bennis, 2007; Kahn, 2014). Positive psychology coaching programmes focus on positive behaviour, thereby excluding leaders' negative experiences, such as loneliness, attacks, envy, narcissism and performance anxiety. These programmes also accentuate personal development, thus denying the shadow side of leadership and toxicity, which often leads to the derailment of leaders (Western, 2012).

Systems Psychodynamics

Systems psychodynamics (SP) has its roots in depth psychology, Freudian systemic psychoanalysis, group and object relations theory and systems thinking (Kets de Vries et al., 2007). Systems psychodynamics is defined as the scientific study towards the understanding of the manifestation of unconscious and dynamic behaviour in organisations, especially about leadership and authorisation (Colman & Bexton, 1975; Colman & Geller, 1985; Cytrynbaum & Noumair, 2004). The SP leadership philosophy is conceptualised in terms of the systemic identity, taking up the role of leader, working on a given primary task and being authorised to manage the self and the other on the boundary between what is inside versus outside (Huffington et al., 2004; Stapley, 2006).

Systems psychodynamics interprets the present voluminous amount of leadership theories and its constant deconstruction as compulsiveness and an unconscious defence against the anxiety of facing the complexity of the leadership role, its relationships and relatedness (Czander, 1993; French & Simpson, 2015). Systems psychodynamics sees leadership as not belonging to an individual or a group and states that it cannot be confined to a set theory of interactions, rules, guidelines or habits. Rather, leadership is seen as a psychosocial influencing dynamic (Kets de Vries, 2006). Western (2013) explains that:

1. 'psycho' refers to the psychodynamics of leadership happening within and between people – leadership and followership stimulate intra-psychic, unconscious and emotional responses within and inter-relational dynamics between employees;

2. 'social' refers to the social construction and relational dynamics of leadership, power and authority, control of material and symbolic resources, use of knowledge and technology as manifesting in organisational history, discourses, culture and politics;

3. 'influencing' refers to the agency to influence the other, drawing on a wide array of resources such as personality and coercive power; and

4. 'dynamic' refers to the forever fluid movement of the social leadership-followership process, which can't be reduced to skills, competencies or a way of being.

Systems Psychodynamic Leadership Coaching

The primary task of SPLC is to provide psycho-educational and developmentally focussed learning opportunities for coachees, to explore the self and the prevailing organisational dynamics as an open system (including structural aspects such as design, division of labour, boundaries, the primary task, levels of authority, reporting relationships and relatedness) and the manifestation of their own unconscious systemic behaviour (primitive, social and system domain defences) (Armstrong & Rustin, 2015; Beck, 2012; Brunning, 2006; Kets de Vries, 2006; Neumann, Kellner & Dawson-Shepherd, 1997; Newton et al., 2006; Sandler, 2011). Systems psychodynamic leadership coaching focuses on conscious-rational, unconscious–irrational and the congruence-incongruence between these, the manifesting anxiety and its defensive structures on the systemic micro- (individual), meso (group) and macro (organisational) levels (Campbell

& Huffington, 2008; Hirschhorn, 1993; Kets de Vries, 2014). Anxiety is accepted as the driving force (dynamo) of the relationship and relatedness between leadership and followership. Defensive structures manifest in the systemic social unconscious as basic assumptions of dependence, fight/flight, pairing (Bion, 1961), me-ness and one-ness or we-ness (Fraher, 2004), as well as defences such as splitting, introjection, suppression, denial, projection, projective identification and transference (Blackman, 2004). The coachee's leadership identity as observed, experienced and represented in the mind, is informed by how the role is taken up and the nature of the experienced authorisation while managing the boundaries between the self and the other in the service of the primary task (Cytrynbaum & Noumair, 2004). 'Task' refers to the basic component of work and can manifest as adhering to the primary task (indicating contained anxiety) or as diversions into off-task and anti-task behaviour (indicating, e.g. performance anxiety) (Czander, 1993). 'Role' refers to the boundary surrounding work and position and between the coachee and the other (Stapley, 2006).

'Authorisation' refers to the formal and official right to perform a task, bestowed from above (the organisation, manager, leader), the side (colleagues), below (subordinates) and from within (self-authorisation) (Hirschhorn, 1997).

'Boundary' refers to the physical or psychological demarcation and differentiation, observable or subjective, acting as the space around and between parts of the system (e.g. time, space and task) (Cytrynbaum & Noumair, 2004). Transactional analysis adds the constructs of the systemic ego states of parent, adult and child, script development and games (Erskine, 2010; Tangolo, 2015; Tudor & Summers, 2014), explaining the coachee's communication in significant relationships.

Operationally, the SP coach provides an emotionally contained and transitional space to the coachee's experiential exploration of the self in the role as leader (Clarke, Hahn & Hoggett, 2008). The coach attends to the coachee's reality testing, cognitive functioning (abstractions, differentiations), affective functioning (emotional relatedness to the self and the other), experienced anxiety and use of individual, social and system domain defensive (differentiated between the neurotic, psychotic and the perverse) and object relations, vertical with authority (based on the transference from parental figures), and horizontal with colleagues (based on the transference from siblings) (Newton et al., 2006). The coachee's role is analysed by differentiating between the three role parts of normative (the rational, objectively measurable content), existential (how they believe they are performing based on their introjections (their unconscious internalised and transferred feelings, attitudes and values that belong to the external environment) and phenomenal roles (how they believe they perform as experienced by colleagues and others based on their received projections) (Obholzer & Roberts, 1994). Incongruence between the three role parts indicates role anxiety, which could manifest as free-floating, survival, performance, paranoid or persecutory anxiety (Blackman, 2004). At the same time, their valence is studied, defined as one's unconscious tendency or propensity to internalise, collude with and respond to the projections of the other and to take on a similar informal role repeatedly in groups dependence on one's object relations and social identity (Beck, 2012; Sandler, 2011). Typically, sessions start with an open invitation such as: 'Tell me about your present experiences in your role as a leader'. Sessions do not have specific agendas – rather, they follow the coachee's conscious and unconscious exploration and stay as close as possible to the coachee's immediate role experiences (Armstrong & Rustin, 2015; Kets de Vries, 2014). Storytelling and drawings may also be included (Western, 2012).

The coach needs to be systems psychodynamically informed, which refers to a high level of training and competence in working with systemic unconscious material, as well as having a dynamic self-insight and being prepared to use the self as an instrument (Huffington et al., 2004; Kets de Vries et al., 2007). The role of the coach is to not take on a guru position but rather a reflective stance from a meta-position (Schafer, 2003), alert to the coachee's conscious and unconscious behaviour and the manifestation of defensive behaviour without judgement, memory or desire (Beck, 2012; Campbell & Huffington, 2008; Sandler, 2011). The coach formulates working hypotheses, defined as an integrative statement of 'searching into' the coachee's experiences, which are constantly revisited in the light of further or new evidence (Campbell, 2007). Coachees are encouraged to be curious, to free-associate, to explore a variety of related feelings, patterns, defences and representations, including the transferences between coach and leader, and to move between different levels of abstraction in thought (Jaques, 1990).

Research on coachees' experiences in SPLC reports in general raised awareness of, insight into and understanding of their leadership role identity in their relationships with and relatedness to the organisational system (Chapman & Cilliers, 2008; Cilliers & Terblanche, 2010; Huffington et al., 2004; Kahn, 2014; Motsoaledi & Cilliers, 2012; Passmore et al., 2013). Coachees experience a change in their thinking about their representative nature and value in the organisational system and how they authorise themselves and their followers in their complex matrix systems with its constantly changing organisational context and conscious and unconscious psychological boundaries within and between conflicting subsystems (Kets de Vries, 2006, 2014; Kets de Vries et al., 2007). Coaching gives them the opportunity to explore the dynamics of taking up their leadership role and the accompanying levels of survival anxiety, feeling disorientated, lost, lonely, doubtful, not good enough and performance anxiety to perform their primary task and manage their relationships with followers effectively (Passmore et al., 2013). Coachees report on working through very real experiences and behaviours as they never expected to play an important role in leadership (Cilliers, 2005; Motsoaledi & Cilliers, 2012). These include their unconscious beliefs, fantasies, wishes, conflicts, defences, preferences, competition, rivalry, jealousy, envy, hostility, narcissism, aggression, regression, repetition of previous relationship patterns, valence for attracting specific projections, collusion with and responses to others' projections and containing feelings or objects on behalf of the system (Beck, 2012; Brunning, 2006; Kets de Vries et al., 2007; Neumann et al., 1997; Newton et al., 2006; Obholzer & Roberts, 1994; Sandler, 2011; Stapley, 2006).

Research Aim and Contribution

The research aim was to explore the experienced impact of SPLC amongst professionals in a financial services organisation and to report on how this impact can be understood in the context of the literature guidelines on coaching and leadership effectiveness. The contribution of this study lies firstly in a rich description of the SPLC experiences of professionals in a financial services organisation. Secondly, this study contributes towards an understanding of the experienced impact of SPLC as a coaching stance, as well as on leadership effectiveness. Thus, the research has intrinsic (in the understanding of the coachees' experiences) and instrumental value (to provide the coaching fraternity with meaningful data about the nature of SPLC as a depth psychology leadership developmental input) (Denzin & Lincoln, 2005).

Methods

Research Design and Approach

The research was qualitative, explorative and descriptive in nature (Thorne, 2016). Participatory action research was performed (Wagner, Kawulich & Garner, 2012) to ensure continuous connectivity, effective communication and good working relationships in the research system, as well as to ensure active researcher involvement. Hermeneutic phenomenology was chosen as the interpretive research paradigm (Clarke & Hoggett, 2009). A multi-case approach was used (McLeod, 2012; Wilson & MacLean, 2011), focussing on coachees' experiences while undergoing SPLC, delimited in time, place and task, and then studied through observation, documented self-report and comparison (Hollway & Jefferson, 2010).

Setting

The study was set in a large South African financial services organisation where the OD division provides professional, logistical and administrative opportunities to financial professionals in need of individual leadership coaching. The researcher was requested to serve on the coaching panel to conduct chemistry meetings (Stout Rostron, 2009), followed by SPLC with interested professional staff members, according to a standard coaching contract consisting of six 90-min sessions over 12 weeks. All sessions were conducted in a boardroom during office hours.

Sampling

Fifteen professionals voluntarily completed the coaching contract. This number became the purposive and convenient sample (Thorne, 2016) for this study. The sample comprised charted accountants appointed on associate director level. There were nine males and six females, five black people, four Indians and six white people, and all were younger than 40 years of age.

Data Collection, Recording and Analysis

Two data collection methods were used, namely coaching field notes (Thorne, 2016) and coachee essays (Wolcott, 2001). The field notes, recorded by the coach during and after each session, provided a detailed rendition of the coachees' verbatim and non-verbal behaviour during each coaching session. The common objection against field notes, namely the researcher's subjective perceptions, was compensated for by the researcher's attention to detail during recording (Denzin & Lincoln, 2005). Halfway through and at the end of the coaching contract, each coachee wrote an essay of about five A4 pages on the question: 'What do you experience and what are you learning through coaching in your role as leader in this organisation?' The two methods in combination provided the text for analysis of the coachees' lived experience (Thorne, 2016). Simple hermeneutics allowed for the understanding of the content of coachees' experiences during coaching and double hermeneutics allowed for the critical interpretation of their experiences from the SP stance (Clarke & Hoggett, 2009) as it manifested in themes.

Ethicality

During each individual chemistry meeting the relevant coaching and research ethical aspects were explained to the coachees (Terre Blanche, Durrheim & Painter, 2006). These aspects were informed consent, voluntary participation and withdrawal, privacy and confidentiality. Participants also gave consent for their data to be included in this research project.

Strategies Employed to Ensure Quality Data

Trustworthiness was based on the following aspects (Wagner et al. 2012). In terms of credibility, the researcher is qualified as a systems psychodynamically informed coach. During the research project, the researcher received coaching supervision (Kets de Vries et al., 2007) to ensure objectivity and self-authorisation. The coaching research was approved and authorised by the organisation, and the OD division assisted in ensuring consistency in logistics and practical arrangements. The research evidenced strong and believable validity in its psychological description, which revealed the complexities of how the SP constructs of task, role, authorisation and boundaries manifested and how the dynamic interaction between the constructs informs the coachees' leadership identity. In this research, triangulation was defined as the process of assessing the outcome of research by viewing it from different perspectives and methods, resulting in a convergence of the data to present rich and valid data (Creswell & Plano Clark, 2011; Denzin & Lincoln, 2005; McLeod, 2012; Wilson & MacLean, 2011). Methodological and data triangulation referred to the inclusion of field notes and essays as raw data to avoid interpreting already interpreted data. Investigator triangulation (Wagner et al., 2012) was ensured in using peer reviewers (Thorne, 2016). Two independent psychologists, not associated with the research project, both SP informed coaches, were asked to review the database and the qualitative findings using their own criteria (Creswell & Plano Clark, 2011). Their positive feedback on the data analysis gave evidence of dependability. Their feedback on saturation provided evidence of internal generalisability (Denzin & Lincoln, 2005). Theory triangulation was attended to by including transactional analysis (as another interpretive stance within the SP paradigm), which added to the richness of ego states operating in the data (see Wagner et al., 2012).

Findings

The emerging themes were anxiety, task, role, boundaries, authorisation and identity.

Anxiety

Coachees experienced free-floating anxiety (Blackman, 2004). They referred to the organisation's demand to 'become more involved in leadership' – a 'job that I know nothing about' and 'I am not even sure I want it'. They expressed performance anxiety (Blackman, 2004) about leadership ('something I have no training in') and existential and separation anxiety in the fear of giving up 'my professional role in thinking about and working with numbers – not with people'). In terms of their dependence on authority figures, they tended to split their authority in the mind (Armstrong, 2005) between the coach as the good object (Klein, 1997) ('the guru' that 'must help' and 'understand', 'help me make sense out of the confusion of relationships' and 'save me' from not knowing) and their organisational leadership role as the bad object ('they are not helping in this chaos', 'they don't seem to know themselves', 'I doubt if they had any leadership training themselves'). They used fight as a defence against the 'cruel' system for 'allowing them to not know' and 'to struggle' with difficult clients and colleagues. They used flight as a defence to get away from difficult relationships ('I avoid getting involved in issues with people'). They exhibited we-ness when they expressed strong feelings (referred to as 'frustration' and 'annoyance') and me-ness when the individual wanted to distance the self from the larger system, who was supposed to be impressed with his or her professional performance. Their defensive structures (Armstrong & Rustin, 2015) consisted of splitting between the (introjection of the) good professional track record, versus the (projection of the) bad of the 'people issues' associated with leadership and regression ('I wish I was still a clerk who [could] just be busy with auditing tasks all the time'). During the sessions, coachees explored these anxieties towards differentiating between their own introjected feeling and thinking behaviour, and what the system was projecting onto them. This resulted in projective identification (Klein, 1997), which was an awareness they had never felt before ('I realise more and more that I take on so much of other people's stuff', 'it is not easy to do this work'). They explored how their awareness of their dependence and 'my blaming of the firm for my issues', 'stand in my way to develop my own potential'.

Task

Coachees split their known professional (Charted Accountant) task from their unknown task of leading people. Originally, they attached (Sievers, 2009) to the 'simplicity' of the management of client projects while they detached from what they experienced as the 'extremely demanding', 'complex' and 'unpredictable' leadership task. They realised their inclination to avoid the complexity of leadership by using 'flight into control' of the task ('I feel more productive when I check my team's work on paper' vs. 'I feel so out of control when I need to address the conflict in my team'). They learned to differentiate between the primary task of a project and when they 'go off-task', especially when they feel out of control ('I realise that when I am anxious, I want to control even the uncontrollable and then I lose perspective of the primary task').

Role

Coachees experienced conflict between their normative, existential and phenomenal roles (Obholzer & Roberts, 1994), indicating their role anxiety. Intellectually they understood their normative role as a combination of and balance between their professional and leadership roles. Emotionally they 'struggled because I wanted to keep them apart', especially in difficult interpersonal situations 'when I feel my stress skyrocketing'. In their existential role, they were proud of how the firm had recognised their work, their career background, accomplishments, values and personality characteristics as professionals ('what I was trained to do', 'what I prefer' and 'love to do'). They started to realise their regression (Blackman, 2004) into the known role was an indication of the anxiety caused by their leadership role. In their phenomenal role, they explored the projections they received from 'the other', such as colleagues, partners and family. This included expectations of being heroes to save the system with their intelligence, 'professionalism', emotional strength and 'resilience', as well as their interpersonal competence and 'empathy'. They learned to become aware when these projections onto them occurred ('when it is not my stuff', 'I am learning that if it feels unreal, I know it is not mine', 'I do not see myself that way', 'it is what people want me to be for them'). The existential-phenomenal role difference indicated to them that their 'identity was under attack', which caused high levels of anxiety. Towards the end, coachees could start to differentiate between what belonged to them (their introjections) and what systemic projections they received from the other.

Boundaries

Coachees consciously understood the role of organisational time, space and task boundaries. Yet they were often surprised at how their unconscious boundaries (in the mind) influenced their leadership behaviour. This included the boundary between their personal self and their organisational role ('these roles are so different'), between financial professional and leader of others ('it is a totally different ball game'), the psychological boundaries between associate director and partner in the firm ('we are treated as professionals' and then 'act like children towards the parents') and the boundaries between professional leader and client ('they treat me so differently when I am in my leader role'). Some coachees explored their valence (Huffington et al., 2004) to contain 'feelings and stuff' for the other ('it may be part of the role, but it is very difficult' to carry others' projections). A few coachees processed how they moved from being over-bounded (and having impenetrable boundaries) (Czander, 1993), which served to contain their performance anxiety, towards using their systemic awareness to 'relax' and try to function with permeable boundaries.

Authorisation

Coachees understood how they consciously self-authorised (Hirschhorn, 1997) and how they were authorised from above by the partners in the firm, from the side by colleagues and from below from their team members. Their 'most significant learning' was the realisation of the frequency and intensity of being unconsciously de-authorised in the system. In their existential role, this happened as a parental transference dynamic (Hindle & Sherwin-White, 2014) in how they heard their superiors (partners in the firm) 'as if he is my controlling father' ('I can hear my parents' voices telling me that I am not good enough', 'I have often been told by my teachers that I will not make it far '). In their phenomenal role, this happened through the processing of their received projections of incompetence ('they withhold important information from me' 'about rules' and 'the right way of doing'). This was often experienced as management's 'type of power play'. Coachees explored the unconscious power dynamics and could start to process their individual systemic valence to play 'the victim' and 'underdog' roles. Good insights were gained from studying how they collude (Armstrong & Rustin, 2015) with systemic power games. For most coachees, significant learning took place in self-authorisation based on the differentiation between what belongs to the self and what not and 'not to take responsibility or guilt for the others'. One coachee mentioned, 'I now understand that what I often see as incompetence is much more a case of not being authorised by leadership'.

Identity

Coachees struggled to differentiate between and integrate their personal, professional and leader part-identities (Vansina & Vansina-Cobbaert, 2008). They experienced 'confusion', 'being overwhelmed' and high levels of performance anxiety in their new leadership role. This role contained a complexity of irrational expectations – introjections of having to be a 'super-competent' 'people's person', as well as unrealistic projections onto them from the organisational system. As young leaders, they became aware of the unconscious dynamic of 'being used' by the organisational system (Campbell & Groenbaek, 2006) to contain and process the organisation's leadership and succession anxiety. Although this caused free-floating anxiety ('it is very confusing', 'I can't process this by myself'), the coachees move towards exploring, disentangling and differentiating between illusion and fantasy on the one hand, and their reality of taking up a leadership role in the context of their own unique personality styles. They were brave to explore and relinquish their ignorance in favour of heightened awareness. They experienced 'relief', 'insight' and authorisation to face the 'below the surface stuff' that 'play such a big role' in their relationships 'at work and at home'.

Discussion

The research findings are discussed with reference to three sets of data seen as significant for coaching effectiveness in this research, namely:

1. the experienced impact of SPLC amongst professionals in this financial services organisation;

2. the experienced impact of SP as a coaching stance; and

3. the experienced impact of SPLC explored against the Kellogg Foundation's indicators for effective leadership (see Kets de Vries, et al. 2007; Nohria & Khurana, 2010; Passmore et al., 2013; Western, 2012).

The Experienced Impact of Systems Psychodynamic Leadership Coaching Amongst Professionals in a Financial Services Organisation

In their normative role coachees had cognitively reconstructed leadership into an accessible and workable behavioural repertoire. This reconstruction was made possible by relinquishing the need to study the voluminous amount of literature on leadership theories and models ('MBA style') and to instead experience leadership as a role with many facets such as rational versus irrational, conscious versus unconscious behaviour on the self–other boundary.

To work with and learn about the self through the exploration of anxiety as an unconscious driving force and its defences was surprising to most coachees ('I thought anxiety and defences were for sick people', and 'here we have spent a whole session on trying to understand my defences against my primitive anxiety'). In their existential role coachees explored their introjections about leadership as the impossible task (Cytrynbaum & Noumair, 2004) often linked to negative past experiences with 'my so-called leaders'. Their introjected values, feelings, thinking and expressive behaviours that manifested as their psychological valence contributed to their most profound learning. The exploration of their transferences of relationships with parental figures and siblings from their family of origin into their present leadership role (Winnicott, 2006), brought surprising insights in terms of repeated patterns and parallel processes. In their phenomenal role, many coachees explored projection as a phenomenon for the first time in their lives. They were intrigued by the power of their own and their received projections and its capacity to influence one's behaviour through projective identification. Applied to their leadership role, they reported on their significant learning about how they formed unconscious ideas and biases in their relationships with and about their colleagues, direct reports and partners in the firm, based on their family of origin experiences. They gave examples of their growing awareness about how they projected their own unconscious emotional survival and performance anxieties onto their colleagues during meetings and in project management. For many, the breakthrough came when they could, in the here-and-now moment, realise and own the projection as 'my own stuff' and even offer an explanation and 'take back my own stuff'. These findings have also been reported in other South African SP coaching research (Chapman & Cilliers, 2008; Cilliers, 2005; Cilliers & Terblanche, 2010; Kahn, 2014; Motsoaledi & Cilliers, 2012).

The coachees learned about their object relations through the transactional analysis interpretations (Tudor & Summers, 2014). They reported how they have framed the construct leadership as the demanding and controlling parent in the mind and how they then, in a defensive reaction, took on a rebellious-child response. It took hard work to disentangle from the hooked parent-child engagement in the mind and to shift to adult–adult communication to ensure a balanced and realistic conceptualisation of leadership. They also reported on using their coaching insights to diagnose their project and team cultures. They realised that the firm's prevailing culture was mainly experienced as the critical parent with almost no caring-parent behaviour manifesting. A few coachees started to address this awareness in their projects by stimulating positive storytelling about leaders and leadership, to deconstruct the negative projections onto leadership as a role, as well as onto leaders as people. No research could be traced where transactional analysis was used as an interpretive stance in leadership coaching.

The Experienced Impact of Systems Psychodynamics as a Coaching Stance

In order to understand the experienced impact of SP as coaching stance, the findings were compared to the following literature on coaching and leadership effectiveness: Bain (1998); Campbell and Huffington (2008); French and Simpson (2015); Meyer and Boninelli (2007); Nohria and Khurana (2010); Passmore et al. (2013); and Sternberg (2007).

Coaching is embedded in contemporary leadership thinking. Systems psychodynamic leadership coaching facilitated aspects of transformational leadership (Avolio, 2007) with reference to individualisation and intellectual stimulation as intra-personal aspects. Systems psychodynamic leadership coaching did not directly address inspirational and idealised influence as interpersonal leadership dimensions. Rather, SPLC focussed on containment leadership (Kilburg & Diedrich, 2007) where leaders become aware of their unconscious representation as the leader in the mind of the system.

Coaching provides a reflectional space. Systems psychodynamic leadership coaching provided opportunities for reflection about leadership (not as only a theory or as competencies, but) as a systemic role managing the boundaries between the rational and irrational, the conscious and unconscious and between the self and the other. Furthermore, SPLC provided a transitional space (Winnicott, 2006) for coachees to (1) develop their awareness of and insight into systemic individual (micro-), group (meso-) and organisational (macro-level) behavioural dynamics and (2) to explore their leadership identity in terms of self-representation, behaviour and relationships. Coachees moved from being mostly ignorant unconscious containers of system domain, socially constructed and personal defences, to an openness to experiment with unconscious personal and leadership behaviour. They learned to take up their leadership roles with significantly more self-authorisation and to manage their boundaries with consciousness and rationality. They started to integrate their normative, experiential and phenomenal roles and reported on experiencing more congruence between their introjections and received projections. This indicates a heightened awareness of anxiety as it happens (in the here and now) and the differentiation between 'what emotionality is mine and what is not mine'. They illustrated an increased capacity to create new thoughts, to process relatively deep feelings and to venture into conscious and rational action (as part of their adult ego state). Thus, leaders developed a dynamic awareness of their individual identity, how they related to others, what they individually represented in the organisational system and the competence to ask critical questions about the dynamic experiences of the other. These behavioural outcomes are congruent to how SPLC is described in the literature (Beck, 2012; Kets de Vries, 2014; Macaux, 2014; Newton et al., 2006; Passmore et al., 2013; Peltier, 2009; Sandler, 2011). Some of the reported insights can be framed as moving towards leadership wisdom (Kilburg & Diedrich, 2007), defined as taking up the role with an openness to experience and a creative exploration of own, team and organisational behaviours towards a cognitive understanding, a strong sense of self and a systemic awareness of process and dynamics.

Coaching enhances an understanding of organisational dynamics. Systems psychodynamic leadership coaching facilitated leaders' macro-level insight into the dynamics of the system domain defences of financial organisations, such as narcissism, envy, competition, rivalry and greed (Long, 2008). On the meso-level they explored socially constructed defences such as the compulsive dependence on rules, regulations and customs (e.g. in auditing as a profession and in the firm's partner structure). On the micro-level, they explored the complexities of their own defensive leadership behaviour, especially their use of denial and projection, and how these dynamics permeated below the surface of consciousness and, as such, influenced their leadership relationships. They explored how they contained emotionality on behalf of the meso-system and practised ways of owning what they experienced as their own.

Coaching facilitates understanding of leadership dynamics and complexity. Systems psychodynamic leadership coaching frames the leadership task as the execution of a dynamic and systemic relational process between leader and follower (Kets de Vries, 2014). Coachees started to integrate dynamic concepts into their daily work, for example, the primary task, off-task and anti-task behaviour. This allowed for increased rational self-regulation (Campbell & Groenbaek, 2006) and a here-and-now awareness and realisation of when they were unconsciously colluding or being seduced into serving irrational systemic agendas.

Coaching facilitates the conceptualisation of leadership and its complexity. Systems psychodynamic leadership coaching facilitated coachees' experiential conceptualisation of leadership as consisting of social and politically conscious and unconscious dynamics. As leaders, their self-awareness and authorisation facilitated their more effective boundary management between self, other and organisational system (Kets de Vries et al., 2007). In terms of Jaques' (1990) stratified systems theory, postulating how leaders need to deal with increasing levels of complexity as they get promoted up the hierarchy, SPLC seems to have stimulated fourth-order complexity and decision-making. Systems psychodynamic leadership coaching facilitated coachees' conceptualisation of leadership as a dynamic relationship with others and an unconscious relatedness with the system as a whole. Systems psychodynamic leadership coaching stimulated third-order complexity and decision-making. It seems that the clearer explication of leadership as a construct in SP was advantageous in coachees' systemic conceptualisation and dealing with leadership complexity.

Coaching facilitates the construction of a leadership identity. Systems psychodynamic leadership coaching facilitated a systemic awareness and strong efforts to establish an own leadership role boundary enhanced with self and others' authorisation towards realising the coachees' leadership identity (Campbell & Groenbaek, 2006).

Coaching facilitates the transference of a leadership competencies and virtues. Systems psychodynamic leadership coaching addressed cognitive, personal and social characteristics and universal leadership virtues such as humanity (kindness, social intelligence) and courage (emotionality, authenticity, bravery, persistence) (Kets de Vries, 2014). Systems psychodynamic leadership coaching facilitated leaders' movement from dependence and the denial of their own systemic impact towards working with their independence and ownership in their leadership roles, with some evidence of interdependence (Stapley, 2006).

They became more robust in their exploration of their own, as well as the behaviour of others as they explored the effect of their defensive behaviours.

The Kellogg Foundation's Indicators for Effective Leadership

The Kellogg Foundation indicators (Development Guild, 2015) are categorised as individual, organisational, community, field (outcome) and systemic. Systems psychodynamic leadership coaching facilitated behavioural awareness in various aspects of all five indicators. One outstanding element was the coachee's openness to use the self as an instrument (Kets de Vries et al., 2007) in the systemic context, meaning to recognise defences such as projections and transferences as they happen. In terms of Sibson Consulting's (O'Malley & Baker, 2012) 12 criteria of effective leadership, SPLC stimulated intent, focus and human significance. Systems psychodynamic leadership coaching additionally stimulated form, representation, imagination, human significance, context and criticism. Less evidence occurred about authenticity, engagement and pleasure (which one would expect to be addressed in positive psychology coaching). It seems that SPLC impacted leadership functioning in terms of self-leadership, leadership of the other (colleagues and followers in dyads and teams) and leadership in the organisation as a system (Greif, 2007).

Conclusion

Professionals in this financial services organisation experienced SPLC as a demanding as well as a fulfilling activity. They explored their own dynamic conscious and unconscious leadership behaviour, how they take up their leadership role, authorise themselves and their colleagues, as well as how they are authorised by the organisational system, manage their boundaries and develop insight into their leadership identity. Systems psychodynamic leadership coaching as methodology created a good-enough container for these professionals to explore, gain a significant level of understanding of and insight into their own anxiety and defensive behaviours to work towards the optimisation of their leader-follower relationships.

The organisation's request for feedback about the impact of SP as a coaching stance is encapsulated in the discussion section of this article. Measured against guidelines for leadership coaching effectiveness, SPLC seems to comply with most of the set criteria. Although SPLC does not subscribe to a specific leadership theory, it seemed necessary to report back in this manner because of the corporate need to compare coaching inputs for purposes of return on investment.

The limitations of this research are as follows. The literature on SP in leadership coaching is limited, which makes the comparison and confirmation of findings difficult. In terms of design, the contractual restriction of working with only six coaching sessions limited the possibility of a deeper study of coachees' transference of learning to more actual leadership interactions. The thickness of the data may imply that this study reported on too many phenomena in the coachees' experiences, as opposed to focussing on fewer phenomena and giving a deeper rendition of their manifestation.

It was recommended that future research include coaching with other professional fraternities and the experienced difference between professions and that different leadership coaching stances be compared in order to illustrate the strengths and most appropriate application of various models. For this specific organisation, it was recommended that the data from this study should be followed up, for example, in interviews to ascertain the long-term impact of SPLC. The last recommendation is that leaders at partner level be included in the SPLC programme. Apart from providing them with the opportunity to learn about their individual and team dynamics, it would also give a gestalt view of the manifesting SP of this kind of financial services organisation.

Acknowledgements

Competing Interests

The author declares that he has no financial or personal relationships that may have inappropriately influenced him in writing this article.

References

Armstrong, D. (2005). *Organisation in the mind. Psychoanalysis, group relations and organisational consultancy.* London: Karnac.

Armstrong, D. & Rustin, M. (2015). *Social defences against anxiety.* London: Karnac.

Avolio, B.J. (2007). Promoting more integrative strategies for leadership theory-building. *American Psychologist*, 62(1):25-33. https://doi.org/10.1037/0003-066X.62.1.25

Bachkirova, T. (2011) *Developmental coaching. Working with the self.* Maidenhead: Open University Press.

Bain, A.(1998). Social defences against organisational learning. *Human Relations*, 51(3):413-429. https://doi.org/10.1177/001872679805100309

Beck, U.C. (2012). *Psychodynamic coaching. Focus and depth.* London: Karnac.

Bennis, W. (2007). The challenges of leadership in the modern world. *American Psychologist*, 62(1):2-5. https://doi.org/10.1037/0003-066X.62.1.2

Bennis, W. & Sample, S.B. (2015). *The art and adventure of leadership.* New Jersey: Wiley.

Bion, W.R. (1961). *Experiences in groups.* London: Tavistock.

Biswas-Diener, R. & Dean, B. (2007). *Positive psychology coaching. Putting the science of happiness to work for your clients.* John Wiley, NJ: Hoboken.

Blackman, J.S. (2004). 101 *Defences. How the mind shields itself.* New York: Brunner-Routledge. https://doi.org/10.4324/9780203492369

Bluckert, P. (2006). *Psychological dimensions of executive coaching.* Maidenhead: Open University Press.

Brown, P. & Brown, V. (2012). *Neuropsychology for coaches. Understanding the basics.* Maidenhead: Open University Press.

Brunning, H. (2006). *Executive coaching. Systems-psychodynamic perspective.* London: Karnac.

Campbell, D. (2007). *The socially constructed organization.* London: Karnac.

Campbell, D. & Groenbaek, M. (2006). *Taking positions in the organization.* London: Karnac.

Campbell, D. & Huffington, C. (2008). *Organisations connected. A handbook of systemic consultation.* London: Karnac.

Chapman, L. & Cilliers, F. (2008). The integrated experiential executive coaching model: A qualitative exploration. *South African Journal of Labour Relations*, 32(1):63-80.

Cilliers, F. (2005). Executive coaching experiences. A systems psychodynamic perspective. *South African Journal of Industrial Psychology*, 31(3):23-30. https://doi.org/10.4102/sajip.v31i3.205

Cilliers, F. (2011). Positive psychology leadership coaching experiences in a financial organization. SA Journal of Industrial Psychology/SA Tydskrif vir Bedryfsielkunde, 37(1):Art. #933, 14 pages. https://doi.org/10.4102/sajip.v37i1.933

Cilliers, F. & Terblanche, L. (2010). The systems psychodynamic leadership coaching experiences of nursing managers. *Health SA Gesondheid*, 15(1):Art #457, 9 pages. https://doi.org/10.4102/hsag.v15i1.457

Clarke, S. & Hoggett, P. (2009). *Research beneath the surface. Psycho-Social research methods in practice.* London: Karnac.

Clarke, S.; Hahn, H. & Hoggett, P. (2008). *Object relations and social relations.* London: Karnac.

Colman, A.D. & Bexton, W.H. (1975). *Group relations reader 1.* Jupiter, FL: The A.K. Rice Institute.

Colman, A.D. & Geller, M.H. (1985). *Group relations reader 2.* Jupiter, FL: The A.K. Rice Institute.

Cooper, C.L. (2005). *Leadership and management in the 21st century: Business challenges of the future.* New York: Oxford University Press.

Creswell, J.W. & Plano Clark, V.L. (2011). *Designing and conducting mixed methods research.* Los Angeles, CA: Sage.

Crevani, L. & Endrissat, N. (2016). Mapping the leadership-as-practice terrain: Comparative elements. In: J.A. Raelin (ed.), *Leadership-as-practice: Theory and application,* pp.21-49. New York: Routledge. https://doi.org/10.4324/9781315684123-2

Cytrynbaum, S. & Noumair, A. (2004). *Group relations reader 3.* Jupiter, FL: The A.K. Rice Institute.

Czander, W.M. (1993). *The psychodynamics of work and organizations.* New York, Guilford,

Denzin, N.K. & Lincoln, Y.S. (2005). *The Sage handbook of qualitative research.* London: Sage.

Development Guild (2015). http://www.devlopmentguild.com [Accessed 14 May 2015].

Dippenaar, M. & Schaap, P. (2017) The impact of coaching on the emotional and social intelligence competencies of leaders. *South African Journal of Economic and Management Sciences,* 20(1):a1460. https://doi.org/10.4102/sajems.v20i1.1460

Elkington, R. & Booysen, L. (2015). Innovative leadership as enabling function within organisations: A complex adaptive systems approach. *Journal of Leadership Studies,* 9(3):78-80. https://doi.org/10.1002/jls.21414

Erskine, R.G. (2010). *Life scripts. A transactional analysis of unconscious relational patterns.* London: Karnac.

Fraher, A. (2004). *A history of group study and psychodynamic organisations.* London: Free Association.

French, R. & Simpson, P. (2015). *Attention, cooperation, purpose. An approach to working in groups using insights from Wilfred Bion.* London: Karnac.

Grant, A.M. (2007). A languishing flourishing model of goal striving and mental health for coaching populations. *International Coaching Psychology Review,* 2(3):250-264.

Greif, S. (2007). Advances in research on coaching outcomes. *International Coaching Psychology Review,* 2(3):222-249.

Hawkins, P. & Smith, N. (2013). *Coaching, mentoring and organisational consultancy. Supervision and development.* Maidenhead: Open University Press.

Hindle, D. & Sherwin-White, S. (2014). *Sibling matters: A psychoanalytic, developmental and systemic approach.* London: Karnac.

Hirschhorn, L. (1993). *The workplace within: Psychodynamics of organizational life.* Cambridge: MIT.

Hirschhorn, L. (1997). *Reworking authority. Leading and following in the post-modern organization.* London: MIT Press.

Hollway, W. & Jefferson, T. (2010). *Doing qualitative research differently.* Los Angeles: CA Sage.

Huffington, C.; Armstrong, A.; Halton, W.; Hoyle, L. & Pooley, J. (2004). *Working below the surface. The emotional life of contemporary organisations.* London: Karnac.

Jaques, E. (1990). *Creativity and work.* Madison, WI: International Universities.

Kahn, M.S. (2014). *Coaching on the axis. Working with complexity in business and executive coaching.* London: Karnac.

Kaiser, R.B.; Hogan, R. & Craig, S.B. (2008). Leadership and the fate of organisations. *American Psychologist*, 63(2):96-110. https://doi.org/10.1037/0003-066X.63.2.96

Kets de Vries, M.F.R. (2006). *The leader on the couch. A clinical approach to changing people and organisations.* Chichester: Jossey-Bass.

Kets de Vries, M.F.R. (2014). *Mindful leadership coaching. Journeys into the interior.* London: Palgrave Macmillan. https://doi.org/10.1057/9781137382337

Kets de Vries, M.F.R.; Korotov, K. & Florent-Treacy, E. (2007). *Coach and couch. The psychology of making better leaders.* London: Palgrave.

Kilburg, R. & Diedrich, R. (2007). *The wisdom of coaching: Essential papers in consulting psychology for a world of change.* Washington, DC: American Psychological Association. https://doi.org/10.1037/11570-000

Klein, M. (1997). *Envy and gratitude and other works, 1946-1963.* PA: Vintage, Reading.

Klein, R.H.; Rice, C.A. & Schermer, V.L. (2009). *Leadership in a changing world: Dynamic perspectives on groups and their leaders.* Lanham: Lexington Books.

Leonard, H.S.; Lewis, R.L.; Freedman, A.M. & Passmore, J. (2013). *The Wiley-Blackwell handbook of the psychology of leadership, change and organisational development.* Malden, MA: John Wiley & Sons. https://doi.org/10.1002/9781118326404

Long, S. (2008). *The perverse organisation and its deadly sins.* London: Karnac.

Macaux, W.P. (2014). Coaching the faltering executive. *Organisational and Social Dynamics*, 14(2):264-284.

Maddi, S.R. & Khoshaba, D.M. (2005). *Resilience at work. How to succeed no matter what life throws at you.* New York: AMACOM.

McKenna, D.D. & Davis, S.L. (2009). Hidden in plain sight: The active ingredient of executive coaching. *Industrial and Organisational Psychology*, 2:244-260. https://doi.org/10.1111/j.1754-9434.2009.01143.x

McLeod, J. (2012). *Case study research in counselling and psychotherapy.* Los Angeles: CA Sage.

Meyer, T.N.A. & Boninelli, I. (2007). Conversations in leadership, *South African perspectives.* Randburg: Knowres.

Motsoaledi, L. & Cilliers, F. (2012). *Executive coaching in diversity from the systems psychodynamic perspective. SA Journal of Industrial Psychology/SA Tydskrif vir Bedryfsielkunde*, 38(2):Art. #988, 11 pages. https://doi.org/10.4102/sajip.v38i2.988

Neumann, J.E.; Keller, K. & Dawson-Shepherd, A. (1997). *Developing organisational consultancy.* London: Routledge.

Newton, J.; Long, S. & Sievers, B. (2006). *Coaching in depth. The organisational role analysis approach.* London: Karnac.

Nohria, N. & Khurana, R. (2010). *Handbook of leadership theory and practice.* Boston, MA: Harvard Business Press.

Northouse, P.G. (2014). *Leadership: Theory and practice*. Thousand Oaks, CA: Sage.

O'Malley, M. & Baker, W.F. (2012). *The 12 criteria of effective leadership, Perspective*, 20 December http://www.sibson.com/publications [Accessed 06 April 2015].

Obholzer, A. & Roberts, V.Z. (1994). *The unconscious at work*. London: Routledge.

Page, N. & De Haan, E. (2014). Does executive coaching work? *The Psychologist*, 27(8):582-586.

Paice, L. (2012). *New coach. Reflections from a learning journey*. Maidenhead: Open University Press.

Passmore, J.; Peterson, D.B. & Freire, T. (2013). *The Wiley-Blackwell handbook of the psychology of coaching and mentoring*. Chichester: Wiley-Blackwell. https://doi.org/10.1002/9781118326459

Peltier, B. (2009). *The psychology of executive coaching. Theory and application*. New York: Brunner-Routledge.

Sandler, C. (2011). Executive coaching. *A psychodynamic approach*. Maidenhead: McGraw Hill.

Schafer, R. (2003). *Insight and interpretation. The essential tools of psychoanalysis*. London: Karnac.

Sievers, B. (2009). *Psychoanalytic studies of organisations*. London: Karnac.

Stapley, L.F. (2006). *Individuals, groups and organisations beneath the surface*. London: Karnac.

Sternberg, R.J. (2007). Foreword to the special issue on leadership. *American Psychologist*, (62(1):1. https://doi.org/10.1037/0003-066X.62.1.1

Stout Rostron, S. (2009). *Business coaching. Wisdom and practice. Unlocking the secrets of business coaching*. Randburg: Knowledge Resources.

Tangolo, A.E. (2015). *Psychodynamic psychotherapy with transactional analysis*. London: Karnac.

Terre Blanche, M.; Durrheim, K. & Painter, D. (2006). *Research in practice. Applied methods for the social sciences*. Cape Town: UCT Press.

Thorne, S. (2016). *Interpretive description. Qualitative research for applied practice*. New York: Routledge. https://doi.org/10.4324/9781315545196

Tudor, K. & Summers, G. (2014). *Co-creative transactional analysis. Papers, responses, dialogues, and developments*. London: Karnac.

Vansina, L.S. & Vansina-Cobbaert, M. (2008). *Psychodynamic for consultants and managers. From understanding to leading meaningful change*. Chichester: Wiley-Blackwell. https://doi.org/10.1002/9780470697184

Veldsman, T.H. & Johnson, A.J. (2016). *Leadership: Perspectives from the front line*. Randburg: KR Publishing.

Wagner, C.; Kawulich, B.B. & Garner, M. (2012). *Doing social research. A global context*. New York: McGraw-Hill.

Western, S. (2012). *Coaching and mentoring. A critical text*. Los Angeles, CA: Sage. https://doi.org/10.4135/9781446251577

Western, S. (2013). *Leadership. A critical text*. Los Angeles, CA: Sage.

Wilson, S. & MacLean, R. (2011). *Research methods and data analysis for psychology*. London: McGraw-Hill.

Winnicott, D.W. (2006). *The family and individual development*. London: Routledge.

Wolcott, B.L. (2001). *Writing up qualitative research*. London: Sage.

Article 5

Leadership Coaching Experiences of Clients with Alexithymia[1]

F Cilliers

Orientation
Leaders who find it difficult to connect emotionally with colleagues are often seen as incompetent, the idea that they may suffer from alexithymia – an inability to feel – is not taken into account. This coaching model seemed to be not successful in changing this behaviour pattern.

Research purpose
The purpose of the research was to describe the coaching experiences of leaders with symptoms of alexithymia and to formulate hypotheses around their leadership experiences.

Motivation for the Study
Effective leadership is strongly associated with emotional connections with colleagues. Leaders suffering from alexithymia, struggle with making these connections. It was thought that coaching might help them bridge the gap towards building effective relationships.

1   Cilliers, F. (2012). Leadership coaching experiences of clients with alexithymia. *SA Journal of Industrial Psychology/SA Tydskrif vir Bedryfsielkunde*, 38(2):Art.#995, 10 pages. https://doi.org/10.4102/sajip.v38i2.995

Research Design, Approach and Method

A qualitative research design using case studies was used. Three participants underwent 10 months of systems psychodynamic leadership coaching, including role analysis. Researcher's field notes and participant essays were discourse analysed. The researcher's unconscious experiences were included in the interpretations.

Main Findings

Five themes manifested themselves namely, leaders' difficult experiences with coaching, the dynamics underlying their normative, experiential and phenomenal roles and the coach's unconscious experiences affecting the relationship. The research hypothesis referred to the differences between the role parts and the resulting anxiety.

Practical/managerial Implications

This coaching model did not provide sufficient opportunities for the participating leaders with regard to emotional reactivity and regulation.

Contribution/value-add

The research created awareness of how alexithymia amongst leaders manifests in organisations. Unfortunately, the coaching was unsuccessful in addressing the emotional task. Other ways need to be explored

Introduction

Some leaders find it difficult to form emotional connections with colleagues because of the presence of alexithymia, an inability to feel emotionally. Such leaders are often seen as incompetent and 'sent for coaching' to address their cold and aloof style and 'lack of empathy'. An in-depth understanding of the behaviour of these leaders and the nature of alexithymia may assist in realising that coaching about emotionality may not be the answer to this leadership matter.

Leadership is popularly defined as a process whereby an individual influence a group of individuals to achieve a common goal (Northouse, 2004). In all its components of process, influence, interpersonal and group context, and goal attainment, leadership is in its essence an interpersonal activity between leader and follower (Nohria & Khurana, 2010). The leadership literature classifies leadership competencies as problem-solving skills, social-judgement skills and knowledge (Northouse, 2004). Where both problem-solving and knowledge rely heavily on intellectual and cognitive abilities, the social aspect refers to the understanding of behaviour and social systems, understanding of attitudes (thinking, feeling and actions), sensitivity to feelings through empathy and effective communication around emotional, social and work matters. Kets de Vries (2006) included the awareness of and effectiveness in dealing with behavioural dynamics such as conflicts, power relations, resistances and other defensive structures.

The above-mentioned emotional competency is defined (Meyer & Boninelli, 2007) as the ability to manage emotions within the self, and between the self and the other, amidst diversity in culture, value, ability and behaviour. The leadership literature (see Hughes & Terrell, 2007) is increasingly linking the above-mentioned competency to emotional intelligence (EQ), which is defined as the ability to perceive, appraise and express emotion accurately and adaptively; the ability to understand emotion and emotional knowledge; the ability to access and/or generate feelings when they facilitate cognitive activities and adaptive action; and the ability to regulate emotions in oneself and others (Goleman, Boyatzis & Mckee, 2008; Snyder & Lopez, 2002). Although many models of EQ exist, it is generally accepted that it consists of high levels of awareness in own intra-personal (including control), interpersonal (empathy) and social (realness, respect) behaviour, and skill in social influence (inspiration) and the experience of purpose (authenticity based on deeply felt intentions and values) (Seligman, 2003; Wall, 2007).

Transformational leadership (Van Eeden, Cilliers & Van Deventer, 2008) as one of the popular theories of the post-modern age (Nohria & Khurana, 2010), embraces EQ as desired leadership quality. It is defined as the process whereby the leader engages with the follower in an emotional connection that facilitates the motivation and morality in both parties towards fulfilling the task beyond their self-interest for the good of the group, organisation or society (Bass, 1997; Bass & Avolio, 1994; Northouse, 2004). The leader's behaviour is characterised by idealised influence, inspirational motivation, intellectual stimulation and individualised consideration (Bycio, Hackett & Allen, 1995). Thus, leadership includes followership's identification with the leader and the forming of a meaningful trusting relationship (Sievers, 2009). The above was integrated in Avolio's (2007) integrative model of authentic leadership based on how leader and follower regulate the translation of their awareness into behaviours based on authenticity (congruence), transparency and ethics.

Measured against the above competence, it was hypothesised that alexithymic leaders would not cope with the emotional demands of the leadership role. The relevant question here is whether their 'inability to feel' emotionally can be addressed in an organisational context, such as in coaching.

Leadership coaching is generally defined as a regular, short-term and highly focussed organisational learning opportunity (compared to therapy and traditional training). This involves a helping relationship between a client who has managerial authority and responsibility in an organisation, and a consultant who uses behavioural techniques and methods to help the client to improve personal insight towards effective leadership performance and consequently, to improve the effectiveness of the client's organisation, all within the boundaries of a formally defined coaching agreement (Kets de Vries, 2007; Kilburg & Diedrich, 2007; McKenna & Davis, 2009). The goal of leadership coaching is to optimise competence in task and people management (Blake & McCanse, 1995; Lowman, 2002; Sperry, 2004). Most of the coaching studies mentioned in management and organisational psychology (Coutu & Kaufman, 2009; Harvard Business Essentials, 2004; McGovern, Lindemann, Vergara, Murohy, Barker & Warrenfeltz, 2001) approach coaching from a mechanistic perspective and report results on cognitive learning about leadership. Coaching in the humanistic paradigm (Stout Rostron, 2009) uses respect and empathy as constructs and reports on the facilitation of self-awareness. Systems psychodynamic coaching includes experiential learning methods (Chapman & Cilliers, 2008) and reports comparatively deeper levels of insight and awareness in the leadership role and a compelling and dynamic connective quality in the human relationships. According to Kets de Vries and Engellau (2007) this awareness builds an *authentizotic organisation*.

The purpose of the research was to describe the coaching experiences of leaders with symptoms of alexithymia and to formulate hypotheses around their leadership experiences. The leadership literature is very clear about the desired emotional characteristics of the effective leader and the misuse of emotions to manipulate and harm others (Babiak & Hare, 2006). Nelson and Hogan (2009) commented on how the dark side of personality can derail occupational performance and leadership competence. On the other hand, there is a gap in its reference to the absence of emotional energy, such as in alexithymia and its effect on the leadership-followership interaction.

Alexithymia

Alexithymia means *no word for emotion* and is referred to as *the deadness within* (Kets de Vries, 2001). Its origin and nature are described in three different ways (Berenbaum & Irvin, 1996; Berenbaum & Prince, 1994; Kets de Vries, 2001; Lumley, Gustavson, Partridge & Labouvie-Vief, 2005; Snyder & Lopez, 2002) namely:

1. *neuro-psychological* (where poor emotional regulation manifests as a physical, psychological and a communication disorder caused by a genetic neuro-physical defect – a disconnect between the left and right brain hemispheres leading to a deficiency in the transmission of messages from the visceral brain to the language centres of the cortex).

2. *a developmental character trait* (where the parents are out of touch with their young child's emotional needs and use the child as a drug to solve their own narcissistic conflicts through the child – the child becomes trapped in an aborted symbiotic relationship where extreme dependence is artificially prolonged and the child's true self has not been allowed to emerge).

3. *a situation-specific type of coping behaviour* (where socio-cultural factors follow on particularly stressful events, or a series of events, or extreme situations, such as imprisonment.

The following symptoms of alexithymia are mentioned in the literature (Abe & Izard, 1999; Apfel & Sifneos, 1979; Berenbaum & Irvin, 1996; Berenbaum & Prince, 1994; Dewaraja, Tanigawa, Araki, Nakata, Kawamura, Ago & Sasaki, 1997; Friedlander, Lumley, Farchione, & Doyal 1997; Izard, 1990; Kauhanen, Kaplan, Cohen, Salonen, & Salonen, 1994; King, 1998; King & Emmons, 1990; Kooiman, 1998; Lane & Schwartz, 1987; Lane, Ahern, Schwartz & Kaszniak, 1997; Lane, Sechrest, Reidel, Weldon, Kaszniak, & Schwartz, 1996; Taylor, Bagby, & Parker, 1997). On the physical level the individual shows a decreased immune response, a variety of ailments such as hypertension and a decrease in the ability to associate physical sensations with emotions. Intellectually the individual reasons in terms of concrete, objective and physical realities, and has a preoccupation with matters external to own experiences and situations, has little understanding of own feelings and of emotional information and may experience judgmental bias. Emotionally the individual is described as numb, blank and cold fish. The individual has an impoverished emotional and fantasy life, is emotionally illiterate, shows an inability to be aware of, identify or differentiate between various emotions, to use metaphors and understand hidden meanings, has a reduced ability to experience emotions consciously, and/or has difficulty in expressing and describing feelings verbally or communicating about them to others. Interpersonally the individual is often in conflict with others and shows an inability to experience or show empathy. Organisationally, alexithymia especially manifests in large systems (such as in government, insurance, banking) with rigid structures and cultures, where emotions are suppressed. Being extremely emotionally cold and detached blends into the culture and becomes seen as normal behaviour.

Based on the above literature review, the following leadership hypothesis was formulated: When leaders exhibit the symptoms of alexithymia of not being able to differentiate between feelings, not to know and share their emotions, not being able to understand or show empathy towards others' feelings and meaning, their colleagues will not be able to make emotional connections with them, which will lead to the breakdown of communication and eventually their relationship.

Systems Psychodynamic Leadership Coaching

This form of leadership coaching was developed by the Tavistock Institute's (Miller, 1993) Group Relations Training events over the last 60 years (Brunner, Nutkevitch & Sher, 2006; Fraher, 2004). It consists of a depth psychology organisational theory (Armstrong, 2005; Gould, Stapley & Stein, 2001) and an organisational development consultancy stance (Neumann, Kellner & Dawson-Shepherd, 1997). The perspective is based on Freudian systemic psychoanalysis, group relations theory, object relations and open systems theory (Colman & Bexton, 1975; Colman & Geller, 1985; Cytrynbaum & Noumair, 2004) and is theoretically informed by five basic behavioural assumptions, namely:

1. dependency,
2. fight/flight,
3. pairing (Bion, 1961; 2003);
4. me-ness (Turquet, 1974); and
5. one-ness/we-ness (Lawrence, Bain & Gould, 1996).

The primary task of systems psychodynamic leadership coaching is to provide developmentally and psycho-educationally focussed reflection and learning opportunities to the leader, and to study, become aware of and gain insight into how task and organisational performance are influenced by both conscious and unconscious behaviour (Brunning, 2006; Huffington, Armstrong, Halton, Hoyle, & Pooley, 2004; Kets de Vries, 2007; Newton, Long & Sievers, 2006).

Consciousness refers to objectivity and rational behaviour, and unconsciousness to *the organisation in the mind*, which contains the system's unconscious defences and irrational behaviours (Armstrong, 2005).

Systems psychodynamic leadership coaching experientially investigates how specific constructs manifest in the leader's behaviour (Armstrong, 2005; Campbell & Groenbaek, 2006; Campbell & Huffington, 2008; Campbell, 2007; Hirschhorn, 1997; Klein, 2005; Vansina & Vansina-Cobbaert, 2008): *anxiety*, defined as the fear of the future and acting as the driving force (dynamo) of the relationship and relatedness between leadership and followership; *task*, the basic component of work, with the leader's adherence to the primary task indicating contained anxiety, and diversions into off-task and anti-task behaviour indicating confusion and anxiety; *role*, the boundary surrounding work and position, and between leader/follower/organisation, where leadership is defined as managing the boundaries between what is inside and what is outside the role; *authority*, the formal and official right to perform the task bestowed from above (the organisation, manager, leader), the side (colleagues), below (subordinates), and from within (self-authorisation); *boundaries* (such as task, time, territory) which act as the space around and between parts of the system, keeping it safe and contained; and *identity*, the nature of the leader's role behaviour and the branding, climate and culture of the organisational system.

Coaching starts with role analysis to explore the leader's behavioural dynamics (Newton, Long & Sievers, 2006). The focus is on the leader in the role within the person-role-organisation interaction (Huffington, Armstrong, Halton, Hoyle & Pooley, 2004). Leaders describe their normative (the objective job description and/or content, measured according to performance management), existential (how they believe they are performing) and phenomenal roles (how they believe they perform as experienced by colleagues around them) (Brunning, 2006; Obholzer & Roberts, 1994). The incongruence between the three parts of the role indicates role anxiety, which is explored to facilitate insight and behavioural change (Newton, et al., 2006). Each subsequent session starts with the open question, 'what is happening with you in your role as leader at the moment'. Coaching sessions do not have specific aims thus ensuring flow of the discourse in the here-and-now (Kets de Vries, 2007).

The coach takes on a reflective stance from a meta-position, attending to the leader's behaviour, interpreting the behavioural dynamics in terms of the above basic assumptions and behavioural concepts without judgement, memory or desire (Campbell & Huffington, 2008). Working hypotheses are formulated, defined as an integrative statement of *searching into* the leader's behaviour and describing the here-and-now behaviour until new evidence appears (Schafer, 2003). Leaders are encouraged to be curious, to freely associate, to explore a variety of related feelings, patterns, defences and representations (including the transferences and counter-transferences between leaders and coach), and to move between different levels of abstraction in thought (Jaques, 1990; Kegan, 1994). In this manner leaders can access their own unexplored conscious and unconscious role experiences, attitudes, beliefs, fantasies, wishes, conflicts, social defences, preferences, competition, rivalry, jealousy, envy, hostility, aggression as well as patterns of relationships and collaboration; investigate how parts of the self are split off and projected onto and into other parts of the organisational system (individuals and groups); explore their valences for receiving and containing specific projections on behalf of the system (their projective identification); and consider what can be done to take back the projections and reclaim the lost parts of the self (Blackman, 2004; Campbell & Groenbaek, 2006; Neumann, et al., 1997; Stapley, 1996; 2006).

The coach's unconscious psychological experiences, specifically transferences and counter-transferences, are seen as part of the coaching relationship (Cilliers, Rothmann & Struwig, 2004). Transference is described as the unconscious shift of memories of past situations and relationships onto the client, then using old defences to forget the past or to master it by living or acting it out again symbolically or by changing the ending thereof (Blackman, 2004). Counter-transference is described as the unconscious response to the client's transference (Hunt, 1989). This positioning is useful in understanding how disavowed experiences are placed in objects, including the coach. The role requires using own subjectivity, curiosity, intrigue and suspicion as vehicles of inquiry into the manifestation of behavioural dynamics in the coaching system (Alvesson & Sköldberg, 2010).

The research problem was formulated as follows: Will leadership coaching offer a good enough containment opportunity for leaders with strong symptoms of alexithymia to significantly increase their emotional awareness and improve the quality of their interpersonal relationships? The first objective was to apply the above coaching model to a group of leaders and to report on their coaching growth experiences. The second objective was to report on the researcher's unconscious experiences as a way of determining the effect of alexithymia on the other in the relationship.

The potential value-add of the research was to make leadership coaches aware of the behavioural dynamics of alexithymia and to hypothesise around the effectiveness of coaching this phenomenon.

The rest of the article is structured as follows. The research design is presented with reference to the research approach and strategy. This is followed by the research method consisting of the setting, roles of the researcher, sampling method, data collection, recording and analysis. Lastly, the strategies employed to ensure quality data are mentioned. Thereafter the findings are presented. In the discussion, the research hypothesis is presented, followed by the conclusion, recommendations, limitations and suggestions for further research.

Research Design

Research Approach

Qualitative and descriptive research was performed (De Vos, Strydom, Fouché & Delport, 2002) according to the psycho-social approach (Clarke & Hoggett, 2009). This included phenomenological reduction (Alvesson & Sköldberg, 2010) in answering the *how* and *why* questions of client experiences in a thick, rich and varied description. Hermeneutics was chosen as a research paradigm (Terre Blanche, Durrheim & Painter, 2006).

Research Strategy

A case study design (Chamberlayne, Bornat & Apitzsch, 2004) was used to empirically investigate the phenomenon of alexithymia in a real-life coaching setting. This allowed for a detailed examination of the manifesting behaviours from multiple sources in a rich description (Creswell, 2003). Three cases were studied individually and then integrated into a collective case study on alexithymia (Hollway & Jefferson, 2010; Stake, 1995). The cases were seen as intrinsic (providing an understanding of the behaviour in the interest of the coaching relationship), as well as instrumental (towards developing knowledge [Denzin & Lincoln, 2005]).

Research Method

Research Setting

The research comprised three individual leadership coaching clients from different organisations in the manufacturing, financial and educational sectors. Each one underwent 10 months of leadership coaching, comprising of monthly sessions that lasted 90 minutes, and conducted in a meeting room in the clients' organisation. Systems psychodynamic coaching, including role analysis (Newton, Long & Sievers, 2006), was used.

Entrée and Establishing Researcher Roles

The researcher took up the roles of consulting psychologist (Lowman, 2002), leadership coach (Brunning, 2006), systems psychodynamically informed analysand (Schafer, 2003) and self as the instrument (Watts, 2009). He is a psychologist with training and experience in this methodology and fulfilled the requirements for this role as stipulated by Brunner, Nutkevitch and Sher (2006). As a researcher, he positioned himself as defended subject (Boydell, 2009), referring to a continuous openness towards his own unconscious and inter-subjective dynamics, such as transference, counter-transference and projective identification, and how these affect the research relationship (Alvesson & Sköldberg, 2010).

Sampling

Convenient (Brewerton & Millward, 2004) and opportunistic sampling (Terre Blanche, Durrheim & Painter, 2006) was used. The three mentioned organisations randomly requested coaching services as part of their standard coaching procedures for the individuals, one Black female (aged 34) and two White males (aged 38 and 43). In their chemistry meetings, they framed their coaching issues as 'not getting along with my direct reports', 'I am seen as too cold' and 'people say I have no empathy'. During the first few coaching sessions, the researcher realised that all three showed strong symptoms of alexithymia (Kets de Vries, 2001) and decided to use the material as a unique opportunity to study the phenomenon of alexithymia in a coaching context.

Data Collection Method

Coaching field notes were made during all coaching sessions, followed up immediately afterwards with detailed comments about the process and dynamics of the session (Hinshelwood & Skogstad, 2005). After the tenth coaching session, participants were asked to 'write a 4-5 page essay on your learning during coaching' (Camic, Rhodes & Yardley, 2003).

Recording of Data

The field notes, process and dynamic comments, and essays were integrated per participant and stored in a secure place.

Data Analyses

Two complementary approaches were used, namely, discursive psychology and psychodynamically informed discourse analysis (Boydell, 2009). Simple hermeneutics served to interpret the discursive, and double hermeneutics allowed for a critical interpretation (Clarke & Hoggett, 2009) of systems psychodynamic behaviour (using Armstrong, 2005; Campbell, 2007; Huffington, et al., 2004; Klein, 2005). Triple hermeneutics allowed for interpretations around the researcher as defended subject (Alvesson & Sköldberg, 2010). This included the researcher's unconscious psychological experiences in terms of transferences, counter-transferences and projective identification and the effect thereof on the research relationship. Firstly, single cases were analysed to stay close to their surprising elements, before moving to cross-case analysis and the emergence of themes (Hollway & Jefferson, 2010).

Strategies Employed to Ensure Quality Data

Ethicality was ensured by obtaining the participants' informed consent, the researcher's concern, care and respect for the participants and their experiences of personal and work-related issues, as well as the responsibility towards scientific data interpretation (Holloway & Jefferson, 2010). The notion of the defended subject was kept in mind during the coaching sessions and data interpretation (Clarke & Hoggett, 2009) by suspending memory, desire and judgement (Cytrynbaum & Noumair, 2004).

Trustworthiness was based on credibility, validity and reliability (Denzin & Lincoln, 2005). Credibility was ensured through the researcher's competence in systems psychodynamic leadership coaching, his authorisation and role differentiation between coach and researcher, and in the data analysis, between object and subject (De Vos et al., 2002). Validity was ensured by the in-depth (psychological) description of the research, which revealed the complexities of the manifesting themes (Clarke & Hoggett, 2009). Reliability was ensured by means of careful and scientific planning and presentation of the coaching sessions, and theoretical reliability through scientific data recording, analysis and deep and rich interpretations (Denzin & Lincoln, 2005). Interpretations were peer-reviewed (Brewerton & Milward, 2004) by an independent psychologist to whom the theoretical model is well known. He reported positively on the dependability of the findings and the saturation of the data.

Reporting

The research findings were reported for the collective case per theme and with reference to the experiences of the individual participants where appropriate.

In the discussion the coaching behaviour of the leaders was interpreted, their growth during coaching assessed and the identity of the alexithymic leader integrated. The above data were integrated in the research hypothesis. This was followed by the conclusions, recommendations, limitations and suggestions for future research.

Findings

Five themes manifested themselves, namely:
1. the leaders experiences of coaching,
2. the normative role,
3. the experiential role,
4. the phenomenal role, and
5. the coach's experiences.

Leaders Experiences of Coaching

The coaching task for all three participants was framed as working towards an increased awareness of feelings and how to use these effectively in interactions with colleagues and followers. Participants seemed detached from the coach as if he was an object in a project. They described him as 'attentive', 'patient', 'sometimes nitpicking', 'going on for so long about so little', and 'krap waar dit nie jeuk nie [scratch where it is not itching]'. One participant remarked, 'halfway through I started to see that he was caring – I think I did not see that at the beginning'. They described the coaching process as 'interesting', 'challenging', 'thought-provoking', 'not quite what I thought it was going to be', 'sometimes too dragged out', and 'helpful towards structuring my work better'. One participant referred to 'those discussions about feelings! I got tired of it. He said I look frustrated, but I don't know how he knows that. Perhaps I was'.

Normative Role

All three participants were intelligent, university and professionally trained and registered with their different professional boards. Two of them served as members of standing committees in their professional societies and one participant received a life membership award from his society. In their organisations, all three were promoted between one and two years ago to director positions in an average of a 50% professional and 50% managerial and/or leadership ratio. Their roles included their professional work in their individual industries and organisations, as well as the management and leadership of their teams of between four and nine direct reports.

Experiential Role

In terms of their background, the participants regarded themselves as having made a good career choice according to their personality, aptitude and temperament. Their choice of employment in their individual organisations was framed as 'a good thing' and 'I thought it would be good for my career'. Cognitively they described their roles and performances by giving lots of information about projects and workflow, which they seemed to be mastering well. Affectively they seemed detached from their colleagues, as well as from their role and task. They sometimes used emotional words ('I was happy when that was completed'; 'I thought one was going to be irritated when one was not allowed to ...') – always with reference to the past. Motivationally they referred to the energy they gained from completing projects successfully and how they used the energy to get more involved in the organisation, which included volume as well as complexity. One participant described himself as 'very serious – perhaps too serious', whilst another said, 'I am here to work and get things done'. They reported on driving themselves hard towards attaining their set project goals and financial targets. They implied high levels of loyalty towards their profession and organisations.

Interpersonally the participants referred to their leaders in a cognitive manner as 'a good manager', 'someone that gets things done' and 'makes fire under those who do not contribute'. One participant described his leader as someone who is always trying 'to make feeling conversation – almost like the coach does – that is strange for me'. They described their direct reports and colleagues in a mechanistic and impersonal manner. In session 5, one participant broke out in tears and declared, 'I should never have become a manager – I also do not want to be a leader – whatever that means'. For this participant the realisation and experience of intense frustration were more important than the matters of career choice. Another said in his essay, 'Sartre said hell is other people. I also think so – in my work anyway'.

The participants described themselves in their professional and organisational roles and the standards and performance targets, very positively. This was congruent with their performance management outcomes. Their description of their 'people skills' was different. Participants described this as 'a minefield', 'something that brings me many headaches' – 'I wish I could work without people, especially the difficult ones – you know, the sensitive people'. One participant was promised a promotion on condition that 'if only I could become friendlier. My manager said I lack empathy. Can you [the coach] teach me that?'

Phenomenal Role

The participants' discourses on how others experience them corresponded with their experiential role. They were positively assessed and respected for their career advancement, intellect and motivation. On the other hand, in terms of emotionality, they were described as 'hard/cold/aloof/like a stone', 'dull' and interpersonally as 'difficult to understand', 'impossible to comprehend'; what makes them 'tick' and 'difficult/impossible to work with'. They were often told that they were inhumane, non-caring, 'treat people as machines' and 'animals', and that they 'have no warmth/compassion/empathy'. The participants used many coaching hours to process 'why others avoid me', 'why my manager only makes contact with me three times a year for my performance reviews', and why 'colleagues exclude me from their after hour's activities'.

The Coach's Experiences

After the chemistry sessions with all three participants, I was consciously looking forward to the coaching, impressed by their corporate positions and associated glamour and affluence, their qualifications and intelligence. Unconsciously, I was comparing my (very different) daily work and social reality to the idealised picture of them in my mind. My transference was about people who have everything which made we feel less worthy and envious of what they had. This resulted in feelings of incompetence which created performance anxiety. As this anxiety became unbearable, I started to project my experienced incompetence onto them as a way to hold on to my competence as their coach.

In working through the dependence of the individual on the couch, I realised that the three individual participants had intense difficulty with emotionality and connection (the primary task of their coaching) and that they resisted my inputs and role. My counter-transference was a form of counter resistance – which manifested as diminished enthusiasm, impatience and helplessness. I experienced the sessions as drawn-out, tedious and tiring, which drained my motivation. I experienced the participants as irritating and projected stupidity onto them. As the coaching progressed, I became aware of my intellectual competition with them by giving clever interpretations of their leadership behaviours and feeling proud of myself. My counter-transference was to take them on as if it was an intellectual coaching examination. After a while, I realised that I won the competition and that I was stupid (owning my previous projection) to compete with my non-coaching and/or psychologist clients! Unconsciously, I could not step out of the competitiveness, although the content of the fight had changed. In trying very hard to make sense of their non-emotional worlds, I tried to be the best Rogerian psychologist I could. My competitive transference became to reflect through deep empathic listening. The participants stayed emotionally aloof, detached and disinterested. I sensed their irritation but it was always disguised by their rational explanations around how things work for them.

Slowly I started to realise that the participants were performing as best they could (*this is as good as it gets*) and that my 'emotional labour' (Clarke & Hoggett, 2009:103), unconscious experiences and excessive conscious strategising, was indicative of *who is doing the work* and in what way *the coaching is not effective*. My learning was that my response to their behaviour was probably indicative of how *their other* experienced them daily. Framing their behaviour in terms of projective identification, I realised that they projected their responsibility to have feelings onto me as an authority figure, which then identified with the projection and thus became the container for their emotional experiences and left them dissociated and isolated from their feelings. I searched for and found evidence in their here-and-now coaching discourses for similarities to their leadership responses with colleagues. I felt sad for their inability to experience their feelings, thinking that they probably never had experienced meaningful emotional connections (because of parental relationships) and probably never would. Later I could see that the sadness was also my projection (the sadness did not belong to them).

The exploration of my experiences facilitated my better understanding of their valence to attract, introject and hold the non-feeling parts of their work environment. This made me think of what their work systems and colleagues projected onto and into them, for example, the lack of any feeling and emotion. Perhaps they were trusted by their work systems (Bion, 2003) to take on and contain the feeling void (a type of nothingness), which allows the other to be emotional and explorative in terms of feelings.

My feelings of incompetence resurfaced associated with more anxiety. Now I had evidence not only of their leadership incompetence but also their inability to react to and regulate their feelings. My counter-transference was about the pity I felt for them (people who do not feel cannot be good leaders) and anger towards their organisations (why were they promoted into positions whilst unable to cope with the emotional demands thereof?). My counter-transference was to avoid this hopeless situation, which was evident during a period of my dissociation from them, and acting emotionally detached. My avoidance defence also manifested itself when I tried to cancel a scheduled appointment with two of the participants.

Through intense reflection and supervision, I regained some realism and objectivity. I could see the issues of the participants separate from mine. I used my rational faculties and studied alexithymia as a behavioural phenomenon. This helped me to realise the extent of the issues of the participants, and I started to emotionally connect with their (assumed) pain and bravery to keep going and tolerate me and the coaching challenges. Working through my field notes I became aware of how often and strongly they told me in different ways that they were not interested in the coaching task, to feel awareness and reactivity, or the process of exploring emotional experiences. My counter-transference was to protect them from the organisation that had (in my mind) manipulated them into a coaching situation which was not within their emotional abilities. In my mind, coaching became the organisation's compensation defence against its frustration and desperation to change the employee. I then realised that I colluded in this manipulation by accepting the coaching task. Then I identified with the participants again which lead to my feelings of shame, for being cruel and torturing them. I decided to see the coaching contract through and spent the remaining sessions on supporting their efforts to try and understand their own leadership styles and their efforts to build relationships with colleagues (albeit mostly intellectual).

Discussion

The purpose of the research was to describe the coaching experiences of leaders with symptoms of alexithymia and to formulate hypotheses around their leadership experiences.

The research was important in its in-depth exploration of the manifestation of alexithymia amongst leaders as well as using the unconscious experiences of the coach in understanding the transferences and projections onto them.

Theme 1 illustrated how leaders experienced coaching as oscillating between being worthwhile and a waste of time. The leaders found it difficult to establish an emotional connection with the coach. Their behaviour was interpreted as a discomfort with psychological intimacy and a desire to maintain psychological independence (Prior & Glaser, 2006). Although they unconsciously expressed a need for caring and attention from the coach, it was as if they experienced a deep uncertainty about their capacity or willingness to respond to such needs (Rholes & Simpson, 2004). Their conflict *to connect or to not connect* was interpreted as an inability to seek and give care, especially under stressful situations. This is described in attachment theory as the inability to form emotional bonds, to self-regulate, express and use emotional resonance, attunement and empathy in their interactions (Colin, 1996; McCluskey, 2005; Prior & Glaser, 2006; Rholes & Simpson, 2004). Their behaviour came across as an anxiety of being rejected, abandoned and unloved which could explain their avoidance of intimacy and interdependence. Theoretically, the origins of the forming of their poor emotional attachment relate to their experienced non-availability of a secure attachment figure (such as a parent) to offer support under threatening situations. They introjected insecurity developed a non-autonomous identity, felt unworthy of affection and saw attachment figures as non-responsive, non-caring, undependable (McCluskey, 2005; Rholes & Simpson, 2004). As leaders, they did not have a memory of how to form significant emotional attachments. It was hypothesised that the quality of the leaders' relationship with the coach was transferred from previous non-caring and thus disappointing authority figures (Gould, Stapley & Stein, 2004; Hirschhorn, 1997).

Given the above attachment forming style, the literature (Colin, 1996) predicted low levels of work satisfaction. These leaders showed the contrary – they experienced seemingly above-average levels of satisfaction.

Theme 2 illustrated the leaders' success in their professional roles, their preference for the rational task and avoidance of people management.

Theme 3 illustrated how the leaders experienced themselves positively in taking up their role in terms of career development, cognitive functioning and drive. Initially, they could not differentiate between cognitive and emotional demands and reasoned about all their experiences (Diamond & Allcorn, 2009). Gradually they learned a basic emotional repertoire, but still used it mechanistically and in reference to past experiences. They attached to the rational and cognitive aspects of their roles and detached themselves from the affective parts. Their natural tendency to avoid their people management role and treat the other as objects in their mind (Armstrong, 2005) did not change significantly.

Theme 4 illustrated how the others experienced the leaders as emotionally unavailable and interpersonally detached, which overshadowed their positive career, intellectual and motivational aspects. This finding supported evidence of how dysfunctional leaders cause misery amongst followers (Nelson & Hogan, 2009).

Theme 5 illustrated the complexity of the unconscious relationship between the leaders and the coach. The coach introjected the emotional labour in the relationship (Clarke & Hoggett, 2009) – whilst he consciously aimed to maintain the well-being of the relationship, he unconsciously took on an assumed position of knowing and valuing what a proper state of mind might be – suppressing the expression of his own true feeling and acting on behalf of the collective unconscious (Diamond & Allcorn, 2009). He became the container of the leaders' projections of incompetence around feeling reactivity and regulation. The coach's experience of professional incompetence was derived from his feelings of envy and repulsion towards the leaders. Working through the complex unconscious interpersonal dynamics he could understand how his own dynamics reflected the unconscious world of alexithymia (see Morgan-Jones, 2010).

The leaders' growth was described as limited. They struggled to attach to the coaching task and to take up the role as learner about their own emotional world (Hirschhorn, 1997). Using the unconscious dynamics as evidence, it was interpreted as the leaders not owning their projections towards learning (Czander, 1993). This may have been based on the nature of alexithymia as an inability.

The identity of the leaders with alexithymia was described as follows. They were professionally trained, well established in their careers and performing well in their rational and technical tasks, and physically they often appeared stiff, distant and lacked facial expressions. Cognitively they were highly intelligent and competent in abstract reasoning and differentiation on content and rational matters. Their focus on the concrete was used as a defence against experiencing feelings. Affectively they had a limited feeling repertoire, seemed emotionally empty and apathetic. They could not differentiate between affective nuances (e.g. between glad, sad, mad and bad – see Kets De Vries, 2001) and did not use any metaphors or fantasy language. Their anxiety was about managing to keep their competent cognitive parts inside their role boundaries and their affective and dynamic experiences outside. This defence was a split between thinking and feeling, introjecting and owning thinking (using their high IQ's, cognitive and rational competence, focussing on the concrete and objective) and disowning, denying and dissociating from their feelings (EQ, affective, irrational and subjective abilities) (see Blackman, 2004). This led to a position where their egos were inhibited to grow to its full potential (Kets de Vries, 2001). In organisational terms, the leaders self-authorised through the introjection of their rational task, could not authorise themselves to take up their emotional and people management roles (see Blake & McCanse, 1995). Motivationally, the leaders seemed tired towards the end of the coaching sessions. It was hypothesised that, although they did not process feelings consciously, the energy they used to cope with the focus on emotional processing indicated how active their emotional energy was, albeit unconsciously. Interpersonally their relationships (including with the coach) were superficial in line with Fromm's (1947) notion of the market orientation. It was also hypothesised that their role anxiety did not originate from the difference between their experiential and phenomenal roles (as is often the case – Obholzer & Roberts, 1994), but from the splits within both the experiential and phenomenal roles (referring to the co-existence of their competence and incompetence within the same role part).

The research question could not be answered positively – the coaching could not offer the leaders with strong symptoms of alexithymia, a containment opportunity to increase their emotional awareness and quality interpersonal relationships. They could often not understand the rationale for coaching and what the coach was on about. One leader realised that the notion of not being able to show feeling, was much deeper than what could be addressed in leadership coaching. He started therapy to work on the exploration of his family dynamics. The findings corresponded with other coaching research (see Nelson & Hogan, 2009) illustrating how the dark side of a leader's personality creates a situation where leaders are derailed and incompetent to form relationships with followers. This situation is also reported on in the transformational leadership literature (Avolio, 2007).

The research hypothesis was formulated as follows. The leaders' background and family dynamics kept them stuck in a borderline culture where emotional distance between objects (and thus also people) needed to be maintained in service of the primary task of survival. Their capacity to form an emotional identity was inhibited to such an extent that they were acting as if they were emotionally illiterate. Their well-developed intellectual, rational and professional competencies facilitated their promotions into leadership positions. All three leaders would have been served better by the organisation if they had been kept functioning in professional and specialist roles. From a personal growth perspective, they were at least exposed to some possibilities towards emotional awareness.

It was concluded that to coach leaders with strong symptoms of alexithymia represents on the one hand feelings of incompetence in the coach, compensated for in emotional labour on behalf of the leader, and on the other hand, minimum growth for the leader. This research showed little evidence of success in coaching alexithymic leaders.

It was recommended that organisations think more rationally about promoting employees into leadership positions. When sent for coaching, leaders who showed symptoms of alexithymia should be informed about the possibilities of low success levels. Alternatively, coaches should explore other coaching models.

A limitation of the research was that the three participants were not neurologically or psychometrically assessed for alexithymia (see Nelson & Hogan, 2009). This could have assisted the coach in realising the presence and severity of the emotional matters of the leaders sooner.

It was suggested that future research use psychometric instruments to assess the strength of the alexithymia behaviour to ensure clear cases of this phenomenon (see Snyder & Lopez, 2002:177 for examples of such instruments).

Acknowledgements

Competing interests

The author declares that he has no financial or personal relationship(s) which may have inappropriately influenced him in writing this paper.

References

Abe, J., & Izard, C. (1999). A longitudinal study of emotion expression and personality relations in early development. *Journal of Personality and Social Psychology*, 77:566-577. http://doi.org/10.1037/0022-3514.77.3.566

Alvesson, M., & Sköldberg, K. (2010). *Reflexive methodology. New vistas for qualitative research*. London: Sage.

Apfel, R. & Sifneos, P. (1979). Alexithymia: Concept and measurement. *Psychotherapy and Psychosomatics*, 32:180-190. http://doi.org/10.1159/000287386

Armstrong, D. (2005). *Organisation in the mind. Psychoanalysis, group relations and organisational consultancy*. London: Karnac.

Avolio, B.J. (2007). Promoting more integrative strategies for leadership theory-building. *American Psychologist*, 62(1):25-33. http://doi.org/10.1037/0003-066X.62.1.25

Babiak, P. & Hare, R. (2006). *Snakes in suits. When psychopaths go to work*. New York: Harper Collins.

Bass, B.M. (1997). Does the transactional-transformational leadership paradigm transcend organizational and national boundaries? *American Psychologist*, 52(2):130-139. http://doi.org/10.1037/0003-066X.52.2.130

Bass, B.M., & Avolio, B.J. (1994). *Improving organizational effectiveness*. Thousand Oaks: Sage.

Berenbaum, H. & Irvin, S. (1996). Alexithymia, anger, and interpersonal behavior. *Psychotherapy and Psychosomatics*, 65:203-208. http://doi.org/10.1159/000289076

Berenbaum, H. & Prince, J.D. (1994). Alexithymia and the interpretation of emotion relevant information. *Cognition and Emotion*, 3:231-244. http://doi.org/10.1080/02699939408408939

Bion, W.R. (1961). *Experiences in groups*. London: Tavistock. http://doi.org/10.4324/9780203359075

Bion, W.R. (2003). *Learning from experience*. London: Karnac.

Blackman, J.S. (2004). *101 Defences. How the mind shields itself*. New York: Brunner-Routledge. https://doi.org/10.4324/9780203492369

Blake, R.R. & McCanse, A.A. (1995). *Leadership dilemmas – grid solutions*. Houston: Griff.

Boydell, L. (2009). Analysing discourse psycho-socially. In: S. Clarke & P. Hoggett (eds.), *Researching beneath the surface. Psycho-social research methods in practice*, pp.241-266. London: Karnac. https://doi.org/10.4324/9780429479564-11

Brewerton, P. & Millward, L. (2004). *Organisational research methods. A guide for students and researchers*. London: Sage.

Brunner, L.D., Nutkevitch, A. & Sher, M. (2006). *Group relations conferences. Reviewing and exploring theory, design, role-taking and application*. London: Karnac.

Brunning, H. (2006). *Executive coaching. Systems-Psychodynamic perspective*. London: Karnac.

Bycio, P.; Hackett, R.D. & Allen, J.S. (1995). Further assessment of Bass's (1985) conceptualization of transactional and transformational leadership. *Journal of Applied Psychology*, 80(4):468-478. http://doi.org/10.1037/0021-9010.80.4.468

Camic, P.M.; Rhodes, J.E. & Yardley, L. (2003). *Qualitative research in Psychology.* Washington: APA.

Campbell, D. (2007). *The socially constructed organisation.* London: Karnac.

Campbell, D. & Groenbaek, M. (2006). *Taking positions in the organisation.* London: Karnac.

Campbell, D. & Huffington, C. (2008). *Organisations connected. A handbook of systemic consultation.* London: Karnac.

Chamberlayne, P.; Bornat, J. & Apitzsch, U. (2004). *Biographical methods and professional practice. An international perspective.* Bristol: Policy Press. https://doi.org/10.1332/policypress/9781861344939.001.0001

Chapman, L. & Cilliers, F. (2008). The integrated experiential executive coaching model: A qualitative exploration. *South African Journal of Labour Relations,* 32(1):63-80.

Cilliers, F.; Rothmann, S. & Struwig, W.H. (2004). Transference and counter-transference in systems psychodynamic group process consultation: The consultant's experience. *South African Journal of Industrial Psychology,* 30(1):72-81. https://doi.org/10.4102/sajip.v30i1.143

Clarke, S. & Hoggett, P. (2009). *Researching beneath the surface. Psycho-social research methods in practice.* London: Karnac.

Colin, V.L. (1996). *Human attachment.* New York: McGraw-Hill.

Colman, A.D. & Bexton, W.H. (1975). *Group relations reader 1.* Jupiter: The A.K. Rice Institute.

Colman, A.D. & Geller, M.H. (1985). *Group relations reader 2.* Jupiter: The A.K. Rice Institute.

Coutu, D. & Kaufman, C. (2009). What can coaches do for you? *Harvard Business Review,* January:91-97.

Creswell, J.W. (2003). *Research design: Qualitative, quantitative and mixed methods.* London: Sage.

Cytrynbaum, S. & Noumair, A. (2004). *Group dynamics, organizational irrationality, and social complexity: Group relations reader 3.* Jupiter: A.K. Rice Institute.

Czander, W.M. (1993). *The psychodynamics of work and organizations.* New York: Guilford.

De Vos, A.S.; Strydom, H.; Fouche, C.B. & Delport, C.S.L. (2002). *Research at grass roots. For the social sciences and human service professions.* Pretoria: Van Schaik.

Denzin, N.K. & Lincoln, Y.S. (2005). *The Sage handbook of qualitative research.* London: Sage. https://doi.org/10.1177/1468794105047237

Dewaraja, R.; Tanigawa, T.; Araki, S.; Nakata, A.; Kawamura, N.; Ago, Y. & Sasaki, Y. (1997). Decreased cytotoxic lymphocyte counts in alexithymia. *Psychotherapy and Psychosomatics,* 66(2):83-86. http://doi.org/10.1159/000289113

Diamond, M.A. & Allcorn, S. (2009). *Private selves in public organizations. The psychodynamics of organisational diagnosis and change.* New York: Palgrave.

Fraher, A. (2004). *A history of group study and psychodynamic organizations.* London: Free Association.

Friedlander, L.; Lumley, M.; Farchione, T. & Doyal, G. (1997). Testing the alexithymia hypothesis: Physiological and subjective responses during relaxation and stress. *Journal of Nervous and Mental Disease*, 184(4):233-239. http://doi.org/10.1097/00005053-199704000-00003

Fromm, E. (1947). *Man for himself.* New York: Holt, Rinehart & Winston.

Goleman, D.; Boyatzis, R. & Mckee, A. (2008). The new leaders. *Transforming the art of leadership into the science of results.* London: Sphere.

Gould, L.J.; Stapley, L.F. & Stein, M. (2001). *The systems psychodynamics of organisations.* London: Karnac.

Gould, L.J.; Stapley, L.F. & Stein, M. (2004). *Experiential learning in organizations. Application of the Tavistock Group Relations Approach.* London: Karnac.

Harvard Business Essentials. (2004). *Coaching and mentoring. How to develop top talent and achieve stronger performance.* Boston: Harvard Business School.

Hinshelwood, R.D. & Skogstad, W. (2005). *Observing organisations. Anxiety, defence and culture in health care.* London: Routledge.

Hirschhorn, L. (1997). *Reworking authority. Leading and following in the post-modern organisation.* London: MIT.

Hollway, W., & Jefferson, T. (2010). *Doing qualitative research differently. Free association, narrative and the interview method.* London: Sage.

Huffington, C.; Armstrong, A.; Halton, W.; Hoyle, L. & Pooley, J. (2004). *Working below the surface. The emotional life of contemporary organisations.* London: Karnac.

Hughes, M. & Terrell, J.B. (2007). *The emotionally intelligent team. Understanding and developing the behaviours of success.* San Francisco: Jossey-Bass.

Hunt, J. (1989). *Psychoanalytic aspects of fieldwork.* London: Sage. https://doi.org/10.4135/9781412985505

Izard, C. (1990). Facial expressions and the regulation of emotions. *Journal of Personality and Social Psychology*, 58:487-498. http://doi.org/10.1037/0022-3514.58.3.487

Jaques, E. (1990). *Creativity and work.* Madison: International Universities.

Kauhanen, J.; Kaplan, G.; Cohen, R.; Salonen, R. & Salonen, J. (1994). Alexithymia may influence the diagnosis of coronary heart disease. *Psychosomatic Medicine*, 56(3):237-244. https://doi.org/10.1097/00006842-199405000-00010

Kegan, R. (1994). *In over our heads. The mental demands of modern life.* Cambridge: Harvard University.

Kets De Vries, M.F.R. (2001). *The leadership mystique.* London: Prentice-Hall.

Kets De Vries. M.F.R. (2006). *The leader on the coach. A clinical approach to changing people and organisations.* New York: Jossey-Bass.

Kets De Vries, M.F.R. (2007). *Coach and couch. The psychology of making better leaders.* London: Palgrave.

Kets De Vries, M.F.R. & Engellau, E. (2007). Organisational dynamics in action. In: R.R. Kilburg, (ed.), *Executive wisdom. Coaching and the emergence of virtuous leaders*, pp.21-52. Washington: APA. https://doi.org/10.1016/j.orgdyn.2007.04.001

Kilburg, R. & Diedrich, R. (2007). *The wisdom of coaching: Essential papers in consulting psychology for a world of change.* Washington: *American Psychological Association.* http://doi.org/10.1037/11570-000

King, L. (1998). Ambivalence over emotional expression and reading emotions in situations and faces. *Journal of Personality and Social Psychology,* 74:753-762. http://doi.org/10.1037/0022-3514.74.3.753

King, L., & Emmons, R. (1990). Conflict over emotional expression: Psychological and physiological correlates. *Journal of Personality and Social Psychology,* 58:864-877. http://doi.org/10.1037/0022-3514.58.5.864, PMid:2348373

Klein, L. (2005). *Working across the gap. The practice of social science in organisations.* London: Karnac.

Kooiman, C. (1998). The status of alexithymia as a risk factor in medically unexplained physical symptoms. *Comprehensive Psychiatry,* 39(3):152-159. http://doi.org/10.1016/S0010-440X(98)90075-X

Lane, R.; Ahern, G.; Schwartz, G. & Kaszniak, A. (1997). Is alexithymia the emotional equivalent of blindsight? *Biological Psychiatry,* 42(9):834-844. http://doi.org/10.1016/S0006-3223(97)00050-4

Lane, R. & Schwartz, G. (1987). Levels of emotional awareness: A cognitive-developmental theory and its application to psychopathology. *The American Journal of Psychiatry,* 144(2):133-143.

Lane, R.; Sechrest, L.; Reidel, R.; Weldon, V.; Kaszniak, A. & Schwartz, G. (1996). Impaired verbal and nonverbal emotion recognition in alexithymia. *Psychosomatic Medicine,* 58(3):203-210.

Lawrence, W.G.; Bain, A. & Gould, L. (1996). *The fifth basic assumption.* London: Tavistock.

Lowman, R.L. (2002). *The handbook of organizational consulting Psychology.* San Francisco: Jossey-Bass.

Lumley, M.; Gustavson, B.; Partridge, R. & Labouvie-Vief, G. (2005). Assessing alexithymia and related emotional ability constructs using multiple methods: Interrelationships amongst measures. *Emotion,* 5(3):329-342. http://doi.org/10.1037/1528-3542.5.3.329

McCluskey, U. (2005). *To be met as a person. The dynamics of attachment in professional encounters.* London: Karnac.

McGovern, J.; Lindemann, M.; Vergara, M.; Murphy, S.; Barker, L. & Warrenfeltz, R. (2001). Maximizing the impact of executive coaching. Behavioural change, organisational outcomes and return on investment. *The Manchester Review,* 6(1):1-10.

McKenna, D.D. & Davis, S.L. (2009). Hidden in plain sight: The active ingredient of executive coaching. *Industrial and Organisational Psychology,* 2(3):244-260. http://doi.org/10.1111/j.1754-9434.2009.01143.x

Meyer, T.N.A., & Boninelli, I. (2007). *Conversations in leadership. South-African perspectives.* Randburg: Knowres.

Miller, E.J. (1993). *From dependency to autonomy: Studies in organization and change.* London: Free Association.

Morgan-Jones, R. (2010). *The body of the organisation and its health.* London: Karnac.

Nelson, E., & Hogan, R. (2009). Coaching on the dark side. *International Coaching Psychology Review,* 4(1):7-16.

Neumann, J.E.; Kellner, K. & Dawson-Shepherd, A. (1997). *Developing organisational consultancy.* London: Routledge.

Newton, J.; Long, S. & Sievers, B. (2006). *Coaching in depth. The organisational role analysis approach.* London: Karnac.

Nohria, N. & Khurana, R. (2010). *Handbook of leadership theory and practice.* Boston: Harvard Business Press.

Northouse, P.G. (2004). *Leadership. Theory and practice.* Thousand Oaks: Sage.

Obholzer, A. & Roberts, V.Z. (1994). *The unconscious at work.* London: Routledge. http://doi.org/10.4324/9780203359860

Prior, V. & Glaser, D. (2006). *Understanding attachment and attachment disorders. Theory, evidence and practice.* London: Jessica Kingsley.

Rholes, W.S. & Simpson, J.A. (2004). *Adult attachment. Theory, research and clinical implications.* New York: Guilford.

Schafer, R. (2003). *Insight and interpretation. The essential tools of psycho-analysis.* London: Karnac.

Seligman, M.E.P. (2003). *Authentic happiness.* London: Nicholas Brealey.

Sievers, B. (2009). *Psychoanalytic studies of organizations. Contributions from the International Society for the Psychoanalytical Study of Organizations (ISPSO).* London: Karnac.

Snyder C.R. & Lopez, A.J. (2002). *Handbook of positive psychology.* New York: Oxford.

Sperry, L. (2004). *Executive coaching. The essential guide for mental health professionals.* New York: Brunner-Routledge. https://doi.org/10.4324/9780203483466

Stake, R. (1995). *The art of case study research.* Thousand Oaks. Sage.

Stapley, L.F. (1996). *The personality of the organisation. A psychodynamic explanation of culture and change.* London: Free Association.

Stapley, L.F. (2006). *Individuals, groups and organisations beneath the surface.* London: Karnac.

Stout Rostron, S. (2009). *Business coaching. Wisdom and practice. Unlocking the secrets of business coaching.* Randburg: Knowledge Resources.

Taylor, G.; Bagby, M. & Parker, J. (1997). *Disorders of affect regulation: Alexithymia in medical and psychiatric illness.* New York: Cambridge University Press. http://.doi.org/10.1017/CBO9780511526831

Terre Blanche, M.; Durrheim, K. & Painter, D. (2006). *Research in practice. Applied methods for the social sciences.* Cape Town: UCT Press.

Turquet, P.M. (1974). Leadership – the individual in the group. In: G.S. Gibbard, J.J. Hartman & R.D. Mann (eds.), *Analysis of groups,* pp.52-67. San Francisco: Jossey-Bass.

Van Eeden, R.; Cilliers, F. & Van Deventer, V. (2008). Leadership styles and associated personality traits: Support for the conceptualisation of transactional and transformational leadership. *South African Journal of Psychology,* 38(2):253-267. https://doi.org/10.1177/008124630803800201

Vansina, L.S.; & Vansina-Cobbaert, M. (2008). *Psychodynamics for consultants and managers. From understanding to leading meaningful change.* Chichester: Wiley-Blackwell. https://doi.org/10.1002/9780470697184

Wall, B. (2007). *Coaching for emotional intelligence.* New York: Amacom.

Watts, L. (2009). Managing self in role: Using multiple methodologies to explore self-construction and self-governance. In: S. Clarke & P. Hoggett (eds.), *Researching beneath the surface. Psycho-social research methods in practice*, pp. 215-239. London: Karnac. https://doi.org/10.4324/9780429479564-10

Article 6

The Robben Island Diversity Experience: An Exploration of South African Diversity Dynamics[1]

M Pretorius, F Cilliers & M May

Orientation

Because of its historic, symbolic and psychological representation, presenting a diversity event on Robben Island posed invaluable opportunities to form an in-depth understanding of South African diversity dynamics. This research focussed on such an event interpreted from the systems psychodynamic perspective.

Research Purpose

The purpose of the research was to describe the experiences of participants attending the Robben Island Diversity Experience (RIDE) in order to understand South African diversity dynamics from a depth psychology perspective.

Motivation for the Study

Of the many and different diversity events presented in South African organisations, RIDE is the only annual systems psychodynamically designed and presented event. This research was an effort to explore the nature of these dynamics which manifest themselves from below the surface.

1   Pretorius, M. Cilliers, F. & May M. (2012). The Robben Island Diversity Experience. An exploration of South African diversity dynamics. *SA Journal of Industrial Psychology/SA Tydskrif vir Bedryfsielkunde*, 38(2):Art.#996, 8 pages. https://doi.org/10.4102/sajip.v38i2.996

Research Design, Approach and Method

Qualitative and descriptive research from a hermeneutic phenomenology paradigm was used. The 15 participants who attended a RIDE event formed a case study. The data from an unstructured interview was content-analysed and interpreted using the systems psychodynamic perspective. The themes were integrated into a research hypothesis.

Main Findings

Five themes manifested themselves, namely, crossing boundaries, engaging the brave new world, ties that bind, being imprisoned and the struggle.

Practical/managerial Implications

The research highlighted the importance of understanding unconscious dynamics in the context of diversity in order to inform consultants about diversity management interventions in organisations.

Contribution/value-add

The research contributed towards how South African diversity dynamics manifest themselves and how that can be addressed in organisations.

Introduction

In the South African context, DIVERSITY can indeed be written in capital letters. The country's history is fraught with differentiation, segregation, exclusion and discrimination (Bekker & Carlton, 1996; Eades, 1999). The replacement of the apartheid regime by the first democratically elected government in 1994 facilitated opportunities for everyone in the rainbow nation towards the celebration of diversity (Beck, 2000; Charlton & Van Niekerk, 1994). This road, to reconstruct the South African society, has been far from smooth (Hunt & Lascaris, 1998; Thompson, 2001).

Organisations realised that diversity often leads to frustration, misunderstandings, unhealthy conflict and an increase in turnover of people if it is not properly managed (Milliken & Martins, 1996; Van Eron, 1995). Often such organisations use mechanistic approaches to diversity (Cilliers & May, 2002). Although these approaches do little more than achieve certain structural and behavioural changes, they seem to create an environment in which consultants and employees can work with diversity. A solitary diversity intervention is however doomed to failure since the emotions and resistance that it elicits, normally fuel various unconscious dynamics that subvert the possibility of true connection between and change in employees. Studying diversity from the systems psychodynamic perspective implies exploring the unconscious dynamics that influence the way similarities and differences amongst employees are viewed and acted upon. The aim of such endeavours would be to gain an in-depth understanding of the dynamics of South African diversity by analysing and interpreting the experiences of participants in such experiential events.

Robben Island as Venue for Diversity Work

The researchers were part of the founding team of the Robben Island Diversity Experience (RIDE). The venue was chosen as an attractive marketing plan, but also because the hosting organisation realised the historical and symbolic significance of Robben Island to study South African diversity dynamics as a phenomenon.

The Robben Island Diversity Experience (RIDE)

The RIDE was planned and presented as a Group Relations Training event (see Brunner, Nutkevitch & Sher, 2006; Cytrynbaum & Noumair, 2004; Fraher, 2004), consisting of plenaries, large and small study groups, intergroup and institutional events, and review and applications events. Table 1 contains the programme.

The primary task of the RIDE was to provide opportunities to individually and collectively study the core concepts of diversity dynamics (identity, reference systems, power, as well as relations and relatedness) in order to understand how they perceive, interpret and act towards individual and collective diversity. Systems psychodynamically informed staff members were employed.

The purpose of the research was to describe the experiences of participants attending the RIDE and to form a depth psychology understanding of South African diversity dynamics.

The Ride Crucible

The South African journey in transforming the country from a minority-driven apartheid regime to a democratic nation is often described as a miracle. Miller (2011) eloquently described it by stating that the miraculous events in South Africa made hope possible again and that the people of South Africa had opened the way for the rest of the world in bringing about peaceful change. The South African miracle collapsed the apartheid system and removed the barriers that separated Black and White people. Beck and Linscott's (1996) metaphor aptly described this coming together of all South Africans in the post-1994 democratic society as a crucible in which, under extreme pressure and conflict, various disparate and volatile human elements were being poured – White people, Black people, Coloured people, Indian people, males, females and people from different religious orientations, ethnic groups and age groups. Although there was recognition that it would be hard to reverse apartheid's legacy, it seemed possible with Mr Nelson Mandela at the helm. The reality is however that the hope of creating the rainbow nation endures as long as it remains a dream. Any talk of the differences between Black and White people's lifestyles, attitudes or expectations was shouted down; no one wanted to wake from the dream (Brown, 2008). The dream of the rainbow nation, in a sense, kept people from dealing with the realities of the South African crucible, and the remnants of the past. The intense emotions, conflicts and (diversity) dynamics that arose through the process of amalgamating the highly segregated South African society were largely not dealt with. In a similar way the RIDE created a crucible which represented a microcosm of the larger South African society, and provided a golden opportunity to study diversity dynamics as it unfolded during the experience. The challenge was to deal with the emotions, conflicts and (diversity) dynamics whilst holding onto the dream of becoming a nation at peace with itself and the world. This research explores the diversity dynamics that shaped and characterised the South African crucible.

The South African Diversity Challenge

Diversity has proved to be a double-edged sword because it is both an opportunity as well as a threat (Booysen, 2005; Cavaleros, Van Vuuren & Visser, 2002; Newell, 2002). Organisations realised that diversity in itself does not lead to a competitive advantage, instead it is more likely to result in frustration, misunderstanding, unhealthy conflict, and an increase in staff turnover if it is not properly managed (Milliken & Martins, 1996; Van Eron, 1995). Thus the diversity sword, if not skillfully wielded, can have major cost implications for organisations in terms of production.

Table 1 **RIDE Programme**

Time	Sunday	Monday	Tuesday	Wednesday	Thursday	Friday
07h00				Breakfast		
08h00		Large group 2	Large group 3	Large group 4	Large group 5	Small group 7
09h30				Break		
10h00		Small group 2	Small group 3	Small group 5	Lecture	RIDE Plenary
11h30	Registration			Break		
12h00	Departing Cape Town Arrival RI	Intergroup plenary	Intergroup 4	Intergroup 6	Small group 6	Application group 2
13h30	Opening plenary			Lunch		Social event
14h30	Tour of RI	Intergroup 2	Free time – Prison tour	Intergroup 7	Large group 6	Departure from RIA
16h00	Large group 1	Break	Intergroup	Break	Break	
17h00		Intergroup 3		Discussion group	Processing group	
17h30–18h00				Dinner		
18h30				Small group 1		
19h00				Processing group		
19h30						

Table 1   RIDE programme (continued)

Time	Sunday	Monday	Tuesday	Wednesday	Thursday	Friday
20h00	Break					
20h30–21h30	Processing group					

Robben Island employee absenteeism, inefficient communication, poor utilisation of resources, low morale, and industrial action (Cox & Beale, 1997; Human, 2005; Oakley-Smith & Winter, 2001).

Organisations can also reap huge benefits and even gain a competitive advantage if diversity is effectively managed (Cavaleros et al., 2002; Laubscher, 2001) resulting from the implementation of a variety of diversity initiatives (Cox & Beale, 1997; Hayles & Russel, 1997; Prasad, Mills, Elmes & Prasad, 1997). Traditional approaches to diversity tended to focus rather more on mobilising mechanistic organisational structures, than on achieving attitudinal and behavioural change at an individual level (Van der Westhuizen, 2001). The focus of diversity training programmes was mostly about facilitating diversity awareness and ensuring that non-discriminatory policies were communicated and understood (Eades, 1999; Thomas, 1996; Van der Westhuizen, 2001). These diversity interventions were usually based on a behaviouristic and socio-cognitive approach. The training programmes were typically presented in a mechanistic, instructional and telling style, extending knowledge and content about the different ways in which different people perceive and approach life. The underlying assumption of this mechanistic approach to diversity seems to be that members could be trained and that once they had undergone the training they could be certified as being able to cope with diversity (Cilliers & May, 2002).

According to Human (2005), the more rational and cognitive approaches to diversity often fail because of an inadequate understanding of the concept of diversity and its unconscious behavioural dynamics (Cavaleros et al., 2002). The systems psychodynamic stance accepts that traditional *talk and chalk training* approaches do little more than share knowledge and enhance dependency. Thus, organisations only study the tip of the *diversity iceberg* if the covert and unconscious social-political issues such as resistance, denial, splitting, projections and projective identifications are neglected (Cilliers & May, 2002; Obholzer & Roberts, 1994). True understanding and awareness develop when organisations take into consideration, both the rational and the irrational forces, conscious and unconscious processes, and overt as well as covert behavioural dynamics (Czander, 1993; Kets De Vries & Balazs, 1998).

The need is therefore to attain a deeper understanding of diversity and the underlying forces that impact on the way diversity is perceived, experienced and acted upon. In this quest, the systems psychodynamic perspective offers the possibility of attaining a deeper learning and understanding of diversity and its accompanying dynamics. Diversity programmes presented from a systems psychodynamic consulting stance using group relations training methodology can be seen as a microcosm of organisational diversity dynamics. This implies that the macro organisational diversity issues will play out in the micro workshop here-and-now events (Campbell & Huffington, 2008). Research of the effect of such programmes indicates some movement towards increasing the awareness of diversity issues on the conscious and unconscious systemic levels. The success of these programmes lies in their focus on the owning of projections onto and into *the other*, authorising the subsystem to take up a leadership role, and to move from the paranoid-schizoid to the depressive position (Cilliers & May, 2002; Cilliers, Rothmann & Struwig, 2004; Coetzee, 2007; Myburg, 2006).

The core research problem was formulated as follows. Although experiential events in diversity dynamics are presented in South African organisations and some information is available about the experiences of participants, more knowledge about South African diversity dynamics is required. The objectives were to describe the experiences of the RIDE participants and to offer systems psychodynamic interpretations towards understanding the unconscious (below the surface) behaviour that organisations are not aware of or do not take seriously in planning human resources or organisational development activities.

The potential value-add of the research is to push the awareness around diversity dynamics beyond the obvious and rational organisational functioning, towards the exploration of behaviours and dynamics below the surface of consciousness. The authors hope that this endeavour could open opportunities for organisations to have more real – albeit difficult – discussions on relationships fraught with diversity anxiety.

The rest of the article is structured as follows. The research design is presented with reference to the research approach and strategy. Then the research method, consisting of the setting, the roles of the researchers, the sampling method, data collection, analysis and interpretation, is discussed. The strategies employed to ensure quality data are mentioned. Thereafter the findings are presented as manifested themes. The discussion contains the hypotheses followed by the conclusion, recommendations, limitations and suggestions for further research.

Research Design

Research Approach

Qualitative and descriptive research (De Vos, Strydom, Fouché & Delport, 2002; Camic, Rhodes & Yardley, 2003) was chosen to allow the researchers to delve deeply into relatively unknown areas of organisational psychology, namely the personal diversity dynamic experiences of participants in an unstructured and experiential diversity experience (see Alvesson & Sköldberg, 2010). Hermeneutic phenomenology (Terre Blanche, Durrheim & Painter, 2006) was chosen as research paradigm, which allowed for the in-depth understanding of the participants' experiences around diversity. The paradigm also enabled us to interpret the data from the systems psychodynamic stance in an attempt to develop knowledge around the conscious and unconscious manifestation of diversity dynamics (see Terre Blanche, Durrheim & Painter, 2006).

Research Strategy

A single case study was used (Chamberlayne, Bornat & Apitzsch, 2004) for its instrumental value, namely to report to South African organisations how employees experience diversity events in the unconscious (below the surface) and in terms of their object relations (see Denzin & Lincoln, 2005).

Research Method

Research Setting

Broadly speaking, the research was set within diversity management as organisational development (OD) activity. More specifically, the November 2000 RIDE was planned and presented as a group relations event on Robben Island with its provocative diversity symbolism and connotations (Cilliers & May, 2002). The authors presented the event, voluntarily attended by employees from different organisations interested in diversity dynamics.

Entrée and Establishing Researcher Roles

All three authors were involved in the planning, presentation and research of the event. Individually, the first author took up the role of director of the hosting organisation and consultant during the event, the second as the director of the RIDE and the third, as the associate director of the RIDE. All three authors are psychologists with special training and experience in Group Relations Training as well as systems psychodynamically informed consultancy and research (as explicated in Cytrynbaum & Noumair, 2004; Fraher, 2004).

Sample and Sampling

A sample of convenience was used (Terre Blanche, Durrheim & Painter, 2006) which consisted of the 15 participants who attended the event voluntarily. They were human resources practitioners working in large organisations, sponsored by their various organisations. Table 2 indicates the diversity characteristics of the sample.

Data Collection Method

One month after the RIDE the first author conducted a one-hour, unstructured interview with the participants. Interviews were conducted by telephone or in-person at a private and silent location (Terre Blanche, Durrhein & Painter, 2006). The interview started with an open question, namely *'It is now one month since the RIDE. Could you tell me about your experience of the event?'* The researcher asked a maximum of three follow-up questions to elicit more responses from the participant if needed, namely:

1. 'What else did you experience?'
2. 'Would you like to add anything else relating to your experience of the event? and
3. 'Are there any other experiences that stood out for you?'

Recording of Data

The interviews were recorded on tape, transcribed and kept secured.

Data Analyses

Content analysis (Brewerton & Millward, 2004) was used from which five themes manifested themselves. Interpretations were made from the systems psychodynamic perspective (Armstrong, 2005; Campbell, 2007; Gould, Stapley & Stein, 2004; Huffington, Armstrong, Halton, Hoyle & Pooley, 2004; Klein, 2005). The emerging themes enabled the researchers to formulate working hypotheses and a research hypothesis about South African diversity dynamics.

Strategies Employed to Ensure Quality Data

Scientific rigour was ensured by focussing on validity, reliability, and ethics (Denzin & Lincoln, 2005; Terre Blanche et al., 2006). Reliability and dependability were ensured through the careful planning, execution and reporting of different aspects of the research project.

The credibility and transferability were ensured by a detailed and accurate description of the design and method (Denzin & Lincoln, 2005). Bias, which could impact credibility, was reduced through critical self-reflection about potential

---

predispositions (see Johnson & Christensen, 2000). The researchers also used themselves as instruments to become aware of intra-personal and interpersonal dynamics that could influence their analyses and interpretations (McCormick & White, 2000). Consensus discussions (Mukherji, 2000) were conducted with colleagues (industrial psychologists) and consultants in the fields of diversity and systems psychodynamics to enhance the credibility of the research.

Ethical requirements were attended to in order not to cause harm to participants or to invade their privacy (Camic, Rhodes & Yardley, 2003). Informed consent was obtained verbally, during the telephone interviews. The privacy, anonymity and confidentiality of participants were protected by not disclosing their identity, but rather by assigning group membership to them (Henning, 2004). Therefore participants' verbatim responses were given by using their alphabetical numbers (e.g. p.4).

Reporting

The research findings were reported and interpreted per theme. In the discussion, the findings were integrated into working hypotheses and eventually into the research hypothesis. This was followed by the conclusions, recommendations, limitations and suggestions for further research.

Table 2 Biographical Information of the Sample

Gender	Black people	White people	Coloured people	Asian people	Total
Female	3	3	1	1	8
Male	3	3	1	-	7
Total	6	6	2	1	15

Findings

Five themes manifested themselves, namely:

∝ crossing boundaries,

∝ engaging the brave new world,

∝ ties that bind,

∝ being imprisoned, and

∝ the struggle.

Crossing Boundaries

The RIDE implied that participants had to cross a physical boundary to get to the island, a methodological boundary to engage in learning from a different perspective (group relations training), as well as various symbolic boundaries in the process of connecting to and relating with *the other*. The latter included the crossing of the boundary from and the elaborate interplay between being a singleton to that of becoming a group member (see Turquet, 1975). During the event, participants were confronted with their own personal identity boundaries and the need to belong.

Engaging the Brave New World

Engaging with the new world (of the RIDE) aroused a great deal of anxiety for participants and resulted in a need for safety and containment. Participants primarily sought containment and created comfort zones for their anxiety by linking with other participants with similar diversity characteristics. It seemed to be difficult, and possibly overwhelming to *face* the new world by oneself. The quest was to find ways in which the *singleton* could link up with and become part of a subgroup. This manifested in various splits within the overall membership based primarily on race and gender. A statement by P4 illustrated this dynamic: *'We clung onto those groups, it was a comfort zone ... people find safety in a group whether it is on the basis of colour or being a woman or man.'* The irony is, that the very act by which participants tried to contain their anxiety by linking to certain similarities (race and gender), created immense anxiety in the RIDE system due to the dynamics of exclusion. The very act of including implies excluding (Patel, Bennet, Dennis, Dosanjh, Mahtani, Miller & Nadirshaw, 2000).

Some participants however dealt with the anxiety of facing the new world in the opposite way – by disassociating themselves from the group. This behaviour, which is typical of the basic assumption of me-ness (Lawrence, Bain & Gould, 1996) emphasises separateness and averts any link with the subgroup's collective.

Within the RIDE fraternity, the focus was predominantly on the primary dimensions of diversity, with priority given to race. As P3 stated *'It was as if this colour-thing was still important for people to survive in the new South Africa.'* This could be an indication of the extent to which the South African society fixates on race. The many unprocessed race-related issues become the frame through which situations and relations are seen. Although gender issues were also dealt with, those played a secondary role and were only seen to be 'women's issues'. The men seemed to divorce themselves from the gender issues by projecting those onto the women. This gender dynamic underscores the notion that the privileged or dominant group (in this case the men) will seldom be motivated to deal with issues concerning the disadvantaged or denigrated group (in this case women). Interestingly, the discussions on the gender issues were derailed and turned into the race-related issues – maybe once again reiterating the perception that South Africans find it difficult to move beyond race.

Ties that Bind

During the RIDE it became apparent that the ties (diversity characteristics) that were used to define the identity of the participants were also used to bind them to a specific subgroup. This leads to complex interactions between people, because of their implied allegiance (ties) to different subgroups. P13 (White female) stated: '*I made a close connection with a Black female ... but in the plenary she sided with the (Black) group and that floored me and I reacted on behalf of my (White) group and she couldn't understand that.*' (P13)

These ties thus not only linked people to a specific group but also brought with it certain unspoken responsibilities. Participants were, for example, expected to be loyal to their groups and to protect co-participants. Breaking this unspoken contract led to severe emotional reactions from other participants of that group. Perhaps this indicates the powerful unconscious impact that the (diversity) ties might have on mobilising intergroup dynamics such as splitting, pairing and fight-flight behaviour (Bion, 1970; Lawrence, 1999).

Being Imprisoned

As with the South African Crucible, the RIDE participants crossed the boundary into the event not with clean slates, but with their personal and collective memories, experiences, reference systems, values and emotions attached. This baggage was subgroup-specific and in a sense imprisoned the participants. Black participants for instance, verbalised a lot of rage and resentment about what had happened in the past. P6 (White male) reflected on '*how deep-seated the hate is amongst the Blacks towards Whites.*' The baggage that Black participants were carrying, despite their political control, is probably linked to emotional scars caused by oppression. The White participants seemed to carry a collective guilt about the past, projected onto them by the RIDE society on behalf of their forefathers. The baggage of Coloured and Indian participants seemed to centre on rejection, the feeling of not being good enough, and the struggle to find a place in the RIDE society. P15 (Coloured female) stated that:' *it awakened a lot of feelings inside me. The most important was my childhood rejection of being coloured. It made me so angry.*'

The (diversity) baggage from the past does not only create ties that bind, but much worse, it seems to have imprisoned participants into specific subgroups, which served as a stumbling block to connect across differences. Thus, unresolved/fixated diversity issues will keep haunting and returning until they are addressed and adequately worked through (Brown & Pedder, 1991; Rutan & Stone, 1993).

The Struggle

The struggle for power and position in RIDE illustrated typical characteristics of the fight-flight basic assumption (Bion, 1961). Within the RIDE, position, power and status were primarily allocated according to subgroup membership, especially with regards to race and gender. The primary position was reserved for Black and White participants, while Coloured and Asian participants were a distant second. In the past, the South African society was characterised by the phenomenon that some people were more equal than others. Ironically the situation seems to be perpetuating itself in the new dispensation with the difference that Black males are now at the top. It seemed that Black people felt entitled to their position because of the pain and suffering they had experienced in the past. The message was clearly communicated that they would not give up their newly found position at the top of the ladder soon. A heated debate about the right to be called 'Black' or 'African' vividly illustrated this struggle. Black participants heavily opposed the notion of White, Coloured or Indian people calling themselves African. In this regard P9 (an Indian female) related her traumatic experience when Black participants denied her her 'blackness' as follows: *'I have never been exposed to such anger in my life … from day one (of this event) I was being told that I am not Black. I lived my whole life knowing that I am Black.'* By refusing other groups the right to be 'African' or 'Black', the Black participants indirectly told the other groups that they would neither share their identity nor their position of power. The dynamics of subgroups looking after themselves and ensuring their own survival seems to be a theme that repeats itself throughout the history of South Africa.

Coloured participants were struggling with issues relating to acceptance, rejection, acknowledgement, and to find a place in the new society. The general experience was that of being caught in the middle – reflecting the biological constitution of being both White and Black. This symbolised being both an object of denigration and idealisation. The denigration was due to impurity as denoted by the mixture. They could not fit into either of the worlds (Black or White), and were therefore rejected by both parties. They however also represented an idealised object due to the integration they present in being both Black and

White. This ability to fit into both worlds made them an object of envy, as well as a crucial variable in the power relations between Black and White participants.

The underlying assumption seemed to be that being good enough is determined by the colour of one's skin, and that Black and White are the only two recognised colours in South African society. The difficult position of being Coloured or Indian, is illustrated by the statement of an Indian participant that '*I am too White to be Black and too Black to be White.*' In the past, South African society projected denigration onto and into Black people. In the new South Africa, with its hypersensitivity towards discrimination against Black people, this is no longer a viable option. It is as if society, in terms of the Coloured and Indian participants, found new scapegoats to carry the denigration label with which it struggles. This tendency to function in a paranoid-schizoid way seems to perpetuate itself. The more things change the more they stay the same – society seems to be caught up in a vicious circle, unable to contain the denigrated parts of the system, thus splitting them off and projecting them into another part of the system.

Discussion

The purpose of the research was to describe the experiences of participants attending the Robben Island Diversity Experience (RIDE), which form a depth psychology understanding of South African diversity dynamics.

The research is seen as important in its in-depth and rich comments on South African diversity dynamics. As such it informs diversity consultants and leaders about the unconscious diversity matters that manifest themselves in their organisations. It also provides a methodology to study these dynamics inside their organisations for use in future human resources and leadership initiatives.

For each manifesting theme working hypotheses were formulated, which were integrated into the research hypothesis.

1. For **theme 1** (crossing boundaries) the following working hypothesis was formulated. In our relations and relatedness with difference (different subgroups and/or diversity), we are continually confronted with the struggle and elaborate interplay between being an individual and also being part of a group. This struggle and interplay are impacted on by crossing symbolic boundaries created by diversity characteristics between us as individuals, between, us as individuals, and our preferred subgroups, as well as between subgroups.

2. For **theme 2** (engaging the brave new world) the following working hypothesis was formulated. South Africans engage with the new diverse society through the process

of linking with those who have similar diversity characteristics as themselves. Race is used as the principal diversity dimension to differentiate between and making connections with others, followed by gender.

3. For **theme 3** (ties that bind) the following working hypothesis was formulated. Linking and subgroup formation based on diversity characteristics give rise to issues of inclusion and exclusion, as well as the processes associated with in-group and out-group dynamics. Being part of a subgroup unconsciously ties the individual to the subgroup, and implies certain unspoken obligations, such as being loyal to the subgroup and to protect it from other subgroups. The South African diversity dynamic struggle is characterised by subgroups based on race and gender.

4. For **theme 4** (being imprisoned) the following working hypothesis was formulated. Black people are imprisoned by their past baggage which is transferred from one generation to the next. In this process, the different subgroups seem to contain different aspects of South Africa's past. Black people seem to carry the anger, hate and aggression, while White people carry the guilt related to an unjust past. The Coloured and Indian people seem to carry the ambiguity of both being rejected for not being good enough and feelings of rejection by not being acknowledged.

5. For **theme 5** (the struggle) the following working hypothesis was formulated. Much of the diversity dynamics is centred on the struggle between the different subgroups in which they tried to find a place for themselves in the new dispensation. This is especially important since the position of the different subgroups seems to determine the amount of acceptance and acknowledgement their members have received and whether they were listened to.

The above was integrated into the research hypothesis, reading as follows: South African diversity dynamics is about the splits and subgroups within the country and the dynamics between these different subgroups. South African diversity dynamics focuses on the dynamics (drives, emotions and needs) that inform subgroup formation, what these subgroups represent and carry on behalf of the total system, as well as the ensuing dynamics between the subgroups. Some of these dynamics could be linked to how projections of the various subgroups give rise to the process of projected identification in which the different subgroups, primarily based on race and gender, are kept in specific roles and/or positions.

It was concluded that South African diversity dynamics is not a rational phenomenon and cannot be treated as one. It is socially constructed and relational in nature. The way that similarities and differences are perceived, interpreted and acted upon is influenced by a host of conscious and unconscious, rational and irrational, as well as overt and covert forces.

The research findings elicited similar findings in other South African diversity dynamic studies (Cilliers & May, 2002; May & Cilliers, 2000). It affirms the presence of high levels of anxiety, which manifest themselves unconsciously in basic assumption behaviour and the paranoid-schizoid systemic position (Stapley, 2006). No similar international diversity research could be traced. In comparison with international group relations training events (see Brunner, Nutkevitch & Sher, 2006) these participants experienced similar types of (free-floating, performance and persecutory) anxiety around authority and the taking up of a leadership role. In comparing the present findings with the theorising about diversity dynamics which manifest themselves in the US (McRae, 2004; McRae & Short, 2010) and in the UK (Foster, 2004; Foster, Dickinson, Bishop & Klein 2006; Nichols, 2004; White, 2006), similarities and differences were found. The similarity lies in the anxiety which is inherent in diversity dynamics. The difference lies in the unique manifestation of diversity dynamics in South Africa because of the past splits between race groups and the resulting experience of entitlement and denigration.

It is recommended that South African organisations approach diversity (instead of in a mechanistic manner using instructional methods such as lectures and presentations) in a dynamic and experiential manner (such as using group relations training and systems psychodynamic thinking. Although participants in such events experience many defensive responses such as resistance and projection, the learning lies in processing the defences and accepting personal responsibility for their roles and actions regarding diversity. It was suggested that South Africans could not go forward if they had not dealt with the past. The vicious circles and destructive interactive patterns around diversity matters which manifest themselves in organisations, can only be broken by following the road less travelled – this implies re-owning projections to repair the broken relationships. In this process, communication and attitude become the stimulating factors on the journey to reconciliation and healing.

A further recommendation is that diversity interventions based on the systems psychodynamic perspective should be used in conjunction with other approaches such as the socio-cognitive and legal imperatives currently used in organisations in order to optimise the management of diversity. It is thus not a case of opting for one or the other approach, but using them together in order to gain a more comprehensive understanding of diversity, and therefore to be able to manage more effectively.

Some limitations are the following. Although the sample was relatively representative, there was no Indian male present during the RIDE. Hence the perspective of an Indian male was excluded in the views on South African diversity dynamics. The second, and probably the principal aspect of the sample was that the members included in the sample could best be described as being affluent. Because of the financial implications to attend the RIDE, organisations generally sent senior human resource personnel or members from middle management to attend the event. Thus, the socio-economic diversity of the group could be seen as a limitation of the study. It could be contended that a more diverse membership in this regard, would probably have led to more dynamics on envy between the *haves* and *have not's*.

It was suggested that future research should focus on more qualitative as well as quantitative research. Qualitative research could focus on and obtain a more in-depth understanding of the specific themes and hypotheses about diversity dynamics generated by this research between specific variables suggested in the themes and hypotheses Quantitative research projects could focus to establish clearer causal or descriptive links generated through this research.

Acknowledgements

Competing Interests

The authors declare that they have no financial or personal relationship(s) which may have inappropriately influenced them in writing this paper.

Authors' Contributions

M.P. (University of South Africa) did the empirical research. F.C. (University of South Africa) and M.M. (University of South Africa) supervised the research. All three authors worked on the formulation of the themes and discussion.

References

Alvesson, M. & Sköldberg, K. (2010). *Reflexive methodology. New vistas for qualitative research*. London: Sage.

Armstrong, D. (2005). *Organisation in the mind. Psychoanalysis, group relations and organisational consultancy*. London: Karnac.

Beck, D.E. & Linscott, G. (1996). *The crucible: Forging South Africa's future*. Denton: New Paradigm.

Beck, R.B. (2000). *The history of South Africa*. London: Greenwood Press.

Bekker, S. & Carlton, D. (1996). *Racism, xenophobia and ethnic conflict*. Durban: Creda.

Bion, W.R. (1961). *Experiences in groups*. London: Tavistock. http://doi.org/10.4324/9780203359075

Bion, W.R. (1970). *Attention and interpretation*. London: Tavistock.

Booysen, L. (2005). *Social identity changes in South Africa: Challenges facing leadership*. Inaugural lecture, Graduate School of Business Leadership, University of South Africa, Pretoria.

Brewerton, P. & Millward, L. (2004). *Organisational research methods. A guide for students and researchers*. London: Sage.

Brown, A. (2008). Rainbow nation – dream or reality? *BBC News*, UK., http://news.bbc.co.uk/s/hi/africa/7512700.stm [Accessed 18 July 2003].

Brown, D. & Pedder, J. (1991). *Introduction to psychotherapy: An outline of psychodynamic principles and practice*. London: Routledge.

Brunner, L.D.; Nutkevitch, A. & Sher, M. (2006). *Group relations conferences. Reviewing and exploring theory, design, role-taking and application*. London: Karnac.

Camic, P.M.; Rhodes, J.E. & Yardley, L. (2003). *Qualitative research in Psychology*. Washington: APA.

Campbell, D. (2007). *The socially constructed organisation*. London: Karnac.

Campbell, D. & Huffington, C. (2008). *Organisations connected. A handbook of systemic consultation*. London: Karnac.

Cavaleros, C.; Van Vuuren, L.J. & Visser, D. (2002). The effectiveness of a diversity awareness training programme. *South African Journal of Industrial Psychology*, 28(3):50-61. https://doi.org/10.4102/sajip.v28i3.68

Chamberlayne, P.; Bornat, J. & Apitzsch, U. (2004). *Biographical methods and professional practice. An international perspective*. Bristol: Policy Press. https://doi.org/10.1332/policypress/9781861344939.001.0001

Charlton, G.D. & Van Niekerk, N. (1994). *Affirming action: Beyond 1994*. Cape Town: Creda.

Cilliers, F. & May, M. (2002). South African diversity dynamics. Reporting on the 2000 Robben Island Diversity Experience. A Group Relations event. *South African Journal of Labour Relations*, 26(3):42-68. https://doi.org/10.4102/sajip.v30i1.143

Cilliers, F.; Rothmann, S. & Struwig, W.H. (2004). Transference and counter-transference in systems psychodynamic group process consultation: The consultant's experience. *South African Journal of Industrial Psychology*, 30(1):72-81.

Coetzee, O. (2007). Exploring interpersonal and inter-group diversity dynamics in South African organisations by means of a theoretical model. Unpublished DCOM thesis. Pretoria: University of South Africa.

Cox, T. & Beale, R.L. (1997). *Developing competency in managing diversity: Readings, cases and activities*. San Francisco: Berrett-Koehler.

Cytrynbaum, S. & Noumair, A. (2004). *Group dynamics, organizational irrationality, and social complexity: Group relations reader 3*. Jupiter: A.K. Rice.

Czander, W.M. (1993). *The psychodynamics of work and organisations. Theory and applications*. New York: Guilford Press.

De Vos, A.S.; Strydom, H.; Fouché, C.B. & Delport, C.S.L. (2002). *Research at grass roots*. Pretoria: Van Schaik.

Denzin, N.K. & Lincoln, Y.S. (2005). *The Sage handbook of qualitative research*. London: Sage. https://doi.org/10.1177/1468794105047237

Eades, L.M. (1999). *The end of apartheid in South Africa*. London: Greenwood Press.

Foster, A. (2004). *Living and working with difference and diversity*. Paper presented at OPUS, London.

Foster, A.; Dickinson, A.; Bishop, B. & Klein J. (2006). *Difference: An avoided topic in practice*. London: Karnac.

Fraher, A. (2004). *A history of group study and psychodynamic organisations*. London: Free Association.

Gould, L.J.; Stapley, L.F. & Stein, M. (2004). *Experiential learning in organisations. Applications of the Tavistock group relations approach*. London: Karnac.

Hayles, V.R. & Russel, A.M. (1997). *The diversity directive: Why some initiatives fail and what to do about it*. London: Irwin Professional.

Henning, E. (2004). *Finding your way in qualitative research*. Pretoria: Van Schaik.

Huffington, C.; Armstrong, A.; Halton, W.; Hoyle, L. & Pooley, J. (2004). *Working below the surface. The emotional life of contemporary organisations*. London: Karnac.

Human, L. (2005). *Diversity management for business success*. Pretoria: Van Schaik.

Hunt, J. & Lascaris, R. (1998). *The South African dream*. Goodwood: Zebra Press.

Johnson, B. & Christensen, L. (2000). *Educational research: Quantitative and qualitative researches*. London: Allyn & Bacon.

Kets De Vries, F.R. & Balazs, K. (1998). The psychodynamics of organizational transformation and change. *European Management Journal*, 16(5):611-621. http://doi.org/10.1016/S0263-2373(98)00037-1

Klein, L. (2005). *Working across the gap. The practice of social science in organisations*. London: Karnac.

Kreeger, L. (1975). (ed.), *The large group*. London: Constable.

Laubscher, C. (2001). Managing diversity. *People Dynamics*, 18(8):16-18.

Lawrence, W.G. (1999). *Exploring individual and organisational boundaries. A Tavistock open systems approach*. London: Karnac.

Lawrence, W.G.; Bain, A. & Gould, L. (1996). *The fifth basic assumption*. London: Tavistock Institute.

May, M.S. & Cilliers, F. (2000). Robben Island: Container for difference. Unpublished manuscript.

McCormick, D.W. & White, J. (2000). Using one's self as an instrument for organizational diagnoses. *Organizational Development Journal*, 18(3):49-62.

McRae, M.B. (2004). Class, race and gender: Person-in-role implications in taking up the directorship. In: S. Cytrynbaum & D.A. Noumair, *Group dynamics, organisational irrationality, and social complexity: Group Relations Reader 3*, pp.225-237. Jupiter: AK Rice Institute.

McRae, M.B. & Short, E.L. (2010). *Racial and cultural dynamics in group and organisational life*. London: Sage.

Miller, A. (2011). Getting along: South Africa's real miracle. *The Daily Maverick*, Tuesday 1 March, p. 5. http://www.thedailymaverick.co.uk/article/2011-03-01-getting-along-south-africas-real-miracle [Accessed 2 March 2011].

Milliken, F.J. & Martins, L.L. (1996). Searching for common threads: Understanding the multiple effects of diversity in organizational groups. *Academy of Management Review*, 21(2):402-433. http://doi.org/10.5465/AMR.1996.9605060217

Mukherji, P.N. (2000). *Methodology in social research: Dilemmas and perspectives*. London: Sage. https://doi.org/10.1557/PROC-612-E8.10.1

Myburg, H.S. (2006). The experience of organisational development consultants working in the systems psychodynamic stance. Unpublished M.A. dissertation. University of South Africa, Pretoria.

Newell, S. (2002). *Creating the healthy organization: Well-being, diversity and ethics at work*. London: Thomson Learning.

Nichols, L. (2004). *When faith eclipses hope; forgiveness within reparation*. Paper presented at OPUS, London.

Oakley-Smith, T. & Winter, V. (2001). Workplace racism. *People Dynamics*, 18(8):19-21.

Obholzer, A. & Roberts, V.Z. (1994). *The unconscious at work: Individual and organizational stress in the human services*. London: Routledge. http://doi.org/10.4324/9780203359860

Patel, N.; Bennet, E.; Dennis, M.; Dosanjh, N.; Mahtani, A.; Miller, A. & Nadirshaw, Z. (2000). *Clinical psychology, "race" and culture: A training manual*. Leicester: BPS Books.

Prasad, P.; Mills, A.J.; Elmes, M. & Prasad, A. (1997). *Managing the organizational melting pot: Dilemmas of workplace diversity*. London: Sage.

Rutan, J.S. & Stone, W.N. (1993). *Psychodynamic group psychotherapy*. New York: Guilford Press.

Stapley, L.F. (2006). *Individuals, groups and organisations beneath the surface*. London: Karnac.

Terre Blanche, M.; Durrheim, K. & Painter, D. (2006). *Research in practice. Applied methods for the social sciences*. Cape Town: UCT Press.

Thomas, R.R. (1996). *Redefining diversity*. New York: American Management Association.

Thompson, L. (2001). *A history of South Africa*. London: Yale University Press. https://doi.org/10.1080/02582470108671409

Turquet, P.M. (1975). Threats to identity in the large group. In: L. Kreeger (ed.), *The large group*, pp.87-144. London: Constable. https://doi.org/10.4324/9780429482267-5

Van der Westhuizen, H. (2001). The evaluation of a diversity training programme in the South African Police Service. Unpublished Master's dissertation. Grahamstown: University of Rhodes.

Van Eron, A.M. (1995). Ways to assess diversity success. *HR Magazine*, 40(8):51-52.

White, K. (2006). *Unmasking race, culture and attachment in the psychoanalytic space. What do we see? What do we think? What do we feel?* London: Karnac.

Article 7

Social Defence Structures in Organisations: How a Lack of Authorisation Keeps Managers from Moving to Transformation Leadership[1]

R van Eeden & F Cilliers

Abstract

The systems psychodynamic perspective was used to explore the functioning of a management team at one of the plants of a South African production company experiencing change. The focus was on the impact of social defences on the leadership style being exercised. During a day-long consultation session with the team a dynamic of control and dependency was observed. The transactional culture that can be regarded as "normal," in this environment, actually became part of a defence strategy, resulting in dependency and a lack of authorisation that limited the use of transformational leadership. A lack of clarity in terms of role and boundary definitions furthermore resulted in a struggle in terms of interrelatedness and a lack of interdependent functioning at a system's level.

The Systems Psychodynamics Perspective

The general management and leadership discourse in the world is focused on the quantitative measurement of mainly conscious behavioral processes and systems, defined from behavioristic and humanistic psychology (Cilliers, 2000).

1   Van Eeden, R. & Cilliers, F. (2009). Social defence structures in organisations: how a lack of authorisation keeps managers from moving to transformational leadership. *International Journal of Organisation Theory and Behaviour*, 12(3):475-501.

On the other hand, systems psychodynamics (with its origins in psychoanalysis) studies the meaning of unconscious behavioral processes to understand the emotional complexity in the world of work. As such, it has influenced and shaped the world in terms of how we think and talk about being human, not only in management and leadership but also in other disciplines concerned with human nature, such as the arts and philosophy. Although systems psychodynamics has not yet fully entered the mainstream of critical thinking in business, it is especially relevant in understanding the organisational system's political and power issues as applied to how managers and leaders are authorised to take up their roles in providing opportunities for followers in order to reach their organisational goals and to grow the business (Hogget, 2006).

Systems psychodynamics refers to the interaction between the structural features of the organisation with its members, which stimulates patterns of individual and group dynamic processes, which, in turn, result in the organisation's culture, role definitions, boundary definitions, and the management and regulation of these roles and boundaries (Czander, 1993; De Board, 1978; Miller, 1993; Miller & Rice, 1967, 1975, 1990; Stokes, 1994). The systems psychodynamic perspective is based on psychoanalysis, group relations theory, and open systems theory. The term "systems" refers to the open systems theory that regards the organisation, the group, and the individual as open systems involved in continuous mutual transactions (Miller, 1993; Miller & Rice, 1967; 1975; 1990). The structural aspects of the organisational system are thus explored in terms of the effect on individuals and groups. The term "psychodynamics" refers to a psychoanalytic perspective on individual experiences, group functioning, and the way these relate to organisational functioning. Object relations theory and the concepts of the paranoid-schizoid and depressive positions, in particular, explain individual functioning and the use of individual defences (Czander, 1993; De Board, 1978; Klein, 1959; 1985). These concepts were applied to groups (Bion, 1961; 1975; De Board, 1978; Rioch, 1970; 1975), thus forming the basis for group relations theory, and also extended to explain the formation of organisational defence structures (De Board, 1978; Stokes, 1994).

Objective anxiety implies the feelings caused by an external source of danger that result in automatic physical reactions. Neurotic anxiety, however, is the result of experienced internal danger resulting from subjective and frequently unconscious feelings. Klein's theory (1959; 1985) explores the paranoid-schizoid and depressive positions typical of the earliest phases of mental life, and explains how the individual, in reaction to psychotic anxiety, regresses to the mechanisms characteristic of these positions. The paranoid anxiety experienced by an infant is dealt with by the mechanisms of splitting and projective identification. Internal persecutory anxiety is projected onto the mother who is then experienced as both an external and internal threatening bad object, resulting in splitting of both the ego and the object. The infantile depressive position develops with the realisation that good and bad objects are in fact aspects of the same thing (the mother and the self). This leads to an experience of guilt and despair (depressive anxiety) at the apparent destruction of the loved object. A paranoid attitude and denial could be adopted to avoid the depressive anxiety. On the other hand, the complexity of the internal and external reality could be faced resulting in work and creativity and often a desire to repair previous injuries.

Bion (1961; 1975) hypothesised that the group responds in a manner similar to that of the individual to psychotic anxiety. The members of the group experience psychotic anxiety and persecutory fear when faced with the reality of their own behavior. To deal with this, the group regresses and resorts to mechanisms such as splitting of the ego and the object, projective identification, and denial. Bion's theory of group behavior deals with the basic assumption groups which are manifestations of these defences (Bion, 1961; 1975; De Board, 1978; Kets de Vries & Miller, 1984; Rioch, 1970; 1975). The manifest aspects of a group (the work group) imply behaviors that are geared towards rational task performance whereas the latent aspects (basic assumption group) refer to those behaviors that are geared towards emotional needs and anxieties, that is, towards the survival of the group. The basic assumption positions are: dependency (the unconscious aim is to obtain security and protection from an authority figure); fight/flight (where survival depends on one of these two options, again involving the authority figure); and pairing (with perceived powerful others, or bonding to create a savior). Two additional basic assumptions were added, namely "me-ness" (Turquet, 1974) that represents the individual's escape into the safety of his or her inner world, and "we-ness" (Lawrence, Bain, & Gould, 1996) which implies that the individual joins into a powerful union, surrendering the self for passive participation. Only one basic assumption is prominent at any one time, although fairly regular changes in assumptions are possible (Bion, 1961; 1975). Once the group recognises and deals with the fact that the rational working of the group is affected by the (often irrational) emotions of its members, it releases its potential (although groups may regress temporarily after having made progress). The group should furthermore be an open system that maintains a balance between what is in and what is outside the group.

The basic assumptions (and related defences) also manifest at group level in organisations due to the interaction of individual dynamics with task-related or situational variables that create anxiety (Kets de Vries & Miller, 1984). Task or work groups use defence mechanisms to deal with difficult experiences and emotions which are too threatening or too painful to acknowledge (Halton, 1994). These defences include denial, avoidance, envy, and regression to a paranoid-schizoid way of functioning (involving splitting, projection, and projective identification). The boundary between what is inside the group and what is in the environment is blurred and reality is distorted (Moylan, 1994). More competent functioning implies integration and cooperation in and between groups, although clear boundaries are still needed to contain anxiety and ensure the survival of the system (Cilliers, 2000; Cilliers & Koortzen, 2000).

Similar dynamics are observed at an organisational level. The individual joins an organisation to try to fulfil unconscious needs and to resolve unconscious conflicts but due to a lack of fit between these needs and conflicts, and the reality of the work situation, anxiety results (Cilliers & Koortzen, 2000). The anxiety is associated with the tasks and responsibilities of the job and with the relationships with others (Obholzer, 2001). The organisation serves as a container for these individual anxieties and is used to reinforce individual defence mechanisms (De Board, 1978), hence the term "social defence system" (Czander, 1993). During organisational transition, changes occur in the structural features of the organisation (including authority structures) and the familiar social defence system is no longer functional (Krantz, 2001). The organisation no longer serves as a reliable container, and organisational conflicts are forced down to the individual and interpersonal levels (Stokes, 1994). To deal with this the organisation has to understand, interpret, and work through collective defences. This will enable the organisation to adapt in a manner appropriate to the task in terms of a rational distribution of authority, clear role and boundary definitions, and the management of these roles and boundaries (Gould, 2001). Boundaries contain anxiety but collaboration between systems requires that the different systems function as open systems that transact with the environment to ensure survival and growth especially during a time of transition (Bar-Lev Elieli, 2001).

Consultation from a Systems Psychodynamic Perspective

The Tavistock approach to group relations training is based on the group relations theory discussed previously (Gould, 2001; Luft, 1984; Smith, 1980). This approach has been expanded to organisational settings. Consultation based on a systems psychodynamic perspective was originally explored by Rice and Miller in their 1967 publication on the systems of organisations (Gould, 2001). The consultant analyses the interrelationships in the organisation and between the organisation and its environment through the selective interpretation of and feedback on the covert and dynamic aspects of this system. Czander (1993) identified aspects of the system that need to be addressed as boundary maintenance and regulation, task analysis, authority and leadership, role definition, inter-organisational relations, and subsystem dependency and autonomy. One needs to differentiate between the content, that is, the particular task, and the different levels of processes occurring simultaneously in the organisation as a whole, in subsystems and in individuals.

One of the main focus areas of the systems psychodynamic consulting stance concentrates on the nature of authority, the exercise of authority, and problems encountered in exercising authority in the context of interpersonal, intergroup, and organisational relationships (Fraher, 2004; Lawrence, 1999; Miller, 1993; Rice, 1965; 1975). Authority in this context is not limited to positions of power, hence the concept of personal authority that is a function of managing oneself in relation to role and task performance (Miller, 1993). A distinction can be made between delegated authority that is derived from an individual's role in the system, sanctioned authority that involves the membership, and personal authority that is the confirmation of authority from within individuals (Obholzer, 1994). Carr (2001) referred to dependency and power as related concepts while interdependence implies an acknowledgement of the fact that despite any autonomy achieved, the individual or group remains interdependent with the environment. This acknowledgement is in itself an exercise in personal authority. Leadership implies a relationship with followers that enables the latter to appreciate the concept of interdependence (Carr, 2001) and that encourages active followership (Obholzer, 2001). The core functions of leadership, according to Obholzer (2001) and Obholzer and Miller (2004), are creating a vision; management of change; boundary-keeping; exploring the dynamics involved in the relationship with followers; and dealing with organisational dynamics and anti-task behaviors resulting from the organisation's role as defence system.

In terms of developments in leadership theory, the preceding stance can be linked to the concept of transformational leadership. The full range model of leadership provides for a transactional–transformational paradigm of leadership (Bass & Avolio, 1994). Transformational leadership is defined in terms of an interpersonal (the functions of idealised influence and individualised consideration) and a visionary aspect (the functions of inspirational motivation and intellectual stimulation). The literature (e.g. Conger, 1999) shows that although behaviors associated with charismatic leadership can also be distinguished in the case of the transformational leader, there is less identification with an individual (that could lead to dependence) and more emphasis on the cause, implying interdependence and an active followership. Central to the latter is the relationship between the leader and individual followers (Atwater & Bass, 1994; Kuhnert, 1994). The full-range model also includes the concepts of laissez-faire or passive leadership and transactional leadership that implies a greater task-focus. An effective leader uses these styles together with the transformational style on occasion in an appropriate manner (Bass, 1997).

According to Avolio (1997), transformational teams and transformational organisational cultures are two additional levels of analysis at which this leadership style can be displayed. These need to be distinguished from individual leadership behaviors. As seen in the present study, the psychodynamics of the group and of related systems affect the individuals' leadership styles and influence the manifestation of these styles at a group level. A more "transformational group" would be expected to have the innovative qualities and openness associated with a visionary outlook (Bass, 1990; Church & Waclawski, 1999; Hogan, 1994; Howell & Higgens, 1990; Miller, Kets de Vries, & Toulouse, 1982; Van Rensburg & Crous, 2000; Wofford, Goodwin, & Whittington, 1998). Interpersonal interactions would be qualified by leaders' self-confidence and self-determination (Bass, 1990; Hogan, 1994; Ross & Offermann, 1997), their adherence to moral standards (Bass, 1990), and their need for affiliation (Van Rensburg & Crous, 2000), together with the support and concern shown towards others (Atwater & Bass, 1994; Ross & Offermann, 1997). The focus on task performance behaviors that characterises the transactional style, implies a practical orientation with a preference for structure and the use of procedures to maintain control (Bass, 1997; Miller et al., 1982). A degree of detachment is possible and the development of others is of less concern.

Consulting to the organisation from a systems psychodynamic stance implies that the leader is assisted in the functions of dealing with change, the management of boundaries, and the exploration of group and organisational dynamics. Psychoanalytic consultation means that conscious as well as unconscious motives are considered and through interpretation and insight, this leads to structural change in terms of the psychic structure of the organisation (Czander, 1993). However, this change affects the very feature of the organisation, namely the defence system, required to make change succeed (Krantz, 2001), and the organisation can no longer provide suitable containment. Bar-Lev Elieli (2001) described how a group involved in organisational change reacted to their fears and need for protection by creating safety in the group (a fantasy of sameness and "family"). The leadership was consequently not allowed to emerge – management members were swallowed by the system and not allowed to function on the boundary as representing inside and outside reality. Through the creation of greater awareness, a psychodynamic intervention facilitates the change needed in a group or team which, in turn, enables successful transition at organisational level (Cilliers, 2000). The reality in terms of what is happening in the group is important, but systemic relationships in the organisation and in terms of the outside environment also need to be analyzed (Miller, 1999).

Consultation in the present study was diagnostic (rather than therapeutic) in that the aim was to explore the social defence structures within a particular organisation and how this prevented the general manager and his management team from taking up their leadership role.

Method

A request was received for an intervention at management level at one of the plants of a South African production company. The company has a board of directors at national level and a general manager with a management team at each plant. Transformation in this organisation was needed due to technological demands and labour relation issues, and a shift from a procedural to a participative approach was indicated. The specific plant furthermore showed inadequate production, leading to the request for intervention.

Consultation to the processes and dynamics in the management team at the plant was aimed at sensitizing the team members with regard to their functioning. It also provided an opportunity to study the leadership style, group processes and dynamics, and the role of related systems in the context of organisational change.

Research Participants

The company has a corporate management and a management team at each plant. The team at the current plant comprised a general manager, a technical expert, managers for the two phases of production, and managers for planning and logistics, quality control, engineering, human resources, finances, and marketing. Based on a confidentiality agreement, details of the primary task of the organisation and biographical information on individual respondents cannot be given. The members of the management team were primarily white, Afrikaans-speaking males. Tenure varied, with some of them having been with the organisation only a few years and others for more than 10 years.

Collection of Research Material

Observation during a group consultation session provided the opportunity for exploring the natural functioning of the management team. The consultants planned the day-long group session in terms of time, task, and role boundaries. Four time periods were planned (the first being one hour and the others one and a half hours) with lunch and two tea breaks in between (each lasting 30 minutes). A time schedule was given to the general manager who, with the help of the human resources manager, made the necessary arrangements.

The group session resembled a team development design (Smith, 1980) where an intact work group meets as before, but the agenda is limited to the improvement of working relationships between those present. The aim is to create an awareness of current working relationships and possible desired change in this regard. The limits are reasonably firm but the process still relies on trust and openness. Boundaries were stated at the beginning of the session but the session itself was unstructured to allow observation of the processes and dynamics in the team. The consultancy team included a primary and secondary consultant and an observer/recorder. Their roles were clear and their inputs moved between active and less active, according to the systems psychodynamic approach. In terms of this approach the consultant analyses the relatedness in the team and with other systems in the organisation (Gould, 2001). This involves selective interpretation of and feedback on covert and dynamic aspects of the systems in the organisation.

Terre Blanche and Kelly (1999) recommended that comprehensive field notes be taken (rather than use of a tape recorder) when observation is used as research method. In the present study it was expected that the respondents would be more comfortable without a tape recorder and that this would contribute to the trust in the group session. In the case of observations, the recording and typing of material are influenced by a degree of subjectivity as qualitative research implies an inseparable relationship between the collection and interpretation of material (De Vos, 2002).

Interpretation of the Research Material

The information in the field notes made during the group session was organised and analytical notes were made on the processes and dynamics observed. Personal experiences and methodological and theoretical issues were also noted. Each time period of the group session was thereupon described in detail, followed by a discussion of the processes and dynamics observed during that period. The systems psychodynamic approach (Cilliers & Koortzen, 1997; Cilliers, Rothmann, & Struwig, 2004; Czander, 1993; De Board, 1978; Gould 2001; Miller, 1993; Miller & Rice, 1967, 1975, 1990; Stokes, 1994) was used in the interpretation. Recurrent themes were subsequently identified and hypotheses on the processes and dynamics in the management team and in relation to the broader context were formulated.

Ethical Considerations

The intervention was requested by corporate management and approval for the publication of the results was obtained from some of the directors and the general manager at the plant. This had implications in terms of informed consent with regard to the rest of the management team at the plant. Participation was nevertheless to some extent voluntary and all efforts were made to ensure confidentiality. The consultation session benefited the team members in the sense that it was not limited to gaining information, but, through feedback, members also gained insight into the team's functioning. However, using an approach that focuses on process in a content-driven environment could have impacted on the progression of events during the consultation session.

A Description of the Group Consultation Session

The focus of this session was on the here and now. It was a learning experience for the members of the consultancy team as well as the members of the management team regarding the functioning of the latter and changes needed in this regard. For the purposes of this article, the original description has been somewhat shortened.

Preparation

The consultants acknowledged feelings of apprehensiveness before the group session. Upon arrival at the plant, a discussion between the consultants and the human resources manager focussed on who should and who would be attending the group session. Specific reference was made to the marketing manager, the technical expert, the quality control manager (who had handed in a resignation), and a temporary manager from head office (who was excluded from the meeting). Team members arrived on time with the exception of the planning and logistics manager about whose initial absence there was some concern. There was familiarity between the team members and some of the consultants whom they had met before, yet reserve about the "new" consultant – this was also reflected in the way the team members seated themselves, pairing two of the consultants. The seating also reflected some pairing in terms of gender and seniority.

Time Period 1

Time, task and role boundaries were stated, and to create a point of departure, a matrix of the team's leadership and personality profile was presented. The general manager asked what had to be achieved and referred specifically to "today." *The consultant responded that the team had to decide for themselves.*

Throughout this session, insecurity about the task was indicated by various people, for example, "do not understand today's process", "in the dark", and "tell us". *The consultant commented that the team seemed dependent and that they believed that the expertise was outside and that they did not value what was inside or realised that the answers were in the system. Their struggle to get started possibly reflected the dynamics of the organisation.*

One of the production managers started a discussion on acceptance of individuals and the conversation focussed on communication, understanding of the self and others, and how members complemented each other to the benefit of the team. Joking occurred and the discussion returned to the team profile. *The consultant referred to them as a needy group. They were furthermore focussed on the future and they experienced pressure to perform, therefore seeing things in terms of right or wrong, confusing production with people and competing rather than listening to each other.* Team members commented that the organisation was results-driven with the team not always delivering. The functioning of the team was affected by splits in it and the self-centeredness of members and there was a need for teamwork. *The consultant noted that the team was results-driven, implying a task leadership focus but that people leadership was more of a struggle. The members of the team furthermore focussed on "me" rather than "us" and they needed to work on their identity as a team, the picture in the mind of us. The phrase "to be honest and open with you" was often used and there was more listening and communication than at the start of the time period.* A member asked: "How do we go forward from here?"

During lunch the consultants and the team members grouped together respectively. The financial manager was absent.

Time Period 2

A task-oriented reflection on the group session almost immediately changed to the expression of feelings such as frustration related to the session and a need for understanding and appreciation as individuals. The general manager expressed the discomfort of dealing with the here and now and the confusion of and personal limitation in trying to understand and deal with soft versus hard issues. *The consultant referred to the split that had to be made between content and process and he identified the members' need to connect and asked them to illustrate this.* There was some confusion and the group returned to a content-related discussion. *The consultant commented that the members did not listen to the painful side and tried to escape from anxiety.*

Work-related frustrations were identified in terms of the workforce and in terms of corporate management. *The consultant commented on the complaining ("moaning and groaning") and that the frustration of the group members was disempowering them. Talking about people who were not in the room could have served as self-protection.* The lack of unity in the team was again discussed ("kamstige team" or so-called team) with reference to a split between services and production. It was thought that a focus on a common organisational goal rather than on personal interests ("own little mountain" and "back-stabbing") would lead to less dependency and greater unity. Work pressure and ineffective communication were again mentioned as well as the difficulty in challenging authority because of a culturally based respect for authority. The general manager responded with "ek is nie jou pa nie" (I am not your father). *The consultant commented that the team members were frustrated by authority but that their fear of challenging authority was disempowering them. The leadership, in turn, resisted the dependency. Ineffective communication made it difficult to relate and the struggle with relatedness in the team was mirrored in their interaction with the total system leading to feelings of isolation.* Previous issues were repeated. *The consultant mentioned that guilt was being placed on someone else rather than realizing that they were all part of a system and needed to carry stuff for each other. They should not expect heaven with no fear, frustration, and anxiety but they should work towards less anxiety and thus not be managed by fear but manage fear.*

The atmosphere was relaxed during the break with greater interaction amongst the consultants and the members of the management team.

Time Period 3

The financial manager and one of the production managers were late (causing some concern). Members continued to express their need for sufficient and open communication, sharing, and mutual support. One of the production managers stated that "he felt scared some mornings". Informal contact as a means for creating better working relationships was discussed. *The consultant said that they should not regard social interaction as separate but do the work in a different manner so as to build respect and trust in the work situation creating a context in which challenging each other was possible.* Talk returned to problems related to production and the planning and logistics manager was at this stage called out. *The consultant commented on the shift to the content away from the process and to the fact that the members did not talk directly to or listen to one another.*

Problems at the plant were partly attributed to perceived incompetence at the lower levels. *The consultant referred to the fantasy that managers were competent and had to make the decisions.* A joke was made. The general manager stated that the team efforts were sufficient to make this the number one plant. *The consultant stated that the general manager was holding onto his "object of authority" role, the result of a system that was not authorizing people to assume their positions as leaders.* It was acknowledged that managers and workers should function more independently. *The consultant commented that there should be greater concern about issues such as growth and trust, otherwise dependency and overprotection would result. The "needy system" seduced the general manager and the management team into a role of being in control, thus keeping others dependent. Management would experience guilt if they did not take responsibility and the subordinates might react with shock and anger. Who was in control of what?* This dynamic was explored but it was concluded that some control was necessary given the capability of the workforce and the need for responsibility to be "pushed down" and people to be lifted up. *The consultant saw the general manager as providing containment and the safety for the team to grow and do their work. However, when the team members overstepped the boundary, it led to overload and feelings of burnout, tiredness, helplessness, and not being connected.* The general manager confirmed this by saying "it takes courage to come to work". Control and constraints from corporate management were mentioned.

Comments were made on the split in the team and a lack of cooperation resulting in feelings of isolation. *According to the consultant, the split in the team mirrored the structure in the plant which played into the room causing isolation and making it difficult to communicate and integrate.* Family matters were discussed during the break.

Time Period 4

This was defined as a review and application session with the focus on task (as opposed to boundaries, authority or role). Each member had to describe his or her job in normative (job description) and existential (how the member sees it) terms, and a phenomenal perspective (how others see it) was also gained. The service departments emphasised their role in service of production, in support of the management team, and in service of the customer. The need for providing reliable and timely information was mentioned as well as the fact that this was not an initiating role. Frustrations in managing subordinates were referred to. Positive feedback (e.g. enthusiasm, willingness, competence) and some criticism (e.g. insufficient sharing of information, not responding soon enough, over-involvement with the customer) were given by the rest of the team. *The consultant wondered how willing the members of the group were to provide feedback despite the need for this.*

The managers who dealt with production emphasised quality, standards, timely delivery, and keeping costs low. The job demanded a task-oriented person. However, involvement in teamwork required not only the ability to delegate effectively but also the ability to coach others. Some frustration in this regard was experienced. Positive feedback (e.g. knowledge, creativity, drive, professionalism, responsible, non-compromising) as well as criticism (e.g. insufficient consideration of others and a lack of trust) were given. *The consultant commented on the need to talk and be heard and talking on behalf of others.*

The general manager saw his role as taking the team "on a journey of improvement to world-class excellence". He preferred to work as part of a creative, winning team and was uncomfortable in a controlling role with the conflict and dependency that this involved ("at times it is a challenge to get out of bed"). The team commented on the general manager's work overload because he did not give others sufficient responsibility, his perfectionism and the fact that although he showed compassion, some people did not experience him as supportive. *The consultant concluded the session by saying that the team was feeling frustration as a result of helplessness, hopelessness, and anger that was not being expressed (me versus the goal).*

Psychodynamics Observed during the Group Session

At the start of the session, anxiety and resultant efforts to create safety through inclusion and closing the system were apparent. This was an unfamiliar situation for both the consultants and the management team and apprehension was to be expected. Efforts to create safety seemed to take the form of maintaining the "family", and issues dealing with belonging and boundaries were prominent. There was specific reference to people on the boundary between the team and the client (marketing manager) and between the team and corporate management (technical expert and replacement manager). The consultants provided some containment and safety for the group to work in by setting boundaries. However, issues of inclusion again surfaced throughout the day and it was clear that the group was still relying on an apparently intact "family," thus reflecting their dependency. The team members did not acknowledge the importance of interaction with the environment and to keep them "safe" the general manager had to form part of the group. This implied that he was not always allowed to fulfill his leadership function on the boundary with the environment. Towards the end of the session, the general manager in fact, indicated a wish to be "swallowed" by the team.

The group members indicated a task focus and a resultant need for a clear task. When this need was not met, they did not create their own structure but reacted to feelings of confusion and frustration by looking for help from outside the group. Flight into feelings such as confusion and frustration could also imply an avoidance of the anxiety associated with having to deal with the task. (These feelings were projected onto the consultants as seen in personal experiences of being out of control and a lack of motivation). The general manager seemed to take up the responsibility for meeting the group's need for dependency by trying to find clarity and providing structure on behalf of the group thus allowing passivity in the group. He also tried to keep the focus on the here and now, possibly not accepting his boundary role, or being allowed by the group to do so. The lack of clarity in terms of the task mirrored a lack of clarity in terms of the plant's primary task resulting in the "struggle to get started." Ultimately, they needed to identify and work on their primary task as a management team (related to the primary task of the organisation).

The consultation provided an opportunity for expressing feelings in the here and now and a need for understanding and acceptance was expressed. As the day progressed, the group members started to explore emotions with less resistance and indicated a greater willingness to do the work required in the group session. The need for trust and support was voiced and an honest expression of feelings of anxiety made it clear that, if they were prepared to acknowledge and show their vulnerability and to respect these feelings in others, interdependence might be possible. However, working in the here and now and dealing with soft issues (the process) made the managers uncomfortable and flight behavior was repeatedly seen. For example, when the discussion returned to task-related and production issues (the content). At one stage this shift required someone to carry the feelings not dealt with as seen in a member leaving the room and a member who commented very little. The confusion in task versus people management was reflected in the group's competitiveness ("me" rather than "us") and the struggle with communication that prevented the development of a team identity. A need for connection was expressed on more than one occasion but the team had to realise that unity requires trust and open communication (including effective confrontation). The lack of integration in the team probably mirrored the situation in the rest of the plant as well as in the organisation. There was a need for greater emphasis on relationships and the development of people skills.

A sense of responsibility and a non-compromising attitude were valued, indicating the need for structure and control. Being results-driven implied little tolerance for uncertainty and ambiguity. This "right/wrong" attitude was appropriate in terms of production but was also applied to people, creating opportunities for splitting and projection. Anxiety about their ability to deal with work-related as well as interpersonal demands, resulted in anti-task behavior such as projection onto other team members (including the general manager), the workers, and corporate management. The split between production and services is an example of this and it seemed as if the latter resented their serving role (were they carrying the less "glamorous" part?). The frustration of the team members was disempowering them (as mirrored in the depression experienced by a member of the consultancy team) and their need for structure and control was restricting the flow of energy. This led to feelings of helplessness, hopelessness, and anger. They had to realise that concepts such as individual responsibility versus group support and individual versus group goals were not mutually exclusive. Role clarity and clarity in terms of group norms had to be established to improve relatedness.

The team members furthermore struggled to challenge authority and to take up personal authority. Dependency prevailed despite resistance from the leadership. The depressive position would have implied that each member had to accept his or her own part in the system and the fact that anxiety results from taking up authority and responsibility. This anxiety had to be managed rather than using defences such as blaming to deal with it. The projection of incompetence onto the workforce resulted in even more pressure because it implied greater responsibility for the management team which, in turn, was resolved by members becoming dependent on the general manager. He was experiencing role overload and feelings of burnout, helplessness, and not being connected as a result of this dependency. "Fathering" by the general manager could also have been a defence against having to discipline. The pattern was repeated in the plant. Instead of authorizing the leadership, the system seemed to be using it to fulfil dependency needs. In turn, subordinates were not trusted to or allowed to take up their authority. Again roles had to be clarified and boundaries managed. Comments indicated that the control and dependency culture originated with corporate management.

The session created anxiety, dealt with by pairing, flight, and dependency. An example is the general manager's flight into the future to escape with an idealistic vision of "world-class excellence".

Integration and Hypotheses

A context of change is associated with anxiety and resistance to change (James & Huffington, 2004; Kranz, 2001). In this study, inadequate production at the plant, in what is clearly an outcomes-driven environment, implied further pressure on the staff and especially on the general manager and his management team. The consultants provided a degree of containment and carried some of the confusion associated with the lack of clarity. This was seen in the increasing attempts by team members to work in the here and now and some willingness to acknowledge (and thus take back) their feelings. The general manager expressed a somewhat vague and idealistic conception of the changes to take place ("world-class excellence") that could have implied that reality testing was to some extent diminished (Krantz, 2001).

The exercise of control in a production environment is a practical necessity, and it was probably used with reasonable success as an organisational defence in the present context (Cilliers & Koortzen, 2000; Czander, 1993; De Board, 1978; French & Vince, 1999; Obholzer, 2001; Stokes, 1994). However, an organisation experiencing change cannot offer the necessary containment (James & Huffington, 2004; Krantz, 2001) and it is hypothesised that containment of anxiety through control was the response in the team, the plant, and at organisational level. Hence the repeated need for structure. In line with a culture of control, a centralised leadership style, a lack of development of personal authority, and the resultant dependency of subordinates characterised different levels of the organisation, starting with corporate management. The basic assumption of dependency was present in the team (Bion, 1961, 1975; De Board, 1978; Kets de Vries & Miller, 1984; Rioch, 1970, 1975) and in the organisation (Kets de Vries & Miller, 1984; Schneider & Shrivastava, 1988). Instead of authorizing leadership to work on the task, the system seemed to be using it to fulfil dependency needs.

In terms of the leadership style practiced by the general manager, transformational elements such as a work ethic, caring, and providing his team with a vision were observed. Transactional elements included taking on a lot of responsibility, reliance on structure, and a controlling manner. The latter behaviors are appropriate in a manufacturing environment but task-management was probably over-emphasised at the expense of people-management to deal with pressure and the resultant anxiety. The general manager was consequently experiencing role overload and showing symptoms of burnout. He provided containment for the management team, which enabled them to work, but which also implied dependency. His style made it difficult for the team members to take up their own authority. They, in turn, resisted efforts to take up personal authority and seemed to be using dependency (and the resultant flight into passivity) as a way of dealing with pressure. Their dependency implied that the general manager had to be one of the team rather than being on the boundary as a representative of the team, the plant, and corporate management (Bar-Lev Elieli, 2001). This is an example of the manipulation of the leader out of his role (Cilliers & Koortzen, 2000). If there is role confusion and authority boundaries are not clearly specified, the leader becomes disempowered (Cilliers, 2001; Cilliers & Koortzen, 2000; Shapiro, 2001). The general manager resisted the dependency upon him but was drawn into this role, wishing to be 'swallowed' by the team.

The management team also used control over both processes and people to deal with anxiety. Elements of a transformational style were present in the team (e.g. references to creativity, knowledge, and conscientiousness) but a task focus was primary. The team members nevertheless struggled to obtain clarity in terms of the primary task of the team and the plant (Miller & Rice, 1967, 1975; 1990) and also did not seem able to create structure, make decisions, and deal with ambiguity. A right-wrong attitude is appropriate in terms of the production process, but when applied to people, this created opportunities for splitting and projection (Halton, 1994). The management team projected onto the workforce in seeing them as incompetent and in need of control ("push down" responsibility). Control was thus even implied in the efforts to "empower" (which means giving power according to Carr [2001]) subordinates. Subordinates were consequently not trusted or allowed to take up their authority which, in turn, resulted in their dependency. It was possible that the workers were comfortable in a position of dependency and might have resented having to take on the responsibility that accompanies personal authority.

The team members experienced insecurity with regard to task management but especially people management (Obholzer, 2001). They struggled with interrelatedness both in the team and in their interaction with the system. A basic assumption acts as a closed system and fears associated with change imply even greater efforts to create safety within (Bar-Lev Elieli, 2001). The efforts were unsuccessful as seen in the splits and projections as well as issues of inclusion and exclusion that threatened the team's unity. Team members showed a need for understanding, acceptance, and connection but a lack of trust prevented open communication and effective confrontation and conflict management. The team had to be sensitised with regard to the concepts of interdependence (that implies interpersonal support) versus dependency (with its lack of personal authority and accountability). Team members furthermore did not adequately acknowledge the importance of interaction with the environment and of the boundary roles of some of its members. A lack of trust and effective communication also seemed to characterise the relationship between the management team and staff (as seen in the projections that took place).

Clarity in terms of authority structures, roles, and boundaries was needed, together with the acceptance of personal authority in terms of one's roles and the management of the anxiety accompanying the responsibility that personal authority implies. Only then was interdependence possible – a dynamic that is crucial when facing change, because the transition involves the whole system, and a group has to acknowledge their relationships with the whole organisation and the outside environment (Bar-Lev Elieli, 2001; Miller, 1999; Stacey, 2001).

A centralised leadership style resulted due to an unconscious effort to contain the anxiety associated with, amongst others, the change experienced in the particular context. The general manager and his management team demonstrated transactional leadership as seen in their efforts to control tasks as well as people and to fulfill the need for structure. Simultaneously, dependency resulted in a lack of authorisation and, especially in the case of the general manager, this kept the managers from moving to transformational leadership.

From a systems perspective, the type of leadership being exercised is a function of the organisational culture and authorisation of the leader depends on the different subsystems. Obholzer (1994) referred to delegated authority, sanctioned authority that involves the membership, and personal authority. Degeling and Carr (2004) also distinguished between institutional authority and the authority assigned by followers. A need for structure and a focus on task performance, in other words, transactional behaviors, are probably not only necessary but also effective in a manufacturing environment. However, by combining leadership theory with a systems psychodynamic perspective, it became clear that reliance on transactional behaviors served as a defence strategy. The resultant dependency prevented the authorisation of the managers to make sufficient use of the visionary and interpersonal components associated with their leadership function, the latter being an essential requirement for management at all levels.

References

Atwater, D.C. & Bass, B.M. (1994). Transformational Leadership in Teams. In: B.M. Bass & B.J. Avolio (eds.), *Improving Organizational Effectiveness*, pp.48-83. Thousand Oaks, CA: Sage.

Avolio, B.J. (1997). A Somewhat Loose Interpretation of the Loose-Tight Distinction. *Applied Psychology: An International Review*, 46(4):439-443. https://doi.org/10.1111/j.1464-0597.1997.tb01251.x

Bar-Lev Elieli, R. (2001). An Organization Looks at Itself: Psychoanalytic and Group Relations Perspectives on Facilitating Organizational Transition. In: L.J. Gould, L.F. Stapley, & M.Stein (eds.), *The Systems Psychodynamics of Organizations: Integrating the Group Relations Approach, Psychoanalytic, and Open Systems Perspectives*, pp.76-90. London, UK: Karnac.

Bass, B.M. (1990). *Bass and Stogdill's Handbook of Leadership: Theory, Research, and Managerial Applications* (3rd ed.). New York: The Free Press/Macmillan.

Bass, B.M. (1997). Does the Transactional-Transformational Leadership Paradigm Transcend Organizational and National Boundaries? *American Psychologist*, 52(2):130-139. https://doi.org/10.1037//0003-066X.52.2.130

Bass, B.M. & Avolio, B.J. (1994). Introduction. In: B.M. Bass & B.J. Avolio (eds.), *Improving Organizational Effectiveness*, pp.1-9. Thousand Oaks, CA: Sage.

Bion, W.R. (1961). *Experiences in Groups*. London: Tavistock.

Bion, W.R. (1975). Selections from: Experiences in Groups. In: A.D. Colman & W.H. Bexton (eds.), *Group Relations Reader 1*, pp.11-20. Washington, DC: A.K. Rice Institute.

Carr, W. (2001). The Exercise of Authority in a Dependent Context. In: L.J. Gould, L.F. Stapley, & M.Stein (eds.), *The Systems Psychodynamics of Organizations: Integrating the Group Relations Approach, Psychoanalytic and Open Systems Perspectives*, pp.45-66. London, UK: Karnac.

Church, A.H. & Waclawski, J. (1999). The Impact of Leadership Style on Global Management Practices. *Journal of Applied Social Psychology*, 29(7):1416-1443. https://doi.org/10.1111/j.1559-1816.1999.tb00146.x

Cilliers, F. (2000). "Team-Building from a Psychodynamic Perspective." *Journal of Industrial Psychology*, 26(1):18-23. https://doi.org/10.4102/sajip.v26i1.694

Cilliers, F. (2001). The Role of Sense of Coherence in Group Relations Training. *Journal of Industrial Psychology*, 27(3):13-18. https://doi.org/10.4102/sajip.v27i3.29

Cilliers, F. & Koortzen, P. (1997). *Course in Group Process Consultation: Reader*. Pretoria, University of South Africa: South Africa: Centre for Industrial and Organizational Psychology.

Cilliers, F. & Koortzen, P. (2000). The Psychodynamic View on Organizational Behavior. *The Industrial Organizational Psychologist*, 38(2):59-67. https://doi.org/10.1037/e576962011-006

Cilliers, F.; Rothmann, S. & Struwig, W. H. (2004). Transference and Counter-transference in Systems Psychodynamic Group Process Consultation: The Consultant's Experience. *Journal of Industrial Psychology*, 30(1):110-119. https://doi.org/10.4102/sajip.v30i1.143

Conger, J.A. (1999). Charismatic and Transformational Leadership in Organizations: An Insider's Perspective on these Developing Streams of Research. *Leadership Quarterly*, 10(2):145-179. https://doi.org/10.1016/S1048-9843(99)00012-0

Czander, W.M. (1993). *The Psychodynamics of Work and Organizations: Theory and Application*. New York: Guilford Press.

De Board, R. (1978). *The Psychoanalysis of Organizations: A Psychoanalytic Approach to Behaviour in Groups and Organizations*. London, UK: Routledge. https://doi.org/10.4324/9780203321812

Degeling, P. & Carr, A. (2004). Leadership for the Systemization of Health Care: The Unaddressed Issue in Health Care Reform. *Journal of Health Organization and Management*, 18(6):399-414. https://doi.org/10.1108/14777260410569975

De Vos, A.S. (2002). Qualitative Data Analysis and Interpretation. In: A.S. de Vos, H. Strydom, C.B. Fouché & C.S.L. Delport (eds.), *Research at Grass Roots: For the Social Sciences and Human Service Professions* (2nd ed.), pp.339-355. Pretoria: Van Schaik.

Fraher, A. (2004). Systems Psychodynamics: The Formative Years (1895 1967). *Organisational and Social Dynamics*, 4(2):191-211.

French, R. & Vince, R. (1999). Learning, Managing, and Organizing: The Continuing Contribution of Group Relations to Management and Organization. In: R. French & R. Vince (eds.), *Group Relations, Management and Organization*, pp.3-19. New York: Oxford University Press.

Gould, L.J. (2001). Introduction. In: L.J. Gould, L.F. Stapley, & M. Stein (eds.), *The Systems Psychodynamics of Organizations: Integrating the Group Relations Approach, Psychoanalytic, and Open Systems Perspectives*, pp.1-15. London, UK: Karnac. https://doi.org/10.1017/CBO9780511497391.002

Halton, W. (1994). Some Unconscious Aspects of Organizational Life: Contributions from Psychoanalysis. In: A. Obholzer & V. Z. Roberts (eds.), *The Unconscious at Work: Individual and Organizational Stress in the Human Services*, pp.11-18. London, UK: Routledge.

Hogan, R. (1994). Trouble at the Top: Causes and Consequences of Managerial Incompetence. *Consulting Psychology Journal*, 46(1):9-15. https://doi.org/10.1037//1061-4087.46.1.9

Hogget, P. (2006). Conflict, Ambivalence and the Contested Purpose of Public Organizations. *Human Relations*, 59(2):175-194. https://doi.org/10.1177/0018726706062731

Howell, J.M., & Higgens, C.A. (1990). Champions of Technological Innovation. *Administrative Science Quarterly*, 35(2):317-341. https://doi.org/10.2307/2393393

James, K. & Huffington, C. (2004). Containment of Anxiety in Organizational Change: A Case Example of Changing Organizational Boundaries. *Organisational and Social Dynamics*, 4(2):212-233.

Kets de Vries, M.F.R. & Miller, D. (1984). Group Fantasies and Organizational Functioning. *Human Relations*, 37(2):111-134. https://doi.org/10.1177/001872678403700201

Klein, M. (1959). Our Adult World and its Roots in Infancy. *Human Relations*, 12:291-303. https://doi.org/10.1177/001872675901200401

Klein, M. (1985). Our Adult World and its Roots in Infancy. In A. D. Colman & M.H. Geller (eds.), *Group Relations Reader 2*, pp.5-19. Washington, DC: A.K. Rice Institute.

Krantz, J. (2001). Dilemmas of Organizational Change: A Systems Psychodynamic Perspective. In: L.J. Gould, L.F. Stapley, & M. Stein (eds.), *The Systems Psychodynamics of Organizations: Integrating the Group Relations Approach, Psychoanalytic, and Open Systems Perspectives*, pp.133-156. London, UK: Karnac. https://doi.org/10.4324/9780429483387-7

Kuhnert, K.W. (1994). Transforming Leadership: Developing People through Delegation. In: B.M. Bass & B.J. Avolio (eds.), *Improving Organizational Effectiveness*, pp.10-25. Thousand Oaks, CA: Sage.

Lawrence, W.G. (1999). Introductory Essay: Exploring Boundaries. In: W.G. Lawrence (ed.), *Exploring Individual and Organizational Boundaries: A Tavistock Open Systems Approach*, pp.1-19. London, UK: Karnac. https://doi.org/10.4324/9780429474453-1

Lawrence, W.G.; Bain, A. & Gould, L. (1996). The Fifth Basic Assumption. *Free Associations*, 6(1):28-55.

Luft, J. (1984). *An Introduction to Group Dynamics* (3rd ed.). Palo Alto, CA: Mayfield.

Miller, D.; Kets de Vries, M.F.R. & Toulouse, J. (1982). Top Executive Locus of Control and its Relationship to Strategy-making, Structure, and Environment. *Academy of Management Journal*, 25(2):237-253. https://doi.org/10.5465/255988

Miller, E. (1993). *From Dependency to Autonomy: Studies in Organization and Change*. London, UK: Free Association Books.

Miller, E.J. (1999). Open Systems Revisited: A Proposition About Development and Change. In W.G. Lawrence (ed.), *Exploring Individual and Organizational Boundaries: A Tavistock Open Systems Approach*, pp.217-233. London, UK: Karnac. https://doi.org/10.4324/9780429474453-15

Miller, E.J. & Rice, A.K. (1967). *Systems of Organization: Task and Sentient Systems and their Boundary Controls*. London, UK: Tavistock.

Miller, E.J. & Rice, A.K. (1975). Selections from: Systems of Organization. In: A.D. Colman & W.H. Bexton (eds.), *Group Relations Reader 1*, pp.43-68. Washington, DC: A.K. Rice Institute.

Miller, E.J. & Rice, A.K. (1990). Task and Sentient Systems and their Boundary Controls. In: E. Trist & H. Murray (eds.), *The Social Engagement of Social Science: A Tavistock Anthology, Vol. I: The Socio-psychological Perspective*, pp.259-271. Baltimore, MD: University of Pennsylvania Press. https://doi.org/10.9783/9781512819748-014

Moylan, D. (1994). The Dangers of Contagion: Projective Identification Processes in Institutions. In: A. Obholzer & V.Z. Roberts (eds.), *The Unconscious at Work: Individual and Organizational Stress in the Human Services*, pp.51-59. London, UK: Routledge.

Obholzer, A. (1994). Authority, Power and Leadership: Contributions from Group Relations Training. In: A. Obholzer & V.Z Roberts (eds.), *The Unconscious at Work: Individual and Organizational Stress in the Human Services*, pp.39-47. London, UK: Routledge.

Obholzer, A. (2001). The Leader, the Unconscious, and the Management of the Organisation. In: L.J. Gould, L.F. Stapley, & M. Stein (eds.), *The Systems Psychodynamics of Organizations: Integrating the Group Relations Approach, Psychoanalytic, and Open Systems Perspectives*, pp.197-216. London, UK: Karnac. https://doi.org/10.4324/9780429483387-10

Obholzer, A. & Miller, S. (2004). Leadership, Followership, and Facilitating the Creative Workplace. In: C. Huffington, D. Armstrong, W. Halton, L. Hoyle, & J. Pooley (eds.), *Working Below the Surface: The Emotional Life of Contemporary Organizations*, pp.33-48. London, UK: Karnac. https://doi.org/10.4324/9780429485237-4

Rice, A. K. (1965). *Learning for Leadership: Inter-personal and Inter-group Relations*. London, UK: Tavistock.

Rice, A.K. (1975). Selections from; Learning for Leadership,. In: A.D. Colman & W.H Bexton (eds.), *Group Relations Reader 1*, pp.71-158. Washington, DC: A.K. Rice Institute.

Rioch, M. J. (1970). The Work of Wilfred Bion on Groups. *Psychiatry*, 33(1):56-66. https://doi.org/10.1080/00332747.1970.11023613

Rioch, M. J. (1975). The Work of Wilfred Bion on Groups. In: A.D. Colman & W.H. Bexton (eds.), *Group Relations Reader 1*, pp.21-3. Washington, DC: A.K. Rice Institute.

Ross, S.M. & Offermann, L.R. (1997). Transformational Leaders: Measurement of Personality Attributes and Work Group Performance. *Personality and Social Psychology Bulletin*, 23(10):1078-1086. https://doi.org/10.1177/01461672972310008

Schneider, S.C. & Shrivastava, P. (1988). Basic Assumptions Themes in Organizations. *Human Relations*, 41(7):493-515. https://doi.org/10.1177/001872678804100701

Shapiro, E. R. (2001). Institutional Learning as Chief Executive. In: L.J. Gould, L.F. Stapley, & M. Stein (eds.), *The Systems Psychodynamics of Organizations: Integrating the Group Relations Approach, Psychoanalytic, and Open Systems Perspectives*, pp.175-195. London, UK: Karnac. https://doi.org/10.4324/9780429483387-9

Smith. P.B. (1980). *Group Processes and Personal Change*. London, UK: Harper & Row.

Stacey, R. (2001). Complexity at the 'Edge' of the Basic-assumption Group. In: L.J. Gould, L.F. Stapley, & M. Stein (eds.), *The Systems Psychodynamics of Organizations: Integrating the Group Relations Approach, Psychoanalytic, and Open Systems Perspectives*, pp.91-114. London, UK: Karnac. https://doi.org/10.4324/9780429483387-5

Stokes, J. (1994). Institutional Chaos and Personal Stress. In: A. Obholzer & V.Z. Roberts (eds.), *The Unconscious at Work: Individual and Organizational Stress in the Human Services*, pp.122-128. London, UK: Routledge.

Terre Blanche, M. & Kelly, K. (1999). Interpretive Methods. In: M. Terre Blanche & K. Durrheim (eds.), *Research in Practice: Applied Methods for the Social Sciences*, pp.123-146. Cape Town: University of Cape Town Press.

Turquet, P.M. (1974). Leadership: The Individual and the Group. In: G.S. Gibbard, J.J. Hartman, & R.D. Mann (eds.), *Analysis of Groups: Contributions to Theory, Research, and Practice*, pp.349-371. San Francisco, CA: Jossey-Bass.

Van Rensburg, C. & Crous, F. (2000). Die Verband tussen Sekere Persoonlikheidseienskappe en Transformasionele Leierskap (The Relationship between Certain Personality Traits and Transformational Leadership). *Journal of Industrial Psychology*, 26(3):39-46. https://doi.org/10.4102/sajip.v26i3.718

Wofford, J.C.; Goodwin, V.L., & Whittington, J.L. (1998). A Field Study of a Cognitive Approach to Understanding Transformational and Transactional Leadership. *Leadership Quarterly*, 9(1):55-84. https://doi.org/10.1016/S1048-9843(98)90042-X

Theme 2 | Systems Psychodynamics in Postgraduate Academic Work

Understanding Implicit Texts in Focus Groups from a Systems Psychodynamic Perspective[1]

B Smit & F Cilliers

Many researchers have been inquiring into focus groups as a qualitative data collection method (Barbour & Kitzinger, 1999; Krueger, 1998; Morgan, 1998), but only a few have been able to analyse the different levels of understanding in focus groups, which we focus on in this article. The guiding research question is how do focus groups offer deeper levels of understandings from a systems psychodynamic perspective. Research participants were purposively sampled using maximum variation (Patton, 2002). Data were collected during the focus group, and group data were analysed during data gathering. Meaning-making and interpretation of data were done from the systems psychodynamic perspective. The main theme of inclusion and exclusion is evidence of hidden texts in focus groups.

Keywords
Diversity; Focus Groups; Inclusion and Exclusion; Race and Systems Psychodynamic Perspective.

Introduction and Background

Many researchers have been inquiring into focus groups as a qualitative data collection method (Barbour & Kitzinger, 1999; Krueger, 1998; Morgan, 1998), but

1   Smit, B., & Cilliers, F. (2006). Understanding implicit texts in focus groups from a systems psychodynamic perspective. *The Qualitative Report*, 11(2):302-316. hppt://www.nova.edu/ssss/QR/QR11-2/smit.pdf

only a few have been able to analyse the different levels of understanding in focus groups. Our broad purpose was to build on research already done regarding focus groups, adding to a deeper and nuanced understanding, using the systems psychodynamic lens (Colman & Geller, 1985; Corey, 1995) to explore and explain more complex issues pertaining to this data collection method. In particular, we report on empirical implicit data elicited from a focus group, which we conducted.

The main research question of this inquiry is how can focus groups offer deeper levels of understandings from a systems psychodynamic perspective? We believe this inquiry is particularly beneficial and important for researchers wishing to deepen their understanding of the added potential of focus groups in interpretive and critical research, and more specifically for those working in the field of organisational and educational change. This perspective of focus groups may add to a comprehensive and process-dynamic knowledge base, contrary to the content levels of knowledge.

The remainder of this article is organised as follows. We look at what focus groups are, state the research problem, and discuss the theoretical framework; the systems psychodynamic perspective. After that, we describe the research methods, data collection and analysis, and interpret the findings. Lastly, we offer our concluding summarised thoughts.

Description of a Focus Group

A focus group can be defined as a carefully planned and organised discussion designed to obtain perceptions on a defined area of interest in a permissive, non- threatening environment by a selected group of participants sharing and responding to views, experiences, ideas, feelings, and perceptions (Krueger, 1994; Litosseliti, 2003; Morgan, 1998; Morgan & Collier, 2002). The purpose of a focus group is to gain information, perspectives, and empirical field texts about a specific research topic. The rationale for the method is to provide a socially-oriented interaction, similar to a real-life situation, in which participants freely influence one another, build on one another's responses and thus stimulate collective and synergistically generated thoughts, feelings, and experiences. The group typically consists of four to twelve participants. The size of the group is a variable that influences opportunities to participate as well as the ease or complexity in managing the event. Focus group data may also be influenced by purposive sampling. For example, biographic and demographic information such as age, gender, race, level of expertise, class, social-and-economic status, and identity need to be carefully considered for group composition.

Depending on the key research question, participants are chosen in terms of biographical and demographic variables to create homogenous or heterogeneous groups. The method is applied in the context of the primary task of the research, and the aim is to produce field texts and to co-construct meaning. As such it has advantages compared to other data gathering methods, such as interviews and participant observation, in the sense that it offers a more natural environment to study behaviour. Technically, as a method of data collection, the focus group is located between in-depth observation and participant observation (Litosseliti, 2003). The group is planned by a moderator who has the primary task of guiding the discussion (Morgan, 1998). The technique includes using a number of interventions in the form of open-ended questions. The moderator observes the group constantly to ensure its consistent focus on discussing the key questions. This role requires planning, management, and interpersonal skills.

Researcher Context

The researchers are academics working in the fields of education (a white female) and organisational psychology (a white male) respectively. Both have been trained and have extensive professional experience in consulting groups in schools and organisations from the group relations training model (also called the systems psychodynamic stance and the Tavistock approach) (Cytrynbaum & Noumair, 2004). Furthermore, both researchers have a wide experience in focus groups. The white male took up the role of moderator, and the female was the observer in this project. Over the last 10 years, the content of their consultations focused increasingly on South African diversity issues around race and gender, as the country is finding its new democratic identity. The research reported in this study referred to their experiences as consultants in the role of moderator and observer to diversity events, which are attended mostly by employees in private organisations. The researchers had no previous knowledge of the participants, except for their biographical background and their willingness to participate in the investigation.

Problem Statement and Research Question

In their focus group experiences in the roles of participants, observers, moderators, and researchers, the researchers have become aware of how the assumptions about unconscious group behaviour and related constructs such as power, leadership, and authority lead focus group outcomes in surprising directions. This resulted in the reasoning that the interaction of the two levels of behaviour, namely the verbatim focus group text (or work group/primary task behaviour) and the manifesting unconscious dynamics (or basic assumption group) (Bion, 1996), were underplayed and not adequately explored or optimised. In order to grasp the full meaning of the participants as individuals, as well as their interactions in the collective group sense, the researchers started to use their experience as systems psychodynamically informed consultants to gain insights into the shared understandings and communal constructions of meaning (Gibbs, 1997). This argument links with the description of a focus group as an endeavour in which the individual's experiences are integrated to make "collective sense" of their understandings, which can be viewed as a collective psychodynamic view as proposed by Jung (1986).

If the above-mentioned manifesting unconscious dynamics (or basic assumption group behaviour) could become part of the interpretation of focus group outcomes, the result could enrich the understanding of the researched phenomenon. Enrichment in this sense refers to linking the group's overt content behaviour to the covert and unconscious behaviour towards understanding the researched phenomenon fully (Koortzen & Cilliers, 2002). No previous studies could be found that researched the impact of systems psychodynamic assumptions and constructs on focus groups and its participants.

When using the systems psychodynamic perspective in understanding focus groups, the epistemological assumptions include unconscious behavioural manifestations as a vehicle of "access" to other peoples' knowledge, views, and attitudes. One example would be a participant's representation in the group, and how that position is used to legitimise authority, which impacts the process and the dynamics of the focus group interaction. We would also look at how positional power; is opposed or supported by personal power; and we ask what this may mean or how this may influence the data. For example, consider an individual who is seen by others as insignificant in an organisation, but is bestowed with admiration (as a form of power) because of strong personal connections to people in authority.

Therefore, we argue that in managing the mechanics of such a focus group event, the moderator also needs to deal with the dynamics of the group. We claim that such demands require training in diverse levels of awareness in order to make sense of the collective layers of meaning constructions. Also, the role of power and authority are issues to which the moderator must be sensitised. Particularly significant are the skills of qualitative data analysis such as discourse and conversation analysis. This means the moderator has to pay attention to issues that are revealed beyond the level of content. The rationale for this is that understanding discourses allows researchers to construct meaning beyond the levels of content concerning the process and the dynamics of the here-and-now of the focus group. Questions regarding what underpinnings of discourse are at play, at any given moment are appropriate to ask and investigate (Cheek, 2000). Observations beyond obvious group behaviour become critical, particularly in deciding what to observe and how to observe.

In sum, the mental preparation and attentiveness to a variety of levels of data gathering, from the systems psychodynamic perspective, requires a unique and sophisticated use of research talents. Having stated the research problem, we now pose the key research question: How can focus groups offer deeper levels of understanding when conducted from a systems psychodynamic perspective? The aim of this inquiry is to study the awareness of systems psychodynamic behaviour and its inclusion in the focus group outcomes, which can lead to deeper levels of understanding of the phenomenon being studied. Furthermore, this inquiry explored and explained the split and pairing dynamic (Bion, 1996; 2003) and its patterns of inclusion and exclusion, as evidence of hidden texts in the focus group (which is made clear in the following section).

Theoretical Framework: The Systems Psychodynamic Perspective

The conceptual origins of the systems psychodynamic perspective stems from classic psychoanalysis (Freud, 1921), group relations theory, and open systems theory (French & Vince, 1999; Miller, 1993). This perspective is based upon the following five assumptions that are the cornerstones for studying relationships in systems (Hirschhorn, 1993; Lawrence, Bain, & Gould; 1996; López-Corvo, 2003; Obholzer & Roberts, 1994).

1. Dependency, referring to the group's unconscious projection for attention and help onto an authority figure as parental object.

2. Fight/flight, referring to defence mechanisms in trying to cope with discomfort involving the authority figure. For example, management or leadership.

3. Pairing, referring to the unconscious connection with perceived powerful others such as the leader, or splitting the authority figure(s) as an individual or as a pair in order to be able to identify with one part as a saviour (Bion, 1970, 1996; Lipgar & Pines, 2003).

4. One-ness or me-ness (Turquet, 1974), referring to the individual's escape into his/her own fantasy and inner safe, comfortable, and good world, whilst denying the presence of the group, seen as the disturbing and bad part.

5. We-ness, referring to the opposite of me-ness, the unconscious need to join into a powerful union with and absorption into an omnipotent force, surrendering the self in passive participation (Lawrence, 1999).

The systems psychodynamic perspective is a developmentally focused, psycho-educational process for the understanding of the deep and covert behaviour in the system. In working from this perspective, one's primary task is to push the boundaries of awareness to better understand the deeper and covert meaning of organisational behaviour, including the challenges of management and leadership (Koortzen & Cilliers, 2002; Miller & Rice, 1976). In addition, one engages in an analysis of the interrelationships of some or all of the following: boundaries, roles and role configurations, structure, organisational design, work culture, and group processes (Miller, 1993; Neumann, Kellner, & Dawson-Shepherd, 1997). The consultant focuses on the covert and dynamic aspects of the organisation and the work group that comprises it, centering on relatedness, representation, and how authority is psychologically distributed, exercised, and enacted overtly and covertly in the here-and-now, in contrast to how it is overtly and formally invested in the there-and-then of the system's official structure.

In practice, the consultant will focus on the covert aspects in terms of how people and objects relate to, and what they represent for one another; how authority is exercised and distributed amongst people and objects in the here-and-now (in contrast to how it is overtly and formally spoken about the system's official structure). An example would be the group that overtly declares a value system of "we are all the same/equal," while the consultant has here-and-now evidence of a pecking order or an inclusion/exclusion dynamic in the conversation. Thus, the consultant notices behaviour such as attitudes, beliefs, fantasies, conflicts, core anxieties, social defences, patterns of relationships, and collaboration as well as how these in turn, may influence task performance, and how the individuals take up their roles as group members. Another example could be when unwanted and negative feelings and experiences (for example, exclusion) are (mostly unconsciously) experienced as painful, then defended against, then split off and projected onto someone else in the group. It is believed (Colman & Bexton, 1975; Colman & Geller, 1985; Cytrynbaum & Lee, 1993) that the person receiving these projections and unconsciously identifying with them may have a specific "valence" (an unconscious preponderance) to receive these projections, and carry them on behalf of the system. This is referred to as the individual's projective identifications and process roles, as distinct from their formally sanctioned roles.

The consultant will monitor movement by being aware of how the group is initially functioning in its basic assumption (see dependence, fight/flight, etc. above) and paranoid-schizoid position; towards interdependence, characterised by work group functioning; and the depressive position, characterised by an openness to and acceptance of differences (Czander, 1993; Gabelnick & Carr, 1989; Gould, Stapley, & Stein, 2001; 2004; Shapiro & Carr, 1991; Stapley, 1996; Wells, 1985).

The stance studies the emotional task of the system, which may be filled with chaos, a lack of control, and difficult experiences such as competition, rivalry, jealousy, envy, hate, hostility, and aggression (Miller, 1976, 1993). As a result, leadership becomes difficult (if not impossible). Furthermore, relationships and relatedness between subsystems as well as the containment of these within boundaries become increasingly complex. As a result, mistrust and distrust increase (indicating the prevalence of paranoid fear, as well as a lack of meaning and hope in the system). Because leaders seem to find themselves de-authorised to negotiate new roles within their organisations directly, the system creates new mechanisms as a defensive compensation for the loss of control (Huffington, Armstrong, Halton, Hoyle & Pooley, 2004). An example could be when a working team who does not trust its designated leader uses an informal leader to create a shadow leadership to (at least on a fantasy level) serve the group and satisfy needs for nurturing and caring.

Method

Participant Selection

The particular focus group that we used for study in this inquiry was formed for understanding how diversity was experienced in the workplace. Permission for participants' attendance was given by their individual managers. The 12 participants were purposively sampled, using maximum variation or heterogeneity sampling (Patton, 2002). They represented diversity with respect to professional background, ages, and racial groups. In general, the participation of focus group members is important in order to optimise the research data gathering. Research participants consented to take part in the focus group after they had been informed about the broad topic, diversity in the workplace. We did not, however, distribute the focus group questions beforehand.

Ethical considerations in focus groups differ somewhat from other data collection methods in terms of consent, confidentiality, anonymity, privacy, and voluntary participation. What was important and different instance, was the responsibility of individual focus group participants' code of conduct regarding confidentiality, anonymity, privacy, and disclosure. The moderator had thus another set of ethical ground rules to which all had to adhere. Focus group data were collective group data and had to be treated as such. The ground rules and reciprocal trust were negotiated upfront for the shared protection of all participants. This was particularly crucial, if not critical because the topic under investigation, diversity in the workplace, was of a sensitive kind and an ethical clearance certificate was obtained from the ethics committee of the university.

Data Collection

The assumptions underlying the data gathering were that focus group data reflect collective notions of understandings of the topic, which are shared and/ or negotiated by group participants, as opposed to interview data, which reflect views and opinions of an individual. It is also assumed that group data do not necessarily imply group consensus. The male researcher acted as moderator and the female researcher as an observer. The moderator role consisted of being psychologically present in the moment, and responding to the content, feelings, and processes, and the group dynamics, while the non-participant observer took copious field notes. Examples of these dynamics were dependency, fight/ flight, pairing, me-ness, and we-ness. Additional dynamics such as silences, turn-taking, and anti-task behaviour were noted. The observer made notes of the conversations and wrote field notes of the observation. For instance, we listened to what had been said and more specifically, how something was said, and most importantly, why it was said.

Data Analysis During and After Data Collection

Empirical data from the focus group discussion, and field notes of observation, including the overt and the covert, were manually analysed for content and discourse. During the content analysis, we elicited some themes, which are later discussed as our findings. Thereafter, we used a variety of analytical questions and analysed the texts for discourse. The assumptions underlying the data analysis were that we took little for granted.

∞ Why were these words chosen and not others?

∞ On which discourses do participants draw to position themselves?

∞ Or, which discourses were afforded presence, how and why?

∞ Who had the voice to speak and who not?

∞ Who was silenced by whom and who broke the silence?

∞ Who needed to speak louder to be heard and who had a silent voice?

∞ At what levels were the discussions; on cognitive rational or emotional levels and at what depth?

∞ What was promoted and what was underplayed?

∞ What was marginalised (on the peripheral) and what was mainframe in the discussion (Cheek 2000)?

Although most of these guiding questions were employed during data analysis, one could also use them as a conceptual frame during data collection in order to make sense of the focus group in the here-and-now. It is helpful to study the use of language in terms of discourse. For instance, what discourses were afforded presence, and which were marginalised? At times participants use jargon or rhetoric to distance themselves from the discussion. Also, highfaluting language is used to define and legitimise position (e.g. "if you look again, I will be president"). The levels at which participants were communicating were studied (e.g. the superficial, game, defensive, or authentic levels). We studied these levels of discussion in which language was used differently because language has the potential of perpetuating division and splits, most visibly on issues such as inclusion and exclusion. This manner of interpretation corresponds with Schafer's (2003) description of the systems psychodynamic consultancy stance. We interpreted the data in their object relations and relatedness. For example, an object can:

1. be an individual from a specific race and gender,
2. speak from a specific positional space in the group,
3. be about an issue, and
4. address another individual representing his/her own race, gender, position, and stance.

The overt level content and the relationships between group members were then linked with the covert processes, dynamics to ascertain the (unconscious) relatedness between objects.

Trustworthiness of the Inquiry

The notion of trustworthiness (i.e. credibility and validity) in our inquiry is based on craftsmanship with precision, care and accountability, open communication throughout the inquiry, together with ethical conduct (Henning, Van Rensburg, & Smit 2004).We claim that this inquiry yielded believable evidence, which was peer-reviewed, and checked by one member of the group. Methodologically, we collected data from various sources, interviews, observations, and non-verbal behaviour, and analysed data for content and discourse. The thick descriptions add to enhanced and deep understanding, beyond the surface, to create a rigorous, believable scholarly product. To sum up, we used multiple ways to establish trustworthiness, multiple methods of data collection, analysis, (also referred to as triangulation of methods) two researchers, peer review, member checking, and thick descriptions.

Findings: Diversity in the Workplace

What follows is a succinct discussion of some properties of inclusion and exclusion (as the most prominent split dynamic that emanated from the data), and a clarification of how these became observable and evident in the focus group. Thus, the theoretical assumptions of the systems psychodynamic approach, described earlier as a suitable lens to shed light on specific behaviour in the group, were used in order to gain a deeper understanding of various levels of discussions and elicit hidden texts in focus groups.

Projections Around Age

To begin with, age differences lead to inclusion and exclusion of participants in the focus group. Older participants used age to label younger participants as ruthless, arrogant, and impatient. Furthermore, they were accused of not taking the time to engage in the process, and not contributing meaningfully. This acquisition was extended into the political realm, saying the younger people do not honour the political struggle and the sacrifices by older citizens. In defence, younger participants described themselves as youthful, with energy and adaptability, and not caring about the past, which added to the hostility amongst the older group participants. The working hypothesis offered was that the older participants were rejecting and splitting off their bad parts (in this case being ruthless, arrogant, impatient, non-engaging, not interested, and non-participative) and projecting that onto the younger ones. The dynamic continued when the younger participants identified with the projection, which meant that the older participants' projection was now not only onto but also into the younger participants as a subsystem of the group. This projective identification (Obholzer & Roberts, 1994) implied that the younger participants were acting out the older participant's bad parts, leaving the older to behave as old people traditionally do. If these unconscious behavioural dynamics are not noted by the researcher, the findings may reflect only the conscious meaning given by individuals. By interpreting the group dynamics, the findings become so much richer in the interpretation that age is used by the group to manage its anxiety, and that it can only engage with diversity issues by splitting of it's younger and older parts and letting its subsystems contain its parts. Ideally, the group should meet over a longer time, if participants can work through their defences, become aware, and own them, then they can become responsible for their own individual opinions.

Projections Around Age and Gender

Next and closely related, the role of gender added tension to the dynamics, particularly in terms of age. For instance, young women were seen as too independent and not obedient enough (especially amongst blacks). On the one hand, some men saw younger women as dominant, but without authorisation, as if older people have to give the younger the permission and authority to act in an adult manner. On the other hand, women saw men as coercing the process and the discussion. This often resulted in conflict and resistance, noticeably in-flight reactions by shifting the discussion from the here-and-now focus to outside and safer topics. Furthermore, the male and female fight for dominance, visibly in assumed roles of father and mother, were directly opposed by the younger participants in the group. Some openly articulated that they did not need a mother or a father in this context, or to be told how the group should proceed or work. It was as if a true family dynamic was playing itself out; the children fighting with the parents about rules for behaviour. The working hypothesis offered was that an intergroup dynamic (between subgroups) had developed, which was characterised by stereotyping, blaming, and suspicion (or paranoia). This is known as the paranoid-schizoid position (Cytrynbaum & Noumair, 2004), which indicates the disintegration of the system where the group functions as a split system. If this unconscious dynamic is not noted by the researcher, the findings may indicate that some individuals have serious issues around age and gender as diversity dimensions, and the group's role in projecting parts of the self onto and into others will be denied.

Splits Caused by Language

In addition, male and female dominance had a tendency to shift from time to time. The working hypothesis was offered that this related to the levels of energy at any given time, as well as to the content of the discussion. Often, when the discussion was male-dominated, the content was by and large at cognitive levels and less personal. Once the level of discussion reached a deeper level of consciousness, emotion, and sensitivity, the women seemed to authorise themselves into the leadership roles. It appeared as if they believed they could handle such conversations better, which the group allowed them to do. The hypothesis was that men did not trust their inner selves to participate on those levels. Furthermore, age and gender difference, and the associated dominance thereof, turned into discourse competition manifesting in different levels of discussion. A variety of discourses, which resulted in the inclusion and exclusion of participants in the group, were seen. For instance, language had the potential of perpetuating division amongst participants through the levels of discussion as well as the content and the usage of language. The dominant language of the group was English. At times this was problematic, particularly when the discussions became highly emotional. During such periods, when some group participants found it difficult to express their feelings in English, which was their 2nd, 3rd and 4th language, they switched to their vernacular. This lead to further divisions and exclusions. This behaviour indicated how the group split itself according to gender, age, and language as a defence against the anxiety of working together as a system. If this unconscious dynamic is not noted by the researcher, the assumption may be that individuals are passionate about their language origins, which denies the role of the group using language as an object to split the system, and to thus manage its anxiety. It would, for example, help to follow up this focus group with groups of only males/females and blacks/whites to hear the opinions of the "purer" configuration and then compare this with the mixed format.

Splits Caused by Status

Another issue concerning language usage was linked to the levels of discussions. Some used their academic status and performed intellectual "gymnastics" in an attempt to apply the rhetoric to exclude and withdraw from other participants. This type of conversation, in which rhetoric was used to bore some in the group, resulted in severe segregation of other participants. Unfortunately, though, only a few participants made an effort to understand why such discourses did take place, and what that meant for the focus group discussion. The impression was that the complexity of the behavioural dynamics created so much anxiety that it was impossible to engage with the content on an equal level. The working hypothesis offered to the group was that status was used to split the system into more manageable and safer parts. It can also be interpreted as flight reactions into status issues as a defence against linking with opposites. As in many of the above examples, this could indicate a lack of safety, trust, and support in the group, making it difficult for the moderator to distinguish between a participant's real answers to the focus group question and the collective and unconscious dynamic anxiety. There was also evidence of boredom as a defence mechanism, meaning that all participants were not involved in the focus group, again devaluing the outcomes. If this unconscious dynamic is not noted by the researcher, the findings may exclude the role of intense anxiety around differences, and the idea that boredom may mean on the content level "I'm not interested", as well as "this is making me so anxious, that I must disengage" on the unconscious and dynamic level.

The Continuous Splitting of the System

There were times when it seemed as if some participants were not capable of engaging at an emotional level: The commitment felt too risky. It was as if the anxiety levels were so high that they had hoped by using complex language they would be able to cope better with the anxious situation: a flight reaction. It was fascinating to observe how some white men used such highfaluting discourse to remove themselves from the process. This was done at times in a hostile manner. This behaviour was interpreted as a distancing phenomenon in defence of linking with opposites. Conversely so, some black men took up the roles of the mature traditional leader, using their "words of wisdom" to tell others in the group what do to and how to keep on with the process. This led to more splits in the group and added to yet more black and white male confrontations, much to the frustration of the women in the group. These behaviours offer evidence of how the group, as a collective, projected different objects (including feelings) onto its different parts; for example, hostility and distance onto the white male and tradition, and leadership onto the black male. This split the males in the group with the females carrying the frustration. The psychodynamic interpretation was that a classic war dynamic was created in which the men fight and the women stay at home deprived and frustrated. This indicated the group's lack of creativity (or procreation). If this unconscious dynamic is not noted by the researcher, the findings may indicate that the group is divided around some issues, but with no idea of what the causes are. This stance elevated the nature of the underlying dynamic of competition and how that can marginalise some individuals who can then not engage with the discourse or the processes.

Hostility Between the Generations

As opposed to the black and white male domination, the older black men often frustrated the younger white females. It appeared that some black younger women were labelled as less "obedient" towards older black men, while the older black women appeared more accepting of older black men. Young black men were at times less opposing or confronting to the elder, while the white women, both young and old, frankly expressed their frustration and disagreement to the older black men. Often the black men dominated the discussion attempting to assume power. This was directly opposed, particularly by younger women, both white and black. The older black women were less challenging or resistant. This became evident in the long speeches by black men, as attempts were made to position themselves; voices were raised in an attempt to be heard, yet they had only a few followers. This was interpreted as a generation split involving the genders in different positions. This was followed by hostility and threats to the group participants, particularly by one black male, who shouted, "if you look again, I will be president." This is a powerful speech act, which ironically, elicited lots of laughter that contributed to added disempowerment and disrespect. It may have been a matter of trying too hard, and only a few really heard him. It could be interpreted as a competition to be the chosen one in the ultimate role of authority, which the group was withholding, and even ridiculing. If this unconscious dynamic is not noted by the researcher, the findings may not include the power play in the system in coping with its splits.

Splits Around Identity

Lastly, the issue of race and colour, as objects of inclusion and exclusion, showed fascinating dynamics, particularly in terms of acceptance and/or the denial of blackness and whiteness. For example, an Indian woman expressed her confusion, "Part of me feels black, part of me feels white." Interestingly, the reactions from some group participants, particularly white men, were to deny seeing her blackness and as such, her identity. The working hypothesis offered was that the anxiety about who belongs where and with whom, and in what identity, was so intense that participants become pseudo colour blind as a defence against really working with the difference between race and gender. If this unconscious dynamic is not noted by the researcher, the findings will not include the dynamics around inclusion/exclusion and denial as a defence against diversity. These behaviours are especially important towards understanding a construct such as diversity with its emotionally charged content.

In this inquiry, the dynamics of inclusion and exclusion were highlighted because it played such a huge role in the focus group participation. In making use of the systems psychodynamic consultancy stance and interpreting the covert here -and-now group behaviour, it became clear that diversity in the organisation was filled with extreme levels of anxiety, which were manifested in all kinds of defensive behaviours. When these data are added to the verbatim focus group information, the research results become extremely rich and add comprehensible colour to the empirical data. This process calls for a reflexive, critical stance, and necessitates a repositioning beyond the obvious or the visible.

Limitations

To begin with, before we draw our conclusions we also make explicit what we did not intend to accomplish, and what the design of this inquiry inherently did not allow. The limitations are those characteristics of design, methodology, and our roles as researchers, which can be regarded as the parameters of the application of interpretations of the data, the constraints on generalisability, and utility of findings. Then, the most obvious limitations would relate to the ability to draw descriptive generalisations. This implies that our particular findings are not representative, and that our identified themes are typical of all. Furthermore, we do not claim to have identified all the possible themes of diversity. Lastly, the theoretical frame in itself, the systems psychodynamic perspective, which assumes understanding covert behaviour as a vehicle of "access" to other peoples' knowledge, views, and attitudes, could be restricting field text interpretations, and ultimate findings of this inquiry.

Conclusion

The above findings illustrate that unconscious behavioural dynamics play a part in focus group functioning, as is believed in the systems psychodynamic perspective. Evidence was given for splits and all kinds of defence mechanisms such as projection, intellectualisation, and denial which adds richness and complexity to the experience of the focus group around diversity.

If these behavioural manifestations were not noted by the researchers, they may stay unaware in the social unconscious (Hopper, 2003). The researchers may interpret the behaviour on the content level and further refer to the specific group as "being difficult" without knowing why. This means that the findings could represent a constraint towards understanding the social and communication nature around diversity.

We suggest that focus group teams are systems psychodynamically trained observers, to note and interpret the unconscious behaviour in order to ascertain the deeper meaning of the group's experience.

References

Barbour, R. S. & Kitzinger, J. (eds.). (1999). *Developing focus group research. Politics, theory, and practice.* London: Sage. https://doi.org/10.4135/9781849208857

Bion, W.R. (1970). *Attention and interpretation.* London: Tavistock.

Bion, W.R. (1996). *Experiences in groups and other papers.* London: Routledge.

Bion, W.R. (2003). *Learning from experience.* London: Karnac.

Cheek, J. (2000). *Postmodern and post-structural approaches to nursing research.* Thousand Oaks, CA: Sage.

Colman, A.D. & Bexton, W.H. (1975). *Group relations reader 1.* Jupiter, FL: The A.K. Rice Institute.

Colman, A.D. & Geller, M.H. (1985). *Group relations reader 2.* Jupiter, FL: A.K. Rice Institute Series.

Corey, G. (1995). *Theory and practice of group counselling* (4th ed.). Pacific Grove, CA: Brooks/Cole.

Cytrynbaum, S. & Lee, S.A. (1993). *Transformations in global and organizational systems.* Jupiter, FL: A.K. Rice Institute.

Cytrynbaum, S. & Noumair, D.A. (2004). *Group dynamics, organizational irrationality, and social complexity: Group relations reader 3.* Jupiter, FL: A.K. Rice Institute.

Czander, W.M. (1993). *The psychodynamics of work and organis.* New York: Guilford Press.

French, R. & Vince, R. (1999). *Group relations, management, and organization.* New York: Oxford University Press.

Freud, F. (1921). *Group psychology and the analysis of the ego. Complete works of Sigmund Freud.* London: Hogarth. https://doi.org/10.1037/11327-000

Gabelnick, F. & Carr, A.W. (1989). *Contributions to social and political science.* Jupiter, FL: A.K. Rice Institute.

Gibbs, A. (1997, Winter). 7. http://www.soc.surrey.ac.uk/sru/SRU19.html [Accessed 4 April 1999].

Gould, L.J.; Stapley, L.F., & Stein, M. (2001). *The systems psychodynamics of organisations.* London: Karnac.

Gould, L.J.; Stapley, L.F., & Stein, M. (2004). *Experiential learning in organisations. Applications of the Tavistock group relations approach.* London: Karnac.

Henning, E.; Van Rensburg, W. & Smit, B. (2004). *Finding your way in qualitative research.* Pretoria, Van Schaik.

Hirschhorn, L. (1993). *The workplace within: Psychodynamics of organizational life.* Cambridge, MA: Massachusetts Institute of Technology Press.

Hopper, E. (2003). *The social unconscious: Selected papers.* London: Jessica Kingsley.

Huffington, C.; Armstrong, A.; Halton, W.; Hoyle, L. & Pooley, J. (2004). *Working below the surface. The emotional life of contemporary organisations.* London: Karnac.

Jung, C.G. (1986). *Psychological reflections.* London: Ark.

Koortzen, P. & Cilliers, F.V.N. (2002). The psychoanalytical approach to team development. In: R. L. Lowman (ed.), *Handbook of organisational consulting psychology,* pp.260-284. San Francisco: Jossey-Bass.

Krueger, R.A. (1994). *Focus groups: A practical guide for applied research.* London: Sage.

Krueger, R.A. (1998). *Moderating focus groups.* Thousand Oaks, CA: Sage. https://doi.org/10.4135/9781483328133

Lawrence, W.G. (1999). *Exploring individual and organisational boundaries. A Tavistock open systems approach.* London: Karnac.

Lawrence, W.G.; Bain, A. & Gould, L. (1996). *The fifth basic assumption.* London: Occasional Paper.

Lipgar, R.M. & Pines, M. (2003). *Building on Bion: Branches.* London: Jessica Kingsley.

Litosseliti, L. (2003). *Using focus groups in research.* London: Continuum.

López-Corvo, R.E. (2003). *The dictionary of the work of W.R. Bion.* London: Karnac.

Miller, E.J. (1976). *Task and organisation.* New York: Wiley.

Miller, E. J. (1993). *From dependency to autonomy: Studies in organization and change.* London: Free Association Books.

Miller, E.J. & Rice, A.K. (1976). *Systems of organisation.* London: Tavistock.

Morgan, D. L. (1998). *Planning focus groups.* Thousand Oaks, CA: Sage. https://doi.org/10.4135/9781483328171

Morgan, D.L. & Collier, P. (2002, April). *Focus groups and symbolic interactionism: A method meets a theory.* Paper presented at the meeting of the Eighth International Qualitative Health Research Conference, Banff, Alberta, Canada.

Neumann, J.E.; Kellner, K. & Dawson-Shepherd, A. (1997). *Developing organisational consultancy.* London: Routledge.

Obholzer, A. & Roberts, V.Z. (1994). *The unconscious at work.* London: Routledge.

Patton, M.Q. (2002). *Qualitative research & evaluation methods (3rd ed.).* Thousand Oaks, CA: Sage.

Schafer, R. (2003). *Insight and interpretation. The essential tools of psychoanalysis.* London: Karnac.

Shapiro, E.R. & Carr, A.W. (1991). *Lost in familiar places: Creating new connections between the individual and society.* London: Yale University Press.

Stapley, L.F. (1996). *The personality of the organisation.* London: Free Association Books.

Turquet, P.M. (1974). The individual and the group. In: G.S. Gibbard, J.J. Hartman, & R.D. Mann (eds.), *Analysis of groups,* pp.337-371. San Francisco: Jossey-Bass.

Wells, L. (1985). The group-as-a-whole: A systemic socio-analytical perspective on interpersonal and group relations. In: A.D. Colman & M.H. Geller (eds.), *Group relations reader 2,* pp.109-126. Jupiter, FL: A.K. Rice Institute Series.

Article 2

Present Challenges and Some Critical Issues for Research in Industrial/Organisational Psychology in South Africa[1]

S Rothmann & F Cilliers

Abstract

The objective of this study was to determine a set of problems and critical issues that researchers in Industrial and Organisational Psychology deem to be important areas for immediate and future enquiry. The changing identity of this field of application is investigated, more relevant paradigms in the study of organisational health and wellness is explored and methods, techniques and interventions suitable to the South African context are suggested. Conclusions are formulated to increase the ability of organisations to work towards economic development while promoting the wellness and quality of life of employees.

Keywords

Industrial/Organisational Psychology, identify, tasks, challenges

The objective of this research was to ascertain some of the present challenges and critical issues in Industrial and Organisational Psychology (I/O Psychology) in South Africa, in order to determine the immediate and long-term foci for researchers. Firstly, the work context in which employees and employers – as the clients of I/O Psychology – are currently functioning, is analysed. Secondly, the identity of I/O Psychology is discussed. Thirdly, the tasks of the I/O psychologist

1   Rothmann, S. & Cilliers, F. (2007). Present challenges and some critical issues for research in industrial/organisational psychology in South Africa. *South African Journal of Industrial Psychology*, 33(1):8-16.

are discussed, with specific reference to implications for research. Lastly, some recommendations for possible future research are formulated.

The Changed Context of Work

Over the last few decades, the occupational arena has undergone remarkable changes. Among these changes are the increased utilisation of information and communication technology, the rapid expansion of the service sector, the globalisation of the economy, the changing structure of the workforce, the increasing flexibility in the world of work, the creation of the 24-hour economy, and the utilisation of new production concepts (e.g. team-based work, tele-work, downsizing, outsourcing and subcontracting) (Barling & Zacharatos, 2002). Increased flexibility and fragmentation of the workforce also present new challenges for management as they seek to coordinate and control activities (Guest, 2004).

Another factor impacting on the world of work is the pervasiveness and urgency of change. Advances in technology lead to the speeding up of the world of work. Speed and flexibility of response form an important basis for a competitive advantage (Guest, 2004). Compared to 20 years ago, modern employees increasingly work in offices (and less in agriculture or industry) with information or clients (and less with tangible objects), in teams (and less in isolation), and with less job security. The nature of work has also changed from manual to having significantly more mental and emotional demands (Barling, 1999; Turner, Barling & Zacharatos, 2002).

Many organisations have implemented practices that attempt to reduce costs and increase productivity, which often leads to a mentality that favours profitability over the welfare of people (Turner et al., 2002). The numbers employed in many workplaces are getting smaller. This makes the trade union job of organising the workforce more difficult. It is easier for managers to establish a more personal relationship with employees (Guest, 2004).

Diversity in the workforce is increasing with a less dominant role for the male breadwinner and a growing interest in work-life balance. This is important, especially considering the efforts of organisations to attract and attain high-quality employees.

Identity of Industrial/organisational Psychology

The above ever-changing world of work and its demands imply increased anxiety in all work systems (Miller, 1993). It is therefore hypothesised that organisations need new ways of thinking and operating to effectively deal with these demands. The same is true for I/O psychology focussing on the application of psychology in the workplace (Cascio, 2001).

In 2001, the South African Journal of Industrial Psychology contributed a special edition to review I/O psychology as profession and discipline, its challenges and responses. The general impression created in this edition was that the profession has developed quite substantially in the realm of bringing about (and facilitating) the needed change in organisations, specifically in medium (group/team) and large (organisational) systems (Moalusi, 2001; Pienaar & Roodt, 2001; Renecle, 2001; Schreuder, 2001; Veldsman, 2001). Less information (or progress) was reported on the development of (1) the profession's role boundaries, and (2) the discipline's (theoretical and professional) development of clear subject identity, and the understanding of (especially) organisational behavioural dynamics.

Referring to its roots, I/O psychology is defined as an applied division of psychology concerned with the study of human behaviour related to work, organisations and productivity (Cascio, 2001). According to Watkins (2001), the denial of this connection with general Psychology, as is occurring in practice as well as in academia, has led to an identity crisis, which in practice manifests in role confusion, for example between being a psychologist versus a human resources practitioner.

This phenomenon can be interpreted as (on the one hand) a seduction by the organisation and its authority structures, and (on the other hand) a disempowerment to apply real and deep psychological knowledge (Stapley, 1996). It is suggested that this confusion be addressed at subject conferences (such as SIOPSA) and university departments of I/O psychology in order to empower practitioners and students alike in order to perform optimally.

I/O psychology may never be able to be called an independent science with its own well thought through perspective on humanity and reality, independent hypothesis and theory formulation, objectivity and sophistication in empirical methodology and data collection (Cilliers, 1991). Matarazzo (1987) stated that in spite of over 100 years of evolution in psychology, there is one core psychology, distinguishing itself from other related disciplines such as physics, economy and history. This implies that the subject has informal de facto recognition for specialist parts of Psychology, although it does not enjoy de jure recognition anywhere in the world. The conclusion can thus be made that there is only one Psychology with different fields of application. It is suggested that I/O psychology should keep studying its own identity within the boundaries of general psychology and as such move towards role clarity in various organisational applications.

This suggestion implies working within the boundaries of psychology as a subject. Kruger (1980) describes psychology as a pre-paradigm science, caught up in establishing itself as a science in the postmodern world (see Gergen, 2001). Further, because of its natural sciences methodology and its uncritical usage of constructs of reality from natural sciences, the Cartesian duality is seen as cancer in psychology (Kruger, 1980). In short, the subject philosophical issues within psychology need to be studied by researchers and practitioners in all fields of psychology in order render a true professional service to organisations.

I/O psychology mainly operates in the analytical, positivistic paradigm, with an almost exclusively analytical-empirical epistemology (Pietersen, 1989). Its locus of knowledge is involved in the epistemological differentiation between the knower or researcher and the known or employee and organisation, with a value-free perspective of the working person (Cilliers, 1991). The range of its research assumes that there is a unique and best description of any chosen aspect of working behaviour. Methodologically there is a preference for quantitative and structured technologies such as questionnaires, tests and structured interviews as opposed to qualitative, unstructured, descriptive case studies, depth interviews and group techniques (Brewerton & Millward, 2004). Where the latter is used, it is often seen as pilot studies. In terms of the process of knowledge development, there is a preference for prediction and control with deductive and differentiated research. Knowledge is measured empirically in predetermined conceptual categories, behavioural models and research hypotheses. Thus, theory is illustrated and validated, rather than defining it. The time perspective is trans-historical with the assumption that findings are the same for all in all circumstances.

It is suggested for researchers and practitioners to study organisational phenomena using quantitative as well as qualitative research designs and to explore the deeper meaning of already established constructs such as leadership and followership, authority, trust, active listening and empathy. This will allow a deeper exploration into organisational dynamics and its effect on employee functioning and wellness. It is interesting that for example, Rogers (in Schneider, Bugental & Pierson, 2001) cautioned that his work should not be trivialised in organisational applications. For example, Kramer (1995) illustrated how active listening is easily forced into a tool to enhance productivity (rather than a skill to build relationships) and Cilliers (1996) illustrated how the concepts of empathy and facilitation are used superficially in training, management and organisational development.

The above identity crises manifest professionally when the industrial psychologist often gets caught up in conflicts between different organisational roles (Campbell, 1995), such as between human resources practitioner and I/O psychologist. On the other hand the I/O psychologist often gets confused about who the client in the organisation is – management or employee, management or board member, individual employee or team. Maybe university departments of I/O psychology can self-authorise more to help resolve this split.

Identity can be defined as a sense of self, a distinctness of differentiation and of the system's own individuality (Huffington, Armstrong, Halton, Hoyle & Pooley, 2004). Identity is formed in the comparison of the self to 'the other'. Thus, any system seeks and/or constructs an opponent against which it can define itself (such as a sibling or 'the other' department, team or organisation) and then learns what makes the self different or unique. The 'other' functions as a repository object into which the system displaces its internal anxieties, fears and hostilities (Cytrenbaum & Noumair, 2004). The system tends to rate the self as more favourable and 'the other' as less favourable, especially in conflict situations which could be filled with survival anxiety, needs and behaviour. This may be where one part of the system finds itself in a position of envy, defined as the desire to spoil something good simply because it is good and does not belong to the self. This dynamic may explain the sometimes 'difficult' relationship between I/O psychology and for example clinical psychology and human resources management.

The next step in identity forming refers to projections onto and into 'the other', using the other to serve as the receptacle for uncomfortable anxiety, splits, aggression and other unwanted feelings. It can be hypothesised that this internal split is indicative of external splits which makes identity-forming difficult, filled with issues around suspicion, power and de-authorisation. When the system can be mature enough to realise and own the projections, it will be able to develop its identity.

In the organisational setting, the role taken up by leadership is important. A mature identity is formed when leadership is experienced by the system as 'good-enough', meaning a nurturing object, providing containment and emotional need satisfaction. This implies that the group will feel safe, cared for, listened to (which are all aspects of transformational leadership).

For I/O psychology, its empowering will need to focus more on the philosophy underlying the psychology of work and in organisations, including the meaning of work. It is suggested that the systems psychodynamic theory and stance, which originated in-depth psychology be used (Bion, 1961; Colman & Bexton, 1975; Colman & Geller, 1985; De Board, 1978; French & Vince, 1999; Hirschhorn, 1993; Miller, 1993; Neumann, Kellner & Dawson-Shepherd, 1997; Obholzer & Roberts, 1994; Stapley, 1996). Furthermore, the scope of I/O psychology is ever increasing, as is evident in the development of new and challenging interpersonal role roles, such as the facilitation of learning, mentorship, coaching and executive coaching (Huffington et al., 2004; Peltier, 2001; Sperry, 2004). This implies continuous training for the I/O psychologist to stay abreast of all relevant applications in theory and in practice.

The Tasks of the Industrial/organisational Psychologist

The primary task of I/O psychology is the application of psychological principles and research to workplace phenomena. I/O psychologists use the scientific approach, characterised by qualitative observation, as well as quantitative measurement and statistics (see Brewerton & Millward, 2004) to conduct research and intervene in the workplace. Furthermore, they are concerned about the effectiveness of the organisation and the wellness of individuals. Lastly, I/O psychologists operate with an implicit multilevel model, i.e. they recognise that in addition to individual influences on individual behaviour and attitudes, higher-order units such as teams and the organisational context have influence (Ryan, 2003). Therefore, four broad tasks of the I/O psychologist are distinguished for the purposes of this paper:

1. explaining individual, group and organisational behaviour and optimising functioning,
2. measuring behaviour and predicting potential,
3. contributing to organisation development, and
4. translating I/O research findings and empowering potential users thereof.

Examples of specific areas that should be researched by I/O psychologists are given in this section. However, this list is not exhaustive and merely suggest some important research needs.

Explaining individual, group and organisational behaviour and optimising functioning I/O psychologists should conduct research about theories and models that could be used to explain individual, group and organisational functioning and the optimisation thereof. Traditionally the health and social sciences have been characterised by a pathogenic paradigm, i.e. an orientation towards the abnormal (Strümpfer, 1990). Knowledge gained by answering this question is then used to find ways of treating and preventing diseases. Diener, Suh, Lucas and Smith (1999) showed that 17 times more articles that are scientific were published on negative feelings and experiences than on the positive. Myers (2000) found a more favourable ratio of 14:1. Burnout, stress, violations of psychological contracts, job insecurity and downsizing remain popular topics for study in I/O psychology (Turner et al., 2002).

Schaufeli and Bakker (2001) concluded that work is often associated with illness. Research in the Netherlands showed that between 4% and 10% of the working population reported serious burnout complaints (Bakker, Schaufeli & Van Dierendonck, 2000). A recent study amongst European workers showed that the most common work-related health problems are backache, stress and fatigue. Pienaar (2002) found that 8,64% of police officers showed serious levels of suicide ideation, while 15% reported stress-related problems. Levert, Lucas and Ortlepp (2000) reported that 54,9% of psychiatric nurses in their study in government hospitals experienced a high level of emotional exhaustion. Compared with international norms (Cartwright & Cooper, 2002), studies in South Africa showed high levels of physical and psychological ill-health for academic and support staff of higher education institutions (Barkhuizen & Rothmann, 2004; Coetzee & Rothmann, 2005), employees in the insurance industry (Coetzer & Rothmann, 2006) and teachers (Jackson & Rothmann, 2006).

Dysfunctional behaviour frequently occurs in the workplace. For example, American military police recently conducted atrocities with Iraq prisoners (McGeary, 2004). It might be true that they lapsed into sadistic behaviour because they had control over prisoners and they might have felt that their behaviour was sanctioned by an authority figure (Milgram, 1963; 1965; 1974). However, the question arises why such sadistic acts were committed by individuals who are part of a society where the field of Psychology and specifically I/O Psychology is more advanced than in any other society. In South Africa, a teacher in a secondary school was recently been charged because he showed pornographic pictures to school-children (Beeld, 22 May 2004). Furthermore, incidences of sexual harassment, bullying, poor quality work, theft, unsafe actions and unethical behaviour are regularly reported in organisations. However, dysfunctional behaviour is not limited to South African organisations.

In contrast with the above-mentioned argument, it seems that work, and more specifically goal-directed, structured activity, translate directly into other mental health outcomes (Kelloway & Barling, 1991; Turner et al., 2002) and indirectly affect employees' life satisfaction (Hart, 1999; Judge & Watanabe, 1993). In addition, research (e.g. Kirchler, 1985) regarding the effects of unemployment, showed that a lack of work has detrimental effects, including depression, alcoholism, psychological complaints and even suicide. Therefore, it can be concluded that either work could contribute towards illness or it could have a therapeutic effect.

One possible reason for the overemphasis on negative aspects of work and life is the failure of I/O psychology research to be responsive to the needs of all potential research stakeholders. The prevailing values perspective in I/O Psychology research, emphasising a utilitarian, cost-benefit approach has strongly influenced the framing and interpretation of research questions (Wright & Wright, 2002). The utilitarian approach regards the achievement of the goals as set forth by one stakeholder group, namely the management of an organisation, as the primary objective of applied research. As a consequence, the employees (as another stakeholder grouping), are considered to be important only to the extent which they are instrumental in fulfilling the organisation's goals. According to utilitarianism, actions and policies should be evaluated based on costs and benefits they impose on the organisation. Therefore, this approach focuses on organisational rather than individual effectiveness.

A consequence of the utilitarian perspective has been that applied research tends to focus unduly on the identification of financial costs to the organisation of distressed, dissatisfied and unhappy employees. The cause of this employee dissatisfaction and unhappiness is typically seen as being deeply embedded in the emotional maladjustment of the employee, as opposed to aspects of the job itself (Wright, 2003). As a result, the cure for this maladjustment usually involves some type of prevention-based employee therapy (Wright & Cropanzano, 2000). According to Wright (2003), a short-run focus on the negative may be less than an optimal strategy. While the utilitarian perspective has provided a significant value-addition for those interested in the so-called bottom line for business success, it has been much less articulate in proposing an agenda to pro-actively assist employees in their pursuit of healthier and more meaningful lives. Therefore, research must not only focus on how to get employees to be more productive but also on employee health and wellness.

During 2000, a whole edition of the American Psychologist focussed on positive psychology (Seligman & Csikszentmihalyi, 2000). According to Seligman (2002), the central objective of positive psychology is to understand and facilitate happiness and subjective well-being. The field of positive psychology at the subjective level is about valued subjective experiences; well-being, contentment, and satisfaction (in the past); hope and optimism (for the future) and flow and happiness (in the present) (Seligman & Csikszentmihalyi, 2000:5).

The field of positive psychology is rapidly gaining momentum in I/O psychology (Snyder & Lopez, 2002; Wright, 2003). Erez and Isen (2002) have shown that inducing positive emotional states in people facilitates flexible, effective problem-solving, decision making and evaluation of events. Fredrickson's (1998) 'broaden-and-build' theory of positive emotions states that positive emotions, including, joy, interest, contentment and happiness all share the ability to 'broaden' an individual's momentary thought-action repertoires. In addition, these positive emotions assist in building a individual's enduring personal resources. The tendency to experience the positive is proposed to be central to one's ability to flourish, mentally prosper and psychologically grow. Therefore, positive emotions have a potentially adaptive and interactive nature and might moderate the relationship between job satisfaction and job performance. Considering the changes employees have to deal with, as well as the deprived background of many South Africans, research about causes, moderators, mediators and effects of positive emotions is of great importance.

Adopting a utilitarian, cost-benefit perspective emphasizing the goal of enhanced workplace performance, Luthans (2002a; 2002b) noted the need for a more relevant, proactive approach to organisational research. He termed this positive organisational behaviour, defined as the study and application of positively oriented human resource strengths and psychological capabilities that can be measured, developed and effectively managed for performance improvement in today's workplace. Therefore, the relationship between happiness and wellness on the one hand, and individual, group and organisational effectiveness on the other hand should be conducted. However, Wright (2003) argues that in addition to a utilitarian perspective, which focuses on the bottom line for business success, the mission of I/O Psychology also includes the pursuit of employee happiness and wellness.

In research with 198 000 employees in 36 companies by the Gallup Organisation, responses to the following question were analysed: "At work, do you have the opportunity to do what you do best every day?" When employees answered 'strongly agree' to this question, they were 50% more likely to work in businesses with a low turnover, 38% more likely to work in productive business units, and 44% more likely to work in business units with high customer satisfaction scores (Buckingham & Clifton, 2001). Furthermore, it was found that globally, only 20% of employees working in large organisations experienced that their strengths are utilised every day. In addition, the longer an employee stays with an organisation and the higher he/she climbs the traditional career ladder, the less likely he/she is to strongly agree that he/she is performing to his strengths. The researchers attributed this finding to the following flawed assumptions about people: (1) each person can learn to be competent in almost anything, and (2) each person's greatest room for growth is in his/her areas of greatest weakness.

Organisations should not only accommodate the fact that employees are different; they must build their enterprises around the strengths of each person. According to Buckingham and Clifton (2001), organisations should change the way they select, measure, develop and channel the careers of individuals. However, this needs change to the following assumptions: (1) each person's talents are enduring and unique, and (2) each person's greatest room for growth is in his/her greatest strength. Research is needed regarding different talents, knowledge and skills that will contribute to individual happiness and organisational performance as well as systems to identify these (Buckingham & Clifton, 2001). Research linking the 6 virtues (and 24 strengths) identified by Seligman (2002) to individual wellness and organisational effectiveness should be conducted. These virtues (and strengths) include the following:

1. wisdom and knowledge (curiosity, love of learning, judgement, ingenuity, emotional intelligence and perspective);
2. courage (valour/bravery, perseverance and integrity);
3. humanity and love (kindness, loving and allowing oneself to be loved);
4. justice (citizenship, fairness, equity and leadership);
5. temperance (self-control, prudence and humility), and;
6. transcendence (appreciation of beauty and excellence, gratitude, spirituality, forgiveness, humour and passion).

Employees bear some responsibility for making healthy work systems succeed (Turner et al., 2002). Constructs related to proactive role orientations and role-breadth self-efficacy could contribute to wellness and individual effectiveness and efficiency (Strümpfer, 1995). These constructs include amongst others a sense of coherence (Antonovsky, 1987), self-efficacy (Bandura, 1977), optimism (Carver & Scheier, 2002; Seligman, 2002), subjective well-being and life satisfaction (Diener, Lucas & Oishi, 2002), resilience (Masten & Reed, 2002), positive affectivity (Watson, 2002), coping strategies (Stanton, Parsa & Austenfeld, 2002) and emotional intelligence (Salovey, Mayer & Caruso, 2002). However, research is needed to evaluate the effects of these constructs in the work situation, the effects of the work situation on these constructs, as well as the effects of interventions directed at building these orientations.

While a positive psychology perspective is necessary, harsh realities exist that contribute to occupational stress, burnout and ill health (Cherniss, 1995). A need exists for behavioural theories and models to integrate positive and negative aspects of human behaviour. For example, Schaufeli and Bakker (2004) developed the Comprehensive Burnout and Engagement (COBE) Model to explain positive and negative behaviour at work. The COBE-model assumes two psychological processes, namely an energetic and a motivational process. The energetic process links job demands with health problems via burnout. The motivational process links job resources via engagement with organisational outcomes. Schaufeli and Bakker (2004) confirmed that job demands were associated with exhaustion, whereas job resources were associated with work engagement. Burnout was related to health problems as well as to turnover intentions, and mediated the relationship between job demands and health problems, while engagement mediated the relationship between job resources and turnover intentions. However, many questions remain about the effectiveness of the model, because their research relied only on self-report measures and cross-sectional data. Furthermore, integrating burnout and work engagement could lead to a new taxonomy which categorise work behaviour according to energy at work (varying from exhaustion to vigour) and identification with work (varying from cynicism to dedication).

Organisational change (including employment equity, layoffs, downsizing, acquisitions, mergers, job relocations and technological innovations at work) have adverse effects on employee well-being. Research should be conducted to determine the effects of such changes on employees in South Africa and assess the effectiveness of interventions to help employees to cope with them (Kalimo, Taris & Schaufeli, 2003).

As the world is becoming a global village, people are increasingly confronted with diversity, especially in South Africa with its multicultural society. Diversity refers to any difference and includes attributes such as gender, social class, ethnicity, culture, age, sexual orientation and lifestyle. On the individual level, the person could have certain limitations making it difficult to deal with diversity (Triandis, 2003). For example, (1) when they process little information, they will have the tendency to use categorisation, and (2) cultures are ethnocentric in nature, that is they use their own culture as standard for judging other cultures. According to Lopez, Prosser, Edwards, Magyar-Moe, Neufeld and Rasmussen (2002:711), research is needed about the following aspects:

1. the magnitude and equivalence of constructs across cultures;
2. the value of religious practices, spirituality and diverse constructions of life meaning;

3. searching for clues to the good life that cultural experiences might provide; and

4. clarifying what works in the life of people.

Although South African research by Cilliers and May (2002) investigated specific diversity manifestations from a systems psychodynamic stance, more such research is needed to understand how diversity issues change over time and how this influences human relationships and organisational climate.

Few attempts have been made to evaluate the cross-cultural equivalence of constructs such as hope, optimism, self-esteem, happiness, subjective well-being and resilience (Lopez et al., 2002). Most of the studies examining positive psychological constructs have focused on Western samples. Relatively little is known about the concurrent and predictive validity of measures of positive constructs. In a review of national differences, Diener et al., (1999) reported that people living in individualistic cultures have higher levels of satisfaction than those in collectivist cultures. While collectivist cultures give priority to the in-group and define the self in relational terms, individualist cultures encourage independence, attention to personal opinions and feelings and autonomy. Subjective well-being, for example, may therefore be more salient to individualists, and attributes traditionally associated with well-being may not be as relevant for members of collectivist cultures. It is important to recognise that what constitutes a good life may be different in different cultural settings.

While a true cross-cultural perspective on workplace wellness is lacking, various cross-national studies have been carried out (Golembiewski, Scherb & Boudreau, 1993; Savicki, 2002). Instead of post-hoc explanations of differences in wellness in multicultural or cross-cultural situations, the testing of a priori formulated cross-cultural hypotheses are needed. For instance, Schaufeli (2003) argued that in individualistic cultures, social exchange relationships between individuals (interpersonal reciprocity) might play a crucial role in causing burnout, whereas in collectivistic cultures social exchange relationships with the group (individual-group reciprocity) might be pivotal. In addition, the effects of stereotypes, prejudice and discrimination on individual wellness and organisational effectiveness should be studied. Furthermore, the role of inter-cultural communication, cultural differences, minority positions and migration in individual wellness and organisational effectiveness should be investigated.

World-wide there seems to be a tendency for organisations to drift from domestic to global, no matter how small the organisation (Furnham, 1997). One of the consequences of South Africa's becoming part of the global business community is that there has been a vast increase in the number of South Africans taking up assignments outside the country (Hawley, 1999). Research has shown that some expatriate managers who are given foreign assignments end them early because of their poor performance or their inability to adjust to the foreign environment. Many of those who do not return early, function at a low level of effectiveness (Fish & Wood, 1997). Congruent to the strategic importance of assignments, failure of an expatriate may be costly and even detrimental to the future of a multinational company in a host country (Gregersen & Black, 1990). Thus, research is needed regarding factors related to the success of expatriate assignments.

Leadership is another area that should be researched in South Africa. Although few academics or business practitioners would argue with the notion that effective leadership contributes to the positive health of an organisation, little research has focussed on the effects of leadership on individual wellness (Turner et al., 2002). This has resulted in a limited appreciation of the value of positive leadership within the context of organisations. Transformational leadership has the potential for enhancing wellness. This occurs when leaders increase followers' awareness of the mission/vision towards which they are working, choose what is right rather than what is simple or expedient, display inspirational motivation and intellectual stimulation, and manifest individualised consideration. Studies (e.g. Barling, Kelloway & Weber, 1996) showed that transformational leadership leads to higher performance and employee morale, although its relationship with performance is mediated by affective organisational commitment. However, superior performance would require transformational leadership to be present above and beyond constructive interactions between employees and management that constitute good management (Turner et al., 2002). The relatively new concepts (Huffington et al., 2004) of containment leadership (stimulating exploration and curiosity) and pro-attainment (including organisational reframing and creativity) need to be researched for its potential in facilitating employee wellness.

Work/life balance is also an important research topic in South Africa. Keyser and Dickinson (2002) introduced the concept of organisational schizophrenia as a condition that exists in organisations due to the opposing pulls of employees' need to have a personal life and the organisation's need to have employees accessible and working on an almost constant basis. More demands (including an increase in the average work hours) are placed on employees in their workplaces. Geurts, Kompier, Roxburgh and Houtman (2003) found that work-home interference mediated the relationship of the workload with depressive mood and health complaints and moderated the relationship with work-related negative affect. It seems that workload exerts its negative effects on wellness through a process of spillover of negative load-effects that impede recovery during non-working hours. Research into emotional work demands and work-home balance is necessary (Kompier, 2002). On the other hand, employees may not just suffer from excessive work demands, but may as well benefit from a work situation that contains support or resources that are relevant to meeting demands.

Sonnentag (2003) studied the work-related outcomes of recovery during leisure time. She found that day-level recovery was positively related to day-level work engagement and day-level proactive behaviour. The results of her study showed that experiences outside work are crucial for feelings and behaviour at work. However, it is not clear what the preconditions of recovery on a specific day are. It is also not clear which factors mediate or moderate the relationship between recovery on and work engagement or proactive behaviour. The long-term effects of recovery should also be researched.

Every year more young people are entering the labour market, seeking jobs. At the same time, South Africa is struggling with an enormous unemployment rate. For a variety of reasons, many of the job seekers in South Africa have attained very low educational levels. Research is needed on the best way to implement career counselling services and life skills training for job seekers. The dilemma facing organisations is that they need to employ job seekers that possess the necessary technical, business and scientific skills to face the challenges posed by the business environment. The fact that many job seekers do not possess the necessary skills implies that research is needed on how to improve the employability of applicants. Because of the use of technology and of the skills required to use the technology, many workers are nowadays less subject to management control systems. This means that non-supervisory personnel need to acquire 'management' skills, which include self-management skills, inter personal skills and problem-solving skills.

Paid work contributes to mental health and affects employees' life satisfaction. Consequently, unemployment has been shown to have detrimental effects on well-being. Individual coping behaviour associated with unemployment depends on certain objective characteristics such as age, level of education, and length of unemployment (Warr, 1984). De Witte (1994) distinguished a typology of coping behaviours, which integrates meaningful patterns of unemployment experiences and adaptive responses, including the attitudes, expectations and experiences of the unemployed (e.g. work motivation, well-being and search behaviour). Research regarding unemployment could be used to plan and implement policies in organisations.

It is not only sufficient to investigate which themes in I/O psychology should be researched. It is also necessary to consider how research should be done. For instance, Kompier (2002) analysed various I/O psychology studies and recommends the following:

1. more general research is not needed,

2. further expansion of the number of studies based on cross-sectional study designs and on employees' self-reports has little added value, and

3. researchers should not try to compensate for weak study designs by increasing the number of sophisticated statistical analyses. There is a need for better designs, such as longitudinal and experimental designs and better quality data (Breverton & Millward, 2004).

More qualitative designs and work across boundaries of paradigm and theory should also be considered. For example, the inclusion of the systems psychodynamic stance (Miller, 1993; Obholzer & Roberts, 1994) would explain the relevant qualitative and deeper, unconscious behaviour. The application of this model often helps in understanding organisational stuckness, non-movement and anti-task behaviour in for example change, transformation and diversity issues.

Measuring Behaviour and Predicting Potential

Over the years psychological tests have become essential tools for implementing change. The term test refers to group and individually administered standardised measures of aptitudes, achievement, intelligence, personality, social, language, perception and motor skills (Oakland, 2004). Strong evidence exists to support the merit of tests for monitoring children in the educational system, providing policy-makers with information for decision making, aiding psychologists in the individual screening and diagnostic process, credentialing and licensing candidates in professions and specialities, and providing organisations with data for employee selection, promotion and evaluation of training (Hambleton & Oakland, 2004).

The cultural appropriateness of psychological tests and their usage were placed in the spotlight with the promulgation of the new Employment Equity Act 55 of 1998, Section 8 (Government Gazette, 1998), which stipulates that: "Psychological testing and other similar assessments are prohibited unless the test or assessment being used – (a) has been scientifically shown to be valid and reliable, (b) can be applied fairly to all employees; and (c) is not biased against any employee or group." Despite the multicultural nature of our society, psychological test development in South Africa has historically been characterised by the development of tests for separate cultural and/or language groups (Claassen, 1997; Foxcroft, 1997). While past apartheid policies and legislation shaped the way in which test development was approached until the 1990s, it is somewhat disturbing to note that subsequent to apartheid's demise, very few new culturally relevant tests have been developed that can be applied to a diverse range of cultural and language groups in South Africa.

Personality variables and issues related to their use, especially in work settings have generated a vast amount of interest, research and publications. The importance of personality too I/O Psychology is now apparent with meaningful relationships between personality variables and criteria, such as job satisfaction, supervisory ratings, the development of job-specific criteria, counterproductive behaviour, and organisational citizenship. Criterion-related validities for predicting work-related constructs reveal the importance of personality variables in understanding and predicting work performance. Various methodological questions should be raised when applying personality assessment, namely:

1. Is paper-and-pencil testing familiar to people in a specific culture?
2. Are respondents proficient in reading English?
3. Is the translation done accurately?
4. Is the translated test equivalent to the original test?
5. Are there cross-cultural differences in the means and distributions of test scores?
6. How can cross-cultural differences in test scores be interpreted? (Cheung, 2004).

Currently, none of the available personality tests used in South Africa has been found to provide a reliable and valid picture of personality for all cultural (and language) groups in this country. Meiring, Van de Vijver, Rothmann and Barrick (2005) clearly demonstrated that psychological instruments imported from abroad could have limited suitability for South Africa. It was only after a series of item adaptations that acceptable psychometric properties were found. In recent years more attention has been paid to the issue of equivalence of tests for the multicultural South-African context (e.g. 1991; Meiring et al., 2005). The results of the examinations were not unequivocally positive. Meiring et al. reported very low internal consistencies for the 15FQ (see Tyler, 2002) in all South-African language groups. In what is known as an etic approach, the currently used tests have been imported from elsewhere (often from Anglo-Saxon countries), while emic personality constructs important in Africa have been omitted. The Chinese Personality Assessment Inventory (CPAI) is cited as an example of indigenous measures that have identified culturally salient dimensions. The unique Interpersonal Relatedness factor of the CPAI measures an aspect of personality which has been absent in the personality tests that are used all over the world (Cheung, 2004). The development of a personality test in South Africa might contribute to the development of an indigenous personality theory.

In the social, behavioural, and medical sciences self-report questionnaires are often used as an efficient and inexpensive method for data collection. However, asking respondents to report on their own personality, attitudes, or behaviour entails a number of problems. Respondents often show tendencies to answer according to certain patterns (response styles) lowering the validity of instruments. The most salient response style is social desirability, which is the tendency of participants to respond to questionnaire items in line with societal norms about what is appropriate (Van Hemert, 2003).

Research regarding the reliability, factorial validity, and predictive validity of assessment tools is needed. Furthermore, more research is needed on the equivalence and bias of assessment tools used in South Africa. Van de Vijver and Leung (1997) make a hierarchical distinction of three types of equivalence, namely:

1. construct equivalence, which indicates the extent to which the same construct is measured across all cultural groups studied;
2. measurement unit equivalence which can be obtained when two metric measures have the same measurement unit but have different origins; and
3. scalar equivalence which can be obtained when two metric measures have the same measurement unit and the same origin.

Equivalence cannot be assumed but should be established and reported in each study (Van de Vijver & Leung, 1997). Item bias should also be computed. An item is an unbiased measure of a theoretical construct if persons from different cultural groups have the same average score on the item (Van de Vijver & Leung, 1997). Item bias can be produced by sources such as incidental differences in appropriateness of the item content and inadequate item formulation.

Contributing to Organisational Development

To contribute to organisational development, researchers and practitioners need to conceptualise organisational effectiveness and develop measures thereof. These measures could then be used as criteria in concurrent and predictive validity studies.

Also, with the current focus on effectiveness in organisations (including state departments), organisation diagnostic measuring instruments (focussing on organisational culture and climate) should be researched.

The effects of individual, group and organisational interventions directed at organisational effectiveness and efficiency should be researched (Rothmann, 2003). Traditionally there was too much focus on changing the individual, without considering the situation in which individuals find themselves (Kompier & Cooper, 1999). One of the most important ways of improving the experience of work is to design jobs such as to encourage workers to engage actively with their tasks and work environment (Turner et al., 2002). By providing workers with autonomy in performing their jobs, challenging work, and the opportunity for social interaction, employee effectiveness and feelings of competence are maximised. The following work design models should be evaluated in the South African context (Kompier, 2003):

1. the job characteristics model;
2. the Michigan organisation stress model;
3. the job demands-control model;
4. the socio-technical approach;
5. the action theoretical approach;
6. the effort-reward imbalance model; and
7. the vitamin model.

The effectiveness and potential cost benefits of interventions (e.g. redesigning jobs and implementing teamwork) have not been rigorously evaluated (Kompier & Cooper, 1999). The few rigorous studies that were conducted showed significant improvements in employee satisfaction and motivation levels, but productivity outputs improved minimally.

Organisational development interventions in general and interventions to influence culture and values should be implemented to contribute to healthier work-places. Furthermore, psycho-educational programmes should be developed and presented to combat burnout and to promote work engagement (Kompier & Cooper, 1999).

New technology (including information technology and new production methods) are continuously introduced by organisations. I/O psychologists should be involved in interdisciplinary teams who plan the implementation of new technology. From a systems perspective, it is necessary that changes in the task subsystem (e.g. technology) must be accompanied by changes in the psycho-social subsystem (knowledge, skills, attitudes and values) (Robbins, Odendaal & Roodt, 2003).

Four dimensions of organisational results should be evaluated when measuring the effects of work wellness interventions, namely financial results, time and personnel resources, customer satisfaction and health and safety (Kompier & Cooper, 1999). Financial results are taken from an organisation's profit and loss account and balance sheet. Time and personnel resources include hours worked, personnel statistics and personnel reports, which show the levels of staffing and competency that have been used to achieve the financial result. Measurement of customer satisfaction shows how effective an organisation has been in satisfying customer's requirements. Health and safety include the physical and psychological working environment, stress, burnout, health, work engagement and job satisfaction. Study of the effectiveness of interventions will require an interdisciplinary approach.

Translating Research Findings and Empowering Potential Users Thereof

Although a large body of research findings exist, potential users often do not react to them. This might be attributed to a lack of knowledge of research findings, a lack of implementation skills, a lack of motivation and/or limitations created by the prevailing organisational culture. According to Watkins (2001), many industrial leaders uphold dysfunctional paradigms, which may profoundly diminish the effectiveness of I/O Psychology teaching and research. Reacting to the opinions of industrial leaders, without at least considering organisational success factors to support their reasoning, may potentially be devastating to the subject.

Recommendations

Next, recommendations are made regarding some important research topics for I/O psychologists. I/O psychology should study its changing identity and dynamics constantly in order to stay relevant in the world of work. This includes responding in a sensitive manner towards organisational efforts to seduce practitioners to become involved in the administration and mechanistic inputs. Research designs should include more qualitative designs across boundaries of paradigm and theory to fit post-modern thinking (Camic, Rhodes & Yardley, 2003). For example, the inclusion of the systems psychodynamic stance (Miller, 1993, Cytrynbaum & Noumair, 2003) would explain the relevant qualitative, deep and unconscious behaviour manifesting in organisational change, transformation, mergers, acquisitions, diversity management and the symptoms of stuck-ness, pain and anti-task behaviour associated therewith.

The philosophy underlying the Psychology of work and in organisations, including the meaning of work, should be studied. In addition, new theories to conceptualise individual, group and organisational behaviour in the work context, based on a continuum of human behaviour (from negative to positive) as expressed in multicultural and cross-cultural environments should be developed and tested. Causal models of behaviour in multicultural and cross-cultural work contexts should be developed and tested. The effects of organisational factors (job demands and job resources) on well-being, work/life balance, as well as the moderating or mediating effects of personality characteristics and strengths should be studied in longitudinal and/or experimental designs. Strategies to improve the work/non-work interface should be researched. Furthermore, the effects of individual wellness on organisational outcomes such as performance, labour turnover, safety behaviour and absenteeism should be studied.

Diversity represents another important area of research for industrial psychologists. The effects of stereotypes, prejudice and discrimination on individual wellness and organisational effectiveness should be studied. Furthermore, research is needed regarding the role of inter-cultural communication, cultural differences, minority positions and migration in individual wellness and organisational effectiveness. Research is needed regarding the reliability, validity, equivalence and bias of psychological tests in the multicultural context of South Africa. These tests could provide policymakers with information for decision making, aid psychologists in the individual screening and diagnostic process and provide organisations with data for employee selection, promotion and evaluation of training. While the cultural appropriateness of internationally developed psychological tests should be evaluated, new tests should be developed based on South African circumstances. The use of psychological tests to predict individual well-being and organisational effectiveness should also be researched.

Strengths and psychological capabilities that can be measured, developed and effectively managed for performance improvement in the workplace should be studied. Such strengths and capabilities include sense of coherence, self-efficacy, optimism, subjective well-being and life satisfaction, resilience, positive affectivity, coping strategies and emotional intelligence. Research regarding the ways organisations could select, measure, develop, and channel the careers of individuals based on their strengths, should be conducted. The magnitude and equivalence of constructs across cultures, the value of religious practices, spirituality and diverse constructions of life meaning, and clues to the good life that cultural experiences might provide should also be studied.

It is clear that the employment relationship has changed. Therefore, changes in psychological contracts and the effects thereof on individual wellness and organisational effectiveness should be studied. The effects of changes in the psychological contract on job security levels, factors which contribute to job insecurity, moderators and/or mediators, as well as outcomes thereof should be investigated. Research is needed on the best way to implement career counselling services and life skills training for job seekers. Furthermore, experiences of unemployment in South Africa should be investigated to determine its impact on the well-being, attitudes and coping behaviours of unemployed individuals in a multicultural context. Psychological profiles of unemployed individuals of different demographic groups could be used as a basis for planning and implementing policies (regarding counselling services, life skills programmes, training programmes and job creation programmes) to solve problems related to the unemployed.

The effectiveness of primary, secondary and tertiary level interventions to promote individual, group and organisational effectiveness should be investigated. Research is needed conceptualise organisational effectiveness and to develop reliable and valid indicators thereof.

Careful consideration should be given to the selection of research designs. Cross-sectional designs might be useful in developing and standardising psychological tests. However, more studies based on cross-sectional study designs and on employees' self-reports have little added value. Relevant and applicable statistics should be used. Better research designs (such as longitudinal and experimental research designs) are needed. It is also important that industrial psychological researchers collaborate with occupational physicians, psychiatrists, psychologists, engineers as well as fellow scholars from such fields as epidemiology, physiology, economics and business administration. However, as a prerequisite for collaborating with researchers and/or practitioners from other disciplines, it is necessary that I/O Psychology solves its identity issues.

References

Antonovsky, A. (1987). *Unravelling the mystery of health: How people manage stress and stay well.* San Francisco: Jossey-Bass.

Bakker, A.; Schaufeli, W.B. & Van Dierendonck, D. (2000). Burnout: Prevalentie, risicogroepen en risicofactoren. In: I.L.D. Houtman, W.B. Schaufeli & T. Taris (eds.), *Psychische vermoeidheid en werk: Cijfers, trends en analyses*, pp.65-82. Alphen a/d Rijn: Samsom.

Bandura, A. (1977). Self-efficacy: Toward a unifying theory of behaviour change. *Psychological Review*, 84:191-215. https://doi.org/10.1037//0033-295X.84.2.191

Barkhuizen, N. & Rothmann, S. (2004, March). *Burnout of academic staff in a higher education institution.* Paper presented at the 2nd South African Work Wellness Conference, Potchefstroom, South Africa.

Barling, J. (1999). Changing employment relations: Empirical data, social perspectives and policy options. In: D.B. Knight & A. Joseph (eds.), *Restructuring societies: Insights from the social sciences*, pp.59-82. Ottawa: Carlton University Press.

Barling, J.; Kelloway, E.K. & Weber, T. (1996). Effects of transformational leadership training on attitudinal and financial outcomes: A field experiment. *Journal of Applied Psychology*, 81:827-832. https://doi.org/10.1037//0021-9010.81.6.827

Bion, W.R. (1961). *Experiences in groups.* London: Tavistock Publications.

Brewerton, P. & Millward, L. (2004). *Organisational research methods.* London: Sage.

Buckingham, M. & Clifton, D.O. (2001). *Now, discover your strengths.* New York: The Free Press.

Camic, P.M.; Rhodes, J.E. & Yardley, L. (2003). *Qualitative research in Psychology. Expanding perspectives in methodology and design.* Washington: APA. https://doi.org/10.1037/10595-000

Campbell, D. (1995). *Learning consultation. A systemic framework.* London: Karnac.

Cartwright, S. & Cooper, C.L. (2002). *ASSET: An Organizational Stress Screening Tool – The management guide.* Manchester, UK: Robertson/Cooper Ltd.

Carver, C.S. & Scheier, M.F. (2002). Optimism. In: C.R. Snyder & S.J. Lopez (eds.), *Handbook of positive psychology*, pp.231-243. Oxford, UK: Oxford University Press.

Cascio, W.F. (2001). Knowledge creation for practical solutions appropriate to a changing world of work. *South African Journal of Industrial Psychology*, 27(4):14-16. https://doi.org/10.4102/sajip.v27i4.798

Cherniss, C. (1995). *Beyond burnout: Helping teachers, nurses, therapists and lawyers recover from stress and disillusionment.* New York: Routledge.

Cheung, F.M. (2004). Use of western and indigenously developed personality tests in Asia. *Applied Psychology: An International Review*, 53:173-191. https://doi.org/10.1111/j.1464-0597.2004.00167.x

Cilliers, F. (1991). *Die veranderende rol van die Bedryfsielkunde in Suid-Afrika.* Pretoria: UNISA.

Cilliers, F. (1996). Facilitator training in South Africa. In: R. Hutterer, G. Pawlowsky, P.F. Schmid & R. Stipsits (eds.), *Client centred and experiential psychotherapy*. Frankfurt am Main: Peter Lang.

Cilliers, F. & May, M. (2002). South African diversity dynamics. Reporting on the 2000 Robben Island Diversity Experience. A Group Relations event. *SA Journal of Labour Relations*, 26(3):42-68.

Claassen, N.C.W. (1997). Cultural differences, politics and test bias in South Africa. *European Review of Applied Psychology*, 47:297-307.

Coetzee, S.E. & Rothmann, S. (2005). Occupational stress in a higher education institution in South Africa. *South African Journal of Industrial Psychology*, 31(1):47-54. https://doi.org/10.4102/sajip.v31i1.179

Coetzer, W.J. & Rothmann, S. (2006). Occupational stress and strain of employees in an insurance company. *South African Journal of Business Management*. https://doi.org/10.4102/sajbm.v37i3.605

Colman, A.D. & Bexton, W.H. (1975). *Group relations reader 1*. Jupiter: A.K. Rice Institute.

Colman, A.D. & Geller, M.H. (1985). *Group relations reader 2*. Jupiter: The A.K. Rice Institute.

Cytrynbaum, S. & Noumair, D. (2004). *Group relations reader 3*. Jupiter: A.K. Rice Institute.

De Board, R. (1978). *The psychoanalysis of organisations*. London: Routledge. https://doi.org/10.4324/9780203321812

De Witte, H. (1994). *Differences in psychological well-being of short-term and long-term unemployed: A cross-sectional study in the Flanders, Belgium*. Katolieke Universiteit Leuven, Belgium.

Diener, E.; Lucas, R.E. & Oishi, S. (2002). Subjective well-being: The science of happiness and life satisfaction. In: C.R. Snyder & S.J. Lopez (eds.), *Handbook of positive psychology*, pp.63-73. Oxford, UK: Oxford University Press.

Diener, E.; Suh, E.M.; Lucas, R.E. & Smith, H.I. (1999). Subjective wellbeing: Three decades of progress. *Psychological Bulletin*, 125:267-302. https://doi.org/10.1037//0033-2909.125.2.276

Erez, A. & Isen, A.M. (2002). The influence of positive affect on the components of expectancy motivation. *Journal of Applied Psychology*, 87:1055-1067. https://doi.org/10.1037//0021-9010.87.6.1055

Fish, A. & Wood, J. (1997). Managing spouse/partner preparation and adjustment. *Personnel Review*, 26:445-466. https://doi.org/10.1108/00483489710188874

Foxcroft, C.D. (1997). Psychological testing in South Africa: Perspectives regarding ethical and fair practices. *European Journal of Psychological Assessment*, 13:229-235. https://doi.org/10.1027/1015-5759.13.3.229

Fredrickson, B.L. (1998). What good are positive emotions? *Review of General Psychology*, 2:300-319. https://doi.org/10.1037//1089-2680.2.3.300

French, R. & Vince, R. (1999). *Group relations, management and organization*. New York: Oxford University Press.

Furnham, A. (1997). *The psychology of behaviour at work: The individual in the organization*. Sussex, UK: Psychology Press.

Gergen, K.J. (2001). Psychological science in a postmodern context. *American Psychologist*, 56:803-813. https://doi.org/10.1037//0003-066X.56.10.803

Geurts, S.A.E., Kompier, M.A.J., Roxburgh, S. & Houtman, I.L.D. (2003). Does work-home interference mediate the relationship between workload and well-being? *Journal of Vocational Behavior*, 63:532-559. https://doi.org/10.1016/S0001-8791(02)00025-8

Golembiewski, R.T.; Scherb, K. & Boudreau, R.A. (1993). Burnout in cross-national settings: Generic and model-specific perspectives. In: W.B. Schaufeli, C. Maslach & T. Marek (eds.), Professional burnout: Recent developments in theory and research. *Series in applied psychology: Social issues and questions*, pp.217-236. Washington: Taylor & Francis. https://doi.org/10.4324/9781315227979-17

Government Gazette. (1998). *Republic of South Africa, 400(19370)*, Cape Town, 19 October 1998.

Gregersen, H.B. & Black, J.S. (1990). A multifaceted approach to expatriate retention in international assignments. *Group and Organizational Studies*, 15:461-485. https://doi.org/10.1177/105960119001500409

Guest, D.E. (2004). The psychology of the employment relationship: An analysis based on the psychological contract. *Applied Psychology: An International Review*, 53:541-555. https://doi.org/10.1111/j.1464-0597.2004.00187.x

Hambleton, R.K. & Oakland, T. (2004). Advances, issues and research in testing practices around the world. *Applied Psychology: An International Review*, 53:155-156. https://doi.org/10.1111/j.1464-0597.2004.00165.x

Hart, P.M. (1999). Predicting employee life satisfaction: A coherent model of personality, work and non-work experiences, and domain satisfaction. *Journal of Applied Psychology*, 84:564-584. https://doi.org/10.1037/0021-9010.84.4.564

Hawley, K. (1999). The expatriate departure-planning period. *Management Today*, 15(3):34-35.

Hirschhorn, L. (1993). *The workplace within: Psychodynamics of organizational life.* Cambridge: MIT Press.

Huffington, C.; Armstrong, A.; Halton, W.; Hoyle, L. & Pooley, J. (2004). *Working below the surface. The emotional life of contemporary organisations.* London: Karnac.

Jackson, L.T.B. & Rothmann, S. (2006). Occupational stress of teachers in the North West Province of South Africa. *South African Journal of Education.*

Judge, T.A. & Watanabe, S. (1993). Another look at the job satisfaction-life satisfaction relationship. *Journal of Applied Psychology*, 78:939-948. https://doi.org/10.1037/0021-9010.78.6.939

Kalimo, R.; Taris, T.W. & Schaufeli, W.B. (2003). The effects of past and anticipated future downsizing on survivor wellbeing an equity perspective. *Journal of Occupational Health Psychology*, 8:91-109. https://doi.org/10.1037/1076-8998.8.2.91

Kelloway, E.K. & Barling, J. (1991). Job characteristics, role stress and mental health. *Journal of Occupational Psychology*, 64:291-304. https://doi.org/10.1111/j.2044-8325.1991.tb00561.x

Keyser, D. & Dickinson, F. (2002). The schizophrenic organization. *The Industrial-Organizational Psychologist*, 39(4):39-41.

Kirchler, E. (1985). Job loss and mood. *Journal of Economic Psychology*, 6(1):9-25. https://doi.org/10.1016/0167-4870(85)90003-0

Kompier, M. & Cooper, C. (1999). *Preventing stress, improving productivity.* London: Routledge.

Kompier, M. (2002). The psychosocial work environment and health: What do we know and where should we go? *Scandinavian Journal of Work Environment Health*, 28(1):14. https://doi.org/10.5271/sjweh.639

Kompier, M. (2003). Job design and well-being. In: M.J. Schabracq, J.A.M. Winnubst & C.L. Cooper (eds.), *The handbook of work and health psychology*, pp.429-454. London: Wiley. https://doi.org/10.1002/0470013400.ch20

Kramer, R. (1995). Carl Rogers meets Otto Rank: The discovery of relationship. In: T. Pauchant & Associates (eds.), *In search of meaning.* San Francisco: Jossey-Bass.

Kruger, D. (1980). Het die Sielkunde as wetenskaplike projek misluk? *South African Journal of Psychology*, 11(1):6-17. https://doi.org/10.1177/008124638101100102

Levert, T.; Lucas, M. & Ortlepp, K. (2000). Burnout in psychiatric nurses: Contributions of the work environment and a Sense of Coherence. *South African Journal of Psychology*, 30:36-43. https://doi.org/10.1177/008124630003000205

Lopez, S.J.; Prosser, E.C.; Edwards, L.M.; Magyar-Moe, J.L.; Neufeld, J.E. & Rasmussen, H.N. (2002). Putting positive psychology in a multicultural context. In: C.R. Snyder & S.J. Lopez (eds.), *Handbook of positive psychology*, pp.700-714. Oxford, UK: Oxford University Press.

Luthans, F. (2002a). Positive organizational behavior: Developing and maintaining psychological strengths. *Academy of Management Executive*, 16:57-72. https://doi.org/10.5465/ame.2002.6640181

Luthans, F. (2002b). The need for and meaning of positive organizational behavior. *Journal of Organizational Behavior*, 23:695-706. https://doi.org/10.1002/job.165

Masten, A.S. & Reed, M.G.J. (2002). Resilience in development. In: C.R. Snyder & S.J. Lopez (eds.), *Handbook of positive psychology*, pp.74-88. Oxford, UK: Oxford University Press.

Matarazzo, J.D. (1987). There is only one Psychology, no specialities, but many applications. *American Psychologist*, 42:893-903. https://doi.org/10.1037//0003-066X.42.10.893

McGeary, J. (2004). The scandal's growing stain. *Time*, 163(20):24-32.

Meiring, D.; Van de Vijver, A.J.R.; Rothmann, S. & Barrick, M.R. (2005). Construct, item, and method bias of cognitive and personality measures in South Africa. *South African Journal of Industrial Psychology*, 31(1):1-8. https://doi.org/10.4102/sajip.v31i1.182

Milgram, S. (1963). Behavioral study of obedience. *Journal of Abnormal and Social Psychology*, 67:371-378. https://doi.org/10.1037/h0040525

Milgram, S. (1965). Liberating effects of group pressure. *Journal of Personality and Social Psychology*, 1:127-134. https://doi.org/10.1037/h0021650

Milgram, S. (1974). *Obedience to authority.* New York: Harper.

Miller, E.J. (1993). *From dependency to autonomy: Studies in organization and change.* London: Free Association Books.

Moalusi, K.P. (2001). Repositioning Industrial Psychology for the creation of new futures in turbulent times. *South African Journal of Industrial Psychology*, 27(4):17-21. https://doi.org/10.4102/sajip.v27i4.794

Myers, D.G. (2000). The funds, friends, and faith of happy people. *American Psychologist*, 55:56-67. https://doi.org/10.1037//0003-066X.55.1.56

Neumann, J.E.; Kellner, K. & Dawson-Shepherd, A. (1997). *Developing organisational consultancy*. London: Routledge.

Oakland, T. (2004). Use of educational and psychological tests internationally. *Applied Psychology: An International Review*, 53:157-172. https://doi.org/10.1111/j.1464-0597.2004.00166.x

Obholzer, A. & Roberts, V.Z. (1994). *The unconscious at work*. London: Routledge.

Peltier, B. (2001). *The psychology of coaching. Theory and application*. New York: Brunner-Routledge.

Pienaar, J. (2002). Coping, stress and suicide ideation in the South African Police Service. Unpublished doctoral thesis. Potchefstroom: Potchefstroom University for CHE.

Pienaar, Y. & Roodt, G. (2001). The current and future roles of Industrial Psychologists in South Africa. *South African Journal of Industrial Psychology*, 27(4):25-33.

Pietersen, H.J. (1989). An epistemological view of industrial/organisational psychology: Some perspectives and implications for future knowledge development. *South African Journal of Industrial Psychology*, 19(2):101-108. https://doi.org/10.1177/008124638901900206

Renecle, S.D. (2001). The relevance of Industrial Psychology as a profession and discipline in South Africa. *South African Journal of Industrial Psychology*, 27(4):22-24. https://doi.org/10.4102/sajip.v27i4.795

Robbins, S.P.; Odendaal, A. & Roodt, G. (2003). *Organisational behaviour: Global and South African perspectives*. Cape Town: Pearson Education.

Robertson, G.J. (1990). A practical model for test development. In: C.R. Reynolds & R.W. Kamphaus (eds.), *Handbook of psychological and educational assessment of children: Intelligence and achievement*, pp.62-85. New York: The Guilford Press.

Rothmann, S. (2003). Burnout and engagement: A South African perspective. *South African Journal of Industrial Psychology*, 29(4):16-25. https://doi.org/10.4102/sajip.v29i4.121

Ryan, A.M. (2003). Defining ourselves: I/O psychology's identity quest. *The Industrial-Organizational Psychologist*, 41(1):21-33. https://doi.org/10.1037/e578792011-002

Salovey, P.; Mayer, J.D. & Caruso, D. (2002). The positive psychology of emotional intelligence. In: C.R. Snyder & S.J. Lopez (eds.), *Handbook of positive psychology*, pp.159-171. Oxford, UK: Oxford University Press.

Savicki, V. (2002). *Burnout across thirteen cultures: Stress and coping in child and youth care workers*. Westport, CT: Preager.

Schaufeli, W.B. (2003). Past performance and future perspectives of burnout research. *South African Journal of Industrial Psychology*, 29(4):1-15. https://doi.org/10.4102/sajip.v29i4.127

Schaufeli, W.B. & Bakker, A.B. (2001). Werk en welbevinden: Naar een positieve benadering in de Arbeids- en Gezondheidspsychologie [Work and wellbeing: Towards a positive occupational health psychology]. *Gedrag en Organizatie*, 14:229-253.

Schaufeli, W.B. & Bakker, A.B. (2004). Job demands, job resources and their relationship with burnout and engagement: A multi-sample study. *Journal of Organizational Behavior*, 25:293-315. https://doi.org/10.1002/job.248

Schneider, K.J.; Bugental, J.F.T. & Pierson, J.F. (2001). *The handbook of humanistic psychology*. Thousand Oaks, CA: Sage.

Schreuder, A.M.G. (2001). The development of Industrial Psychology at South African Universities: A historical overview and future perspective. *South African Journal of Industrial Psychology*, 27(4):2-7. https://doi.org/10.4102/sajip.v27i4.792

Seligman, M.E.P. & Csikszentmihalyi, M. (2000). Positive psychology: An introduction. *American Psychologist*, 55:5-14. https://doi.org/10.1037//0003-066X.55.1.5

Seligman, M.E.P. (2002). *Authentic happiness: Using the new positive psychology to realize your potential for lasting fulfillment*. London: Nicholas Brealey.

Snyder, C.R. & Lopez, S.J. (2002). *Handbook of positive psychology*. Oxford, UK: Oxford University Press.

Sonnentag, S. (2003). Recovery, work engagement, and proactive behavior: A new look at the interface between non-work and work. *Journal of Applied Psychology*, 88:518-528. https://doi.org/10.1037/0021-9010.88.3.518

Sperry, L. (2004). *Executive coaching. The essential guide for mental health professionals*. New York: Brunner-Routledge. https://doi.org/10.4324/9780203483466

Stanton, A.L.; Parsa, A. & Austenfeld, J.A. (2002). The adaptive potential of coping through emotional approach. In: C.R. Snyder & S.J. Lopez (eds.), *Handbook of positive psychology*, pp.148-158. Oxford, UK: Oxford University Press.

Stapley, L.F. (1996). *The personality of the organisation*. London: Free Association Books.

Strümpfer, D.J.W. (1990). Salutogenesis: A new paradigm. *South African Journal of Psychology*, 20:265-276. https://doi.org/10.1177/008124639002000406

Strümpfer, D.J.W. (1995). The origins of health and strength: From 'salutogenesis' to 'fortigenesis'. *South African Journal of Psychology*, 25:81-89. https://doi.org/10.1177/008124639502500203

Triandis, H.C. (2003). The future of workforce diversity in international organizations: A commentary. *Applied Psychology: An International Review*, 52:496-495. https://doi.org/10.1111/1464-0597.00146

Turner, N.; Barling, J. & Zacharatos, A. (2002). Positive psychology at work. In C.R. Snyder & S.J. Lopez (eds.), *Handbook of positive psychology*, pp.715-728. Oxford, UK: Oxford University Press.

Tyler, G. (2002). *A review of the 15FQ+ Personality Questionnaire*. Pulloxhill, UK: Psychometrics Limited. https://doi.org/10.1108/pr.2002.31.1.114.1

Van de Vijver, F. & Leung, K. (1997). *Methods and data-analysis for cross-cultural research*. Thousand Oaks, CA: SAGE.

Van Hemert, D. A. (2003). Patterns of cross-cultural differences in psychology: A meta-analytic approach. Unpublished doctoral dissertation, Tilburg University, The Netherlands.

Veldsman, T. (2001). A new playing field, game and/or different rules? Into the future with Industrial Psychology as a discipline and profession. *South African Journal of Industrial Psychology*, 27(4):34-41. https://doi.org/10.4102/sajip.v27i4.797

Warr, P. (1984). Economic recession and mental health: A review of research. *Tijdschrift voor Sociale Gezondheidszorg*, 62:298-308.

Watkins, M.L. (2001). Industrial Psychology: An identity crises and future direction. *South African Journal of Industrial Psychology*, 27(4):8-13. https://doi.org/10.4102/sajip.v27i4.793

Watson, D. (2002). Positive affectivity: The disposition to experience pleasurable emotional states. In: C.R. Snyder & S.J. Lopez (eds.), *Handbook of positive psychology*, pp.106-119. Oxford, UK: Oxford University Press.

Wright, T.A. & Cropanzano, R. (2000). The role of organizational behaviour in occupational health psychology: A view as we approach the millennium. *Journal of Occupational Health Psychology*, 5:5-10. https://doi.org/10.1348/096317900167065

Wright, T.A. & Wright, V.P. (2002). Organizational researcher values, ethical responsibility, and the committed to participant perspective. *Journal of Management Inquiry*, 11:173-185. https://doi.org/10.1177/10592602011002012

Wright, T.A. (2003). Positive organizational behavior: An idea whose time has truly come. *Journal of Organizational Behavior*, 24:437-442. https://doi.org/10.1002/job.194

Article 3

The Systems Psychodynamic Role Identity of Academic Research Supervisors[1]

Abstract

Research on the unconscious role behaviour of academic research supervisors is limited. The aim of this research was to study and describe the systems psychodynamic role identity of a group of academic research supervisors. A qualitative in-depth socio-analytic interview was used as the data-gathering instrument. A convenient and purposive sample was drawn consisting of 11 supervisors at a large South African university. Systems psychodynamic role analysis was used as the method of data analysis. The findings indicated an experienced difference between the normative, existential and phenomenal roles demonstrating high levels of anxiety amongst academic research supervisors, being introjected by them and projected onto them. Recommendations for the institution and further research were formulated.

Keywords

anxiety, normative role, existential role, introjections, phenomenal role, projections, projective identification

1   Cilliers, F. (2017). The systems psychodynamic role identity of academic research supervisors. *South African Journal of Higher Education*, 31(1), 29-49.

Introduction

The conceptualisation of master's/doctoral degree academic research supervision has changed significantly in the last few years (Armstrong, Allinson & Hayes, 2004:4145; Emilsson & Johnsson, 2007:163-165; Mackinnon, 2004:395-399; Petersen, 2014:823-828). The previous strong focus on policy development is now not only accompanied by increased competition, pressure on resources (such as time and funding) and increased research outputs, but also by a focus on the quality of the supervisor-student relationship. In this, the characteristics and experiences of successful students have been well documented (Adler & Adler, 2005:13-15; Conrad, Duren & Haworth, 2002:67-70; Emilsson & Johnsson, 2007:165-169; Gordon, 2003:156-157; Marcketti, Mhango & Gregoire, 2006:65-70; Murphy & Coleman, 2004:3-7; Popov, 2009:3-5; White, 2007:596-601), whereas comparatively less research is available on the characteristics and experiences of academic research supervisors. Waghid (2015:7, 15-22) refers to this aspect as a largely unstudied aspect of pedagogical work in academia.

Academic Research Supervision

For the purpose of this research, this concept was defined as an interpersonal relationship in which students develop as critically thinking, creative problem-solving and autonomous researchers and professional scholars towards gaining research competence to complete a higher (master's and doctoral) degree research project under the guidance of academics authorised in their roles as academic research supervisors and with relevant subject and research competence (Denholm & Evans, 2007; Green & Lee, 1995:41; Lee, 2012:10-12; Oost & Sonneveld, 2007:15; Trafford & Leshem, 2010:111-112; Wright, Murray & Geale, 2007:459). Originally, effective academic research supervisors were described simplistically as either being born or trained (Emilsson & Johnsson, 2007:165), after which the focus changed to their personality profile. Specifically, their intra-personal characteristics of knowledge, understanding of complexity, interest in supervision and interpersonal characteristics of effective teaching skills, trusting others, dealing with complex relationships and knowing the impact of their own power, were studied (Lepp, Remmik, Leijen & Karm, 2010:51; Mackinnon, 2004:396-401). Research shows that many academic research supervisors have negative experiences of their task – they report on not having enough or adequate training, development, time and institutional support, feeling alone, overwhelmed and stressed, and being intimidated by university policies and procedures (Chiappetta-Swanson & Watt, 1999:48; Grossman, 2016; Mackinnon, 2004:399; McNamara, 2014:3). As a consequence, these characteristics are being addressed in various training and accreditation courses focusing on professionalism, standards, supervision for the supervisor and ensuring effective performance outcomes for students (Armstrong, Allinson & Hayes, 2004:45; Kam, 1997:83-85; Lizzio & Wilson, 2004:471-475).

Most researchers agree that the supervisor-student relationship is the most important factor influencing the quality and timeous completion of students' research projects (Halse & Bansel, 2012:378; Sonn, 2016:226-241; Waghid, 2015:7; Wright, Murray & Geale, 2007:459). The description of this relationship and its quality varies, depending on the researcher's philosophical and academic focus. For some, the optimal relationship is framed as a socially constructed collaborative partnership between supervisors, students and other members of the academic community, based on their lived experiences (Armstrong, 2004:561; Ferris, 2002:186; 2003:377). For others, supervision is seen as constituting a learning alliance between multiple institutional agents or stakeholders (Van Biljon & De Villiers, 2013:1) grounded in a relational ethic of mutual responsibility (Halse & Bansel, 2012:381). Also, the relationship is seen as being embedded in the compatibility between student and supervisor (Armstrong, Allinson & Hayes, 2004:45). The preferred characteristics of supervisors are listed as cognitive (understanding, boundary setting), affective (encouragement, warmth, honesty, trust, rapport, empathy) and behavioural (collaboration, support) academic (commitment, expectations of the work and its outcomes) and ethical (Chikte & Chabilall, 2016; Lepp et al., 2010:5; Mackinnon, 2004:399-403). Supervision is also seen as a dynamic relationship because of the academic research supervisors' professional identity changes in the eyes of the student during the research project (Haamer, Lepp & Reva, 2012:112). An ineffective academic supervision relationship is characterised by personality differences and clashes, a lack of guidance and direction in structuring, planning, organising and time scaling, and a situation where the academic research supervisors' knowledge and interests do not match the research topic (Adler & Adler, 2005:12; Aguinis & Nesler, 1996:267).

From an organisational psychology stance, the academic supervision relationship is seen as comprising two roles. According to Grant (2003:177) and implied by Chikte and Chabilall (2016), the academic research supervisor assumes the role of the senior partner with the credentials of relevant qualifications, often professional registration, subject knowledge and experience in teaching and research. In terms of personality, academic research supervisors should preferably be sensitively aware of their own intellectual, functional and subjective motivations (Hockey, 1996:493) and be able to give support, show enthusiasm, facilitate quality, innovate, integrate, direct, coordinate, guide and mentor students as future researchers (Chikte & Chabilall, 2016:60-65; Wright et al., 2007:461). In their managerial role, academic research supervisors need to define the task of supervision according to the situation and the students' needs (Kam, 1997:85-89; Lee, 2012:38) and focus on structuring and controlling the training and development of the students' competencies (Wright et al., 2007:467). Students assume the role of the junior partner which is described as receiving encouragement towards academic freedom in their exploration of knowledge (Hockey, 1996:493-499).

Almost all research on the academic research supervisors' role focuses on conscious behaviour from a behaviouristic, humanistic, social and positive psychology perspective and using quantitative research (Mmako & Schultz, 2016). For example, Govender and Ramroop (2013) found that supervisors' perception of organisational climate influences their perception of the quality of the supervision. Still, within these perspectives, interesting qualitative research showed how the use of narrative enquiry (through listening and responding to one another's stories) enhances supervisors' self-belief, resourcefulness and interpersonal support, all contributing to become better academics (Pithouse-Morgan, Masinga, Naicker, Hlao & Pillay, 2016:224-244). Van Laren, Pithouse-Morgan, Chisanga, Harrison, Meyiwa, Muthukrishna, Naicker and Singh (2014:1) used metaphor drawings and imaging towards understanding and optimising the supervision role. Coldwell, Papageorgiou, Callaghan and Fried (2016:80-105) provided evidence of the communality of role experiences amongst South African and Swedish academic supervisors in terms of the nature of the helping relationship, academic citizenship and experiences of well-being.

Hardly any research could be found on and little is known about how the role is experienced unconsciously and how it affects the academic research supervisor. Some studies refer to depth psychology constructs but without directly studying unconscious role behaviour. For example, Damonse and Nkomo (2012) referred to the role of leadership amongst academic research supervisors and showed how academic role modelling serves as a positive influencer in the intellectual development of researchers. Mackinnon (2004:395-400) and Wright et al. (2007:458) refer to role complexity, Aguinis and Nesler (1996:267-280) to power, and Hammer et al. (2012:110) to how the academic research supervisors' professional identity changes in the eyes of the student during the research project. All of these studies argue that as long as the unconscious behaviour remains unknown, it will influence the relationship mostly negatively and possibly even destructively. In his impressive narrative on doctorate supervision Waghid (2015:15-27) describes his own journey as a student and promoter. This is based on the philosophy of education and specifically, democratic education theory focussing on amongst others the individualisation of knowledge, socialisation into the doctorate study and pragmatism leading to doctorate work as a manifestation of a creative consensus through establishing a democratic encounter aimed as scholarly and intellectual growth (Waghid, 2015:62-67). In this vein, the role of the supervisor is seen as establishing a socially just democratic encounter consisting of rationality, attention to emotions, attachment, compassion, friendship (to love in view of knowledge), inclusivity, responsibility and hope. Although not specifically referring to or interpreting unconscious behavioural dynamics, Waghid (2015:15-27) refers to concepts such as attachment, implying using the self as a psychological instrument and taking on an object relations position.

The present research links with the above and further focuses on the unconscious role behaviour of the academic research supervisor while using systems psychodynamics as a theoretical container (Sievers, 2009:87). Various authors have confirmed the gravitas of this stance to provide an understanding of systemic unconscious role behaviour from a depth psychology perspective and to translate that into action in order to move the system along towards self-insight and higher levels of productivity (Czander 1993:18; Diamond & Allcorn, 2009:1-9; Kets de Vries, Korotov & Florent-Treacy, 2007:3-13).

Systems Psychodynamics

Systems psychodynamics (SP) is theoretically informed by Freudian social and systemic psychoanalysis, family psychology, group and object relations, and systems thinking (Colman & Bexton, 1975:1-43; Colman & Geller, 1985:1-127; Cytrynbaum & Noumair, 2004:1-117). SP consists of depth psychology, developmentally focused, psycho-educational organisational theory and an interpretive stance towards the understanding of systemic conscious and unconscious behaviour (Brunner, Nutkevitch & Sher, 2006:3-13; Huffington, Armstrong, Halton, Hoyle & Pooley, 2004:109; Klein, 2005). Consciousness (the 'tip of the iceberg') refers to rational day-to-day behaviour in the self and human relationships while working on the sophisticated organisational task (López-Corvo, 2003:39-41). Unconsciousness refers to systemic behaviour below the water in the iceberg metaphor and contains the experienced anxiety, irrationality and its defensive structures (Klein, 1997:61-88) while working on the basic assumption task (López-Corvo, 2003:39-41). Anxiety is defined as fear of the future, the experience underlying any systemic experience of intense emotions, mental anguish, anticipation and dread about something unexpected, unpleasant and unwanted, such as the loss of love objects and desired parts of the system's identity (Armstrong & Rustin, 2015:39-48; Curtis, 2015:31-35). Anxiety can be categorised as free-floating (not linked to a specific object), survival (being physically or emotionally threatened), performance (having to execute a task), persecutory (feeling victimised) or paranoid (feeling threatened) (Long, 2006:280-285). Coping with anxiety implies using defence mechanisms (Blackman, 2004:1-16) with the purpose of protection and survival. Defences can be classified as realistic (real danger that needs responding to), neurotic (repression, regression, sublimation, transference), psychotic (splitting, projection, projective identification) and perverse (denial of reality, acting in an entitled manner, displacing objects) (Long, 2008:15-38).

Anxiety serves as the driving force of workplace systemic relatedness and manifests as follows at all systemic levels (Armstrong & Rustin, 2015:151; Huffington et al., 2004:107-118; Cytrynbaum & Noumair, 2004:389): Micro-level: personal anxiety associated with coping with complex emotional factors, task anxiety generated by work; meso-level: role anxiety associated with systemic representation, group anxiety generated by organisational structures manifesting as the basic assumptions of dependence (the need for a perceived strong parental object or saviour), fight/flight (responses towards or away from danger towards survival), pairing (merging with similarity as defence against alienation and loneliness), me-ness (differentiation from the system), and we-ness (relinquishing individuality to merge with groupishness); macro level: existential anxiety associated with organisational survival.

To take up an organisational role is defined as consciously being appointed in a task position, as well as unconsciously managing the complexity where person and institution meet in the exercise of representation of self and other (Campbell & Groenbaek, 2006:13-32). Role consists of the normative, experiential and phenomenal parts (Obholzer & Roberts, 1994:30), and the experienced difference between these represents systemic anxiety (Armstrong & Rustin, 2015:151). The normative contains the conscious, rational and measurable work components. The existential contains the system's introjections defined as unconscious incorporation of external ideas, feelings, attitudes and values into the system's mind and behaviour – the external is taken into the inner self (Klein, 1997:9-11). The phenomenal contains the unconscious projections and projective identifications about competence received from the other, as well as the projections made onto the other. Projection refers to unconscious transferences of the system's own impressions and feelings (often unwanted, disowned, denied, unacceptable, undesired, unrecognised or ambivalent experiences) to external objects or persons. The capacity to attribute certain mental contents from one system to another can alter the behaviour of that system through the identification with the contents, which is referred to as projective identification (French & Vince, 1999:58). The system's valence (disposition) determines the projections it identifies with.

Role identity comprises the following domains: Task is the basic component of role where the primary task contains anxiety, and off-task/anti-task behaviour indicates high levels of free-floating anxiety (Neumann, Kellner & Dawson-Shepherd, 1997:160). Boundaries (e.g. ego, time, task, territory, organisational structure) refer to the either tight or loose permeable space around and between parts of the role system, keeping it safe and contained or causing vulnerability or suspicion (Diamond & Allcorn, 2009:4, 35). Authority refers to the right given to be working on the primary task as a result of rank or office occupancy, to issue commands and to punish violations (Czander, 1993:266-293). Authority is bestowed (in terms of the organigram in the mind) from above (the organisation, leadership), the side (colleagues), below (subordinates) and from within (self-authorisation). Containment refers to holding one's own and others' transformational anxiety as a potential space where thinking can move from elementary to complex (Clarke, Hahn & Hoggett, 2008:141-160; Zinkin, 1989:227-230). Role identity is seen as the integration of the above elements making the system similar to and different from others (Campbell & Groenbaek, 2006:80). Identity manifests in how the system consciously (normatively) and unconsciously (existentially, phenomenally) assumes its role, manages the primary task and the different relevant boundary conditions, authorises itself and others, and contains anxiety towards rational thinking (Sievers, 2009:58-61).

Applied to academic research supervisors, SP can be used to study their role behaviour in terms of contradictory thoughts that generate tensions in the mind and inhibit authenticity, creativity and keep the system in control and in a pleasing mode (Campbell & Huffington, 2008:143-146; Neumann et al., 1997:117-118). Lucey and Rogers (2007:16-25) hypothesised about how the above unconscious power dynamics negatively influence the supervisor-student relationship and inhibit research project progress. Gordon (1995:154-160) studied the unconscious symbolic representation of academic research supervisors to students and reported on how idealised transference leads to positive identification, whereas negative identification may lead to narcissistic injury, resulting in a negative supervision experience. Grant (2003:174-186) and Lepp et al. (2010:1-5) studied how the present supervision behaviour of academic research supervisors is unconsciously impacted by their past experiences. Through regression as defence, they unconsciously allow their own past student-in-supervision feelings of gratitude, frustration, resentment and disappointment to enter into their present role as supervisor. Although previous research provides valuable insights into some psychodynamic behaviour of academic research supervisors, their SP role identity has not yet been studied. It also needs to be mentioned that when research studies the conscious relationship between supervisor and student, the student is normally included as a subject and a person. In this systems psychodynamic research, the student is not studied as a person but as an unconscious object representation in the mind of the supervisor (Armstrong, 2005:1-9). Moreover, the student is one of many such objects, including colleagues and the institution as a whole.

Research Purpose, Question, Aim and Contribution

The purpose of this study was to extend academia's understanding of the systems psychodynamic role identity of academic research supervisors. The aim of the research was to study and describe the systems psychodynamic role identity of a group of academic research supervisors. The contribution of the research lies in the explication of how academic research supervisors are unconsciously taking up their role and how that can assist in the understanding of what they bring to their role, what they project onto and into the other (students, colleagues, management) and what systemic behaviours are projected onto and into them.

Methodology

In this study, systems psychodynamics served as the disciplinary relationship (Huffington et al., 2004:11-27). Qualitative research in the psychosocial tradition (Clarke & Hoggett, 2009:1-22) was chosen to describe the lived experiences of the researched (Leavy, 2014:30). Hermeneutic phenomenology was chosen as the interpretive stance defined as the interpretation of text-based the epistemological assumption that empathetic listening allows for deep understanding of shared experiences (Alvesson & Sköldberg, 2010:91-140). The study allowed for an in-depth description of the academic research supervisors' unconscious behaviour when working in role as a contemporary and real-life experience in a bounded system (Clarke & Hoggett, 2009:1-22).

The research was set in a large South African university where the researcher was a staff member. He assumed the role of participant-observer using the self as the research tool or instrument (Clarke & Hoggett, 2009:145-163).

Sampling was convenient and purposive (Wagner, Kawulich & Garner, 2012:86-99) and included 11 academics (average age of 48, four women, seven men) with between seven and 16 years of master's and doctoral supervision experience in three colleges at the University (Economic and Management Sciences, Humanities, Education).

Congruent to the behavioural assumptions of SP and the hermeneutic lenses, data gathering was conducted by means of a 90-minute socio-analytic interview (Long, 2013:91-104). This is defined as a qualitative in-depth interview operating according to an existential and phenomenological approach to uncover, understand and hypothesise about thoughts and feelings related to unconscious systemic processes and dynamics that support, obscure and influence experiences. The planning and execution of the interview entailed putting mechanistic boundaries in place (preparation, room setup, note-taking, ethics) as well as dynamically ensuring a safe contained space. The interview consisted of the introduction (explaining purpose, conditions and participant consent), the questions and the review of the conversation. The opening question was framed as follows: 'The primary task of the interview is to explore your experiences of taking up the role as an academic research supervisor at this university. Where would you like to start?' The interviewer's responses include observation, active listening, clarifying, challenging, empathising, encouraging free association and note-taking. The participant is provided with the space to 'think the unknown known' and to access the unconscious infinite (López-Corvo, 2003:301). The interviews were tape-recorded and transcribed.

Data analysis consisted of systems psychodynamic role analysis incorporating the following hermeneutic steps (Alvesson & Sköldberg, 2010:91-105):

1. studying the text for understanding and the discovery of themes, patterns, trends, narratives and critical incidents;

2. identifying the systems psychodynamic behaviours with the focus on role behaviour; and

3. interpreting role experiences differentiated as normative, existential and phenomenal (Obholzer & Roberts, 1994:30).

Data interpretation took the hermeneutic circle into account (Alvesson & Sköldberg, 2010:105) where each unique individual experience was considered in relation to its meaning in the collective, which again could only be understood in respect of its constituent parts.

Scientific rigour and trustworthiness were ensured as follows (Graneheim & Lundman, 2004:105-108). Dependability was ensured in the process of enquiry and the rigour applied in the planning and execution of the research project. Credibility was ensured through a relatively intense research engagement and the authorised involvement of all parties (Hirschhorn, 1997:2-13). Because of his own involvement in supervision and working with colleagues, the researcher was especially aware of the insider-outsider dialogue in his mind and consequently tried to stay true to the voices of the researched while at the same time trying to answer the research question (Terre Blanche, Durrheim & Painter, 2006:399). Internal generalisability and conformability were attended to by having an independent psychologist (practising in SP) scrutinise the interpretation. She declared the research dependable and agreed on its richness (Hollway & Jefferson, 2010:26-38). The thick and detailed data description of the experiences served the purpose of transferring the meaning to different and yet similar contexts. Conformability was established through the author's attempts to examine the product to attest that the findings, interpretations and recommendations were supported by the theoretical data. Ethicality referred to informed consent and anonymity negotiated with all participants during the data-gathering phase (De Vos, Strydom, Fouché & Delport, 2002:65-66).

The findings are presented for the three conscious and unconscious role parts. The discussion explicates the manifested individual, social and system domain defences, and concludes with the integrated role identity. Lastly, the limitations and recommendations are formulated.

Findings

The manifesting normative (conscious), existential and phenomenal (unconscious) role behaviour was as follows:

Normative Role

Participants described the academic research supervisor role with reference to the university policies on supervision and explained the role and its relevant procedures, expectations and outcomes clearly and logically. Some had attended training workshops and conferences in academic supervision at various universities. Most participants proudly described their role as of great academic importance to ensure master's and doctoral student throughput, to develop students' research competence and to create and publish knowledge in their subjects. Some referred to supervision as a key performance indicator of senior academics being assessed in their annual performance review.

Existential Role

Participants described their introjections as a conflict between 'wanting to do it well', 'be the best academic supervisor to the student' and 'our subject/ department', versus 'I am often uncertain whether I am doing it right', 'not always knowing the real what and how' of supervision, 'doubting my competence', having 'a fear of failure', 'humiliation' and 'embarrassment in case my student fails'.

Participants' anxiety about their role content related to the process and outcome of supervision. The process was experienced as 'daunting' and 'almost threatening' to 'my self-image' 'in spite of having done my own master's and doctorate' and 'my own publishing record'. The research topics represented an unknown to many participants ('they are all very different', 'you can't know everything about all of them'). The research design represented a threat to their own knowledge and experience ('I often struggle with knowing which method fits the research question', 'although you may know theoretically what to do', 'you don't always cope in practice'). Most participants expressed a longing for structure ('if only we can follow a template' 'to make it controllable'). The research projects' outcome was experienced as anxiety-provoking, especially with regard to the acceptance of the students' dissertation/theses by examiners (before the student hands in 'I know I have to judge the research content' and 'make a decision about the quality and the standard', but 'the criteria are so vague!').

Participants' relationships with their students were described as 'stressful', 'unpredictable', 'sometimes overwhelming', and 'the aspect of my work that puts me off most' ('I am always nervous about a new student', 'I wonder if I will be able to cope with the content', 'design' and 'the communication issues'). They referred to how they 'hate it when a student sends in a chapter' for review, 'let alone a full thesis' (because 'it disrupts my whole life', 'planning' and 'schedule'). They would often procrastinate 'which does not work' – 'you just feel guilty' and 'shameful' for 'not being a good supervisor'. They mentioned their 'intense frustration' when students do not understand the complexity of the research or academic style ('where do you draw the line between my role as supervisor and the students' task to do the research themselves?'). Many participants mentioned that they often 'think that I am not up to this topic' or 'to deal with a student'.

Some participants coped with the situation by 'over-preparing for a student feedback appointment', because 'you do not want to make a mistake' or 'be seen as stupid'. One participant reminded herself of occasions where 'my own issues and nervousness just confused the student more'. Some participants mentioned how their supervision task reminded them of being at school and university – where 'tight time deadlines' and 'performance criteria' were set by the authorities, and 'you just have to sink or swim'. These defences of regression and transference tie in with previous research (Grant, 2003:174; Lepp et al., 2010:1) on how present supervision behaviour is unconsciously impacted by experiences.

Phenomenal Role

Participants experienced projections of competence and incompetence from below (students), from the side (colleagues) and from above (authority figures representing the department, college and university).

From below, the projections of competence onto the participants were about the students' dependence on the supervisor as the authority figure ('sometimes the students want us to do everything for them', 'even rescue them in case their examiners disapprove of their work', 'one student said in the class how glad she was that I am her promoter because I will do the work for her', 'they think I know it all'). Projections of incompetence were as follows: Students projected their anger about their incompetence to cope with the demands of research ('she was very angry at me when she realised that I will not search the references'/'provide the measuring instruments', and 'that I could not arrange her respondents for her'). Students also projected their fears of being confronted with their research incompetence onto the supervisor ('at conferences I see students duck and dive when they see me', 'they often do not answer my e-mails'). The above projections stimulated strong feelings amongst participants ('somehow I like it when they think I know so much', 'I get frustrated when they do not finish in spite of all my efforts to help', 'I get so angry when they do not follow simple rules', 'I wish I could tell them to grow up' yet 'one needs to be careful in what you say' – 'It would be terrible if a student accuses me of wrongdoing and get into more trouble').

From the side, the projections of competence were about support from colleagues ('they tell me that I am a good supervisor', 'they often ask me my opinion about supervision', 'young colleagues have asked to co-supervise with me'). The projections of incompetence were about denigration ('I have been told that I take all the distinction students', 'that I make the students work extra hard', 'when a colleague realised that we will jointly supervise a doctorate student, he retracted saying that then he will have to do all the work and only get half the recognition').

Participants projected onto their colleagues. Projections of competence were about praise ('she is just so good at doing this', 'he helps students to produce far beyond their capacity'). Projections of incompetence were about anger, resentment, competition, rivalry, jealousy and envy ('some colleagues have only one or two students and they do not even finish', 'I have supervised and delivered more students than any of my colleagues', 'he has been here for ages and has never delivered a doctoral student', 'she always complains about struggling with incompetent students', 'some seem to deliver M and D's like a sausage machine', 'everybody is putting her on a pedestal – I don't understand the fuss').

From above, the projections of competence were about assuming the role of a supervisor with knowledge of the subject, intelligence, rationality, responsibility and loyalty to the subject and the university in order to successfully deliver higher degree research projects ('I suppose they trust me to do the job', 'they seem to appreciate what I do', 'my COD always acknowledges me when one of my students graduates'). The projections of incompetence were about doubt and mistrust ('the system doesn't believe that we can do proper/professional supervision', 'we often get asked how many M and D students we have', 'why the students are working so slowly', 'why our throughput is so low', 'whether we can work harder' and 'take on more students', 'they are always checking up on us', 'especially on school and college-level' – 'I had a dream where I lost my job because of this'). For some, the projections of incompetence were about confusion ('I sometimes get confused about what supervision is', 'there are so many side-shows' 'distracting me from doing supervision'); and for others about paranoia ('I don't know who to believe anymore', 'I wonder what they want from me', 'it is as if they watch you make a mistake'). Some participants referred to a combined and conflicting competence/incompetence projection from the institutional authorities ('they use empowerment language like "you know what to do"', but 'the moment there is a hiccup' they 'come down on you like a ton of bricks' – 'supervision has become the stick to hit us with').

Discussion

The aim of this research was to study and describe the systems psychodynamic role identity of a group of postgraduate research supervisors.

In their normative role, the academic research supervisors in this study gave convincing evidence of consciously and intellectually understanding the role boundaries of research supervision within academia. It was interpreted that they took up their sophisticated task with consciously managed authority (Cytrynbaum & Noumair, 2004:43-45) from above (management) and from below (students), based on their training and experience in their academic role.

The significant differences in the content of their conscious (normative) and unconscious (existential/phenomenal) role parts illustrated a high level of free-floating anxiety (Armstrong & Rustin, 2015:144). This was interpreted as a conflict between their intellectual understanding of the work content and their emotional coping with the complexity of managing the self in the role and coping with the other in the system (Obholzer & Roberts, 1994:30).

In their existential role, academic research supervisors experienced high levels of performance anxiety where their good intent and a realistic sense of own competence were in conflict with their self-doubt and fear of failure. They struggled to differentiate between their own competence and the success of the student. They over-identified with and personalised their supervision role, which led to taking the outcome as a personal success or failure. The failure often resulted in experiencing guilt and shame (Mollon, 2004). Even the variety of research topics, designs and methods were turned into an internal fight about competence and a compulsive need for over-structure to contain their anxiety. The outcome of their students' examination became a test of their own psychological coping. These intra-personal behaviours had a negative effect on their relationships with their students. Their high levels of performance anxiety led to a compulsive avoidance of the bad object (e.g. the irritating student) (Klein, 1997:3). The academic research supervisors introjected an exaggerated (almost dramatising – Blackman, 2004:71) position of not being good enough in the role (Klein, 1997:61-68). Although the above could relate to previous research (Lucey & Rogers, 2007:16) on how unconscious power dynamics negatively influence the supervisor-student relationship, the present findings did not measure if and how research project progress is influenced.

In their phenomenal role, the academic research supervisors received projections of competence when they pleased the needs of the other and of incompetence when they stood up for academic and ethical principles different from the others' needs. This was interpreted as the system using the academic research supervisor as an object to have its personal needs met, while it disregards the academic research supervisor as a subject with its humanity, honesty and scientific principles and drive. Most of the academic research supervisors in this research found it difficult to not identify with the projections (Cytrynbaum & Noumair 2004:35-36). This manifested as irritation, frustration, anger and fear of failure. On a larger systemic level, it was interpreted that the university system used the academic research supervisors to contain these negative feelings on its behalf (Cytrynbaum & Noumair, 2004:62; Stapley, 2006:34-39). In terms of projections from students, these findings relate to the research by Akala & Backhouse (2015). Although they did not interpret unconscious dynamics their findings suggest the powerful effect of students' gossiping on supervisors.

Unconsciously, the academic research supervisors experienced conflict about whether they are competent and good enough to assume the role. The role seems to contain free-floating, survival, performance, paranoid and persecutory anxiety, which they defended against by using various primitive and sophisticated defensive structures – splitting (the good self from the bad other), regression into childlike behaviour, denial of their qualifications, experience and evidence of their competence, suppression of their aggression towards students, colleagues and management, projection of their fears onto colleagues and rationalisation of the seriousness of not feeling competent to do their work. These experiences are congruent with what the SP literature describes as symptomatic of being under intense emotional pressure in systems working on the primary task of securing specialised excellence (Czander, 1993:294-308), and in this instance, in the academic system domain (Bain, 1998:413).

In terms of basic assumption behaviour, the academic research supervisors expressed their 'longing' dependence on an understanding and parental supportive university leadership system. In its absence, they expressed their counter-dependence by offloading their anger onto and blaming the university system for their difficult situation. They tried to pair with colleagues in similar situations and formed cliques, which for some, became a support group (Cytrynbaum & Noumair, 2004:143). Their fight responses indicated their anxiety about failing and ways to establish a clean record and track record (Stapley; 2006:210) and their flight responses manifested as a wish to avoid difficult students, to do more graduate and honours teaching and to leave academia. We-ness manifested in how they referred to themselves in the plural (indicating the fantasy that many colleagues experience the same and are united in doing so) (Cytrynbaum & Noumair, 2004:361). Me-ness manifested mostly when they received 'positive' projections about competence and excellence. The above was interpreted as evidence of the academic research supervisors' high levels of free-floating, performance and paranoid anxiety in performing their task and staying in the role (Clarke, Hahn & Hoggett, 2008:166-176).

Furthermore, the academic research supervisors experienced conflict between being competent and incompetent at the same time, using their own sense of good enough academic decision making and relationship management versus what the other expects and projects onto them (Czander, 1993:274-275). Their primary task of supervising the work of their designated individual students was under attack by their introjections of not being good enough for this 'prestigious role' and the incapacitating projections of incompetence onto their role. Some of them illustrated off-task behaviour by worrying about their performance, procrastinating and spending time on checking students' spelling and references. Two academic research supervisors, who described themselves as 'having been doing this for a long time', reported on their boredom, which was interpreted as the defence against seeing the opportunities of excitement and novelty in each task or project (Armstrong & Rustin, 2015:70-87). The academic research supervisors' time and ego boundaries were under attack, which caused them performance and survival anxiety. They experienced being de-authorised by the system in various ways – personally, technically, academically and managerially (Cytrynbaum & Noumair, 2004:153-154). The above was interpreted as follows: Academic research supervisors' high level of internal (introjected) and relational (projected) conflict caused high levels of free-floating, performance and paranoid anxiety, which manifested in spells of off-task behaviour, role confusion, difficulty in managing the boundaries of self, time and task, and feeling de-authorised by others using them as containers of their issues.

Using SP guidelines (Armstrong & Rustin, 2015:300-314), the academic research supervisors' experience of survival, performance and paranoid anxiety can be seen as suspiciously intense. Although anxiety amongst individual supervisors is to be expected, the concern is about its collective intensity leading to such a strong position (Campbell & Huffington, 2008, 80-83) of not being good enough (Klein, 1997:268-274) in role (in spite of qualifications, experience, publication records and status in academia). It was hypothesised that these anxiety experiences were projections from the larger university system onto and into (Huffington et al., 2004:67-82) its academic research supervisors, based on the following argument: As a macro-system, the university's primary task and normative role is about (economic and financial) survival, performance (of staff and students) and sustainability (Diamond & Allcorn, 2009:13-91). Its unconscious task is to act as a container, holding potential space for its staff and students as clients (Clarke, Hahn & Hoggett, 2008:185-193) to assume (in this case) their academic and supervision roles towards the transformation of the system-as-a-whole (Armstrong, 2005:1-9). Although not directly studied in this research, the participants implied that the large university system expressed anxiety about their performance and its effect on the institution's 'financial bottom line'. Therefore, the present findings suggest that the academic research supervisors' intense anxiety in their phenomenal role about containing a primary task that does not fit their organisational level, does not belong to them, but that it is the larger system's uncontained anxiety being projected. The academic research supervisors as the target of the projection are significant in that their primary task is to secure higher degree throughput, implying large government subsidies. It needs to be mentioned here that projections are seen as unconsciously based on trust towards the receiver to preserve the precious projected material and possibly even transform this before it can be owned again (Cytrynbaum & Noumair, 2004:173-174). It is therefore interpreted that through projective identification, the academic research supervisors were used by university leadership to (in addition to their normative and existential roles) carry and process the extremely important large system (university) anxiety about survival, performance and sustainability on behalf of the institution.

In their study of the conscious behaviour of academics Pihouse-Morgan et al. (2016) suggested that collegial relationships are critical to the growth of self-belief and self-resourcefulness in becoming and being academics. The above findings suggest that the well-intended conscious functioning and assumed self-reliance could be eroded by unconscious projective attacks by the larger system.

Conclusion

The systems psychodynamic role identity of academic research supervisors can be characterised as follows: Consciously, they seem to be clear about their roles and they cope with its rational demands by applying their intelligence and relevant training. Unconsciously, they experience different kinds and intensities of anxiety. These refer to their introjected incompetence and not-good-enough-position which has a negative effect on their relationships with their students. Furthermore, they receive conflicting projections – about competence when it serves the other and about incompetence where the other projects their unwanted anxieties onto and into the academic research supervisors.

The implication of these findings can be framed as follows. It is clear that academic supervision creates strong (unconscious) anxiety amongst supervisors that are not addressed or processed in the day-to-day execution of the work towards catharsis and understanding of what this says about themselves (their introjections) or where it could possibly come from (their received projections), they become stuck in a system domain position of acting as containers of the larger university's projected anxiety as well as what students and colleagues unconsciously represent for them as objects. It can be hypothesised that this scenario keeps supervisors trapped in irrational and impersonal object relations with their students, colleagues and the university as a system.

Limitations

The sample in this study was from one institution with its limiting broader application.

Hopefully the findings can be transferred to similar institutions – which the readers will have to decide on. The researcher, as an academic and involved in academic research supervision, had to guard against being seduced out of the researcher role. The inputs from the independent psychologist (see above) and the rationality of the SP stance hopefully provided sufficiently effective containers for interpretation purposes. It could also be argued that the supervisors' students needed to be included in this research project, to which the SP stance would comment as follows. The students, colleagues, management and the institution mentioned by the academic supervisors are studied in their unconscious object representation and not as subjects (people or individuals).

Recommendations

For this and similar universities, it was recommended that leadership reflect on the findings in a facilitated session to ensure their understanding of and insight into the unconscious dynamics. The outcome of such a session could be for leadership to introspect on their own survival anxiety as an institution, and to own that in the differentiation of what research supervisors' roles hold. Thus, leadership will be assisted in taking back their projections from the academic research supervisors as containers of larger systemic anxiety which will hopefully facilitate insight into the larger systemic dynamics belonging to the senior institutional roles.

For academic research supervisors, it was recommended that systems psychodynamic experiential sessions be incorporated in their continuous training to facilitate awareness of how they are unconsciously impacted by the other objects-in-the-mind (students, colleagues, management) and vice versa. These sessions can focus on how the individual supervisor takes up the unconscious part of the role while they are encouraged to explore (1) the origin of their introjections as unconscious patterns which have developed in childhood and are presently manifesting as repetition compulsions and transferences, and (2) the nature of their received projections and their valence to act on specific kinds of projections which they contain (as 'dumping grounds') on behalf of the system, which also represents their own authority and sibling objects. In exploring and processing these unconscious experiences the supervisors can see themselves, their students and the university system less as irrational unconscious objects and more as realistic subjects in need of forming authentic relationships with. It was hypothesised that this 'new' position would avail the supervisor as more objective and rational facilitators of learning to their students and the university.

It was also recommended that more research be conducted on the academic research supervisors' role as an SP object to ascertain its unconscious representation in a university as a complex organisational system. It is suggested that the role has become pivotal in ensuring systemic survival and that it may have developed a valence for containing systemic anxiety relating to rivalry, competition and envy.

References

Adler, P.A. & Adler, P. (2005). The identity career of the graduate student: Professional socialisation to academic sociology. *The American Sociologist*, 36(2):11-17. https://doi.org/10.1007/s12108-005-1002-4

Aguinis, H. & Nesler, M.S. (1996). Power bases of faculty supervisors and educational outcomes. *Journal of Higher Education*, 67(3):267-297. https://doi.org/10.1080/00221546.1996.11780261

Akala, B. & Backhouse, J. (2015). They can't even agree! Student conversations about their supervisors in constructing understanding of the PhD. *South African Journal of Higher Education*, 29(4). https://doi.org/10.20853/29-4-507

Alvesson, M. & Sköldberg, K. (2010). *Reflexive methodology: New vistas for qualitative research*. London: Sage.

Armstrong, D. (2005). *Organisation in the mind: Psychoanalysis, group relations and organisational consultancy*. London: Karnac.

Armstrong, D. & M. Rustin. (2015). *Social defences against anxiety: Explorations in a paradigm*. London: Karnac.

Armstrong, S.J. (2004). The impact of supervisors' cognitive styles on the quality of research supervision in management education. *British Journal of Educational Psychology*, 74(4):599-617. https://doi.org/10.1348/0007099042376436

Armstrong, S.J.; Allinson, C.W. & Hayes, J. (2004). The effects of cognitive style on research supervision: A study of student-supervisor dyads in management education. *Academy of Management Learning and Education*, 3(1):41-63. https://doi.org/10.5465/amle.2004.12436818

Bain, A. (1998). *Social defences against organisational learning. Human Relations*, 51(3):413-429. https://doi.org/10.1177/001872679805100309

Blackman, J.S. (2004). *101 Defences: How the mind shields itself*. New York: Brunner-Routledge. https://doi.org/10.4324/9780203492369

Brunner, L.D.; Nutkevitch, A. & Sher, M. (2006). *Group relations conferences: Reviewing and exploring theory, design, role-taking and application*. London: Karnac.

Campbell, D. & Groenbaek, M. (2006). *Taking positions in the organisation*. London: Karnac.

Campbell, D. & Huffington, C. (2008). *Organisations connected: A handbook of systemic consultation*. London: Karnac.

Chiappetta-Swanson, C. & Watt, S. (1999). *Good practice in the supervision and mentoring of postgraduate students: It takes an academy to raise a scholar*. New York: McMaster University.

Chikte, U.M.E. & Chabilall, J.A. (2016). Exploration of supervisors and student experiences during master's students in a health science faculty. *South African Journal of Higher Education*, 30(1):57-79. https://doi.org/10.20853/30-1-559

Clarke, S.; Hahn, H. & Hoggett, P. (2008). *Object relations and social relations: The implications of the relational turn in psychoanalysis*. London: Karnac.

Clarke, S. & Hoggett, P. (2009). *Researching beneath the surface: Psycho-social research methods in practice*. London: Karnac.

Coldwell, D.; Papageorgiou, E; Callaghan, C. & Fried, A. (2016). Academic citizenship and wellbeing: An exploratory cross-cultural study of South African and Swedish academic perceptions. *South African Journal of Higher Education*, 30(1):80-105. https://doi.org/10.20853/30-1-555

Colman, A.D. & Bexton, W.H. (1975). *Group relations reader 1.* Jupiter, FL: A.K. Rice Institute.

Colman, A.D. & Geller, M.H. (1985). *Group relations reader 2.* Jupiter, Fl: A.K. Rice Institute.

Conrad, C.F.; Duren, J. & Haworth, J.G. (2002). Student's perspectives on their master's degree experiences: Disturbing the conventional wisdom. *New Directions in Higher Education*, 101:65-76. https://doi.org/10.1002/he.10106

Curtis, H. (2015). *Everyday life and the unconscious mind: An introduction to psychoanalytic concepts.* London: Karnac.

Cytrynbaum, S. & Noumair, A. (2004). *Group dynamics, organisational irrationality, and social complexity: Group relations reader 3.* Jupiter, FL: A.K. Rice Institute.

Czander, W.M. (1993). The psychodynamics of work and organisations. New York: Guilford.

Damonse, B. & Nkomo, M. (2012). Leading fromm the front: Exploring the professional and personal nature of research leadership. *South African Journal of Higher Education*, 26(3).

De Vos, A.S.; Strydom, H.; Fouche, C.B. & Delport, C.S.L. (2002). *Research at grass roots: For the social sciences and human service professions.* Pretoria: Van Schaik.

Denholm, C.T. & Evans, T. (2007). *Supervising doctorates down under.* Camberwell, Australia: ACER.

Diamond, M.A. & Allcorn, S. (2009.) *Private selves in public organisations: The psychodynamics of organisational diagnosis and change.* New York: Palgrave Macmillan.

Emilsson, U.M. & Johnsson, E. (2007). Supervision of supervisors: On developing supervision in postgraduate education. *Higher Education Research and Development*, 26(2):163-179. https://doi.org/10.1080/07294360701310797

Ferris, W.P. (2002). Students as junior partners, professors as senior partners, the B-school as the firm: A new model for collegiate business education. *Academy of Management Leading and Education*, 1(2):185-193. https://doi.org/10.5465/amle.2002.8509373

Ferris, W.P. (2003). Why the partnership model's usefulness far exceeds that of the client model: *Reply to Armstrong. Academy of Management Learning and Education*, 2(4):375-377. https://doi.org/10.5465/amle.2003.11901966

French, R. & Vince, R. (1999). *Group relations, management and organisation.* Oxford: Oxford University Press.

Gordon, P.J. (2003). Advising to avoid or to cope with dissertation hang-ups. *Academy of Management Learning and Education*, 2(2):181-187. https://doi.org/10.5465/amle.2003.9901674

Gordon, R.M. (1995). The symbolic nature of the supervising relationship: Identification and professional growth. *Issues in Psychoanalytic Psychology*, 17(2):154-166.

Govender, K.K. & Ramroop, S. (2013). The relationship between the postgraduate research climate, role clarity and research service quality: exploring the supervisors' and students' perceptions. *South African Journal of Higher Education,* 27(1). https://doi.org/10.20853/27-1-231

Graneheim, U.H. & Lundman, B. (2004). Qualitative content analysis in nursing research: Concepts, procedures and measures to achieve trustworthiness. *Nurse Education Today,* 24:105-112. https://doi.org/10.1016/j.nedt.2003.10.001

Grant, B. (2003). *Mapping the pleasures and risks of supervision. Discourse: Studies in the Cultural Politics of Education,* 24(2):174-190. https://doi.org/10.1080/01596300303042

Green, B. & A. Lee. (1995). Theorising postgraduate pedagogy. *Australian Universities Review,* 38:40-45.

Grossman E.S. (2016). 'My supervisor is so busy ...'. Informal spaces for postgraduate learning in the health sciences. *South African Journal of Higher Education,* 30(2):94-109. https://doi.org/10.20853/30-2-643

Haamer, A.; Lepp, L. & Reva, E. (2012). The dynamics of professional identity of university teachers: Reflecting on the ideal university teacher. *Studies for the Learning Society,* 2(2-3):110-120. https://doi.org/10.2478/v10240-012-0010-5

Halse, C. & Bansel, P. (2012). The learning alliance: Ethics in doctoral supervision. *Oxford Review of Education,* 38(4):377-392. https://doi.org/10.1080/03054985.2012.706219

Hirschhorn, L. (1997). *Reworking authority: Leading and following in the post-modern organisation.* London: MIT.

Hockey, J. (1996). Motives and meaning amongst PhD supervisors in the social sciences. *British Journal of Sociology of Education,* 17(4):489-506. https://doi.org/10.1080/0142569960170405

Hollway, W. & Jefferson, T. (2010). *Doing qualitative research differently: Free association, narrative and the interview method.* Los Angeles: Sage.

Huffington, C.; Armstrong, D.; Halton, W.; Hoyle, L. & Pooley, J. (2004). *Working below the surface: The emotional life of contemporary organisations.* London: Karnac.

Kam, B.H. (1997). Style and quality in research supervision: The supervisor dependency focus. *Higher Education,* 34(1):81-103. https://doi.org/10.1023/A:1002946922952

Kets de Vries, M.F.R.; Korotov, K. & Florent-Treacy, E. (2007). *Coach and couch: The psychology of making better leaders.* London: Palgrave.

Klein, L. (2005). *Working across the gap: The practice of social science in organisations.* London: Karnac.

Klein, M. (1997). *Envy and gratitude and other works 1946-1963.* London: Vintage.

Leavy, P. (2014). *The Oxford handbook of qualitative research. Oxford: Oxford University Press.* https://doi.org/10.1093/oxfordhb/9780199811755.001.0001

Lee, A. (2012). *Successful research supervision: Advising students doing research.* London: Routledge. https://doi.org/10.4324/9780203816844

Lepp,L.; Remmik, M.; Leijen, A. & Karm, M. (2010). *Through hardships to the stars: Experiences of doctoral thesis supervisors about their doctoral studies and connections with their supervising practice.* http://eha.ut.ee/wp-content [Accessed 20 January 2016].

Lizzio, A. & Wilson. K. (2004). Action learning in higher education: An investigation of its potential to develop professional capability. *Studies in Higher Education*, 4:469-488. https://doi.org/10.1080/0307507042000236371

Long, S. (2006). Organisational defences against anxiety: What has happened since the 1995 Jaques paper? *International Journal of Applied Psychoanalytic Studies*, 3(4):279-295. https://doi.org/10.1002/aps.111

Long, S. (2008). *The perverse organisation and its deadly sins.* London: Karnac.

Long, S. (2013). *Socio-analytic methods: Discovering the hidden in organisations and social systems.* London: Karnac. https://doi.org/10.1039/c3ay40783g

López-Corvo, R.E. (2003). *The dictionary of the work of W.R. Bion.* London: Karnac.

Lucey, H. & Rogers, C. (2007). Power and the unconscious in doctoral-supervisor relationships. In: V. Gillies (ed.), *Institutional is political*, pp.16-36. London: Palgrave Macmillan. https://doi.org/10.1057/9780230287013_2

Mackinnon, J. (2004). Academic supervision: Seeking metaphors and models for quality. *Journal of Further and Higher Education*, 28(4):395-405. https://doi.org/10.1080/0309877042000298876

Marcketti, S.B.; Mhango, M.W. & Gregoire, M.B. (2006). The experiences of African graduate students in a College of Human Sciences. *Journal of Family and Consumer Sciences Education*, 24(1):63-72.

McNamara, C. (2014). *Typical experiences of a first-time supervisor. Online integrated library for personal, professional and organisational development.* http://www.academic.supervisors [Accessed 16 December 2014].

Mmako, M. & Schultz, C. (2016). An employee engagement framework for technical vocational education and training colleges in South Africa. *South African Journal of Higher Education*, 30(2):143-163. https://doi.org/10.20853/30-2-606

Mollon, P. (2004). *Shame and jealousy: The hidden turmoils.* London: Karnac.

Murphy, E. & Coleman, E. (2004). Graduate students' experiences of challenges in online asynchronous discussions. *Canadian Journal of Learning and Technology*, 30(2):1-9. https://doi.org/10.21432/T27G7N

Neumann, J.E.; Kellner, K. & Dawson-Shepherd, A. (1997). *Developing organisational consultancy.* London: Routledge.

Obholzer, A. & Roberts, V.Z. (1994). *The unconscious at work.* London: Routledge.

Oost, H. & Sonneveld, H. (2007). *Selected readings on PhD supervision.* Amsterdam: Netherlands Centre for Research Schools and Graduate Schools.

Petersen, E.B. (2014). Re-signifying subjectivity? A narrative exploration of 'non-traditional' doctoral students' experience of subjective formation through two Australian cases. *Studies in Higher Education*, 39(5):823-834. https://doi.org/10.1080/03075079.2012.745337

Pithouse-Morgan, K.; Masinga, L.; Naicker, I.; Hlao, T. & Pillay, D. (2016). Sink or swim?: Learning from stories of becoming academics within a transforming university terrain. *South African Journal of Higher Education*, 30(1):224-244. https://doi.org/10.20853/30-1-561

Popov, O. (2009). Teacher's and student's experiences of simultaneous teaching in an international distance and on-campus master's programme in engineering. *International Review of Research in Open and Distance Learning*, 10(3):1-8. https://doi.org/10.19173/irrodl.v10i3.669

Sievers, B. (2009). *Psychoanalytic studies of organisations. Contributions from the International Society for the Psychoanalytical Study of Organisations (ISPSO)*. London: Karnac.

Sonn, R.(2016). The challenge for a historically disadvantaged South African university to produce more postgraduate students. *South African Journal of Higher Education*, 30(2):226-241. https://doi.org/10.20853/30-2-601

Stapley, L.F. (2006). *Individuals, groups and organisations beneath the surface*. London: Karnac.

Terre Blanche, M.; Durrheim, K. & Painter, D. (2006). *Research in practice: Applied methods for the social sciences*. Cape Town: UCT Press.

Trafford, V. & Leshem, S. (2010). *Stepping stones to achieving your doctorate: Focusing on your viva from the start*. Maidenhead, UK: Open University Press.

Van Biljon, J.A. & De Villiers, M.R. (2013). Multiplicity in supervision models: The supervisor's perspective. *South African Journal of Higher Education*, 27(6). https://doi.org/10.20853/27-6-307

Van Laren, L.; Pithouse-Morgan, K.; Chisanga, T.; Harrison, L.; Meyiwa, T.; Muthukrishna, N.; Naicker, I. & Singh, L. (2014). Walking our talk: Exploring supervision of postgraduate self-study research through metaphor drawing. *South African Journal of Higher Education*, 28(2). https://doi.org/10.20853/28-2-346

Waghid, Y. (2015). *Dancing with doctoral encounters. Democratic education in motion*. Stellenbosch: African Sun Media. https://doi.org/10.18820/9781920689490

Wagner, C.; Kawulich, B. & Garner, M. (2012). *Doing social research: A global context*. London: McGraw-Hill.

White, N.W. (2007). *The customer is always right? Student discourse about higher education in Australia. High Education*, 54:593-604. https://doi.org/10.1007/s10734-006-9012-x

Wright, A.; Murray, J.P. & Geale, P. (2007). *A phenomenographic study of what it means to supervise doctoral students. Academy of Management Learning and Education*, 6(4):458-474. https://doi.org/10.5465/amle.2007.27694946

Zinkin, L. (1989). The group as container and contained. *Group Analysis*, 22:227-234. https://doi.org/10.1007/BF01473155

Article 4

The Psychological Well-Being Manifesting Amongst Master's Students in Industrial and Organisational Psychology[1]

F Cilliers & A Flotman

Orientation

Psychological well-being amongst master's students is seen as a contributing factor towards having a meaningful, enjoyable and productive experience as a student.

Research Purpose

The purpose of this study was to provide a qualitative description of the psychological well-being experiences of first-year students in a part-time coursework master's degree in Industrial and Organisational Psychology (IOP) in order to foster an empathetic understanding of their experiences.

Motivation for the Study

The understanding of their master's students' psychological well-being experiences will assist university IOP departments in facilitating the appropriate psychological containment to students and the optimisation of their resilience towards meaningfully completing their first year and perhaps also their master's degree.

1   Cilliers, F. & Flotman, A.P. (2016). The psychological well-being manifesting amongst master's students in industrial and organisational psychology. *SA Journal of Industrial Psychology/SA Tydskrif vir Bedryfsielkunde*, 42(1): a1323. http://doi.org/10.4102/sajip.v42i1.1323

Research Design, Approach and Method

Qualitative research was conducted within a hermeneutic interpretive stance. Data were gathered from a focus group with 10 conveniently chosen participants. Thematic content analysis provided eight themes, which were interpreted and linked to the literature on psychological well-being.

Main Findings

Student distress caused by job demands leads to languishing and feeling overwhelmed. In contrast, student eustress resulting from job resources leads to flourishing, consisting of self-efficacy, locus of control and optimism.

Practical Implications

University IOP departments can use the information towards understanding their master's students' psychological well-being experiences, which could assist in the students' successful and timeous completion of their studies.

Contribution

The study contributes to the literature on master's students' real negative and positive experiences and psychological well-being, which university departments often deny or dismiss as idiosyncratic.

Introduction

Industrial and organisational psychologists often consult to the optimisation of psychological well-being amongst individuals, groups and organisations as their clients. Effective performance in this task requires that psychologists not only know the relevant theory but also illustrate psychological well-being in their professional roles and personal lives (Lowman, 2002). This research studied the psychological well-being of first-year part-time coursework master's degree students in IOP as the platform for their last formal educational endeavour towards learning to consult on psychological well-being.

IOP is the scientific study of human behaviour in the workplace. It applies psychological theories and principles to organisations, towards the optimisation of individual, group and organisational performance (Cummings & Worley, 2015; Van Tonder & Roodt, 2008). According to South African law, an industrial psychologist requires a bachelor's degree, honours, a coursework master's degree and a 12-month internship in IOP. These degrees are all regularly inspected for approval by the Board for Psychology, a division of the Health Professions Council of South Africa (HPCSA). The successful completion of all the above parts leads to the students' professional registration as an industrial psychologist (HPCSA, 2016).

This research focussed on the first-year part-time coursework master's degree in IOP at a large South African university. The selection criteria included full-time employment in an organisation in an IOP role, previous academic performance, numeracy, literacy, personality and other relevant competencies assessed in a structured assessment centre. The degree is presented over three academic years. The first year consists of coursework in five academic modules, namely Career, Organisational and Personnel Psychology, Psychometrics and Psychological Research Methods, as well as a practical module in Personal Growth. In this practical module, students keep track of and process their personal experiences with one another through blogging. Students attend compulsory residential on-campus workshops in all six modules, totalling 18 full days spread over the academic year and presented by 14 staff members who act as facilitators. The students' assignment and examination marks in the modules contribute 50% to the degree mark. The second and third academic years consist of a dissertation of limited scope under the supervision of a designated supervisor and contribute the other 50% to the degree mark.

In the researchers' discussion with the master's programme manager, the following data came to the fore. Whereas most students pass the first year, only 60% complete their dissertation and thus complete the master's degree. This statistic is of concern on many levels. On the macro level, the university authorities are concerned about throughput, especially because of the labour intensity of the degree (a ratio of 14 lecturers to 20 students), which has subsidy implications. On the meso level the lecturing staff, who are also assigned as supervisors for students' dissertations in the first year, do not have the advantage of publishing the research project with the student. On the professional level, the university is not able to deliver the desired number of industrial psychologists to take up their roles in practice. To solve this systemic problem of low throughput and loss of research, publications and professional registration opportunities, the discussion turned to the coping behaviours of the first-year part-time coursework students. These students seem to cope well cognitively – their intellectual competence serves as a selection criterion, they rate the coursework content and the facilitator inputs as cognitively challenging, and they have an above-average pass rate. In contrast, in terms of emotional coping, a recent systems psychodynamic study (Cilliers & Harry, 2012) on students in this specific first-year part-time coursework master's degree programme illustrated their high levels of performance anxiety, emotional exhaustion, introjected emotional and relational incompetence, a sense of not being good enough and therefore pretending to be happy, resilient and coping well to impress their lecturers. The above was interpreted as evidence that students experience their first-year part-time coursework as extremely emotionally demanding in terms of their endurance to stay in the programme, self-efficacy to manage the academic matters and resilience to balance their academic, organisational and personal roles. The researchers and the programme manager agreed on the importance of conducting research to study these matters in order to understand the lived emotional coping experiences of the first-year students.

The purpose of the research was to provide a qualitative description of the psychological well-being of first-year students undertaking a part-time coursework master's degree in IOP, in order to foster an empathetic understanding of their experiences. It is anticipated that the findings may in future serve as an entry into the facilitation of appropriate psychological containment to students and the optimisation of their resilience towards meaningfully completing their first year and eventually their master's degree.

Psychological Well-being

The 21st-century world of work is known for its increasing levels of stress, caused by the demands of the new economy, continuous change, transformation, globalisation, complexity, uncertainty and alienation (Bennis, 2007; Botha & Mostert, 2014). Non-coping with these demands results in negative stress, or distress, manifesting amongst employees as negativity, poor decision-making, emotional alienation, ineffective process and people management, and an increase in autocratic and bureaucratic leadership (Worrall & Cooper, 2014; Youssef & Luthans, 2012). Coping with these demands results in positive stress, or eustress, manifesting as employees' psychological well-being (Weinberg & Cooper, 2007), defined as having a proactive stance towards achieving optimal physical, mental and emotional well-being (Rothmann & Cooper, 2015). This field of study is embedded in positive psychology and a number of recently developed positive organisational models.

Positive psychology is described as the scientific paradigm studying what enables individuals and institutions to flourish by focussing on the expression of potential through positive well-being, positive traits, positive emotions, strengths, virtues and values towards optimal human functioning (Linley, Joseph, Harrington & Wood, 2007; Seligman & Csiksztmihalyi, 2000; Seligman, Steen, Parks & Peterson, 2005; Snyder & Lopez, 2009). As a focus area within positive psychology, positive organisational psychology is defined as the scientific study of positive subjective experiences and traits in the workplace and positive organisations and its application to improve the effectiveness and quality of life in organisations (Donaldson & Ko, 2010). Additionally, positive organisational scholarship and behaviour (Spreitzer & Soneneshein, 2003) are defined as the study and application of positively oriented human resource strengths and psychological capacities that can be measured, developed and effectively managed for performance improvement (French & Holden, 2012; Luthans, 2002b).

Various behavioural models of optimal human functioning in the workplace have been developed in the last 15 years (Rothmann & Cooper, 2015) that collectively describe positive institutional functioning on the individual, team and organisational levels. The effort-reward imbalance model states that imminent or delayed rewards significantly reduce the adverse impact This means that employees would be prepared to make significant sacrifices if they had a perception of possible future reward (Schaufeli & Bakker, 2004; Siegrist, 1996). The demand and control model states that autonomy over tasks and responsibilities safeguards employees from excessive work strain, thereby fulfilling a buffering role (Demerouti & Bakker, 2011; Karasek, 1998). The conservation of resources model offers a general approach to coping, stating that employees are primarily concerned with the maintenance, accumulation and conservation of resources (Hobfoll, 2002; Hobfoll, Dunahoo & Monnier, 1995). These resources could be accumulated because they can serve as a gateway to other values or simply because they are inherently and objectively of immense value (Hobfoll, 2001).

Positive organisational scholarship focuses on the positive characteristics of an organisation that facilitate its ability and function (Cameron & Spreitzer, 2012). Positive organisational behaviour is described as the study and application of positively oriented human resources strengths and psychological capacities that can be measured, developed and effectively managed for performance improvement (Luthans, 2002b). The following three models were assessed to be especially relevant to this research because of their clear explication of relevant behavioural constructs.

Psychological Capital

Psychological capital (PsyCap) is defined as the employee's positive psychological state of development focusing on four distinct psychological capacities, namely self-efficacy, optimism, hope and resilience (Carver & Scheier, 2002; Luthans, Avolio, Avey & Norman, 2007; Luthans & Youssef, 2007; Weick & Quinn, 1999).

1. **Self-efficacy** refers to the employee's ability to mobilise the motivation and cognitive resources of action needed to successfully execute a specific task within a given context (Stajkovic & Luthans, 1998). Research reports that a positive relationship exists between self-efficacy and organisational commitment (Harris & Cameron, 2005).

2. **Optimism** refers to a generalised positive expectancy and an optimistic expectancy style (Carver & Scheier, 2002; Luthans, 2002b). Research reports that a positive relationship exists between optimism and employee engagement and subsequently employee performance (Medlin & Faulk, 2011).

3. **Hope** refers to a positive motivational state based on an interactively derived sense of successful agency (goal-directed energy) and pathways (planning to meet goals) (Snyder, Irving & Anderson, 1991). Research reports that hope predicts job performance and contributes to employee well-being (Peterson, Walumbwa, Byron & Myrowitz, 2009; Weick & Quinn, 1999).

4. **Resilience** refers to the positive psychological capacity to rebound, to bounce back from adversity, uncertainty, conflict, failure and even positive change, progress and increased responsibility (Luthans, 2002b; Wagnild, 2012). Research reports that a strong positive relationship exists between resilience and positive emotions in the face of adverse conditions (Philippe, Lecours & Beaulieu-Pelletier, 2008).

The Job Demands Resources Model

The job demands-resources (JD-R) model states that every occupation has specific characteristics, described as *job demands* and *job resources* (Bakker & Demerouti, 2007). *Job demands* refer to physical, psychological, social or organisational aspects of the job representing a risk to psychological well-being;

job demands require sustained physical and/or psychological effort or skill associated with cost. *Job resources* refer to physical, psychological, social or organisational aspects of the job that may be functional in achieving work goals, reducing job demands and stimulating motivation, personal growth, development and psychological well-being (Demerouti & Bakker, 2011).

Positive Institutions

The positive institutions model comprehensively includes many aspects of the above and can be described as the study of organisations and institutions who have a purpose and a vision (of the moral goal of the institution); provide safety against threat, danger and exploitation; ensure fairness in having rules governing reward and punishment and humanity in providing care, concern and dignity; and where individuals, groups, organisations, communities and society are all treated as equals (Rothmann, 2014; Rothmann & Cooper, 2015). The model includes various positive psychology constructs differentiated into four dimensions.

1. **Flourishing** is defined as the appraisals individuals make regarding the quality of their lives as expressed in terms of multidimensional indicators (Keyes & Annas, 2009; Rothmann, 2013; Seligman, 2011). Flourishing consists of two dimensions, namely feeling good and functioning well. Flourishing employees show the following behaviours: hope, efficacy, optimism and resilience (linked to the PsyCap model); engagement in their work – a positive and fulfilling work-related state of mind characterised by vigour, dedication and absorption (Schaufeli & Bakker, 2004) (linked to the JD-R model); the experience of purpose – having a sense of desired end states to work; the experience of meaning – the perceived significance of the employees' experience of work; an intrinsic motivation based on one's autonomy, competence and relatedness satisfaction; the experience of high levels of work-related emotional well-being, which includes job satisfaction – a pleasurable or positive emotional state resulting from the appraisal of one's job or job experiences (Locke, 1976) – and positive emotions such as joy, interest, contentment and happiness. These behaviours facilitate the ability to broaden momentary thought-action repertoires, generativity and behavioural flexibility based on the employee's enduring personal resources (Rothmann, 2014). As the opposite of flourishing, languishing employees do not feel or function well in their work.

2. Strengths and virtuousness: **Strengths** refer to pre-existing capacities for a particular way of behaving, thinking or feeling that is authentic and energising (Linley & Joseph, 2004), and **virtuousness** refers to an abundance culture characterised by positive deviance, well-intended virtuous practice and an affirmative bias (Lewis, 2011).

3. **Positive relationships** are defined as short-term connections between employees that are positive, as indicated by the subjective experiences in and between them and the structural features of the connection (Cameron & Spreitzer, 2012). This also includes the reciprocity, social exchanges, trust and trustworthiness.

4. **Positive institutional** and human resources practices include work design, organisational support from management and leadership, co-worker relationships, positive communication, role clarity, positive leadership, and training, development, performance management and career development.

Related Research

Based on the above theoretical explication, Rothmann and Cooper (2015) designed an integrative diagnostic model for psychological well-being for people in the work context. This model describes how negative (distress) and positive (eustress) experiences manifest due to outside forces (social and technological change; family, race, gender, social class and community; environmental factors), organisational forces (job demands and job resources) and moderating forces (perception, experience, self-efficacy, locus of control, optimism and coping). Next, the application of the model for employees in organisations, as well as for students, is illustrated. Both are relevant to this study as the participants here were both (full-time) employees and (part-time) students.

All the above psychological well-being models have been quantitatively researched in many organisational settings internationally (Avey, Reichard, Luthans & Mhatre, 2011; Luthans, 2012; Schaufeli & Bakker, 2004) and in South Africa (De Beer, 2012; Rothmann & Rothmann, 2010; Rothmann, Strydon & Mostert, 2006). The research indicates that many positive organisational psychological constructs (such as emotional intelligence, engagement and resilience) contribute towards coping with stress, commitment, satisfaction, career adaptability, retention and general mental health amongst employees (Harry, 2015; Mayer & Van Zyl, 2013; Mendes & Stander, 2011; Shelton & Renard, 2015; Simons & Buitendach, 2013). The PsyCap model has been researched in terms of its validity (Görgens-Ekermans & Herbert, 2013) and its statistical relationships with various constructs such as engagement, organisational commitment (Simons & Buitendach, 2013), resistance to change, organisational citizen behaviour (Beal, Stravros & Cole, 2013), reward preference and satisfaction (Shelton & Renard, 2015). Research on the JD-R model has shown that the strengthening of job resources facilitates employee well-being (Tremblay & Messervey, 2011) and that job demands relate to toxic feelings and organisational phenomena such as bullying (Van den Broeck, Baillien & De Witte, 2011). The broad overarching concept of a positive organisation/institution is used increasingly to describe a positive work environment characterised by a positive climate, effective leadership and functioning on high relevant constructs such as engagement, sense of coherence and staff retention (Mayer & Van Zyl, 2013; Mendes & Stander, 2011; Van Zyl & Stander, 2013).

Research on the psychological well-being of students is limited compared to employees and typically focuses on quantitative measures of their experience of course content (Murphy & Coleman, 2004; Popov, 2009; Stiwne & Jungert, 2010) and cognitive learning (Rautenbach, 2007). Positive psychology constructs such as personal growth, emotional intelligence, self-efficacy, resilience, strengths and hope have shown to relate to academic success and satisfaction amongst, for example, nursing, medical and first-year students (Ahmed, Kameshwari, Mathew, Ashok, Shaikh & Muttappallymyalil, 2011; Görgens-Ekermans, Delport & Du Preez, 2015; Marcketti, Mhango & Gregoire, 2006; Stander, Diedericks, Mostert & De Beer, 2015; Taylor & Reynes, 2012). Research on master's students, in general, has shown how they have grown in the subject matter as well as in personal accomplishment during their programmes (Conrad, Duren & Haworth, 2002). A South African longitudinal qualitative study on master's students in Clinical Psychology evidenced how positive psychology coping and resilience contributed towards academic success and how these behaviours increase during the programme (Edwards, Ngcobo & Edwards, 2014). The students' coping related to support from others, time management and study skills, exercise and recreation, spiritual/religious activities and relaxation, while their resilience related to struggle, personal, life management and study experiences. The JD-R model was adapted and tested as the study demands-resources (SD-R) model in two quantitative studies. Mokgele and Rothmann (2014) found that the availability of study resources was positively associated with psychological well-being and engagement. Basson (2015) found that psychological well-being amongst students manifested as liking most parts of one's personality, being good at managing daily responsibilities, having challenging experiences that foster growth, being confident about ideas and opinions and feeling that life has meaning and direction.

Research Question, Aim and Contribution

The research question was framed as, what aspects of psychological well-being as described in the above theoretical explication manifest amongst students undertaking a part-time coursework master's degree in IOP? The aim of the research was to qualitatively describe the psychological well-being of first-year students in this master's degree programme. The contribution of the research consisted of providing this university and other similar IOP departments with qualitative research evidence of students' psychological well-being, which may in future serve as a point of departure towards the understanding of, empathy for and emotional support of the students, even beyond their first year in the programme.

Next, the research design, findings and discussion are presented.

Research Design

Research Approach

Psychological well-being served as the disciplinary relationship (Rothmann, 2014). Qualitative research within the interpretive paradigm (Terre Blanche, Durrheim & Painter, 2006) was chosen in order to describe the lived experiences of the research subjects (Leavy, 2014). Hermeneutics (Clarke & Hoggett, 2009) served as the interpretive stance, defined as the interpretation of a text based on the epistemological assumption that close and empathic listening to the other allows for a deep understanding of shared experiences (Alvesson & Sköldberg, 2010; Salkind, 2012). The acknowledgement of the hermeneutic circle between part and whole (Terre Blanche *et al.*, 2006) implied that the meaning of the parts was considered in relation to the meaning of the whole, which could only be understood with respect to its constituent parts.

Research Method

Research Setting

The research was set in the first-year part-time coursework master's degree in IOP at a large South African university (as explicated in the introduction), specifically in the module on Psychological Research Methods consisting of workshops in quantitative and qualitative research methods. In the qualitative research workshop, students are exposed to various individual and group data gathering methods. As a group method, a focus group (FG) is used as an experiential illustration, with the students taking up various FG roles. There is no written examination in this module. Students may or may not use their learning in their research projects (the second-year dissertation). Thus, the effect of the FG on their performance as students cannot be measured.

Entrée and Establishing Researcher Roles

Both researchers were psychologists and lecturers in this master's degree programme in IOP and were tasked to present the qualitative research workshop. This entailed the academic planning and presentation of the workshop. Apart from this academic role, they were both authorised by the chair of the department and the university's ethical committee to take up the role of researchers in this master's degree workshop. This role entailed the sub-roles of managers of the research project, convenors of the FG, analysts and interpreters of the research data.

Sampling

Convenient and purposive sampling (Brewerton & Millward, 2004) was used. The sample was the 2013 first-year students in the part-time coursework master's degree in IOP (N=20). Ten students volunteered to take up a role as participants in the FG – eight females, two males; four black, one coloured, two Indian and three white students. Their average age was 28 years.

Data Collection

A *focus group* can be defined as a research interview conducted with a group who share a similar type of experience but are not a naturally constituted social group (Litosseliti, 2003). FG preparation concerns the procedure, interaction, content and recording (Terre Blanche et al., 2006). The FG was structured in terms of space and roles of participant, convenor and scribe. Chairs were placed in two concentric circles. In the inner circle, the 10 volunteering students took up their role as FG participants. They were joined by both researchers in their role of FG convenors, which was framed as reflecting the content presented by participants using respect (a positive, accepting and non-judgemental orientation) and empathy (providing verbal and non-verbal emotional support, checking for understanding and stimulating self-exploration) (Egan, 1990), while also making field notes consisting of group dynamic and non-verbal behaviour. In the outer circle, the remaining 10 students took up their role as FG scribes, which was framed as recording the data verbatim. The convenors started the FG with an explanation of the procedure and what would be required from the participants (Terre Blanche et al., 2006). They were also reminded to be honest in their responses on the FG question. Next, the convenors posed the FG question, namely, 'Describe your experiences as a first-year part-time coursework master's degree student in IOP'. The FG lasted 90 minutes. The researchers integrated the two sets (convenor and scribe notes), which were framed as the research data.

Data Analysis and Interpretation

Thematic content analysis was used (Brewerton & Millward, 2004; Camic, Rhodes & Yardley, 2003) following a five-step procedure, as espoused by Terre Blanche et al. (2006), namely:

1. familiarisation and immersion;
2. induction of themes;
3. codin;
4. elaboration; and
5. interpretation and checking.

Categorisation and coding, therefore, led to elaboration and interpretation, text analysis, possible recategorisation, and finally the development of clusters, which were translated into themes. The themes emerged out of the data and were then interpreted in terms of the comprehensive diagnostic well-being at work factors designed by Rothmann and Cooper (2015).

Strategies Employed to Ensure Quality Data

Scientific rigour was ensured through focussing on trustworthiness, credibility, dependability, transferability and ethics (Denzin & Lincoln, 2005; Terre Blanche et al., 2006). Trustworthiness and the richness of the data could only partially be ensured, mainly because only one FG was used. The researchers compensated for this limitation as follows. (1) Peer reviews were used (Brewerton & Milward, 2004; Camic et al., 2003) – two independent psychologists, to whom the research design was known, were asked to assess the richness of the data and the worthiness of the interpretations. Both agreed that the work showed sufficient trustworthiness for interpretation. (2) Both verbatim data (collected by the scribes) and field notes (made by the convenors) were used – thus verbal, non-verbal and group dynamic data could be integrated for interpretation. Credibility was ensured through the authorised involvement of all parties (Hirschhorn, 1997). Drawing on Appleton's (1995) propositions, credibility was further enhanced by providing a detailed description of the research process and appealing to the reader to confirm the credibility of the study. Dependability was ensured through the scientific rigour applied in the planning and execution of the research project. Transferability referred to ensuring a scientific link between the FG data and the interpretive stance (Denzin & Lincoln, 2005; Eisner, 1998). As psychologists, both researchers are trained in this stance as applied to research and as stipulated by positive psychology scholars (Donaldson & Ko, 2010; Luthans, 2002a; Lyubomirsky, 2013; Seligman & Csikszentimihalyi, 2000). As accentuated in the hermeneutic approach, the researchers stayed aware of the insider-outsider tension and dialogue in their own minds (Terre Blanche et al., 2006). They tried to stay true to the voices of the research subjects, while at the same time trying to answer the research question. In terms of ethics, all participants gave their informed consent, their identities were protected, and the researchers adhered to the Belmont ethical principles of beneficence, non-maleficence and justice (Bernhofer, 2011; De Vos, Strydom, Fouché & Delport, 2002). The researchers were granted the necessary ethical clearance according to the academic institution's ethics policy.

Next, the findings are presented by theme, followed by a discussion using the well-being diagnostic model and the research hypothesis mentioned.

Findings

Participants spent about one-third of the time on their negative experiences of being a first-year part-time coursework master's degree student in IOP. It was as if they used the FG opportunity to offload their stress while having an audience with representatives of the department who were instrumental to their difficulties. Three themes manifested, namely, not coping, doubting own competence and multiple roles.

Not Coping

Participants described their experience as 'hard', 'intense', 'like being on a roller coaster', 'isolated from the rest of the world', being on a 'lonely journey', 'my worst nightmare' and 'not coping well' with 'my current stress'.

Doubting Own Competence

Participants doubted their academic competence, with questions such as 'have I done the right thing', 'will I be able to measure up', and 'will I be good enough to be' and 'stay in the programme', all compared to the other 'clever and intellectual' students.

Multiple Roles

Participants expressed how they were overwhelmed being in the different roles of student, employee and family member. They struggled to 'balance my roles' – 'I am a master's student, I am a wife, I am a mom, I recently had another baby' and having 'a very demanding job'. They referred to how their 'different roles make me feel numb', how 'it is difficult to balance all of these', 'I had no feeling ... I felt emotionally drained ... I wanted to quit'. As a *student*, one participant said, 'compared to honours and undergrad I am putting a lot more effort into my master's'. They referred to how they 'underestimated the work', 'how colossal the assignments are', 'it ends up being an iceberg' (in the discovery of the unexpected complexity), 'all structure has been lost ... it is difficult for people to thrive without structure', 'your daily planning changes all the time', 'I am going through experiences I never had before', 'what do you do when you see your performance levels are not that good' and 'you have to constantly think on your feet'. They felt out of control when they realised that their 'time and how I manage' and 'usually plan things', 'are all gone'. They realised that 'no-one could provide me with support'. They became 'very critical of my own views'. One participant 'dreamt that I failed the exam', one considered 'to drop out' while another 'asked myself – how is this making me more competent?'

They complained about the library, unclear assessment criteria, unhelpful and unmotivated lecturers, lecturers' inconsistent ways of marking, and rude lecturers saying, 'you are an M-student, you should be able to deal with it'. They expressed being overwhelmed by the study content – 'the conflicting instructions, multiple theories' and 'putting everything into five pages – all of it with references – I mean come on'. In terms of their student colleagues, they complained about group assignments in terms of the vast geographical distance between students, 'having to change my style to accommodate others' and 'having other students' use of language in my assignments'. With reference to the Personal Growth module, they described their blogging inputs as 'not working', 'time wasted', 'nothing in it for me', 'it is like constipated feelings', and 'so mechanical'. One participant said, 'I blogged 33 times, all sincerely from the bottom of my heart', and another noted, 'people did not comment as promised – I have not received any comments'. As *employees*, they expressed a wish 'to be rich enough' to resign and to study full time, 'to have more time to do it properly'. They referred to their job demands in terms of newness, complexity and time consumption – all associated with distress. As *family members*, they referred to how their studies affected their relationships. One participant said, 'My family do not understand what I am doing' and another '... why am I doing this'. This made them feel disconnected from their significant support structures. One female participant mentioned that she 'had to undergo an emergency operation' and another that she 'was supposed to have reconstructive surgery on my leg'. Some of these examples were linked to financial difficulties.

After the offloading of their distress, participants started to share their positive challenges in the programme, or eustress. Five themes manifested, namely, a support system, self-realisation, coping, self-efficacy and/or resilience and hope and/or optimism.

A Support System

Participants mentioned using others for emotional support, specifically fellow students ('he became my roller-coaster buddy', 'I felt alone until I found her as a support'), the university department and family members (although for some the families 'often do not understand what I am going through'). They normalised their difficult experiences ('this is normal, I am not alone' – 'I know that everyone is going through the same thing') through having meaningful emotional connections with others ('it is a relief, learning that we all feel the same'), learning cognitively from others ('in the group assignments, I have learned so much from how others write, their sentence construction)' and 'being motivated by others'.

Self-realisation

Participants reported on how they had grown through the experience ('although you are not always aware of it'). They 'appreciate small things', 'love myself more', 'know that this is where I want to be', 'driving my goal' and 'understand my limits so much better '. They learnt to explore their 'own emotions and defences' and started to 'talk to myself'. Several participants mentioned a spiritual awareness of getting 'closer to God', 'the harder it got the more I would ask God to carry this burden for me'.

Coping

Participants mentioned that they coped firstly by using their intellectual ('IQ'), 'critical analysis', 'focussing' and 'reframing' skills. Thus, some learned 'a deeper appreciation' for the complexity of psychology. Emotionally, they coped by working through their frustrations and guilt and trying to 'view it from a different point of view'. Motivationally, they had learned to periodically 'disengage/detach from' and 'step out of the difficult situation', 'gather energy and then re-engage', 'sometimes take a day off', 'prioritise', and 'look at the bigger picture'. This assisted them to 'deal with things as they come', 'otherwise I would be too stressed'; 'plan better and start earlier with an assignment'; and 'self-motivate'. Interpersonally, they had learned to listen to others differently in order to understand their own situation better. Towards the end of the session, a participant said, 'in retrospect, I think that it was actually manageable, it was not that bad – if only you plan wisely and use the inter-relatedness'.

Efficacy and/or Resilience

Participants expressed their competence in performing the task effectively ('I am on auto-pilot') when they 'reflect', 'take charge' and keep the goal in mind. They were energised to 'deal with things as they come' and 'bounce back' because 'I do not want to be a coward and pull out'.

Hope and/or Optimism

Hope was expressed by four participants – 'when I get my marks, I feel good again', 'knowing that there is hope'. It helped to 'focus on the positive and not let the other stuff slow you down'. Some participants declared that 'I am doing well' when 'I have role models' to 'keep me optimistic'. They referred to some of the lecturers, who engaged with them in a way that they found meaningful, admirable and inspiring.

Discussion

The purpose of the research was to provide a qualitative description of the psychological well-being of first-year students undertaking a part-time coursework master's degree in IOP, in order to foster an empathetic understanding of their experiences. Using the integrative diagnostic model (Rothmann & Cooper, 2015), the following interpretations were made.

Outside Forces

The students did not refer to the *rate of social and technological change* as a stressor. Most students experienced distress in having to cope with their *family's* lack of understanding and support in their efforts towards completing this advanced professional degree. They experienced being disengaged from loved ones, which manifested in loneliness and anger. This finding is consistent with research on the absence of a support system during stressful times (Wissing, Potgieter, Guse, Khumalo & Nel, 2014). *Race* was never mentioned as a stressor, perhaps because of the balanced configuration in the selection of the students in the programme as well as in this FG. *Gender* manifested as a differentiator in how female students experienced being overwhelmed in trying to balance their role as a student with being a wife and a mother of young children. This links with the existential anxiety manifesting among professional women (Naik, 2015). *Social class, community* and *environmental factors* were experienced as stressors in terms of not having the financial resources to study full time and not neglecting their organisational work in favour of their academic work (see Snyder & Lopez, 2009).

Organisational Forces: Job Demands

The students experienced distress due to *role demands*, which manifested as conflict, ambiguity and overload (Demerouti & Bakker, 2011). Their role conflict related to the experience that their master's student role was much more demanding than their previous academic degree roles, as well as that their roles of employee, spouse, parent and citizen (in their community involvement and hobbies) became unmanageable in terms of time and energy. Their role ambiguity related to their split loyalties between the student role which absorbed their resources of time and energy and limited the same for use in their organisational and family systems. Their role overload related to feeling overwhelmed with the demands of time, complexity, lack of predictability and containment, physical and emotional exhaustion. A couple of students contemplated quitting as a flight response because of these role demands. Distress was experienced due to the students feeling *responsible for others* (Snyder & Lopez, 2009). Some of the female students mentioned their responsibility in caring for their families and children as stressors, which is consistent with the experiences of professional women in stressful situations (Naik, 2015). Others mentioned feeling responsible for not disappointing their student colleagues (in the Personal Growth module). Whereas the conscious purpose of the relationship was about mutual academic and emotional support, the students seem to have created an unconscious authority object to deal with their own fear of failure (Hirschhorn, 1997). The students' *interpersonal demands* caused distress in their relationship with lecturers, whom they sometimes experienced as non-supportive, and with their fellow students, whom one student referred to as non-responsive (see Linley & Joseph, 2004). The *organisational structure* did not cause significant distress. The evidence showed that they experienced the structure of student-lecturer-academic departments and the professional body as logical and meaningful. The *nature of the task* caused distress in terms of the highly structured and regulated way the course content, assignments, assessments and research proposals were presented and controlled. The students experienced this as inhibiting their individual decision-making, freedom and creativity (as supported by Czander, 1993). The students mentioned *physical problems* (e.g. an emergency operation, reconstructive surgery on a leg), which were interpreted as the symbolic sense of immobilisation of the students (Linley et al., 2007). Psychological *stress symptoms* manifested as a sense of irritation towards the university system for not listening and containing their issues, anger towards the lecturers for not treating them as adults, and a sense of boredom during the FG. In terms of psychosomatic symptoms, some participants mentioned having problems sleeping (which had a sense of being overstimulated) as well as oversleeping (interpreted as avoidance of working on an academic task) (Czander, 1993). No cognitive symptoms such as problems with concentration or decision-making were reported.

Organisational Forces: Job Resources

The students' *relations with management* (the lecturers and academic department) were experienced as supportive. The significant personal growth that students experienced could relate to the programme and management's focus on well-being and self-realisation in the Personal Growth module as well as that by various staff members who actively do research in positive psychology. This relates to Guse's (2010) suggestion to teach positive psychology in psychology master's courses. The above resulted in the stimulation of the students' level of engagement and intention to stay in the programme (Rothmann, Diedericks & Swart, 2013). The identity and *nature of the task* were experienced as a conflict. On the one hand, most students experienced eustress – finding the task clear and purposeful in terms of the focus on becoming a psychologist working in organisations, the variety as well contained, balanced between too little and too much and being allowed to work autonomously. The student-task interaction was interpreted as consisting of flow (Csikszentmihalyi, 1990) with reference to the synchronisation of and harmony between thought, feeling and action. In contrast, a few students experienced distress manifesting as irritation and being inhibited in having to adapt to the strict and detailed academic rules in research conceptualisation, conversation and documentation. This was interpreted as due to the crossing of the boundary into a different systemic domain (Bain, 1998), in this case taking up a dependent position as a learner with the primary task of knowledge creation and sharing, and being assessed according to vague and unknown academic, professional and ethical criteria. The identity and *nature of the social context* facilitated the students' flourishing (Rothmann & Cooper, 2015). According to Rothmann's (2014) model, this includes the student's emotional (job satisfaction, positive affect balance) and psychological well-being (self-determination in the satisfaction of psychological needs, meaningfulness, purpose, engagement and harmony). The students illustrated flourishing in (1) their experiences of emotional well-being – their positive assessment of their task as master's student and the positive affect – their positive and pleasurable emotions overshadowed their negative emotions, such as feeling overwhelmed and out of control, and (2) their psychological well-being – their autonomy, competence, relatedness, experience of meaningfulness, purpose and engagement. Their *interpersonal relationships* with other students were experienced as supportive, respectful and appreciative, which created their sense of identity as a group, belonging to a significant system. Interestingly, the students defended against the diversity between them by creating a fantasy that all students have exactly the same experiences. *Communication* upward was experienced by most students as having role models as psychologists and facilitators of growth, although one student mentioned lectures being rude. The students' *performance management* (assignment feedback) was experienced as timeous, accurate and thought-provoking. This encouraged engagement (Schaufeli & Bakker, 2004).

Moderators

The students shared the *perception* that being a master's student was a voluntary and challenging academic endeavour involving theoretical, practical, professional and personal learning towards attaining a professional qualification and career advancement and becoming an optimally functioning human being and psychologist. Some students expressed their own individual reality of struggling with the demands of working with unsupportive lecturers and fellow students. This indicated a differentiation in reality testing amongst students; this finding was interpreted to mean that the well-being of students is perhaps distributed normally between high and low (Hirschhorn, 1997) – even for such a carefully psychologically selected group of candidates. Their *experience of the programme* was about being confronted with something momentous in their careers, initially emotionally overwhelming, but with time and exposure, their stress levels normalised. The students' *self-efficacy* varied between doubting and realising their capabilities. They doubted their potential to get into and stay in the programme, compared to the other students and their perceived superior intelligence. They realised their capabilities to mobilise their cognitive resources, motivation and courses of action needed to meet given academic demands. The text also gave evidence of their task-specific efficacy in how they could in advance judge the likelihood and expectation of passing the degree and fulfilling their dreams of becoming a psychologist. In this process, they used resilience to overcome setbacks, such as work demands, time constraints and below-expected assignment marks (Stajkovic & Luthans, 1998), as well as to counter guilt (I have done something wrong) and shame (there is something wrong with me) (Mollon, 2004). The students' external *locus of control* manifested in a limited manner in how they blamed lecturers and fellow students, yet their internal locus of control manifested strongly in the way in which they took control over their work, personal environment and success without ascribing this to the power of the other or to chance (Rothmann & Cooper, 2015). The students illustrated both learned and dispositional *optimism* – in how they explained their situation in detail, owned their choices and behaviour, had a global sense of taking responsibility for their choices, mobilised their strengths to secure a future and a career filled with promise and success in spite of the occasional pitfall. Thus, their optimism illustrated how they lessened their stress levels by engaging with the task, experiencing and verbalising the stress involved (Medlin & Faulk, 2011). The students experienced *non-coping* behaviour in how difficult and overwhelming the programme was experienced. It was as if students who worked in isolation, avoiding the demands and interpersonal contact, expressed more distress, while those who worked in collaboration with fellow students and lecturers experienced less stress. Coping behaviour was described as keeping stressors at bay through applying perceptual, cognitive, emotional and motivational behaviour to focus on the task and to focus on positive expectations and outcomes (Edwards et al., 2014).

Conclusion

The psychological well-being models used in this research served as good-enough containers (Czander, 1993) for the description of the master's students' experiences.

1. The effort-reward imbalance model facilitated an understanding of how students' imminent and delayed rewards significantly reduced the impact of their academic investments in terms of time, energy and family relations.

2. The demand and control model illustrated how the students' sense of autonomy over tasks and responsibilities safeguarded them from distress.

3. The PsyCap constructs of self-efficacy, optimism, hope and resilience all manifested in the students' coping profiles.

4. The JD-R model was functional in differentiating between the students' distress and eustress.

5. The positive instruction constructs of languishing and flourishing acted as a core description of the students' experiences and the role of both in describing the nature of the students' relationships were valuable.

6. The Rothmann and Cooper (2015) integrative diagnostic model for psychological well-being provided validity for the analysis and interpretation of psychological well-being as a construct.

The psychological well-being manifesting among master's students in IOP can be integrated as follows. Physically, the students coped well with the course demands. Two students were exposed to surgery but seem to have recuperated. Cognitively, they seem to have coped well with the course demands. This is not surprising, seeing that the students were scientifically selected in terms of academic performance.

Affectively, the students struggled with balancing the demands from their different roles. Female students felt overwhelmed in their family and mother roles. Otherwise, most students experienced high levels of optimism and flourishing behaviour. Motivationally, the students experienced high levels of coping and self-efficacy from an internal locus of control. Interpersonally, the students felt unsupported by their families, some lecturers and some fellow students. Overall, their relationships were characterised by effective and meaningful contacts between them and the university department, lecturers and fellow students. Their task behaviour was characterised by a positive experience of the structures and a sense of flow in how they integrated the demands of the assignments.

It was concluded that the psychological well-being manifesting amongst first-year students in this part-time coursework master's degree in IOP is characterised by distress and eustress. Their distress is caused mostly by outside factors and job demands, leading to a sense of languishing and feelings of being overwhelmed. Their eustress is caused by job resources and the moderating factors of self-efficacy, locus of control and optimism, leading to flourishing behaviour. They use their eustress to manage their distress, and their interpersonal distress in one area is compensated for by investing more energy into another area.

Limitations

Although not an academic or examined input, the masters' programme's Personal Growth module could have made the students sensitive towards their own psychological well-being, which may have had an effect on their experiences and the research data. In terms of the research design, the lecturers working with their own students could have created subjectivity, in spite of the researchers keeping this in mind throughout the study. This aspect could have inhibited the students' responses by creating suspicion or the desire to impress authority figures.

Recommendations

It is recommended that the above information be used by IOP departments at this and other universities to understand the experiences of their master's students and to gain empathy for their positions as learners. It is not recommended that the course content or academic procedures be changed, because that was not studied in this research and would be seen as a reactive and mechanistic approach to this qualitative study. Rather, the programme management is urged to engage with the master's students about their psychological well-being experiences, often in a dynamic manner, for example at the beginning (emotionally checking in) and end (emotionally checking out) of workshops, as well as in regular psychological well-being engagement sessions (see Guse, 2010). Thus, the staff could act as containers and role models of well-being. It is suggested that this research be replicated biannually in a longitudinal approach to monitor students' experiences, including the generational aspect in the teaching of psychology. Lastly, it is recommended that this study design be applied amongst second-year students in the part-time dissertation master's degree programme in IOP as measurement and support in the completion of their master's degrees.

Acknowledgements

Competing Interests

The authors declare that they have no financial or personal relationships that may have inappropriately influenced them in writing this article.

Authors' Contributions

F.C. and A.F. were equally responsible for the whole research project, including the planning, data gathering and analysis, as well as the writing up and interpretation of the findings.

References

Ahmed, M.; Kameshwari, A.; Mathew, E.; Ashok, J.; Shaikh, R.B., & Muttappallymyalil, J. (2011). Intrinsic component of resilience among entry-level medical students in the United Arab Emirates. *Australasian Medical Journal*, 4(10),548-554. https://doi.org/10.4066/AMJ.2011.826

✓Alvesson, M. & Sköldberg, K. (2010). *Reflexive methodology. New vistas for qualitative research*. London: Sage.

Appleton, J.N. (1995). Analysing qualitative interview data: Addressing issues of validity and reliability. *Journal of Advanced Nursing*, 22:993-997. https://doi.org/10.1111/j.1365-2648.1995.tb02653.x

Avey, J.B.; Reichard, R.J.; Luthans, F. & Mhatre, K.H. (2011). Meta-analysis of the impact of positive psychological capital on employee attitudes, behaviours and performance. *Human Resource Development Quarterly*, 22:127–152. https://doi.org/10.1002/hrdq.20070

Bain, A. (1998). Social defences against organisational learning. *Human Relations*, 51-(3):413-429. https://doi.org/10.1177/001872679805100309

Bakker, A.B., & Demerouti, E. (2007). The Job Demands-Resources model: State of the art. *Journal of Managerial Psychology*, 22:309-328. https://doi.org/10.1108/02683940710733115

Basson, M.J. (2015). *Pathways to flourishing of pharmacy students*. PHD thesis. Vanderbijlpark: North-West University.

Beal, L. III; Stavros, J.M. & Cole, M.L. (2013). Effect of psychological capital and resistance to change on organisational citizenship behaviour. *SA Journal of Industrial Psychology*, 39(2):Art.#1136, 11 pages. https://doi.org/10.4102/sajip.v39i2.1136

Bennis, W. (2007). The challenge of leadership in the modern world: Introduction to special issues. *American Psychologist*, 62(1):2-5. https://doi.org/10.1037/0003-066X.62.1.2

Bernhofer, E., (2011). Ethics and pain management in hospitalized patients. *OJIN: The Online Journal of Issues in Nursing*, 17(1):11-15.

Botha, C. & Mostert, K. (2014). A structural model of job resources, organisational and individual strengths use and work engagement. *SA Journal of Industrial Psychology/SA Tydskrif vir Bedryfsielkunde*, 40(1):Art. #1135, 11 pages. https://doi.org/10.4102/sajip.v40i1.1135

Brewerton, P., & Millward, L. (2004). *Organisational research methods. A guide for students and researchers.* London: Sage.

Cameron, K.S. & Spreitzer, G.M. (2012). *Oxford handbook of positive organizational scholarship.* New York: Oxford University Press. https://doi.org/10.1093/oxfordhb/9780199734610.001.0001

Camic, P.M.; Rhodes, J.E. & Yardley, L. (2003). *Qualitative research in Psychology.* Washington, DC: APA.

Carver, C.S. & Scheier, M. (2002). Optimism. In: C.R. Snyder & S. Lopez (eds.), *Handbook of positive psychology,* pp.231-243. Oxford, UK: Oxford University Press.

Cilliers, F. & Harry, N. (2012). The systems psychodynamic experiences of first-year Master's students in Industrial and Organisational psychology. *SA Journal of Industrial Psychology/SA Tydskrif vir Bedryfsielkunde,* 38(2):Art. #992, 9 pages. https://doi.org/10.4102/sajip.v38i2.992

Clarke, S. & Hoggett, P. (2009). *Research beneath the surface. Psychosocial research methods in practice.* London: Karnac.

Conrad, C.F.; Duren, J. & Haworth, J.G. (2002). Students' perspectives on their master's degree experiences: Disturbing the conventional wisdom. *New Directions in Higher Education,* 101:65-76. https://doi.org/10.1002/he.10106

Csikszentmihalyi, M. (1990). *Flow: The psychology of optimal experience.* New York: Harper Perennial.

Cummings, T.G. & Worley, C.G. (2015). *Organization development and change* (10th edn.). Stamford, CT: South-Western Cengage Learning.

Czander, W.M. (1993). *The psychodynamics of work and organizations.* New York: Guilford.

De Beer L.T. (2012). *Job demands-resources theory, health and well-being in South Africa.* PhD thesis. Potchefstroom: North-West University.

Demerouti, E. & Bakker, A.B. (2011). The job-demands-resources model: Challenges for future research. *SA Journal of Industrial Psychology/SA Tydskrif vir Bedryfsielkunde,* 37(2):Art. #974, 9 pages. https://doi.org/10.4102/sajip.v37i2.974

Denzin, N.K. & Lincoln, Y.S. (2005). *The Sage handbook of qualitative research.* London: Sage. https://doi.org/10.1177/1468794105047237

De Vos, A.S.; Strydom, H.; Fouche, C.B. & Delport, C.S.L. (2002). *Research at grass roots. For the social sciences and human service professions.* Pretoria: Van Schaik.

Donaldson, S.I. & Ko, I. (2010). Positive organisational psychology, behaviour and scholarship: A review of emerging literature and the evidence base. *The Journal of Positive Psychology,* 5:177-191. https://doi.org/10.1080/17439761003790930

Edwards, D.J.; Ngcobo, H.S.B. & Edwards, S.D. (2014). Resilience and coping experiences among master's professional psychology students in South Africa. *Journal of Psychology in Africa,* 24(2):173-178. https://doi.org/10.1080/14330237.2014.903065

Egan, G. (1990). *The skilled helper. A systematic approach to effective helping.* Pacific Grove, CA: Brooks/Cole.

Eisner, E.W. (1998). *The enlightened eye: Qualitative inquiry and the enhancement of educational practice.* Toronto: Macmillan.

French, S. & Holden, T. (2012). Positive organisational behaviour: A buffer for bad news. *Business Communication Quarterly*, 75(2):208-220. https://doi.org/10.1177/1080569912441823

Görgens-Ekermans, G.; Delport, M. & Du Preez, R. (2015). Developing emotional intelligence as a key psychological resource reservoir for sustained student success. *SA Journal of Industrial Psychology*, 41(1):Art.#1251, 13 pages. https://doi.org/10.4102/sajip.v41i1.1251

Görgens-Ekermans, G. & Herbert, M. (2013). Psychological capital: Internal and external validity of the Psychological Capital Questionnaire (PCQ-24) on a South African sample. *SA Journal of Industrial Psychology*, 39(2):Art.#1131, 12 pages. https://doi.org/10.4102/sajip.v39i2.1131

Guse, T. (2010). Positive psychology and the training of psychologists. Students' perspectives. *SA Journal of Industrial Psychology*, 36(2):Art.#848, 6 pages. https://doi.org/10.4102/sajip.v36i2.848

Harris, G.E. & Cameron, J.E. (2005). Multiple dimensions of organisational identification and commitment as predictors of turnover intentions and psychological well-being. *Canadian Journal of Behavioral Science*, 37(3):159-169.https://doi.org/10.1037/h0087253

Harry, N. (2015). Constructing a psychological coping profile in the call centre environment: Wellness-related dispositions in relation to resiliency-related behavioural capabilities. *SA Journal of Industrial Psychology*, 41(1):Art. #1265, 11 pages. https://doi.org/10.4102/sajip.v41i1.1265

Hirschhorn, L. (1997). *Reworking authority. Leading and following in the post-modern organisation.* London: MIT.

Hobfoll, S.E. (2001). The influence of culture, community, and the nested-self in the stress process: Advancing conservation of resources theory. *Applied Psychology: An International Review*, 50:337-370. https://doi.org/10.1111/1464-0597.00062

Hobfoll, S.E. (2002). Social and psychological resources and adaptation. *Review of General Psychology*, 6:307-324. https://doi.org/10.1037/1089-2680.6.4.307

Hobfoll, S.E.; Dunahoo, C.A. & Monnier, J. (1995). Conservation of resources and traumatic stress. In: J.R. Freedy & S.E. Hobfoll (eds.), *Traumatic stress: From theory to practice*, pp.29-47. New York: Plenum Press. https://doi.org/10.1007/978-1-4899-1076-9_2

HPCSA. (2016). *Health Professions Council of South Africa*, 2015. http://www.hpcsa.co.za [Accessed 26 October 2015].

Karasek, R.A. (1998). Demand/Control Model: A social, emotional, and physiological approach to stress risk and active behaviour development. In: J.M. Stellman (ed.), *Encyclopaedia of occupational health and safety*, pp.34.6-34.14). Geneva: ILO.

Keyes, C. & Annas, J. (2009). Feeling good and functioning well: Distinctive concepts in ancient philosophy and contemporary science. *Journal of Positive Psychology*, 4(3):197-201. https://doi.org/10.1080/17439760902844228

Leavy, P. (2014). *The Oxford handbook of qualitative research*. Oxford: Oxford University Press. https://doi.org/10.1093/oxfordhb/9780199811755.001.0001

Lewis, A. (2011). The management of childhood stress. *Child Abuse Research in South Africa (CARSA)*, 12(1):14-25.

Linley, P.A. & Joseph, S. (2004). *Positive psychology in practice.* Hoboken, NJ: John Wiley. https://doi.org/10.1002/9780470939338

Linley, P.A.; Joseph, S.; Harrington, S. & Wood, A.M. (2007). Positive psychology: Past, present and possible future. *Journal of Positive Psychology*, 1(1):3-16. https://doi.org/10.1080/17439760500372796

Litosseliti, L. (2003). *Using focus groups in research.* London: Continuum.

Locke, M. (1976). Organizational behaviour: Affect in the workplace. *Annual Review of Psychology*, 53:279-307. https://doi.org/10.1146/annurev.psych.53.100901.135156

Lowman, R.L. (2002). *Handbook of organisational consulting psychology. A comprehensive guide to theory, skills and techniques.* San Francisco, CA: Jossey-Bass. https://doi.org/10.1037/1061-4087.54.4.213

Luthans, F. (2002a). Positive organisational behaviour: Developing and managing psychological strengths. *The Academy of Management Executive*, 16(1):57-72. https://doi.org/10.5465/ame.2002.6640181

Luthans, F. (2002b). The need for and meaning of positive organisational behaviour. *Journal of Organisational Behaviour*, 23:695-706. https://doi.org/10.1002/job.165

Luthans, F. (2012). Psychological capital: Implications for HRD, retrospective analysis and future directions. *Human Resource Development Quarterly*, 23(1):1-8. https://doi.org/10.1002/hrdq.21119

Luthans, F.; Avolio, B.J.; Avey., J.B. & Norman, S.M. (2007). Psychological capital: Measurement and relationship with performance and satisfaction. *Personnel Psychology*, 60:541-572. https://doi.org/10.1111/j.1744-6570.2007.00083.x

Luthans, F., & Youssef, C.M. (2007). Emerging positive organisational behaviour. *Journal of Management*, 33(3):321-349. https://doi.org/10.4135/9781446212752.n2

Lyubomirsky, S. (2013). *The myths of happiness: What should make you happy, but doesn't, what shouldn't make you happy, but does.* New York: Penguin Press.

Marcketti, S.B.; Mhango, M.W. & Gregoire, M.B. (2006). The experiences of African Graduate students in a College of Human Sciences. *Journal of Family and Consumer Sciences education*, 24(1):63-72.

Mayer, C-H. & Van Zyl, L.E. (2013). Perspectives of female leaders on sense of coherence and mental health in an engineering environment. *SA Journal of Industrial Psychology*, 39(2):Art. #1097, 11 pages. https://doi.org/10.4102/sajip.v39i2.1097

Medlin, B. & Faulk, L. (2011). The relationship between optimism and engagement: The impact on student performance. *Research in Higher Education Journal*, 13:1-9.

Mendes, F. & Stander, M.W. (2011). Positive organisation: The role of leader behaviour in work engagement and retention. *SA Journal of Industrial Psychology*, 37(1):Art. #900, 13 pages. https://doi.org/10.4102/sajip.v38i1.900

Mokgele, K.R.F. & Rothmann, S. (2014). A structural model of student well-being. *South African Journal of Psychology*, 44(4):514-527. https://doi.org/10.1177/0081246314541589

Mollon, P. (2004). *Shame and jealousy. The hidden turmoils.* London: Karnac.

Murphy, E. & Coleman, E. (2004). Graduate students' experiences of challenges in online asynchronous discussions. *Canadian Journal of Learning and Technology*, 30(2):1-9. https://doi.org/10.21432/T27G7N

Naik, B. (2015). The systems psychodynamics underlying the work-family interface amongst managerial women in the public sector. Unpublished doctoral thesis. University of South Africa.

Peterson, S. J.; Walumbwa, F.O.; Byron, K. & Myrowitz, J. (2009). CEO positive psychological traits, transformational leadership, and firm performance in high technology start-up and established firms. *Journal of Management*, 35:348-368. https://doi.org/10.1177/0149206307312512

Philippe, F.L.; Lecours, S. & Beaulieu-Pelletier, G. (2008). Resilience and positive emotions: Examining the role of emotional memories. *Journal of Personality*, 77(1):139-176. https://doi.org/10.1111/j.1467-6494.2008.00541.x

Popov, O. (2009). Teacher's and student's experiences of simultaneous teaching in an international distance and on-campus master's programme in engineering. *The International Review of Research in Open and Distance Learning*, 10(3):1-8. https://doi.org/10.19173/irrodl.v10i3.669

Rautenbach, I. (2007). An electronic learning (e-learning) readiness model for distance education in the workplace. Unpublished Doctoral Thesis. Potchefstroom: University of North West.

Rothmann, S. (2013). From happiness to flourishing at work: A southern African perspective. In: M.P. Wissing (ed.), *Well-being research in South Africa: Cross-cultural advances in positive psychology*, Vol. 4, pp.123-152. Dordrecht, Netherlands: Springer. https://doi.org/10.1007/978-94-007-6368-5_7

Rothmann, S. (2014). Positive institutions. In: M.P. Wissing, J.C. Potgieter, T. Guse, I.P. Khumalo, & L Nel (eds.), *Towards flourishing. Contextualising positive psychology*, pp.221-261. Pretoria: Van Schaik.

Rothmann, I. & Cooper, C.L. (2015). *Work and organisational psychology.* London: Routledge.

Rothmann, S.; Diedericks, E. & Swart, J.P. (2013). Manager relations, psychological need satisfaction and intention to leave in the agricultural sector. *SA Journal of Industrial Psychology*, 39(2):11. https://doi.org/10.4102/sajip.v39i2.1129

Rothmann, S. & Rothmann, S., Jr. (2010). Factors associated with employee engagement in South African organisations. *SA Journal of Industrial Psychology*, 36(1):1-12. https://doi.org/10.4102/sajip.v36i2.925

Rothmann, S.; Strydom, M. & Mostert, K. (2006). A psychometric evaluation of the Job Demands-Resources Scale in South Africa. *SA Journal of Industrial Psychology*, 32(4):76-86. https://doi.org/10.4102/sajip.v32i4.239

Salkind, N.J. (2012). *Exploring research* (8th ed.). Englewood Cliffs, NJ: Pearson Prentice-Hall.

Schaufeli, W.B. & Bakker, A.B. (2004). Job demands, job resources, and their relationship with burnout and engagement: A Multi-sample study. *Journal of Organisational Behavior*, 25:293-315. https://doi.org/10.1002/job.248

Seligman, M.E.P. (2011). *Flourish: A visionary new understanding of happiness and well-being*. New York: The Free Press.

Seligman, M.E.P. & Csikszentimihalyi, M. (2000). Positive psychology. *American Psychologist*, 55:5-14. https://doi.org/10.1037//0003-066X.55.1.5

Seligman, M.E.P.; Steen, T.A.; Parks, N. & Peterson, C. (2005). Positive psychology progress: Empirical validation of interventions. *American Psychologist*, 60(5):410-421. https://doi.org/10.1037/0003-066X.60.5.410

Shelton, S.A. & Renard, M. (2015). Correlating nurses' levels of Psychological Capital with their reward preferences and reward satisfaction. *SA Journal of Industrial Psychology*, 41(1):Art.#1271, 14 pages. https://doi.org/10.4102/sajip.v41i1.1271

Siegrist, J. (1996). Adverse health effects of high effort-low reward conditions. *Journal of Occupational Health Psychology*, 1:27-41. https://doi.org/10.1037//1076-8998.1.1.27

Simons, J.C. & Buitendach, J.H. (2013). Psychological capital, work engagement and organisational commitment amongst call centre employees in South Africa. *SA Journal of Industrial Psychology*, 39(2):Art.#1071, 12 pages. https://doi.org/10.4102/sajip.v39i2.1071

Snyder, C.R.; Irving, L. & Anderson, J. (1991). Hope and health: Measuring the will and the ways. In: C.R. Snyder & D.R. Forsyth (eds.), *Handbook of social and clinical psychology*, pp.285-305. Elmsford: Pergamon.

Snyder, C.R. & Lopez, S.J. (2009). *Oxford handbook of positive psychology*. New York: Oxford University Press.

Spreitzer, G. & Soneneshein, S. (2003). Positive deviance and extraordinary organisation. In: K. Cameron, J.K. Dutton & R. Quinn (eds.), *Positive organisational scholarship*, pp.207-224. San Francisco, CA: Berrett Koehler.

Stajkovic, A.D. & Luthans, F. (1998). Social cognitive theory and self-efficacy. *Organisational Dynamics*, 26:62-74. https://doi.org/10.1016/S0090-2616(98)90006-7

Stander, F.W.; Diedericks, E.; Mostert, K. & De beer, L.T. (2015). Proactive behaviour towards strength use and deficit improvement, hope and efficacy as predictors of life satisfaction amongst first-year university students. *SA Journal of Industrial Psychology*, 41(1):Art.#1248, 10 pages. https://doi.org/10.4102/sajip.v41i1.1248

Stiwne, E.E. & Jungert, T. (2010). Engineering students' experiences of transition from study to work. *Journal of Education and Work*, 23(5):417-437. https://doi.org/10.1080/13639080.2010.515967

Taylor, H. & Reyners, H. (2012). Self-efficacy and resilience in baccalaureate nursing students. *International Journal of Nursing Education Scholarship*, 9(1):1-12. https://doi.org/10.1515/1548-923X.2218

Terre Blanche, M.; Durrheim, K. & Painter, D. (2006). *Research in practice. Applied methods for the social sciences*. Cape Town: UCT Press.

Tremblay, M.A. & Messervey, D. (2011). The Job Demands-Resources model: Further evidence for the buffering effect of personal resources. *SA Journal of Industrial Psychology*, 37(2):Art.#876, 10 pages. https://doi.org/10.4102/sajip.v37i2.876

Van den Broeck, A.; Baillien, E. & De Witte, H. (2011). Workplace bullying: A perspective from the Job Demands-Resources model. *SA Journal of Industrial Psychology*, 37(20):Art.#879,12 pages. https://doi.org/10.4102/sajip.v37i2.879

Van Tonder, C. & Roodt, G. (2008). *Organisation development. Theory and practice*. Pretoria: Van Schaik.

Van Zyl, L.E. & Stander, M.W. (2013). A strengths-based approach towards coaching in a multicultural environment. In: J.H. Cornelius-White, R. Motschnig-Pitrik & M. Lux (eds.), *Interdisciplinary handbook of the person-centered approach*, pp.245-257. New York: Springer. https://doi.org/10.1007/978-1-4614-7141-7_17

Wagnild, G. (2012). *The resilience scale*. http://resiliencescale.com/usersguide.html [Accessed 10 October 2015].

Weick, K.E. & Quinn, R.E. (1999). Organizational change and development. *Annual Review of Psychology*, 50:361-386. https://doi.org/10.1146/annurev.psych.50.1.361

Weinberg, A., & Cooper, C. (2007). *Surviving the workplace: A guide to emotional well-being*. London: Thomson.

Wissing, M.P.; Potgieter, J.C.; Guse, T.; Khumalo, I.P. & Nel, L. (2014). *Towards flourishing. Contextualising positive psychology*. Pretoria: Van Schaik.

Worrall, L., & Cooper, C.L. (2014). The effect of the recession on the quality of working life of UK managers: An empirical study. *International Journal of Management Practice*, 7(1):1-18. http://doi.org/10.1504/IJMP.2014.060540

Youssef, C.M., & Luthans, F. (2012). Positive global leadership. *Journal of World Business*, 47, 539–547. http://doi.org/10.1016/j.jwb.2012.01.007

Article 5

The Systems Psychodynamic Experiences of First-year Master's Students in Industrial and Organisational Psychology[1]

F Cilliers & N Harry

Orientation

The researchers described the experiences of first-year master's students in industrial and organisational psychology in terms of their anxiety and basic assumption behaviour. Apart from their academic tasks, they seem to be unconsciously involved in many relationships and relatedness matters.

Research Purpose

The purpose of this research was to describe the systems psychodynamic experiences of first-year master's students in Industrial and Organisational Psychology.

Motivation for the Study

Academic staff members tend to forget their own experiences as master's students, lose touch with their students' experiences, lose empathy and treat student groups in mechanistic ways. Although the students' conscious tasks and roles are relatively clear, very little is known about their unconscious experiences.

1   Cilliers, F. & Harry, N. (2012). The systems psychodynamic experiences of first-year Master's students in Industrial and Organisational psychology. *SA Journal of Industrial Psychology/SA Tydskrif vir Bedryfsielkunde*, 38(2):Art. #992, 9 pages. http://doi.org/10.4102/sajip.v38i2.992

Research Design, Approach and Method

The researchers used qualitative research involving a case study. They collected the data and conducted their analyses by administering a Listening Post (LP) and discourse analysis. Two themes emerged, from which the researchers formulated their working and research hypotheses.

Main Findings

The themes related to anxiety and basic assumption behaviour. The research hypothesis referred to students' introjections of emotional incompetence. This resulted in exhaustion.

Practical/managerial Implications

More focused attention on the students' emotional experiences, by themselves and by academic staff members, could conserve students' energy for their academic work and relationships.

Contribution/value-add

Being masters' students consumes emotional energy that jeopardises students' academic work and forming relationships. Being aware of these and managing them could help students to achieve better academically.

Introduction

After completing their honours degrees, master's students in industrial and organisational psychology (IOP) move into the master's programme with high hopes of becoming professionally registered psychologists. From a rational and conscious perspective, the students perform and cope well with the academic demands within the prescribed time limit. On the other hand, academic staff members often speculate about the unconscious dynamics that manifest in the students. The researchers tried to explore the students' behavioural dynamics by entering their experiences and trying to put their minds into the students' space and, by being empathetic, report more specifically on 'what is going on below the surface'.

The university has presented its master's programme for more than 25 years. The degree has a two-year programme and the university requires its students to complete it in a maximum of four years. The first-year consists of six modules. They cover the fields of organisational, personnel and career psychology, psychometrics, psychological research methods and personal growth. The university presents the modules in workshops, on campus, in four five-day blocks (20 working days). Students have to hand in and pass 15 assignments in the various modules and pass the examination in November. It constitutes 50% of the first-year assessment.

The second-year consists of a dissertation with a limited scope. It constitutes the other 50%. The Health Professions Council of South Africa has accredited the programme. It gives students access to internships and registration as industrial psychologists. Twelve staff members are involved in the programme. All are registered industrial, counselling, clinical or research psychologists.

The university selects students using the criteria of previous academic performance, literacy, numeracy, personality and other relevant skills (measured in an assessment centre). Approximately 20 students enter the programme every year. About 50% have honours degrees from this university. Others come from other South African universities. On average, 12 students graduate each year (calculated for 2000-2010). This is a 60% throughput. Very few students finish their degree in two years. Most students spend between three and four years to complete it. Most students complete the first year successfully, whilst the largest fallout occurs during their work on the dissertation. Over the last five years, measured feedback on the students' first year of study showed their satisfaction with the academic content, standard, practical application possibilities of the work and the competence of the lecturers.

The researchers became curious about possible underlying and unconscious themes that are presently unknown. They could assist students and staff members to a more holistic understanding of the students' experiences. This line of thought is consistent with Bion's (2003) notion of integrating knowing with not knowing to improve performance. On the surface, students are well selected, academically informed and sufficiently emotionally resilient to begin master's studies. However, if one explores below the surface behaviour (see Huffington, Armstrong, Halton, Hoyle & Pooley, 2004), it seems that students' resilience changes during their first year. This influences their 'groundedness'. Arrogant expressions like 'we are the best of the best' turn into realisations of the hard intellectual and emotional work the students need to do to stay in and move through the programme.

This often manifests in child-like behaviour. An example is a student who phoned a professor to inform him impatiently that she was still waiting for him to send her the instruments she needed for her research. Another student wanted to know when his newly appointed supervisor was going to re-write his research proposal and whether it would be in time for the deadline. Within the first few months of the start of the programme, students approach lecturers to ask what would happen if they did not complete the first year successfully or wanted to postpone their studies to the following calendar year. Students tend to contact the research module lecturers much more frequently than they contact the other lecturers, especially about the due dates for their dissertations.

One could use these vignettes to hypothesise about the students':

∞ narcissism that turns to arrogance,

∞ anxieties that turn into defences like regression and projection or into a strong dependence on staff members as authority figures, and

∞ performance anxiety about their dissertations (see Blackman, 2004; Sandler, Person & Fonagy, 2004).

Without substantial evidence, these hypotheses become risky. We cannot be sure which of these behaviours belong to individuals and which belong to the student system or even to the student-lecturer-departmental system. To access these below the surface behaviours, the researchers decided to work from the systems psychodynamic perspective because this would allow them to study the students' unconscious behaviour and the relatedness between the students as a system (Campbell, 2007).

Research Purpose

The purpose of the research was to describe the systems psychodynamic experiences of first-year master's students in industrial and organisational psychology. It seems to be an unresearched topic. There has been plenty of research on cognitive learning and the relationship between learner and instructor from a rational and conscious perspective (Rautenbach, 2007). Educationists have conducted most of the qualitative research that focuses on students' affective experiences, but they report little psychological behaviour (see Conrad, Duren & Haworth, 2002; Marcketti, Mhango & Gregoire, 2006; Murphy & Coleman, 2004; Popov, 2009; Stiwne & Jungert, 2007).

The systems psychodynamic literature reports on learners' behaviour in group relations training events (Brunner, Nutkevitch & Sher, 2006; Fraher, 2004), in organisations as part of staff development, in coping with change (Czander, 1993) and in consulting (Neumann, Keller & Dawson-Shepherd, 1997). The researchers could not trace any related research in the literature on systems psychodynamic enquiry into student experiences during a teaching programme.

Trends from the Research Literature

The literature on the systems psychodynamic perspective uses research at the Tavistock Institute (Miller, 1993) as its basis and group relations training (Brunner, Nutkevitch & Sher, 2006). Theoretically, it incorporates Freudian (1921) systemic psychoanalysis, the work of Klein (1988) on family psychology, Ferenczi on object relations and Bertalanffy on systems thinking (Colman & Bexton, 1975; Colman & Geller, 1985; Cytrynbaum & Noumair, 2004). As a research perspective, systems psychodynamics offers a depth psychology organisational theory and a developmentally focused, psycho-educational process for understanding conscious and unconscious behaviour (Campbell, 2007; Campbell & Huffington, 2008; Huffington et al., 2004; Klein, 2005). The systems psychodynamic perspective accepts anxiety as the basis for, and driving force (dynamo) of, relationship and relatedness behaviour (Armstrong, 2005). One can define it as fear of the future.

People use defence mechanisms (Blackman, 2004) against the anxiety to ensure emotional safety. Examples of primitive defences people use often are splitting, introjections, projection and projective identification. Ones that are more sophisticated are rationalisation and intellectualisation. In an organisation, any system (person, group or organisation) unconsciously needs something or someone (managers or leaders) to contain the anxiety on its behalf. The organisation does this through structures like laws, regulations, procedures, organograms, job descriptions and idiosyncratic ways of solving problems.

The system acts out its anxiety in various ways. Five basic behavioural assumptions encapsulate them. They are dependency, fight or flight, pairing (Bion, 1961; 1970; 2003), me-ness (Turquet, 1974) and one-ness or we-ness (Lawrence, Bain & Gould, 1996). These behaviours manifest unconsciously and systemically in a kind of group mentality, described as a unanimous expression of the will of the group. People contribute to it in ways of which they are unaware and which invariably influence them again.

'Dependency' refers to the system's anxiety about its need for security and structure that it projects onto a perceived strong or parental object. It becomes an unconscious dependence on this object (Campbell, 2007). When the object does not meet these needs, the system experiences frustration, helplessness, powerlessness and de-authorisation (Czander, 1993; Stapley, 2006) that manifest as counter-dependence.

'Fight or flight' refers to the system's performance anxiety in the here-and-now. It defends itself by fighting the imagined enemy or removing the self physically or emotionally from the danger (Cytrynbaum & Noumair, 2004). Fight responses manifest in aggression against the self, peers (through envy, jealousy, competition, elimination, boycotting, sibling rivalry, fighting for a position in the system or an assumed privileged relationship with authority figures) or against authority itself (Klein, 2005). Flight responses manifest physically in, for example, avoiding others, being ill or resigning. Psychological flight responses include defence mechanisms like avoiding threatening situations or emotions in the here-and-now, rationalising and intellectualising (Gould, Stapley & Stein, 2004).

'Pairing' manifests in order to cope with anxiety about alienation and loneliness. The system tries to pair with an object (person, subgroup or idea) it perceives as powerful (Colman & Bexton, 1975). The unconscious fantasy is that creation will happen in pairs and will protect the system against threat (Colman & Geller, 1985).

'One-ness' refers to the system's efforts to join a powerful union or omnipotent force. It surrenders the self for passive participation and lives in the fantasy of well-being and wholeness (Turquet, 1974). We also refer to one-ness as we-ness. 'Me-ness' refers to survival and solace in the own inner world, avoiding the outer world and its reality (Lawrence, Bain & Gould, 1996). The importance of the individual is greater than that of the group (Cilliers & Koortzen, 2005).

These basic assumption behaviours manifest on different levels of work that Cilliers and Koortzen (2005) integrated as the CIBART model (conflict, identity, boundaries, authority, role and task). For the sake of this research, the researchers changed the sequence (to conflict, task, role, authority, boundary and identity) to fit the findings.

'Conflict' refers to the split between differences, like between two or more parts of a system. Conflict can manifest intra-personally (in the individual between ideas and feelings), interpersonally (between two or more team members), intra-group (between factions or sub-groups) and inter-group (between one team or department and others in the larger system). See Cilliers and Koortzen (2005).

'Task' is the basic component of work. The leader adheres to the primary task, indicating contained anxiety. Diversions into off-task and anti-task behaviour show confusion and free-floating anxiety (Cytrynbaum & Noumair, 2004).

'Role' is the centre of individual activity. A series of boundaries delineate and define the behaviour (actual, implied or potential), authority, structure, culture, duties and responsibilities under a formalised title that others recognise and more or less value. It manifests as normative, experiential and phenomenal experiences (Cytrynbaum & Noumair, 2004; Czander, 1993; Obholzer & Roberts, 1994).

'Authority' refers to the right one has, because of one's rank or office, to issue commands and to punish violations (Czander, 1993). Authority comes from above (the organisation, manager or leader), the side (colleagues), below (subordinates) and from within (self-authorisation).

'Boundaries' refer to the space around and between parts of the system. They keep the system safe and contained (Cilliers & Koortzen, 2005). Examples are the boundaries of task, time and territory.

'Identity' refers to the aspects that make the system the same as, and different from, others (Campbell & Groenbaek, 2006). It is also the system's climate, cultural characteristics and whether it identifies with the self (Cytrynbaum & Noumair, 2004; Klein, 2005; Hirchhorn, 1997).

Research Problem and Objectives

The researchers formulated the research problem as 'would the systems psychodynamic perspective give the researchers access to enter and explore student experiences, to enable them to understand the depth psychology of being master's students and to lead students towards different ways of containment in future?'. The research objectives were to explore the behaviour the researchers recorded and to analyse it qualitatively.

The Potential Value-add of the Study

The researchers saw the potential value of the research as an in-depth understanding of the experiences students have as master's students and building knowledge around them.

What will Follow

The structure of the rest of the article follows. The researchers present the research design, the research approach and research strategy. The research method follows. It consists of the research setting, the roles of the researchers, their sampling method, data collection, recording and analysis. The strategies the researchers used to ensure quality data follow. They then present the findings as manifested themes. The discussion contains the research hypotheses. The article concludes with the conclusion, recommendations, limitations and suggestions for further research.

Research Design

Research Approach

The researchers chose qualitative and descriptive research (De Vos, Strydom, Fouché & Delport, 2002) within the hermeneutic paradigm (Terre Blanche, Durrheim & Painter, 2006). Whilst interpreting the data, the researchers used themselves as instruments (Watts, 2009) using the epistemological assumption that empathetic listening allows for a deep understanding of shared experiences (Alvesson & Sköldberg, 2010).

Research Strategy

The researchers used a single case study (Chamberlayne, Bornat & Apitzsch, 2004). They treated it as a collective narrative event (Breverton & Millward, 2004) to elicit a richly descriptive account of the stories in their real contexts. They saw the case study as intrinsic (intended to interpret and understand) and instrumental (as feedback to their academic department). See Denzin and Lincoln (2005).

Research Method

Research Setting

The researchers set the study in the master's student programme in industrial and organisational psychology (IOP) at a large university. During the qualitative research module, the university exposes students to an experiential event so that they can learn about research processes and roles.

Entrée and Establishing Researcher Roles

Both researchers are academic staff members in the IOP department. Whilst collecting the data, the first researcher was the convenor of the event. The second researcher was a participant-student in the event. The first researcher conducted the data analysis, interpreted it and structured the research. The second researcher assisted in interpreting and structuring the research.

Sampling

The researchers used convenience (Breverton & Millward, 2004) and opportunistic sampling (Terre Blanche, Painter & Durrheim, 2006). The case study comprised the 2009 master's students (N=23). Whilst collecting the data, the researchers divided the students into two groups. Eight volunteers participated in the event. Seven were women and one was a man. All were between 25 and 38 years of age and worked full time in different organisations. The remaining students acted as scribes.

Data Collection Methods

The researchers used a systems psychodynamic LP (Stapley, 1996; 2006). The Organisation for Promoting Understanding of Society (OPUS) developed it for use in research and consulting (Neumann, Keller & Dawson-Shepherd, 1997; Stapley & Rickman, 2010). Its design is unstructured, allowing one hour for exploring a specific matter experientially through thinking and free association (Stapley & Collie, 2005). In the next hour, researchers process the conscious and unconscious aspects of the matter into working hypotheses (Terre Blanche, Durrheim & Painter, 2006). A system psychodynamically informed convenor manages the time and task boundaries (Dartington, 2000). Research validity depends on the convenor's ability to provide a contained space without judgement, memory or desire (Miller, 1993). The volunteers sat around a table, surrounded by the scribes. The convenor introduced LP matter, stated as 'explore your experience as a master's student'.

Recording of Data

The scribes recorded the data verbatim and the convenor made field notes. In the second hour, the whole group, divided into five subgroups, formulated the working hypotheses. The researchers integrated the verbatim material with the hypotheses the group and the convenor's field notes generated. This integration was the research text.

Data Analyses

The researchers used thematic analysis (Breverton & Millward, 2004; Camic, Rhodes & Yardley, 2003). They applied simple hermeneutics to the text in order to understand the participants' meaning. Two themes emerged. The researchers applied double hermeneutics (Clarke & Hoggett, 2009) to interpret the data from the systems psychodynamic stance (using Armstrong, 2005; Campbell, 2007; Cilliers & Koortzen, 2005; Huffington et al., 2004; Klein, 2005). Congruent with the group relations notion of group-as-whole and the LP assumption of the individual speaking on behalf of the system, the researchers analysed the data and reported them (Stapley, 2006). For each theme, the researchers formulated a working hypothesis. They integrated them into the research hypothesis (see Schafer, 2003).

Strategies Employed to Ensure Quality Data

The researchers ensured scientific rigour by focusing on credibility, dependability, transferability and ethics (Denzin & Lincoln, 2005; Terre Blanche, Durrheim & Painter, 2006). They ensured credibility through the authorised involvement of all parties (Hirschhorn, 1997). They ensured dependability using the scientific rigour they applied in planning and executing the research project. Transferability referred to ensuring a scientific link between the LP data and the systems psychodynamic stance (Denzin & Lincoln, 2005; Eisner, 1998).

The first researcher is a psychologist with training in systems psychodynamics – as it applies to consulting and research, according to the conditions of Brunner, Nutkevitch and Sher (2006). Ethicality referred to obtaining the informed consent of all participants, keeping the identities of the eight volunteers confidential, not causing them harm or invading their privacy (De Vos, Strydom, Fouché & Delport, 2002).

Reporting

The researchers reported their findings in terms of the manifested basic assumption themes.

Findings

Two themes emerged. They were anxiety and basic assumption functioning.

Anxiety

Participants experienced crossing the boundary into the master's programme and the selection as 'intimidating', 'overwhelming' and 'daunting'. They were pessimistic ('I did not think I would make it'). They found the selection 'surprising' and saw the procedure as an obstacle to their dreams of becoming psychologists. On the other hand, their acceptance in the programme led to 'excitement' and 'feeling very special' to know 'that I was successful'. Once participants started engaging with the task of handing in assignments, their excitement faded. They became 'surprised that this was not the same as honours'. They described the work as 'hard', 'difficult', 'pressuring' and 'unstructured'. It made them feel 'out of my comfort zone' and 'out of control'. They realised that they would have to 'juggle everything', 'strike a balance' and use skills that they had never used before.

Most participants considered leaving the programme at some point. They reported feeling despondent and having thoughts of 'giving up'. Their anxiety about failure brought compulsive coping methods to the fore: 'I just worked harder' and 'put in more hours'. Many had to make a decision 'to go or to stay', to 'get stuck in fear' or 'make a paradigm shift' and become 'flexible'. Their possible failure did not relate to their dreams of becoming psychologists. Their anxiety was about survival. They approached it by competing ('I know I was stronger than some of the others'), guilt (leaving would 'rob another person from participation'), projection ('I am doing this for my family'), personal growth ('I have to lift myself and be strong') and self-motivation ('I know I am much more resilient than I thought').

Once they began to get their marked assignments back, they realised that lecturers commented on their performance and marked in different ways. They experienced this as 'an inconsistency' and 'a disappointment'. Some suggested that the complexity of the course content was unexpected and difficult to deal with. Participants coped with the work and the split experience by relying on their own resilience or by becoming rebellious, ('I just wanted to give it up, and get my life back'). Participants expressed 'how naive' their expectations were to think that 'the master's would be easy'. They 'realised how little I know' about what the programme was about in terms of academic content.

Participants experienced a split between various aspects relating to their competence. On the one hand, they said that they knew what they needed to do. They had the energy to do the work and had been successful up to that point in time. On the other hand, they did not know what they needed to do, were unsure and experienced a lack of confidence about doing anything ('I thought I just can't do this'). Their naiveté was connected to 'not knowing' the content of the programme, 'not knowing what I got myself in to' and not having any idea what master's study was about ('no one in my family did such a degree before'; 'I never thought of what a psychologist really does').

Basic Assumption Functioning

Dependence

Participants expressed their strong dependence on predictability, form and structure. They often referred to the master's programme as 'having no structure' and how 'unexpected' that was. They expressed their need for emotional security as a 'soundboard', 'a mentor or life coach' to 'give perspective'. Participants continuously referred to their dependent coping mechanism of needing to be self-reliant and resilient, as if this had become their religion (Blackman, 2004) – something to guide them through difficult times in the programme. Counter dependence manifested in the participants' implied love-hate relationships with the lecturers. They saw the lecturing staff members as 'intimidating', 'inconsistent' and as causes of confusion in the different ways they gave feedback on assignments. Comments on how lonely they were usually followed these comments. Instead of working with their loneliness in an authorised manner (Hirschhorn, 1997), they became stuck in their lonely child ego state (James, 1977). It was as if their need to stay reactive and childlike was stronger than their need to step into adult roles of pushing boundaries (Cytrynbaum & Noumair, 2004).

Fight and Flight

Fight responses manifested in participants' excuses for not having enough time and resources. It was as if they were fighting something outside of themselves in order to avoid taking responsibility for being out of control. In a way, they were fighting the primary task of being a student and learning (Bion, 2003). They said they were 'overwhelmed' and thus de-authorised (Campbell & Groenbaek, 2006).

The participants did not allow themselves to express any negative feelings. Yet, below the surface, their aggressive tendencies appeared in their projections onto the 'rigid programme', 'limited time' and the 'inconsistent lecturers'. It was as if they contained the students' survival anxiety. It seemed that the conflict they were fighting was to stay in the programme and keep their family relationships and marriages intact.

Flight responses manifested as flight into-past and into-future. In their fantasy, the past was an ideal place where the students 'had time to attend to their families' and when they were in a 'much more structured' and less complex honours IOP course. At the same time, they fantasised about the future as a place where they would complete their studies and be professional psychologists. In this future flight, they also negated their second-year dissertation. Another flight response was avoiding feelings of anger and hostility towards authority figures (including the lecturers in the room) – it was as if the students desperately needed to impress them. This avoidance extended to their search for their own identities (Campbell & Huffington, 2008).

Pairing

Participants tried to pair with authority: the lecturers, the department and the programme. Because authority did not reciprocate, the participants projected their anger back and described authority as distant, cold, inefficient and unstructured. As compensation, they expressed the need for a soundboard, mentor and coach, which they always linked to expressions of 'God's grace'. It was as if they projected their lonely struggle onto an imagined connection with a force that would save them miraculously and gracefully from the anxiety of coping on their own. Therefore, they did not address their high level of performance anxiety successfully.

As another compensation, they started (through their assignments) to pair with their tasks. This happened in their singleton roles based on their individual resilience, about which they became quite proud. The evidence showed that the participants, as a collective, struggled with building any kind of relationship. This might be a result of their high levels of interpersonal competition and the accompanying performance anxiety (Blackman, 2004).

One-ness

The researchers did not refer to the participants as objects of togetherness or cohesion. They framed the relatedness identity of the participants in their connection with outsiders and imagined authority figures (mentors). Therefore, their emotional attachment was with their known and fantasy relationships and their detachment towards those in the same boat as themselves. The researchers hypothesised that the intensity of the competition in the group led to the participants avoiding internal intimacy. This could also have happened to keep the fantasy of winning the competition alive (Czander, 1993).

Me-ness

Participants' one-ness as group members manifested in their relatedness to their families. One participant referred to doing the studies 'for my family'. Me-ness also manifested in the many references to 'me', 'myself', 'I', 'my studies', 'I'd rather do it myself' – as if the participants were fighting to have an effect and be heard as individuals. Participants also referred to their 'loneliness' and 'alienation'. This linked to working on assignments late at night. It was as if the master's programme had become the participants' life partners with whom they spent many intimate nights. One participant referred to a recent divorce. This showed that me-ness compensated for the loss of meaningful relationships. Participants expressed their loneliness in the first person singular – as if they could not even make emotional connections with loss.

The importance of personal growth followed most references to loneliness. It was as if personal growth, as an individual endeavour, became a defence against connecting with others. Participants conceptualised personal growth as toughness in coping with difficult circumstances. This framing did not include the relationship interdependency that personal growth models, like self-actualisation (Rogers, 1985) or individualisation (Jung, 1986), describe. On another level, it was as if participants attached to their singleton roles strongly as a defence against the anxiety of sharing and letting others see their vulnerability.

Discussion

The purpose of the study was to describe the system psychodynamic experiences of first-year master's students in industrial and organisational psychology. The research was important because of its rich description of students' unconscious experiences. Accessing these behaviours could assist students and academic departments to manage students' expectations and demands during master's studies.

Theme 1: Anxiety

This theme illustrated the extent and depth of the students' unconscious experiences. They projected their paranoid anxiety (Czander, 1993) about failure and leaving the programme onto the selection procedure and the lecturers. Their performance anxiety (Menzies, 1993) became arrogance, implying that they knew more than the authority figures did about assessment. The researchers interpreted this as narcissistic tendencies the students used as a defence against their vulnerability (Sandler, Person & Fonagy, 2004).

The students idealised (Blackman, 2004) their membership of the programme and becoming psychologists. At the same time, they felt under attack from the demands of the programme. The researchers interpreted this as feelings of being inadequate (Klein, 1988). This suggested that the students projected their narcissism to relieve their shame about their inadequacy (Freud, 1921). This defence was a turning into the self. Instead of being angry at the objects of their anger (like the department), they introjected the anger (Blackman, 2004). The researchers interpreted this behaviour as perfectionism – an obsessive narcissistic wish (Blackman, 2004). This suggests that their wish for narcissistic perfection acted as a defensive distortion of reality (an affectionately labelled fantasy based on the originally perfect self-object bliss of the symbiotic phase). See Czander (1993).

The researchers interpreted the students' surprise and naiveté as a denial of the complexity inherent in a master's programme and psychology training – a disavowal of a reality despite the overwhelming evidence of its existence (Blackman, 2004). The researchers interpreted the students' need to leave the programme as regression (Campbell & Huffington, 2008) because of their insecurity and because parental figures were not meeting their need for acceptance. This was a defence against their perceived incompetence and the introjections thereof.

Reaction formation (Blackman, 2004) manifested as individual resilience to cover for their unexpressed anger, incompetence and vulnerability. They split the good (positive) from the bad (negative) as a symptom of their denial of autonomy (Czander, 1993). They could not move out of this ambiguity. This means that they could not move to a position where they projected only good feelings and parts onto an object in order to idealise it and subsequently to develop superior-subordinate relations, integrate and bond (Vansina & Vansina-Cobbaert, 2008). It was as if their child ego state functioning (James, 1977) and its primitive defences of splitting and projection (Blackman, 2004) had trapped them.

Working Hypothesis 1

Their anxiety to impress, and get acceptance from, their authority-in-the-mind de-authorise master's students when they enter the programme. They introject incompetence, project competence onto the academic staff and rivalry onto student colleagues. This leaves them stuck in their singleton roles with only individual resilience as a coping mechanism.

Theme 2: Basic Assumption Functioning

This theme illustrated the intensity of master's students' anxiety about the content and structure of the programme. They split their previous ability to use structure from their present incompetence about not coping with lack of structure. They became dependent on various objects that did not satisfy their performance needs and acted out their counter dependence on staff members as parental figures. They used fight to get attention and flight when it did not happen. They had limited resources to connect with one another as support systems. Therefore, they had to use their individual resilience to cope. If this carries on for long, one can expect symptoms of burnout (Cilliers, 2003), as in their expressed helplessness.

The researchers interpreted the students' tendency to avoid building relationships with others as their over-identification with authority (as parental figures). It is a defence against building relationships with peers. This may connect to their performance anxiety about research when they pair with a supervisor and the dissertation becomes the result (a baby). Playing out their intimacy needs in relatedness with authority could help them to achieve their ultimate goal of qualifying as psychologists.

Working Hypothesis 2

Master's students' performance anxiety and inability to form new relationships lead to experienced incompetence with individual resilience as their only available coping mechanism.

The researchers integrated these findings using the adapted CIBART model (Cilliers & Koortzen, 2005). Because all of the interpretations imply conflict, the researchers did not treat it as a separate theme.

Task

In terms of their primary task, students expressed their realistic cognitive understanding of what they need to do. Emotionally, they felt overwhelmed and exhausted. Motivationally, they experienced high levels of performance anxiety and a need to over-control (Sievers, 2009). This derailed the task emotionally. The students replaced it with survival (originally a secondary task) as the new primary task. The researchers linked their performance anxiety and narcissism and thought that the department, by referring to the master's programme as the department's flagship, projected their performance anxiety onto the students. The department unconsciously tasked them with keeping the ship sailing on its behalf but without authorising them to do so. This could explain the student's irrationality and lack of (sibling) relationships.

Role

In their normative roles (Obholzer & Roberts, 1994), the students were cognitively and emotionally unclear about entering the programme and managing their academic tasks. Their previous academic skills did not help them. In their experiential roles, they introjected pressure and incompetence. The researchers interpreted this as the method the students used to contain the shadow side of the system, allowing the lecturers to keep the competence. This left the students in the adapted child ego state with its anxiety about unclear boundaries. In their phenomenal roles, the students carried and identified with, the systemic projections about learners or children performing academically well whilst remaining personally resilient. This made the parents (the department) look good but not good enough and they authorised themselves to be regarded as adults (Vansina & Vansina-Cobbaert, 2008).

Authorisation

The students experienced their authorisation as a roller coaster of high and low expectations, hope and despair, competence and incompetence. They experienced low emotional authorisation from the authority figures (the academic staff members) but could not manage effective and supportive inter-relationships. This meant that they had to self-authorise as a defence against the withholding of the authority figures (Vansina & Vansina-Cobbaert, 2008). The authority-in-the-mind (Armstrong, 2005) disappointed them. This meant that they had to contain everything that was authoritative and rely on resilience.

The researchers interpreted their way of self-authorisation as the next wave of dependence on authority. This was to use many positive psychology constructs in their discourse. This started a new wave of competition amongst them, albeit to argue whom the most resilient student would be (Stapley, 2006).

Boundaries

The students experienced high levels of anxiety about task and time boundaries (Lawrence, 1999). The researchers interpreted the lack of clarity about task boundaries as their limited authorisation, especially from within. With regard to the students' struggle to manage time, the researchers felt that it was because the students were emotionally out of control and struggling to differentiate and integrate (Fox & Spector, 2005). They tried hard not to let the emotional toxicity (see Porter-O'Grady & Malloch, 2007) spill over into their work and family lives. References to God and the church surrounded these responses. The researchers interpreted them as the students' guilt feelings about not attending to their families well enough. It was as if the students used their guilt and shame (Mollon, 2004) to hide their anger about being away from their loved ones – the anger that they could not express at the programme authorities.

The participants interpreted their anxiety about the time and task boundaries as their incompetence and 'not making it'. The turned the challenge of managing boundaries into opportunities to be resilient and to compete by being strong, self-reliant, independent and, eventually, lonely. It was as if holding tight boundaries around the self-became their formula for survival (Obholzer & Roberts, 1994).

Identity

The students' identity consciously contained their rational attachment (Rholes & Simpson, 2004) to their academic tasks and their boundary demands. Their work became unconsciously counterproductive (Fox & Spector, 2005) because their anxiety about balancing intellectual and emotional demands, differentiating and integrating (Sievers, 2009) preoccupied them. The split between academic performance and personal development drained their emotional and, sometimes, intellectual energy. Nevertheless, their self-idealisation and quest for perfection motivated them – if not to achieve academic excellence then at least to become more resilient (see Sievers, 2009).

Working Hypothesis 3

The split between holding on to their intellectual and academic competence, whilst struggling to stay emotionally grounded, characterises students' identity. They introject the adapted child ego state with frustrated attachment needs and use flight into an obsessive search for personal growth.

Research Hypothesis

The researchers formulated the research hypothesis that follows. After a period of adaptation, master's students seem to cope with most of the intellectual demands of the programme. They introject incompetence. This leads to their feeling stuck because they do not have access to a wide repertoire of feelings and ways of connecting. It eventually drains their energy. Their compensatory defence is a quest for personal growth to cope and to impress authority.

Conclusions

The researchers concluded that, although most IOP master's students seem to perform well academically, it seems that the programme unconsciously acts as an attack on their emotional and relational coping mechanisms. This is a conflict between being competent and feeling incompetent. As a defence against the attack, students compensate by using flight into personal growth for the sake of coping, and not – as the positive psychology literature suggests (Snyder & Lopez, 2002) – to achieve the most favourable life experiences, happiness and meaning. The compensation impressed the department. The evidence suggested that the notion of growth that the students acted out actually serves the department's agenda and narcissistic fantasy.

Recommendations

The researchers recommend that the findings are shared with academic staff members to study the manifestation and depth of the unconscious experiences of master's students in IOP. Practices could be built into the selection and training to make these experiences more real, to counteract the high levels of anxiety and as learning opportunities for students.

Possible limitations of the study

A limitation of the study was that the researchers were part of the system they studied (see Hinshelwood & Skogstad, 2005). This suggests that subjective experiences influenced the trustworthiness of the data.

Suggestions for Further Research

The researchers suggest that future research focuses on system domain defences (Bain, 1998) that manifest in higher education teaching and learning as well as in master's training in psychology. Although it was not the aim of this research, the researchers became aware of parallel processes and the mirroring that manifested between the students and the staff (see Kets de Vries, 1991). One could hypothesise that the student subsystem contained the projected performance anxiety on behalf of the academic staff. This needs to be researched further.

Acknowledgements

Competing interests

The authors declare that they have no financial or personal relationship(s) that may have inappropriately influenced them when they wrote this paper.

Authors' contributions

F.C. (University of South Africa) was responsible for planning and conducting the empirical research as well as interpreting the data. N.H. (University of South Africa) helped to gather data and with the literature search.

References

Alvesson, M. & Sköldberg, K. (2010). *Reflexive methodology. New vistas for qualitative research.* London: Sage.

Armstrong, D. (2005). *Organisation in the mind. Psychoanalysis, group relations and organisational consultancy.* London: Karnac.

Bain, A. (1998). Social defences against organisational learning. *Human Relations,* 51(3):413-429. https://doi.org/10.1177/001872679805100309

Bion, W.R. (1961). *Experiences in groups.* London: Tavistock.

Bion, W.R. (1970). *Attention and interpretation.* London: Tavistock.

Bion, W.R. (2003). *Learning from experience.* London: Karnac.

Blackman, J.S. (2004). *101 Defences. How the mind shields itself.* New York: Brunner-Routledge. https://doi.org/10.4324/9780203492369

Breverton, P. & Millward, L. (2004). *Organisational research methods. A guide for students and researchers.* London: Sage.

Brunner, L.D.; Nutkevitch, A. & Sher, M. (2006). *Group relations conferences. Reviewing and exploring theory, design, role-taking and application.* London: Karnac.

Camic, P.M.; Rhodes, J.E. & Yardley, L. (2003). *Qualitative research in Psychology.* Washington: APA.

Campbell, D. (2007). *The socially constructed organisation.* London: Karnac.

Campbell, D. & Groenbaek, M. (2006). *Taking positions in the organisation.* London: Karnac.

Campbell, D. & Huffington, C. (2008). *Organisations connected. A handbook of systemic consultation.* London: Karnac.

Chamberlayne, P.; Bornat, J. & Apitzsch, U. (2004). *Biographical methods and professional practice. An international perspective.* Bristol: Policy Press. https://doi.org/10.1332/policypress/9781861344939.001.0001

Cilliers, F. (2003). A systems psychodynamic perspective on burnout. *South African Journal of Industrial Psychology,* 29(4):26-33. https://doi.org/10.4102/sajip.v29i4.120

Cilliers, F. & Koortzen, P. (2005). Conflict in groups. The CIBART model. *HR Future,* October:52-53.

Clarke, S. & Hoggett, P. (2009). *Researching beneath the surface. Psycho-social research methods in practice.* London: Karnac.

Colman, A.D. & Bexton, W.H. (1975). *Group relations reader 1.* Jupiter: The A.K. Rice Institute.

Colman, A.D. & Geller, M.H. (1985). *Group relations reader 2.* Jupiter: The A.K. Rice Institute.

Conrad, C.F.; Duren, J. & Haworth J.G. (2002). Student's perspectives on their master's degree experiences: Disturbing the conventional wisdom. *New Directions in Higher Education,* 101:65-76. https://doi.org/10.1002/he.10106

Cytrynbaum, S. & Noumair, A. (2004). *Group dynamics, organizational irrationality, and social complexity. Group relations reader 3.* Jupiter: A.K. Rice.

Czander, W.M. (1993). *The psychodynamics of work and organizations.* New York: Guilford.

Dartington, T. (2000). The pre-occupation of the citizen – reflections from the OPUS Listening Posts. *Organisational and Social Dynamics*, 1:94-112.

De Vos, A.S.; Strydom, H.; Fouche, C.B. & Delport, C.S.L. (2002). *Research at grass roots. For the social sciences and human service professions*. Pretoria: Van Schaik.

Denzin, N.K. & Lincoln, Y.S. (2005). *The Sage handbook of qualitative research*. London: Sage. https://doi.org/10.1177/1468794105047237

Eisner, E.W. (1998). *The enlightened eye: qualitative inquiry and the enhancement of educational practice*. Toronto: Macmillan.

Fox, S. & Spector, P.E. (2005). *Counterproductive work behaviour. Investigations of actors and targets*. Washington: APA. https://doi.org/10.1037/10893-000

Fraher, A. (2004). *A history of group study and psychodynamic organisations*. London: Free Association.

Freud, S. (1921). *Group psychology and the analysis of the ego. Complete works of Sigmund Freud*. London: Hogarth. https://doi.org/10.1037/11327-000

Gould, L.J.; Stapley, L.F. & Stein, M. (2004). *Experiential learning in organizations. Application of the Tavistock Group Relations Approach*. London: Karnac.

Hinshelwood, R.D. & Skogstad, W. (2005). *Observing organisations. Anxiety, defence and culture in health care*. London: Routledge.

Hirschhorn, L. (1997). *Reworking authority. Leading and following in the post-modern organisation*. London: MIT.

Huffington, C.; Armstrong, A.; Halton, W.; Hoyle, L. & Pooley, J. (2004). *Working below the surface. The emotional life of contemporary organisations*. London: Karnac.

James, M. (1977). *Techniques in transactional analysis for psychotherapists and counsellors*. Reading: Addison-Wesley.

Jung, C.G. (1986). *Psychological reflections*. London: Collins.

Kets de Vries, M.F.R. (1991). *Organizations on the coach. Clinical perspectives on organizational behaviour and change*. San Francisco: Jossey-Bass.

Klein, L. (2005). *Working across the gap. The practise of social science in organisations*. London: Karnac.

Klein, M. (1988). *Envy and gratitude and other works 1946-1963*. London: Hogarth.

Lawrence, W.G. (1999). *Exploring individual and organisational boundaries. A Tavistock open systems approach*. London: Karnac.

Lawrence, W.G.; Bain, A. & Gould, L. (1996). *The fifth basic assumption*. London: Tavistock.

Marcketti, S.B.; Mhango, M.W. & Gregoire, M.B. (2006). The experiences of African Graduate students in a College of Human Sciences. *Journal of Family and Consumer Sciences education*, 24(1):63-72.

Menzies, I.E.P. (1993). *The functioning of social systems as a defence against anxiety*. London: Tavistock.

Miller, E.J. (1993). *From dependency to autonomy. Studies in organization and change*. London: Free Association.

Mollon, P. (2004). *Shame and jealousy. The hidden turmoils*. London: Karnac.

Murphy, E. & Coleman, E. (2004). Graduate students' experiences of challenges in online asynchronous discussions. *Canadian Journal of Learning and Technology*, 30(2):1-9. https://doi.org/10.21432/T27G7N

Neumann, J.E.; Keller, K. & Dawson-Shepherd, A. (1997). *Developing organisational consultancy.* London: Routledge.

Obholzer, A. & Roberts, V.Z. (1994). *The unconscious at work.* London: Routledge.

Popov, O. (2009). Teacher's and student's experiences of simultaneous teaching in an international distance and on-campus master's programme in engineering. *The International Review of Research in Open and Distance learning*, 10(3):1-8. https://doi.org/10.19173/irrodl.v10i3.669

Porter-O'Grady, T. & Malloch, K. (2007). *Quantum leadership. A resource for health care innovation.* Boston: Jones & Bartlett.

Rautenbach, I. (2007). An Electronic Learning (e-learning) Readiness Model for Distance Education in the workplace. Unpublished Doctoral Thesis, University of North West, Potchefstroom, South Africa.

Rholes, W.S. & Simpson, J.A. (2004). *Adult attachment. Theory, research and clinical implications.* New York: Guilford.

Rogers, C. (1985). *Carl Rogers on personal power. Inner strength and its revolutionary impact.* London: Constable.

Sandler, J.; Person, E.S. & Fonagy, P. (2004). *Freud's 'On narcissism: An introduction'.* London: International Psychoanalytical Association.

Schafer, R. (2003). *Insight and interpretation. The essential tools of psychoanalysis.* London: Karnac.

Sievers, B. (2009). *Psychoanalytic studies of organizations. Contributions from the International Society for the Psychoanalytical Study of Organizations (ISPSO).* London: Karnac.

Snyder C.R. & Lopez, S.J. (2002). *Handbook of positive psychology.* Oxford: Oxford University Press.

Stapley, L.F. & Collie, A. (2005). Global dynamics at the dawn of 2005. *Organizational and Social Dynamics*, 5(1):111-133.

Stapley, L.F. & Rickman, C. (2010). Global dynamics at the dawn of 2010. *Organisational and social dynamics*, 10(1):118-141.

Stapley, L.F. (1996). *The personality of the organisation. A psychodynamic explanation of culture and change.* London: Free Association.

Stapley, L.F. (2006). *Individuals, groups and organisations beneath the surface.* London: Karnac.

Stiwne, E.E. & Jungert, T. (2007). Engineering students' experiences of the transition from study to work. *Proceedings of the 3rd International CDIO Conference*, MIT, Cambridge, Massachusetts, USA, 11-14 June.

Terre Blanche, M.; Durrheim, K. & Painter, D. (2006). *Research in practice. Applied methods for the social sciences.* Cape Town: UCT Press.

Turquet, P.M. (1974). Leadership – the individual in the group. In: G.S. Gibbard, J.J. Hartman & R.D. Mann. *Analysis of groups*, p.357. San Francisco: Jossey-Bass.

Vansina, L.S. & Vansina-Cobbaert, M. (2008). *Psychodynamics for consultants and managers. From understanding to leading meaningful change.* Chichester: Wiley-Blackwell. https://doi.org/10.1002/9780470697184

Watts, L. (2009). Managing self in role: Using multiple methodologies to explore self-construction and self-governance. In: S. Clarke & P. Hoggett (eds.), *Researching beneath the surface. Psycho-social research methods in practice,* pp.215-239. London: Karnac. https://doi.org/10.4324/9780429479564-10

Theme 3 | Systems Psychodynamics in Team Formation

Article 1

Team-Building from a Psychodynamic Perspective[1]

F Cilliers

Abstract

The aim of this research is to measure the impact of a psychodynamic Tavistock stance, team-building event. Its task is to provide opportunities for learning about team behaviour and dynamics. Consultants offer interpretations in the form of working hypotheses about what is happening in the here-and-now: This refers to the basic assumptions (dependency, fight/flight, pairing) and its relevant dynamic concepts. Post measured, qualitative research findings, indicate an increase in knowledge about the team's unconscious behaviour, a realisation of own identity, boundaries, potential and a strong sense of empowerment to act collectively in problem-solving,

According to many predictions, future organisational success will rely increasingly on effective group behaviour and team-building (Robbins, 1998). Most large South African organisations have started building effective work and management teams over the last decade (Kruger, 1999). This task is performed by industrial/organisational psychologists and Human Resources practitioners acting as internal and/or external consultants, and who are traditionally trained to work from the functionalistic and for humanistic paradigm(s).

The functionalistic approach (Morgan, 1980) is regulative and pragmatic in orientation and it tries to understand behaviour in a way which generates

1   Cilliers, F. (2000). Team-building from a psychodynamic perspective. *South African Journal of Industrial Psychology*, 26(1):18-23.

useful empirical knowledge. Its assumptions are that society has a real and concrete existence and a systematic character oriented to produce an ordered and regulated state of affairs. Behaviour is seen as being contextually bound in a real-world of concrete and tangible social relationships. Within this approach, the ream would be exposed to predetermined exercises where after typical roles, generally played in groups, would be ascribed to participants, for example, according to the Belbin (1993) theory. The focus on order, regulation and concreteness, makes this a mechanical approach to team-building, in the sense that the team's behaviour is measured against expected behaviour. Furthermore, because the so-called facilitator tells the team how it should behave, dependence on outside authority is created, which disempowers the team (Miller, 1993).

The humanistic approach (Quitmann, 1985) sees the person as more than the sum of his/her parts, being principally good, existing in a human context, acting in awareness, making choices and living purposefully. Within this approach, the team would focus on its development through the theoretically predicted group processes of forming, storming, norming and performing (Bergh & Theron, 1999:262-263), as well as on membership skills of listening to and giving one another feedback (Luft, 1984). Although this approach refers to growth in terms of self-actualisation, respect and openness as core values (Rogers, 1975; 1982), the focus is more on individual growth and interpersonal effectiveness (Cilliers, 1995a; 1995b; Cilliers & Wissing 1993), than on team behaviour. Sometimes, in working forms these assumptions, reference is made to "group dynamics" (Kruger, 1999:50-52), which in further investigation, refers to the processes of the group and not its dynamic behaviour (such as the teams' – collective – unconscious behaviour with its underlying anxiety, splits and defence mechanisms – Miller, 1993).

As an alternative to the above mentioned traditional team building approaches, this research suggests the Tavistock stance, which originated at the Tavistock Institute in the UK (Miller, 1989; 1993), and the AK Rice Institute in the USA (Coleman & Bexton, 1975; Coleman & Geller, 1985). This approach has become synonymous with the study of organisational behaviour and consulting to organisations form the psychodynamic approach.

Although Freud and Jung – as the fathers of psychoanalysis – did not comment directly on the application of psychodynamic principles in the world of work (Czander, 1993:11), especially Freud's theories were used as basis for this purpose, incorporating the work of Melany Klein on child and family psychology (De Board, 1978:25-34), Ferenczi on object relations (De Board, 1978:22-24; Hugg et al., 1993:138-

146) and Bertalanffy on systems thinking, developing into the open systems model (Czandcl, 1993:43; De Board, 1978:86-111; Hirshhorn, 1993; Hugg et al., 1993:130-137; 193-197). This has been used in group relations working conferences for over 50 years (Cytrynbaum & Lee, 1993:125-133; Lawrence, 1979:1-19; 53-68), developed into a workable organisational theory (Bion, 1961; 1970; Lawrence, 1979; Miller, 1976; 1983; 1993), as well as an organisational Consultancy stance (French & Vince, 1999; Gabelnick & Carr, 1989:97-104; Lawrence, 1979; Neumann et al., 1997).

The above-mentioned psychodynamic stance is well known and used in Psychiatry in Europe and the USA (Menzies, 1993; Miller, 1976; 1980; Obholzer & Roberts, 1994:49-118; Rioch, 1970). Its application in organisational psychology is growing internationally. In South Africa however, very few Industrial/ Organisational psychologists and/or Human Resources practitioners know about this stance or have been exposed to such training. Research from this stance in team building situations have been reported (Cytrynbaum & Lee, 1993:44-54; French & Vince, 1999; Gabelnick & Carr, 1989:103-113; Kets de Vries, 1991). However, these studies are conceptual in nature and no impact studies could be found in the existing literature.

Aim of this Research

The aim of this research is to measure the impact of a team building event presented from the psychodynamic approach or Tavistock stance.

Rationale and Hypothesis for Presenting Team-Building from the Psychodynamic Approach

The rationale for studying team behaviour from the psychodynamic approach can be stated as follows (Coleman & Bexton, 1975; Czander, 1993:123-143; French & Vince, 1999; Gabelnick & Carr, 1989:175-179; Hirschorn, 1993; Kets de Vries, 1991; Lawrence, 1979; Miller, 1993; Obholzer & Roberts, 1994). Some team behaviour is clear and explicit. Others have to do with needs and anxieties that are unconscious. When this is discovered, team members find themselves unexpectedly resistant to change. The team usually assumes that there is a right way of behaving or a set of rules for its conduct, when in fact these are conventions that the team has developed collectively. These are then used to disguise unexamined relationships of power and authority.

From the same above-mentioned sources on the Tavistock stance, a few basic hypotheses about team behaviour can be formulated.

∞ Team members approach the work situation with unconscious and unfulfilled family needs which manifest in the work situation. An example is when unfulfilled needs for recognition or affection expected from parents, are played out in the relationship with the manager, who represents male or female authority.

∞ Team members bring unconscious and unresolved conflict, for example with parental authority, into the team. Because the role of the manager excludes relating to the team member in the way a father or mother would, the team member experiences frustration.

∞ Team members unconsciously play out unfulfilled past needs for power over and competition with siblings and the parental figure. Because colleagues are not siblings or parents, the need does not fit the reality of the here-and-now work situation. This leads to confusion, anxiety, anger and aggression.

The Basic Assumptions of the Psychodynamic Approach to Team-Building

Bion's (1961) three basic assumptions explain individual (the micro-system), team (the meso system) and organisational (the macro-system) behaviour as well as the dynamics between them. These assumptions are generally accepted as the corner-stones of psychodynamic group work (French & Vince, 1999; Kets de Vries, 1991; Miller, 1993; Rice, 1963; Rioch, 1970).

Dependency

The assumption is that team members, in the same way as children in a family, unconsciously experience dependency from (imaginative) parental figures or systems. Because these needs are irrelevant in the workplace, and thus not met, team members experience frustration, helplessness, powerlessness and disempowerment. Typical remarks in this regard are, "why is the boss not giving us more attention?" and "what do you want us to do?" These expressions are seen as projections of own anxiety and insecurity and indicate work and emotional immaturity. Organisationally it manifests in the need for structure in remarks such as "we need a committee to "investigate" or "we need to structure this department more": This defence against anxiety results in the manipulation of the authority figure out of its role, for example from supervisor to parental figure in view of the fantasy of then "we will be safe/cared for":

Fight/flight

The assumption is that the here-and-now of teamwork is filled with anxiety. In trying to get away from this discomfort, team members unconsciously use fight or flight as defence mechanisms. Fight reactions manifest in aggression against the self, colleagues (with envy, jealousy, competition, elimination, boycotting, sibling rivalry, fighting for a position in the group and for privileged relationships) or the authority figure. Flight reactions manifest physically in for example avoidance of others, being ill or by resigning from the team or organisation. Psychological flight reactions would include defence mechanisms such as avoidance of threatening situations or feelings, rationalisation and intellectualisation. In a meeting, for example, this would mean talking about "them "and "out there" issues, and thus avoiding taking ownership of "what this behaviour is saying about us".

Pairing

The assumption is that in order to cope with anxiety, alienation and loneliness, the team member tries to pair with perceived powerful team members and/or subgroups. The unconscious need is to feel secure and to create. The unconscious fantasy is that creation will take place in pairs. Pairing also implies splitting up (Hugg et al., 1993:31-43), which may happen because of experienced anxiety in a diverse workplace. Examples are the splits between black and white, male and female, senior and junior and old and new. Unconsciously the individual or the team tries to split up the whole and build a smaller system, to which he/she can belong and feel seconding. It also manifests in ganging up against the perceived aggressor or authority figure. Intra and intergroup conflict may for example result from pairing.

Psychodynamic Team Behaviour

These include anxiety, boundaries, taking up a role, representation, authority, leadership and followership, relationship and relatedness and group as a whole.

Anxiety

Anxiety is accepted as the basis of all team (and organisational) behaviour (French & Vince, 1999; Lawrence, 1979:206-208; Menzies, 1993). In order to cope with this discomfort, the team unconsciously needs something or someone to contain the anxiety on its behalf (Gabelnick & Carr, 1989:5-22).This is done by means of defence mechanisms, serving the purpose of gaining a sense of safety, security and acceptance in the workplace. Projection may be used to blame management for what goes wrong. For example, the team may expect the manager to contain its anxiety about losing jobs, securing jobs in a difficult labour market or negotiating with the union on its behalf (The team may also expect the existing structures like laws, regulations, procedures, organograms, job descriptions and idiosyncratic ways of solving problems, to act as containers for anxiety. The moment the level of anxiety in the system rises, the need for structure is expressed in for example "let's make a rule about …: "why don't you put this on paper" and "let's discuss this in future … : Projective identification takes place when feelings or other behaviours are projected into another team member or subsystem, who then accepts and internalises the behaviour – influencing the self as well as the other (Neumann et al., 1997:145). An example would be when the team is unconsciously making the human resources manager carry the feelings -or so-called "soft issues" – on behalf of the team, and then this person becomes a soft-spoken and caring team member. Rationalisation and intellectualisation are used to stay emotionally uninvolved and to feel safe and in control (Miller, 1993).

Boundaries

In the same way psychoanalysis refers to ego boundaries, distinguishing between the individual and the environment, the team member, the team and the organisation as interactive parts of the total system, operate inside and across its boundaries (Cytrynbaum & Lee, 1993:55-62; Czander, 1993:203; Hirschhorn, 1993:31-39; Kets de Vries, 1991; Lawrence, 1979; Miller, 1993; Neumann et al., 1997). The purpose of setting organisational boundaries is to contain anxiety, thus making the workplace controllable and pleasant. Examples of boundary management in teams are time, space and task (Miller, 1989).

Time boundaries are used to structure the working day (starting, going home, meetings) in an endeavour to order, structure and contain. The space boundary refers to the workplace itself, for example, to know exactly where to sit or stand whilst working, having an own desk, cabinet, locker, office or building. It may be argued that having to work in an open-plan office, creates anxiety because of the lack of dear space boundaries. The task boundary refers to knowing what the work content entails. The anxiety about not knowing what to do and according to what standard, is contained in structures such as the job description and organogram. Another example of a boundary issue is the forming of team identity (Miller, 1993), which, if nor managed effectively, creates a lot of anxiety in team members. Also important is the desire to be in (for example the manager's "good books" for acceptance) versus the anxiety of being out, rejected or ostracised.

Taking up a Role

To take up a team role (Czander, 1993:294; French & Vince, 1999:209-223; Gabelnick & Carr, 1989:205-210; Hirschhorn, 1993:40-56; Kets de Vries, 1991; Lawrence, 1979:235-249), implies uncertainty and risk. Anxiety is not simply rooted in the team member's internal "voices" or private preoccupations, but it reflects real threats to professional identity. If the team member's anxiety becomes too difficult to bear, he/she may escape by stepping out of the role. An example would be when the "professionally caring" human resources practitioner expresses frustration and anger in a real way. Anxiety is transformed along a chain of interaction through the psychological process of projection and introjection (Hirschhorn, 1993). Psychological violence happens inside the individual as a result of the inter-play between anxiety created by real uncertainty, and anxiety created by threatening "voices" within. These mostly parental voices are punishing the team member, and paradoxically, he/she can feel bad even before he/she has failed in reality. This anxiety chain leads team members to violate boundaries and other team members. When anxiety mobilises behaviour, the team member experiences others not as they are, but as he/she needs them to be, so that the others can play a role in the individual's internal drama (Hirschhorn, 1993:50).

Representation

This occurs when a team member or the whole team crosses a boundary (Lawrence, 1979:103-109; Kets de Vries, 1991). The crossing of individual (micro-system) boundaries happens in interpersonal communication. The crossing of meso-system boundaries happens in meetings between teams or departments. An example would be when the human resources department has a planning meeting about training with the production department. The crossing of macro-system boundaries happens when a team member or whole team meets with an individual or group from another organisation. The issue of representation refers to the authority given to the person crossing the boundary on behalf of someone else, the team or the organisation (Obholzer & Roberts, 1994). Unclear authority boundaries seem to immobilise and disempower representatives in other parts of the system.

Authorisation

This approach distinguishes between three levels of authorisation (Czander, 1993:266; Obholzer & Roberts, 1994), namely observing, delegated and plenipotentiary authority. Observing authority implies being restricted in giving and sharing information about the team across the boundary. Delegated authority refers to more freedom in sharing, but with a clear boundary around the content there (Plenipotentiary authority gives the team member total freedom to cross the boundary and to use own responsibility in decision making and conduct. The argument is that when a team member is sent to communicate, negotiate or sell across the boundary of the own team without a clear indication of level of authority, it creates anxiety which hinders rational decision making and reporting back to colleagues inside the team boundary (Cytrynbaum & Lee, 1993:63-73; 134-138; French & Vince, 1999:112-126; Hugg et al.,1993:15-30; 86-88; West et al., 1995:47-56; 195-202).

Leadership and followership in relation to what is outside (Gabelnick & Carr, 1989:23-29; 139-143; Obholzer & Roberts, 1994; West et al., 1995:57-70). For example, a team member takes individual leadership when negotiating on his/her own behalf for a salary increase. Leadership of followers applies when an individual – not necessarily the designated leader or manager – acts or negotiates on behalf of others in the team. This role has its own boundary within the team and is experienced as very powerful by the member as well as the group.

Relationship and Relatedness

The Tavistock stance is based on the study and understanding of human relations. This implies the relationships between team members, which refers to face-to-face or telephonic interaction in the team, as it happens in the here-and-now of the event (French & Vince, 1999; Gabelnick & Carr, 1989:166-170; Neumann et al., 1997; Shapiro & Carr, 1991). On an unconscious level, the team (and the organisation) is always in the mind of the team member, influencing behaviour as such. This is referred to as relatedness or "the organisation in the mind" (Shapiro & Carr, 1991). This concept originated from basic child cognisance of the family he or she belongs to. In organisational context, it seems that the team member's fantasies about the team and the rest of the organisation, act as a driving force for a lot of its behaviour.

Group as a Whole

Originating from analytical psychology, the concept of collectivism is used (Cytrynbaum & Lee, 1993:144-146; Hugg et al., 1993:165-187; Wells, 1980). It refers to one part of the system acting, or carrying emotional energy, on behalf of another. For example, the production department (or blue-collar workers) may work under appalling and dirty conditions and thus "carrying the filth': so that the office staff (or white-collar workers) may have good-looking and air-conditioned offices, "carrying the cleanliness and order" on behalf of the total system. Another explanation is to say that these two sections manage different organisational boundaries, each with its own rules and appearances.

Collectivism also implies that no event happens in isolation and that there is no co-incidence in the behaviour of any team (or organisation).

The Psychodynamic Team-Building Event

The Tavistock (Leicester) model (Gabelnick & Carr, 1989:1-4; Higgin & Bridger, 1965; Lawrence, 1979:1-19; Miller, 1989; 1993) is used a base for structuring the team-building event. The event consists of team and staff members and is seen as a temporary institution, developing its own dynamics, rituals, ways of working and culture. The primary task of the event is to provide opportunities for the team to study its own behaviour in the here-and-now of the event. This task is educational – each participant uses own authority to accept what proves valid and reject what is not.

Staff members are not observers of the learning taking place, but are actively involved in it (Cytrynbaum & Lee, 1993:1-7; 92-97; Gabelnick & Carr, 1989:53-58: Hugg et al., 1993:57-70; Lawrence, 1979:116; West et al., 1995:71-74).They act as consultants to the process and the dynamics, taking place in the here-and-now. Based on their own observations and experience, they offer working hypotheses in the format of interpretations, about the manifesting assumptions and psychodynamic team behaviour (as discussed above). Further, they take responsibility and authority to provide the boundary conditions – task, space and time – in such a way that all participants can engage with the primary task of the team-building event.

The total team-building event consists of intense experiential learning sub-events, namely plenaries, large, small and inter-group events, discussions, review and applications events. The description and task of these events are as follows:

∝ Plenary. The team and 3 staff members are present. The total event opens and ends in plenary, as well as the intergroup event. This provides the opportunity to share information about the learning.

∝ Large group event. All team and three staff members, in the role of consultant, are present. The primary task is to provide opportunities for the team to learn about their team's behaviour as it happens in the here-and-now of the total system. Chairs are placed in a spiral formation.

∝ Small group event. The team is divided by the staff members into subgroups of between six and ten with one staff member, in the role of consultant. The primary task is to provide opportunities for the team to learn about their subgroup's behaviour in the here-and-now of a small ream system.

∞ Intergroup event. The team has the opportunity to form subgroups amongst themselves and to interact with other groups so formed. The primary task is to provide opportunities for the team to learn about authority, leadership, followership and representation over team boundaries. Consultancy is offered by staff members.

∞ Discussion. The team and three staff members are present. The primary task is to provide opportunities for the team to learn about the concepts in the Tavistock stance to team-building.

∞ Review/application group event. The team is divided by the staff members into groups of between six and ten with one staff member, in the role of consultant. The primary task is to provide opportunities for the team to review their learning during the team building event. Then to work towards the application of the learning to roles in the team's everyday working life.

Method

Sample

Convenient sampling was used (Kerlinger, 1986). Four existing management teams, who have been working together for at least two years, consisting of between 18 and 23 top and middle managers (total N=83), from four large (N=1.500+) South African organisations, were approached to participate in the research. Attendance was voluntary. The mean age was 37 years.

The gender ratio was 6 (male)/4 (female). Blacks, Coloureds. Indians and Whites were included, although this was (understandably) not representative of the present South African demographic scene.

The Team Building Event

The event was presented as discussed above. The same three staff members were present throughout. They are Psychologists (category Industrial) and have extensive training and experience in the Tavistock stance through attending working conferences at the Tavistock Institute in the UK, the A.K. Rice Institute in the USA and through presenting such training in South America.

Programme

The team building event is structured over three days of eight hours each (a total of 24 hours). The programme is laid out in Table1.

Table 1 Team-Building Programme

TIME	DAY 1	DAY 2	DAY 3
08:00 - 09:30	Plenary Large group 1	Large group 2	Large group 1
09:30 - 10:00	Tea		
10:00 - 11:30	Small group 1	Small group 2	Small group 4
11:30 - 13:00	Plenary Inter-group 1	Inter-group 3 Plenary	Review group 2
13:00 - 14:00	Lunch		
14:00 - 15:30	Inter-group 2	Small group 3	Application group
15:30 - 16:00	Tea		
16:00 - 17:00	Discussion 1	Review group I	Discussion 2 Plenary

Procedure

The team building event was presented according to the programme, for each of the four teams separately, at a venue away from the workplace. Afterwards, a 30-minute, semi-structured, tape-recorded interview was conducted with each participant by the author (who also acted as a consultant in the team-building event) and then transcribed. The aim of the interview was to measure the impact of the team-building event. A single question was asked. namely: "What was the impact of the team building event on you and your team?': Hereafter the interviewer only encouraged the interviewee by summarising and reflecting (Egan, 1990) on already given material. The interview was analysed by means of content analysis (Strauss & Corbin, 1990), and specifically open coding (a process of breaking down, examining, comparing, conceptualising and categorising of data). Thus, the main and sub-themes and their relationships were determined Jones, 1996; Kerlinger, 1986). Reliability was ensured by having the results examined by a psychologist. to whom this technique is well known.

Results

The results are reported in terms of the manifesting main and sub themes, and their frequencies (given in percentages for easier interpretation). The main themes are cognitive, affective, conative, interpersonal and group behaviour.

Cognitive Behaviour

1. Broad knowledge about team behaviour and dynamics

   This was reported by all team members (100%), referring to the three basic assumptions of team building, as well as "all the" relevant psychodynamic team building concepts. Especially the concept of the here-and-now (which was new to some team members – 55%), helped to focus on having an open mind in learning about "what is happening in the team at the moment?" (29%).

2. Understanding own behaviour and role in the team

This was reported by many team members (88%), referring to a better understanding of their own style (28%) within the team boundary. Some referred to a better understanding of what is projected upon them as individuals (58%), and what they project upon other team members (37%). Some (26%) reported a clearer understanding of why and how this is happening in their workplace (27%).

3. Understanding own symbolic behaviour

Team members (29%) referred to understanding "what I represent for the team and play out on their behalf': Some (18%) referred to the realisation of how and why they symbolically keep the team, the manager or the total organisation in their subconscious minds, which leads to a better understanding of their reaction to authority figures. Reference was made to the manager as symbolic authority figure (6%): "I hate it when my manager does exactly what my father did to me': Some team members (34%) stated that they have tried during the event, to put boundaries between past experiences and the present learning event, and not to project that on the poor boss" (4%).

4. Difficulty in understanding some concepts

A few members (14%) struggled in understanding the dynamics of the collective unconscious and the principle of no coincidence. The concept of group as a whole was mentioned as the strangest concept within this way of team building. It was called "an intriguing phenomenon" which they have never been aware of in terms of their own team functioning (9%).

Affective Behaviour

1. Increased awareness of own feelings

Most team members (94%) reported this awareness, referring to a wide variety of feelings – from excitement about the team (56%) and its accomplishments (76%), to pain and sadness (41 %). There is now less fear of openly expressing these feelings within the team boundary (67%) – "I can now be myself more than ever before': These include "unpopular feelings" such as anxiety (72%), hostility (27%), anger (68%), jealousy (13%) as well as showing aggression (18%).

2. Increased awareness of own defences against anxiety and their meaning

Team members (52%) reported this awareness referring to projections onto others (46%), especially the manager (35%) and team members whom they envy (19%). Other defences are rationalising (63%) and intellectualising (37%) about team issues ("hoping they will go away" – 11 %) and denial of issues (61%) ("because it is too big to handle" – 28%). in this regard, the learning in the team building event was about becoming aware of own defences as they happen and owning them (42%).

3. Acceptance

Team members (74%) reported experiencing more acceptance towards their own team behaviour, other members as well as acceptance by others in the team.

Conative Behaviour

1. External versus internal locus of control

Most team members (84%) referred to how their team always work from an external locus of control in blaming colleagues, consultants and the manager/leader for not helping them. Some members (20%) named this collective unconscious dependency and its effect, as the most important learning in the team building event.

2. Disempowerment versus empowerment

Many members (76%) referred to their realisation that they have been acting from a disempowered base for very long, which is seen to be emotionally taxing on management. They would like to use the insights from this event in future, whenever dependency and disempowerment arise, to be aware of their own feelings of anxiety (for example – 30%) in the here-and-now and to act upon them in order to empower the self and the system (71%).

Interpersonal Behaviour

1. Learning about own interpersonal style

Team members (65%) report an enhanced insight into their own interpersonal style and dynamics after the event. They refer to the concepts of relatedness (43%) (a new concept for many – 32%) as providing an explanation of fantasies towards others – colleagues as well as managers. Learning about their fantasies. helps the team to understand its own projections (33%).

2. Openness towards the self and others

Team members (55%) report being more willing and able to challenge the self and others, as well as organisational systems and boundaries. This manifests in giving others and receiving feedback, in a responsible way (33%). A few team members (8%) referred to the realisation that feedback must sometimes also be understood as a projection of the person who gives it.

Group Behaviour

1. Learning about own team dynamics

Team members (86%) mentioned the manifestations of the basic assumptions as the greatest team learning. This way of experiential learning with psychodynamic interpretations by the consultants, facilitated the knowledge and awareness about the real culture (or "personality") of the team. The focus on conscious and unconscious team behaviour, helps to understand the behavioural dynamics of the team (28%) – "its ups and downs".

2. Dependency

Team members (72%) referred to how their dependence on authority figures (their own manager – 44%, as well as topmanagement – 31%) inhibits their performance. A few (9%) referred to how the manager sometimes (unconsciously) wants to keep them dependent on him like children. They became aware of the team's need to work through their counter dependence and independence, to eventually reach interdependence. They realise that only then the team can really function fully.

3. Flight/fight reactions

Team members (68%) referred to how difficult it is for the team to stay working in the here-and-now. In the past they have collectively learned to cope with difficult issues and anxieties, by cleverly steering away from it through intellectualising, denying and talking about anything else but the "real issues': Some (51%) referred to their learning about how the team fights in all kinds of sophisticated ways. Through this team building event, they have learned to stay aware in the here-and-now, however difficult it may be, to acknowledge their defences and to be more real in their feelings.

4. Pairing/split

Team members report on their awareness (94%) and learning (79%) about how the team continuously splits itself into subsystems, making working together very difficult (57%). The concept of boundaries helps them to become sensitive towards establishing honest and clear relationships with other members and sections in the larger team and the organisation (42%). Especially the splits of gender, race and hierarchy create communication breakdowns (87%). They have learned about their unconscious need to split, in order to cope with the difficulty of diversity (43%). They are now much more aware of manifesting splits, the unconscious reasons for this and how to react upon this phenomenon (70%).

5. The symbolic role of authority

Team members (53%) reported their realisation about the symbolic role played by authority figures in the mind. In this event, they tried to own their feelings of fear for (25%) and rejection (43%) by these perceived powerful figures.

6. Building team identity

Team members (82%) reported on how the event helped in becoming aware of the absence of a clear identity in their team, because of vague boundaries. In this team-building event they consciously and unconsciously started working (82%) on the establishment of an own identity in terms of boundaries (67%) and potential (32%), owning of own behaviour (38%) and an experience of empowerment to act collectively in problem-solving (62%). Thus, the team started working on operationalising its own plans for coping with change (61%), transition (45%) and diversity (63%).

Conclusions

The above results indicate that the team-building event from the Tavistock stance, impacts on the individual as well as on the team. The individual team member gains knowledge about and understanding of team behaviour and about the self (He/she is more aware of own feelings in the here-and-now. how to recognise defences and what to do about them. External motivation and taking up a disempowered role are replaced by operating from an internal locus of control and acting in an empowered way. Interpersonally the team member is more inclined to risk new behaviour and challenge existing boundaries.

On the team level, there is clear evidence that the team is more aware of the manifestation as well as understanding the basic assumptions and concepts of group dynamics. This includes the symbolic meaning of team behaviour and being empowered to work with and through it when it occurs. The team is more open and accepting towards its own unconscious behaviour, using the manifestations thereof as learning opportunities. The team strengthened its boundaries towards establishing a strong team identity

Recommendations

In terms of the research design, follow-up team-building needs to be conducted to ascertain the long-term effect of the event and to ensure the transition of the learning into the workplace. These should be measured with pre, post and post-post interviews and the results should be compared to traditional team-building approaches, to ascertain the difference in impact. In this research, the interviewer was also involved as a consultant in the team-building event. On the one hand, this was done in order to have a better understanding of the group member's experience. On the other hand, this may have led to transference and countertransference. influencing the validity of the results. In future research, the two tasks should be performed by different people.

Industrial/Organisational psychologists and Human Resources practitioners should be exposed to and trained in the psychodynamic approach and the Tavistock stance. This will enable them to understand the complexity of team behaviour and to interpret this in the context of change and diversity as part of the learning and teaching processes in the institution (West et al., 1995:87-104). This represents a challenge because of the needed extensive knowledge about depth psychology and dynamic behaviour. Using the Tavistock stance for organisational analysis and diagnosis should also be pursued, as described by Gabelnick and Carr (1989:59-73), Kets de Vries (1991) and West et al. (1995:138-160; 169-175).

References

Belbin, R.M. (1993). *Team roles at work.* Oxford: ButterworthHeinemann.

Bergh, Z.C. & Theron, A.L. (1999). *Psychology in the work context.* Johannesburg: Thomspson International. https://doi.org/10.1037/001990

Bion, W.R. (1961). *Experiences in groups.* London: Tavistock Publications.

Bion, W.R. (1970). *Attention and interpretation.* London: Tavistock Publications.

Cilliers, F.v.N. (1995a). Die effek van 'n groeigroepervaring op predikante. *NG Teologiese Tydskrif,* XXXVI(4):630-642.

Cilliers, F.v.N. (1995b). Fasiliteerderopleiding. *Journal.for Industrial psychology,* 21(3):7-11. https://doi.org/10.4102/sajip.v21i3.592

Cilliers, F.v.N. & Wissing, M.P. (1993). Sensitiewe relasievorming as bestuursdimensie: Die evaluering van 'n ontwikkelingsprogram. *Journal for Industrial psychology,* 19(1):5-10. https://doi.org/10.4102/sajip.v19i1.549

Colman, A.D. & Bexton,W.H. (1975). *Group relations reader 1.* Jupiter: The A.K. Rice Institute.

Colman, A.D. & Geller, M.H. (1985). *Group relations reader 2.* Jupiter: The A.K. Rice institute.

Cytrynbaum, S. & Lee, S.A. (1993). *Transformations in global and organizational systems.* Jupiter: A.K. Rice Institute.

Czander, W.M. (1993). *The psychodynamics of work and organizations.* New York: Guilford Press.

De Board, R. (1978). *The psychoanalysis of organisations.* London: Routledge.

Egan, G. (1990). *The skilled helper. A systematic approach to effective helping.* Pacific Grove: Brooks/Cole.

French, R. & Vince, R. (1999). *Group relations management and organization.* New York: Oxford University Press.

Gabelnick, F. & Carr, A.W. (1989). *Contributions to social and political science.* Jupiter: A.K. Rice Institute.

Higgin, G. & Bridger, H. (1965). *The psychodynamics of an intergroup experience. Tavistock pamphlet no.10.* London: Tavistock Publications.

Hirschhorn, L. (1993). *The workplace within: Psychodynamics of organizational life.* Cambridge: MIT Press.

Hugg, T.W.; Carson, N.M. & Lipgar. R.M. (1993). *Changing group relations. The next twenty-five years in America.* Jupiter: A.K. Rice Institute.

Jones, R.A. (1996). *Research methods in the social and behavioural sciences.* Sunderland: Sinauer.

Kerlinger, F.N. (1986). *Foundations of behavioural research.* New York: Rinehart & Winston.

Kets De Vries, M.F.R. (1991). *Organisation on the couch: Handbook of psychoanalysis and management.* New York: Jossey-Bass.

Kruger, P. (1999). *Understanding the dynamics of a group.* People Dynamics, 17(3):50-52.

Lawrence, W.G. (1979). *Exploring individual and organizational boundaries. A Tavistock open systems approach.* London: Karnac.

Luft, J. (1984). *Group processes. An introduction to group dynamics.* Mountain View: Mayfield.

Menzies, I.E.P. (1993). *The functioning of social systems as a defence against anxiety*. London: The Tavistock Institute of Human Relations.

Miller, E.J. (1976). *Task and organisation*. New York: Wiley.

Miller, E.J. (1980). The politics of involvement. *Journal of Personality and Social Systems*, 2(2-3):37-50.

Miller, E.J. (1983). *Work and creativity. Occasional paper no.6*. London: Tavistock Institute of Human Relations.

Miller, E.J. (1989). *The "Leicester" Model: Experiential study of group and organisational processes. Occasional paper no. 10*. London: Tavistock Institute of Human Relations.

Miller, E.J. (1993). *From dependency to autonomy: Studies in organisation and change*. London: Free Association Books.

Morgan, G. (1980). Paradigms, metaphors and puzzle-solving in organisational theory. *Administrative Science Quarterly*, 25(4):605-622. https://doi.org/10.2307/2392283

Neumann, J.E.; Kellner, K. & Dawson-Shepherd, A. (1997). *Developing organisational consultancy*. London: Routledge.

Obholzer, A. & Roberts, V.Z. (1994). *The unconscious at work*. London: Routledge.

Quitmann, H. (1985). *Humanistische Psychologie*. Gottingen: Verlag fur Psychologie.

Rice, A.K. (1963). *The enterprise and its environment*. London: Tavistock.

Rioch, M.J. (1970). The work of Wilfred Bion on groups. *Psychiatry*, 33(1):56-66.

Robbins, S.P. (1998). *Organizational behaviour. Concepts, controversies, applications*. Upper Saddle River: Prentice-Hall.

Rogers, C.R. (1975). *Encounter groups*. London: Penguin.

Rogers, C.R. (1982). *Freedom to learn for the 80's*. Columbus: Charles E. Merrill.

Shapiro, E.R. & Carr, A.W (1991). *Lost in familiar places: Creating new connections between the individual and society*. London: Yale University Press.

Strauss, A. & Corbin, J. (1990). *Basics of qualitative research: Grounded theory. Procedures and techniques*. Newbury Park: Sage.

Wells, L. (1980). Th e group-as-a-whole: A systemic socio-analytical perspective on interpersonal and group relations. In: C.P. Alderfer & C.L. Cooper (ed.), *Advances in experiential social processes*, 2:165-198.

West, K.L.; Hayden, C. & Sharrin, R.M. (1995). *Community and chaos*. Proceedings of the eleventh scientific meeting of the A.K. Rice Institute.

The Impact of Silo Mentality on Team Identity: An Organisational Case Study[1]

F Cilliers & H Greyvenstein

Orientation

Organisational silos do not only refer to conscious structures, but also to an unconscious state of mind and mentality that takes on a life of its own. Silos result in the splitting of organisational artefacts and relationships, and impact negatively on relationship, fanning between individuals and within teams.

Research Purpose

The purpose of this research was to describe how the silo mentality impacts on team identity.

Motivation for the Study

During a recent organisational consultation, the researchers realised that a so-called silo phenomenon had much more unexplained unconscious behaviour than was traditionally realised in terms of organisational development. It is hoped that findings from this qualitative study could give consultants entry into what happens below the surface in the silos' unconscious.

1   Cilliers, F. & Greyvenstein, H. (2012). The impact of silo mentality on team identity. *An organisational case study. SA Journal of Industrial Psychology/SA Tydskrif vir Bedryfsielkunde*, 38(2), Art.#993, 9 pages. http://doi.org/10.4102/sajip.v.382is.993

Research Design, Approach and Method

A qualitative and descriptive research design using a case study strategy was used. Data gathering consisted of 25 narrative interviews. Using discourse analysis four themes manifested, integrated into four working hypotheses and a research hypothesis. Trustworthiness and ethical standards were ensured.

Main Findings

Themes that emerged were the physical environment and structure, intra-group relations, experiences of management, and intergroup relations.

Practical/managerial Implications

Consulting on silo behaviour as physical structures only may not be successful in changing organisational behaviour. The silo resembles an iceberg – the largest part is below the surface.

Contribution/value-add

The findings evidenced silo behaviour to be an unconscious phenomenon influencing team identity negatively. Consultants are urged to study these manifestations towards understanding silos and their effect on team identity better.

Introduction

We have all heard jibes such as 'Oh don't bother trying to find HR after four o'clock ...' or 'Senior management still has no clue what's really happening on the plant!'. Inherent to any hierarchical organisation is a vertical and horisontal specialisation which is often looked upon with disdain, and which contains to-and-fro projections across boundaries (Vansina & Vansina-Cobbaert, 2008). The vertical specialisation exists between the various functional areas, such as production and marketing, whilst the horisontal segmentation exists between the positional power levels of leadership, management and employees. To understand the depth psychology of organisational silos necessitates an appreciation of the unconscious dynamics and symbolism inherent in silos (whether vertical or horisontal), and how this influences the formation of team identity.

Group and organisational identity are well researched in different fields of specialisation, including marketing (Amy, 2002; Gupta & Ogden, 2009; Grier & Rohit, 2001), education (Hartnett, 2007; Gurim & Nagda, 2006; Stark-Rose, Lokken & Zargharni, 2009), anthropology (Torres-Rouff, 2008), sociology (Wade & Brittan-Powell, 2000; Yount, 2004; Heaven, 1999a; Purdie-Vaughns & Eibach, 2008; Swann, Kwan, Polzer & Milton, 2003) and psychology (Anthony, 2005; Lipponen & Leskinen, 2006; Mali, 2006; Noels & Clement, 1996; Heaven, 1999b; Volkan, 2009). Organisational psychology yields a substantial amount of research in this field (Randel, 2002; Hatch & Schultz, 2002; Meyer, Barttmek & Lacey, 2002), mostly conceptualised from the humanistic view.

Research on group and organisational identity often regard the two constructs as being similar. This is evident in the work of Blomback and Brunninge (2009), He and Baruch (2009), Kovoor-Misra (2009), Reza (2009) and Sato (2010), where the literature on group identity implies organisational behaviour. This is seldom the case the other way around. Both group and organisational identity are well differentiated from individual behaviour (Diamond & Allcorn, 2009). This research approached the impact of silo behaviour on team identity from a meso (group) perspective, as distinct from an individual (micro) or organisational (macro) perspective.

Volkan defines group identity as 'the subjective experience of people linked by a persistent sense of sameness' (2009:6). This view resonates with Whetten's (2006) seminal work on organisational identity, where the latter is defined as 'the central and enduring attributes of an organisation that distinguishes it from other organisations' (2006:220). This definition incorporates a phenomenological component where any identity-related inquiry' was most likely to be observed in conjunction with profound organisational experiences '(Whetten, 2006:220). This implies that the construct of team identity refers to rational and conscious organisational behaviour.

The concept of organisational silos is often used in practice but has not been thoroughly researched. It is thought that Neebe (1987) made the first reference to silos as a metaphor in organisational behaviour, with reference to grain silos as an example of how parts of organisations function in a manner disconnected from the others. The general organisational psychology literature refers to the concept based on the traditional view and mechanistic manner in which organisations are structured (Diamond & Allcorn, 2009; Head, Yaeger & Sorensen, 2010; Stone, 2004; Sy & Cote, 2004; Weisbord & Janoff, 2005). This implies a hierarchical organisation structure whereby positions flow downward – vertically, from those with the most organisational power and authority to those with the least. These are typically depicted on an organisational chart or organogram.

The top-most position carries definitive responsibility for the organisation's performance along with ultimate decision-making power and final authority (Greenberg & Baron, 2003). As one descends the hierarchy, decision-making power and authority diminish to the point where employees have little if any authority (Hirschhorn, 1997). The above literature also distinguishes vertical areas of functional specialisation, where organisations' horisontal axes are divided into specialised divisions and manageable work groups (e.g. marketing, human resources, legal, operations, production, research and development).

Traditionally the organisational psychology literature views silos as conscious, rational and objective entities. Yet the effect of silo behaviour seems to relate also to behaviour happening below the surface (see Huffington, Armstrong, Halton, Hoyle & Pooley, 2004) in terms of its unconscious, irrational, symbolic and representative meaning, implications and impact.

This led researchers to systems psychodynamics as a paradigm to investigate such unconscious dynamics. This theory is based on classic psychoanalysis (Freud, 1921), object relations (Klein, 1948, 1997), open systems theory (Von Bertalanffy, 1968), social systems as defences against anxiety (Jaques, 1970; Menzies, 1993), group relations theory (Bion, 1961) and various relevant dynamic constructs (Cilliers, 2005; Cilliers & Koortzen, 2005). Generally, organisational psychodynamics can be defined as the study of unconscious patterns of work relations (Adams & Diamond, 1999) and their influence on leadership, role formation, conflict, identity, boundaries and authority. Such unconscious patterns include ego defence mechanisms like splitting, where the subject gains relief from internal conflicts by peeling off (usually negative, unwanted) parts of the self as if they were not of the self, and projection, whereby these split-off parts are attributed to another to carry on behalf of the subject, thereby providing containment for its own anxiety (Czander, 1993; Hinshelwood, Robinson & Zarate, 1997; Klein, 1997). Such behaviour can also be understood against Bion's framework for analysing the irrational features of unconscious group life, consisting of dependency, fight and/or flight, pairing (Bion, 1961) and, more recently, also 'one-ness' (Turquet, 1974) and 'we-ness' (Gabelnick & Carr, 1989; Hirschhorn, 1988).

The purpose of this research was to describe how silo mentality impacts team identity. Whereas group and/or team identity, as well as silo behaviour, have been studied in organisational psychology from different paradigms, the effect of what is referred to as silo mentality in systems psychodynamic thinking has never been linked to team behaviour or identity forming. The research objectives were to explore the meaning of silo mentality from a systems psychodynamic stance, to describe a case study in terms of its silo behaviour and to present a hypothesis of how silo mentality influenced the team identity in this organisational system as a guideline for consultants working in the area.

The psychodynamic view of organisations holds that, apart from their conscious and physical aspects, organisations also exist in the unconscious minds of people. This construct is referred to as the 'organisation-in-the-mind' (Armstrong, 2005; Turquet, 1974) and contains the individual and collective fantasies and projections in and about the workplace (Czander, 1993; Gabriel, 1999; Gould, Stapley & Stein, 2001).

Collective meaning and identity are given to these unconscious fantasies and emotions through exploring and studying intra-personal and intra-subject object-relational patterns. By doing so meaning is derived about organisations. Therefore, to know, understand and appreciate an organisation, more than traditional behavioural, empirical and positivistic analysis methods are required (Gould, Stapley & Stein, 2004; Hirschhorn, 1988; Huffington et al., 2004). Unconscious patterns of relations between individuals and their image of the organisation-in-the-mind need to be elicited.

Since the 1950s most organisations have been structured hierarchically (Greenberg & Baron, 2003). Typically an organisation would have layers of positions flowing downward from the top position with the most power and influence to those at the bottom with less. Another characteristic is the vertical areas of specialisation – human resources (HR), marketing and operations. Hence horisontal and vertical silos are created. As parts of the organisation, silos too are in-the-mind and have their own unconscious patterns of relations between individuals. As an image of the organisation-in-the-mind, silos influence work behaviour (Diamond & Allcorn, 2009).

Mainstream literature on organisational behaviour (Greenberg & Baron, 2003) uses the silo metaphor to denote organisation dysfunction and fragmentation. It refers to feelings of disconnection – the left hand not knowing what the other is doing, stuckness, isolation and powerlessness, lack of trust, respect, collaboration and collegiality. The image is one of silos in opposition internally or with other silos. Allcorn, Diamond and Stein (2002) introduced silos as an organisational metaphor in the systems psychodynamic literature (Diamond & Allcorn, 2004, 2009; Diamond, Stein & Allcorn, 2002; Diamond, Allcorn & Stein, 2004). They defined organisational silos as vast psychological spaces of compartmentalisation, segregation and differentiation.

Psychodynamically, silos represent the phallic characteristics of male dominance, submission and persecution. They are characterised by intra- and intergroup anxiety followed by the infantile and regressive defensive structures of splitting (dividing the external world into good and bad objects), introjection (taking the good into one's inner reality), projection (putting the bad onto the other), and projective identification (putting the bad onto the other with the unconscious intent of using, coercing or manipulating the object). This has consequences for work performance on the personal, group and/or team and organisational levels – the micro, meso and macro levels. Thus, silos become a split-in-the-mind, serving as an invisible barrier to contain the collective unconscious team and organisational fantasies and emotions.

It can be hypothesised that through studying the unconscious silo behaviour in organisations, important information can be gained about what the silo represents for the team (what keeps the silo intact), how teams struggle to find their identity, and to differentiate between the within silo and outside of the silo aspects of identity.

Silo as Invisible Barrier

Silos are not really physically present in organisations – they exist in the mind of employees who have a shared impression of its reality (Diamond & Allcorn, 2004; 2009). In the mind, they provide safety and comfort by keeping the others out, those who are 'not like us'. In doing so, silos as barriers fragment organisations. These barriers create an 'us and them' mentality which makes boundary-crossing difficult and often causes major anxiety in employees having to attend meetings with or visiting other departments, sites or teams.

These various parts of the organisation become delineated to the extent that those inside feel threatened by those outside the invisible barrier and view them with suspicion, fear and disdain (Diamond et al., 2004). When teams or groups exhibit silo mentality it refers to a position where systemic thinking and the vision of the larger organisation are absent (Burge, 1993). In the unconscious such denial of a part of the whole brings about splitting, usually followed by projection and high levels of free-floating, survival and persecutory anxiety (see Blackman, 2004).

Silo as Container

As container, silos serve to facilitate primitive reaction forms of fight and flight – fight whatever is outside and flee to the inside of the container with its presumed safety (Czander, 1993). This represents the paranoid–schizoid position (Klein, 1948) and object-to-object communication in that the container as an invisible barrier furthers 'us and them' fragmenting. As a container, the silo enables group-think, which indicates the presence of basic assumption we-ness. We-ness leads to self-aggrandisement as a defence, which further supports the notion that 'everything out there is bad and everything in here is good'. To be the container and the contained at the same time leads to silo inhabitants becoming all-knowing and manic (see Huffington et al., 2004).

In sum, silos represent a near-absence of depressive whole-object connections and are dominated by paranoid-schizoid part-object experiences (Diamond & Allcorn, 2009). Through reification, the silo itself is seen as the source of the experiences rather than its projective surface (Blackman, 2004), often followed by introjection and projective identification where employees in the silo take that silo inside of themselves and think of themselves as teams, departments or sections, unaware of a whole – as if it does not exist. The purpose of the reification is to assure silo members that the problem is outside rather than inside and related to themselves (Diamond & Allcorn, 2009). In the mind, the team in a silo then becomes the whole. Important to note is that whether for the silo or for a part of the silo, the same dynamic manifests, such as for an organisational development (OD) team within an HR silo.

A single team or group will also feel safe within the team and view the other silos and teams in the organisation not just as the other, but as the enemy other – to be distrusted, feared and fought. The bad in the mind (such as the incompetent, not understanding, infighting, slow to react) is then split off and projected onto those silos or teams, for them to carry. The team then becomes the whole seeing itself as only good, and the centre and reason for the existence of the entire organisation. In terms of its own identity (the central and enduring attributes that distinguish it from other teams), the team will then assume attributes of omnipotence, camaraderie and knowledge. Silo mentality can, therefore, be described as a phenomenon where employees unconsciously treat (perceive and act) the organisation, and those in other departments and divisions, as part-objects (see Diamond & Allcorn, 2009).

The research problem was formulated as follows: How does the presence of the silo mentality impact on a team's sense of identity? The research objectives were to describe and understand silo mentality and to hypothesise how this impacted on a specific team's identity.

No evidence of previous research findings studying the effect or impact of silo behaviour on team functioning or identity could be traced. This research could, therefore, be seen as a contribution towards extending the knowledge around this impact and specifically within the South African context. As such it could assist organisational psychologists and consultants to understand the underlying dynamics manifesting in their client systems whenever there is a tendency to silo-ing.

The research design is presented next, with reference to the research approach and strategy. This is followed by a description of the research method, consisting of the setting, roles of the researchers, sampling method, data collection, recording and analysis. Lastly, strategies employed to ensure quality data are outlined. Thereafter the findings are presented in four themes. In the discussion, the findings are integrated in the research hypothesis, which is followed by the conclusion, recommendations, limitations and suggestions for further research.

Research Design

Research Approach

Qualitative research was used (Camic, Rhodes & Yardley, 2003), set within psychosocial organisational studies (Clarke, 2006) and organisational anthropology (Levinson, 2002). The research position allowed for the application of a cluster of methodologies, working beyond the purely discursive and beneath the surface (Clarke & Hoggett, 2009). As an epistemology, the hermeneutic interpretive stance was used (Geertz, 2000), which allowed for rich and meaningful interpretations of the observed occurrences (Alexandrov, 2009).

Research Strategy

A departmental case study (Chamberlayne, Bornat & Apitzsch, 2004) with three sub-cases was used to investigate the phenomenon of silo behaviour empirically in a real-life context (Creswell, 2003). Sub-case analysis was used to facilitate individual understanding, followed by cross-case analysis and the emergence of themes (Hollway & Jefferson, 2010) for the department as a whole (Wells, 1980). This allowed for an in-depth examination of the manifesting behaviours from multiple sources of information (Creswell, 2003). This strategy was seen as intrinsic to gain an understanding of the organisation's dynamics and instrumental to in building the knowledge base on silo behaviour (Denzin & Lincoln, 2005; Stake, 1995).

Research Method

Research Setting

The research was set in a large corporate head office in Gauteng, specifically one department rendering a technical service to internal clients. A project team, which consisted of the head of the OD division, the departmental manager and the first researcher, was tasked to investigate the department's declining performance rating.

Entrée and Establishing Researcher Roles

The first researcher was authorised by the organisation to take up the role of consultant (Lowman, 2002) and researcher (Alexandrov, 2009). During data collection he took the role of the interviewer (Alvesson & Sköldberg, 2010), and during the analysis the role of systems psychodynamic consultant (Neumann, Kellner & Dawson-Shepherd, 1997). The first and second researchers were involved in the data analysis, interpretation and integration.

Sampling

Opportunistic sampling was used (Terre Blanche, Durrheim & Painter, 2006). The department as an organisational case study consisted of three cases, namely the manager (N=1), his staff (N=14) and two representatives each from five internal client departments (N=10). The manager was a 55-year-old White male with 30 years' experience in this organisation. The 24 staff members were all technically qualified and almost equally distributed in gender and race, with a mean age of 38 years.

Data Collection Method

A one-hour, unstructured, individual narrative interview was used (Clarke & Hoggett, 2009). This took place in a boardroom in close proximity to the department's location. The interview started with the question: 'What is it like to be a member of this department?' (Diamond & Allcorn, 2009). Hereafter the interviewer responded to the respondents' ordering and phrasing – carefully listening in order to make follow-up comments using the respondents' own words and phrases without offering interpretations, becoming an almost invisible facilitating catalyst to the respondents' stories (Hollway & Jefferson, 2010).

Recording of Data

The interviews were tape-recorded. Afterwards, the first researcher used 10 minutes to add data around the participant's body language, the ambience in the room, and his own subjective experience during the interview (see Van Manen, 1990). The data were transcribed and stored safely.

Data Analyses

Discourse analysis was used (Breverton & Millward, 2004; Cilliers & Smit, 2006). Simple hermeneutics allowed for the understanding of individuals' subjective and inter-subjective reality and meaning and double hermeneutics facilitated critical interpretation of unconscious processes from the systems psychodynamic stance (Clarke & Hoggett, 2009). The assumption was that unconscious communication dynamics and defences influence subjects' construction of their reality (Alvesson & Skoldberg, 2005; Hunt, 1989).

Strategies Employed to Ensure Quality Data

Ethicality (Terre Blanche et al., 2006) was assured by formally contracting the consulting and research activities with the head of the OD division, the departmental head, and individual participants. This included voluntary participation, informed consent and confidentiality of shared data. In terms of the research project, ethicality was ensured through thorough design, planning, conducting and analysis of the interviews, presentation of the data in this document and feedback to the head of the OD division.

Trustworthiness is based on validity and credibility (Denzin & Lincoln, 2005). The study evidenced strong and believable validity in its depth psychological description, which revealed the complexities of the systems' defensive behaviours. The interpretations were peer-reviewed (Brewerton & Millward, 2004) by an independent systems psychodynamically informed psychologist, who evaluated the dependability and saturation of the findings favourably. Credibility was assured in the competence of the researchers – both are trained in systems psychodynamic consulting and research (according to the requirements stated by Brunner, Nutkevitch & Sher, 2006).

Reporting

The findings are reported according to discourse theme. In the discussion working hypotheses (Terre Blanche et al., 2006) are formulated for each theme, integrated into the research hypothesis (Schafer, 2003). Finally, the conclusion, recommendations, limitations and suggestions for future research are presented.

Findings

Four themes manifested namely:

1. physical environment and departmental structure;
2. intra-group relations;
3. experiences of management; and
4. intergroup relations.

Physical Environment and Departmental Structure

The department was situated in the basement of a large midtown building, filling a large open-plan space, with boxes of green plants between workstations. Participants described their work environment as 'our space', 'where we can be different/like fish in water', 'we need to be separate' and 'out of the way', 'even though we feel forgotten sometimes'. Participants voiced their resistance to a rumour that the department would move to another part of the building by saying 'that would frustrate us', 'will expose us to the noise in the business', 'we will get sucked into the politics there', 'it will lead to chatting' and 'time wasted'. Some of the younger participants called the basement 'the dungeon', 'where we hide and 'pretend that we are the world'. Participants were clear about the departmental strategy, structure, primary task and job content. One participant remarked that the departmental structure 'keeps people hostage', whilst another made a (Freudian) slip, referring to 'my colleague's parole', whilst referring to his promotion.

Intra-group Relations

Participants described their work performance as follows: 'we are specialists', 'proud of our work and delivering a remarkably efficient and surprisingly effective service'. They mentioned that 'we are well trained', have 'state of the art' technical equipment and electronic hard- and software. Participants described their work relationships amongst the team members, excluding the manager, as 'positive/calm/serene/friendly/helpful/creative 'and the nature of the internal relationships as 'united/secure/together/cohesive', 'almost spiritual', and like a family'.

Experiences of Management

The departmental manager was described positively by some participants in terms of his 'intelligence', 'good corporate insight' and 'extroversion'. Thereafter, all participants described him in an extremely negative way as emotionally immature, inflexible, rigid, not trustworthy, defensive, moody and with little insight into his own behaviour. His management style was described as centralised, making all the decisions, controlling, enforcing his view, pretending to care and listen but not doing so, making people dependent, disempowering and confusing them, managing by fear, causing stress, derailing our work and creating animosity amongst us with his double messages and 'contradictions'. One participant said 'he is dangerous because he is unaware of his impact on people'. His department experienced stress; people said they were 'living in fear', anxious 'to not make mistakes', feel 'like to be on a rollercoaster', 'not getting recognition', 'don't have work-life balance', and the department 'is in serious need of team-building and integration'. One participant said that 'we have learned to work around him'.

During his own interview, the manager was apprehensive about the interviews and the involvement of the head of OD in the project. He defensively justified his behaviour, often using numbers and figures to strengthen his arguments. He was nervous and tried to sell himself as a good and caring manager, whilst at the same time not listening to the interviewer's inputs. He created an image of independence, aloofness and detachment as if he feared being out of control. He voiced his inputs in a grandiose manner by referring to 'my department that I have built up over 12 years', 'my very sophisticated equipment' and to the staff as 'my family that I have picked by hand'.

Intergroup Relations

The department's experience of their internal client is negative. In terms of work performance, participants referred to the client managers as 'not being skilled' and the staff as 'they don't know what they do', 'don't take pride in their work', 'they have no realisation of time', 'always do last-minute changes', 'supply incorrect information', and 'deliver poor and incomplete demands'. In terms of behaviour on the boundary with the client, participants said 'they don't understand our work/what we do/how we think', 'they don't know what to do with us/how to handle us', 'we only see them when they demand something', 'they put pressure on us', 'they always demand', 'they compete with us/don't respect us/treat us with hostility/appreciation', 'treat us like idiots', and 'they anger and frustrate us'.

The client's experience of the department always started with a positive remark – and was immediately followed by an outpouring of negative aspects. Positively, the department is giving 'excellent service', produces 'effective work/has good delivery', has 'their procedures in place', 'maintains deadlines', 'gives quality', 'renders good client service', and 'the work gets done'. They described the departmental staff as 'well qualified', 'skilled', and 'working hard'. These positive remarks were followed by negative comments about the department's management, work performance and behaviour. The department's management was experienced as 'poor', ineffective and 'not providing a clear strategy/direction', and 'we are not sure of what we are working towards'. Management is 'not available', 'don't provide resources' and can't ensure that their staff have the 'relevant skills to service us'. Projects are 'mismanaged' in terms of planning, control, tracking and feedback.

'Their work processes are ambiguous', 'They demand impossible deadlines' and 'the matrix lines' through which the department and the business-related 'are filled with difficulties' resulting in 'a disconnection'.

Their work performance 'has been going down over time' 'they don't know what they do', 'they are incompetent', 'they are getting used to the same old thing', 'their work has become rigid over time', 'they misinterpret instructions', 'the pace has become slower due to volume', 'there are delays/slackness/bottlenecks', 'there are limited updates about progress or changes'. Their work 'has become inconsistent', for example, when 'they prefer to service the more corporate glamorous/affluent parts of the business' when 'our requests were first and more urgent', 'they have become risk/change-averse', 'they have tunnel vision' and 'there is a lack of transparency' in how they operate. Some people 'do not make sure they get the correct information', sometimes they 'report our mistakes to management', 'they gossip about us', 'get us into trouble with our bosses', 'act behind our backs' in 'collusion with my line manager', to the extent that 'the information will then unexpectedly pop up in my performance discussion'.

The department's behaviour is 'negative', 'not good at all', 'they think they are in charge of us', 'some people highjack information and power', 'they act defensively', 'they use power to control us', 'they use emotional power over us', 'we handle them with gloves' because 'we are afraid that we may sound confrontational'. The relationship is 'unfriendly', 'it feels like a madam and servant talking', 'it is as if they only think of themselves', 'we often have to stand on our knees, begging', 'you need to be very careful in how you communicate', 'we often are fearful when we enter the basement', 'you feel as if you hit an iron wall'. It was also stated that 'all kinds of negative feelings are between us' such as 'irritation/anger/frustration/jealousy'.

An additional dynamic manifested amongst seven young Black women amongst the client participants. During the interviews they appeared hurried, rushed and uninterested, saying 'I am only here to work', 'if they can just leave me alone', 'I am doing my best', 'I need to get along with everyone', and 'I don't want to get involved in the politics'. Halfway through their interviews, three of these participants asked the researcher 'can I go now – I need to get back to my desk'. Four participants volunteered information about being the first in their families to have tertiary education and to work in a corporate environment. They spoke about their exhaustion, a sense of 'losing myself', 'not knowing why I am here' and of thinking of resigning. Their stories revealed that they have approached their corporate careers with excitement, curiosity and hope – idealising the corporate world and its promises of endless opportunities. Their previous positive experiences have disappeared, their energy was depleted and they appeared disillusioned and even burnt-out.

Discussion

The purpose of this research was to describe how silo mentality impacts on team identity. The research is important in that it reveals that manifestations of unconscious defensive structures in the organisation act as symptoms of silo mentality. The findings also illustrate how the silo mentality plays such a significant part in identity forming. Themes that emerged from the findings were the physical environment and departmental structure, intra-group relations, experiences of management, and intergroup relations.

Theme 1: Physical Environment and Departmental Structure

The first theme evidenced the department's basic assumption functioning (Bion, 1961). It split the clear techno (structure) from the troubled socio (relationship) aspects (Miller, 1993). The system was obsessively dependant on its boundaries of separateness. In their flight into one-ness, the basement became their boundary in the mind (Lawrence, 1999) – their fantasised, safe, detached and untouchable silo-bunker (as a psycho-geographical silo – see Stein, 1987). Here they experienced inner support, protection and preservation, but also imprisonment; and outer incompetence characterised by noise, politics and time wastage. The department used the primitive defences (Blackman, 2004) of splitting off the bad and owning the good, regression (into the basement), resistance (staying in the basement), introjection (of the good and their preservation), projection (of the incompetence) and flight (away from the other) (Vansina & Vansina-Cobbaert, 2008).

Working Hypothesis 1

The system functioned in a split between light, represented by the technical and/or structure, and darkness, represented by the poor human relations in the basement. It has introjected a prison-like smugness, authorised (Hirschhorn, 1997) by self-righteousness, and projected its incompetent shadow onto the other, who identified with the projection. The use of primitive defences indicated the system's experience of being under attack (probably by the manager), which explains the need to hide in the basement with limited social connections. These unconscious dynamics lead to the department's primary role as service rendering being denied and de-authorised, which manifested as off-task survival, to the point of self-imprisonment.

Theme 2: Intra-group Relations

This theme evidenced the department's extreme introjected goodness in terms of tasks and relationships. Their relationships were characterised by a flight into one-ness almost to the point of incestuous cohesion (Gutmann, 2003). The boundary around the department (excluding the manager) was tightly contained, almost impenetrable, and their relatedness inside was idealised to the point of becoming a spiritual sanctuary (see Lawrence, 1999).

Working Hypothesis 2

The system functioned in extreme one-ness characterised by the preservation of goodness elevated into a fantasy of holiness.

Theme 3: Experiences of Management

The theme was evidenced by the departmental staff's strong negative experiences of the manager, and their attack on his management and personal style (with a few less personal cognitive aspects framed as positive). It was as if the staff put a clear boundary between themselves and the manager. On the inside (according to theme (2) they associated themselves with and have introjected love (Eros), whilst they have excluded and dissociated themselves from the manager and projected their aggression (Thanatos) onto him (Cytrynbaum & Noumair, 2004). Consciously the manager presented himself as a clever, strong and well-managing hero. Unconsciously he defended against his anxiety (Blackman, 2004) through denial (of staff's hate), detachment (being out of touch), projection (making the head of OD the enemy), suspicion (making the interviews the enemy), compensation (presenting himself as hero), rationalisation (explaining) and narcissism (referring to his possessions and people) (Obholzer & Roberts, 1994).

Working Hypothesis 3

In the split between staff and manager, the staff attached to the good and denied and detached from the bad, living safely in a utopian fantasy. As staff could not identify with the manager's style, he became the target of their projection of all bad. It was as if the manager was emotionally taken hostage and given an impossible (double) task of containing the bad as well as denying it in trying to keep up appearances.

Theme 4: Intergroup Relations

This theme was evidenced by intergroup conflict between the department and its clients, with to-and-fro projections of incompetence (Campbell, 2007). The client system's limited positivity illustrated their dependence (as a client). The discourse of the seven Black females indicated how they as a subsystem identified with the projections of attack and became the container of detachment. It was as if they became the representation of the obliterated, burnt-out ashes of the system.

Working Hypothesis 4

The intergroup dynamic in the system is fraught with splits and projections as if the war was in a deadlock, causing extreme emotional confusion and exhaustion. Black women represent the hopelessness in the fight.

Silo Mentality

The findings strongly suggested the manifestation of silo mentality in this organisational case study (Diamond & Allcorn, 2009; Stein, 1987). The employees treated one another as part-objects as if they were the whole, as a defence against not coping with the integrated organisation-as-whole and its systemic complexity and hostility (see Wells, 1980). High levels of anxiety created defences which formed invisible barriers in and between subsystems and in the mind. The silos manifested horisontally in the aggressive split between staff and manager and vertically between the department and the internal client.

The discourse was filled with metaphors of danger, hostage-taking, dominance and control, opposition, isolation, stuckness, imprisonment, inclusion-exclusion, separation, segregation, compartmentalisation, differentiation, fragmentation, lack of collaboration, denigration and the balkanisation of parts. The manifesting primitive defensive behaviours were split (between owning and not-owning), projection, projective identification, detachment, regression and resistance (Campbell & Huffington, 2008). As a 'silo within a silo,' the White male manager and the Black females mirrored one another's behaviour as evidence of how the system brought diverse opposites together through aggression. It was hypothesised that the silo mentality acted as: (1) an invisible boundary between the self and the other; as well as (2) a container of safety for the self and protection against the hostile other (Klein, 2005).

Team Identity

The findings strongly suggested a team identity characterised by high levels of anxiety and basic assumption functioning (Bion, 1961; 2003). As a whole, the system was caught up in its dependence on territory and toxicity (Fox & Spector, 2005) followed by counter-dependence manifesting as projections of aggression. The department was fighting the enemies-in-the-mind as well as their own projected identification around incompetence. They used flight into fantasies of security and competence as a defence against their experienced threat and chaos (Campbell & Gronbaek, 2006). The team's we-ness was manifesting in an extreme spiritual and familial togetherness, as an indication of how strong the sense of threat was. It was hypothesised that their behaviour of we-ness was based on guilt (Speziale-Bagliacca, 2004) and/or a sense of delusional grandiosity (Schwartz, 1990). In his isolated superiority, the manager played out the systemic me-ness.

The above basic assumption functioning was supported by defence mechanisms (Blackman, 2004; Klein 2005), namely, resistance (to relinquish the image of superiority, creativity), splitting (of task and relationships), introjection (of own beliefs about the self), introjective identification (which hindered their objectivity about reality), splitting off and projection (of incompetence), and regression (into family dynamics of rebellious children).

From a systems psychodynamic role-analysis perspective (Newton, Long & Sievers, 2006), the team's identity was interpreted as follows (Obholzer & Roberts, 1994). The normative role was relatively clear, although negatively influenced by the projections from the client. The experiential role contained the team's introjected poor-child ego state of not being cared for and having to grow up alone (James, 1977) and the manager's all-knowing and competent parental ego state. These two states functioned as the base of the split in the relationship. The phenomenal role of the staff contained strong projections of incompetence from the client, the manager from the staff and the young Black women from the whole system.

The team's identity can be summarised as a detached, acting- in and autistic differentiation (Czander, 1993; Gould et al., 2001; Stapley, 2006) stuck in its own confined, demarcated and schizoid mind space. Silo mentality is described in the same manner.

The research hypothesis was formulated as follows: the silo mentality with its destructive splitting into the compartmentalisation of part objects, impacted negatively on team identity and manifested in similar symptoms of destructive, autistic and schizoid functioning. The silo mentality acted as a defence against mature connection between people.

It was concluded that silo mentality and a disengaged team identity are similar in their destructive differentiation and breaking down of connection. Both showed the characteristics of the paranoid-schizoid position with its object relations, thus keeping the system in basic assumption functioning.

It is recommended that organisational psychologists and consultants take note of the destructive impact of silo mentality on team identity, the breaking down of connections, relationships and relatedness for not only the part object but presumably for the whole organisation. It is recommended that role analysis be used in a formal consulting project for teams such as these. This may replace the narrowly specialised single mindset (Kaeter, 1993) towards an integrated and well-connected system.

Limitations of this research relate to the use of one collective case study. If more cases in the same organisation were used, a clear idea of the organisational climate and culture could have been integrated into the findings.

It is suggested that future research focuses on replicating this study in other organisations and settings for comparison and towards the building of knowledge across organisational types.

References

Adams, G.B. & Diamond, M.A. (1999). Psychodynamic perspectives on organizations: identity, politics and change. *American Behavioral Scientist*, 43(2):221-224.

Adams, G.B. & Diamond, M.A. (1999). Psychodynamic perspectives on organizations: identity, politics and change. *American Behavioral Scientist*, 43(2):221-224. https://doi.org/10.1177/00027649921955227

Alexandrov, H. (2009). *Experiencing knowledge: the vicissitudes of a research journey.*

Clarke, S. & Hoggett, P. (2009). (eds.), *Researching beneath the surface. Psycho-social research methods in practice*, pp.29-49. London: Karnac.

Alvesson, M. & Skoldberg, K. (2010). *Reflexive methodology. New vistas for qualitative research.* London: Sage.

Amy, E.R. (2002). Identity salience: A moderator of the relationship between group gender composition and work group conflict. *Journal of Organizational Behavior*, 23(6):749. https://doi.org/10.1002/job.163

Anthony, D. (2005). Cooperation in Microcredit Borrowing Groups: Identity, Sanctions, and Reciprocity in the Production of Collective Goods. *American Sociological Review*, 70(3):496. https://doi.org/10.1177/000312240507000307

Armstrong, D. (2005). *Organization in the mind: Psychoanalysis, group relations, and organizational consultancy.* London: Karnac Books.

Bion, W.R. (1961). *Experiences in groups.* London: Tavistock Publications.

Bion, W.R. (2003). *Learning from experience.* London: Karnac.

Blackman, J.S. (2004). *101 Defences. How the mind shields itself.* New York: Brunner-Routledge. https://doi.org/10.4324/9780203492369

Blombäck, A. & Brunninge, O. (2009). Corporate identity manifested through historical references. *Corporate Communications*, 14(4):404. https://doi.org/10.1108/13563280910998754

Breverton, P. & Millward, L. (2004). *Organisational research methods. A guide for students and researchers.* London: Sage.

Brunner, L.D.; Nutkevitch, A. & Sher, M. (2006). *Group relations conferences. Reviewing and exploring theory, design, role-taking and application.* London: Karnac.

Burge, F.J. (1993). Silo commanders and the enterprise-wide vision. *Electronic Business Buyer*, 19(10):188.

Camic, P.M.; Rhodes, J.E. & Yardley, L. (2003). *Qualitative research in Psychology.* Washington: APA.

Campbell, D. (2007). *The socially constructed organisation.* London: Karnac.

Campbell, D. & Gronbaek, M. (2006). *Taking positions in the organisation.* London: Karnac.

Campbell, D. & Huffington, C. (2008). *Organisations connected. A handbook of systemic consultation.* London: Karnac.

Chamberlayne, P.; Bornat, J. & Apitzsch, U. (2004). *Biographical methods and professional practice. An international perspective.* Bristol: Policy Press. https://doi.org/10.1332/policypress/9781861344939.001.0001

Cilliers, F. (2005). Executive coaching experiences. A systems psychodynamic perspective. *South African Journal of Industrial Psychology*, 31(3):23-30. https://doi.org/10.4102/sajip.v31i3.205

Cilliers, F. & Koortzen, P. (2005). Working with conflict in teams – the CIBART model. *HR Future*, October, 52.

Cilliers, F. & Smit, B. (2006). A systems psychodynamic interpretation of South African diversity dynamics: A comparative study. *South African Journal of Labour Relations*, 30(2):5-18.

Clarke, S. (2006). *From enlightenment to risk: Social theory and contemporary society*. New York: Palgrave Macmillan. https://doi.org/10.1007/978-1-137-07500-0

Clarke, S. & Hoggett, P. (2009). *Researching beneath the surface. Psycho-social research methods in practice*. London: Karnac.

Creswell, J.W. (2003). *Research design: Qualitative, quantitative and mixed methods*. London: Sage.

Cytrynbaum, S. & Noumair, A. (2004). *Group dynamics, organizational irrationality, and social complexity: Group relations reader 3*. Jupiter: A.K. Rice.

Czander, W.M. (1993). *The psychodynamics of work and organizations – theory and application*. New York: Guilford Press.

Denzin, N.K. & Lincoln, Y.S. (2005). *The Sage handbook of qualitative research*. London: Sage. https://doi.org/10.1177/1468794105047237

Diamond, M.A. & Allcorn, S. (2004). Moral violence in organisations: Hierarchic dominance and the absence of potential space. *Organisational & Social Dynamics*, 4(1):22-45.

Diamond, M.A. & Allcorn, S. (2009). *Private selves in public organizations – The psychodynamics of organizational diagnosis and change*. New York: Palgrave Macmillan. https://doi.org/10.1057/9780230620094

Diamond, M.A.; Allcorn, S. & Stein, H.F. (2004). The surface of organizational boundaries: A view from psychoanalytic object relations theory. *Human Relations*, 57(1):31-53. https://doi.org/10.1177/0018726704042713

Diamond, M A.; Stein, H.F. & Allcorn, S. (2002). Organizational silos: Horizontal organizational fragmentation. *Journal of the Psychoanalysis of Culture and Society*, 7(2):280-296.

Fox, S. & Spector, P.E. (2005). *Counterproductive work behaviour. Investigations of actors and targets*. Washington: APA. https://doi.org/10.1037/10893-000

Freud, F. (1921). *Group psychology and the analysis of the ego. Complete works of Sigmund Freud*. London: Hogarth. https://doi.org/10.1037/11327-000

Gabelnick, F. & Carr, A.W. (1989). *Contributions to social and political science*. Jupiter: A.K. Rice Institute.

Gabriel, Y. (1999). *Organizations in depth*. Thousand Oaks: Sage.

Geertz, C. (2000). *Interpretation of cultures*. New York: Basic.

Gould, L.J.; Stapley, L.F. & Stein, M. (2001). *The systems psychodynamics of organisations*. London: Karnac.

Gould, L.J.; Stapley, L.F. & Stein, M. (2004). *Experiential learning in organizations. Application of the Tavistock Group Relations Approach*. London: Karnac.

Greenberg, J. & Baron, R.A. (2003). *Behavior in organizations*. (8th edn.). Thousand Oaks: Upper Saddle River.

Grier, S. & Rohit, D. (2001). Social dimensions of consumer distinctiveness: The influence of social status on group identity and advertising persuasion. *Journal of Marketing Research*, 38(2):216. https://doi.org/10.1509/jmkr.38.2.216.18843

Gurim, P. & Nagda, B A. (2006). Getting to the What, How, and Why of Diversity on Campus. *Educational Researcher*, 35(1):20. https://doi.org/10.3102/0013189X035001020

Gupta, S. & Ogden, D.T. (2009). To buy or not to buy? A social dilemma perspective on green buying. *Journal of Consumer Marketing*, 26(6):376. https://doi.org/10.1108/07363760910988201

Hartnett, S.P.D. (2007). Does Peer Group Identity Influence Absenteeism in High School Students? *High School Journal*, 91(2):35. https://doi.org/10.1353/hsj.2008.0000

Hatch, M.J. & Schultz, M. (2002). The dynamics of organizational identity. *Human Relations*, 55(8):989. https://doi.org/10.1177/0018726702055008181

He, H. & Baruch, Y. (2009). Transforming organizational identity under institutional change. *Journal of Organizational Change Management*, 22(6):575. https://doi.org/10.1108/09534810910997014

Heaven, P.C.L. (1999a). Attitudes towards women's rights: Relationships with social dominance orientation and political group identities. *Sex Roles*, 41(7/8):605.

Heaven, P.C.L. (1999b). Group identities and human values. *Journal of Social Psychology*, 139(5):590. https://doi.org/10.1080/00224549909598419

Hinshelwood, R.; Robinson, S. & Zarate, O. (1997). *Introducing Melanie Klein*. Cambridge: Icon Books.

Hirschhorn, L. (1997). *Reworking authority. Leading and following in the post-modern organisation*. London: MIT.

Hollway, W. & Jefferson, T. (2010). *Doing qualitative research differently. Free association, narrative and the interview method*. London: Sage.

Huffington, C.; Armstrong, A.; Halton, W.; Hoyle, L. & Pooley, J. (2004). *Working below the surface. The emotional life of contemporary organisations*. London: Karnac.

Hunt, J. (1989). *Psychoanalytic aspects of fieldwork*. London: Sage. https://doi.org/10.4135/9781412985505

James, M. (1977). *Techniques in transactional analysis for psychotherapists and counsellors*. Reading: Addison-Wesley.

Jaques, E. (1970). *Work, creativity and social justice*. New York: International Universities Press.

Kaeter, M. (1993). The age of the specialised generalist. *Training*, 30(1):48-53.

Klein, L. (2005). *Working across the gap. The practice of social sciences in organisations*. London: Karnac.

Klein, M. (1948). *Contributions to psychoanalysis, 1921–1945*. London: Hogarth Press.

Klein, M. (1997). *Envy and gratitude and other works 1946-1964*. London: Vintage.

Kovoor-Misra, S. (2009). Understanding perceived organizational identity during crisis and change. *Journal of Organizational Change Management,* 22(5):494. https://doi.org/10.1108/09534810910983460

Lawrence, W.G. (1999). *Exploring individual and organisational boundaries. A Tavistock open systems approach.* London: Karnac.

Levinson, H. (2002). *Organizational assessment.* Washington: APA.

Lipponen, J. & Leskinen, J. (2006). Conditions of contact, common in-group identity, and in-group bias towards contingent workers. *Journal of Social Psychology,* 146(6):671. https://doi.org/10.3200/SOCP.146.6.671-684

Lowman, R.L. (2002). *The handbook of organizational consulting Psychology.* San Francisco: Jossey-Bass. https://doi.org/10.1037/1061-4087.54.4.213

Mali, A.M. (2006). The formation and development of individual and ethnic identity: insights from psychiatry and psychoanalytic theory. *American Journal of Psychoanalysis,* 66(3):211. https://doi.org/10.1007/s11231-006-9018-2

Menzies, I.E.P. (1993). *The functioning of social systems as a defence against anxiety.* London: Tavistock.

Meyer, J.P.; Bartunek, J.M. & Lacey, C.A. (2002). Identity change and stability in organizational groups: A longitudinal investigation. *International Journal of Organizational Analysis,* 10(1):4. https://doi.org/10.1108/eb028942

Miller, E.J. (1993). *From dependency to autonomy: Studies in organization and change.* London: Free Association.

Neumann, J.E.; Kellner, K. & Dawson-Shepherd, A. (1997). *Developing organisational consultancy.* London: Routledge.

Newton, J.; Long, S. & Sievers, B. (2006). *Coaching in depth. The organisational role analysis approach.* London: Karnac.

Noels, K.A. & Clement, R. (1996). Communicating across cultures: social determinants and acculturative consequences. *Canadian Journal of Behavioural Science,* 28(3):214. https://doi.org/10.1037/0008-400X.28.3.214

Obholzer, A. & Roberts, V.Z. (1994). *The unconscious at work.* London: Routledge.

Purdie-Vaughns, V. & Eibach, R. (2008). Intersectional invisibility: The distinctive advantages and disadvantages of multiple subordinate-group identities. *Sex Roles,* 59(5–6):377. https://doi.org/10.1007/s11199-008-9424-4

Randel, A.E. (2002). Identity salience: A moderator of the relationship between group gender composition and work group conflict. *Journal of Organizational Behavior,* 23(6):749-766. https://doi.org/10.1002/job.163

Reza, E. (2009). Identity constructs in human organizations. *Business Renaissance Quarterly,* 4(3):77.

Sato, T. (2010). Organizational identity and symbioticity: Parco as an urban medium. *Journal of Management History,* 16(1):44. https://doi.org/10.1108/17511341011008304

Schafer, R. (2003). Insight and interpretation. *The essential tools of psychoanalysis.* London: Karnac.

Speziale-Bagliacca, R. (2004). *Revenge, remorse and responsibility after Freud.* New York: Brunner-Routledge.

Stake, R. (1995). *The art of case study research.* Thousand Oaks. Sage.

Stapley, L.F. (2006). *Individuals, groups and organisations beneath the surface.* London: Karnac.

Stark-Rose, R.; Lokken, J. & Zarghami, F. (2009). Increasing awareness of group privilege with college students. *College Student Journal*, 43(2):537.

Stein, H.F. (1987). *Developmental time, cultural space.* Norman: University of Oklahoma Press.

Stone, F. (2004). Deconstructing silos and supporting collaboration. *Employment Relations Today*, 31(1):11. https://doi.org/10.1002/ert.20001

Swann, W.B.; Kwan, V.S.Y.; Polzer, J.T. & Milton, L.P. (2003). Waning of stereotypic perceptions in small groups: Identity negotiation and erosion of gender expectations of women. *Social Cognition*, 21(3):194. https://doi.org/10.1521/soco.21.3.194.25341

Sy, T. & Cote, S. (2004). Emotional intelligence: A key ability to succeed in the matrix organization. *The Journal of Management Development*, 23(5/6):437. https://doi.org/10.1108/02621710410537056

Terre Blanche, M.; Durrheim, K. & Painter, D. (2006). *Research in practice. Applied methods for the social sciences.* Cape Town: UCT Press.

Torres-Rouff, C. (2008). The influence of Tiwanaku on life in the Chilean Atacama: Mortuary and bodily perspectives. *American Anthropologist*, 110(3):325. https://doi.org/10.1111/j.1548-1433.2008.00042.x

Turquet, P.M. (1974). Leadership: The individual and the group. In: G.S. Gibbard, J. Harman & L. Wells (eds.), *Analysis of groups*, pp.349-371. San Francisco: Jossey-Bass.

Vansina, L.S. & Vansina-Cobbaert, M. (2008). *Psychodynamics for consultants and managers. From understanding to leading meaningful change.* Chichester: Wiley-Blackwell. https://doi.org/10.1002/9780470697184

Van Manen, M. (1990). *Researching lived experience.* Toronto: State University of New York.

Volkan, V. (2009). Large-group identity: 'Us and them' polarizations in the international arena. *Psychoanalysis, Culture & Society*, 14(1):4. https://doi.org/10.1057/pcs.2008.50

Von Bertalanffy, L. (1968). *General systems theory: Foundations, development, applications.* New York: George Braziller.

Wade, J.C. & Brittan-Powell, C.S. (2000). Male reference group identity dependence: Support for construct validity. *Sex Roles*, 43(5/6):323.

Weisbord, M. & Janoff, S. (2005). Faster, shorter, cheaper may be simple; it's never easy. *The Journal of Applied Behavioral Science*, 41(1):70. https://doi.org/10.1177/0021886304273248

Wells, L. (1980). The group-as-a-whole: A systemic socio-analytical perspective on interpersonal and group relations. In: C.P. Alderfer, & C.L. Cooper (eds.), *Advances in experiential social processes*, pp.165-198. Washington DC: A.K. Rice Institute.

Whetten, D.A. (2006). Albert and Whetten Revisited: Strengthening the concept of organizational identity. *Journal of Management Inquiry*, 15(3):219. https://doi.org/10.1177/1056492606291200

Yount, K.M. (2004). Symbolic gender politics, religious group identity, and the decline in female genital cutting in Minya, Egypt. *Social Forces*, 82(3):1063. https://doi.org/10.1353/sof.2004.0062

Article 3

Working with Boundaries in Systems Psychodynamic Consulting[1]

H Struwig & F Cilliers

Orientation

The researcher described the systems psychodynamics of boundary management in organisations. The data showed how effective boundary management leads to good holding environments that, in turn, lead to containing difficult emotions.

Research Purpose

The purpose of the research was to produce a set of theoretical assumptions about organisational boundaries and boundary management in organisations and, from these, to develop a set of hypotheses as a thinking framework for practising consulting psychologists when they work with boundaries from a systems psychodynamic stance.

Motivation for the Study

The researcher used the belief that organisational boundaries reflect the essence of organisations. Consulting to boundary managers could facilitate a deep understanding of organisational dynamics.

1   Struwig, H & Cilliers, F. (2012). Working with boundaries in systems psychodynamic consulting. *SA Journal of Industrial Psychology/SA Tydskrif vir Bedryfsielkunde*, 38(2):Art.#987, 10 pages.

Research Design, Approach and Method

The researcher followed a case study design. He used systems psychodynamic discourse analysis. It led to six working hypotheses.

Main Findings

The primary task of boundary management is to hold the polarities of integration and differentiation and not allow the system to become fragmented or overly integrated. Boundary management is a primary task and an ongoing activity of entire organisations.

Practical/managerial Implications

Organisations should work actively at effective boundary management and balancing integration and differentiation. Leaders should become aware of how effective boundary management leads to good holding environments that, in turn, lead to containing difficult emotions in organisations.

Contribution/value-add

The researcher provided a boundary-consulting framework in order to assist consultants to balance the conceptual with the practical when they consult.

Introduction

Background of the Study

Consultants have given far too little attention to organisational boundaries in consulting psychology. In this study, the researcher studied dynamic boundary management as a primary activity in organisations. It yielded very interesting findings. Every part of organisational systems operates within and across their own boundaries (Cilliers & Koortzen, 2005; Koortzen & Cilliers, 2002). By focusing on boundaries, consultants will always work with organisations as systems of interrelated parts and relationships between people (Diamond & Allcorn, 2009).

Lawrence (1999) explained that boundaries are necessary in order for human beings to relate to each other and to their organisations. If there are no boundaries, relatedness and relationships are impossible because we become one, lost in each other, lost in organisations and lost in societies. By focusing on relationships and boundaries, consultants work directly with the essence of organisations.

Over the last few decades, the consulting literature has criticised positivism for its confined and narrow thinking, its focus on simplified cause and effect relationships (Lewis & Kelemen, 2002) as well as its simplistic and deterministic constructs (Goldkuhl, 2002). There is a growing awareness that the social, economic and cultural realities of life in organisations are complex and multi-dimensional (Kegan, 1994). This requires an interpretive stance toward understanding and making meaning.

The movement of social science from simple exclusive paradigms towards complex inclusive paradigms that take into account the holistic, systemic, dynamic and chaotic aspects of behaviour in organisations mirror this awareness (Fuqua & Newman, 2002). Organisational consulting psychology will remain relevant as long as it can draw on thinking frameworks and consulting processes that are able to deal with complexity and the depth of the human experience (Haslebo & Nielsen, 2000). The systems psychodynamic perspective provides such a paradigm. It deals with complexity and relationships on a systemic, dynamic and psychological level (Colman & Geller, 1985; Czander, 1993; Gould, Stapley & Stein, 2001).

A key concept in systems psychodynamics is that of individual, group and organisational boundaries (Lawrence, 1999; Diamond & Allcorn, 2009). They seem to be more relevant than ever in our time. Vansina and Vansina-Cobbaert (2008:390) wrote that 'Collaboration and partnership are popular discourse in the 21st-century ... working across boundaries has become increasingly important in a world where organisations are intertwined and interdependent'. They made the point that the task of working across the boundaries of business units, departments, disciplines and hierarchical levels challenges organisations and institutions. Boundary management seems to be a substantial part of everyday organisational life. Consultants who work in organisations cannot ignore this reality.

Lawrence (1999) makes the point that the trend in society to move away from categorising people has de-emphasised boundaries. In his view, one needs to recognise boundaries, but they must remain open to inquiry. The role of consultants is to work with managing boundaries and to make teams and leaders aware of boundary management issues (Cilliers & Koortzen, 2005).

When consulting about boundaries, many boundary-related issues face psychologists. They include unclear boundaries, boundaries that are too small, too loose, too tight, shared, or well defined (Haslebo & Nielsen, 2000). Clients may be concerned that they have compromised their boundaries, that they have been excluded from a boundary or that certain boundaries are conflicted. They might want to cross a boundary, push it, form one, change one, remove it, understand it, share it, question it or break it down. Organisational boundaries seem to be a logical focal point for consultants who wish to approach organisations from a complex and systemic paradigm, whilst systems psychodynamics provide an approach to boundary-related issues in organisations.

Research Purpose

The purpose of the research was to produce a theoretical set of assumptions about organisational boundaries and boundary management and, from these assumptions, to develop a set of hypotheses as a thinking framework for practising consulting psychologists when they work with boundaries from a systems psychodynamic stance. The study focused on individual, group and organisational boundaries as consultants' points of engagement with organisations. More specifically, it focused on boundary management as a phenomenon in organisations and a focus of consultation.

The rationale was to work towards applying boundary management practically to the field of organisational consulting psychology as an applied science. According to Loveridge, Willman and Deery (2007), after 60 years of publication, the focus is still on multi-disciplinary approaches that connect social theory to social practice, which can contribute towards the well-being of employees and the effectiveness of organisations. Although the systems psychodynamic paradigm and theory is complex, it allows consultants entry into organisations' below the surface behaviour (Campbell & Huffington, 2008; Huffington, Armstrong, Halton, Hoyle & Pooley, 2004). Heracleous (2004) makes this point when he calls for grounded research on organisational boundaries that focus on the first-order perceptions of stakeholders in an organisational context.

According to the literature, the systems psychodynamic view of organisations looks beyond the rational and economic view of work (Sievers, 2009). It focuses on organisations as living systems that are both conscious and unconscious (Colman & Bexton, 1975; Colman & Geller, 1985; Cytrynbaum & Noumair, 2004). Fraher (2004) traces the roots of the approach to classical psychoanalysis, group relations theory and open systems theory. The systemic aspects of this paradigm give obvious importance to the concept of boundaries, because these define what is inside or outside of systems or any parts of them (Campbell & Huffington, 2008; Churchman, 1968; Diamond & Allcorn, 2009). Boundaries help us to make sense of the world. They give us a way of classifying and categorising, without which the here-and-now would be chaotic and intolerable (Stapley, 1996; 2006). Boundaries, seen in this way, provide people with a sense of safety and control. Boundary management concerns working with what is inside versus what is outside through internal integration and external adaptation (Gould, 1993; Klein, 1959; 1997; Schein, 2004).

Trends from the Research Literature

The systems psychodynamic literature review provided the researcher with eight assumptions about organisational boundaries and boundary management. The first is that 'boundary management happens between people and in the minds of people. Therefore, boundary management is a social and psychological process'.

In the context of organisations, groups and people, boundaries are related and inter-related (Hernes, 2004; Lawrence, 1999; Stapley, 1996; 2006). The interplay and tension between people and groups, groups and organisations, as well as between organisations and their environments are the contexts of boundary management. Boundaries are social constructs that exist in the minds of people. These conceptualisations may be individual or shared. The psychological and social view of boundaries means that boundary management concerns learning and negotiating. For effective functioning, the subsystems of organisations (including people) need to learn what their boundaries are and negotiate these with other parts of their organisations. The processes of learning and negotiating occur at the same time. Because boundaries are socially constructed, they can also be socially deconstructed, unlearned and re-negotiated.

The second is that 'there are five key differentiating constructs that define boundaries in the minds of people and in organisations. These are identity, role, task, authority and capability'. Identity, role, task, authority, and capability are primarily psychological constructs (Koortzen & Cilliers, 2002; Hayden & Molenkamp, 2002; Hirschhorn & Gilmore, 1992; Santos & Eisenhardt, 2005). In other words, they exist in the minds of people (Diamond, Allcorn & Stein, 2004; Hirschhorn & Gilmore, 1992). The idea of 'organisation in the mind' (Armstrong, 2005) extrapolates to 'boundaries in the mind'. The constructs of capability, identity, authority, role and task are the building blocks of these boundaries. For example, authority in the mind may refer to the construction of people's own authority as they understand or perceive it. This construction is a psychological one about people's relationships with, and relatedness to, others. This construction in the mind carries inherent boundaries with it. One can argue that people, groups and organisations use the constructs of identity, authority, capability, role and task to answer the question 'who am I and not I, us and not us' (Hirschhorn & Gilmore, 1992; Stapley, 2006).

The third is that 'each boundary construct contains conscious and unconscious aspects'. If the proposed boundary constructs are essentially psychological ones, then they will also have psychological properties, in this case both conscious and unconscious constructions in the mind of people (Stapley, 2006). One can define the boundary between leaders and followers in conscious terms by using the proposed constructs. Team leaders might have titles, job descriptions, role descriptions, formal responsibilities and distinct abilities that would clearly differentiate them from followers. On an unconscious level, the same relationship might also have, under the surface, a parent-child construction. The unconscious emotional needs of followers might define different roles and tasks for team leaders and vice versa (Lawrence, 1999).

The fourth is that 'there are two aspects to each boundary. These are in-lines and out-lines'. The in-line consists of the identity, role, task, authority and ability that A (people, groups or organisations) thinks it has, whereas the out-line consists of how B (other people, groups or organisations) perceives the identity, role, task, authority and ability of A (Miller, 1985a). This principle brings the social aspect of boundary management into play. If one sees it in this way, one may share or not share a boundary, recognise or not recognise it. This also suggests that a boundary may exist for one but not for the other. This aspect of the theory provides an understanding of boundary confusion and conflict.

The fifth is that 'people, groups or organisations can only control their in-lines. They need to negotiate their out-lines'. If a boundary exists for particular people, teams or organisations, others will not automatically recognise, accept, authorise or support it (Miller, 1985b). Sometimes they need to explain, negotiate, agree to or even enforce a boundary before others authorise or recognise it.

The sixth is that 'for people in the same team or organisation to share an in-line, negotiation is necessary between them'. A shared understanding of the boundary of a team requires a meeting of minds between the people in the team (Gundlach, Zivnuska & Stoner, 2006; Roberts & Dutton, 2009). A shared set of assumptions about identity, role, task, authority and ability is an in-line (or shared) concept of the team's own boundary.

The seventh is that 'physical and psychological boundaries are related and interrelated'. It is the belief that psychological boundaries result in physical boundaries or barriers and vice versa (Diamond, Allcorn & Stein, 2004; Hirschhorn & Gilmore, 1992). People, who identify with each other, will, more often than not, see themselves as a group in some way or another, for example in language, dress or proximity. These physical artefacts are the result of their psychological boundaries. On the other hand, if people create a physical boundary between or around others, they will respond to it psychologically more often than not. In the same manner, boundaries are spilling over into organisations and vice versa. They also reflect one-another (Campbell & Huffington, 2008).

The eighth is that 'integration and differentiation are interrelated and complementary activities in organisations and lie at the centre of boundary management'. Lewis and Kelemen (2002:251) observed that organisations face 'contradictory demands for control and autonomy, coordination and individuality, expansion and contraction'. Theories of integration and differentiation in organisations explain how they deal with these paradoxical demands. Integration refers to the process by which the members of groups or organisations create shared psychological beliefs that relate and connect. Differentiation is the social and psychological process by which people, groups and organisations draw distinctions between themselves and others. Organisations that have high levels of integration and differentiation at the same time perform better than those who do not (Lawrence, 1999). Managing these two antagonistic states seems to be an essential task for the performance and survival of organisations.

These are theoretical assumptions about organisational boundaries and boundary management. The boundaries are multi-dimensional and dynamic. They are multi-dimensional because they are physical and psychological, individual and collective (shared), conscious and unconscious. They are dynamic because they are related and interrelated.

This applies to each of the boundary dimensions mentioned earlier. For example, people's personal moral boundaries relate to, and interrelate, with the moral boundaries of society. The conscious aspects of those moral boundaries will also relate to, and interrelate with, unconscious beliefs and assumptions. These psychological conceptualisations will lead, in turn, to physical or artefactual behaviour (Schein, 2004). These boundaries also consist of central concepts or differentiators.

In this study, the researcher sees identity, role, task, authority and capability as the primary differentiators of boundaries and as boundaries in their own right – they are multi-dimensional. This means that each of the differentiators has conscious, unconscious, physical, psychological, individual and collective attributes. This understanding of boundaries and boundary management led to the research questions that follow:

- ∞ what is the primary task of boundary management?
- ∞ what does the systems psychodynamics of boundary management in organisations mean?

The Potential Value-add of the Study

The value of this study lies in its offer of a set of qualitatively verified assumptions about organisational boundaries and boundary management as a way of making sense of anxiety and chaos in organisations. The study addressed the typical scenario of a range of experiences that confront consultants. They need to distinguish, compare and connect them to make sense (Oliver, 2005). Here consultants ask questions like:

- ∞ What part of the organisations should they work with?
- ∞ Where do consulting assignments start and where do they end?
- ∞ Who are the clients?
- ∞ What do the scopes include and what do they exclude?
- ∞ What is really going on?
- ∞ What should they work with and what should they not work with? (See Dillon, 2003).

This sifting process helps consultants to change holistic and systemic insights about organisations into practical consulting work. Without this process, consultations will never move from the conceptual to the practical. It is here that this research focuses on the interface between relationships in organisations, that is, on their boundaries. This gives consultants a useful and practical platform that might assist them to balance the complex conceptual world with the practical consulting one.

What will Follow

The structure of the rest of the article follows. The researcher presents the research design, the research approach and research strategy. The research method follows. It consists of the setting, the roles of the researchers, the sampling method, data collection, recording and analysis. The researcher then mentions the strategies he used to ensure quality data. He then presents the findings for cases A and B, the themes that emerged and the working hypotheses. The discussion contains the answers to the two research questions. The conclusion follows and the article concludes with recommendations, possible limitations of the study and suggestions for further research.

Research Design

Research Approach

The approach was qualitative (Terre Blanche, Durrheim & Painter, 2006) and interpretive (Gorton, 2006; Yanow & Schwartz-Shea, 2006). Hermeneutics was the research paradigm (Scott & Keetes, 2001). The researcher chose this paradigm because of his belief that reality and truth are internal and subjective. Using these approaches, the study tried to answer the 'how' and 'why' questions of boundary management in a thick, rich and varied description (Alvesson & Sköldberg, 2010).

Research Strategy

The researcher used a two case study design (Woodside & Wilson, 2003). This is 'the description of an ongoing event in relation to a particular outcome of interest over a fixed time in the here and now' (Brewerton & Millward, 2001:53). The case studies were instrumental (Denzin & Lincoln, 2000) to gain an understanding of boundary management and to elaborate on and extend the relevant theory.

Research Method

Research Setting

The researcher conducted the research in the South African head office of an international specialist banking group with global divisions. It served a niche client base. Its organisational model balanced centralisation with decentralisation to facilitate control and provide focus to its business units. The two case studies are from different autonomous specialist business units. The organisation is structured for nimbleness, flexibility, a high level of decision-making authority – that is rarely overridden – and decentralised support functions.

Entrée and Establishing Researcher Roles

The first researcher played three distinct roles. The first was as a consultant (Lowman, 2002) to the organisation. The second was as a participant observer (Brewerton & Millward, 2001) who witnessed, described, recorded and made sense of the consultation whilst being part of it at the same time (Dewalt & Dewalt, 2002). The third was as discourse researcher (Cilliers & Smit, 2006) who analysed the research data. He used the orientation of self as the instrument of analysis (Clarke & Hoggitt, 2009; McCormick & White, 2000). The second researcher was the supervisor (see Clarke & Hoggett, 2009).

Sampling

The researcher used convenience and purposive sampling to 'examine particular instances of the phenomenon of interest' (Teddle & Tashakori, 2009:177) in order to define and elaborate on the manifestation of boundary management. The researcher chose the two cases to yield different organisational-level data. Case A happened on a micro-level. It focused on the intergroup dynamics (Brunner, Nutkevitch & Sher, 2006) of specific teams in a single division and with the same geography. Case B occurred on a macro group-as-whole scale (Brunner et al., 2006; Wells, 1985). It included divisions of the whole organisation with different geographies. It had several support functions throughout the organisation. As Teddle and Tashakori (2009) suggested, Case B supplemented Case A in its scale and holistic nature. All role players were present and the conversation involved the whole organisation.

Data Collection Methods

The researcher used the diary method (Brewerton & Millward, 2003) during the consulting sessions. He made detailed written field notes (of thoughts, feelings, realisations and insights) during and after each consulting session. He conducted ethnographic interviews (Flick, 2009) for case A, with its head and his team leaders. He used focus groups (Bernard, 2006) for Case B with each team after ending the consultation. The question he asked for both techniques was 'what is your experience of your division?'

Recording of Data

The researcher used the diary material in its original form. During the interviews and the focus groups, he recorded the verbatim material in detail and immediately afterwards transcribed it to ensure that he had captured all the detail. He kept and stored the data safely.

Data Analyses

The researcher used discourse analysis (Camic, Rhodes & Yardley, 2003; Denzin & Lincoln, 1994), which he interpreted from the systems psychodynamic stance (see Cilliers & Smit, 2006; Armstrong, 2005; Campbell, 2007; Cilliers & Koortzen, 2005; Gould et al., 2001; Huffington, et al., 2004; Klein, 1997). The researcher categorised the case study data into themes that relate to boundary management. He formulated working hypotheses for each of the two cases and viewed them in relation to one other (Terre Blanche et al., 2006). He then finalised the hypotheses for each case study by merging the hypotheses that built on each other or by separating the hypotheses that needed more focus. This yielded a set of hypotheses for each of the two cases. The next step was to accumulate findings from both cases. He checked the coherence of the hypotheses (Terre Blanche, 2006) that emerged from the two cases and followed the process of merging and separating once more. A final set of hypotheses emerged. The researcher checked it against the data from the two case studies and finally correlated it with the existing literature.

Strategies Employed to Ensure Quality Data

The researcher ensured validity and reliability by following the suggestions of Denzin and Lincoln (1994), Riege (2003) and Terre Blanche et al., (2006). Construct validity refers to using several sources of evidence, establishing a chain of events and reviewing a draft case study report. The internal validity of findings refers to crosschecking data during analysis.

Reliability refers to giving a full account of the theories and ideas for each research phase, assuring congruence between research issues and the features of the study, recording actions and observations in writing, as well as using peer reviews.

Ethicality refers to informed consent and confidentiality in terms of contracts with managers and team members. The researcher tried to show respect for the participants and their shared personal information in the cases and in the analysis of the data (Holloway & Jefferson, 2010).

Reporting

The researcher presented the findings by case study, followed by the five manifested themes. He gave answers to the research questions in the discussion.

Findings

The researcher reported the findings for cases A and B by referring to the consulting context and his experience.

Case A: Leadership in Business Support Services

The client was the operations unit of the investment banking division. The primary task of this business unit was to generate income by growing and preserving the assets of clients. Its structure was a front and a back office that operated in different office areas to facilitate its undivided attention on its primary tasks.

The primary task of the front office was to offer clients relevant advice and portfolio management services by focusing on protecting capital and growth in local and international investments. The primary task of the back office was to support the front office through information technology (IT), administrative support and solutions.

The focus of this case study was the functions of the back office, called Business Support Services (BSS). It provided full support to the securities division, and services to third parties, in an attempt to generate its own income. As this strategy interfered with the level of service to internal clients, management decided to split it into two separate entities, one with a focus on internal clients only.

'Settlements' became an area on its own whilst the operational support area became a separate entity called BSS. BSS comprised several teams that were mostly IT related. They included:

∞ business analysis;
∞ service desk and statements;
∞ development infrastructure; and
∞ an incentive scheme.

Each of these teams had its own team leader who, in turn, reported to the head of BSS. He, in turn, reported to the head of the securities division through the chief operating officer (COO) of Securities, who was responsible for all back-office areas.

Case A: Consultation

The consultation sessions focused on the inability of different teams and areas within BSS to relate and collaborate. There were several splits in the area. They led to fragmentation and ultimately inhibited the unit from performing its primary task. The consultant's analysis of the collaboration issues suggested poorly negotiated boundaries in the area. More specifically, the consultant believed that the identity, role and primary task of the back office were not clearly defined and negotiated with the front office. This led to conflict and discrepancies in expectations and delivery. This also resulted in the de-authorisation of the back office.

For example, developers in the IT department were seen as service providers rather than as strategic partners. Therefore, they were often excluded from business strategy meetings. This led to unrealistic development requests that the IT department could not meet. This, in turn, frustrated the front office that needed speedy IT delivery in order to improve its work. The consultant gave the leaders of the back office an opportunity to understand clearly their own identities, roles and primary tasks. Once these became shared concepts in their own minds, they were able to negotiate boundaries with their colleagues in the front office.

This work enabled leaders of the back office to redefine their leadership roles. They made a significant shift from being essentially managers to leaders of their division. This shift led to a watershed strategy session for the division. The leadership team presented the BSS strategy as a journey, starting with the state of affairs 20 months into the history of the function and ending with plans for the new quarter. Not only did the team leaders show their intention to lead the division during this process but they also started to contain anxiety in the system. They communicated their philosophy about people and their intention to create a much more caring environment: 'We do regard the people as our most important asset'. They also communicated the relationship that they intended to create with the front office, which was 'to be strategic partners with our clients'. This change helped the leaders to get closer to their staff. The head of the area was stunned by the impact of the session. The staff for the first time seemed to be more aligned. He described it as a sense of solidarity.

The consultant ultimately approached the entire consultation as boundary work. The back office renegotiated the boundary between itself and the front office along with the parameters of identity, role and task. The leaders in the back office also created a shared concept of their own boundary with each other (in-line). The leaders also re-negotiated the boundary between themselves and their staff. During this process of alignment and re-negotiation, the consultant worked with both conscious and unconscious material relating to boundaries. The consultant assisted the team leaders to redefine their role from 'task-masters' who drove tasks to that of 'leaders' who gave direction, built relationships and provided a context for performance to their staff. The leaders communicated this shift in intention clearly to their staff. They also assisted the staff to bring to the surface their own inabilities, which they had previously denied.

The consultant then helped the leaders in the back office to align their capabilities with their newly negotiated boundaries. The interplay between identity, role, task, authority and capability formed the central theme of the consulting work. The consultant treated these constructs as the building blocks of the boundaries. Here, the team leaders made an identity shift from 'service providers' to 'strategic partners' and from 'managers of tasks' to 'leaders of people'. These identity shifts led to consultation on how they played their roles in the organisation. This, in turn, led to new tasks they needed to perform, which raised new competency challenges. Negotiating authority for this shift in roles and tasks then came into play.

Case B: Information Security in an International Specialist Banking Group

The client was the international specialist banking group. The particular consulting process occurred on an organisational level. It pivoted on the theme of information security. Information was a key asset to the organisation. Therefore, it needed to manage its information appropriately and protect it from a wide range of risks to ensure competitive advantage and business continuity. Implementing an appropriate set of controls, which comprised policies, standards, procedures, structures and technology configurations, would improve information security.

This organisation allocated the task and responsibility for managing and protecting information to the group information security officer (GISO). The GISO operated with a small team of people, the Information Security Team (known as the Info-Sec team). The primary task of the Info-Sec team was to manage and protect the organisation's information. The GISO and his team were ultimately responsible for producing policies, standards and procedures related to information security. The business units had to implement them. Some of the GISO team members acted as consultants to the business units, assisting them to implement these policies and helping them to identify specific threats to the business units.

The structure of IT in this organisation is largely decentralised. Each business unit has an IT division. A separate division, known as Central IT (CIT), was responsible for the IT infrastructure (including hardware, servers and voice technology) whilst a small team of people shouldered the responsibility of Group IT. Group IT takes strategic leadership. It is accountable for the whole IT domain in the organisation, including information security. Other role players and forums of significance to this case study included:

- ∞ Group Risk
- ∞ Internal Audit
- ∞ The Technical Architecture Board (TAB)

Group Risk performed the primary task of reducing the organisation's exposure to risk. The Internal Audit function helped the organisation to achieve its stated goals by analysing business processes, activities and procedures, highlighting problems and providing solutions. TAB was an advisory and decision-making forum that focused on all technical and architectural aspects of IT. It comprised key members of the Group IT Management Committee (Manco) and other technical experts.

Case B Consultation

The consultation process focused on the de-authorisation of the Info-Sec team. The identity, role and task of this team had not been clearly communicated to, and negotiated with, the organisation. The Info-Sec team described its primary task (Rice, 1963) as 'to protect the organisation's information'. However, the IT divisions in the business units saw this task as their responsibility. They were not interested in the proposals of the Info-Sec consultants, nor did they support the role of the GISO. This led to misalignment and conflict with the business units that they were supporting. The business units said that Group IT and the GISO were 'telling them what to do'. The initial consulting sessions focused on re-negotiating the identity, role and primary task of the Info-Sec team with the rest of the organisation. However, as the consultation progressed, the focus shifted towards information security as an activity.

A three-day institutional event (Brunner, Nutkevitch & Sher, 2006) followed. The role players agreed and negotiated their roles and responsibilities in relation to information security in the group. Two very distinct primary tasks emerged for the Info-Sec team and the business units. The primary task for the Info-Sec team was 'oversight and promotion of information security within the group'. They were not authorised to execute tasks on behalf of the business units and they were not responsible for implementation or 'product selection'.

The business units, on the other hand, now had to 'ensure that the group's environment is secure'. This was a fundamental shift in their primary task.

Integration

The researcher used the constructs of identity, role, task, authority and capability as the parameters that defined the boundary negotiations throughout. Five themes emerged from the data.

Theme 1: Interaction between authority, capability, identity, role and task: Both cases showed that the constructs of authority, capability, identity, role and task were related and interrelated.

Theme 2: Differentiation and boundaries: There was substantial evidence in each of the cases that the organisation's subsystems differentiate themselves from others based on authority, capability, identity, role and task.

Theme 3: Integration and boundaries: The data suggested that the subsystems of the organisation, like teams and divisions, integrate through sharing a collective conceptualisation of their own authority, capability, identity, role and task.

Theme 4: Misalignment and fragmentation: Both cases showed that misalignment between the different subsystems of the organisation, in terms of authority, capability, identity, role and task, might lead to its fragmentation.

Theme 5: The adverse effects of boundary problems: The data suggested that boundary problems may lead to conflict and stress that might adversely affect the functioning of the organisation.

Using these themes, the researcher formulated the six working hypotheses that follow:

∞ **Working hypothesis 1:** There is a natural balance between capability, authority, identity, role and task. When the balance is disturbed, the system will re-organise to restore the equilibrium.

∞ **Working hypothesis 2:** When one part of a system differentiates itself from another in terms of capabilities, authority, identity, role and task, a psychological boundary forms between them.

∞ **Working hypothesis 3:** When one part of a system shares capabilities, authority, identity, role or tasks with another, they share a psychological boundary.

∞ **Working hypothesis 4:** Misalignment between different parts of organisations, in terms of capability, authority, identity, role and task, can lead to their fragmentation.

∞ **Working hypothesis 5:** Alignment between different parts of organisations, in terms of capability, authority, identity, role and task, can lead to integration.

∞ **Working hypothesis 6:** Boundary management can reduce conflict and stress, as well as their dysfunctional effects.

Discussion

The first purpose of the research was to produce a theoretical set of assumptions about organisational boundaries and boundary management. Using these assumptions, its second purpose was to develop a set of hypotheses as a thinking framework for practising consulting psychologists when they work with boundaries from a systems psychodynamic stance. The findings could provide a useful and practical consulting platform that might help consultants to balance the complex conceptual world with the practical consulting one when it comes to boundary management consulting.

The researcher answered the first research question ('what is the primary task of boundary management?'). It is 'to hold the polarities of integration and differentiation and not allow the system to become fragmented or overly integrated'. The researcher answered the second research question ('what does the systems psychodynamics of boundary management in organisations mean?'). It 'is an activity in organisations that happens continuously at all levels and involves whole organisations' (also see Fuqua & Newman, 2002).

The tendency of organisations to move through repeating cycles of centralisation and decentralisation is proof that there is no ideal point of balance between integration and differentiation (Lawrence & Lorsh, 1967; Schneider, 1985; Schein, 2004). In practice, this refers to the continuous processes of aligning and negotiating that happens between people and groups (Hirschhorn & Gilmore, 1992). The ultimate task of boundary management is to create a balance between being flexible, adaptable (necessary for the survival of postmodern organisations) – see Lewis & Kelemen (2002) – and connected. Without relationships and collaboration, there is no organisation (Gundlach et al., 2006; Hernes; 2004).

Subsystems of organisations, like teams and divisions, differentiate and integrate according to their distinct identities, roles and tasks. They also do this through the ways that they are authorised and the capabilities that they have (Koortzen & Cilliers, 2002; Hayden & Molenkamp, 2002; Hirschhorn & Gilmore, 1992; Santos & Eisenhardt, 2005). Organisations make sense of the complex range of tasks and activities they need to perform by differentiating, thereby giving them focus. Clear differentiation helps people to know what their responsibilities are and what they need to do. They also contain unconsciously on behalf of their organisations (Hyde, 2006). Without differentiation, being aware of boundaries, as well as the classification and categorisation that they provide, organisations would be unmanageable – and working in them would be untenable (Stapley, 1996; 2006).

Different teams and divisions focus on different strategic areas. Each develops its own special skills and knowledge (Dosi, Faillo & Marengo, 2009). They continuously discover who they are, what they should be doing and who should be in charge in relation to others in their organisations (Hirschhorn & Gilmore 1992; Schein, 2004). In case A, this form of functional differentiation was very apparent between the front office staff and their back-office support. However, too much differentiation can lead to disconnected organisations. This could happen when teams and divisions become so differentiated that they break off, or become completely disassociated, from the rest of their organisations (Gundlach et al., 2006). This is precisely what happened in Case A. Important role players were excluded from business strategy discussions. It led to strategic decisions that were difficult to implement.

Shared capabilities, authority, identity, roles and tasks integrate teams and subsystems in organisations (Gundlach et al., 2006). It brings people together, focuses their collective efforts and creates a sense of belonging. In Case A, the leaders of BSS used a two-day dialogue session to create a shared sense of identity, role and task. This helped them to create a leadership team coming from 'a group of individual leaders who each do their own thing'. When organisations become too integrated, they become rigid, overly controlled and inflexible (Lawrence & Lorsch, 1967).

The interrelated nature of the constructs of capability, authority, identity, role and task was apparent in these research findings. This showed face validity. Tasks and roles are intricately entangled in organisations. Every role has a task and all tasks seem to belong to a role. People in organisations identify themselves according to their roles and tasks because they relate to their primary tasks and, therefore, to the very essence of their organisations. Furthermore, in order to perform tasks or play roles, there needs to be a set of related abilities.

Finally, all people and teams in organisations exist in relation to each other. Roles and tasks are not possible if they are not authorised. The interrelatedness of these constructs gives consultants several points from which to work when boundaries are involved. In theory, boundary management can start with any of the constructs. Working with one will activate the others and bring them into the consulting process.

In Case B, the consultant worked with several different subsystems of the organisation to re-negotiate their responsibilities in relation to information security. These re-negotiations of responsibilities related closely to the authority, role, identity and capability boundaries of each area. Conflict arises when the subsystems of organisations do not agree on their boundaries. Conflict leads to splits and splits lead to breakdowns in communication, relationships, collaboration and ultimately in the organisations' ability to perform their primary tasks (Hyde, 2006). Both case studies showed this clearly.

In Case A, boundary disagreements between the front and back office created much animosity. In Case B, boundary confusion left the team de-authorised and incapable of performing its tasks. In this research, the constructs of capability, authority, identity, role and task were boundaries in their own right. It seems that people and teams constantly need to manage their boundaries in their organisations through negotiating these constructs with each other. Without this, misalignment and breakdown will happen. This reinforces the need for alignment (Haslebo & Nielsen, 2000). In order for the differentiated parts of organisations to connect with each other, there must be alignment (Gundlach et al., 2006). This alignment across boundaries happens when two or more parts of organisations have similar 'organisations in the mind'. When different parts of organisations have aligned ideas of the identities, roles and tasks of others, and when these subsystems have corresponding abilities, they are able to authorise each other, communicate, build relationships, collaborate and ultimately perform their primary tasks. All of this helps to integrate organisations.

In both cases, the consultant helped the different subsystems of the organisation to understand and agree on their boundaries in relation to, and with, others. These interventions helped the organisation to integrate and made greater collaboration and performance possible.

Conclusions

The researcher concluded that effective boundary management leads to good holding environments that, in turn, lead to containing difficult emotions in organisations. Staff members negotiate organisational boundaries. They exist in the minds of the staff rather than in the formal structures of organisations' hierarchies. Identity, role, task, capability and authority are prominent concepts in the individual and collective minds of people. They comprise the boundaries in organisations. The principles of boundary management consulting the researcher reached in this research will assist consultants to work with organisational boundaries in a multi-dimensional way. Consultants who operate from this perspective can engage with organisational boundaries as physical, psychological, individual, collective, conscious and unconscious phenomena. The multi-dimensional focus of the principles makes them flexible. It also accounts for complexity but makes the work manageable at the same time.

Recommendations

The researcher recommends that organisations work at managing their boundaries effectively. This suggests that organisations need to create environments where people are relatively free to negotiate their own boundaries with each other and where hierarchy and power do not interfere with this process. Organisations must try very hard to create spaces and practices for communication that will improve effective boundary management.

The researcher also recommends that teams and departments invest the necessary time to talk about their own identities, roles, tasks, authority and abilities. These discussions will facilitate shared understanding about these internal boundaries, which would enable them to negotiate those same boundaries more effectively with other areas of the organisations in which they work. Organisations should become aware of the balance between integration and differentiation if they want to succeed. Organisations that are overly controlled and bureaucratic should differentiate themselves more, whilst organisations that seem to be fragmented and misaligned should integrate themselves more fully.

Possible Limitations of the Study

The researcher identified the limitations that follow. Firstly, the researcher chose five constructs as primary boundary differentiators based on the literature, as well as his knowledge, experience and intuition. Although he found enough empirical evidence to support the relevance of these constructs, future research could investigate the existence of other constructs. For example, Hirschhorn and Gilmore (1992) included political boundaries.

Secondly, using working hypotheses as a tool of analysis has inherent limitations because they do not present absolute truths – they are only applicable and usable until someone proves that they are not. Amado (1995) believes that working hypotheses as research tools always require researchers to check the assumptions.

Thirdly, the consultant and researcher was the same person. This was a limitation because the qualitative research instrument had very human limitations. Therefore, it is difficult, if not impossible, to comment on how the levels of knowledge, insight and experiences of the consultant-researcher, as well as his unconscious processes, influenced the consultation and research processes.

Suggestions for Further Research

In terms of future research, the researcher suggests that researchers explore the working hypotheses presented in this research in other organisations or in different consulting contexts.

Researchers could also test the consulting framework with different consultants. Researchers could apply different research designs to test these findings and hypotheses. For example, they could use them in a group relations training event. This would provide a semi-controlled environment for testing and analyses. Researchers could also use a longitudinal study to test the effect of the consulting intervention. Lastly, researchers could add more elements to authority, ability, identity, role and task as boundary constructs. For example, researchers could explore the political elements of boundaries more fully as the present study almost totally omitted them.

Acknowledgements

Competing Interests

The authors declare that they had no financial or personal relationship(s) which may have inappropriately influenced them when they wrote this paper.

Authors' Contributions

Both researchers planned the research project. H.S. (University of South Africa) conducted the literature review and the empirical study. F.C. (University of South Africa) acted in a supervisory role and took responsibility for publishing the material and the academic editing.

References

Alvesson, M. & Sköldberg, K. (2010). Reflexive methodology. *New vistas for qualitative research*. London: Sage.

Amado, G. (1995). Why psychoanalytical knowledge helps us understand organisations: a discussion with Elliot Jaques. *Human Relations*, 48(4):351-357. https://doi.org/10.1177/001872679504800402

Armstrong, P. (2005). *Organisation in the mind*. London: Karnac.

Bernard, H.K. (2006). *Research methods in anthropology*. Oxford: Alta Mira Press.

Brewerton, P. & Millward, L. (2001) *Organizational research methods: A Guide for students and researchers*. London: Sage Publications Ltd. https://doi.org/10.4135/9781849209533

Brunner, L.D.; Nutkevitch, A. & Sher, M. (2006). *Group relations conferences. Reviewing and exploring theory, design, role-taking and application*. London: Karnac.

Camic, P.M.; Rhodes, J.E. & Yardley, L. (2003). *Qualitative research in Psychology*. Washington: APA.

Campbell, D. (2007). *The socially constructed organisation*. London: Karnac.

Campbell, D. & Huffington, C. (2008). *Organisations connected. A handbook of systemic consultation*. London: Karnac.

Churchman, C.W. (1968). *The systems approach*. New York: Doubleday Dell Publishing Group.

Cilliers, F. & Koortzen, P. (2005). Conflict in groups: The CIBART model. *HR Future*, 113(10):52-53.

Cilliers, F. & Smit, B. (2006). A systems psychodynamic interpretation of South African diversity dynamics: a comparative study. *South African Journal of Labour Relations*, 30(2):5-18.

Clarke, S. & Hoggett, P. (2009). *Researching beneath the surface. Psycho-social research methods in practice*. London: Karnac.

Colman, A.D. & Bexton, W.H. (1975). *Group relations reader 1*. Jupiter: The A.K. Rice Institute.

Colman, A.D. & Geller, M.H. (1985). *Group relations reader 2*. Jupiter: The A.K. Rice Institute.

Cytrynbaum, S. & Noumair, A. (2004). *Group dynamics, organizational irrationality, and social complexity: Group relations reader 3*. Jupiter: A.K. Rice.

Czander, W.M. (1993). *The psychodynamics of work and organizations*. New York: Guilford.

Denzin, N.K. & Lincoln, Y.S. (1994). *Handbook of qualitative research*. Thousand Oaks: Sage.

Dewalt, K.M. & Dewalt, B.K. (2002). *Participant observation: a guide for fieldworkers*. Oxford: Alta Mira Press.

Diamond, M.A. & Allcorn, S. (2009). *Private selves in private organizations. The psychodynamics of organisational diagnosis and change*. New York: Palgrave Macmillan. https://doi.org/10.1057/9780230620094

Diamond, M.A.; Allcorn, S. & Stein, H. (2004). The surface of organizational boundaries: a view from psychoanalytical object relations theory. *Human Relations*, 57(1):31-49. https://doi.org/10.1177/0018726704042713

Dillon, J.T. (2003). The use of questions in organizational consulting. *The Journal of Applied Behavioral Science*, 39(4):438-452. https://doi.org/10.1177/0021886303260503

Dosi, G.; Faillo, M. & Mrengo, L. (2008). Organizational capabilities, patterns of knowledge accumulation and governance structures in business firms: an introduction. *Organization Studies*, 19(8&9):1165-1185. https://doi.org/10.1177/0170840608094775

Flick, U. (2009). *An introduction to qualitative research*. (4th edn.). London: Sage.

Fraher, A. (2004). *A history of group study and psychodynamic organisations*. London: Free Association.

Fuqua, D.R. & Newman, J.L. (2002). The role of systems theory in consulting psychology. In: Lowman, R.L. (ed.), *Handbook of organizational consulting psychology*. San Francisco: Jossey-Bass. https://doi.org/10.1037/1061-4087.54.2.131

Gould, L.J. (1993). Contemporary perspectives on personal and organisational authority: the self in a system of work relationships. In: L. Hirschhorn & C.K Barnett (eds.), *The psychodynamics of organisations* Philadelphia: Temple University Press.

Gould, L.J.; Stapley, L.F. & Stein, M. (2001). *The systems psychodynamics of organisations*. London: Karnac.

Goldkuhl, G. (2002). *Anchoring scientific abstractions: ontological and linguistic determination following socio-instrumental pragmatism*. European Conference on Research Methods in Business Management (ECRM 2002), 29-30 April 2002.

Gorton, W.A. (2006). *Karl Popper and the social sciences*. New York: State University of New York Press.

Gundlach, M.; Zivnuska, S. & Stoner, J. (2006). Understanding the relationship between individualism-collectivism and team performance through an integration of social identity theory and social relations model. *Human Relations*, 59(12):1603-1632. https://doi.org/10.1177/0018726706073193

Haslebo, G. & Nielsen, K.S. (2000). *Systems and meaning: consulting in organisations*. London: Karnac.

Hayden, C. & Molenkamp, R. (2002). *Tavistock Primer*, London: Tavistock.

Heracleous, L. (2004). Boundaries in the study of organization. *Human Relations*, 57(1):95-103. https://doi.org/10.1177/0018726704042716

Hernes, T. (2004). Studying composite boundaries: a framework of analysis. *Human Relations*, 57(1):9-29. https://doi.org/10.1177/0018726704042712

Hirschhorn, L. & Gilmore, T. (1992). The new boundaries of the "boundaryless" company. *Harvard Business Review*, 70(3):104-115.

Holloway, W. & Jefferson, T. (2000). *Doing qualitative research differently. Free association, narrative and the interview method*. London: Sage. https://doi.org/10.4135/9781849209007

Huffington, C.; Armstrong, A.; Halton, W.; Hoyle, L. & Pooley, J. (2004). *Working below the surface. The emotional life of contemporary organisations*. London: Karnac.

Hyde, P. (2006). Managing across boundaries: identity differentiation and interaction. *Journal of Innovation and Learning*, 3(4):349-362. https://doi.org/10.1504/IJIL.2006.009560

Kegan, R. (1994). *In over our heads: the mental demands of modern life.* Cambridge, MA: Harvard University Press.

Klein, M. (1959). Our adult world and its roots in infancy. *Human Relations,* 12:291-303. https://doi.org/10.1177/001872675901200401

Klein, M. (1997). *Envy and gratitude and other works, 1946-1963.* London: Hogarth.

Koortzen, P. & Cilliers, F. (2002). The psychoanalytical approach to team development. In: R.L. Lowman (ed.), *Handbook of organizational consulting psychology.* San Francisco: Jossey-Bass.

Lawrence, P. & Lorsch, J. (1967). Differentiation and integration in complex organizations. *Administrative Science Quarterly,* 12:1-30. https://doi.org/10.2307/2391211

Lawrence, W.G. (1999). Exploring individual and organisational boundaries. Tavistock open systems approach. London: Karnac.

Loveridge, R.; Willman, P. & Deery, S. (2007). 60 years of Human Relations. *Human Relations,* 60(12):1873-1888. https://doi.org/10.1177/0018726707084917

Lewis, M.W. & Kelemen, M.L. (2002). Multiparadigm inquiry: Exploring organizational purism and paradox. *Human Relations,* 55(2):251-275. https://doi.org/10.1177/0018726702055002185

Lowman, R.L. (2002). *The handbook of organizational consulting Psychology.* San Francisco: Jossey-Bass. https://doi.org/10.1037/1061-4087.54.4.213

McCormick, D.W. & White, J. 2000. Using one's self as instrument for organisational diagnosis. *Organisational Development Journal,* 18(3):49-62.

Miller, E.J. (1985a). Organisation development and industrial democracy. In: A.D. Colman & M.H. Geller (eds.), *Group relations reader 2,* pp.243-271. Jupiter: A.K. Rice Institute.

Miller, E.J. (1985b). The politics of involvement. In: A.D. Colman & M.H. Geller (eds.), *Group relations reader 2,* pp.383-397. Jupiter: A.K. Rice Institute.

Oliver, C. (2005). Reflexive inquiry: *A framework for consultancy practice.* London: Karnac.

Rice, A.K. (1963). *The enterprise and its environment.* London: Tavistock.

Riege, A.M. (2003). Validity and reliability tests in case study research: A literature review with "hands-on" applications for each research phase. *Qualitative Market Research: An International Journal,* 6(2):75-86. https://doi.org/10.1108/13522750310470055

Roberts, L.M. & Dutton, J.E. (2009). *Exploring positive identities and organizations: Building a theoretical and research foundation.* New York: Routledge. https://doi.org/10.4324/9780203879245

Santos, F.M. & Eisenhardt, K.M. (2005). Organizational boundaries and theories of organization. *Organization Science,* 16(5):491-508. https://doi.org/10.1287/orsc.1050.0152

Schein, E.H. (2004). *Organizational culture and leadership.* San Francisco: Jossey-Bass.

Schneider, S.C. (1985). Managing boundaries in organisations. In: A.D. Colman & M.H. Geller (eds.), *Group relations reader 2,* pp.231-241. Jupiter: The A.K. Rice Institute.

Scott, J.W. & Keetes, D. (2001). *Schools of thought.* Woodstock: Princeton University Press.

Sievers, B. (2009). *Psychoanalytic studies of organizations. Contributions from the International Society for the Psychoanalytical Study of Organizations (ISPSO)*. London: Karnac.

Stapley, L.F. (1996). *The personality of the organisation: A psychodynamic explanation of culture and change*. London: Free Association.

Stapley, L.F. (2006). *Individuals, groups and organisations beneath the surface*. London: Karnac.

Teddle, C. & Tashakkori, A. (2009). *Foundations of mixed method research: Integrating quantitative and qualitative approaches in the social and behavioural sciences*. San Francisco: Sage.

Terre Blanche, M.; Durrheim, K. & Painter, D. (2006). *Research in practice. Applied methods for the social sciences*. Cape Town: UCT Press.

Vansina, L.S. & Vansina-Cobbaert, M. (2008). *Systems psychodynamics for consultants and managers*. Chichester: John Wiley & Sons. https.//doi.org/10.1002/9780470697184

Wells, L. (1985). The group-as-a-whole perspective and its theoretical roots. In: A.D. Colman & M.H. Geller (eds.), *Group relations reader 2*. Washington, DC: A.K. Rice Institute.

Woodside, A.G. & Wilson, E.J. (2003). Case study research methods for theory building. *Journal of Business & Industrial Marketing*, 18(6/7):493–508. https://doi.org/10.1108/08858620310492374

Yanow, D., & Swartz-Shea, P. (2006). *Interpretation and method: Empirical research methods and the interpretive turn*. NY: M.E. Sharpe.

Article 4

The Role of Sense of Coherence in Group Relations Training[1]

F Cilliers

Abstract

This research measured the role that sense of coherence (SOC) plays on an individual and group level during group relations training, presented to fifty-eight managers, using Antonovsky's scale and an semi-structured interview. The individual measuring high on SOC showed more understanding of group dynamics, made more use of own existing resources to cope with anxiety and found the experience challenging and meaningful, than the low measuring individual. On the group level, the split between high and low led to projective identification: the high SOC individuals contain competence and the low, incompetence. Recommendations for future group relations training are formulated.

Group relations training originated about 60 years ago (Miller, 1989) and has its philosophical and theoretical roots in psychodynamics. It is based upon Freud's writings as the father of psychoanalysis (Czander, 1993), and incorporates the work of Melanie Klein on child and family psychology (De Board, 1978), Ferenczi on object relations (De Board, 1978) and Bertalanffy on systems thinking (Czander, 1993; De Board, 1978; Hirshhorn, 1993).

As a therapeutic stance it is well known and used in Psychiatry in Europe and the USA (Menzies, 1993; Miller, 1976; Obholzer & Roberts, 1994; Rioch, 1970), has been applied in working conferences by the Tavistock Institute (Miller, 1989), developed

---

1   Cilliers, F. (2001). The role of sense of coherence in Group relations training. *South African Journal of Industrial Psychology*, 27(3):13-18.

into an organisational theory (Bion, 1961; 1970; Miller, 1976; 1983; 1993), as well as an organisational consultancy stance (Gabelnick & Carr, 1989; Neumann et al., 1997). Internationally, its application in organisational psychology is growing amongst Industrial/Organisational psychologists, applying the stance to team-building (Cilliers, 2000; Cytrynbaum & Lee, 1993; Gabelnick & Carr, 1989; Kets de Vries, 1991), as well as organisational consultation (Cilliers & Koortzen, 2000a).

True to its psychodynamic nature, group relations training focuses on anxiety as the driving force of individual and group behaviour, and the unconscious defences against unwanted anxiety. As such, the model offers no clear view on psychological well-being what Wissing and Van Eeden (1994, 1997a, 1997b) refer to like the challenge presently being presented in Industrial Psychology in the training of managers and employees. This research endeavours to introduce sense of coherence as one such model of psychological well-being (Cilliers, 1988) into group relations training in order to understand its elect on individual and group behaviour.

Group relations training This training model accepts group behaviour to be both conscious and unconscious (Miller, 1993). Conscious behaviour is clear and explicit, for example, the group's set rules and observable behaviour. On the other hand, the unconscious is filled with unknown, unwanted and sometimes threatening needs and feelings, for example, about relationships of power, authority and leadership, developed collectively by the group. When this disguised and unexamined material surfaces into consciousness, the group defends against it, for example in resisting change (Coleman & Bexton, 1975; Czander, 1993; Requests for copies should be addressed to: T Groenewald, Technikon SA, Private Bag X6, Florida, 1710 Gabelnick & Carr, 1989; Hirschhorn, 1993; Kets de Vries, 1991; Miller, 1993; Obholzer & Roberts, 1994).

The Basic Assumptions of Group Relations Training

Bion's (1961) three assumptions are seen as the cornerstones of group relations training (Kets de Vries, 1991; Miller, 1993; Rice, 1965; Rioch, 1970).

1. **Dependency.** Group members unconsciously project their dependency upon (imaginative) parental figures or systems, representing authority. If these authority figures do not respond the way the group wants them to, anger develops manifesting in counter dependence. Later the group develops to independence and interdependence.

2. **Fight/fight**. These are defence mechanisms the group unconsciously uses in trying to cope with discomfort. Fight reactions manifest in aggression against the self, colleagues (with envy, jealousy, competition, elimination, boycotting, rivalry, fighting for a position in the group and for privileged relationships) or the authority figure.

Flight reactions manifest in the avoidance of others, threatening situations or feelings, or in rationalisation and intellectualisation.

3. **Pairing.** In order to cope with the anxiety of alienation and loneliness, group members try to pair with perceived powerful others or subgroups. The unconscious need is to feel secure and to create. Pairing also implies splitting up, which may happen because of experienced anxiety in a diverse work place. Typical examples of splits are black/white, male/female, senior/junior and competent/incompetent. Unconsciously the group tries to split up the whole and build a smaller system, to which the individual can belong safely and securely.

Concepts in Group Relations Training

During group relations training, the following concepts and its behavioural dynamics are studied and learned about (Cilliers & Koortzen, 2000b).

∞ Anxiety is accepted as the basis of all group behaviour (Menzies, 1993). In order to cope with its discomfort, the group unconsciously needs something or someone to contain the anxiety on its behalf, especially initially in the group's life.

∞ Defence mechanisms against anxiety are used in order to gain a sense of safety, security and acceptance. Rationalisation and intellectualisation may be used to stay emotionally uninvolved and in control (Gabelnick & Carr, 1989; Neumann et al., 1997). Projection refers to the intra-system defensive process, where one part of the system denies and rejects feelings inherent in the unconscious image (fantasy) of the situation. It then tries to alter the uncomfortable experience by imagining that part of it belongs to another part of the system rather than to the self. It then puts good or bad (unwanted) material onto the other, thus distancing itself from the discomfort. This has no eject or influence on the target. Projection may be used to blame management for what goes wrong without management being influenced.

∞ Projective identification as an anxiety-reducing process (Coleman & Geller, 1985; Czander, 1993; Kets de Vries, 1991; Obholzer & Roberts, 1994), is one of the most elusive and complicated concepts in group relations training. It refers to an intersystem, object-relational interaction and process, where one part of the system (as subject) projects material into the other part (as object), who identifies with the projection (taking it on). This results in changes in both parts. The dynamics of projective identification are as follows. The subject experiences anxiety either because of its primitive envy of the object's idealised qualities and its consequent urge to destroy, spoil, dominate, devalue and control, or its wish to refuse with the object, or as a form of parasitism to be part of the object. It tries to relieve itself of this anxiety by externalising it, splitting oǃ parts and internal objects of the self, leaving the selfless aware of its whole and diminished by the projective loss of important aspects of itself. It requires or assigns the object to receive, identify with and contain these aspects of the self, as if it belongs to the object, but still keeps a closeness to the object. Depending on how subtle the projection is, the object may experience being manipulated into a particular role.

When this behaviour predominates in the group, it becomes difficult to and other ways of coping, because it is almost impossible to think clearly, to locate sources of problems and to find appropriate and creative solutions.

∞ Boundaries refer to the physical and psychological borders around the group in order to contain its anxiety, thus making the group controllable, safe and contained (Cytrynbaum & Lee, 1993; Czander, 1993; Hirschhorn, 1993; Kets de Vries, 1991; Miller, 1993; Neumann et al., 1997).

∞ Representation refers to when a member consciously or unconsciously negotiates a boundary, acting on behalf of the group (for example in crossing, resisting or erecting a boundary). If the individual's authority boundaries are unclear, the high level of anxiety tends to immobilise and disempower him/her. The group learns firstly how it normally disempowers representatives and secondly, new ways of empowering them in order to work more effectively on behalf of the group (Kets de Vries, 1991; Obholzer & Roberts, 1994).

∞ Authorisation refers to empowering a group member to act on behalf of the group in the role of observer, delegate or plenipotentiary (Czander, 1993; Obholzer & Roberts, 1994).

∞ Leadership is described as managing what is inside the boundary in relation to what is outside. This can happen inside the individual (without followers) or by one group member on behalf of the followership (Gabelnick & Carr, 1989; Obholzer & Roberts, 1994).

∞ Relationship between group members, refers to any type of face-to-face interaction, as it happens in the here-and-now. Unconsciously, the group member is always in relatedness to the group, also called "the group in the mind" (Gabelnick & Carr, 1989; Neumann et al., 1997; Shapiro & Carr, 1991).

∞ Group as a whole refers to collectivism – one part of the system acting, or containing emotional energy, on behalf of another. This implies that no event happens in isolation and that there is no co-incidence but rather synchronicity in the behaviour of the group (Wells, 1980).

The group relations training event namely the Tavistock (also called Leicester) model (Miller, 1989, 1993) is used in structuring the group relations training event. The primary task of the event is to provide opportunities for the group to study its own behaviour in the here-and-now. This is an educational task consisting of experiential learning sub-events, namely (for example in this research) plenaries, small, discussion, review and application groups, each with its own task, described as follows.

∞ **Plenary** – to provide the opportunity for all members to share information about the learning within the group experience.

∞ **Small group** –to provide opportunities for the group to learn about its own behaviour in the here-and-now.

∞ **Discussion group** – to provide opportunities for the group to learn about the concepts in the group relations training model and to relate theory to practice.

∞ **Review/application group** – to provide opportunities for the group to review their learning during the total event and then to work towards the application of the learning to their roles in their everyday working life.

The group relations training consultant is actively involved in the event, formulating working hypothesis and interpreting behaviour processes and dynamics in the here-and-now, on the basis of his/her own observations, experience and expertise. He/she also takes responsibility and authority to provide the boundary conditions of task, space (also called territory) and time, in such a way that all participants can engage with the primary task (Miller, 1989, 1993).

Sense of Coherence (SOC)

The salutogenic paradigm (Antonovsky, 1979, 1984) focuses on the origins of health and wellness, the locating and developing of personal and social resources and adaptive tendencies which relate to the individual's disposition, allowing him/her to select appropriate strategies to deal with confronting stressors and anxieties. Sense of coherence is defined (Antonovsky, 1984, 1987) as a global orientation that expresses the extent to which the individual has a pervasive, enduring, though dynamic feeling of coherence, that"

1. the stimuli deriving from his/her internal and external environments in the course of living are structured, predictable, and explicable;

2. the resources are available to meet the demands posed by these stimuli; and

3. these demands are challenges worthy of investment and engagement.

The strength of the SOC is connected to a variety of coping mechanisms, called generalised resistance resources (GRR's) (Antonovsky, 1979), defined as any characteristic of the individual, a group, or the environment that can facilitate effective tension management. This enhances the disposition to select appropriate strategies in dealing with and confronting stress and anxiety. A high SOC indicates readiness and willingness to tap into these resources at his/her potential disposal, leading to a cognitive and emotional appraisal of the world, again leading to effective coping, health enhancement and social adjustment.

SOC consists of the following three dimensions (Antonovsky, 1987).

1. Comprehensibility refers to the extent to which the individual perceives confronting stimuli deriving from the internal and external environments, as making cognitive sense, as information that is ordered, consistent, structured and clear, rather than as noisy, chaotic, disordered, random, accidental and inexplicable.

2. Manageability refers to the extent to which the individual perceives that resources at his/her disposal are adequate to meet the demands posed by the bombarding stimuli, events are perceived as bearable that can be coped with and that challenges can be met.

3. Meaningfulness refers to the extent to which the individual feels that life makes emotional sense. In terms of motivation, problems and anxieties posed by life are seen as challenges, providing stimulation to invest energy and in turn elicit commitment and engagement. The individual sees life as meaningful, and problems/events are viewed as challenges worthy of emotional investment and commitment.

Integration

Working in and learning about groups is often confusing and stressful (Rugel & Meyer, 1984) particularly in unstructured situations when sometimes, seemingly no one knows what is going on. Central to this learning process is the repeated discovery of the presence of irrational and unconscious processes that interfere with attempts to manage oneself, the group, tasks and roles in a conscious and rational way (Obholzer & Roberts, 1994). Uncomfortable and threatening feelings are painful to acknowledge and stirs up a high level of anxiety which the group defends against (for example by avoiding), exacerbating stress rather than alleviating it.

For the individual, this can be an overwhelming, as well as an empowering experience. The mental pains experienced in working from a group relations stance have to be dealt with by the individual, each with his/her own personal history of having developed ways of managing or evading situations of anxiety, pain, fear, confusion and depression (Obholzer & Roberts, 1994).The ability to contain a spectrum of painful emotions generated in this way is psychologically difficult. Conversely, this experience facilitates an opportunity to understand the deep and complex group dynamics in terms of authority and leadership, which is essential to the understanding of organisational functioning and dynamics. It illuminates some of the difficulties in managing oneself, managing the self at work, as well as in being managed and managing others (Obholzer & Roberts, 1994).

Although there are certain stress situations that are likely to induce anxiety no matter what coping mechanisms an individual has at his/her disposal or to what extent he/she has a disposition to respond with anxiety (Antonovsky & Sagy, 1986), evidence exist within the salutogenic paradigm, that a high level of SOC facilitates the individual's psychological and/or physiological coping responses to a controlled stressful situation (McSherry & Holm, 1994). Antonovsky

(1987) adds that it is the strength of the SOC of the person experiencing such events that will determine whether the outcomes will be noxious, neutral, or salutary. He emphasises that the strength of an individual's SOC is central to the regulation of emotional tension generated by confrontation with stressors. No research findings could be traced linking group relations training to salutogenic functioning or SOC. From the above it can be expected that an individual with a high SOC will cope differently, hopefully "better" with the stress and anxiety of a group relations training event, than an individual with a low SOC. Proof about this expectation can contribute towards an understanding of how employees cope in stressful relational work situations (see Obholzer & Roberts, 1994).

Research question, aim, research design and hypothesis The research question can be stated as, what role does SOC play in coping with the demands of a group relations training event?

The aim of the research is to ascertain the extent of this role in an actual group relations training event and to formulate recommendations from the findings for application in the fields of group and interpersonal training and development.

Action research will be done in the presentation of a group relations training event, quantitative research in the measurement of SOC and qualitative research in the form of an interview with the participants. The independent variable is the group relations training event and the dependent variable is SOC. The research hypothesis is that there is a relationship between a low SOC score and experienced non-coping with the demands of group relations training, or between a high SOC score and experienced coping.

Method

The Sample

Convenient sampling was used (Anastasi & Urbina, 1997). A general invitation to managers to participate in a group relations training event was addressed to the Human Resources Departments of 12 large semi-government and private organisations in Gauteng. Of the 82 who responded, 58 could attend the event.

The mean age was 33 years. The gender ratio was 25 (male – 43%) /33 (female – 57%). Blacks, Coloureds, Indians and whites were included, although not representative of the total South African demographic scenario.

The Group Relations Training Event

The event was structured and presented as discussed above.

This took place over three working days, each consisting of four sessions of 90 minutes each and a 30 minute end-of-day integration session, totalling 19, 5 hours as set out in Table 1. The author (having had extensive training and experience in the Tavistock stance) acted in the role of consultant.

Table 1   **The Group Relations Training Event Programme Time**

Time	Day 1	Day 2	Day 3
08:30 - 10:00	Opening plenary Small group 1	Small group 5	Small group 8
10:00 - 10:30	Tea		
10:30 - 12:00	Small group 2	Discussion 2	Review group 2
12:00 - 13:00	Lunch		
13:00 - 14:30	Small group 3	Small group 6	Application group
14:30 - 1500	Tea		
15:00 - 16:30	Small group 4	Small group 7	Discussion 2
16:30 - 17:00	Discussion 1	Review group I	Closing Plenary

Measurement

(1) SOC was measured by means of Antonovsky's (1987) 29 – item Sense of Coherence Scale. This provides a total as well as sub-scores for the three dimensions. The scale has satisfactory levels of reliability and validity (Antonovsky, 1987). (2) Afterwards, a 30 minute tape recorded and unstructured interview was conducted by the author. The aim of the interview was to ascertain the training experience of the individual by asking a single question, namely: "What was your experience of the group relations training event?". The interview was transcribed and a content analysis (Strauss & Corbin, 1990) and open coding (breaking down, examining, comparing, conceptualising and categorising of data) were done. The manifesting main and sub themes were determined (Jones, 1996; Kerlinger, 1986) for each individual, distinguishing between the absence and presence of SOC characteristics. Validity and reliability was ensured by having the results examined by a psychologist, to whom this technique is well known. It was declared correct.

Procedure

The sample of 58 was divided (1) randomly and (2) to find their work schedules, into find groups. Thus, the group relations training event was presented five times with groups ranging between nine and 12 members. The SOC scale was administered to each participant beforehand and then the group relations training event was presented. The day after, the interview was conducted with each participant. Next, the SOC scales were marked (this was done after the training event, to ensure that the outcome did not influence the experience of participants or consultants during the event). Individual participant's total SOC scores were ranked from low to high (resulting in a fairly normal distribution). The ten individual scores on the lower end of the continuum were subgrouped and called the "low SOC subgroup' 'and the ten individual scores on the high end of the continuum were sub-grouped and called the "high SOC subgroup". The rest is referred to as the "middle group". Then, tests were done by means of the SAS programme (SAS, 1985) to ascertain the significance of indifference between the low and the high subgroups. Lastly, each individual participant's total as well as dimension SOC scores were matched with his/her interview themes and interpreted.

Results

The qualitative interpretation of the middle group's experience and learning is that low SOC is associated with confusion and difficulty in learning and high SOC with meaningfulness and insight into group dynamics and personal learning. Table 2 contains the test results, indicating a significant difference between the low and high subgroups. This meant that the low and high interview results could be interpreted with validity.

The interviews elicited the themes of anxiety, defence mechanisms, feelings, making sense out of the experience and learning outcomes.

Table 2   Test Results; the Significance of the Difference Between the Low and High Soc Subgroups

Subgroup	N	T	DF	Probability
Low SOC	10	-16.89	7.8	0.00
High SOC	10	-16.89	8.1	0.00

Individuals in the low SOC subgroup reported the following experiences.

1. **Anxiety.** They described the event as filled with confusion and difficulty (anxiety). It was as if the total group had put them within a boundary and made them contain the anxiety on its behalf. Thus, they became powerless to move out of the boundary.

2. **Defence mechanisms**. They used flight and fight reactions. During the event, they projected their anger onto the consultant – this behaviour continued during the

interviews afterwards. They projected their fear of punishment, being rejected, judged and not being trusted, onto the group and its members. Their communication was cognitive, focused on the self and presented in there-and-then terms. This defence took up a lot of energy which resulted in further difficulty to focus on and learn about what was happening in the group. They became the representation of passive resistance for the group.

3. **Feelings**. They experienced uncomfortable feelings of confusion, fear, being lost, conflict, suspicion, jealousy, guilt, irritation, frustration, reluctance, powerlessness, paralysis, they were drained of energy and had a lack of confidence. They were preoccupied with their own individual needs and struggles, which made it difficult to see "the bigger group picture". They reported a sense of being pushed by outside (of their control) forces into doing and even saying things on the group's behalf.

4. **Making sense out of the experience**. They reported difficulty in making sense, describing the event as unfulfilled, a waste of time, and not meeting their expectations. As individuals in this subgroup, they got stuck in dependence which bonded them together and gave them some identity and boundary. It may be that they became the dumping ground for the group's ineffectiveness.

5. **Learning outcomes**. They mentioned their learning in vague and general terms, for example "to listen more carefully" (which could indicate heightened suspicion), "to try to get more in contact with myself" (indicating a lack of coherence), "to learn more about boundaries" (indicating not being able to manage their own learning during the event), and "different things mean different things to different people" (indicating anxiety, confusion and difficulty to become part of the event, struggling to integrate the experience). It is as if they got stuck in the role of follower as well as in the splits manifesting in the group.

Individuals in the high SOC subgroup reported the following experiences.

1. **Anxiety**. Initially a high level of anxiety was experienced, but differently from the previous subgroup, these individuals started to show insight into the group's behaviour and dynamics as well as the own life it was creating – this started happening about halfway through the event. They managed to work with the concept of "group as whole", thus understanding the object relations in the group. After they have started to own and verbalise their anxiety in the group experience, they could start listening to themselves and to other group members.

2. **Defence mechanisms**. They were inclined to intellectualise (more than project) and their fight and flight reactions decreased as the event progressed.

3. **Anxiety,** anger, frustration, insecurity and stress, and at the same time tried to stay positive, being intrigued by what is happening in the group, and feeling adventurous. Thus, they could own their feelings and start taking personal responsibility for their learning.

4. **Making sense out of the experience**. They focused on the behavioural processes which facilitated their understanding of the dynamic nature of the group's behaviour. They authorised themselves to shift their boundaries and to work with the consultant

(instead of against him) towards interdependence. Thus they could start attending to other objects and splits in the group, such as the talking versus the silent members, and the learning versus the "not understanding" members.

5. **Learning outcomes**. They reported an increased awareness of how to build relationships within the group boundary, finding their own role in the group as well as in groups they belong to outside of the event. They referred to having more insight into their own working groups and feeling more empowered to work more effectively in them. They reported their awareness about having to make important career decisions with less fear and disempowerment.

The following integration in terms of the SOC dimensions can be made.

1. Comprehensibility

∝ The low SOC subgroup had difficulty in coping with the event – it did not make cognitive sense to them, it was without direction, disordered, chaotic, unpredictable and a waste of time. They focussed on the content and rejected many of the consultant's interpretations of symbols, metaphors and the manifesting group dynamics – for them it was coincidental, accidental, irrelevant and it had nothing to do with the group's unconscious.

∞ The high SOC subgroup expressed surprise and intrigue at the group's dynamics. Initially they found it difficult to understand, but focussing on their own authority issues increased their ability to work with (instead of against) the interpretations of the consultant as an authority figure. This facilitated an understanding of the dynamics and an experience of the event as clear, ordered and meaningful. They reported more confidence in venturing their own interpretations of the dynamics towards the end of the event, including working with complex terminology such as the splits, defences, boundaries, relatedness, group as a whole as well as the manifesting object relationships.

2. Manageability

∝ The low SOC subgroup experienced a high level of anxiety which led to the immobilisation of their resistance resources. They felt powerless to influence the course of events and their own learning. This finding is consistent with Antonovsky's (1987) view that a low sense of manageability will lead to feelings of victimisation (vexed and irritable) and a sense that life is treating one unfairly.

∝ The high SOC subgroup started to make use of their own and the group's resistance resources, helping them to meet the demands of this difficult kind of training with its focus on the unconscious. Their framing of the event as a challenge and the trusting of their own resources, turned the event into a manageable learning experience.

3. Meaningfulness

∝ The low SOC subgroup could not make a lot of emotional sense out of the experience. It is as if their emotional energy was consumed and they were immobilised by the high

369

level of anxiety. Therefore they did not show a commitment or strong engagement in the group's activities and found the event not to be meaningful.

∞ The high SOC subgroup saw the initial difficulty and uncomfortable feelings as a challenge. Because they invested emotional energy into the event, their commitment and engagement increased. They reported that the training event was meaningful on a personal, a group, as well as on an organisational learning level. The experience of emotional sensibility lead to a sense of empowerment to shape their own experiences as well as their destiny.

Discussion

The results indicate a qualitative difference between the individual with low and high SOC. The latter reports more learning from the group relations training in terms of an understanding of the group's behaviour and dynamics, the employment of his/her own existing resources and the finding of meaning in the nature of group dynamics, than the first mentioned. Therefore, the research hypothesis is accepted.

On the group level the results indicate that projective identification as a group dynamic phenomenon, had a strong influence on the experience and learning of both the extremely low and high SOC individuals as designated subgroups. The total group's anxiety around performance and competitiveness in the training situation was externalised, splitting of parts of the total and leading to a loss of synergy and integrative learning for the whole group. The less the low SOC subgroup copes and learns, the more the high SOC subgroup does. According to Knapp (1989), the part of the system most susceptible to projections will be most dependent, needy, or the least differentiated. This means that the learning about group relations during this event was probably equally difficult for both extremes of low and high SOC and relatively easier for the middle group.

∞ In the collective unconscious, the low SOC subgroup's lack of comprehensibility, manageability and meaningfulness upon entrance into the event, became an object of non-coping, receiving projections of what was unacceptable in the competition, and was then manipulated into containing powerlessness, stuckness, resistance and eventually incompetence. The resulting discomfort in representing the dark side of the system lead to envy towards the opposite position, and a consequent urge to reunite with the high SOC subgroup as an object of competence in order to learn from it. But this was resisted by the object of competence, increasing the frustration about not learning.

∞ In the collective unconscious, the high SOC subgroup's comprehensibility, manage-ability and meaningfulness upon entrance into the event, became an object of coping, receiving projections of what was acceptable in the competition, and was then manipulated into containing power and competence. This privileged, envious, powerful and heroic position lead to a resistance to fuse with the incompetent object and resulted in becoming even more competent.

This defence against the pain of identifying with the incompetence in the self, restricts one's own learning. It can be interpreted as "feeling on a high" about one's own leaning, but because it was projected (not earned) it cannot be fully owned, internalised or valued.

The above mutual projected and emotional dependence of the low and the high SOC subgroups, indicate that both carried a burden on behalf of the other. This may result in restricted learning for both, although clearly more restricted and even prohibitive for the low SOC subgroup. The middle group seem to have played a pivotal role in the incompetence/competence split. These individuals reported an expected variety of learning about themselves and group behaviour, congruent to their level of SOC. They probably learned most of all the participants in the group relations training event.

This research illustrates that the individual's SOC acts as a facilitating condition in learning within group relations training. At the same time the individual's learning is influenced by group dynamic factors beyond his/her control. These projections need to be discussed and processed during the event in order for the individual to optimise his/her own learning. The individual needs to become aware of what characteristics (needs, expectations, personality traits) he/she came into the training event with, and that he/she can distinguish between what his/her own and personal learning experience is, and what is projected ("dumped") onto and into him/her by the group's unconscious (to carry as a container). In terms of group behaviour as applied to team building for example, it illustrates that a training group may split itself between low and high functioning and performance, leading to the impression that one subgroup is not working, while others are star performers. In reality, both may have difficulty in performing their tasks. Consultants should be aware of this dynamic behaviour and ensure that the group addresses its polarisations, relating to competence and contribution. Only when these projections are owned, taken back and processed, the group can work towards synergy, finding new ways of coping, clear thinking, problem-solving leading to clear and creative solutions and work performance.

It is recommended that future research includes the role of other salutogenic constructs (as mentioned by Strümpfer, 1990; 1995), as well as psychological optimality constructs (as mentioned by Cilliers, 1988).

References

Anastasi, A. & Urbina, S. (1997). *Psychological testing*. Upper Saddle River: Prentice-Hall.

Antonovsky, A. (1979). *Health, stress and coping*. San Francisco: Jossey-Bass.

Antonovsky, A. (1984). A call for a new question – salutogenesis – and a proposed answer – The sense of coherence. *Journal of Preventive Psychiatry*, 2:1-13.

Antonovsky, A. (1987). *Unraveling the mystery of health: How people manage stress and stay well*. San Francisco: Jossey-Bass.

Antonovsky, H. & Sagy, S. (1986). The development of a sense of coherence and its impact on responses to stress situations. *Journal of Social Psychology*, 126(2):213-225.

Bion, W.R. (1961). *Experiences in groups*. London: Tavistock Publications.

Bion, W.R. (1970). *Attention and interpretation*. London: Tavistock Publications.

Cilliers, F. (1988). The concept psychological optimality in management. *IPM Journal*, 7(5):15-18.

Cilliers, F. (2000). Team building from a psychodynamic approach. *Journal of Industrial Psychology*, 26(1):18-23. https://doi.org/10.4102/sajip.v26i1.694

Cilliers, F. & Koortzen, P. (2000a). *Consulting from a psychodynamic stance*. Paper presented at the national congress of the Society for Industrial Psychology. Pretoria.

Cilliers, F. & Koortzen, P. (2000b). The psychodynamic view on organisational behaviour. *The Industrial-Organizational Psychologist*, 38(1):59-67. https://doi.org/10.1037/e576962011-006

Colman, A.D. & Bexton,W.H. (1975). *Groups Relations Reader 1*. Jupiter: A.K. Rice Institute.

Colman, A.D. & Geller, M.H. (1985). *Group relations reader 2*. Jupiter: The A.K. Rice Institute.

Cytrynbaum, S. & Lee, S.A. (1993). *Transformations in global and organizational systems*. Jupiter: A.K. Rice Institute.

Czander, W.M. (1993). *The psychodynamics of work and organisations*. New York: Guilford Press.

De Board, R. (1978). *The psychoanalysis of organisations*. London: Routledge. https://doi.org/10.4324/9780203321812

Gabelnick, F. & Carr, A.W. (1989). *Contributions to social and political science*. Jupiter: A.K. Rice Institute.

Hirschhorn, L. (1993).*The workplace within: Psychodynamics of organizational life*. Cambridge: MIT Press.

Jones, R.A. (1996). *Research methods in the social and behavioural sciences*. Sunderland: Sinauer.

Kerlinger, F.N. (1986). *Foundations of behavioural research*. Hong Kong: Holt, Rinehart & Winston.

Kets De Vries, F.R. (1991). *Organizations on the couch: Handbook of psychoanalysis and management*. New York: Jossey-Bass.

Knapp, H. (1989). Projective identification: Whose projection – whose identity. *Psychoanalytic Psychology*, 6(1):47-59. https://doi.org/10.1037/0736-9735.6.1.47

McSherry, W.C. & Holm, J. (1994). Sense of coherence: Its effects on psychological and physiological processes prior to, during, after a stressful situation. *Journal of Clinical Psychology*, 50(4):476-487. https://doi.org/10.1002/1097-4679(199407)50:4<476::AID JCLP2270500402>3.0.CO;2-9

Menzies, I.E.P. (1993). *The functioning of social systems as a defence against anxiety.* London: Tavistock Institute of Human Relations.

Miller, E.J. (1983).*Work and creativity. Occasional Paper No 6.* London: Tavistock Institute of Human Relations.

Miller, E.J. (1989). *The "Leicester" Model: Experiential study of group and organisational processes. Occasional Paper No. 10.* London: Tavistock Institute of Human Relations.

Miller, E.J. (1993). *From dependency to autonomy: Studies in organization and change.* London: Free Association Books.

Neumann, J.E.; Kellner, K. & Dawson-Shepherd, A. (1997). *Developing organisational consultancy.* London: Routledge.

Obholzer, A. & Roberts, V.Z. (1994). *The unconscious at work.* London: Routledge.

Rice, A.K. (1965). *Learning for leadership.* London: Tavistock Publications.

Rioch, M.J. (1970). Group relations: Rationale and technique. *International Journal of Group Psychotherapy*, 20:340-355. https://doi.org/10.1080/00207284.1970.11491769

Rugel, R.P. & Meyer, D.J. (1984). The Tavistock group experience, findings and implications for group therapy. *Small Group Behaviour*, 15(3):361-374. https://doi.org/10.1177/104649648401500305

SAS Institute. (1985). *SAS user's guide: statistics,* version 5 edn. Cary: SAS Institute.

Shapiro, E.R. & Carr, A.W. (1991). *Lost in familiar places: Creating new connections between the individual and society.* London: Yale University Press.

Strauss, A. & Corbin, J. (1990) *Basics of qualitative research: Grounded theory. Procedures and techniques.* Newbury Park: Sage.

Strümpfer, D.J.W. (1990). Salutogenesis: A new paradigm. *South African Journal of Psychology*, 20(4):265-276. https://doi.org/10.1177/008124639002000406

Strümpfer, D.J.W. (1995). The origins of health and strength: From 'salutogenesis' to 'fortigenesis'. *South African Journal of Psychology*, 25 (2):81-89. https://doi.org/10.1177/008124639502500203

Wells, L. (1980). The group-as-a-whole: A systemic socio-analytical perspective on interpersonal and group relations. In: Alderfer, C.P. & Cooper, C.L. (eds.), *Advances in experiential social processes*, 2:165-198.

Wissing, M.P. & Van Eeden, C. (1994). *Psychological wellbeing: Measurement and construct clarification.* Paper presented at the 23rd international congress of Applied Psychology, Madrid.

Wissing, M.P. & Van Eeden, E. (1997a). *Facing the challenge to explicate mental health salutogenically: Sense of coherence and psychological well-being.* Paper presented at the 55th annual convention of the International Council of Psychology, Graz.

Wissing, M.P. & Van Eeden, E. (1997b). *Psychological well-being: A fortigenic conceptualisation and empirical clarification.* Paper presented at the congress of the Psychological Society of South Africa, Durban.

Theme 4 | **Systems Psychodynamics and Organisational Wellness**

Article 1

The Role of Spirituality in Coping
with the Demands of the Hospital
Culture Amongst Fourth-Year
Nursing Students[1]

F Cilliers & L Terblanche

Abstract

The aim of this research was to describe the role of spirituality in coping with
the demands of the hospital culture amongst fourth-year nursing students.
Qualitative, descriptive, hermeneutic interpretive research was done. A case
study of 14 female Canadian nursing students was asked to write an essay on
their experiences of the demands of the hospital culture. Content analysis was
used and positive psychology served as the interpretive lens. Trustworthiness
and ethicality were ensured. The findings indicated that although the nursing
students expressed themselves in religious and spiritual words, they did not
significantly illustrate the theoretically required intra-, interpersonal and
sacred behaviours to be referred to as being spiritual in their experience as
a care-giver in the hospital culture. They also did not illustrate behaviours
linked to other positive psychology constructs such as sense of coherence,
resilience, engagement or emotional intelligence. Rather, the nursing students
experienced identity crises. Recommendations for the inclusion of mentoring in
the curriculum of nursing students were formulated.

1   Cilliers, F. & Terblanche, L. (2014). The role of spirituality in coping with the demands of the hospital
     culture amongst fourth-year nursing students. *International Review of Psychiatry*, 26(3):279-288.

Keywords

hospital culture, spirituality, positive psychology, intra-personal, interpersonal, sacred, case study, mentoring

Introduction

Organisational culture can be defined as the customs, ways, rituals, rules and regulations implemented by a system to preserve its identity (Robbins, Judge, Odendaal & Roodt, 2009). As institutions, hospitals are seen as different from most other types of organisations because of its unique primary task of attending to illness, pain, dying and death (Katz & Kahn, 1978). This has resulted in a worldwide hospital culture of strict hierarchy and control in order to preserve order in reporting lines, obedience to methodology and technique, and cleanliness and sterility for the survival of patients, their families, communities and hospital staff. Menzies' (1993) research on hospital organisational dynamics, found that hospitals as systems compensate for its manifesting institutionalised, survival (amongst patients) and performance (amongst staff) anxieties by enforcing these strict people and procedural control mechanisms.

It is generally accepted in the nursing fraternity that student nurses experience emotional difficulty upon entering the hospital culture (Lanzetta, 2010). As less information is available on their spiritual experiences, this study investigated how they cope from a spiritual perspective.

Literature Review

Nursing science view and study nurses as whole people and it is believed that their professional and work performance depend on the level of integration of their physical, psychological (including cognitive, emotional, motivational), social, cultural, environmental and spiritual functioning (Duke, 2013; Lanzetta, 2010; Meier, O'Connor & Van Katwyk, 2005; Reimer-Kirkham, Grypma & Terblanche, 2012; Young & Koopsen, 2005). Of these domains, research on spirituality is limited and controversial (Wissing & Fourie, 2000) due to the multidimensionality of spirituality, its confusion with religiosity or religious activities, as well as the diverse research methodologies being applied.

Spirituality inputs have been studied amongst various patient groups (Bauer & Barron, 1995; Brillhart, 2005; Hampton & Weinert, 2006; Lovanio & Wallace, 2007; Meraviglia, 2004; Reynolds, 2006; Tuck, McCain & Eiswick, 2001). Although the results are inconsistent, it has shown to facilitate patients' coping with pain, hopelessness and despair. Research on the spirituality of nursing students showed that especially females, regard themselves as having high levels of spirituality characterised by religious activities (discussions, church attendance) and experiencing meaning in life (Shores, 2010). Spiritual sensitivity increase with age and experience (Callister, Bond, Matsumura & Mangum, 2004), especially after inputs containing self-reflection (Catamzaro & McMullen, 2001), and increases the nurse's competence in patient care-giving (Mitchell, Bennett & Manfrin-Ledet, 2006; Pesut, 2002). Nursing students' spirituality at Christian universities do not differ significantly from students at public universities (Garner, McGuire, Snow, Grey & Wright, 2002).

Conceptualising Spirituality

The existing literature on spirituality does not provide a clear and comprehensive conceptualisation or clear behavioural characteristics on the construct (Pargament, 2013a; 2013b). It was therefore decided to create a profile from the existing positive psychology literature.

Psychology in general and organisational psychology specifically, has for a long time ignored, pathologised and reduced spirituality as a part of many underlying psychological functions (Snyder & Lopez, 2009). Organisational psychology is increasingly exploring the role of spirituality in leadership, ethical behaviour, communication, motivation and sustainability (Pargament, 2013b). Since the popularisation of positive psychology (Seligman & Csiksztmihalyi, 2000), spirituality was recognised as a psychological construct (Pargament, 2013a; 2013b). Positive psychology is defined as the scientific study of strengths, virtues, positive emotions, traits and values towards enabling individuals, organisations and communities to thrive and positive organisational psychology as the study of the nature of and enhancement of coping behaviour (Azar, 2011; Linley & Joseph, 2004; Lopez & Lyubomirsky, 2008; Seligman & Csikszentmihalyi, 2000; Seligman, Steen, Park & Peterson, 2005; Sheldon & King, 2001; Sheldon, Kashdan & Steger, 2011; Snyder & Lopez, 2009; Strümpfer, 2005). Coping behaviour is operationalised in constructs such as respect, mindfulness, emotional intelligence, happiness, hardiness, resilience, engagement, self-efficacy, sense of coherence and learned resourcefulness as well as some less well known constructs such as positive character strengths, positive emotions, flourishing, curiosity, hope and joy (Snyder & Lopez, 2009).

Spirituality is derived from the Latin *spiritus* meaning breath and refers to the essence of who and how people are in life. As a multidimensional phenomenon, spirituality has no universally accepted definition (Duke, 2013; Meier, O'Connor & Van Katwyk, 2005; Young & Koopsen, 2005). The World Psychiatric Association

(Verhagen, Van Praag, Lopez-Ibor, Cox & Moussaoui, 2010) defines spirituality as a personal belief in ideas of religious significance such as God, the soul or heaven. The Canadian Nursing Association (CNA, 2010) endorsed Wright's (2005) definition, namely that spirituality refers to whatever or whoever gives ultimate meaning and purpose in one's life that invites particular ways of being in the world in relation to others, oneself and the universe. Pargament (2013a; 2013b) presents an impressive, extensive and recent rendition of the history and psychology of spirituality with reference to relevant paradigms, social contexts, methodological and psychometric data.

In positive psychology, spirituality is defined as a pervasive, basic human, personal, individualistic, subjective, life-enhancing and growth stimulating force indicative of psychological well-being, in search of the sacred (Linley & Joseph, 2004; Meier, O'Connor & Van Katwyk, 2005; Pargament, 1999; 2013a; 2013b; Peterson & Seligman, 2004; Snyder & Lopez, 2009; Young & Koopsen, 2005). The search refers to the ongoing life journey and process of discovery of something sacred (such as personal accomplishments or revelations), conservation (holding on to the discovery, building and sustaining the connection) and transformation (the purification and reframing of the individual's tie and connectedness to the sacred). Sacred refers to what is set apart from the ordinary, worthy of veneration and respect, the individual's concept of God as well as the manifestations of the divine. The individual experiences transcendence (the felt presence of a reality or a being that is wholly different from ordinary experience), immanence, boundlessness and ultimacy (the experience of something as fundamental to the nature of reality, at the heart of the mystery of the universe and of all human experience).

Spirituality has always been connected to religion (a belief system towards a specific concept such as a god) and religiosity (an ideology based on the belief that right and wrong behaviour exist) (Duke, 2013). On the other hand religiousness is seen as a socially, culturally and collectively shared, external, institutional, structural, administrative (often bureaucratic and hierarchical) structure, confined to predefined and cognitively justified beliefs, dogma, creeds and rituals of a particular organised religion (e.g. Christian, Judaism, Islam, African, Eastern) (Pargament, 1999; 2013a; 2013b; Robertson, 2006; Wissing & Fourie, 2000). Spirituality and religion are increasingly differentiated and even polarised. This is evident in popular expressions such as 'being spiritual, not religious' which favours spirituality as more in vogue than religion (Pargament, 2013b). It is as if in comparison, spirituality represents a more basic and inherent human characteristic that precedes religion and is used as an escape from religious servitude towards personal development (Pargament, 2013b).

Spirituality is described in terms of intelligence, coping and well-being. Spiritual intelligence can be defined as a mental capacity to think, reason and dream about, and strive towards meaning, value, vision, holistic integration, joy, happiness and transcendence, while knowing that the whole as greater than the sum of their parts (Meier, O'Connor & Van Katwyk, 2005). Spiritual coping refers to dealing effectively with stressful contexts and demands through self-empowerment based on meaning-making (positive and negative re-appraisal), control (active and passive ways of gaining mastery), comfort (spiritual connection and support), intimacy (religious support with the others) and self-transformation (Pargament, 2013a). Spiritual well-being follows from spiritual intelligence and coping. It refers to a harmonious interconnectedness with the self, the other, community, environment and a deity/the divine in the experience of gratitude, forgiveness, existential purpose, meaning, hope and transcendence, and is connected to psychological well-being through constructs such as happiness and quality of life (Frankl, 1969; Pargament, 2013a; Young & Koopsen, 2005).

Operationalising Spirituality

The operationalisation of spirituality is complex. The popular and scientific literature are filled with lists and descriptions of desired characteristics of what constitutes being spiritual, of which the following is an abbreviated categorisation, integrated for purposes of this research (Fowler, Reimer-Kirkham, Sawatzky & Johnston-Taylor, 2012; Frankl, 1969; Jung, 1955; Kashdan, 2009; Linley & Joseph, 2004; Nasser & Overholser, 2005; Pargament 2013a; 2013b; Robertson, 2006; Snyder & Lopez, 2009; Young & Koopsen, 2005).

1. The self (intra-personal behaviour and inner resources)
   The individual illustrates a high level of subjective, flexible and dynamic self-awareness and consciousness supported by a constant intelligent re-appraisal of the spiritual self. The prevailing value system consists of respect and compassion for the self, personal boundaries, simplicity, solitude, submission, the exploration of all emotional experiences including love, suffering, forgiveness, grace, mystery, curiosity, courage, bravery, a search for the higher purpose and meaning of life, motivated by inner strength, strong beliefs and hope (desire accompanied by expectations of fulfilment), taking control towards personal mastery, individualisation and self-actualisation.

2. The other (interpersonal behaviour, relationships)
   The individual is motivated by the belief in a universal and growth stimulating human inter-connectedness and inter-dependence. The prevailing value system is based on the above inner resources to build deep relationships across difference. These relationships are characterised by social intelligence, respect for interpersonal boundaries, kindness, realness and authenticity, grace (an understanding of the gifts of life that are often contributed to providence), support, comfort, love (an acknowledged

mystery that is experienced and expressed in caring acts, both given and received), intimacy, justice (civic strengths that underlie healthy and fair teamwork, leadership, citizenship and community life) and temperance (modesty, humility, prudence, forgiveness, self-control, regulation and protection against excess).

3. The sacred (connectedness with the universe)

   The individual is energised by the above mentioned intra- and interpersonal awareness to explore its continuous connectedness with the larger, higher and permanent power outside of and beyond the self. This includes the un-understandable, not rationally explainable, universal and unified, existential essence of being, evolution and mystery, all as various concepts of God and the divine. The individual is 'inspirited' through specific experiential activities such as asking existential questions, having conversation and discourse about fundamental matters, reframing questions, reading, rituals, prayer, confession, worship, celebration, solitude, meditation, guided imagery, visualisation, fasting, spending time in nature, viewing and engaging in art, storytelling and service to others. The prevailing value system is a search for purpose, meaning, happiness, gratitude, wisdom, fulfilment, transformation, harmony, peace and being strengthened by religious beliefs, hope, awe and transcendence. The individual values sacred objects such as time (for the self, the other, the sacred), space (nature, a spiritual place), events (birth, graduation, marriage, death), culture (visual art, music, literature) and roles (spouse, parent, employee, leader).

Not being spiritual can be described as being dispirited (Young & Koopsen, 2005). This state consists of spiritual distress, the disruption of life principles that pervades every aspect of the individual's being, and spiritual disequilibrium (Jung, 1955), being in inner chaos when cherished beliefs are challenged, and the lack of integration of good and bad which hinders individuation. Frankl (1969) referred to noogenic neuroses to describe the experienced lack of meaning, manifesting as existential frustration and spiritual emptiness.

Many positive psychology constructs have been explicated in terms of their conceptualisation (Linley & Joseph, 2004; Snyder & Lopez, 2009), their psychometric properties (Strümpfer, 2005; Wissing & Van Eeden, 2002), their inter- and relationships with organisational constructs such as well-being, commitment and satisfaction (Basson & Rothmann, 2002; Breed, Cilliers & Visser, 2006; Cilliers & Coetzee, 2003; Feldt, 1997; Naudé & Rothmann, 2006; Pretorius, 2007; Rothmann & Van Rensburg, 2002; Ryan & Deci, 2000; Storm, 2002; Strümpfer, Eiselen, Meiring & Phalatse, 2010; Van Zyl, Deacon, & Rothmann, 2010; Wright, 2005). The same can't be said about spirituality, mostly because of the lack of differentiation between mental (ill)health and psychological well-being (Wissing & Fourie, 2000). Some behavioural aspects of spirituality such as meaning of work, hope, religiosity, religious orientation and coping showed relationships with other positive psychology constructs such as sense of coherence (Wissing & Fourie, 2000), work engagement (Beukes & Botha, 2013), psychological well-being (Wissing & Van Eeden, 2002) and organisational constructs such as organisational commitment (Beukes & Botha, 2013). Research in nursing on spirituality conceptualised from positive psychology is scarce, although a relationship between spirituality, sense of coherence and hope as inner resources was established (Gibson, 2003) as well as with work engagement (Van der Colff & Rothmann, 2009).

The Research Question, Aim and Purpose of the Research

This research question was framed as follows: Upon being less dependent on and contained by their clinical group lead by the clinical supervisor/instructor, and becoming more independent and functioning increasingly as professionals in the hospital culture, what is the nature of fourth-year nursing students' spiritual coping? The aim of this research was to describe the role of spirituality in coping with the demands of the hospital culture amongst fourth-year nursing students. The purpose of the research was for this description to serve as normalising information for future nursing students entering the hospital culture, and for university and hospital staff as basis for student mentoring.

Methods

Research Design and Strategy

Qualitative and descriptive research was chosen (Brewerton & Millward, 2004) using the hermeneutic interpretive approach (Clarke & Hoggett, 2009). During the data interpretation the researchers used their selves as instrument (McCormick & White, 2000) based on the epistemological assumption that empathetic listening allows for deep understanding of shared experiences (Clarke & Hoggett, 2009). The strategy involved a single case study (Babbie & Mouton, 2001) used for its intrinsic (to gain theoretical and practical understanding of experiences) and instrumental (to provide feedback) values (Denzin & Lincoln, 2005).

Research Setting

The researchers experienced that most nursing students enter their career oblivious of the demands of the hospital culture. Some students are motivated by their spiritual and selfless needs to help and care for the less fortunate – including those in third world countries. Others are driven by an external locus of control (Rotter, 1966) filled with romantic images and stereotypes of nurses being admired as women by attractive and well-behaved doctors as portrayed in films and TV series such as *ER, Scrubs, Grey's Anatomy* and *Call the Midwife*. For these students the experience of the harsh reality of the hospital culture could be devastating and a space where they may need to rely on their inner spiritual strength.

The research was performed within a collaborative university and hospital setting. The University's Nursing School is primarily responsible for the students' academic training and various hospitals (and care facilities) where the students were placed, for their clinical training. The student's four year tertiary education is professionally regulated and structured according to specific and relevant competencies of which the development of clinical skills and critical thinking in the various areas of nursing, and quality care-giving to patients are the most important (see Fowler, Reimer-Kirkham, Sawatzky & Johnston-Taylor, 2012). Although spiritual development is desirable it is seldom directly addressed in the curriculum. The students received their clinical education firstly in a laboratory (e.g. in their first year) after which they were increasingly exposed to real clinical experiences during their placements in various hospital divisions. Here, they worked in groups with a clinical supervisor/instructor.

Sample

The population was the fourth-year Bachelor of Nursing Science students in a Canadian University's Nursing School. A convenient and opportunistic sample (Terre Blanche, Durrheim & Painter, 2006) was used – the 14 Caucasian female students between 21 and 27 years of age who responded on the invitation for participation. The sample represented 70% of the total enrolled fourth-year students. The data was seen as rich enough without having to extend the sample.

Instrument, Procedure and Analysis

As data collection instrument a self-report essay was used (Clark & Hoggett, 2009) using the following question: *Write an essay of maximum 5 pages on your experiences of the demands of the hospital culture by referring to your personal and academic experiences*. Students were asked to send their essays per e-mail to the second author. The data was content analysed, focussing on latent content and using whole interviews as unit of analysis (Graneheim & Lundman, 2004). Simple hermeneutics was used to understand participants' subjective and inter-subjective experiences and double hermeneutics to allow for the critical interpretation of their experiences from a positive psychology perspective (Snyder & Lopez, 2009). The process of interpretation (Terre Blanche et al., 2006) involved familiarisation, immersion, crystallisation and categorisation of experiences into positive psychology constructs. Lastly, the data was integrated into a research hypothesis (Schafer, 2003).

Ensuring Quality Data

Scientific rigour and trustworthiness was attended to (Graneheim & Lundman, 2004; Johnson & Waterfield, 2004). Dependability was ensured in the process of enquiry and the scientific rigour applied in the planning and execution of the research project. Credibility was ensured through a relative intense research engagement and the authorised involvement of all parties (Hirschhorn 1997). Internal generalisability and confirmability were attended to. The two researchers performed separate analyses, integrated these and submitted the findings to two independent, theoretically informed academics for peer-review. They declared the research dependable and agreed on its richness (Denzin & Lincoln, 2005). The thick and detailed data description of the experiences served the purpose of transferring the meaning to different and yet similar contexts. Confirmability was also established through the authors' attempts to examine the product to attest that the findings, interpretations and recommendations were supported by the theoretical data. Ethicality referred to informed consent and anonymity negotiated with all participants during the data-gathering phase (De Vos, Strydom, Fouché & Delport, 2002).

Findings

The participants' experiences of the demands of the hospital culture contained a limited positive and an intense negative content. The following excerpt serves as a typical participant experience. "Driving home my mind was everywhere. I thought back to all the kids I had seen that day, all the charts and stories I read. I didn't know how to process everything. I think that we are incredibly vulnerable to burnout and developing an attitude of bitterness, as it can be easy to get overwhelmed not only with a heavy workload, but also because of stress and demands that came with a new job. In addition, we can also become easily influenced by other's attitudes as we seek to gain the acceptance of our co-workers. I left the shift feeling very disheartened. I am a sensitive person and people's words and attitudes rub off on me. As I hold the hand of a woman dying, I wonder if these precious, yet traumatizing moments will ever cease to break my heart. Will I ever become the nurse that is not impacted by a patients' death? Will I come home this physically and emotionally tired after every shift for the rest of my career? … When managing the care of two patients I had the time to do the job I entered nursing to do. I had the time to invest into my patients and truly take the time to ask them questions about their lives, to grow to understand them, and to take the time to care for them. Yet when running after four sick patients, some of whom are dependent for all physical care, the list of things to do becomes overwhelming, we become rushed, patients become frustrated, and we are able to just get the job done. But the job done was never the job I wanted to do."

The Hospital Context

Before and on crossing the boundary into the hospital culture, all the participants idealised (Blackman, 2004) the hospital environment and the nursing profession. They referred to "the ideals we have been taught", how they "felt honoured" to be involved in "such a beautiful vocation", and their expectations of having "meaningful" and "caring interactions". Motivationally, they were "willing" and "eager", to "connect with suffering patients" and to "make a difference" in the "lives of others who are suffering". After a while of being exposed to the hospital culture, they experienced a "culture shock" where the ideal was replaced by "the actual realities of practice" and a "hard", "cold" and "clinical" culture surrounded by "pain ... suffering ... and death". They experienced disappointment, disillusionment, confusion and intense conflict about being in the hospital ("I love it ... I hate it", it is "the best job ... it is the worst job", "it is a hopeless job"). Nursing became "an immense" and "overwhelming challenge" – they were stressed by the "actual realities of practice", the "business", the "heavy workload", the "very strict routine" and "rules" which resulted in "limited time for myself", "my own activities" and "other meaningful activities".

Interpretation. Intellectually, the participants realised that the hospital is an institutional system managing its primary task of caring and secondary task of containing high levels of anxiety for all involved, and with an in-scripted systemic role for each, including the student nurse (Cilliers & Terblanche, 2010). Emotionally, they experienced overwhelming shock when they realised that they need to adapt to the culture, which implied the deconstruction of the idealised picture in the mind about nursing, and facing the reality of the shadow side of the profession and the institution (Nelson & Hogan, 2009). No participant mentioned the hospital as a space for spiritual togetherness or support which was interpreted as indicative of how the shocking experience caused their spiritual disequilibrium and dispirited state (Shores, 2010; Young & Koopsen, 2005).

The Self

Intra-personally, participants described their physical experiences as being "exhausted", having "difficulty to sleep" and suffering from "compassion fatigue" and "burnout" ("I gave all of myself, there is nothing left of me"). Their emotional experiences were described as "disheartening" ("my heart has been taken out", "cut into pieces", "dispersed to various people"), a constant "struggle" and "moral" "conflict between "acting responsibly" versus "suffering", "feeling vulnerable" and "inadequate". They experienced "paralysing fear", frustration ("since I don't have enough time to get the job done"), blame ("for not doing more"), guilt ("not able to give more to others" and "not fulfilling my responsibility"), "numbness" (and at "a loss of words"), "weakness", "helplessness", sadness ("I cry every time I drive home"), "a brokenness" and strong vulnerability ("I need to respect"/"protect myself right now", "we need to be gentle on ourselves"). Motivationally they struggled to "get by" while they are actually "striving for more" and having a "desire to change the situation". For some it was as if they were losing "balance in my life" and "parts of myself" ("I have become one with" ... "inseparable from my work", "when looking at the patients, I have problems in knowing the difference between my professional identity and personal identity", "I take the patients home with me").

Interpretation. All the participants illustrated their physical and emotional self-awareness (Naudé & Rothmann, 2006) about the content and intensity of their pain and suffering. Their experiences expressed their need for respect for and protection of their personal boundaries as if they were weak, caught up in the moment and even under attack to the point of losing the self (Cytrynbaum & Noumair, 2004). This inhibited their capacity to take control and intelligently appraise their spiritual self to experience solitude, submission, courage and curiosity in search for a higher purpose and meaning in the suffering towards personal mastery (Meier, O'Connor & Van Katwyk, 2005).

The Other

Interpersonally, most participants reported on the prevailing conflict and stress in their relationships with family and friends. Although some found "these conversations meaningful" and "feeding the soul", for others "the connection gets lost", "because of limited time and "they finding it disagreeable" to hear "about my work situation". They described the connection with hospital authority figures as "unfamiliar" and "strange". While two participants reported on having had positive peer conversations described as "promoting camaraderie", "without gossiping", most peer relationships are characterised as comparatively superficial ("we just joke around", "discuss current events", "TV-shows"), non-trusting (not providing a "safe", "private" or "confidential enough" space "for venting work frustrations") and disturbing ("in the way they treat patients", "I am concerned that I will be influenced by their negative attitude"). Participants' relationships with patients were split between caring ("especially for the little babies" by "knowing that God has been with them every step of the way") and negative sentiments ("I am uncertain ..." – "patients treat nurses poorly", "how do I tolerate the abuse?", feeling "vulnerable" and "scared" when faced with "pain and death" – their confusion, frustration, anger, sadness "breaks my heart"). Most participants acknowledged that they were interpersonally not coping well. They expressed hopelessness ("how can I offer hope to hurting people when I do not have it?") and withdrawal from friends, family, colleagues and patients. One participant expressed the difficulty "to choose service over self-interest" – we need "mentorship" to learn about "the practice of servant leadership". Some participants expressed their awareness of a complex emotional interconnectedness with patients, but they did not elaborate on what this meant and how this affected them.

Interpretation. Although some participants illustrated an awareness of their spiritual interconnectedness and some made use of interpersonal opportunities to debrief (Pargament, 2013a), most participants did not build significant, supportive and interdependent relationships. It was as if the intensity of the negative experience inhibited them to access their inner resources such as social intelligence, realness, authenticity, respect, kindness, comfort, grace, intimacy and love across the interpersonal boundary. It is ironic that when they had the first opportunity to exercise their initial nursing quest to help and care for others in need, they seemed so in tangled in their own painful experiences that they could not illustrate the higher order spiritual values of self-regulation, protection against excess, intimacy, temperance, humility and forgiveness. Perhaps they could not move beyond their own anger and hurt resulting in their helplessness to see the same in the other (Cytrynbaum & Noumair, 2004). This was interpreted as their lack of intra-personal sophistication inhibiting their interpersonal values and skills to explore and foster spiritual connections, firstly with the patients (those in immediate need) and colleagues (in the same situation as themselves) (Duke, 2013; Meier, O'Connor & Van Katwyk, 2005; Pargament, 2013a; 2013b, Young & Koopsen, 2005).

The Sacred

Participants illustrated their awareness of the existence ("I am thankful to have an amazing God") and trust in "the greater power of God's strength" ("He will send others to continue to care for our/His patients", "it is only God that gives us strength to care for others", "I find it comforting – being a Christian, to know that God gives us strength when we need it the most and that His hand is in all of this"). They expressed their need "to nurture my spiritual life", to build "an ultimate relationship with God" and "to glorify God", motivated by "to not be alone in our journey". Participants reported on their involvement in a limited number of inspirited activities – they were asking existential questions ("why does God allow these things to happen?"), prayed to God ("between shifts", "in the park", "to put me where He wants me to be", "to help me to step outside of my fear"), and mentioned the possibility of meditation. They relied on hope to counteract despair ("we need to cling on every little bit of hope we can find", "there is always hope").

Interpretation. Participants showed their spiritual awareness and connection with the higher power (Pargament, 2013b). They expressed their strong beliefs, hope, religiosity and an inner need towards searching for some meaning which came across as a dependent way to call upon God to save them from their difficulties (Young & Koopsen, 2005). On the next level of spiritual values, they did not show evidence of a state of being inspirited, dynamically accessing the required intra- and interpersonal resources and energy to make a divine connection towards an understanding of their situation, as a comfort for their painful experiences, or to reach out to the spiritual experiences of the other in their environment (Pargament, 2013a) – the un-understandable, not rationally explainable, universal, existential and mysterious essence of being in the hospital and being exposed to these experiences. Their limited use of experiential activities may indicate their spiritual inhibition towards realising the spiritual values of purpose, meaning, gratitude, fulfilment, harmony and transcendence (Brillhart, 2005).

The Research Hypothesis

The nursing students' dominant experience of the hospital culture was one of being dispirited. Their initial idealisation of being a helping and caring nurse, was followed by emotional shock caused by the hard cultural realities. Intra-personally they illustrated their capacity for physical, intellectual and emotional awareness, but they could not access their inner energy required for spiritual self-exploration, meaning making and control. Interpersonally, they could not spiritually reach out to the other in similar (colleagues) or different (patients) circumstances towards building comforting, real, respectful and intimate connections towards striving for purpose, meaning, hope and transcendence. The hospital culture was not experienced as a potential space for spiritual connection with the self, the other and the sacred.

Discussion

The aim of this research was to describe the role of spirituality in coping with the demands of the hospital culture amongst fourth-year nursing students. The purpose of the research was for this description to serve as normalising information for future nursing students entering the hospital culture, and for university and hospital staff as basis for student mentoring.

The research text contained many references to religiosity and spiritual matters which gave the impression that the nursing students were spiritually inclined. The analysis showed that the students' words on the surface showed a respect for God and his power, but not deep and lived through spiritual experiences, a search for something sacred, transformative, transcendental or out of the ordinary.

The students did not illustrate spiritual intelligence. They showed a lack of spiritual guidance in decision making, meaning making, maintaining their self-confidence, self-worth, quality of their relationships and coping behaviour with the stress and anxiety (Meier, O'Connor & Van Katwyk, 2005). On the contrary, their behaviour indicated an existential conflict (Frankl, 1969) between their idealised representation of nursing and their assumed competence to do good, versus their real experiences of the hospital culture which overwhelmed them with a fragile sense of responsibility, doubt in their competence and questioning their career choice. It was as if they were confronted with an impossible task (Cytrynbaum & Noumair, 2004). They struggled to manage their task and ego boundaries – it was almost as if they became depressed (Nasser & Overholser, 2005; Robertson, 2006).

The students did not illustrate spiritual coping or well-being in their lack of harmonious interconnectedness with the self, the other, community, environment and a deity characterised by a creative energy, the wholeness, strength, gratitude, forgiveness in life-affirming relationships (Meier, O'Connor & Van Katwyk, 2005). In terms of other related positive psychology constructs the following was interpreted. In terms of a spiritual way of being in the world, they were not driven by an ongoing life process of discovery of something sacred (personal accomplishments, revelations), conservation (holding on, building, sustaining connections) and transformation (purifying, reframing the connectedness to the sacred) (Pargament, 2013b). In terms of sense of coherence (Antonovsky, 1987) they did show some ability to comprehend and intellectually understand their experiences, but they struggled to make emotional sense out of the experiences and to manage the situation towards spiritual well-being. Limited emotional intelligence (Bar-On, 2010) manifested in their some self-awareness but not their empathy with the hospital culture, authorities, colleagues and patients. They did not access positive emotions (Frederickson, 2001). Their work engagement (Simpson, 2009) such as vigour and dedication did not manifest. Their lack of resilience and hardiness (Maddi & Khoshaba, 2005) meant that they could not access or develop attitudinal patterns to cope nor could they turn distress into eustress, courage and motivation, use their skills of social support and self-care. They did not show high levels of self-efficacy (Bandura, 1977), learned resourcefulness (Rosenbaum, 1990), psychological and character strengths (Peterson & Seligman, 2004), curiosity (Kashdan, 2009), self-authorisation (Hirschhorn, 1997), optimism (Peterson, 2000) or happiness (Buss, 2000). In the text, some students mentioned having to be mindful (Pargament, 2013b), but the data did not reveal their internal integration, coherence, openness, receptivity, attunement and attachments. In terms of individuation, Jung (1955) mentioned that real spiritual integration only manifests from 60+ year of age, which means that this group of students are far away from having the insights, emotional experiences and spiritual maturity to be individualised.

It was concluded that the only spiritual coping mechanisms with the hospital culture amongst these fourth-year nursing students were limited amounts of self-awareness, a search for meaning and hanging on to hope. Their behaviour did not reflect their capacity to be described as being spiritually inclined as employees in the hospital culture, nor did they illustrate any learned spiritual resourcefulness over three year of nursing education.

In revisiting the research question, it was concluded that becoming more independent as professionals working in the hospital culture, these fourth-year nursing students did not make sense of their difficult experiences through inner spiritual resources. Maybe the strong emphasis in nursing students' education on cognitive and clinical development, and medical care for patients, do not include time and energy for the spiritual development. It would then be unfair to expect of them to "be spiritual" especially at such a young age.

As limitation it needs to be mentioned that the spiritual experiences of students were measured in a general manner as part of their holistic experiences in the hospital. Maybe a more specific and directed way of questioning (e.g. using open ended questions or an interview) would have elicited more exact spiritual experiences.

It was recommended that the description of nursing students' behaviour (not only the spiritual) can be used as information for future nursing students entering the hospital culture. Thus, they may learn from pervious colleagues what the exposure of the hospital culture may be like. It was recommended that nursing schools take note of the experiences in fostering a learning climate focussing on the spiritual development of students. More specific inputs may be included in the curriculum such as mentoring into the culture of the hospital (Cilliers & Terblanche, 2010) to provide students with intellectual, emotional and spiritual insight into their own experiences (see Catamzaro & McMullen, 2001; Rankin & DeLashmutt, 2006; Pesut, 2002; 2003).

Follow up and even longitudinal research was recommended to ascertain the spiritual growth of the students in preparation for, and during the rest of the academic education. Research on systems psychodynamic role analysis is recommended to study the dynamics aspects of the student nurse's role, e.g. what the new nurse represents in the hospital culture, what the student introjects and what is projected onto the student to contain on behalf of the hospital system.

Declaration of Interest

The authors report no conflict of interest. The authors alone are responsible for the content and writing of the paper.

References

Antonovsky, A. (1987). *Unraveling the mystery of health: How people manage stress and stay well.* San Francisco: Jossey-Bass.

Azar, B. (2011). Positive psychology advances, with growing pains. *Monitor on Psychology*, 42(4):32-36. https://doi.org/10.1037/e529422011-014

Babbie, E. & Mouton, J. (2001). *The practice of social research.* Cape Town: Oxford University Press.

Bandura, A. (1977). Self-efficacy: Toward a unifying theory of behaviour change. *Psychological Review*, 84:191-215. https://doi.org/10.1037//0033-295X.84.2.191

Bar-On, R. (2010). Emotional intelligence: An integral part of positive psychology. *South African Journal of Psychology*, 40(1):54-62. https://doi.org/10.1177/008124631004000106

Basson, M.J. & Rothmann, S. (2002). Sense of coherence, coping and burnout of pharmacists. *South African Journal of Economic and Management Sciences*, 5(1):35-62. https://doi.org/10.4102/sajems.v5i1.2664

Bauer, T. & Barron, C.R. (1995). Nursing interventions for spiritual care. Preferences of the community-based elderly. *Journal of Holistic Nursing*, 13:268-279. https://doi.org/10.1177/089801019501300308

Beukes, I. & Botha, E. (2013). Organisational commitment, work engagement and meaning of work of nursing staff in hospitals. *SA Journal of Industrial Psychology*, 39(2):Art. #1144, 10 pages. https://doi.org/10.4102/sajip.v39i2.1144

Blackman, J.S. (2004). *101 Defences. How the mind shields itself.* New York: Brunner-Routledge. https://doi.org/10.4324/9780203492369

Breed, M.; Cilliers, F. & Visser, D. (2006). The factor structure of six salutogenic constructs. *South African Journal of Industrial Psychology*, 32(1):73-85. https://doi.org/10.4102/sajip.v32i1.226

Breverton, P. & Millward, L. (2004). *Organisational research methods. A guide for students and researchers.* London: Sage.

Brillhart, B. (2005). A study of spirituality and life satisfaction amongst persons with spinal cord injury. *Rehabilitation Nursing*, 30:31-34. https://doi.org/10.1002/j.2048-7940.2005.tb00353.x

Buss, D.M. (2000). The evolution of happiness. *American Psychologist*, 55(1):15-23. https://doi.org/10.1037//0003-066X.55.1.15

Callister, L.; Bond, A.E.; Matsumura, G. & Mangum, S. (2004). Threading spirituality throughout nursing education. *Holistic Nursing Practice*, 18:160-166. https://doi.org/10.1097/00004650-200405000-00008

Catamzaro, A.M. & McMullen, K.A. (2001). Increasing nursing students' spiritual sensitivity. *Nursing Educator*, 26:221-226. https://doi.org/10.1097/00006223-200109000-00011

Cilliers, F. & Terblanche, L. (2010). The systems psychodynamic leadership coaching experiences of nursing managers. *Health SA Gesondheid*, 15(1):Art #457, 9 pages. https://doi.org/10.4102/hsag.v15i1.457

Cilliers, F. & Coetzee, S.C. (2003). The theoretical-empirical fit between three psychological wellness constructs: Sense of coherence, learned resourcefulness and self-actualisation. *South African Journal of Labour Relations*, 27(1):4-24.

Clarke, S. & Hoggett, P. (2009). *Research beneath the surface. Psycho-Socail research methods in practice.* London: Karnac.

CNA (Canadian Nurses Association). (2010). Position statement. Spirituality, health and nursing practice. Ottawa: CNA.

Cytrynbaum, S. & Noumair, A. (2004). *Group dynamics, organizational irrationality, and social complexity: Group relations reader 3.* Jupiter: A.K. Rice.

De Vos, A.S.; Strydom, H.; Fouché, C.B. & Delport, C.S.L. (2002). *Research at grass roots.* Pretoria: Van Schaik.

Denzin, N.K. & Lincoln, Y.S. (2005). *The Sage handbook of qualitative research.* London: Sage. https://doi.org/10.1177/1468794105047237

Duke, G. (2013). Spirituality in the last days of life in persons born in Japan. *The Qualitative Report,* 18(87):1-16.

Feldt, T. (1997). The role of sense of coherence in well-being at work: Analysis of main and moderator effects. *Work and Stress,* 11:134-147. https://doi.org/10.1080/02678379708256830

Fowler, M.S.; Reimer-Kirkham, S.; Sawatzky, R. & Johnston-Taylor, E. (2012). *Religion, Religious Ethics, and Nursing.* New York: Springer

Frankl, V.E. (1969). *The will to meaning: Foundations and applications of logotherapy.* New York: world Publishing.

Fredrickson, B.L. (2001). The role of positive emotions in positive psychology. *American Psychologist,* 56(3):218-226. https://doi.org/10.1037//0003-066X.56.3.218

Garner, L.; McGuire, A.; Snow, D.M.; Grey, J. & Wright, K. (2002). Spirituality amongst baccalaureate nursing students at a private Christian university and a public state university. *Christian Higher Education,* 1:371-384. https://doi.org/10.1080/15363750214577

Gibson, L.M. (2003). Inter-relationships amongst sens of coherence, hope and spiritual perspectives (inner resources) of African American and European-American breast cancer survivors. *Applied Nursing Research,* 16:236-244. https://doi.org/10.1016/S0897-1897(03)00053-3

Goleman, D. (1995). *Emotional intelligence.* New York: Bantam.

Graneheim, U.H. & Lundman, B. (2004). Qualitative content analysis in nursing research: Concepts, procedures and measures to achieve trustworthiness. *Nurse Education Today,* 24:105-112. https://doi.org/10.1016/j.nedt.2003.10.001

Hampton, J.S. & Weinert, C. (2006). An exploration of spirituality in rural women with chronic illness. *Holistic Nursing Practice,* 20:27-33. https://doi.org/10.1097/00004650-200601000-00007

Hirschhorn, L. (1997). *Reworking authority. Leading and following in the post-modern organisation.* London: MIT.

Johnson, R. & Waterfield, J. (2004). Making words count: the value of qualitative research. *Physiotherapy Research International,* 9(3):121-131. https://doi.org/10.1002/pri.312

Jung, C.G. (1955) *Psychology and religion.* New Haven. Yale University Press.

Kashdan, T. (2009). *Curious? Discover the missing ingredient to a fulfilling life.* New York: William Morrow.

Katz, D. & Kahn, R.L. (1978). *The social psychology of organisations.* New York: McGraw-Hill.

Linley, P.A. & Joseph, S. (2004). *Positive psychology in practice.* Hoboken: John Wiley. https://doi.org/10.1002/9780470939338

Lopez, S.J. & Lyubomirsky, F.S. (2008). *Positive psychology. Exploring the best in people.* Westpoint: Praeger. https://doi.org/10.1080/17439760701760575

Lovanio, K. & Wallace, M. (2007). Promoting spiritual knowledge and attitudes: A student nurse education project. *Holistic Nursing Practice,* 21:42-47. https://doi.org/10.1097/00004650-200701000-00008

Lyubomirsky, S. (2001). Why are some people happier than others? The role of cognitive and motivational processes in well-being. *American Psychologist,* 56(3):239-249. https://doi.org/10.1037//0003-066X.56.3.239

Maddi, S.R. & Khoshaba, D.M. (2005). *Resilience at work. How to succeed no matter what life throws at you.* New York: AMACOM.

McCormick, D.W. & White, J. (2000). Using one's self as an instrument for organizational diagnosis. *Organizational Development Journal,* 18(3):49-62.

Meier, M.; O'Connor, T.St.J. & Van Katwyk, P. (2005). *Spirituality and health. Multidisciplinary explorations.* Waterloo, ON.: Wilfred Laurier University Press.

Menzies, I.E.P. (1993). *The functioning of social systems as a defence against anxiety.* London: Tavistock.

Meraviglia, M.G. (2004). The effects of spirituality on well-being of people with lung cancer. *Oncology Nursing Forum,* 31:89-94. https://doi.org/10.1188/04.ONF.89-94

Mitchell, D.L.; Bennett, M.J. & Manfrin-Ledet, L. (2006). Spiritual development of nursing students: Developing competence to provide spiritual care to patients at the end of life. *Journal of Nursing Education,* 45:365-370. https://doi.org/10.3928/01484834-20060901-06

Nasser, E.H. & Overholser, J.C. (2005). *Recovery from major depression. The role of support from family, friends, and spiritual beliefs.* Acta Psychiatrica Scandinavica, 111(2):125-132. https://doi.org/10.1111/j.1600-0447.2004.00423.x

Naudé, J.L.P. & Rothmann, S. (2006). Work-related well-being of emergency workers in South Africa. *South African Journal of Psychology,* 36(1):63-81. https://doi.org/10.1177/008124630603600105

Nelson, E. & Hogan, R. (2009). Coaching on the dark side. *International Coaching Psychology Review,* 4(1):7-17.

Pargament, K.I. (1999). The psychology of religion and spirituality? Yes and no. *International Journal of the Psychology of Religion,* 9:3-16. https://doi.org/10.1207/s15327582ijpr0901_2

Pargament, K.I. (ed.). (2013a). *APA Handbook of psychology, religion, and spirituality. Volume 1. Context, theory, and research.* Washington: American Psychological Association. https://doi.org/10.1037/14045-000

Pargament, K.I. (ed.). (2013b). *APA Handbook of psychology, religion, and spirituality. Volume 2. An applied psychology of religion and spirituality.* Washington: American Psychological Association. https://doi.org/10.1037/14046-000

Pesut, B. (2002). The development of nursing students' spirituality and spiritual care-giving. *Nurse Education Today*, 22:128-135. https://doi.org/10.1054/nedt.2001.0664

Persut, B. (2003). Developing spirituality in the curriculum: World views, intra-personal connectedness, interpersonal connectedness. *Nursing Education Perspectives*, 24:290-294.

Peterson, C. (2000). The future of optimism. *American Psychologist*, 55(1):44-55. https://doi.org/10.1037//0003-066X.55.1.44

Peterson, C. & Seligman, M.E.P. (2004). *Character strengths and virtues: A handbook and classification*. New York: American Psychological Association.

Pretorius, L. (2007). Resilience, self-efficacy and burnout of employees in a chemical organisation. Unpublished Masters dissertation, North-West University, Potchefstroom.

Rankin, E.A. & DeLashmutt, M.B. (2006). Finding spirituality and nursing presence. The student's challenge. *Journal of Holistic Nursing*, 24:282-288. https://doi.org/10.1177/0898010106294423

Reimer-Kirkham, S.; Grypma, S. & Terblanche, L. (2012). Religion and ethics in pluralistic healthcare contexts. Conference proceedings for the *Faith and Nursing Symposium: Religion and Ethics in Pluralistic Healthcare Contexts*, Trinity Western University, Langley, BC, Canada, 10-12 May.

Reynolds, D. (2006). Examining spirituality amongst women with breast cancer. *Holistic Nursing Practice*, 20:118-121. https://doi.org/10.1097/00004650-200605000-00005

Robbins, S.P.; Judge, T.A., Odendaal, A. & Roodt, G. (2009). *Organisational behaviour: Global and Southern African perspectives*. Cape Town: Pearson Education.

Robertson, A.C. (2006). Spirituality and depression: A qualitative approach. Unpublished Doctorate thesis. University of South Africa.

Rosenbaum, M. (ed.). (1990). *Learned resourcefulness: On coping skills, self-control and adaptive behaviour*. Springer: New York.

Rothmann, S. & Van Rensburg, P. (2002). Psychological strengths, coping and suicide ideation in the South African Police Services in the North West province. *South African Journal of Industrial Psychology*, 28(3):39-49. https://doi.org/10.4102/sajip.v28i3.64

Rotter, J. (1966). Generalized expectations for internal versus external control of reinforcements. *Psychological monographs: General and applied*, 80(1):1-28. https://doi.org/10.1037/h0092976

Ryan, R.M. & Deci, E.L. (2000). Self-determination theory and the facilitation of intrinsic motivation, social development and well-being. *American Psychologist*, 55(1):68-78. https://doi.org/10.1037//0003-066X.55.1.68

Schafer, R. (2003). *Insight and interpretation. The essential tools of psychoanalysis*. London: Karnac.

Seligman, M.E.P. & Csikszentmihalyi, M. (2000). Positive psychology. An introduction. *American Psychologist*, 55(1):5-14. https://doi.org/10.1037//0003-066X.55.1.5

Seligman, M.E.P.; Steen, T.A.; Park, N. & Peterson, C. (2005) Positive psychology progress. Empirical validation of interventions. *American Psychologist*, 60(5):410-421. https://doi.org/10.1037/0003-066X.60.5.410

Sheldon, K.M. & King, L. (2001). Why positive psychology is necessary. *American Psychologist*, 56(3):216-217. https://doi.org/10.1037//0003-066X.56.3.216

Sheldon, K.M.; Kashdan, T.B. & Steger, M.F. (2011). *Designing the future of positive psychology*. Oxford: Oxford University Press. https://doi.org/10.1093/acprof:oso/9780195373585.001.0001

Shores, C.I. (2010). Spiritual perspectives of nursing students. *Nursing Education Perspectives*, 8-11 February.

Simpson, M.R. (2009). Engagement at work: A review of the literature. *International Journal of Nursing Studies*, 46:1012-1024. https://doi.org/10.1016/j.ijnurstu.2008.05.003

Snyder, C.R. & Lopez, S.J. (2009). *Oxford handbook of positive psychology*. New York: Oxford University Press.

Storm, K. (2002). Burnout and work engagement of teachers in the South African Police Services. Unpublished Doctoral thesis, Potchefstroom University, Potchefstroom.

Strümpfer, D.J.W. (2005). Standing on the shoulders of giants: Notes on early positive psychology (Psychofortology). *South African Journal of Psychology*, 35(1):21-45. https://doi.org/10.1177/008124630503500102

Strümpfer, D.J.W.; Eiselen, R.J.; Meiring, D. & Phalatse, J.S. (2010). Validating measures of psychological well-being by contrasting samples employees in hazardous and less hazardous work. *Journal of Psychology in Africa*, 20(1):23-32. https://doi.org/10.1080/14330237.2010.10820339

Terre Blanche, M.; Durrheim, K. & Painter, D. (2006). *Research in practice. Applied methods for the social sciences*. Cape Town: UCT Press.

Tuck, I.; McCain, N.L. & Elswick, R.K. (2001). Spirituality and psychosocial factores in persons living with HIV. *Journal of Advanced Nursing*, 33:776-783. https://doi.org/10.1046/j.1365-2648.2001.01711.x

Van Der Colff, J.J. & Rothmann, S. (2009). Occupational stress, sense of coherence, coping, burnout and work engagement of registered nurses in South Africa. *South African Journal for Industrial Psychology*, 35(1):Art. #423, 10 pages. https://doi.org/10.4102/sajip.v35i1.423

Van Zyl, L.E.; Deacon, E. & Rothmann, S. (2010). Towards happiness: Experiences of work-role fit, meaningfulness and engagement of industrial/organisational psychologists in South Africa. *South African Journal of Industrial Psychology*, 36(1):Art #890, 10 pages. https://doi.org/10.4102/sajip.v36i1.890

Verhagen, P.J.; Van Praag, H.M.; Lopez-Ibor J.J. Jr.; Cox, J.L. & Moussaoui, D. (2010). *Religion and psychiatry: Beyond boundaries*. West Sussex: Wiley-Blackwell. https://doi.org/10.1002/9780470682203

Wissing, M.P. & Fourie, A. (2000). Spirituality and psychological well-being. Paper presented at the *First South African National Wellness Conference*, Port Elizabeth, 2-5 May.

Wissing, M.P. & Van Eeden, E. (2002). Empirical clarification of the nature of psychological well-being. *South African Journal of Psychology*, 32(1):32-44. https://doi.org/10.1177/008124630203200105

Wright, L.M. (2005). *Spirituality, suffering, and illness: Ideas for healing.* Philadelphia: Davis Company.

Young, C. & Koopsen, C. (2005). *Spirituality, health and healing.* Sudbury, MA.: Jones and Bartlett.

Article 2

Constructing a Systems Psychodynamic Wellness Model[1]

S Henning & F Cilliers

Orientation

The researchers constructed a Systems Psychodynamic Wellness Model (SPW) by merging theory and concepts from systems psychodynamics and positive psychology. They then refined the model for application in organisations during a Listening Post (LP) that comprised experienced subject experts.

Research Purpose

The purpose of the research was to construct and refine the SPW in order to understand psychological wellness at the individual, group and organisational levels.

Motivation for the Study

There is no psychological wellness model that integrates the principles of systems psychodynamics and positive psychology. Systems psychodynamics traditionally focuses on so-called negative behaviour whilst positive psychology tends to idealise positive behaviour. This research tried to merge these views in order to apply them to individual, group and organisational behaviour.

1   Henning, S. & Cilliers, F. (2012). Constructing a systems psychodynamic wellness model. *SA Journal of Industrial Psychology/SA Tydskrif vir Bedryfsielkunde*, 38(2):Art.#989, 9 pages. http://doi.org/10.4102/sajip.v38i2.989

Research Design, Approach and Method

The researchers used qualitative, descriptive and conceptual research. They conducted an in-depth literature study to construct the model. They then refined it using the LP.

Main Findings

The researchers identified 39 themes. They categorised them into three different levels. Three first-level themes emerged as the highest level of integration: identity, hope and love. The nine second-level themes each consisted of three more themes. They were less complex and abstract than the first-level themes. The least complex 27 third-level themes followed.

Practical/managerial Implications

One can apply the SPW as a qualitative diagnostic tool for understanding individual, group and organisational wellness and for consulting on systemic wellness.

Contribution/value-add

The SPW offers a model for understanding individual, group and organisational wellness and for consulting on systemic wellness

Introduction

Kets de Vries (2007) stated that 'wellness' seems typical of the *Zeitgeist* of our age. One can describe it as a preoccupation with health, wealth and happiness. The key focus of the current study was to explore the concept of psychological wellness and provide insights that go beyond trendy buzzwords. The researchers envisaged that consultants would apply the deeper insights they gained from the research to the practice of consulting psychology.

The psychological paradigms of this study were systems psychodynamics and positive psychology. Throughout the research, the researchers highlighted the emerging themes in an appropriate colour (see Figure 1), indicating to which level of analysis the theme belongs in the final psychological wellness model. A brief overview of the two paradigms follows.

Systems Psychodynamic Theory

The systems psychodynamic paradigm evolved at the Tavistock Institute in the United Kingdom in the 1950s and 1960s (Miller, 1993). It is a combination of the 'working outside in' (systems) perspective and the 'working inside out' (psychodynamic) perspective (Czander, 1996). The two different perspectives merge to provide a unique framework because it integrates the concepts of systems thinking and psychoanalysis to understand the unconscious processes in people, groups, organisations and societies better (Gould, Stapley & Stein, 2004).

From a systems psychodynamic perspective, wellness is a relational concept. Object relation theory postulates that the periods of loving care must exceed those of frustration and deprivation during childhood for wellness to develop and be sustained (Klein, 1975). If all goes relatively well and the child experiences a budding faith in primary caretakers, the child eventually develops the ability and courage to integrate the opposing feelings of love and hate (Klein, 1975).

Traditional psychological approaches reduced human beings to a bundle of sensations, drives, innate and learned reactions. In contrast to this mechanistic approach, systems theory proposes that humans link inextricably to the greater web of life. One cannot study them in isolation. The universe is a hierarchy of systems, where each higher level of a system comprises systems at lower levels (Keeney, 1983). One can regard the psychological wellness of any person, group or organisation as an open system, consisting of numerous subsystems that interact across different system boundaries (Keeney, 1983). According to O'Connor and Lubin (1990), psychological wellness is the result of constant interpersonal (between people) and intra-personal (within a person) change and variety.

Positive Psychology

Positive psychology is a sub-discipline of psychology that studies the nature, manifestations and ways of improving positive subjective experiences that link to strengths and virtues (Snyder & Lopez, 2005). It aims to change the focus of theory and practise in some fields of psychology from a preoccupation with disease and healing to well-being and improving strengths and virtues. Treatment is not just fixing what is wrong. It is also building what is right. Psychology is not just about illness or health. It is also about work, education, insight, love, growth and play. This perspective implies an active human that is constantly adapting to the environment to ensure wellness (Lopez, 2008).

One can regard humanistic psychology theorists as the founders of positive psychology (Cilliers & May, 2010). As a field of study, it recognises the importance of learning and optimistically focuses on a person's future rather than on the past. It is concerned with concepts like love, hope, creativity, values, meaning and self-actualisation. Positive psychology encourages buffering strengths like courage, interpersonal skill, curiosity, the capacity for pleasure, future-mindedness and, from psychoanalytic theory, a mature identity (Peterson & Seligman, 2006).

Research Purpose

According to Els and De la Rey (2006), there is a growing trend in organisations worldwide to acknowledge the importance of the so-called human factor as various disciplines highlight the importance of a 'good life', work-life balance and of attending to the total wellness of employees. At the same time organisational consultants are increasingly expressing their need to understand the deeper levels of individual, group and organisational behaviour that manifest 'below the surface' (Huffington, Armstrong, Halton, Hoyle & Pooley, 2004) and to address them. Nevertheless, theorists have never integrated these two perspectives into a model that aims to understand the deeper levels of wellness behaviour and its effects at the individual, group and organisational levels. The purpose of this study was to construct such an integrative model, called the Systems Psychodynamic Wellness Model, and to refine the model in an experiential event, namely a LP, that comprised experienced subject experts.

Trends from the Research Literature

Scholars from different psychological paradigms attempted to define psychological wellness. They contributed to several theories on the topic. Freud (1947:31) believed that one must change unconscious material into conscious material before a person will experience wellness: 'Where Id is there Ego shall be'. He went on to propose that having work to do and someone to love is necessary for a person to be well adjusted. For Jung (1950), one achieves individual wellness through individuation and self-realisation. Erikson (1968:52) remarked that, to understand how a person grows towards wellness, it is necessary to remember the epigenetic principle that derives from the growth of organisms in vitro:

> this principle states that anything that grows has a ground plan, and that out of this ground plan the parts arise, each part having its time of special ascendancy, until all parts have arisen to form a functioning whole.

To Erikson (1968), basic trust is the cornerstone of a well-adjusted adult personality. Antonovsky (1987), the founder of the 'salutogenesis' paradigm, described wellness as an 'ease-disease' continuum. Any person, group or organisation at any given time can oscillate between the two extremes on the continuum. The psychoanalyst Janov (1991:316) stated that the hallmark of psychological wellness is a person's ability to be satisfied with life:

> The neurotic is often dissatisfied with almost everything. Such an individual is missing something, so there is never enough money, security, love, sex, power, prestige or fame. Just feeling satisfied with one's life is an enormous achievement.

He went on to say that a person, who is psychologically well, is authentic and naturally cares because such a person has access to feelings and can really empathise with others.

Strümpfer (1995), as well as Wissing and Van Eeden (1997), proposed that wellness is a dynamic construct on a continuum of extremes where optimal wellness is on the one pole of the continuum and illness is on the other. It is at this point that the researchers challenged the idea of a linear wellness continuum in favour of a systems approach. This describes psychological wellness using concepts like circularity, interdependency and interrelationship. The emphasis shifted from a deterministic understanding of linear causality towards a holistic understanding of context, complexities and paradox.

The researchers introduced chaos theory into the study as a branch of systems thinking. The old Newtonian scientists had an image of the world that one can compare to a big clock (Wilber, 2000). Knowledge about how the clock worked would enable one to predict what could happen at any point in time. They believed in certainties and not probabilities. The modern science of chaos shows that causality does not apply everywhere. Chaos seems to be the creative force behind the emergence of new life forms. It appears in texts from Asian and Egyptian mythology (Butz, 1997). People often use 'chaos' in a negative sense and associate it with incompetence. However, chaos theory assumes that chaos exists within limits. One can describe orderly chaos as 'bounded instability'. It sustains all forms of life through constant change and variety (Stacey, 2003). Chaos theory offers a new way of looking at options for responding to unstable conditions. This new understanding does not anticipate disintegration and panic because of a lack of structure, but is open to the emergence of novel and more creative outputs. In this sense, the constant change and variety makes hope a central theme in chaos theory. For the purpose of this research, chaos theory was valuable as a metaphor to describe the complexity embedded in psychological wellness in a person, group or organisation.

Glass and Mackey (1988) stated that the world is not a gigantic, mechanical clock that is merely winding down, but a game of chance and choice. It allows room for free will, individuality and unpredictable creativity through self-organising properties. The process of flux is an intrinsic part of natural processes in all living systems. Bounded instability is necessary for flexibility, innovation and the capacity for finding new solutions in rapidly changing and unpredictable situations (Stacey, 2003). In laymen's terms, one can conclude that there is no growth without a little chaos.

Jung (1960:467) held that the tension of opposites contains wellness or wholeness, like a swinging pendulum, and that one cannot find it in a static condition:

> When the opposites unite, all energy ceases: there is no more flow. The waterfall has plunged to its full depth in that torrent of nuptial joy and longing; now only a stagnant pool remains, without wave or current.

All life is a marriage of opposites and true wellness is a form of wholeness (Bradshaw, 1992). Holistic thinking is central to a systems perspective. Changes in one part lead to changes to all parts and to the system itself. One cannot understand the system as a whole by analysing its separate parts: 'The essential properties of a system are lost when it is taken apart; for example a disassembled automobile does not transport and a disassembled person does not live' (Patton, 1990:79).

Bateson (2000) stated that there is 'a pattern that connects' living systems to one another, (that is, similar systemic concepts repeat in different contexts). The brilliant colours and shapes of fractal geometry illustrate this idea. Fractal geometry is a feature of chaos theory. It provides the graphic 'container' for the theoretical content of the model. It is also the 'pattern that connects' and is evident in human behaviour.

The Fractal Geometry of Human Behaviour

Chaos theory offers an organic view of human life and a philosophy of hope (Patton, 1990) because of the underlying assumptions of continuous and rapid change, chance and endless variety. Therefore, it provides an important parallel with positive psychology, where the adaptive potential of humans, groups and organisations, their growth and concepts, like creativity and variety of experiences, are central (Snyder & Lopez, 2005).

Gilgen (1995:182) stated that hope is the understanding that, because flux underlies all that is, nothing is unchangeable or fixed: '... the will to happiness is the ultimate strange attractor in human experience' and '... the universe in its unfolding will never stop at any one informational level'. The implication is that humans have the freedom to choose and creatively weave themselves and their universe. Therefore, hope is inherent in chaos theory as people, groups and organisations graph their own existence randomly and unpredictably through chance and choice.

Another characteristic of fractals is the uniqueness of the pattern of each individual fractal as it presents an ever-evolving identity (Mandelbrot, 2005). This reflects the evolving identity of humans, groups and organisations. They all have their own developmental trajectory that gives rise to a special and unique identity.

A third characteristic of fractals is the evolving 'patterns that connect' (Bateson, 2000), implying some form of relatedness between subsystems within a bigger system. Fractals are patterns within patterns within patterns that develop over time, ad infinitum. People are parts of groups that form parts of organisations, which again form parts of a greater society. It is a continuous process of increasing complexity. In human relationships, the 'pattern that connects' may become what Klein (1975) referred to as object relations from the psychodynamic paradigm. Here, patterns of attachment, that is, feelings of love and hate for 'objects' are central. Humans, as living fractals, co-create each other through their relatedness to each other. Love makes psychological wellness attainable to all (Janov, 1991). Psychological wellness is complex and evolving. It is always in process and is never a static state to which one should aspire. The freedom to choose and the desire for happiness are central to psychological wellness:

> Living and choosing is an aesthetic process; so a beautiful life is a truthful life lived out of one's happiness, one's open-ended consonance with the implicit order's subtle promptings. (Gilgen 1995:183)

Core Research Problem and Specific Research Objectives

Els and De la Rey (2006) believed that existing conceptual foundations, models and theories of wellness had a limited effect on wellness research. It seems that the current wellness research seldom led to the phrasing of vital research questions or to the determination of programme contents, their design and development in meaningful ways. The primary research objective was to construct a psychological wellness model that merges the theories and concepts of systems psychodynamics with those of positive psychology to apply at the individual, group and organisational levels.

The secondary research objective was to refine the model by using a LP that comprised experienced subject experts.

The Potential Value-add of the Study

The potential value-add of the study is that consultants can use the SPW as a qualitative diagnostic tool for understanding individual, group and organisational wellness and for consulting on systemic wellness. It includes various organisational development inputs, like executive and leadership coaching for people and teams, team building and change management. In addition, one can apply the SPW to the market research environment because its wellness concepts might reflect the social dynamics of a particular social context.

What Will Follow

The next sections of the article describe the research design, the graphic construction of the model, the findings and discussion of the findings. Finally, the researchers made recommendations for future research.

Research Design

Research Approach

The researchers used a qualitative research approach. They framed it as a non-numeric examination and interpretation of observations to discover underlying meanings and patterns of relationships (Babbie, 2007) in psychological wellness. The research was descriptive and conceptual in nature (Denzin & Lincoln, 2005). The researchers approached the study from an artistic and metaphoric perspective and described it as a process with phases that connect to different forms of behaviours, their interpretation and presentation.

Research Strategy

The strategy consisted of two phases. Phase 1 comprised an extensive literature study and several content analyses to identify patterns of psychological wellness within systems psychodynamics and positive psychology. The researchers explored the potential of fractal geometry as the graphic design for the model and constructed the model theoretically. Phase 2 comprised administering the LP and refining the SPW.

Research Method

Research Setting

The researchers set the study within the organisational psychology fraternity, especially practitioners familiar with systems psychodynamics and positive psychology.

Entrée and Establishing Researcher Roles

The first researcher had two distinct roles. The first was to be the qualitative researcher, to construct the SPW, to analyse the data and refine the model (Terre Blanche, Durrheim & Painter, 2006). The second was to be a participant observer (Brewerton & Millward, 2004) during the LP, to witness, describe, record and make sense of the data whilst being part of it (Clarke & Hoggett, 2009). The second researcher was the research supervisor (Clarke & Hoggett, 2009) and convenor of the LP. Both researchers used the orientation of self as the instrument of analysis (McCormick & White, 2000). Both are psychologists with doctorate degrees and know about positive psychology. They both have specific training, theoretical knowledge and experience in systems psychodynamic consulting and research that conforms to the requirements that Brunner, Nutkevitch and Sher, (2006) set.

Sampling

The first researcher used purposive sampling of the literature (in phase 1) and the participants (in phase 2) to select information-rich data for an in-depth study (Fisher, 2006). In phase 2, the second researcher selected 15 participants based on their substantial local or global group relations and systems psychodynamic consulting experience.

Data Collection Methods

In phase 1, the first researcher analysed the literature on psychological wellness from the systems psychodynamics and positive psychology perspectives and constructed the SPW. In phase 2, the second researcher administered the LP. The LP is a systems psychodynamic organisational consultancy method (Gould, Stapley & Stein, 2004; Neumann, Kellner & Dawson-Shepherd, 1997) that the Organisation for Promoting Understanding of Society (OPUS) developed (Stapley, 2006a; 2006b). It focuses on a specific matter that has an unstructured design (Stapley & Collie, 2005). Consultants use the first hour to process a set question and a second to formulate hypotheses based on the previous processing (Dartington, 2000).

A system psychodynamically informed convenor controls the time boundaries firmly, introduces and closes the event. The quality of the LP depends on the convenor's ability to allow participants to share their experiences in a contained space without judgement, memory or desire (Czander, 1997) and to manage the boundaries between the two roles of convenor and member. The second researcher invited the selected participants to attend the LP. The second researcher presented the SPW to them and set the question: 'does the SPW make sense as a conceptual model for understanding individual, group and organisation wellness?' To allow the 15 participants to process the material freely, the second researcher administered the LP in two sessions. One had eight and the other seven participants.

Recording of Data

The researchers followed the guidelines of Hinshelwood and Skogstad (2005). These were to make an audio recording of the LP with the consent of the participants and to take descriptive field notes during and after the event.

Data Analyses

Bateson (2000) referred to the 'drawing of distinctions' to describe how a person constructs reality. One can describe developing the theoretical content of the model as the continuous 'drawing of distinctions' from the literature on psychological wellness. Pirsig (1987:75) used sorting sand as a metaphor for the way humans draw distinctions or gain knowledge from their world:

> We take a handful of sand from the endless landscape of awareness around us and call that handful of sand the world. The handful of sand looks uniform at first, but the longer we look at it the more diverse we find it to be. We form the sand into separate piles on the basis of this similarity and dissimilarity. Shades

of colour in different piles – sizes in different piles – subtypes of colours in different piles, and so on, and on, and on.

This metaphor appropriately describes what the first researcher experienced when she analysed the literature. During phase 1, using several levels of content analyses (Miles & Huberman, 1994) was the method she chose to 'map' the psychological wellness territory. From the literature on systems psychodynamics and positive psychology, different themes emerged. She integrated them into three different levels of analysis. Each level categorised themes at a progressively higher level of abstraction. In phase 2, the researchers used the LP data to confirm the themes, their progressive nature and to refine the definitions of some of the themes.

Strategies Employed to Ensure Quality Data

The knowledge one gains from research is only a description of reality and is not reality in itself (Bateson, 2000). The first researcher was aware of her own subjective reality and ensured that self-reflection occurred through continuous discussion with others and by diarising her experiences. Bogdan and Bilken (2003) referred to self-reflection as a strategy to improve researcher credibility. Fisher (2006) referred to witness validity and touchpoint validity as ways of improving the trustworthiness of qualitative data. Witness validity confirms that readers of the data (in this research, the participants of the LP) and findings reach conclusions that are similar to those the researchers do. Touchpoint validity confirms that the findings connect with theory and with other studies productively. Researchers affirm, reconcile and expand previous understandings of the topic (Fisher, 2006:6). The researchers were careful to remain within the chosen paradigms throughout the research.

Reporting

Firstly, the researchers reported the findings of the multi-level content analysis. They then completed the graphic construction of the wellness model (the Sierpinski Triangle). Finally, they integrated them into the System Psychodynamic Wellness Triangle.

Findings

Thirty-nine themes emerged from the literature review and created patterns (three first-level themes) within patterns (nine second-level themes) and within patterns (27 third-level themes). Each of the three first-level themes consisted of three second-level themes, which again consisted of three third-level themes. Figure 1 illustrates them. The first-level analysis describes three themes at the highest level of abstraction. The second-level analysis consists of nine second-level themes, which are less abstract and complex. The third-level analysis consists of 27 themes that are the most concrete. One can describe them as behavioural manifestations.

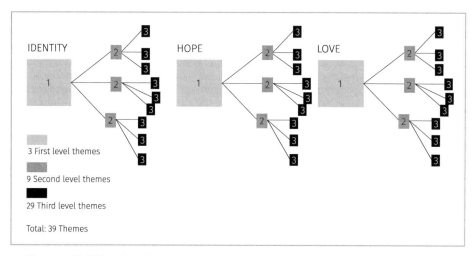

Figure 1 **Multi-level content analysis**

First-level analysis

Theme 1: Identity

Identity is all about becoming and being someone and answers the question 'who am I?' It aims to explain how people, groups and organisations develop an identity, a unique personality, and how they maintain it:

∞ second-level analysis, theme 1: the sources of self

∞ third-level analysis, theme 1: evolution of self

∞ third-level analysis, theme 2: self-image

∞ third-level analysis, theme 3: narcissism

∞ second-level analysis, theme 2: ego

∞ third-level analysis, theme 1: ego structure

∞ third-level analysis, theme 2: ego ideal

∞ third-level analysis, theme 3: ego defences

∞ second-level analysis, theme 3: boundary management

∞ third-level analysis, theme 1: space boundaries

∞ third-level analysis, theme 2: task boundaries

∞ third-level analysis, theme 3: time boundaries.

Theme 2: Hope

Hope addresses the question 'why am I?' Themes that explore the search for meaning and direction for the future of people, groups and organisations are:

∞ second-level analysis, theme 1: wisdom
∞ third-level analysis, theme 1: open-mindedness
∞ third-level analysis, theme 2: curiosity
∞ third-level analysis, theme 3: creativity
∞ second-level analysis, theme 2: meaning
∞ third-level analysis, theme 1: attachment
∞ third-level analysis, theme 2: goal-seeking
∞ third-level analysis, theme 3: authenticity
∞ second-level analysis, theme 3: paradox
∞ third-level analysis, theme 1: reparation
∞ third-level analysis, theme 2: mastery
∞ third-level analysis, theme 3: optimism.

Theme 3: Love

Love refers to the question 'how do I relate?' It illustrates relational aspects, particularly one's relationship with oneself and with others:

∞ second-level analysis, theme 1: mirror gazing – self
∞ third-level analysis, theme 1: self-knowledge
∞ third-level analysis, theme 2: self-acceptance
∞ third-level analysis, theme 3: self-actualisation
∞ second-level analysis, theme 2: window watching – others
∞ third-level analysis, theme 1: social acceptance
∞ third-level analysis, theme 2: social integration
∞ third-level analysis, theme 3: social actualisation
∞ second-level analysis, theme 3: transcendence
∞ third-level analysis, theme 1: beyond boundaries
∞ third-level analysis, theme 2: transformation
∞ third-level analysis, theme 3: aesthetics.

In summary, the researchers used a hierarchical approach to construct the model. Third-level themes are not disjointed fragments but form a network of mutual interactive themes, each valid in their own right. The 39 themes are all relevant on individual, group and organisational levels of consultation. Henning (2009) discusses them in detail.

Graphic Construction of the Systems Psychodynamic Wellness Model:
Fractal Geometry

Mandelbrot (2005) coined the term 'fractal geometry' from the Latin *fractua*, which means 'irregular'. Fractal geometry is a visual way of understanding the natural sciences and a way of showing how things often display the same structure when one looks at the same things on bigger and bigger or smaller and smaller scales. The whole is also always within each part and each part is also the whole. One finds patterns repeatedly at descending scales, so that their parts, at any scale, are similar in shape to the whole. One can see self-similarity in cauliflowers, snowflakes, Gothic arches in European cathedrals, branches of lightning, leitmotifs in operas, the distribution of galaxies, weather patterns and coastlines.

The Sierpinski Triangle

Symbols are universal and pervade all cultures as they resonate with the fundamental aspects of human nature (Jung, 1950). They speak of shared wisdom whose truths we recognise but can never quite put into words. The triangle is the universal symbol of change and transformation. Religion, myth, folk tales, science and art tenaciously reiterate the importance of trinities because of their deep roots in every part of us: 'They have powerful psychological effects on us because the tripartite universe connects us with its archetypal root within us' (Schneider, 1994:144). The Sierpinski Triangle is a fractal named after Sierpinski, who described it in 1915 (Mandelbrot, 2005).

It offers a graphic design whilst reflecting the process of multi-level content analysis. In addition, it contained all 39 themes, as they emerged from the data, in one complete structure. It is one of the most basic examples of self-similar sets. That is, it is a mathematically generated pattern that one can reproduce at any magnification or reduction (see Figure 2). The geometric simplicity of the triangle makes it an appropriate symbol with which to construct a complex theoretical model. The original triangle consisted of a hierarchical set of triangles, which again consists of another set of triangles. Mathematically, the process can keep on generating triangles at deeper and deeper levels, ad infinitum.

Figure 2   **The Sierpinski Triangle**

Sierpinski (Mandelbrot, 2005) referred to the original, white triangle as the 'generator triangle' because it repetitively generates, according to fractal geometry, more similar shapes or, in this case, more triangles. Similarly, the 'generator' theme of 'psychological wellness' generated qualitative themes within themes within themes, each theme describing a specific aspect of the original theme. The complete structure comprises 40 triangles. Jung (1950) noted that the number 40 symbolises 'wholeness', 'totality' and 'completeness'.

Thirty-nine themes emerged from this research. Mathematically, one can calculate the number of themes as follows: $(3 \times 1) + (3 \times 3) + (3 \times 3 \times 3) = 39$. The 40th triangle gives the name of the psychological wellness model, which is the Systems Psychodynamic Wellness Triangle. Figure 3 below illustrates it.

Discussion

The primary research objective was to construct the Systems Psychodynamic Wellness Model and to refine the model conceptually in order to understand psychological wellness at the individual, group and organisational levels. Existing models are mostly insensitive to the systemic properties of living systems. People, groups and organisations are systems within systems within systems that are connected and interdependent. One needs to explore them in context. From a systems perspective, individual parts of any living system are important and one cannot disregard them. However, it is understanding the relationships between the parts of the system and how they fit into the whole that enables deeper insights into the phenomena.

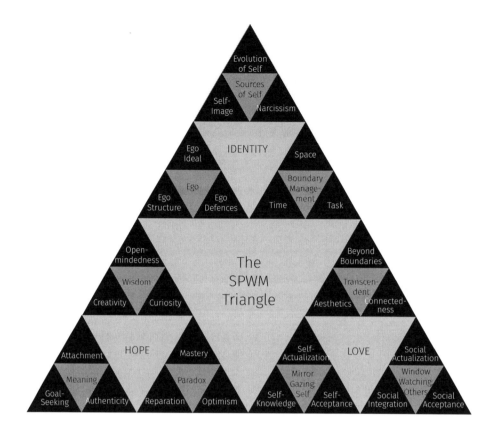

Figure 3 **The Systems Psychodynamic Wellness Model**

The SPW Triangle integrates systems psychodynamic thinking and positive psychology, thereby offering a more holistic and optimistic perspective for studying human behaviour as opposed to the traditional, mechanistic perspectives that focused mainly on disease and pathology. The researchers achieved the primary research objective in constructing the SPW Triangle, where the first-, second- and third-level themes display a logical flow from simple to complex.

The theoretical paradigms (systems psychodynamics and positive psychology) contained the themes that the researchers identified to describe psychological wellness at individual, group and organisational levels. The first-level analysis themes have the highest level of abstraction. The three first-level themes reflect this integration. Identity is a central concept in systems psychodynamics whilst hope and love are inherent to positive psychology. In the graphic design of the model, a fractal called the Sierpinski Triangle provided the container for the emerging themes. It is significant that the themes of hope and love are at the left and right base corners of the triangle, whilst the theme identity is at the top corner. These symbolic positions show that identity is a product of hope and love.

This research challenged the linear wellness continuum (Wissing & Van Eeden, 1997), where illness and wellness are at the opposite extremes, in favour of a systems approach. One expects psychological wellness and the wellness of any living system in conditions where there are change and variety, a tendency to move towards greater differentiation, detail, complexity, paradox and bounded instability (Stacey, 2003). In addition, one can state that positive psychology is a transitional object (Winnicot, 1951). It focuses on the ease-disease model towards an integrated system psychodynamic model of psychological wellness.

Von Bertalanffy (1973) stated that life is not a comfortable settling down in pre-ordained grooves of being. Instead, it inexorably drives all living systems towards higher forms of existence. It is along these lines of systemic thinking that a new model or image of man as an 'active personality system' seems to emerge. One can see systems thinking as an inherently hopeful theory because it describes dynamic, ever-changing systems and not closed, deterministic systems that cannot learn and adapt. Like living fractals, people, groups and organisations evolve. How well they evolve, that is, who they become, why they became and how they relate, is a matter of chance and many choices over a period.

The researchers confirmed witness and touchpoint validity (Fisher, 2006). It led them to conclude that the SPW makes sense as a systemic wellness model that organisations can use. They acknowledged the potential of the model as a diagnostic tool in organisational psychology and for managing customer relationships.

Conclusions

The researchers concluded that one could use the SPW Triangle as a conceptual qualitative diagnostic tool for understanding individual, group and organisational wellness. One can also use the model in a market research environment because its wellness concepts could reflect the social dynamics of a particular social context. Knowing what matters to customers, and taking care to align their needs to strategies, will enable targeted advertising and communication initiatives.

Recommendations

The researchers recommend that consultants use the SPW as 'a model in the mind' (Armstrong, 2005) to guide their discussions and generate interactive communication when they are working with people, groups or organisations. They also recommend that researchers validate the model in qualitative and quantitative research in various organisational settings, like individual and team coaching.

Possible Limitations of the Study

The SPW Triangle reflects significant complexity around the topic of psychological wellness. However, one can never capture all of its complexity. The descriptive nature of the research leads to many questions that the researchers could not answer in the current research. Although the systems psychodynamic literature is substantial, the availability of literature that explores psychological wellness from this paradigm is extremely limited. The conceptual meaningfulness of the model depends to some extent on the user's understanding of the systems psychodynamic paradigm and concepts from positive psychology. The researchers have completed the conceptualisation of the model. However, they have not explored the operational aspects of the model.

Suggestions for Further Research

Future research possibilities include structural equation modelling to construct a quantitative model. This could lead to identifying key drivers that could affect the overall psychological wellness of a system. They might enable business leaders to spend money more wisely on targeted interventions, thereby improving their return on investments. The SPW Triangle could assist businesses to transform customer service transactions into customer service engagements. They could design a unique customer relationship management questionnaire using sound theoretical principles. They could also use it for customer research to explore customers' service expectations as well as the quality of their relationships with a specific brand.

Acknowledgements

Competing Interests

The authors declare that they have no financial or personal relationship(s) that may have inappropriately influenced them when they wrote this paper.

Authors' Contributions

Both authors planned the research project. S.H. (University of South Africa) conducted the literature review and the empirical study. During the LP, F.C. (University of South Africa) was the convenor and S.H. (University of South Africa) was the participant observer. F.C. (University of South Africa) was also the supervisor for the whole research project.

References

Antonovsky, A. (1987). *Unraveling the mystery of health: How people manage stress and stay well.* San Francisco: Jossey-Bass.

Armstrong, D. (2005). *Organisation in the mind. Psychoanalysis, group relations and organisational consultancy.* London: Karnac.

Babbie, E. (2007). *The Practice of Social Research.* (7th ed.). Belmont: Wadsworth.

Bateson, G. (2000). *Steps to an ecology of mind.* London: University of Chicago Press. https://doi.org/10.7208/chicago/9780226924601.001.0001

Bogdan, R.C. & Bilken, S. (2003). *Qualitative research for education: An introduction to theory and method.* Boston: Alyn & Bacon.

Bradshaw, J. (1992). *Home Coming: Reclaiming and championing your inner child.* London: Bantam Doubleday Dell.

Brewerton, P. & Millward, L. (2004). *Organisational research methods. A guide for students and researchers.* London: Sage.

Brunner, L.D.; Nutkevitch, A. & Sher, M. (2006). *Group relations conferences: Reviewing and exploring theory, design, role-taking and application.* London: Karnac.

Butz, M.R. (1997). *Chaos and complexity: implications for psychological theory and practice.* Washington, DC: Talyor & Francis.

Cilliers, F. & May, M. (2010). The popularisation of Positive Psychology as a defence against behavioural complexity in research and organisations. *South African Journal of Industrial Psychology,* 36(2):Art. #917, 10 pages. https://doi.org/10.4102/sajip.v36i2.917

Cilliers, F. & Smit, B. (2006). A systems psychodynamic interpretation of South African diversity dynamics: A comparative study. *South African Journal of Labour Relations,* 30(2):5-18.

Clarke, S., & Hoggett, P. (2009). *Researching beneath the surface. Psycho-social research methods in practice.* London: Karnac.

Czander, W.M. (1997). *The psychodynamics of work and organisations: Theory and application.* New York: Guilford Press.

Dartington, T. (2000). The pre-occupation of the citizen – reflections from the OPUS Listening Posts. *Organisational and Social Dynamics,* 1:94-112.

Denzin, N.K. & Lincoln, Y.S. (2005). *The Sage handbook of qualitative research.* London: Sage publications. https://doi.org/10.1177/1468794105047237

Els, D.A. & De la Rey, R.P. (2006). Developing a holistic wellness model. *South African Journal of Human Resource Management,* 4(2):46-56. https://doi.org/10.4102/sajhrm.v4i2.86

Erikson, E.H. (1968). *Identity and the life cycle.* New York: International Universities Press.

Fisher, C.T. (2006). *Qualitative research methods for psychologists.* London: Elsevier.

Freud, S. (1947). *Het ik in de psigologie der massa.* Amsterdam: Wêreld bibliotheek N.V.

Gilgen, A.R. (1995). *Chaos theory in psychology*. New York: Greenwood Press.

Glass, L. & Mackey, M.C. (1988). *From clocks to chaos: The rhythms of life*. New York: Princeton.

Gould, L.J.; Stapley, L.F. & Stein, M. (2004). *Experiential learning in organisations. Applications of the Tavistock group relations approach*. London: Karnac.

Henning, S. (2009). Towards a system psychodynamic model of psychological wellness. Unpublished DPhil thesis, University of South Africa, Pretoria, South Africa.

Hinshelwood, R.D. & Skogstad, W. (2005). *Observing organisations. Anxiety, defence and culture in health care*. London: Routledge.

Huffington, C.; Armstrong, A.; Halton, W.; Hoyle, L. & Pooley, J. (2004). *Working below the surface. The emotional life of contemporary organisations*. London: Karnac.

Janov, A. (1991). *The new primal scream: primal therapy twenty years on*. London: Abacus Books.

Jung, C.G. (1950). *CW 18: The symbolic life*. New York: Bollingen series.

Jung, C.G. (1960). *On the nature of the Psyche*. New York: Bollingen series. https://doi.org/10.4324/9780203278819

Keeny, B.P. (1983). *Aesthetics of change*. New York: Guilford.

Kets de Vries, M.F. (2007). *The Happiness Equation*. Lincoln: Universe.

Klein, M. (1975). *Envy and Gratitude and other works*. New York: Delacorte Press.

Lopez, S.H. (2008). *Positive psychology: exploring the best in people*. London: Praeger perspectives. https://doi.org/10.1080/17439760701760575

Lowman, R.L. (2002). *The handbook of organisational consulting psychology*. San Francisco: Jossey-Bass. https://doi.org/10.1037/1061-4087.54.4.213

Mandelbrot, B.B. (2005). *The (mis)behaviour of markets: a fractal view of risk, ruin and reward*. London: Profile books.

McCormick, D.W. & White, J. (2000). Using one's self as instrument for organisational diagnosis. *Organisational Development Journal*, 18(3):49-62.

Miles, M.B. & Huberman, A.B. (1994). *Qualitative data analysis: An expanded sourcebook*. (2nd ed.) London: Sage.

Miller, E.J. (1993). *From dependency to autonomy: Studies in organisation and change*. London: Free Association Books.

Neumann, J.E.; Kellner, K. & Dawson-Shepherd, A. (1997). *Developing organisational consultancy*. London: Routledge.

O'Connor, W. & Lubin, B. (1990). *Ecological approaches to clinical and community psychology*. Miami: Robert Krieger.

Patton, M.Q. (1990). *Qualitative evaluation and research methods*. New Bury Park: Sage.

Peterson, C., & Seligman, M.E.P. (2004). *Character strengths and virtues: a handbook and classification*. New York: Oxford University Press.

Pirsig, R.M. (1999). *Zen and the art of motorcycle maintenance*. London: Vintage.

Schneider, M.S. (1994). *A beginners' guide to constructing the Universe: The Mathematical archetypes of nature, art and science*. New York: Harper Perennial.

Snyder, C.R. & Lopez, S.J. (2005). *Handbook of Positive Psychology*. New York: Oxford University Press.

Stacey, R.D. (2003). *Strategic management and organisational dynamics: The challenge of complexity.* (4th ed.). Harlow: Pearson Education.

Stapley, L.F. (2006a). Global dynamics at the dawn of 2006. *Organisational and Social Dynamics,* 6(1):111-142.

Stapley, L.F. (2006b). *Individuals, groups and organizations beneath the surface.* London: Karnac.

Stapley, L.F., & Collie, A. (2005). Global dynamics at the dawn of 2005. *Organizational and Social Dynamics,* 5(1):111-133.

Strümpfer, D.J.W. (1995). The origins of health and strength: From 'salutogenesis' to 'fortigenesis'. *South African Journal of Psychology,* 25(2):81-89. https://doi.org/10.1177/008124639502500203

Terre Blanche, M.; Durrheim, K. & Painter, D. (2006). *Research in practice. Applied methods for the social sciences.* Cape Town: UCT Press.

Von Bertalanffy, L. (1973). *General Systems Theory.* London: Penguin Books.

Wilber, K. (2000). *Sex, ecology, spirituality: The spirit of evolution.* London Shambhala.

Winnicot, D.W. (1951). Transitional objects and transitional phenomena. *In Through paediatrics to psycho-analysis,* pp.229-242. New York: Basic Books.

Wissing, M.P., & Van Eeden, C. (1997). *Psychological wellbeing: a fortigenic conceptualisation and empirical clarification.* Paper presented at the 3rd Annual Congress of the Psychological Society of South Africa, Durban, South Africa, 10–12 September.

Article 3

A Systems Psychodynamic Description of Organisational Bullying Experiences[1]

F Cilliers

Introduction

Bullying has a fascinating and damaging unconscious life of its own that works below the surface of its conscious psychological manifestation and its effect in organisations. This life functions below the surface of individual, dyadic, team and organisational behaviour, and is filled with anxiety that is projected to and fro between the role players. The purpose of this projected anxiety is to avoid feelings of badness.

Bullying has been researched in education (Blase & Blase, 2002; Cemalogly, 2007; De Wet & Jacobs, 2008; Johnson, Thompson, Wilkinson, Walsh, Balding & Wright, 2002), nursing (Hutchinson, Vickers, Jackson & Wilkens, 2006; Lewis, 2006; Yildirim, Yildirim & Timucin, 2007), universities (Lewis, 2004) and even in cyber-space (Kowalski, Limber & Aqatston, 2007). The extensive literature on organisational bullying is reported in daily newspapers (Beeld, 2010), popular management journals (Lewis, 2009; Naidoo, 2008; Ncongwane, 2010a; 2010b), voluminous textbooks (Bassman, 1992; Fox & Spector, 2005), as well as in subject journals (Chamberlin, Novotney, Packard & Price, 2008; Crawford, 1999; Djurkovic, McCormack & Casimir, 2006; Duffy & Sperry, 2007; Harvey, Heames, Richey & Leonard, 2006; Lewis, 1999; Liefooghe & Olafsson, 1999; Marais & Herman, 1997; Martin, 2000; Meyers, 2006a; 2006b; Oade, 2009; Pietersen, 2007; Randall, 1997; Rayner, 1999; Rayner, Sheehan & Barker, 1999; Stambor, 2006; Zapf, 1999).

1 Cilliers, F. (2012). A systems psychodynamic description of organisational bullying experiences. *SA Journal of Industrial Psychology/SA Tydskrif vir Bedryfsielkunde*, 38(2). Art.#994,11 pages. http://.doi.org/10.4102/sajip.v38i2.994

Although workplace bullying manifested itself in primitive times, research about it has tripled since the 1990s (Agervold, 2007; Chamberlin, Novotney, Packard & Price, 2008). This is ascribed to the demands, in the 21st century, of work focussed on high performance, organisational re-design, re-structuring, re-engineering, alignment and sustainability, which formed a new breeding ground for systemic bullying (Meyers, 2006b). The international prevalence and impact of bullying came to the fore when the US President, Barack Obama, addressed the American Psychological Association (APA) at the White House Bullying Conference on 10 March 2011 (Munsey, 2011). He strongly supported the prevention of and intervention into bullying as ways to secure hope for victims of bullying.

The literature on bullying before 2000 tended to describe it in a linear manner as learned and socially reinforced behaviour, manifesting itself as a deliberate intent to cause physical and or psychological distress, through the aggressive exercise and misuse of power for psychological gratification at the expense of the other (Agervold, 2007; Marais & Herman, 1997; Randall, 1997). The bully is described as an individual in an elevated hierarchical position such as a supervisor, manager or leader, alternatively the bully is represented as a group. The victim is also described as an individual or a group. The bully's behaviour is interpreted as an acting out of his or her low self-esteem, frustrated growth needs or hostility, as opposed to their complementary behaviour of friendliness. This behaviour manifests itself as physical, mental, emotional and/or verbal abuse, for example, irrational, unacceptable, disrespectful, offensive, humiliating and intimidating behaviour towards the victim, that often occurs in front of others. This includes shouting, using bad language, and disrupting the victims' work life and workflow. The intended result is to render the victim powerless, ridiculed and incompetent, and to strip them of self-esteem and self-confidence (Bassman, 1992; Marais & Herman, 1997; Randall, 1997). The literature on the personality traits of the bully is vast (Adams, 2000), although relatively little is published on the behaviour of the victim.

A relatively new dynamic discourse on organisational bullying refers to the power relations between the bully and the victim (Martin, 2000; Meyers, 2006a; 2006b; Rayner, 1999; Rayner, Hoel & Cooper, 2002). This discourse researches the dark side of leadership (Blase & Blase, 2002), by either framing the relationship as two independent parts (Adams, 2000; Archer, 1999), or studying the parts as a systemic whole (University of London, 2011; Rayner, Hoel & Cooper, 2002; White, 2004). The last-mentioned research follows the systems psychodynamic tradition that suggests that bullying represents a complex interconnectedness between different objects, which is acted out by the bully and contained by the victim, both in their organisational roles. This bullying takes place in an organisational culture and climate filled with emotional toxicity (Fox & Spector, 2005). The underlying assumption is that employees unconsciously act out larger organisational systemic issues. The evidence suggests that bullying can be institutionalised and that the phenomenon needs to be understood as a representation of organisational culture.

The systems psychodynamic perspective, that is mentioned, studies the extraordinary and sometimes seemingly odd and out-of-place behaviour in the organisation, and also its meaning and deep motives, wherein anxiety leads to the blurring of boundaries between the rational and irrational (Lawrence, 1999; Sievers, 2009; Vansina & Vansina-Cobbaert, 2008). This is the behaviour that normally hurts the system (individual, team or larger parts of the organisation) which may lie in the nature of the (unconscious) group dynamics and in the organisational factors such as culture, structure, processes and systems which could create conditions in which bullying is fostered. This focus provides clues with which to understand the underlying and unconscious anxieties which are theoretically informed by the manifesting defences, power relationships, envy, collusion, transitional space, transference and counter-transference (Armstrong, 2005; Gould, Stapley & Stein, 2001; 2004). This perspective and its research outcomes have added to the understanding of bullying in education. On the other hand, relatively little research has been undertaken on the experiences of victims of bullying in organisations (Stapley, 2006; White, 2004). No related South African research could be traced.

The purpose of this research was to describe organisational bullying experiences from the system psychodynamic perspective. In instances where individual psychology framed bullying as a problem with one person's misbehaviour, the systemic perspective is interested in how the whole organisation is involved, and how the system's dynamics play out between the bully and the victim in their relationships and relatedness.

The systems psychodynamic literature describes bullying as a macro-systemic competition for power, privilege and status played out as an interpersonal and intergroup behavioural dynamic (on the meso level) between a bully and a victim, with valences to become involved in a process of testing and matching power against others to establish, enhance and protect a place in a system (Rayner, Hoel & Cooper, 2002; White, 1999). The destructive nature of the bullying system causes high levels of anxiety in the organisation, which is defended against through a complex splitting dynamic between attachment – detachment, inclusion – exclusion and acceptance – repulsion (Stapley, 1996; 2006).

The defensive process entails the following:

1. Splitting
2. Denial
3. Projection
4. Projective identification

Splitting. This is a defence against persecutory anxiety, which manifests itself when the system experiences performance anxiety and fear of failure (Sievers, 2009), that often results in shame (Lewis, 2004; Mollon, 2004). Anxiety is reduced by differentiating between good and bad parts of the self (Stapley, 2006).

Denial. This is a defence against the bad parts in the self or an external danger (Freud, 1921) that functions by disowning the bad part of the experience by using the fantasy, that it no longer exists. Anxiety is reduced only temporarily because in reality the so-called bad remains part of the system's unconscious (Stapley, 1996).

Projection. Following on splitting and denial, projection refers to the ejection of the unwanted or disowned parts, feelings, behaviours and experiences inherent in the system's unconscious, *onto* another object, and then the projector imagines that the part belongs to the other (Huffington, Armstrong, Halton, Hoyle & Pooley, 2004).

Projective identification. Following on from projection onto an object, this is a defence of projecting the disowned parts *into* the other. The projector's unwanted parts enter the other's psychic system, leading to the recipient's identification with the thoughts, feelings and behaviour of these parts that are perceived by the projector as belonging to the recipient. Thus the behaviour of the receiver is altered according to the needs of the projector (Campbell & Huffington, 2008; Stapley, 2006).

Bully Dynamics

The bully's dynamics manifest themselves as masochism, sadism, narcissism, rivalry and envy (Gaitanidis, 2007; Kets de Vries, 2006; 2007; Rayner, Hoel & Cooper, 2002; Sandler, Person & Fonagy, 2004; Schwartz, 1990). The bully's position, as the receiver of hostility in the masochistic position from parents, formed the grounds for him or her to become the bully in the sadistic position. In masochism, the individual is not satisfied unless the pattern of being hurt is repeated. On the unconscious and irrational levels the individual experiences satisfaction in the realisation that they deserve to be treated badly. In sadism the impression is that no matter what the child did wrong, in the parent's eyes they were always loved. Thus, children learned that they were the centre of the world, accepted by all and successful. From this position the need develops to control others and make them subservient. This implies a fusion in the mind of the phenomenal role (how others see the individual) with the experiential role (how the individual sees the self) (Obholzer & Roberts, 1994). Narcissism leads to the projection of anger onto the other who does not comply in his or her own drama around competition for acceptance (Gaitanidis, 2007). The individual feels threatened by any real or imagined opposition for popularity and acceptance which sparks dynamics of envy (Huffington, et al., 2004). This insecurity, which they experience about their own competence, is projected onto and into their perceived rivals, who are then used to contain the psychic material on their behalf (Adams, 2000).

Although bullies exhibit psychopathic tendencies, they are not classified as such (Babiak & Hare, 2006). The profile of the organisational bully excludes the qualities of the aggressive psychopath (being totally egocentric and almost beyond help), but includes those of the creative psychopath (being successful in work, interpersonal relationships and with some capacity for emotional involvement). Bullies are unable to realise the effect of their actions on others, do not see the self as others do, and do not realise that others may think differently to them. It may be hypothesised that they do not have access to their phenomenal role or projections onto them (Obholzer & Roberts, 1994). Their narcissism manifests itself as self-righteousness, making them immune against guilt if they hurt others, and not take responsibility for their own thoughts and actions (Speziale-Bagliacca, 2004). The driving force is the desire to have one's needs met at all times and in all circumstances (Schwartz, 1990).

Victim Dynamics

The victim dynamic is embedded in childhood (White, 2004). The residual experiences of childhood psychological aggression, are repeated in adulthood. The aggression is experienced as hurt and humiliation, ranging from overt outbursts of anger to covert and subtle hostility, for example where one child is preferred above the other (White, 1999; 2004). The individual develops a valence to take on the role of emotional victim by picking up the weaknesses of the other and become influenced by them. These weaknesses remind the individual of their parents' traits and a repetition compulsion follows (Blackman, 2004). The buried injustices carried from the past, erupt in the present, placing victims in a double bind with their out-of-control dynamics.

On the one hand, victims experience being filled up with the bully's projected feelings of worthlessness, incompetence, self-doubt, powerlessness, despair and even that they need to be treated badly as evidence of a form of inner madness (Kets de Vries, 2006). On the other hand, victims experience their own and more real feelings of rage, anger, bewilderment, shock and disbelief about what is happening to them, followed by self-blame (White, 2001). The victims become preoccupied with revenge and whishing the bully away. Flight (silence, turning the aggression in on the self, sucking up, resentment, quitting, hoping the situation will pass) and fight (fear, anger, confrontation, whistle-blowing, grievance procedures) are the victim's coping options (Cytrynbaum & Noumair, 2004). Unfortunately, both methods represent a sense of failure and enforce the double bind (Schwartz, 1990). The victim's control of their resulting anger leads to inhibition, lethargy, paralysis, hopelessness and depression (White, 2004). Victims generally receive limited systemic support – colleagues tend to pacify rather than take action. The fantasy is that appeasing the bully will cease the attack, whereas, in reality this response increases the likelihood of more attacks (White, 2001).

Systemic Dynamics

In their unconscious search for recognition and containing relationships, both bully and victim do not realise the futility of their behaviour – they are searching for the same thing (Adams, 2000; Lawrence, 1999). As a result, these behaviours manifest themselves as a cycle of conflict. White (2001; 2004) refers to this cycle as mirroring the patterns of a biological life cycle from embryo to death and back to the embryonic (University of London; 2011), manifesting as follows:

1. the embryonic stage;
2. the trigger;
3. loyalty; and
4. dance of death.

The Embryonic Stage

Before the bullying starts, there is a potential (embryonic) bully and a potential (embryonic) victim – both are vulnerable in their unfulfilled need for recognition. Within specific dynamic environmental conditions, both develop into their predestined and entrapped roles in the bullying relationship, idealising their need for control, domination and recognition. The victim experiences independence of mind as loneliness and then seeks recognition through subservience and submission.

The Trigger

Both embryonic objects are awakened by a triggering event in the system which causes frustration, unhappiness, envy and hate. The bully's loss of control and frustration is exaggerated into thoughts of impending crises and overwhelming anxiety. As a means of psychic defence, the bully splits the experience into a good – bad relationship, which Adams (2000) refers to as Jekyll and Hyde. Bullies need a container for their anxiety and target various objects to test their ability to contain the anxiety, for example a vulnerable colleague with a valence for recognition seeking. Once identified, the attack begins. Consciously the victim may be set up to fail (through criticism, exclusion, or denying him or her information). Unconsciously, the bully's split-off undesirable parts are projected onto and into the victim, to the extent that the victim feels the pain on the bully's behalf.

Loyalty

The victim's strong need for recognition leads to their use of loyalty as a defence against the attack (Oade, 2009) in the fantasy that their boundaries will thus be restored. This implies a persistent effort to please the bully and deny the reality. In an attempt to possess the seemingly good object, the victim starts to idealise the bully.

Dance of Death

The bully and the victim are psychically intertwined as if in a frenetic and parasitic dance (White, 2004). The exhausted victim gives up his or her idealisation and experiences the bully as persecutory. As their interpersonal boundaries blur, their identities become intertwined and the bully now experiences the victim as persecutory. The bully introjects innocence, projects guilt into the victim who identifies with the projection and starts blaming the self for the bullying. Thus the bully has successfully isolated the victim who now contains the bad and incompetent projections.

Although the bully may seem to cope well, the constant repression of guilt and shame (Lewis, 2004) brings feelings of psychic deadness, and further splitting between good and bad as a continuing defence (Speziale-Bagliacca, 2004). The bully's unsuccessful effort to be relieved of the self-hatred causes a repetition compulsion to find another victim. White (2004) showed how these feelings may manifest themselves in depression and even suicidal tendencies. Victims experience a loss of identity (White, 1999) and without psychological support they may fall into a post-traumatic cycle of reliving the experiences. White

(2004) mentioned that bullies may continue the fight because of the previous successful bullying experience and thus bully and victim are trapped in the repetition compulsion.

The prevailing literature on organisational bullying points to various contextually determined and socio-technical actions towards breaking the above cycle and to establish firm boundaries and contain anxiety (Cytrynbaum & Noumair, 2004). The technical inputs, mentioned in the literature, refer to structural changes, role re-defining and job re-analysis. The socio-inputs refer, on the macro level, to interventions by senior management, providing a reflective space for all involved colleagues, efforts to understand the manifesting group dynamics by involving the collective and psychological health and safety programmes; and on the micro level they refer to counselling, giving positive feedback, taking a holiday and meditation (Randall, 1997; White, 2004).

The research problem was formulated as follows: how do the above characteristics of bullying, and their cycle, manifest themselves in the experiences of employees being bullied by their managers? The objective was to describe the victim's experiences of their own behaviour, the bully's behaviour, as well as the organisational system's involvement.

The potential value contributed by this research was to add to the systemic knowledge about bullying as experienced by the victim, instead of simplifying bullying to a random and individual activity performed by an angry person, who is often out of control and who needs to be tolerated until he or she feels different.

The rest of the article is structured as follows: the research design is presented with reference to the research approach, and strategy. This is followed by the research method consisting of the setting, roles of the researcher, sampling method, data collection, recording and analysis. Lastly, the strategies employed, to ensure quality data, are mentioned. Thereafter the findings are presented in three themes. In the discussion the findings were integrated within the research hypothesis, which were followed by the conclusion, recommendations, limitations and suggestions for further research.

Research Design

Research Approach

A qualitative and descriptive research approach was chosen (De Vos, Strydom, Fouché & Delport, 2002) in order to study the manifestation of bullying as a behavioural phenomenon, thus answering the *how* and *why* questions of the experience in a thick description. Hermeneutics was chosen as the research paradigm (Terre Blanche, Durrheim & Painter, 2006) applied towards the interpretation of bullying experiences, and double hermeneutics (Clarke & Hoggett, 2009) was applied towards interpreting the data from the systems psychodynamic stance and to develop knowledge.

Research Strategy

Case studies (Chamberlayne, Bornat & Apitzsch, 2004) were used to empirically investigate the phenomenon of bullying in a real-life context. This strategy allowed for a detailed examination of the manifesting behaviours involving multiple sources of information that are rich in the research context (Creswell, 2003). Cases were seen as intrinsic (providing an understanding of the behaviour for the interest of the researcher and the organisation) and as instrumental (towards developing knowledge) (Denzin & Lincoln, 2005).

Research Method

Research Setting

The research was set within various organisations and focussed on individuals who had experienced being bullied by their immediate line managers.

Entrée and Establishing Researcher Roles

The researcher took up the roles of systems psychodynamic interviewer (Alvesson & Sköldberg, 2010) and analysand (Schafer, 2003), using the self as instrument (Watts, 2009). He is a psychologist with training and experience in this methodology and fulfilled the requirements for this role as stipulated by Brunner, Nutkevitch and Sher (2006).

Sampling

Convenient (Breverton & Millward, 2004) or opportunistic sampling (Terre Blanche, Durrheim & Painter, 2006) was used. The first two participants contacted the researcher with the request to speak to a psychologist about their experiences with their 'difficult bosses' and to find out what they should do about their situations. Through them, another three participants come to the fore. The last participant approached the researcher at a conference. The six participants included two academics (both were White, one male and one female), one Afrikaans Church minister (a White male), and three senior managers (a White male from a bank and two Black females, one from a private hospital and the other from a government department).

Data Collection Method

For each participant, a 90 minute interview was scheduled in a boardroom in their organisations. Free association narrative interviewing (FANI) was used (Boydell, in Clarke & Hoggett, 2009), based on four principles (Holloway & Jefferson, 2010): firstly, only using open ended questions; secondly, eliciting stories towards analysing the unconscious processes of transference, projection and projective identification; thirdly, avoiding clichéd, counter intuitive why – questions thereby avoiding explanations about facts; and fourthly, using the participants' ordering and phrasing which demands careful listening, and follow-up questions without offering interpretations and imposing structure onto the story. The aim of the interview was to understand the relationship between the participant and his or her line manager, and it started with the invitation to 'tell me about your relationship with your manager'. The method allows participants to structure the interview and its content whilst moving between the paranoid-schizoid (the splitting of the object) and the depressive positions (the good parts being preserved in the self) (Holloway & Jefferson, 2010). Included in the interview method is the notion of the defended subject (Clarke & Hoggett, 2009) which acknowledges the unconscious merging of identities between interviewer and participant.

Recording of Data

Following Hinshelwood and Skogstad's (2005) guidelines, each participant's interview narrative was tape recorded, followed immediately afterwards with the researcher making notes on the interview process, and his subjective experiences during and after the interview. The data was typed and kept securely.

Data Analysis

Two complementary approaches were used, namely, discursive psychology and psychodynamically informed discourse analysis (Boydell, in Clarke & Hoggett, 2009). Simple hermeneutics was used to interpret the discursive data and double hermeneutics to interpret the systems psychodynamic behaviour (Alvesson & Sköldberg, 2010). Firstly, single cases were analysed to stay close to its surprising elements before, secondly, moving to cross-case analysis and the emergence of themes (Holloway & Jefferson, 2010).

Strategies Employed to Ensure Quality Data

At the start of each interview, the aim of the project, the method of interviewing, the tape recording, manner of interpretation, and the confidential treatment of the data were explained (Terre Blanche, et al., 2006). All six participants gave their informed consent to the research.

Ethicality, in the interviews, refers to concern, care and respect for the participants and their thoughts and feelings about their personal (and sometimes contentious) and work-related issues, as well as their responsibility towards scientific data interpretation (Holloway & Jefferson, 2010). Clarke and Hoggett (2009) mentioned the impact of the defended subject and the defended researcher. Because both participant and researcher were anxious about the content and its implications, the researcher needed to consider his own emotional responses to each participant and to not let parts of one merge with the other. It was therefore important to suspend memory, desire and judgement during the interviews (Cytrynbaum & Noumair, 2004).

The notion of trustworthiness was based on credibility and validity (Denzin & Lincoln, 2005). Credibility was assured in terms of the competence of the researcher in systems psychodynamic research. The study evidenced strong and believable validity in its in-depth (psychological) description, which revealed the complexities of the manifesting themes.

The interpretations were peer reviewed (Brewerton & Milward, 2004; Camic, Rhodes & Yardley, 2003). Two independent psychologists, to whom the theoretical model is well known, were asked to investigate the dependability of the findings (which were found to be positive). Both peer reviewers agreed that the data reached a point of saturation and were responsibly interpreted according to the above strategy and method.

Reporting

The research findings were reported per manifesting theme. In the discussion, the themes were interpreted and a hypothesis formulated for bullying as an organisational phenomenon, for the bully and for the victim. This was followed by the conclusions, recommendations and limitations.

Findings

Three themes manifested themselves, namely, snakes and hyenas, a complex interconnected dyad, and the institutionalisation of bullying.

Snakes and Hyenas

The managers' behaviour corresponded to what Babiak and Hare (2006) referred to as *snakes in suits* and Marais and Herman (1997) as *hyenas at work*. Intrapersonally they exhibited high levels of 'irritation and/or frustration' and 'lots of anger'. Participants described their behaviour as 'you could see the anger in his eyes', 'he looked quite scary', 'he acted like a schoolboy and/or a *prima donna*'. Interpersonally the managers acted with high levels of insensitivity and hostility, and violated the other's personal boundaries as if 'he wanted to dominate' and 'control me' – 'he always had to be right' and 'have the last word'. Participants reported how they were being 'humiliated', 'shouted at', 'in my own office' and 'in meetings', 'blamed for things that went wrong' in aspects 'that [were] not even my job'. Then they started to feel 'bad about things' – 'I was not quite sure about what' or 'why'.

A Complex Interconnected Dyad

Participants' stories gave significant evidence of the cycle of conflict as proposed by White (2004).

The embryonic stage was described as 'like a pregnancy' which 'I only realised the impact of much later' when 'the thing was beyond return'. Participants reported that before the bullying started, they received accolades and prizes for exceptional performance, which the manager congratulated them for in public. At that time they were not suspicious at all, but in hindsight, they started to 'put 2 and 2 together' and realised that the 'air was brewing with something'.

Triggers were described as 'related to technical issues' such as the 're-design of the department', introducing a 'fairly large change in the committee's work' and/or based on relational aspects, such as 'the employment of a new colleague', the choosing of a new departmental representative and 'when I asked for being [sic] relieved from a specific divisional task'. Participants described how a supposedly 'emotional non-event' turned into their managers' 'losing it', and 'exploding in a fit of rage'. The evidence suggested that managers were threatened by participants' competence, mostly in maintaining good relationships. The managers responded either covertly by 'subtly isolating' and 'excusing' participants 'from a new committee', 'a tea room conversation', or by 'denying my inputs in a standard report', or overtly by 'attacking me out of nowhere', 'completely by surprise' which 'left me speechless'– 'he just went berserk'. After the trigger event, participants felt 'amazed' and 'bewildered' – 'I constantly asked myself, what happened here'. They reported feeling 'violated', but 'unable to feel anything else', such as frustration, anger or hurt. Two participants reported seeing the manager afterwards 'just going on as if nothing happened', 'joking with others', and 'not perturbed by his behaviour'. They called this not knowing whether he is Dr Jekyll or Mr Hyde (Adams, 2000). Next, participants experienced overwhelming fear of 'him repeating the outburst', 'me being humiliated again' and 'being overlooked in a meeting again'.

After most attacks participants were 'left on my own' by the manager as well as colleagues which 'was perhaps the worst, they just turned away and went on as of [sic] nothing happened'. Participants reported on their surprise and bewilderment at the attacks, as well as their powerlessness to defend themselves ('I could not think of anything to say'; 'I am a good person', 'wanting to do good', 'progress in my career' and 'I like to work here').

Participants reported being unaware of other colleagues being targeted in the same way. 'It was as if she only singled me out'. One participant remembered that someone else was treated badly some time ago ('humiliated in front of us all') but 'nothing came from that – now I'm not surprised'.

In terms of their interpersonal relationships, participants shared the following. 'I had to get away', 'take a walk', and 'sit in a quiet place' to 'regain my sanity'. Their colleagues who witnessed the attack acted by ignoring the event and the impact – they 'just went on as if nothing happened'. It was as if they 'conveniently forgot' about 'what was so shocking to me'. It was as if 'no-one remembered or cared about what she did'. Some participants voiced their experiences to other colleagues, friends and family who were seemingly shocked, and then they started to defend their inability to help, in their own different ways. For example, they challenged the participant ('what are you going to do about this'), blamed ('she told me I am to be blamed because I was looking for trouble' – which 'felt like a double humiliation' and 'salt in the wound'), and defended the manager (with reference to his or her stress and difficulties). Two participants reported the triggering event to a senior manager – they were told 'to forget the incident', that 'I was overreacting' and 'oversensitive'.

Responses by colleagues and even friends made participants realise that they will 'not be supported by anyone' – even 'those who were present' and 'heard everything'. Participants reported their realisation that they needed to 'pull myself together', and 'move forward'. In hindsight, they realised that they colluded with the systems defences, 'denied the issue' and 'turned it into support' for the organisation. Thus, in looking for help, they turned towards people who were loyal to the system and even the manager. In hindsight participants reflected on their 'fear of another *klap* (smack)' and as a defence, they started to 'think positive thoughts' about the manager. They reported trying to 'put myself in his shoes' to understand what happened with them – 'now I find that bizarre'.

Finally, participants reported their exhaustion, 'being worn down', confusion, isolation, hopelessness and worthlessness. They reported reliving the experiences regularly and vividly, and that their minds 'just keep going round and round'. They felt trapped as if 'I can't move to the left or the right'. Another reported feeling as if 'I have lost parts of myself' and another felt 'unsure of what is expected of me'. They reported being ignored by their manager, feeling disappointed and guilty but not knowing 'what I did wrong'. One said that she should have tried harder to please the manager and repair the relationship. Some reported feeling incompetent in their work as if they had been stripped of their worth. Participants reported the persistence of the behaviours – it happened 'again and again' even after 'I have reported him to his manager'. 'He stayed so mad for a long time over something so small'. One participant reported that the manager made an appointment to talk about the incidents, but 'he was just trying to tell me that it was not as bad as I thought'.

Participants reported that their manager 'was cashing in on the poor relationship' as if he 'knew it was bad' and 'fragile', and that 'he could just keep going at me'. It was as if the participant's fragility 'was exploited further'. One participant referred specifically to the relationship 'spinning round and round' which is reminiscent of compulsivity.

Another participant showed signs of an inability to re-establish his individual identity and another showed acute signs of learned helplessness – as if 'I just can't get myself out of this thing'. It was suggested that this individual receive therapy.

Linking with White's (2004) suggestion about the bully's emotional position, participants shared how they started to see 'cracks' in the manager's behaviour which they framed as 'I hope it is his guilt', 'I hope he feels ashamed' and 'no person can get (emotionally) away with this'.

The Institutionalisation of Bullying

The evidence suggested a similarity in all the represented organisations. Participants referred to how their management (the manager and his or her next higher level) 'drive performance hard'. Participants were often not sure of the criteria for success and succession, and there was either no performance management system or the existing one was non-effective and/or not trusted. Management was described as lacking 'care' and 'respect for people'. The climate was described as 'sometimes threatening' and 'strangely toxic' – colleagues preferred to work on their own or in very small groups. Trust in management was limited and people's experience of meaning was 'in doing it yourself'. Administrative support was limited, fluctuating and not dependable. Managers' criteria for reward and persecution were inconsistent as if there was a new 'favourite person every month'. It seemed that management injected anxiety into the system which left the participants' colleagues de-authorised and with a sense of not being productive. All five of the diagnostic criteria for organisational bullying mentioned by Fox and Spector (2005) manifested themselves in the findings. These were the enactment of:

1. intra,
2. interpersonal bullying behaviour;
3. victims experienced high levels of anxiety and emotional damage;
4. victims labelled themselves as bullied and acted as emotional containers; and
5. experienced difficulty defending the self against the strong and unconscious attack.

Discussion

The purpose of the research was to describe organisational bullying experiences from the system psychodynamic perspective.

The research was important for its rich illustration of bullying as not only an individual psychological phenomenon about the bully and his or her one-way destructive behaviour but rather a complex, systemic phenomenon involving the interpersonal relationship between bully and victim as well as the organisational culture and climate.

Theme 1 illustrated the bullies' neurotic and narcissistic defensive structures (Gaitanidis, 2007) played out in their relationships with the victims. Building on their individual neurotic need for recognition, the bullies used their valence to introject the system's performance anxiety and fear of failure, to avoid shame and persecutory anxiety (Lewis, 2004; White, 2001). Their narcissism and survival anxiety lead to them taking control of their relationships with the victims. This they did by splitting objects as all good or all bad. The unwanted and bad in the self was denied and projected onto another psychologically willing object in the belief that these belong to the other (Klein, 2005). According to Freud (1921) this process can be so effective that the bully lives as if these bad parts no longer exist. This was carried out to impress the authority in the bullies' mind (Hirschhorn, 1997), which becomes a projection of dependence onto their *good* colleagues and leaders in the system. The bullies experience a sense of triumph from having exported the bad and are left all good and the hero in the minds of their significant other. But, because in reality the bad remains part of the system's unconscious (Stapley, 1996; 2006), their defences are only temporarily effective – when the anxiety returned, the next outburst took place.

The bullies' script became a hysterical and egocentric modification of character to externalise the pain. The projections were performed in a powerful, hostile, domineering and alienating manner (Czander, 1993). Interpersonally, the victims were now dragged into the bullies' control drama as targets for the strong and aggressive projections, which resulted in their identification with the projection (Campbell, 2007; Klein, 2005). The bullies' effective *cleansing* of their own unwanted parts and placing these in the victims' psychic system as containers, changed their thinking, feeling and acting behaviour as if it belonged to their victims (Stapley, 2006).

Theme 2 illustrated the complex and unconsciously interconnected dyad between bully and victim in line with White's (2001; 2004) cycle theory of bullying.

In stage 1, the system prepared itself for an eruption. The bullies were stroking (James, 1977) their victims with positive feedback, and hooking them into a comfortable and loyal position (Campbell & Groenbaek, 2006) based on their need for recognition. The bullies' suppressed need for recognition was orchestrating the build-up towards the triggering event.

In Stage 2, the bullies turned a usual, conscious and rational transaction into an unconsciously planned argument, and anxiety-provoking testing ground for the victims' readiness to become their strong (maybe resilient) container for their anxiety. The bullies' suppressed feelings of anger erupted into envious attacks (Kets de Vries, 2006). They now effectively split and projected their undesirable experiences, their inner sense of being out of control and their incompetence to deal with these things, onto their victims. The unconsciously selected victims with their own dynamics for serving others were offered a way of satisfying their need for recognition. It was as if the proposition was attractive on some level, albeit it was powerful, hostile and humiliating. These victims identified with the projections and now carried the bullies' badness and they also carried the characteristics of the triggering moment, namely the bullies' lack of control, incompetence, isolation, confusion and amazement (Armstrong, 2005; Huffington, et al., 2004).

In stage 3, the bullies were in control of the bully-victim dyad. They had emotionally entered the victims' emotional boundary (Lawrence, 1999), isolated them from their own experiences and their support from others. In this complex knot (White, 2004) the victims became the bullies' loyal psychic container – almost property. The victims' behaviour was interpreted as their irrational seeking for recognition and love from authority figures (possibly as a compensation for not experiencing love and establishing firm boundaries during childhood) (Oade, 2009; Strandmark & Hallberg, 2007). Some victims continued to please the bully as if their desired acceptance for authority overshadowed the harsh reality of being abused. This strong unconscious need to stay loyal in spite of pain was interpreted as their counter-transference onto a significant person in authority who abused them (Klein, 2005).

Also, the victims introjected the seemingly good object by idealising the bullies. The victims' obsession with boundaries (Lawrence, 1999) was interpreted as their seeking for protection which resembled a post-traumatic experience (Kets de Vries, 2007; White, 2004). Their denial of the reality and their *defence on a defence* was interpreted as their idealisation of the bullies as objects of authority and as an effort to introject the fantasised good object (Glasø, Matthiesen, Nielsen & Einarsen, 2007). The victim's experiences of their colleagues were filled with bewilderment and amazement. It was hypothesised that their colleagues used their own defences to avoid involvement in dealing with the bullying, which indicated that they were already involved, albeit through defences such as denial and suppression (Oade, 2007).

In stage 4, the boundaries between bullies and victims were obliterated (Lawrence, 1999) – psychically intertwined to the extent of confused identities, and trapped in a frenetic and parasitic dance (White, 2004). The bullies, as the aggressors in the strange dyad, seemed to have experienced themselves as innocent and projected their guilt effectively into the victims. The victims illustrated how the second-order projective identification (White, 2004) lead to their blaming themselves for the bullying, based on feelings of worthlessness. They were effectively isolated and felt incompetent by accepting the bullies' description of them (Campbell, 2007). They seemed to have given their sense of self over to the bully.

One victim appeared quite vulnerable and damaged with no sense of support from any colleague or family. The suggestion of resilience therapy for this individual seemed in order (Sheehan, 1999; Sheehan & Barker, 1999). It was hoped that the victims would learn to be more suspicious towards positive feedback by becoming more conscious of the hostile edge of stroking (James, 1977). Although the bullies appeared to be coping well in the eyes of the victims, the evidence in the stories suggested that they were experiencing persecutory anxiety through fear of being reported or caught out (Speziale-Bagliacca, 2004).

Theme 3 illustrated that bullying triggers could not be explained as a simple cause and effect relationship – it seemed to be characterised by multiple causalities in the micro (individual), meso (collegial) and macro-systems (Hutchinson, Vickers, Jackson & Wilkens, 2006; Oade, 2009). The evidence suggested that bullying was institutionalised in these organisations in the presence of a valence towards fostering emotional abuse (Archer, 1999; Bain, 1998; Koonin & Green, 2004; Lewis, 2006) and post-traumatic stress disorder (Matthiesen & Einarsen, 2004). Using Fox and Spector's (2005) five criteria, the data confirmed the manifestation of organisational bullying. The findings suggested a sixth criterion of such bullying, namely an exceptionally negative, toxic and demoralising climate infiltrating work structures and processes (Fox & Spector, 2005; Salin, 2003). This was characterised by:

- high levels of performance and prosecutor anxiety and fear of failure (Lipgar & Pines, 2003).
- breeding violence just below the surface, called paranoia-genesis (Gould, Stapley & Stein, 2001; 2004).
- this violence being projected by the manager onto colleagues whilst distancing the self from the same rules in an entitled manner (Campbell, 2007).
- the splitting of ideas (between good and bad) (Klein, 2005).
- power and people separated into friend – versus – enemy camps where individuals experience isolation and their bad parts situated within the other, who then becomes the enemy and the receiver of the unwanted projections (Duffy & Sperry, 2007).
- selected over-authorisation of some and de-authorisation of others.
- a silo mentality (Diamond & Allcorn, 2009).
- a traumatised me-ness (Morgan-Jones, 2010).
- a denial of what is going on by the organisational system (Ferris, 2004).
- a lack of formal motivational, incentive or reward systems where workload is experienced as non-equal and performance standards are kept ambiguous (Hauge, Skogstad & Einarsen, 2007; Rayner, Hoel & Cooper, 2002).

This sixth criterion resembles the description of the paranoid-schizoid organisation (Diamond & Allcorn, 2009) (the avoidance of personal accountability), the perverse state of mind (Sievers, 2009) (primary narcissism with individual need satisfaction at the expense of others) and the opposite of the authentizotic organisation (Kets de Vries, 2006) (characterised by trust, reliance, connectivity, a sense of flow, wholeness, appreciation, recognition, effectiveness, competence, autonomy and creativity).

The research hypothesis was formulated for bullying as an organisational phenomenon, for the bully and for the victim:

- ∞ **Hypothesis 1**. Organisational bullying acts as a powerful organisational embryonic domain phenomenon, erupting out of the organisational fabric in the presence of persecutory anxiety in the climate, intergroup and interpersonal behaviour, that thus causes psychological damage to the system.

- ∞ **Hypothesis 2**. Bullies defend against their personal anxieties concerning recognition by splitting good and bad, introjecting the good and sadistically projecting the bad onto and into another object with a specific valence, in the fantasy (which becomes the reality) that they will contain, hold and transform the content on behalf of the system.

- ∞ **Hypothesis 3**. Victims of bullying act from their valence for recognition seeking, masochistically offering themselves to identify with the projections of bullies around badness, and contain these on behalf of the organisational system.

It was concluded that below the surface, bullying consists of the very specific, complex and dynamic interpersonal and organisational dynamics of splitting and projective identification, thus containing the organisational pain in different objects where it does not belong.

It was recommended that organisational psychologists, consultants, coaches and counsellors should take notice of bullying as an organisational and dynamic domain phenomenon on the macro level, manifesting in specific roles taken up in an unconsciously structured drama.

The limitations were formulated with reference to the method and the findings. The method of data gathering allowed participants to structure the interview which could have excluded specific important data. The method also included the notion of the defended subject. Although the researcher tried to remain aware of the mutual unconscious influences between the self and participant, it will remain unclear how this aspect influenced the data (Clarke & Hoggett, 2009).

It was suggested that future research focuses on the refinement of the hypothesis especially about the organisation's valance for breeding bullying as a systemic defence. Also, that identified bullies are used as defended subjects, possibly each with an identified victim.

Acknowledgements

Competing Interests

The author declares that he has no financial or personal relationship(s) which may have inappropriately influenced him in writing this paper.

References

Adams, A. (2000). *Bullying at work. How to confront and overcome it.* London: Virago.

Agervold. M. (2007). Bullying at work. A discussion of definitions and prevalence, based on an empirical study. *Scandinavian Journal of Psychology*, 48:161-172. https://doi.org/10.1111/j.1467-9450.2007.00585.x

Alvesson, M. & Skoldberg, K. (2010). *Reflexive methodology. New vistas for qualitative research.* London: Sage.

Archer, D. (1999). Exploring "bullying" culture in the para-military organisation. *International Journal of Manpower*, 20(1/2):94-105. https://doi.org/10.1108/01437729910268687

Armstrong, D. (2005). *Organisation in the mind. Psychoanalysis, group relations and organisational consultancy.* London: Karnac.

Babiak, P., & Hare, R. (2006). *Snakes in suits. When psychopaths go to work.* New York: Harper Collins.

Bassman, E.S. (1992). *Abuse in the workplace.* London: Management.

Bain, A. (1998). Social defences against organisational learning. *Human Relations*, 51(3):413-429. https://doi.org/10.1177/001872679805100309

Beeld. (2010). Boelies soek na werk mag. *Beeld*, 13 October, p.3.

Blackman, J.S. (2004). *101 Defences. How the mind shields itself.* New York: Brunner-Routledge. https://doi.org/10.4324/9780203492369

Blase, J. & Blase, J. (2002). The dark side of leadership: Teacher perspectives of principal mistreatment. *Educational Administration Quarterly*, 38(5):671-727. https://doi.org/10.1177/0013161X02239643

Boydell, L. (2009). *Analysing discourse psycho-socially. In: S. Clarke & P. Hoggett. Researching beneath the surface*, pp.241-266. London: Karnac. https://doi.org/10.4324/9780429479564-11

Breverton, P. & Millward, L. (2004). *Organisational research methods. A guide for students and researchers.* London: Sage.

Brunner, L.D.; Nutkevitch, A. & Sher, M. (2006). *Group relations conferences. Reviewing and exploring theory, design, role-taking and application.* London: Karnac.

Camic, P.M.; Rhodes, J.E. & Yardley, L. (2003). *Qualitative research in Psychology.* Washington: APA.

Campbell, D. (2007). *The socially constructed organisation.* London: Karnac.

Campbell, D. & Groenbaek, M. (2006). *Taking positions in the organisation.* London: Karnac.

Campbell, D. & Huffington, C. (2008). *Organisations connected. A handbook of systemic consultation.* London: Karnac.

Cemalogly, N. (2007). The exposure of primary school teachers to bullying: An analysis of various variables. *Social Behaviour and Personality*, 35(6):789-801. https://doi.org/10.2224/sbp.2007.35.6.789

Chamberlayne, P.; Bornat, J. & Apitzsch, U. (2004). *Biographical methods and professional practice. An international perspective.* Bristol: Policy Press. https://doi.org/10.1332/policypress/9781861344939.001.0001

Chamberlin, J.; Novotney, A.; Packard, E. & Price, M. (2008). Enhancing worker well-being. *Monitor on Psychology*, 39(5):26-29.

Clarke, S. & Hoggett, P. (2009). *Researching beneath the surface. Psycho-social research methods in practice.* London Karnac.

Crawford, N. (1999). Conundrums and confusion in organisations: The etymology of the word "bully". *International Journal of Manpower*, 20(1/2):86-93. https://doi.org/10.1108/01437729910268678

Creswell, J.W. (2003). *Research design: Qualitative, quantitative and mixed methods.* London: Sage.

Cytrynbaum, S. & Noumair, A. (2004). *Group dynamics, organizational irrationality, and social complexity: Group relations reader 3.* Jupiter: A.K. Rice.

Czander, W.M. (1993). *The psychodynamics of work and organizations.* New York: Guilford.

De Vos, A.S.; Strydom, H.; Fouche, C.B. & Delport, C.S.L. (2002). *Research at grass roots. For the social sciences and human service professions.* Pretoria: Van Schaik.

De Wet, C. & Jacobs, L. (2008). Kosgangers se ervarings van bullebakkery: 'n Gevallestudie (Hostel inhabitants' experiences of bullying: A case study]. *Acta Academica*, 40(1):197-235.

Denzin, N.K. & Lincoln, Y.S. (2005). *The Sage handbook of qualitative research.* London: Sage. https://doi.org/10.1177/1468794105047237

Diamond, M.A. & Allcorn, S. (2009). *Private selves in public organizations. The psychodynamics of organisational diagnosis and change.* New York: Palgrave. https://doi.org/10.1057/9780230620094

Djurkovic, N.; McCormack, D. & Casimir, G. (2006). Neuroticism and psychosomatic model of worksplace bullying. *Journal of Managerial Psychology*, 21(1):73-88. https://doi.org/10.1108/02683940610643224

Duffy, M. & Sperry, L. (2007). Workplace mobbing: Individual and family health consequences. *The Family Journal*, 15(4):398-404. https://doi.org/10.1177/1066480707305069

Ferris, P. (2004). A preliminary typology of organisational response to allegations of workplace bullying: See no evil, hear no evil, speak no evil. *British Journal of Guidance & Counselling*, 32(3):389-395. https://doi.org/10.1080/0306988041000 1723576

Fox, S. & Spector, P.E. (2005). *Counterproductive work behaviour. Investigations of actors and targets.* Washington: APA. https://doi.org/10.1037/10893-000

Freud, S. (1921). *Group psychology and the analysis of the ego. Complete works of Sigmund Freud.* London: Hogarth. https://doi.org/10.1037/11327-000

Gaitanidis, A. (2007). *Narcissism. A critical reader.* London: Karnac.

Glasø, L.; Matthiesen, S.B.; Nielsen, M. & Einarsen, S. (2007). Do targets of workplace bullying portray a general victim personality profile? *Scandinavian Journal of Personality*, 48:313-319. https://doi.org/10.1111/j.1467-9450.2007.00554.x

Gould, L.J.; Stapley, L.F. & Stein, M. (2001). *The systems psychodynamics of organisations.* London: Karnac.

Gould, L.J.; Stapley, L.F. & Stein, M. (2004). *Experiential learning in organizations. Application of the Tavistock Group Relations Approach.* London: Karnac.

Harvey, M.G.; Heames, J.T.; Richey, R.G. & Leonard, N. (2006). Bullying: From the playroom to the boardroom. *Journal of Leadership and Organizational Studies*, 12(4):1-11. https://doi.org/10.1177/107179190601200401

Hauge, L.J.; Skogstad, A. & Einarsen, S. (2007). Relationships between stressful work environments and bullying: Results of a large representative study. *Work & Stress*, 21(3):220-242. https://doi.org/10.1080/02678370701705810

Hinshelwood, R.D. & Skogstad, W. (2005). *Observing organisations. Anxiety, defence and culture in health care.* London: Routledge.

Hirschhorn, L. (1997). *Reworking authority. Leading and following in the post-modern organisation.* London: MIT.

Hollway, W. & Jefferson, T. (2010). *Doing qualitative research differently. Free association, narrative and the interview method.* London: Sage.

Huffington, C.; Armstrong, A.; Halton, W.; Hoyle, L. & Pooley, J. (2004). *Working below the surface. The emotional life of contemporary organisations.* London: Karnac.

Hutchinson, M.; Vickers, M.; Jackson, D. & Wilkens, L. (2006). Workplace bullying in nursing towards a more critical organisational perspective. *Nursing Inquiry*, 13(2):118-126. https://doi.org/10.1111/j.1440-1800.2006.00314.x

James, M. (1977). *Techniques in transactional analysis.* Reading: Addison-Wesley.

Johnson, H.R.; Thompson, M.J.J.; Wilkinson, S.; Walsh, L.; Balding, J. & Wright, V. (2002). Vulnerability to bullying: Teacher-reported conduct and emotional problems, hyperactivity, peer relationship difficulties, and prosocial behaviour in primary school children. *Educational Psychology*, 22(5):553-556. https://doi.org/10.1080/0144341022000023626

Kets De Vries. M.F.R. (2006). *The leader on the coach. A clinical approach to changing people and organisations.* New York: Jossey-Bass.

Kets De Vries, M.F.R. (2007). *Coach and couch. The psychology of making better leaders.* London: Palgrave.

Klein, L. (2005). *Working across the gap. The practice of social science in organisations.* London: Karnac.

Koonin, M. & Green, T.M. (2004). The emotionally abusive workplace. *Journal of Emotional Abuse*, 4(3/4):71-79. https://doi.org/10.1300/J135v04n03_05

Kowalski, R.; Limber, S. & Aqatston, P.W. (2007). *Cyber-bullying.* New York: Wiley. https://doi.org/10.1002/9780470694176

Lawrence, W.G. (1999). *Exploring individual and organisational boundaries. A Tavistock open systems approach.* London: Karnac.

Lewis, D. (1999). Workplace bullying – interim findings of a study in further and higher education in Wales. *International Journal of Manpower*, 20(1/2):106-118. https://doi.org/10.1108/01437729910268696

Lewis, D. (2004). Bullying at work: The impact of shame amongst university and college lecturers. *British Journal of Guidance & Counselling*, 32(3):281-299. https://doi.org/10.1080/0306988041000 1723521

Lewis, M.A. (2006). Nurse bullying: Organisational considerations in the maintenance and perpetration of health care bullying cultures. *Journal of Nursing Management*, 14:52-58. https://doi.org/10.1111/j.1365-2934.2005.00535.x

Lewis, S. (2009). Corporate bullying bad for business. *HR Future*, 7:33.

Liefooghe, P.D. & Olafsson, R. (1999). "Scientists" and "amateurs": Mapping the bullying domain. *International Journal of Manpower*, 20(1/2):39-49. https://doi.org/10.1108/01437729910268623

Lipgar, R.M. & Pines, M. (2003). *Building on Bion: Branches. Contemporary developments and applications of Bion's contributions to theory and practice*. London: Jessica Kingsley.

Marais, S. & Herman, M. (1997). *Corporate hyenas at work: How to spot and outwit them by being hyenawise*. Pretoria: Kagiso.

Martin, B. (2000). Insight and advice about workplace bullying. *Journal of Organizational Change Management*, 13(4):410-408.

Matthiessen, S.B. & Einarsen, S. (2004). Psychiatric distress symptoms of PTSD amongst victims of bullying at work. *British Journal of Guidance & Counselling*, 32(3):335-356. https://doi.org/10.1080/03069880410001723558

Meyers, L. (2006a). Still wearing the 'kick me' sign? *Monitor on Psychology*, 37(7):68-70. https://doi.org/10.1037/e521142006-032

Meyers, L. (2006b). Worrying for a living. *Monitor on Psychology*, 37(7):74-75. https://doi.org/10.1037/e521142006-035

Mollon, P. (2004). *Shame and jealousy. The hidden turmoils*. London: Karnac.

Morgan-Jones, R. (2010). *The body of the organisation and its health*. London: Karnac.

Munsey, C. (2011). APA is front and center at White House bullying conference. *Monitor on Psychology*, 42(5):18-19. https://doi.org/10.1037/e545582011-012

Naidoo, K. (2008). Bullies at work. Eradicating bullying and harassment in the workplace. *HR Future*, 1:30-31.

Ncongwane, S. (2010a). Bullying and violence in the workplace. Part Two. *HR Future*, 11:25.

Ncongwane, S. (2010b). Stop bullies in their tracks. Part Three. *HR Future*, 12:28-29.

Oade, A. (2009). *Managing workplace bullying. How to identify, respond to and manage bullying behaviour in the workplace*. London: Palgrave. https://doi.org/10.1057/9780230249165

Obholzer, A.; & Roberts, V.Z. (1994). *The unconscious at work*. London: Routledge.

Pietersen, C. (2007). Interpersonal bullying behaviours in the workplace. *South African Journal of Industrial Psychology*, 33(1):59-66. https://doi.org/10.4102/sajip.v33i1.256

Randall. P. (1997). *Adult bullying: Perpetrators and victims*. London: Routledge.

Rayner, C. (1999). From research to implementation: Finding leverage for prevention. *International Journal of Manpower*, 20(1/2):28-38. https://doi.org/10.1108/01437729910268614

Rayner, C.; Hoel, H. & Cooper, C.L. (2002). *Workplace bullying. What we know, who is to blame, and what can we do?* London: Taylor& Francis. https://doi.org/10.1201/b12811

Rayner, C.; Sheehan, M. & Barker, M. (1999). *International Journal of Manpower*, 20(1/2):11-15. https://doi.org/10.1108/01437729910268579

Salin, D. (2003). Ways of explaining workplace bullying: A review of enabling, motivating and precipitating structures and processes in the work environment. *Human Relations*, 56(10):1213-1232. https://doi.org/10.1177/00187267035610003

Sandler, J.; Person, E.S. & Fonagy, P. (2004). *Freud's "On narcissism: An introduction"*. London: International Psychoanalytical Association.

Schafer, R. (2003). *Insight and interpretation. The essential tools of psychoanalysis*. London: Karnac.

Schwartz, H.S. (1990). *Narcissistic process and corporate decay. The theory of the organization ideal*. New York: New York University Press.

Sheehan, M. (1999). Workplace bullying: Responding with some emotional intelligence. *International Journal of Manpower*, 20(1/2):57-69. https://doi.org/10.1108/01437729910268641

Sheehan, M. & Barker, M. (1999). Applying strategies for dealing with workplace bullying. *International Journal of Manpower*, 20(1/2):50-56. https://doi.org/10.1108/01437729910268632

Sievers, B. (2009). *Psychoanalytic studies of organizations. Contributions from the International Society for the Psychoanalytical Study of Organizations (ISPSO)*. London: Karnac.

Speziale-Bagliacca, R. (2004). *Guilt. Revenge, remorse and responsibility after Freud*. New York: Brunner-Routledge.

Stambor, Z. (2006). Bullying stems from fear, apathy. *Monitor in Psychology*, 37(7):72-73. https://doi.org/10.1037/e521142006-034

Stapley, L.F. (1996). *The personality of the organisation. A psychodynamic explanation of culture and change*. London: Free Association.

Stapley, L.F. (2006). *Individuals, groups and organisations beneath the surface*. London: Karnac.

Strandmark, M. & Hallberg, L.R. (2007). The origin of workplace bullying: Experiences from the perspective of bully-victims in the public sector. *Journal of Nursing Management*, 15:332-341. https://doi.org/10.1111/j.1365-2834.2007.00662.x

Terre Blanche, M.; Durrheim, K. & Painter, D. (2006). *Research in practice. Applied methods for the social sciences*. Cape Town: UCT Press.

University of London. (2011). *Vulnerable selves, disciplining others: New approaches to bullying and conflict at work*. www.bbk.ac.uk/bullying [Accessed 11 May 2011].

Vansina, L.S. & Vansina-Cobbaert, M. (2008). *Psychodynamics for consultants and managers. From understanding to leading meaningful change*. Chichester: Wiley-Blackwell. https://doi.org/10.1002/9780470697184

Watts, L. (2009). Managing self in role: Using multiple methodologies to explore self construction and self-governance. In: S. Clarke & P. Hoggett. Researching beneath the surface. *Psycho-social research methods in practice*, pp.215-239. London: Karnac. https://doi.org/10.4324/9780429479564-10

White, S. (1999). *Bullying at work – from definition to preventative action.* Proceedings of the Second Annual Conference of the International Harassment Network at the Harris Conference Park. Preston: Merchant.

White, S. (2001). A life cycle theory of bullying: Persecutory anxiety and a futile search for recognition in the work-place. *Socio-Analysis. The Journal of the Australian Institute of Socio-Analysis,* 3(2):137-154.

White, S. (2004). A psychodynamic perspective of workplace bullying: Containment, boundaries and a futile search for recognition. *British Journal of Guidance & Counselling,* 32(3):269-280. https://doi.org/10.1080/0306988041000 1723512

Yildirim, D.; Yidirim, A. & Timucin, A. (2007). Mobbing behaviours encountered by nurse teaching staff. *Nursing Ethics,* 14(4):447-463. https://doi. org/10.1177/0969733007077879

Zapf, D. (1999). Organisational, work group related and personal causes of mobbing/bullying at work. *International Journal of Manpower,* 20(1/2):70-85. https://doi. org/10.1108/01437729910268669

Article 4

A Systems Psychodynamic Perspective on Burnout[1]

F Cilliers

Abstract

The aim of this research was to explore burnout from a systems psychodynamic perspective. A qualitative design, using focus groups, was used. Burnout can be seen as a phenomenon resulting from the psychodynamic relatedness between subsystems in the organisation. The macro-system disowns and projects its unacceptable behaviour onto and into an individual with a specific valence, who identifies with the behaviour. Through counter-transference, the individual experiences and contains the behaviour on behalf of the system. Coping with burnout implies that the total system will try to become aware of its projections and own its good and bad parts alike.

Burnout is generally described as a condition happening only to the individual employee. When he/she cannot cope with work demands anymore, remedies are prescribed to either help the individual personally to get back on track or out of the organisation (Maslach & Jackson, 1984; Schaufeli & Enzmann, 1998). This research argues from a systems psychodynamic perspective (French & Vince, 1999), that burnout involves the individual as micro, as well as the group as meso and the organisation as macro-systems. Coping with burnout thus becomes a total system endeavour.

---

1   Cilliers, F. (2003). A systems psychodynamic perspective on burnout. *South African Journal of Industrial Psychology*, 29(4):26-33.

Burnout

Burnout occurs within a specific job-related context – it refers to a particular type of prolonged job stress, the final step in a progression of unsuccessful attempts by the individual to cope with a variety of negative stress conditions (Maslach & Jackson, 1984; Schaufeli & Enzmann, 1998). Burnout differs from depression, which refers to the individual's symptoms across all life situations (Basson & Rothmann, 2001).

Burnout can be defined (Cherniss, 1995; Golembiewski & Munzenrider, 1988; Jackson, Schuler & Schwab, 1986; Maslach, 1982a; 1982b; Maslach & Jackson, 1984; 1986; Pines, Aronson & Kafry, 1981; Schaufeli & Enzmann, 1998) as a persistent, negative, work-related state of mind (or syndrome) developing over time in a so called "normal" individual, characterised by an array of physical, psychological and attitudinal symptoms, primarily exhaustion, accompanied by distress, a sense of reduced effectiveness, decreased motivation and the development of dysfunctional personal and societal attitudes and behaviours at work. This psychological condition develops gradually but may remain unnoticed for a long time. It results from a misfit between intentions and reality in the job.

The syndrome is described in terms of its self-perpetuating characteristics within the individual and his/her inadequate coping strategies, and especially three conceptually distinct characteristic or dimensions, namely emotional exhaustion, de-personalisation and low personal accomplishment (Cherniss, 1995; Jackson, Schuler & Schwab, 1986; Maslach, 1982a; 1982b; Maslach & Jackson, 1984; 1986; Schaufeli & Enzmann, 1998). The specific physical, cognitive, affective, motivational, behavioural, interpersonal and work symptoms are mentioned (Dubrin, 1990; Juntunen, Asp, Olkinuora, Arimaa, Strid & Kautt u, 1988; Pines et al., 1981; Schaufeli & Enzmann, 1998). The causes of burnout are classified in terms of the individual's profile and the work situation (Cherniss, 1995; Corrigan, Holmes, Luchins, Buican, Basit & Parks, 1994; Freudenberger, 1989; Golembiewski & Munzenrider, 1988; Landsbergis, 1988; Miller, Ellis, Zook & Lyles, 1990; Pines et al., 1981; Schaufeli & Enzmann, 1998). Coping with burnout is discussed in the literature on three levels, namely the individual, the interpersonal and the organisational levels (Cox & Ferguson, 1991; Muldary, 1983; Pines & Aronson, 1988; Schaufeli & Janczur, 1994). (The symptoms, causes and coping with burnout are mentioned as part of the results below.)

The Systems Psychodynamic Perspective

The systems psychodynamic perspective does not address individual behaviour per se, but rather the systemic group and organisational behaviour influencing various systems, such as the individual. The primary task of this paradigm is formulated as pushing the boundaries to better understand organisations, including the challenges of management and leadership. It serves as a praxis for work group and organisational education, training and consultation (Miller & Rice, 1976).

The central tenet of the systems psychodynamic perspective is contained in the conjunction of these two terms (French & Vince, 1999; Miller, 1993; Neumann, Kellner & Dawson-Shepherd, 1997; Obholzer & Roberts, 1994; Stapley, 1996).

1. The systems designation refers to the open systems concepts that provide the dominant framing perspective for understanding the structural aspects of an organisational system. These include its design, division of labour, levels of authority and reporting relationships, the nature of work tasks, processes and activities, its mission and primary tasks and in particular the nature and patterning of the organisation's task, sentient boundaries and the transactions across them. It is accepted that human beings create social institutions to satisfy their (sometimes irrational, primitive and childlike) needs to experience pleasure and avoid pain, as well as to accomplish required tasks. Institutions become external realities, comparatively independent of individuals. These affect individuals in significant emotional and psychological ways, which offers enormous learning opportunities.

2. The psychodynamic designation refers to psychoanalytic perspectives (Freud, 1921) on individual experiences and mental processes (such as transference, resistance, object relations and fantasy) as well as to the experience of unconscious group and social processes, which are simultaneously both a source and a consequence of unresolved or unrecognised organisational difficulties. The observable and structural features of an organisation – even quite rational and functional ones – continually interact with its members at all levels in a manner that stimulates particular patterns of individual and group dynamic processes. In turn, such processes may determine how particular features of the organisation come to be created, such as its distinctive culture, how work is conceived, structured, organised and managed.

On the psychodynamic level, a central feature of this view stresses the existence of primitive anxieties – of a persecutory and depressive nature – and the mobilisation of social defence systems against them. The nature of such defences is conceptualised as either impeding or facilitating task performance and readiness for change. Interventions based on this perspective typically involve understanding, interpreting and working through such collective defences. This will hopefully result in enlarging the organisation's capacity to develop task appropriate adaptations such as a rational distribution of authority, clear role and boundary definitions, as well as their management.

The conceptual origins of the systems psychodynamic perspective stem from classic psychoanalysis, group relations theory and open systems theory (De Board, 1978; French & Vince, 1999; Hirschhorn, 1993; Miller, 1993; Neumann et al., 1997; Obholzer & Roberts, 1994; Stapley, 1996). Bion's (1961) three basic assumptions are seen as its cornerstones (Kets de Vries, 1991; Miller, 1993; Rice, 1965; Rioch, 1970).

1. **Dependency.** Group members unconsciously project their dependency upon (imaginative) parental objects or systems, representing authority. If these authority symbols do not respond in the way the group wants them to, anger develops which manifests in counter dependence. Later the group develops through independence to interdependence, which represents maturity and wisdom.

2. **Fight/flight.** These are defence mechanisms the group unconsciously uses in trying to cope with discomfort. Fight reactions manifest in aggression against the self, colleagues and authority figures, accompanied by envy, jealousy, competition, elimination, boycotting, rivalry, fighting for a position in the group and for privileged relationships. Flight reactions manifest in the avoidance of others, threatening situations or feelings, and defences such as rationalisation and intellectualisation.

3. **Pairing.** In order to cope with the anxiety of alienation and loneliness, group members try to pair with perceived powerful others or subgroups. The unconscious need is to feel secure and to create. Pairing also implies splitting, which may happen because of experienced anxiety in a diverse workplace. The need is to experience relief of internal conflicts. Typical examples of splits could be seeing management as both good and bad, dividing colleagues between black/white, male/female, senior/junior and competent/incompetent. Unconsciously, the group tries to split up the whole and build a smaller system, to which the individual can belong safely and securely.

During the 1990s the following two basic assumptions were added (see Lawrence, Bain & Gould, 1996).

1. **Me-ness**. This assumption refers to the risk of living in contemporary, turbulent society. The individual is increasingly pressed into his/her own inner reality in order to exclude and deny the perceived disturbing reality of the outer environment. The inner world becomes the comfortable place and the outer the one to be avoided. The group works on the tacit, unconscious assumption that the group is to be a non-group. Only people present can be related to, because their shared construct in the mind of what the group is about, is of an undifferentiated mass.

   They, therefore, act as if the group has no existence because if it did exist, it would be the source of persecuting experiences. The idea of a group is contaminating, taboo, impure – all that is negative. The members act as if the group has no reality – the only reality is that of the individual. It exists in a culture of selfishness where the individual is only aware of own personal boundaries which have to be protected from others. This leads to mechanistic transactions with no room for affect (which is seen as dangerous because one would not know where feelings may lead to).

2. **We-ness**. As the opposite of me-ness, this assumption is that group members seek to join into a powerful union with an omnipotent force, surrendering the self for passive participation, thus experiencing existence, well-being and wholeness. It is as if the individual group member gets lost within oceanic feelings of unity. This wish for "salvationist inclusion" can be seen in a team striving towards cohesion and synergy where it is believed that problems will be solved by this strong united force.

The most relevant concepts in this model (in understanding burnout) are the following (Cilliers & Koortzen, 2000; Koortzen & Cilliers, 2002):

1. **Conflict.** The systems psychodynamic perspective towards organisational behaviour is, in essence, a conflict model. The assumption is that behaviour is determined by two or more conflicting powers, for example, the system's instinctive needs opposed to the demands of society (a classic id-superego conflict – De Board, 1978).

2. **Anxiety**. This is accepted as the basis of all system (group and organisational) behaviour. French and Vince (1999) refer to primitive anxiety (the all-pervasive anxiety that is the fate of mankind), anxiety arising from the nature of work (that which the institution defends itself against in such a way that the emphasis of the structure is on defense-related rather than work-related functioning – thus neglecting the primary task and shifting from "on task" to "off-task" functioning such as revisiting job descriptions, organigrams, appointing committees), and personal anxiety (triggered by external societal and work issues, stimulated by conscious and unconscious past personal experiences).

3. **Defence mechanisms**. These are used to act against anxiety in order to avoid pain and to gain a sense of safety, security and acceptance. Rationalisation and intellectualisation may be used to stay emotionally uninvolved and in control (Gabelnick & Carr, 1989; Neumann et al., 1997). Projection refers to the intra-system defensive process, where one part of the system denies and rejects feelings inherent in the unconscious image (fantasy) of the situation. It then tries to alter the uncomfortable experience by imagining that a part of it belongs to another subsystem rather than to the self. It then puts good or bad (unwanted) material onto the other, thus distancing itself from the discomfort. This has no effect or influence on the target. Projection may be used to blame management for what goes wrong without management being influenced.

4. **Projective identification**. This is an anxiety-reducing process (Coleman & Geller, 1985; Czander, 1993; Kets de Vries, 1991; Obholzer & Roberts, 1994), and is one of the most elusive and complicated concepts in group relations theory. It refers to an inter-system, object-relational interaction and process, where one part of the system (as subject) projects material into the other part (as object), who identifies with the projection (taking it on). This results in changes in both parts. The dynamics of projective identification can be described as follows. The subject experiences anxiety either because of its primitive envy of the object's idealised qualities and its consequent urge to destroy, spoil, dominate, devalue and control, or its wish to refuse with the object, or as a form of parasitism to be part of the object. It tries to relieve itself of this anxiety by externalising it, splitting off parts and internal objects of the self, leaving

the self-less aware of its whole and diminished by the projective loss of important aspects of itself. It requires or assigns the object to receive, identify with and contain these aspects of the self, as if it belongs to the object, but still keeps a closeness to the object. Depending on how subtle the projection is, the object may experience being manipulated into a particular role. When this behaviour predominates in the group, it becomes difficult to find other ways of coping, because it is almost impossible to think clearly, to locate sources of problems and to find appropriate and creative solutions.

5. **Counter-transference**. This refers to the state of mind in which other people's feelings are experienced as one's own (Miller, 1993; Neumann et al., 1997; Obholzer & Roberts, 1994). Projective identification frequently leads to the recipient's acting out the counter-transference deriving from the projected feelings. Also, through projective identification, one group/member on behalf of another group/member, can come to serve as a kind of sponge for all the anger, depression or guilt of the one group towards another. The angry members can be used to attack management or a depressed member may be unconsciously manoeuvred into breaking down and leaving the organisation. This individual not only expresses or carries something for the group but may be used to export something which the rest of the system then need not to feel in themselves. Sometimes the organisation imports a consultant to carry these feelings on its behalf.

6. **Valence**. Bion (1961) borrowed this concept from chemistry to designate a part of the system's tendency-cum-unconscious-vulnerability or predisposition to being drawn into one or other basic assumption type of functioning. For example, these may be to become the fighter, spokesperson, the counter dependant, the one referring to the past or to act out specific feelings such as guilt, shame, envy or satisfaction (French & Vince, 1999).

7. **The paranoid-schizoid position**. In the young or immature system, splitting and projection are the prominent defences for avoiding pain, which Klein referred to as the paranoid-schizoid position. Paranoid refers to badness being experienced as coming from outside oneself, and schizoid to splitting (Colman & Bexton, 1975; Colman & Geller, 1985). Schizoid splitting is normally associated with the splitting off and projecting outwards of parts of the self-perceived as bad, thereby creating external figures who are both hated and feared. The projection of feelings of badness to the outside of the self helps to produce a state of illusionary goodness and self-idealisation. This black and white mentality simplifies complex issues and may produce a rigid culture in which growth is inhibited. Splitting and projection exploit the natural boundary between insiders and outsiders which every system has. This often leads to fragmentation because contact was lost between parts of the system which belong together inside its boundary. If no contact or dialogue takes place between conflicting parts or points of view, change and development are frustrated (Czander, 1993; Miller, 1993; Obholzer & Roberts, 1994; Shapiro & Carr, 1991).

8. **The depressive position**. When the system recognises that its painful feelings come from projections, it is a natural response to re urn these feelings to their source, saying: "These are your feelings, not mine". This gives rise to blaming and the ricocheting

of projections back and forth. However, if the system can tolerate the feelings long enough to reflect on them, and contain the anxieties they stir up, it may be possible to bring about change (Bion, 1970). When the timing is right and some of the projections can be re-owned, splitting decreases and there is a reduction in the polarisation and antagonism. This promotes integration and co-operation within the group and a shift from the paranoid-schizoid to the depressive position. When the group is functioning in the depressive position, every point of view will be valued and a full range of emotional responses will be available to explore. The group will be more able to encompass the emotional complexity of the work in which they all share, and no one member will be left to carry his/her fragment in isolation. However, the depressive position is never attained once and for all. Whenever survival or self-esteem are threatened there is a tendency to return to a more paranoid-schizoid way of functioning (Czander, 1993; Miller, 1993; Shapiro & Carr, 1991).

9. **Boundaries**. These refer to the physical and psychological borders around and spaces between parts of the system. Its function is to contain anxiety, thus making life controllable, safe and contained (Cytrynbaum & Lee, 1993; Czander, 1993; Hirschhorn, 1993; Kets de Vries, 1991; Miller, 1993; Neumann et al., 1997).

10. **Representation**. This refers to when a member consciously or unconsciously negotiates a boundary, acting on behalf of the group (for example in crossing, resisting or erecting a boundary). If the individual's authority boundaries are unclear, the high level of anxiety tends to immobilise and dis-empower him/her (Kets de Vries, 1991; Obholzer & Roberts, 1994).

11. Authorisation. This concept refers to empowering a group member to act on behalf of the group in a specific role (Czander, 1993; Obholzer & Roberts, 1994).

12. **Relationship and relatedness.** The relationship between group members refers to any type of face-to-face interaction, as it happens in the here-and-now. Unconsciously, the group member is always in relatedness to the group, keeping "the group in the mind" (Gabelnick & Carr, 1989; Neumann et al., 1997; Shapiro & Carr, 1991).

13. **Containment.** In order to cope with discomfort, the system unconsciously needs something or someone to contain the anxiety on its behalf (Menzies, 1993). Bion's (1970) container-contained model identifies and describes a basic dimension of human experience, namely the relationship between emotion and its containment – the ways in which it is experienced or avoided, managed or denied, kept in or passed on, so that its effects are either mitigated or amplified. The container (1) can absorb, filter or manage difficult or threatening emotions or ideas (the contained) so that they can be worked with, or (2) it can become a rigid frame or shell that restricts and blocks. The contained, whether emotion, idea or person, can, therefore, be experienced as an overwhelming threat or as the welcome messiah.

14. **Taking up a role**. Role is defined as the conscious and unconscious boundary describing the way to behave. Miller (1993) refers to three types of roles, namely:

   1. the existential role (the role ascribed to the individual by the organisation – what the person must do);

2. the phenomenological role (the role that the individual fulfils as seen by others); and

3. the experiential role (the role as seen by the incumbent). Congruence between the three types facilitates harmony, but incongruence leads to anxiety within the individual and between him/her and colleagues.

15. **Group as a whole**. This concept refers to collectivism – one part of the system acting or containing emotional energy, on behalf of another. This implies that no event happens in isolation and that there is no co-incidence but rather synchronicity in the behaviour of the group (Wells, 1980).

The Systems Psychodynamic Perspective as a Consultancy Stance

This stance is not a form of counselling or psychotherapy for problem managers (Obholzer & Roberts, 1994). Rather, it is a developmentally focussed, psycho-educational process for key staff, at any level, whose roles are critical to the organisation's functioning. The systems psychodynamic consultant engages in an analysis of the interrelationships of some or all of the following: boundaries, roles and role configurations, structure, organisational design, work culture and group process (Miller, 1989; 1993; Neumann et al., 1997). The consultant is alert to and interprets the covert and dynamic aspects of the organisation and the work group that comprise it, with the focus on relatedness and how authority is psychologically distributed, exercised and enacted, in contrast to how it is formally invested. This work would include a consideration of attitudes, beliefs, fantasies, core anxieties, social defences, patterns of relationships and collaboration, and how these, in turn, may influence task performance. The consultant will work with how unwanted feelings and experiences are split off and projected onto particular individuals and groups that carry them on behalf of the system – that is their process roles as distinct from their formally sanctioned roles. Also, how work roles are taken up. Menzies (1993) emphasised the analysis of social defence aspects of structure and its relationship to task and process, thus trying to understand how unconscious anxieties are reflected in organisational structures and design (which function to defend against them).

Aim and Research Design

The aim of this research was to explore burnout as a phenomenon (within the above boundaries) from a systems psychodynamic perspective. A qualitative design, using focus groups, was used.

Method

Participants

Eight psychologists were chosen because of their knowledge of both burnout and the systems psychodynamic perspective towards group and organisational behaviour.

The Focus Groups

Two 60 minute focus groups (Brilhart & Galanes, 1992) were conducted, with the researcher in the role of facilitator. Each participant received a copy of the literature on burnout as discussed above. The task of the group was as follows: In the role as systems psychodynamic consultant, (1) give your interpretation of the burnout behaviour and (2) formulate a working hypothesis based on your interpretation.

Results

The results are structured according to the burnout context, the definition, the characteristics, the individual's profile, the causes of and coping with burnout. The burnout behaviour is typed in italics, followed by the systems psychodynamic interpretations and the resultant working hypothesis.

The Burnout Context

1. **"Burn-out".** Fire serves as a symbol of both purification and destruction, and ashes symbolise nothingness – being beyond death. Burnout as a syndrome represents the conflict between life and death, and indicates that something in the system is being killed off or pushed out, and which is regarded as worthless.

2. **Individual behaviour.** By focussing on the individual alone, the larger system is defending against its relatedness to its parts. It denies the unconscious connections between the individual as micro-system and the group/organisation he/she belongs to. It rationalises the causes of burnout as only an individual issue, excluding the rest of the system from carrying any responsibility for the illness.

3. **In a team/organisation.** Burnout manifests within an immature system, experiencing splitting and paranoia. The system defends against this (rather than owning and trying to change or improve it).

4. **Focus on overt organisational behaviour.** This rational and conscious part of organisational functioning (human resources management, strategy, vision, mission, goals, structures, jobs, tasks, roles, culture, climate, procedures), which Bion (1961) referred to as the working group, is incongruent to the covert and unconscious part, containing the unspoken motives and drives (Miller, 1993). This Bion (1961) referred to

as the basic assumption group. This means that the system is consciously trying to manage its task in a rational way, whilst unconsciously, it undermines an individual's performance in a destructive and anti-task manner.

Working Hypothesis 1

Based upon the above interpretations of the burnout context, the following hypothesis is formulated. Because of its unrecognised difficulties, the system has created a social institution to satisfy its irrational, primitive and childlike needs. The burnt-out individual is containing the pain, which leaves the rest of the system to experience the pleasure.

The Definition of Burnout

1. A persistent, negative, work-related state of mind. The negative issues belong to the system as a whole. Unconsciously, this creates anxiety which cannot be faced and dealt with. As a result, the system is projecting its negative (evil/bad) issues onto the individual and making him/her carry these on behalf of the rest of the system.

2. Behaviour developing gradually and remaining unnoticed for a long time. The nature of the (unconscious) projection is such that it isolates the negative system issues, targets the individual and then dumps this energy in a subtle way and over a long period of time. Thus, the "game" stays out of consciousness for the whole system and creates the impression that it is the individual's issue and suffering.

3. Behaviour manifesting in "normal" individuals. It is not clear what is meant with "normal" individual. It may rather be a "special" individual, being unconsciously trusted and chosen by the system to carry negative energy on its behalf, thus fulfilling an important role in order for the whole system to survive. The individual is either trusted to transform part of the system into something more acceptable, or seen as a threat to the system – by eliminating the individual, the system's fantasy is that its threat will disappear.

4. Exhaustion, distress, reduced effectiveness, decreased motivation. Instead of the system facing and owning these experiences of incompetence within itself, which could lead to its death, it dumps it onto the individual. Thus, the pain is isolated and disowned, creating the fantasy of competence in the rest of the system.

5. The development of dysfunctional personal and societal attitudes and behaviours at work. The powerful projection of dysfunctional attitudes and behaviours:

    1. onto;

    2. into the individual, leads to his/her identification with these projections; and

    3. experiencing these as his/her own.

    Counter-transference takes place – the system's fear for extinction/incompetence/lack of meaning is now carried and experienced by the individual alone. Further, the system can now control, dominate or even destroy the badness.

6. Burnout results from a misfit between intentions and reality in the job. The system is putting the projection into an individual in conflict (a "soft" target) – someone who is not managing boundaries effectively and has a valance for receiving these projections. The individual's leadership is challenged and he/she is de-authorised.

7. Self-perpetuating because of inadequate coping strategies. The projection from the system is very strong and the individual identifies with it well. It leads to further non-coping behaviour.

8. Helplessness, hopelessness, disillusionment, a negative self-concept, negative attitudes towards work, people and life itself. These are the feelings of the system being contained by the individual. The fantasy is that now the rest of the system does not "suffer" from this illness anymore, it can relax in a quasi-state of effectiveness, hope, positive self-image and attitudes, and effective relationships. The system is in denial and caught up in its own split between competence and incompetence.

Working Hypothesis 2

Based upon the above interpretations on the definition of burnout, the following hypothesis is formulated. The system develops work performance and relational conflicts over time, which is not adequately addressed consciously and openly. This creates discomfort (such as pain, free-floating and persecutory anxiety), which is suppressed into the collective unconscious. Here the conflicts become the unspoken objects. When these are not opened up and voiced/aired, the anxiety around them becomes unbearable and uncontainable. Consequently, the system needs relief of the energy, gets dependent upon someone and starts defending by using flight. It finds an object to project the conflict onto in order to "function normally again". The discomfort, with all that it represents, is split off and projected onto a ready recipient. An individual is chosen who is seen as a hard worker, who achieves well and wants to progress. This becomes an object of envy and he/she becomes the target of the projected discomfort. This individual is ready for challenges and offers his/her valance for more work and the dumping of more anxiety. This may also serve as a confirmation of what he/she thinks and expects to represent for the system – a willing worker. This may also satisfy the individual's neurotic need for acceptance. He/she identifies with the projection and moreover, starts experiencing the system's conflicts as his/her own. The system is relieved from its burden and the targeted individual is taking up the important role of processing the unwanted issues until he/she is "dead". The system's fantasy is that it has exported its conflicts. Unfortunately, this does not happen by playing unconscious games. The system has lost one of its competent resources, and the conflicts get projected onto and into the next "victim". If the pattern continues the system falls into a repetition compulsion and it will lose all its competence.

Characteristics of Burnout

1. **Emotional exhaustion**, reduction in emotional resources, feeling drained, used up. These experiences in the individual act as evidence for the system's dependence upon the individual. The individual identifies with the system's strong projections and now contains the unwanted behaviour. The counter-transference lies in the individual experiencing the system's incompetence. This leaves the rest of the system free to experience the opposite – for example, positive emotions, creativity, initiative, pro-activity and competence. In this process, the system is splitting itself into a bad and good part (because both cannot be contained at the same time in an immature system). The system believes that one individual cannot cope with demands, and this behaviour "has nothing to do with us".

2. **Depersonalisation.** The increase in negative, cynical and insensitive attitudes towards work (reduced work goals, loss of idealism, heightened self-interest), colleagues and clients (an increasing emotional detachment), and the judging of others as deserving their troubles, can be seen as a form of coping and protecting the self against further emotional draining. The individual experiences a loss of individual distinctiveness – a defence occurring in the disregard of own needs and capacities. This stems from needs and contributions not being recognised and the lack of importance attached to personal contributions to work. This may be what the system wants to avoid happening to itself and what the individual is now carrying on its behalf.

3. **Low personal accomplishment** – a feeling of being unable to meet other's needs and to satisfy essential elements of job performance. The individual is seduced by colleagues to meet their needs, thus becoming the object of need fulfiller and container of confusion between sets of needs. This may result from unconscious fears amongst colleagues that the same could happen to them and which could then interfere with organisational productivity and creativity.

4. **Physical symptoms** – distress, headaches, nausea, dizziness, restlessness, muscle pain, hyper ventilation, sexual problems, sleep disturbances, sudden loss or gain of weight and chronic fatigue; psychosomatic disorders such as ulcers, gastric-intestinal disorders, coronary heart disease, prolonged colds and flu and a susceptibility to viral infections; physiological reactions such as increased heart rate and respiration rate, hypertension and high levels of serum cholesterol. The individual identified with the system's strong projections and now contains its physical pain. The counter-transference manifests in the individual experiencing the painful gut issues and heart-throb for the system. This indicates the severity of the system's issues – it needs a part of it to act out its pain on a physical level because it cannot accept responsibility for its own behaviour.

5. **Cognitive symptoms** such as poor concentration, forgetfulness, making mistakes in complex and multiple tasks, rigid thinking, intellectualising problems, difficult decision making. Here, the counter-transference manifests in the individual experiencing cerebral incompetence in order for the rest for the system to act rationally and to make effective decisions.

6. **Affective symptoms** such as helplessness, hopelessness, powerlessness, a tearful and depressed mode, low spirits, dim mood, exhausted emotional resources because too much energy has been used for too long, decreased emotional control leading to undefined fears, anxiety and nervous tension, irritability, over sensitivity, cool, unemotional, bursts of anger, intellectualising personal and emotional problems, daydreaming, fantasising and a low frustration tolerance leading to aggressiveness. These already strong projected feelings may have another deeper layer, namely the system's anger and hurt being suppressed over a long time. The counter-transference manifests in the individual experiencing and acting out the system's madness and unacceptable rebellious child behaviour.

7. **Motivational symptoms** such as lessened intrinsic motivation, lessened initiative, enthusiasm, interest and idealism, increased disillusionment, disappointment and resignation. Here, the counter-transference manifests in the individual experiencing and acting out the system's lack of interest, stagnation and inability to move dynamically.

8. **Behavioural symptoms** such as hyperactivity without knowing what to do about it, impulsiveness without carefully considering alternatives, procrastination, doubt, indecisiveness, excessive consumption of stimulants such as coffee, tobacco, alcohol, tranquillisers, barbiturates, drugs, under and overeating and accident proneness. Here, the counter-transference manifests in the individual experiencing and acting out the system's childish behaviour as well as emotional, physical and substance dependency. On the superficial level, the system is caring for "the poor colleague by offering cures" which clearly indicates where the sickness and non-coping are located in the system.

9. **Interpersonal symptoms** such as decreased involvement with others characterised by isolation, withdrawal, negativism, irritability, hostility, suspicion, lessened interest, in-difference, discouragement, empathy and stereotyping, as well as aggression because of weakened impulse control. Here, the counter-transference manifests in the individual experiencing and acting out the system's paranoia, lack of connection, isolation and non-relatedness. By "breaking down" the individual's connections with colleagues, the system is securing the containment of its incompetence and at the same time maintaining the split in itself. This behaviour may relate to the philosophy made popular by Sartre (McNeill & Feldman, 1998) that "hell is other people".

10. **Work behaviour** such as reduced effectiveness, minimal productivity, accident proneness, low work motivation, resistance in going to and doing work, low job satisfaction, a sense of failure and that work has no meaning, as well as forgetting appointments. The counter-transference manifests in the individual experiencing, containing and acting out the system's poor work performance and anti-task behaviour. This could mean that the rest of the system is stuck in its non-creative and irrational ways.

Working Hypothesis 3

Based upon the above interpretations on the characteristics of burnout, the following hypothesis is formulated. The unacceptable parts of the system's identity are projected into the individual, infiltrating his/her ego boundaries, and robbing him/her from his/her own identity, individualism and real self. Because of the individual's prevailing me-ness assumption and valence for these projections, he/she acts as a sponge for the systems feelings, creating the impression that non-coping is located in one individual. It is clear that the projective process was successful and the individual is de-authorised to take up his/her role as a "normal" employee. For the individual to survive this process is very difficult. He/she is manipulated into the role of representing a messiah figure – someone who is serving the people (the system), carry the burden or sins (containing many projections), is crucified (emotionally drained), and goes to hell (burning out). Where the real messiah re-appeared in a transformed state and represents hope and everlasting life, the mortal individual will not survive. It may be impossible for a human being to accomplish this without realising the role of the larger system from a psychodynamic and collective unconscious perspective.

The Individual's Profile, the Causes of and Coping with Burnout

1. **Highly motivated,** achieving well, having high expectations, who is not compromising, who has striven hard to reach a goal, and who has been stretching the self beyond the normal work boundaries for too long in the quest for the experience of meaning. The system is unconsciously robbing itself from high performance and output and is replacing this with pain and suffering. This may indicate envy towards outstanding performance, achievement and competence.

2. **Good intentions**, an external control, Type A behaviour and neuroticism. This represents the individual's valence to receive the projections from the system. The profile makes it easy for the individual to act as a container because of the need to work very hard and to satisfy others.

3. **High and unrealistic expectations**. These characteristics are used by the system to set the individual up for failure.

4. **Work overload**, role conflict, role ambiguity, poor collegial support, lack of feedback in decision making and autonomy. Because of unclear authority boundaries, the individual feels dis-empowered and immobilised. He/she becomes an easy target for seduction into taking on more, stretching the self to achieve more and better, then to be rejected and isolated and "killed off". This indicates the system's paranoid-schizoid position.

5. **The individual to take responsibility** to recognise the signs and symptoms of burnout. The system is operating from the basic assumption of me-ness, where the belief is that the pain belongs to the individual and has got nothing to do with the rest of the system. Even after it has successfully projected its bad parts into the individual, the system requires the individual to take responsibility to change him/herself as well as the rest of the system. This is a set up for failure.

6. **To manage environmental** and internal demands and conflicts amongst them which tax or exceed a person's resource, intra-personally the individual uses such strategies as awareness. This is another set up. The system is powerfully and cruelly ensuring that its agenda is played out whilst not accepting responsibility for its own difficult issues.

7. **Taking responsibility** to do something about it, understanding the issue and developing new tools for improving the range and quality of old tools. No individual (micro) effort will be successful if the total system cannot accept responsibility for what is happening on the macro level.

8. **Direct action**, in which the individual tries to master the stressful transaction with the environment. It is impossible for the individual to do the work of the whole. The system is now projecting the curing role onto the individual who is already containing the system's illness. This can be seen as a further de-authorisation and dis-empowerment of the individual.

9. **Palliation**, in which the person attempts to reduce the disturbance when he/she is unable to manage the environment, or when action is too costly for the individual. This indicates the system's cruel and setting-up agenda for requiring the individual as micro-system to accept responsibility to move macro issues on his/her own.

10. **The interpersonal level** – having and using social support systems. It will be crucial to use support system(s) in a very responsible way. The individual will have to gain insight into the behavioural dynamics up to the point of saying, "these are your feelings, not mine". The system will have to become aware of its projections, own them, take them back and process the unconscious events until the burnout symptoms have disappeared. Studies (Burke & Greenglass, 1995; House, 1981; Kasl & Wells, 1985; Russel, Altmaier & Van Velzen, 1982; Wells, 1982) have indicated the valuable contribution of social support as a buffer against job-related stress and burnout. This implies movement and growth amongst members of the support system as well.

11. **The organisational level** – the quality of the organisation, of the work environment, and of work itself can affect the experience of stress and employee health and work performance. A mature and wise organisation will be able to own and process its projections, moving to the depressive position of experiencing and living out feelings. Consultancy to this process will need insight into psychodynamics as described above.

12. **Offers a chance of promoting occupational health** through organisational development. OD programmes can be introduced aimed at the system being sensitively and responsibly aware of what psychodynamic behaviour is happening in the here and now.

Working Hypothesis 4

Based upon the above interpretations on the individual's profile, the causes of and coping with burnout, the following hypothesis is formulated. In order to move from the paranoid-schizoid position to the depressive position, the total system needs to become mature and wise in facing its own projections of collective issues, process them and own them. It would be the task of the Industrial and Organisational Psychologist in the role of systems psychodynamic consultant to be sensitively aware of the dynamics and its effects on all parts of the system. These can be done officially through individual counselling with a focus on the individual's valence for specific projections, team development and growth facilitation with the focus on what the specific team represents for the larger system, as well as (on the macro level) by means of OD and health-promoting programmes.

Integration

The systems psychodynamic perspective sees burnout as a phenomenon involving the whole organisational system. The macro-system is splitting off its bad and unwanted parts and projecting these into an individual who has a need to perform well and a valence to attract projections of overload. He/she then identifies with the strong projections and acts as a container of the pain (on behalf of the system) while becoming emotionally and physically incapacitated. The system's fantasy is that if he/she leaves the group or the organisation, the badness will be exported successfully. The reality of the matter is that projections don't make problems disappear, but maybe consultation does. The outcome of the consultation should be awareness in the system towards ownership of the projections and including its good and bad parts. Thus, the role and task boundaries can be maintained and managed clearly and empowering of everyone in the system can take place towards a more effective and competent work force.

References

Basson, M. & Rothmann, S. (2001). *Sense of coherence, coping and burnout of pharmacists*. Paper presented at the Annual Conference of the Society of Industrial Psychology, Pretoria.

Bion, W.R. (1961). *Experiences in groups*. London: Tavistock Publications.

Bion, W.R. (1970). *Attention and interpretation*. London: Tavistock Publications.

Brilhart, J.K. & Galanes, G.J. (1992). *Effective group discussions*. Dubuque: Wm. C. Brown.

Burke, R.J. & Greenglass, E. (1995). A longitudinal study of psychological burnout in teachers. *Human Relations*, 48(2):187-202. https://doi.org/10.1177/001872679504800205

Cherniss, C. (1995). *Beyond burnout*. New York: Routledge.

Cilliers, F. & Koortzen, P. (2000). The psychodynamic view on organisational behaviour. *The Industrial-Organizational Psychologist*, 38(2):59-67.

Colman, A.D. & Bexton, W.H. (1975). *Groups Relations Reader 1*. Jupiter, FL: A.K. Rice Institute.

Colman, A.D. & Geller, M.H. (1985). *Group Relations Reader 2*. Jupiter, FL: The A.K. Rice Institute.

Corrigan, P.W.; Holmes, E.P.; Luchins, D.; Buican, B.; Basit, A.J. & Parks, J. (1994). Staff burnout in a psychiatric hospital: A cross-lagged panel design. *Journal of Organizational Behavior*, 15:65-74. https://doi.org/10.1002/job.4030150107

Cox, T. & Ferguson, E. (1991). Individual differences, stress and coping. In: C.L. Cooper & R. Payne (eds.), *Personality and stress: Individual differences in the stress process*. Chichester: John Wiley & Sons.

Cytrynbaum, S. & Lee, S.A. (1993). *Transformations in global and organizational systems*. Jupiter, FL: A.K. Rice Institute.

Czander, W.M. (1993). *The psychodynamics of work and organisations*. New York: Guilford Press.

De Board, R. (1978). *The psychoanalysis of organisations*. London: Routledge. https://doi.org/10.4324/9780203321812

Dubrin, A.J. (1990). *Effective business psychology*. Englewood Cliffs, NJ: Prentice-Hall.

French, R. & Vince, R. (1999). *Group relations, management and organization*. New York: Oxford University Press.

Freud, F. (1921). *Group psychology and the analysis of the ego*. Complete works of Sigmund Freud. London: Hogarth. https://doi.org/10.1037/11327-000

Freudenberger, H.J. (1989). Burnout: Past, present and future concerns. In: D.T. Wessells, Jr., A.H. Kutscher, I.B. Seeland, F.E. Selder, D.J. Cherico & E.J. Dlark (eds.), *Professional burnout in medicine and the helping professions*. New York: Haworth.

Gabelnick, F. & Carr, A.W. (1989). *Contributions to social and political science*. Jupiter, FL: A.K. Rice Institute.

Golembiewski, R.T. & Munzenrider, R.F. (1988). *Phases of burnout: Development in concepts and applications*. New York: Praeger.

Hirschhorn, L. (1993). *The workplace within: Psychodynamics of organizational life.* Cambridge, MA: MIT Press.

House, J.S. (1981). *Work stress and social support.* Reading, MA: Addison Wesley.

Jackson, S.E.; Schuler, R.S. & Schwab, R.L. (1986). Toward an understanding of the burnout phenomenon. *Journal of Applied Psychology*, 71:630-640. https://doi.org/10.1037/0021-9010.71.4.630

Juntunen, J.; Asp, S.; Olkinuora, M.; Arimaa, M.; Strid, L. & Kauttu, K. (1988). Doctors' drinking habits and consumption of alcohol. *British Medical Journal*, 297:951-954. https://doi.org/10.1136/bmj.297.6654.951

Kasl, S.V. & Wells, J.A. (1985). Social support and health in middle years. In: S. Cohen & S. Syme (eds.), *Social support and health.* Orlando, FL: Academic Press.

Kets De Vries, M.F.R. (1991). *Organizations on the couch: Handbook of psychoanalysis and management.* New York: Jossey-Bass.

Kets De Vries, M.F.R. (2001). *The leadership mystique.* London: Prentice-Hall.

Koortzen, P. & Cilliers, F. (2002). The psychoanalytical approach to team development. In: R.L. Lowman (ed.), *Handbook of organizational consulting psychology.* San Francisco: Jossey-Bass.

Landsbergis, P.A. (1988). Occupational stress amongst health care workers: A test of the job demands – control model. *Journal of Organizational Behaviour*, 9:217-239. https://doi.org/10.1002/job.4030090303

Lawrence, W.G.; Bain, A. & Gould, L. (1996). *The fifth basic assumption.* London: Occasional paper.

Maslach, C. (1982a). *Burnout: The cost of caring.* Englewood Cliffs, NJ: Prentice-Hall.

Maslach, C. (1982b). Understanding burnout: Definitional issues in analysing a complex phenomenon. In: W.S. Paine (ed.), *Job stress and burnout: Research, theory and intervention.* Beverly Hills, CA: Sage.

Maslach, C. & Jackson, S.E. (1984). Patterns of burnout amongst a national sample of public contact workers. *Journal of Health and Human Resources Administration*, 7:184-212.

Maslach, C. & Jackson, S.E. (1986). *The Maslach Burnout Inventory* (2nd ed.). Palo Alto, CA: Consulting Psychologists Press.

McNeill, W. & Feldman, K.S. (1998). *Continental philosophy. An anthology.* Malden, MA: Blackwell.

Menzies, I.E.P. (1993). *The functioning of social systems as a defence against anxiety.* London: Tavistock Institute of Human Relations.

Miller, E.J. (1989). *The "Leicester" Model: Experiential study of group and organisational processes. Occasional Paper No. 10.* London: Tavistock Institute of Human Relations.

Miller, E.J. (1993). *From dependency to autonomy: Studies in organization and change.* London: Free Association Books.

Miller, E.J. & Rice, A.K. (1976). *Systems of organisation.* London: Tavistock Publications.

Miller, K.I.; Ellis, B.H.; Zook, E.G. & Lyles, J.S. (1990). An integrated model of communication, stress, and burnout in the work place. *Communication Research*, 17:200-326. https://doi.org/10.1177/009365090017003002

Muldary, T.D. (1983). *Burnout amongst health professionals: Manifestations and management.* Norwalk: Appleton-Century-Crofts.

Neumann, J.E.; Kellner, K. & Dawson-Shepherd, A. (1997). *Developing organisational consultancy.* London: Routledge.

Obholzer, A. & Roberts, V.Z. (1994). *The unconscious at work.* London: Routledge.

Pines, A.M. & Aronson, E. (1988). *Career burnout: Cases and cures.* New York: Free Press.

Pines, A.M.; Aronson, E. & Kafry, D. (1981). *Burnout: From tedium to personal growth.* New York: Macmillan.

Rice, A.K. (1965). *Learning for leadership.* London: Tavistock Publications.

Rioch, M.J. (1970). Group relations: Rationale and technique. *International Journal of Group Psychotherapy,* 20:340-355. https://doi.org/10.1080/00207284.1970.11491769

Russel, D.W.; Altmaier, E. & Van Velzen, D. (1982). Job-related stress, social support and burnout amongst classroom teachers. *Journal of Applied Psychology,* 72:269-274. https://doi.org/10.1037/0021-9010.72.2.269

Schaufeli, W.B. & Enzmann, D. (1998). *The burnout companion to study and practice: A critical analysis.* London: Taylor & Francis.

Schaufeli, W.B. & Janczur, B. (1994). Burnout amongst nurses: A Polish-Dutch comparison. *Journal of Cross Cultural Psychology,* 25:95-113. https://doi.org/10.1177/0022022194251006

Shapiro, E.R. & Carr, A.W. (1991). *Lost in familiar places: Creating new connections between the individual and society.* London: Yale University Press.

Stapley, L.F. (1996). *The personality of the organisation.* London: Free Association Books.

Wells, J.A. (1982). Social support as a buffer of stressful job conditions. *Journal of Organizational Behavior,* 2:218-226.

Wells, L. (1980). The group-as-a-whole: A systemic socio-analytical perspective on interpersonal and group relations. In: C.P. Alderfer & C.L. Cooper (eds.), *Advances in experiential social processes,* 2:165-198.

465

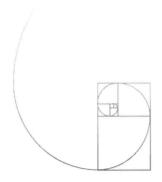

Frans Cilliers
Curriculum Vitae

Academic Qualifications

Degrees completed at the Potchefstroom University (now North-West University):

- ∞ B.A. Psychology/History
- ∞ Honours B.A. Industrial & Organisational Psychology (IOP)
- ∞ M.A. Industrial & Organisational Psychology. Dissertation: The psycho-diagnostic value of the TAT-Z in measuring achievement motivation amongst employees.
- ∞ D.Phil. Industrial & Organisational Psychology. Thesis: A developmental programme in sensitive relationship forming as managerial dimension.

Professional Registrations

- ∞ Psychologist (cat. Industrial). Health Professions Council of South Africa.
- ∞ Master Human Resources Practitioner. South African Council for Personnel Practice.
- ∞ Coaching Psychologist. Professional Development and Supervision Network.
- ∞ Business Coach. World Association of Business Coaches (CAN).
- ∞ Analytic-Network Advanced Coach. Analytic-Network International Coach Network.

Professional Training Courses

1983-1986	Rogerian Facilitation. Centre for the Studies of the Person (US), National Training Laboratories, (US), Esalen Institute (US), Eigenwelt Institute (UK).
1990-2014	Systems Psychodynamic Consultancy/Coaching. Tavistock Institute (UK), AK Rice Institute (US), OPUS (UK), National Training Laboratories (US).
1995	Hypnotherapy. South African Association for Hypnotherapy.
2011	Qualitative research - beneath the surface. University of the West of England (UK).
2016	Advanced Analytic-Network Coaching. AN Coaching International.

Professional Society Membership

South Africa

SIOPSA	Society for Industrial and Organisational Psychology South Africa (Honorary Life Member, EXCO Member, Founding member IGSPO (Interest Group in the Systems Psychodynamics of Organisations).
PsySSA	Psychological Society of South Africa.
COMENSA	Coaching and Mentoring Society South Africa.

Abroad

APA	American Psychological Association (USA).
SIOP	Society for Industrial and Organisational Psychology (USA).
ISPSO	International Society for the Psychoanalytic Study of Organisations (USA).
OPUS	Organisation for Promoting Understanding of Society (UK) (South African National representative).
ADPCA	Association for the Development of the Person-Centred Approach (USA).
PDSN	Professional Development and Supervision Network – Coaching.
ANC	Analytic-Network International Coach Network.
ICF	International Coach Federation.

Employment History

1974-1976	Human Resources Officer. Naschem/Pretoria Portland Cement.
1977-1979	Lecturer, Department of Industrial & Personnel Psychology, Potchefstroom University.
1980	Psychology Internship. South African Transport Services.
1981	Personnel Officer, EBES/ELECTRABEL (electrical supply company), Ghent, Belgium.

1981-1986	Senior Lecturer, Department of Industrial and Personnel Psychology, Potchefstroom University.
1987-2017	Professor, Department of Industrial & Organisational Psychology, University of South Africa (UNISA).
2018	Emeritus Professor. Department of Industrial Psychology, University of South Africa (UNISA).
2015	Professor Extraordinaire. Optentia. North-West University.

Part-Time Lecturing/coaching/examination in I/O Psychology

South Africa

Nelson Mandela Metropolitan University, North-West University, Post-graduate School for Business Leadership UNISA, University of Fort-Hare, University of the Free State, University of Johannesburg, University of KwaZulu-Natal, University of Pretoria, University of Stellenbosch, University of Stellenbosch Business School, University of the Witwatersrand.

Abroad

∞ INSEAD, Paris, France.
∞ Middlesex University, UK.

Private Practice (1987 >)

Individual Work

Psychometric assessment, professional and career guidance and counselling, psychological growth counselling for top/middle management, individual executive/leadership coaching.

Group Work

∞ Management assessment centres, managerial workshops in self-development, facilitation skills, team building, comprising of experiential learning, sensitivity training, T-groups, encounter groups.
∞ Systems Psychodynamic/group relations experiential learning events including large, small and intergroup sessions (working with South African staff e.g. Lorna Brown, Sylvia Poss, Michelle May and international staff e.g. Evelyn Clevely, Herbert Hahn, Eric Miller, Anton Obholzer, Manny Sher and Leslie Brissett).

South African Clients

ABSA, Accenture, AGSA, Aluvani, Anderson Consulting, Anglo American, Auditor General, Boston Consulting, Bowmans, Deloitte & Touche, Distell, EDCON, Gauteng Government, Intercape, Investec, ISCOR, Lechibile, Liberty, Mercedes Benz, MMI, Omnia, RMB, SABC, SABS, SASOL, Shell, Spoornet, Standard Bank, T-Systems, TILT, TUT, UBank.

International Clients

INSEAD Business School (France), Namdeb (Namibian Diamonds), Tavistock Institute (UK) (consulting at the Annual Leicester Group Relations event), Wharton School (University of Pennsylvania, USA).

Academic Tuition Role

- ∞ Lecturing from First-year to Doctorate level covering the full spectrum of IO Psychology
- ∞ Manager of the UNISA Directed Master's in Industrial Psychology programme
- ∞ Manager of the UNISA PHD Consulting Psychology programme

Academic Research Role

National and International Academic Papers Presented Research Topics

Psychological assessment, positive psychology, psychofortology, psychological growth, optimal functioning, salutogenesis, group process, group dynamics, systems psychodynamics, facilitating skills training, consulting skills training, leadership coaching.

Research Awards

- ∞ Department of Industrial & Organisational Psychology, UNISA. 2000-2017. Various awards for Best Researcher/Outstanding Research Contribution
- ∞ School of Management Sciences, UNISA. 2010-2016. Various awards for Researcher of the year/Contribution towards research/Contribution towards Doctoral Student supervision
- ∞ College of Economic and Management Sciences, UNISA. 2010-2017. Various awards for 1st prize Researcher of the year category Maters and Doctorate outputs/1st prize, Researcher of the year award category Accredited Research Outputs/Researcher of the year/Research outputs
- ∞ UNISA Chancellor's prize for Research. 2006 & 2014. Awards for Research Excellence/ Outstanding Research bearing testimony of intensive scientific enquiry, received both national and international recognition, and has been recommended for the award after careful evaluation)
- ∞ Society for Industrial & Organisational Psychology South Africa. Honorary Life Membership. 2006. Award for distinguished and meritorious service to Industrial & Organisational Psychology

∞ South African National Research Foundation. NRF Rated Researcher C3 (2015-2021)

∞ Nominated for the Emerald Africa Academy of Management Trailblazer Award, US (2015)

Involvement in Master's and Doctorate Research Projects

∞ Supervised Master's dissertations - 60 / external examination - 56

∞ Supervised Doctoral theses - 40 / external examination - 40

Committees

∞ Member UNISA College Research Committee

∞ Chairperson UNISA Department of Industrial & Organisational Psychology Research Committee

Journal Editing/reviewing of Accredited Journal Articles

∞ Acta Academica

∞ Communicatio

∞ Consulting Psychology Journal

∞ Health SA - Gesondheid

∞ Human Sciences Research Council, Pretoria

∞ International Journal of Qualitative Methods

∞ Journal of Business Ethics

∞ Journal of Industrial Psychology

∞ South African Board for Psychology

∞ South African Journal for Labour Relations

∞ South African Journal for Psychology

∞ Southern African Business Review

Editorial Committee

∞ Health SA - Gesondheid

∞ South African Journal of Industrial Psychology

∞ South African Journal of Labour Relations

Guest Editorships

2012. South African Journal of Industrial Psychology (Topic: Systems psychodynamic in South African organisations). Co-edited with Pieter Koortzen.

Students Research Projects Supervised

Masters Students

Nel, C.J. (1988). *Selection criteria for black supervisors in a motor plant*. UNISA.

Goddard, B.A. (1989). *An investigation into managers' power over their supervisors in a manufacturing organisation*. UNISA.

Benade, J.M. (1991). *Die verband tussen selfaktualisering en prestasiemotivering*. UNISA.

Marshall, D. (1991). *Selfhandhawing en interne lokus van kontrole as determinante van sukses in 'n keuringsonderhoud*. UNISA.

Van den Berg, B. (1992). *Die evaluering van 'n spanbouprogram*. UNISA.

Elliott, C.A.E. (1994). *Graphology as an assessment technique in industry*. UNISA.

Pheiffer, J. (1994). *Psychological optimality as a concept in industrial psychology*. UNISA.

Scholtz, D.T. (1994). *Die fasilitering van selfaktualisering*. UNISA.

Schulz, G.M. (1994). *Reliability and validity of the Personal Orientation Inventory in South Africa*. UNISA.

Visser, C. (1994). *'n Psigometriese ondersoek na psigologiese optimaliteit*. UNISA.

Cilliers, H.J. (1995). *Trainer competency and psychological optimality*. UNISA.

Geldenhuys, D.J. (1995). *Selfaktualisering as voorspeller van bestuursukses*. UNISA.

Hanekom, A.N. (1995). *Persoonlikheid, selfaktualisering en toesighouersvaardigheid as voorspellers van toesighouersukses*. UNISA.

Ludik, B.E. (1996). *Individuele aanpassing binne die integrasieproses van die Suid-Afrikaanse Nasionale weermag*. UNISA.

Wilmans, L. (1995). *Ouderdom en geslag as veranderlikes in die salutogenese paradigma*. UNISA.

Marais, C.P. (1997). *Salutogenesis as a paradigm in change management*. UNISA.

Wilden, M. (1997). *Die verband tussen prestasiemotivering en interpersoonlike style*. UNISA.

Smit, H.S. (1998). *Self-actualisation and acculturation amongst Black personnel practitioners*. UNISA.

Botha, M.M.M. (1999). *Die validering van 'n gerekenariseerde simulasietegniek vir die meting van kliëntediensvaardighede*. UNISA.

Marx, M. (1999). *Affirmative action success as measured by job satisfaction*. UNISA.

Rabichund, S. (1999). *The role of sense of coherence in group relations training*. UNISA.

Schultz, C.M. (1999). *Psychological optimisation and training competence*. UNISA.

Baloyi, J. (2000). *Confirmatory factor analysis on the measurement of six salutogenic constructs*. UNISA.

Britton, M. (2000). *A group dynamic interpretation of a team building event - a case study.* UNISA.

Ferreira, H. (2000). *'n Bedryfsielkundige ondersoek na groepseffektiwiteits-dimensies.* UNISA.

Freedman, G. (2000). *Validity of measures of cognitive ability for predicting literacy and numeracy performance.* UNISA.

Levy, K. (2000). *Individual behaviour towards authority.* UNISA.

Omar Carrim, S. (2000). *Working women in their multiple role environment. A salutogenic perspective.* UNISA.

Maloa, F. (2001). *Employee perception of a performance management system.* UNISA.

Motshele, V.M. (2001). *The relationship between salutogenic functioning and sick leave.* UNISA.

Bullen, G.N. (2003). *A psychodynamic view of the consulting relationship: A case study.* UNISA.

Dhaniram, N. (2003). *Stress, burnout and salutogenic functioning amongst community service doctors in KwaZulu-Natal hospitals.* UNISA.

Fourie, J.C.J. (2003). *The relationship between burnout and intro/extraversion at middle-management level.* UNISA.

Hammond, V.J. (2003). *The relevance of group dynamics in management meetings.* UNISA.

Jacobs, M. (2004). *Organisasiekultuur in die chemiese bedryf.* UNISA.

Pretorius, M. (2004). *An exploration of South African diversity dynamics.* UNISA.

Abrahams, F. (2005). *A systems psychodynamic perspective on dealing with change amongst different leadership styles.* UNISA.

Van Jaarsveld, J.J. (2005). *The relationship between burnout, coping and sense of coherence amongst engineers and scientists.* UNISA.

Myburg, H.S. (2006). *The experience of organisational development consultants working in the systems psychodynamic stance.* UNISA.

Du Buisson-Narsai, I. (2006). *The relationship between personal meaning, sense of coherence and organisational commitment.* UNISA.

Mtsweni, S.H. (2007). *Salutogenic functioning amongst University administrative staff.* UNISA.

Greyvenstein, H. (2008). *Understanding current South African leadership dynamics from the systems psychodynamic paradigm.* (MBL). UNISA.

Naidoo, V. (2008). *The effect of a corporate diversity workshop.* UNISA.

Scholtz, M.J. (2008). *Die verband tussen verskeie positiewe sielkunde konstrukte by onderwysers.* UNISA.

Mitonga Monga, J.M. (2011). *The relationship between leadership style, employee participation and positive psychology functioning in a manufacturing company in the Democratic Republic of the Congo.* UNISA.

Patrick, M.A. (2011). *Positive psychological functioning amongst civil servants.* UNISA.

Steyn, M.G. (2015). *A systems psychodynamic description of support staff's experiences of organisational transformation.* UNISA.

Bartlett, C. (2016). *The relationship between emotional intelligence, work engagement, creativity and demographic variables.* UNISA.

Students presently finishing off their dissertations.

∞ Pillay, K.

Doctorate Students

Universities include UNISA/Potchefstroom University/University of North-West/University of Johannesburg/University of Middlesex (UK)

Rall, J.H. (1986). *Bestuursevaluering met behulp van 'n verfynde evalueringsentrum en die benutting van evalueringsresultate vir mannekragbeplanning.* Potchefstroom University.

Terblanche, L. (1995). *'n Intra- en interpersoonlike verrykingsprogram vir verpleegkundiges.* Potchefstroom University.

Esterhuizen, P.M. (1997). *'n Selfaktualiseringsbenadering tot bestuursukses binne 'n finansiele instelling.* UNISA.

Viviers, A.M. (1997). *Salutogenese in organisatoriese konteks.* UNISA.

Breed, M. (1998). *Bepalende persoonlikheidskenmerke in die Salutogeniese paradigma.* UNISA.

Erasmus, M.P.A. (1998). *Coping: 'n Salutogenese benadering.* UNISA.

Kossuth, S.P. (1998). *Team building and salutogenic orientations contextualised in a performance model.* UNISA.

Cronje, M. (1999). *Lewenssin van Suid-Afrikaanse sakelui: 'n Bedryfsielkundige perspektief.* UNISA.

De Wet, C.F. (1999). *A salutogenic perspective of burnout in the nursing profession.* UNISA.

Elliott, C.A.E. (1999). *Standardisation of the Seven Graphology Factors Scale for application in industry.* UNISA.

Vosloo, S.E. (2000). *Rolkonflik by die werkende moeder - 'n geestesgesondheids-perspektief.* UNISA.

Hattingh, S.P. (2002). *A model for the training of peer debriefers in the emergency services.* UNISA.

Olivier, L.D. (2002). *An investigation of Locke's model of work motivation for the financial services industry.* UNISA.

Schmidt, L. (2002). *Narrative technique as a tool for perspective transformation in management development*. UNISA.

De Jager, W. (2003). *Leadership development from a systems psychodynamic consultancy stance*. University of Johannesburg.

Austin, R.K. (2005). *The relationship between career thinking and salutogenic functioning*. UNISA.

Bredell, D. (2005). *A developmental programme in salutogenic functioning*. UNISA.

Geldenhuys, D.J. (2005). *Die bydrae van psigodinamiese groepintervensies tot organisasie-ontwikklieng*. UNISA.

Chapman, L.A. (2006). *Integral coaching*. University of Middlesex, UK.

Van Eeden, R. (2006). *Group processes and dynamics in relation to transactional and transformational leadership*. UNISA.

Vinger, M.J.G. (2006). *Effective transformational leadership behaviours for managing change*. Johannesburg University.

Coetzee, O. (2007). *Exploring interpersonal and inter-group diversity dynamics in South African organisations by means of a theoretical model*. UNISA.

Freedman, G. (2007). *The string model. A Gestalt approach to consulting psychology*. UNISA.

Bezuidenhout, A. (2009). *Burnout work, engagement and sense of coherence in female academics at two tertiary education institutions in South Africa*. UNISA.

Henning, S. (2009). *Towards a system psychodynamic model of Psychological wellness*. UNISA.

May, M.S. (2010). *The unconscious at work in a historically black university: The (k)not of relationship between students, lecturers and management*. UNISA.

Motsoaledi, L. (2010). *Executive coaching in diversity from a systems psychodynamic perspective*. UNISA.

Struwig, W.H. (2010). *Boundary management: A model for Organisational Consulting Psychologists*. UNISA.

Dahl, A.D. (2011) *The relationship between cognitive ability, emotional intelligence and negative career thoughts: a study of career-exploring adults*. UNISA.

Van Niekerk, E. (2011). *The Systems Psychodynamic world of the fund manager*. UNISA.

Shongwe, M. (2014). *Systems psychodynamic experiences of professionals in acting positions*. UNISA.

Naik, B. (2015). *The systems psychodynamics underlying the work-family interface amongst managerial women in the public sector*. UNISA.

Mitonga-Monga, J. (2015). *The effects of ethical context and behaviour on job retention and performance-related factors*. UNISA.

Diedericks, J.C. (2017). *Positive work and organisational psychological functioning of academics in the open distance learning work environment.* UNISA.

Madurai, M. (2017). *The systems psychodynamic role analysis of the 21st-century leader.* UNISA.

Goldin, N. (2018). *Systems psychodynamic coaching for leaders in career transition.* UNISA.

Students Presently Finishing off their Theses

∞ Abrahams, F.

∞ Greyling, L-A.

∞ Parsadh, A.

∞ Van der Linde, E-K.

∞ Van der Westhuizen, S.

Academic Publications

1   Cilliers, F. (1978). The TAT-Z and the measurement of achievement motivation. *People and Profits,* 6(3), September.

2   Cilliers, F. (1979). The TAT-Z as a predictor of achievement motivation. *Perspectives in Industrial Psychology,* 5(2).

3   Cilliers, F. (1979). *Social Psychology.* Potchefstroom: Wesvalia.

4   Cilliers, F. (1980). *Introduction to experimental Industrial Psychology.* Potchefstroom: Wesvalia.

5   Cilliers, F. (1980). *Report writing in Industrial Psychology.* Potchefstroom: Wesvalia.

6   Cilliers, F. (1981). The personnel department in Belgium. *People and Profits,* 8(12), June.

7   Cilliers, F. (1982). Personnel development: An introduction. *Curationis. South African Journal for Nursing,* 5(2), June. https://doi.org/10.4102/curationis.v5i2.395

8   Cilliers, F. (1983). *Personality Psychology.* Potchefstroom: Wesvalia.

9   Cilliers, F. (1985). Managerial skill evaluation. *Curationis. South African Journal for Nursing,* 8(4), December.

10 Cilliers, F. (1986). Development, conflict and creativity. In: J. Kroon (ed.), *General Management.* Pretoria: HAUM.

11 Cilliers, F. (1988). The concept psychological optimality in management. *Institute of Personnel Management Journal,* 7(5), October.

12 Cilliers, F. (1988). Personality characteristics of the effective therapist. *South African Journal of Music Therapy,* 6(4).

13   Cilliers, F. (1989). A self-development programme for ministers. *NG Theological Journal*, 30(7), July.

14   Cilliers, F. (1990). Ontwikkeling, konflik, spanning en kreatiwiteit. In: J. Kroon (ed.), *Algemene Bestuur.* (2nd Ed.). Pretoria: HAUM.

15   Cilliers, F. (1990). Development, conflict, stress and creativity. In: J. Kroon (ed.), General Management. Pretoria: HAUM.

16   Oelofse, L. & Cilliers, F. (1990). A self-development programme for obese female students. *Curationis*, 13(3/4):30-32.

17   Cilliers, F. (1991). Facilitating: making a process available. *Human Resource Management*, 7(2), February.

18   Cilliers, F. (1991). *The changing role of Industrial Psychology in South Africa.* Pretoria: UNISA.

19   Cilliers, F. (1992). The (ir)relevance of empathy as concept in management. *Human Resource Management*, 8(3), April.

20   Cilliers, F. (1992). A facilitating skills programme for lecturers in nursing. *Curationis*, 15(2):19-23. https://doi.org/10.4102/curationis.v15i2.356

21   Cilliers, F. & Wissing M.P. (1993). Sensitive relationship forming as managerial dimension: the evaluation of a developmental programme. *South African Journal for Industrial Psychology*, 19(1):5-10.

22   Cilliers, F. (1994). The self-actualization profile of UNISA supervisors. Progressio, 16(2):96-105.

23   Cilliers, F. (1995). Konflik, spanning, innovasie en kreatiwiteit. In: J. Kroon (ed.), *Algemene Bestuur.* (3rd Ed.). Pretoria: Kagiso.

24   Cilliers, F. (1995). Conflict, stress, innovation and creativity. In: J. Kroon (ed.), *General Management.* (2nd Ed.). Pretoria: Kagiso.

25   Cilliers, F. (1995). The effect of a growth group experience on ministers. *NG Theological Journal*, 36(4):630-642.

26   Cilliers, F. (1995). Facilitator training. *South African Journal for Industrial Psychology*, 21(3):7-11. https://doi.org/10.4102/sajip.v21i3.592

27   Viljoen, R.P.; Erasmus, B.J. & Cilliers, F. (1995). The non-professional training needs of lecturers in the faculty of economic and business sciences at UNISA: empirical findings. *South African Journal of Higher Education*, 9(2):92-99.

28   Cilliers, F. (1996). Experiences with facilitation in industry. *Human Resource Management*, 11(10):36-38.

29   Cilliers, F. (1996). Facilitator training in South Africa. In: R. Hutterer, G. Pawlowsky, P.F. Schmid & R. Stipsits. (ed.), *Client Centred and Experiential Psychotherapy.* Frankfurt am Main: Peter Lang.

30   Cilliers, F. (1997). *Group behaviour : An introduction.* Department of Quantitative Management, UNISA. Pretoria: UNISA.

31   Cilliers, F. (1998). Group behaviour. In: Z.C. Bergh & A.L. Theron. (ed.), *Psychology in Work Context*. Johannesburg: International Thompson.

32   Cilliers, F. & Viviers, A.M. (1998). Self-actualisation, academic performance and biographical variables amongst a group of UNISA students. *Progressio*, 20(1):78-94.

33   Rothman, S.; Sieberhagen, G.v.d.W. & Cilliers, F. (1998). The qualitative effect of a group facilitation course. *South African Journal of Industrial Psychology*, 24(3):7-13. https://doi.org/10.4102/sajip.v24i3.656

34   Cilliers, F.; Viviers, A.M. & Marais C.P. (1998). Salutogenesis: A model to understand coping with change. *UNISA Psychologia*, 25(2):32-39. https://doi.org/10.4102/sajip.v25i2.676

35   Cilliers, F. & Koortzen, P. (1998). The Psychodynamics of Organisations. *UNISA Psychologia*, 25(2):8-16.

36   Cilliers, F. (1999). Konflik, spanning, innovasie en kreatiwiteit. In J. Kroon. (ed.), *Algemene Bestuur*. (4th Ed.). Pretoria: Kagiso.

37   Cilliers, F. (1999). Conflict, stress, innovation and creativity. In J. Kroon. (ed.), *General Management*. (3rd Ed.). Pretoria: Kagiso.

38   Viviers, A.M. & Cilliers, F. (1999). The relationship between salutogenesis and work orientation. *South African Journal of Industrial Psychology*, 25(1):27-32. https://doi.org/10.4102/sajip.v25i2.676

39   Cilliers, F. (1999). The essence of team building. *Management Today*, 15(9):26-30. https://doi.org/10.4102/sajip.v26i1.694

40   Cilliers, F. (2000). Team building from a psychodynamic perspective. *South African Journal of Industrial Psychology*, 26(1):18-23. https://doi.org/10.4102/sajip.v26i1.694

41   Cilliers, F. (2000). Facilitation skills for trainers. *South African Journal of Industrial Psychology*, 26(3):21-26. https://doi.org/10.4102/sajip.v26i3.715

42   Cilliers, F. (2000). Consulting for the African Renaissance. *People Dynamics*, 18(3):39-41.

43   Cilliers, F. & Elliott, C. (2000). Insight from handwriting. Personnel assessment by means of graphology: The 8GFS. *People Dynamics*, 18(9):28-33.

44   Cilliers, F. & Koortzen, P. (2000). *Facilitation skills*. Pretoria: ISCOR. https://doi.org/10.4102/curationis.v23i4.762

45   Cilliers, F. & Koortzen, P. (2000). The psychodynamic view on organisational behaviour. *The Industrial-Organizational Psychologist*, 38(2):59-67. https://doi.org/10.1037/e576962011-006

46   Marx, M. & Cilliers, F. (2000). Affirmative action success as measured by job satisfaction. *South African Journal of Labour Relations*, 24(1&2):55-71.

47   Cilliers, F. & Terblanche, L. (2000). Facilitation skills for nurses. *Curationis*, 23(4):90-97. https://doi.org/10.4102/curationis.v23i4.762

48   Rabichund, S. & Cilliers, F. (2001). Group Relations Training. What does it entail? *People Dynamics*, 19(1):28-30.

49   Rabichund, S. & Cilliers, F. (2001). Who benefits most from Group Relations Training? *People Dynamics*, 19(2):24-26.

50   Coetzee, S. & Cilliers, F. (2001). Psychofortology: Explaining coping behaviour in organisations. *The Industrial-Organisational Psychologist*, 38(4):62-68. https://doi.org/10.1037/e576972011-007

51   Cilliers, F. (2001). The role of sense of coherence in group relations training. *South African Journal of Industrial Psychology*, 27(3):13-18. https://doi.org/10.4102/sajip.v27i3.29

52   Cilliers, F. & Kossuth, S. (2002). The relationship between organisational climate and salutogenic functioning. *South African Journal of Industrial Psychology*, 28(1):8-13. https://doi.org/10.4102/sajip.v28i1.42

53   Kossuth, S.P. & Cilliers, F. (2002). The relationship between leadership dimensions, cultural beliefs and salutogenic functioning. *South African Journal of Labour Relations*, 26(1):65-95.

54   Koortzen, P. & Cilliers, F. (2002). The psychoanalytical approach to team development. In: R.L. Lowman (ed.), *Handbook of organizational consulting psychology*. San Francisco: Jossey-Bass.

55   Cilliers, F. & May, M. (2002). South African diversity dynamics. Reporting on the 2000 Robben Island Diversity Experience. A Group Relations event. *South African Journal of Labour Relations*, 26(3):42-68.

56   Cilliers, F. (2002). Salutogenic coping with burnout amongst nurses: A qualitative study. *South African Journal of Labour Relations*, 26(4):61-85. https://doi.org/10.4102/curationis.v26i1.1296

57   Cilliers, F. (2003). Group behaviour. In: Z.C. Bergh & A.L. Theron (eds.), *Psychology in the work context*. Cape Town: Oxford.

58   Cilliers, F. & Coetzee, S.C. (2003). The theoretical-empirical fit between three psychological wellness constructs: Sense of coherence, learned resourcefulness and self-actualisation. *South African Journal of Labour Relations*, 27(1):4-24.

59   Van Wyk, R.; Boshoff, A.B. & Cilliers, F.V.N. (2003). The prediction of job involvement for pharmacists and accountants. *South African Journal of Industrial Psychology*, 29(3):61-67. https://doi.org/10.4102/sajip.v29i3.118

60   Cilliers, F. (2003). Burnout and salutogenic functioning of nurses. *Curationis*, 26(1):62-74. https://doi.org/10.4102/curationis.v26i1.1296

61   Cilliers, F. (2003). A systems psychodynamic perspective on burnout. *South African Journal of Industrial Psychology*, 29(4):26-33. https://doi.org/10.4102/sajip.v29i4.120

62 Cilliers, F.; Rothmann, S. & Struwig, W.H. (2004). Transference and counter-transference in systems psychodynamic group process consultation: The consultant's experience. *South African Journal of Industrial Psychology*, 30(1):72-81. https://doi.org/10.4102/sajip.v30i1.143

63 De Jager, W.; Cilliers, F. & Veldsman, T. (2004). Leadership development from a systems psychodynamic consultancy stance. *South African Journal of Human Resource Management*, 1(3):85-92. https://doi.org/10.4102/sajhrm.v1i3.23

64 Cilliers, F. (2004). Coaching. A systems Psychodynamic approach. *HR Future*, September:41-42.

65 Cilliers, F. (2004). A Person-Centered view of diversity in South Africa. *The Person-Centered Journal*, 11(1-2):33-47.

66 Cilliers, F.; Koortzen, P. & De Beer, M. (2004). Confirmatory factor analysis on the personal orientation inventory (POI). *South African Journal of Labour Relations*, 28(2):33-58.

67 Cilliers, F. & Kossuth S.P. (2004). The reliability and factor structure of three measures of salutogenic functioning. *South African Journal of Labour Relations*, 28(2):59-76.

68 Cilliers, F. & Naidoo, Vijay. (2005). Organisational diversity. Part 1. *HR Future*, January:31.

69 Cilliers, F. & Naidoo, Vijay. (2005). Organisational diversity. Part 2. *HR Future*, February:33-34.

70 Cilliers, F. & Koortzen, P. (2005). Working with conflict in teams: The CIBART model. *HR Future*, October:52-52.

71 Cilliers, F. & Stone, K. (2005). Employment equity practices in three South African Information Technology Organisations: A systems psychodynamic perspective. *South African Journal of Industrial Psychology*, 31(2):49-57. https://doi.org/10.4102/sajip.v31i2.193

72 Cilliers, F. (2005). Executive coaching experiences. A systems psychodynamic perspective. *South African Journal of Industrial Psychology*, 31(3):23-30. https://doi.org/10.4102/sajip.v31i3.205

73 Cilliers, F. & May, M.S. (2006). Exploring the psychodynamic meaning of organisational trust. *HR Future*, March:38-39.

74 Cilliers, F. & Ngokha. G. (2006). Confirmatory factor analysis on the measurement of five salutogenic constructs. *Southern African Business Review*, 10(1):17-34.

75 Cilliers, F. (2006). Leader and team behaviour during organisational change: A systems psychodynamic stance. *South African Journal of Industrial Psychology*, 32(1):33-41. https://doi.org/10.4102/sajip.v32i1.224

76 Breed, M.; Cilliers, F. & Visser, D. (2006). The factor structure of six salutogenic constructs. *South African Journal of Industrial Psychology*, 32(1):73-85. https://doi.org/10.4102/sajip.v32i1.226

77   Cilliers, F. (2006). Group Behaviour. In: Bergh, Z. & Theron A. *Psychology in the work context*. Cape Town: Oxford.

78   Smit, B. & Cilliers, F. (2006). Understanding implicit texts in focus groups from a systems psychodynamic perspective. *The Qualitative Report*, 11(2):302-316.

79   Cilliers, F. (2006). South Africa at the dawn of 2006. *Psycho-analytic Psychotherapy in South Africa*, 14(2):66-76.

80   Cilliers, F. & Smit, B. (2006). A systems psychodynamic interpretation of South African diversity dynamics: a comparative study. *South African Journal of Labour relations*, 30(2):5-18.

81   Vinger, G. & Cilliers, F. (2006). Effective transformational leadership behaviours for managing change. *South African Journal of Human Resources Management*, 4(2):1-9. https://doi.org/10.4102/sajhrm.v4i2.87

82   Rothmann, S. & Cilliers, F.V.N. (2007). Present challenges and some critical issues for research in industrial/organisational psychology in South Africa. *South African Journal of Industrial Psychology*, 33(1):8-16. https://doi.org/10.4102/sajip.v33i1.262

83   Cilliers, F. (2007). A systems psychodynamic exploration of diversity management. *South African Journal of Labour Relations*, 31(2):32-50.

84   Cilliers, F. & Koortzen P. (2007). Symbolism associated with leadership: A system-psychodynamic perspective. *Myth & Symbolism*, 4:28-45. https://doi.org/10.1080/10223820701673981

85   Cilliers, F. (2008). The role and competencies of the OD Consultant. In: C.L. van Tonder & G. Roodt. *Organisational Development*. Pretoria: Van Schaik.

86   Geldenhuys, D.J. & Cilliers, F. (2008). Individual-focussed interventions. Chapter in C.L. van Tonder & G. Roodt. *Organisational Development*. Pretoria: Van Schaik.

87   Chapman, L. & Cilliers, F. (2008). The integrated experiential executive coaching model: A qualitative exploration. *South African Journal of Labour Relations*, 32(1):63-80

88   Van Eeden, R. Cilliers, F. & Van Deventer, V. (2008). Leadership styles and associated personality traits: Support for the conceptualisation of transactional and transformational leadership. *South African Journal of Psychology*, 38(2):253-267. https://doi.org/10.1177/008124630803800201

89   Van Eeden, R. & Cilliers, F. (2009). Social defence structures in organisations: how a lack of authorisation keeps managers from moving to transformational leadership. *International Journal of Organisation Theory and Behaviour*, 12(3):475-501. https://doi.org/10.1108/IJOTB-12-03-2009-B004

90   Cilliers, F. & Terblanche, L. (2010). The systems psychodynamic leadership coaching experiences of nursing managers. *Health SA Gesondheid*, 15(1):Art #457, 9 pages. https://doi.org/10.4102/hsag.v15i1.457

91   Bezuidenhout, A. & Cilliers, F.V.N. (2010). Burnout, work engagement and sense of coherence in female academics in higher-education institutions in South Africa. *South African Journal of Industrial Psychology*, 36(1):Art. #872, 10 pages. https://doi.org/10.4102/sajip.v36i1.872

92   Cilliers, F. & May, M. (2010). The popularisation of Positive Psychology as a defence against behavioural complexity in research and organisations. *South African Journal of Industrial Psychology*, 36(2):Art. #917, 10 pages. https://doi.org/10.4102/sajip.v36i2.917

93   Bezuidenhout, A. & Cilliers, F. (2011). Age, burnout, work engagement and sense of coherence in female academics at two South African universities. *South African Journal of Labour Relations*, 35(1):61-80. https://doi.org/10.4102/sajip.v36i1.872

94   Cilliers, F. (2011). Positive psychology leadership coaching experiences in a financial organisation. *SA Journal of Industrial Psychology/SA Tydskrif vir Bedryfsielkunde*, 37(1):Art. #933, 14 pages. https://doi.org/10.4102/sajip.v37i1.933

95   Austin, K. & Cilliers, F. (2011). The psychometric relationship between career thinking and salutogenic functioning amongst unemployed adults. *SA Journal of Industrial Psychology/SA Tydskrif vir Bedryfsielkunde*, 37(1):Art. #969, 11 pages. https://doi.org/10.4102/sajip.v37i1.969

96   Cilliers, F. (2011). Individual diversity management and salutogenic functioning. International *Review of Psychiatry*, 23(6):501-507. https://doi.org/10.3109/09540261.2011.637911

97   Greyvenstein, H. & Cilliers. F. (2012). Followership's experiences of organisational leadership. A systems psychodynamic perspective. *SA Journal of Industrial Psychology/SA Tydskrif vir Bedryfsielkunde*, 38(2):Art. #1001, 10 pages. https://doi.org/10.4102/sajip.v38i2.1001

98   Cilliers, F. & May, M.S. (2012). The director's roles in containing the Robben Island Diversity Experience (RIDE). *SA Journal of Industrial Psychology/SA Tydskrif vir Bedryfsielkunde*, 38(2):Art. #986, 10 pages. https://doi.org/10.4102/sajip.v38i2.986

99   Coetzee, O. & Cilliers, F. (2012). Humour as defence against the anxiety manifesting in diversity experiences. *SA Journal of Industrial Psychology/SA Tydskrif vir Bedryfsielkunde*, 38(2):Art. #990, 9 pages. https://doi.org/10.4102/sajip.v38i2.990

100   Motsoaledi L. & Cilliers, F. (2012). Executive coaching in diversity from the systems psychodynamic perspective. *SA Journal of Industrial Psychology/SA Tydskrif vir Bedryfsielkunde*, 38(2):Art. #988, 11 pages. https://doi.org/10.4102/sajip.v38i2.988

101   Cilliers, F. (2012). A systems psychodynamic description of organisational bullying experiences. *SA Journal of Industrial Psychology/SA Tydskrif vir Bedryfsielkunde*, 38(2):Art.#994,11 pages. https://doi.org/10.4102/sajip.v38i2.994

102   Pretorius, M. Cilliers, F. & May M. (2012). The Robben Island Diversity Experience. An exploration of South African diversity dynamics. *SA Journal of Industrial Psychology/SA Tydskrif vir Bedryfsielkunde*, 38(2):Art.#996, 8 pages. https://doi.org/10.4102/sajip.v38i2.996

103   Cilliers, F. & Greyvenstein, H. (2012). The impact of silo mentality on team identity. An organisational case study. *SA Journal of Industrial Psychology/SA Tydskrif vir Bedryfsielkunde*, 38(2):Art.#993, 9 pages. https://doi.org/10.4102/sajip.v38i2.993

104   Struwig, H, & Cilliers, F. (2012). Working with boundaries in systems psychodynamic consulting. *SA Journal of Industrial Psychology/SA Tydskrif vir Bedryfsielkunde*, 38(2):Art.#987, 10 pages. https://doi.org/10.4102/sajip.v38i2.987

105   May, M.S.; Cilliers, F. & Van Deventer, V. (2012). Exploring the (k)not of relationship between lecturers and management at a historically Black university: The lecturer's perspective. *SA Journal of Industrial Psychology/SA Tydskrif vir Bedryfsiekunde*, 38(2):Art.#998, 10 pages. https://doi.org/10.4102/sajip.v38i2.998

106   Henning, S. & Cilliers, F. (2012). Constructing a systems psychodynamic wellness model. *SA Journal of Industrial Psychology/SA Tydskrif vir Bedryfsielkunde*, 38(2):Art.#989, 9 pages. https://doi.org/10.4102/sajip.v38i2.989

107   Cilliers, F. & Harry, N. (2012). The systems psychodynamic experiences of first-year Master's students in Industrial and Organisational psychology. *SA Journal of Industrial Psychology/SA Tydskrif vir Bedryfsielkunde*, 38(2):Art. #992, 9 pages. https://doi.org/10.4102/sajip.v38i2.992

108   Cilliers, F. (2012). Leadership coaching experiences of clients with alexithymia. *SA Journal of Industrial Psychology/SA Tydskrif vir Bedryfsielkunde*, 38(2):Art.#995, 10 pages. https://doi.org/10.4102/sajip.v38i2.995

109   Geldenhuys, D.J. & Cilliers, F. (2012). Transforming a small business: A learning intervention. *SA Journal of Industrial Psychology/SA Tydskrif vir Bedryfsielkunde*, 38(2):Art. #1028, 8 pages. https://doi.org/10.4102/sajip.v38i2.1028

110   Mitonga-Monga, J.; Coetzee, M. & Cilliers, F.V.N. (2012). Perceived leadership style and employee participation in a manufacturing company in the Democratic Republic of Congo. *African Journal of Business Management*, 6(15):5389-5398. https://doi.org/10.5897/AJBM11.2443

111   Dahl, D. & Cilliers, F. (2012). The relationship between cognitive ability, emotional intelligence and negative career thoughts: A study of career exploring adults. *SA Journal of Human Resource Management/SA Tydskrif vir Menslikehulpbronbestuur*, 10(2):Art. #461, 14 pages. https://doi.org/10.4102/sajhrm.v10i2.461

112   Cilliers, F. & Coetzee, M. (2013). Personality type, self-actualisation and deep-seated values: A psychological profile of leaders in a financial organisation. *South African Journal of Labour Relations*, 37(2):69-96.

113   Cilliers, F. & Terblanche, L. (2014). The role of spirituality in coping with the demands of the hospital culture amongst fourth-year nursing students. *International Review of Psychiatry*, 26(3):279-288. https://doi.org/10.3109/09540261.2014.890922

114   Henning, S. & Cilliers, F. (2014). The voyage of the dawn treader: The world at the dawn of 2006-2011. Understanding societal themes. *African Journal of Hospitality, Tourism and Leisure*, 3(1):1-12.

115 Cilliers, F. & Pienaar, J.W. (2014). The career psychological experiences of academic department chairpersons at a South African University. *Southern African Business Review*, 18(3). https://doi.org/10.25159/1998-8125/5684

116 Mitonga-Monga, J. & Cilliers, F. (2015). Ethics culture and ethics climate in relation to employee engagement in a developing country setting. *Journal of Psychology in Africa*, 25(3):242-249. https://doi.org/10.1080/14330237.2015.1065059

117 Mitonga-Monga, J. & Cilliers, F. (2016). Perceived ethical leadership: Its moderating influence on employees' organisational commitment and organisational citizenship behaviours. *Journal of Psychology in Africa*, 26(1). https://doi.org/10.1080/14330237.2015.1124608

118 Cilliers, F. & Flotman, A.P. (2016). The psychological well-being manifesting amongst master's students in industrial and organisational psychology. *SA Journal of Industrial Psychology/SA Tydskrif vir Bedryfsielkunde*, 42(1):a1323. https://doi.org/10.4102/sajip.v42i1.1323

119 Pienaar, J.W. & Cilliers, F. (2016). The Janus effect: Contradictory demands placed on the academic chairperson. *South African Journal of Higher Education*, 30(2):184-204. https://doi.org/10.20853/30-2-579

120 Mitonga-Monga, J.; Flotman, A-P. & Cilliers, F. (2016). Workplace ethics culture and work engagement: The mediating effect of ethical leadership in a developing world context. *Journal of Psychology in Africa*, 26(4):326-333. https://doi.org/10.1080/14330237.2016.1208928

121 Mitonga-Monga, J. & Cilliers, F. (2016). Perceived ethical leadership in relation to employees' organisational commitment in an organisation in the Democratic Republic of Congo. *African Journal of Business Ethics*, 10(1):36-51. https://doi.org/10.15249/10-1-122

122 Steyn, M. & Cilliers, F. (2016). The systems psychodynamic experiences of organisational transformation amongst support staff. *South African Journal for Industrial Psychology*, 42(1):a1367. https://doi.org/10.4102/sajip.v42i1.1367

123 Mitonga-Monga, J.; Flotman, A-P. & Cilliers, F. (2016). The relationship between job satisfaction and organisational citizenship behaviour: A Democratic Republic of Congo organisational Perspective. *Journal of contemporary Management*, 13:1064-1084.

124 Cilliers, F. (2017). The systems psychodynamic role identity of academic research supervisors. *South African Journal of Higher Education*, 31(1):29-49. https://doi.org/10.20853/31-1-784

125 Mitonga-Monga, J.; Flotman, A. & Cilliers, F.V.N. (2017). Organisational citizenship behaviour amongst railway employees in a developing country: effects of age, education and tenure. *Southern African Business Review*, 21:385-406.

126 Mitonga-Monga, J.; Flotman, A-P & Cilliers, F. (2018). Job satisfaction and its relationship with organisational commitment: A Democratic Republic of Congo organisational perspective. *Acta Commercii*, 18(1): a578. https://doi.org/10.4102/ac.v18i1.578